Artificial Intelligence, Machine Learning and Blockchain in Digital Twin Computing

This series, **Advances in Digital Twin Computing and Sensor Networks**, presents insights into digital twin and sensor network technologies as they become embedded in human activity, such as healthcare, city planning, manufacturing, distribution, and security. Digital twin computing allows researchers to replicate objects (human or things) in digital form, by capturing real-time data from sensor networks. The real and virtual/digital worlds are synchronized in real time, enabling the model to be used for planning, research, and a wider understanding of healthcare, the built environment, etc.

The series features contributions from a diverse group of authors, including experts from various geographical regions, academic backgrounds, and professional experiences. It covers topics such as smart city, smart education, smart healthcare, smart agriculture, smart manufacturing, smart grids, and smart transport.

The series is edited by **Dr. Tuan Anh Nguyen**, a Senior Principal Research Scientist at the Institute for Tropical Technology, Vietnam Academy of Science and Technology, Vietnam. Dr Nguyen received a Ph.D. in Chemistry from the Paris Diderot University (France) in 2003. His research activities include smart sensors, smart networks, smart hospitals, smart cities and advanced nanomaterials.

Dr Nguyen was the volume editor for several Elsevier titles: *Sensors and Nanosensors for Smart Hospitals*; *Digital Twin and Blockchain in Smart Cities*; *Digital Twin and Blockchain in Smart Hospitals; Sensor Networks for Smart Hospitals; Digital Twin, Blockchain, and Sensor Networks in the Healthy and Mobile City; and Blockchain and Digital Twins for Smart Hospitals*.

Advances in Digital Twin Computing and Sensor Networks

Artificial Intelligence, Machine Learning and Blockchain in Digital Twin Computing

Edited by

Parikshit Narendra Mahalle

Department of Artificial Intelligence & Data Science, Vishwakarma Institute of Technology, Pune, Maharashtra, India

Vijay Sonawane

Department of Computer Engineering, Pune Vidyarthi Griha's College of Engineering & Shrikrushna S. Dhamankar Institute of Management, Nashik, Maharashtra, India

Series Editor

Tuan Anh Nguyen

ELSEVIER

Elsevier
Radarweg 29, PO Box 211, 1000 AE Amsterdam, Netherlands
125 London Wall, London EC2Y 5AS, United Kingdom
50 Hampshire Street, 5th Floor, Cambridge, MA 02139, United States

ISBN: 978-0-443-43914-8

Publisher: Mara Conner
Acquisitions Editor: Craig Smith
Editorial Project Manager: Bhavya Rattan
Production Project Manager: Aishwarya R
Cover Designer: Raman Kumar

Printed in England by CPI Group (UK) Ltd
Croydon CR0 4YY
United Kingdom

Typeset by Integra Software Services

Contents

Part 3: Emerging applications

Contributors

Yogesh Ahirwar Department of Computer Science, Indira Gandhi National Tribal University, Amarkantak, Madhya Pradesh, India

Neha Sharad Bhagwat Department of Computer Engineering, Nutan Maharashtra Institute of Engineering & Technology, Pune, India

Pankaj Chandre Computer Science and Engineering, MIT Art Design and Technology University Pune, Pune, India

Sujata Deshmukh Department of Computer Engineering, Fr. C. Rodrigues College of Engineering, Bandra, Mumbai, Maharashtra, India

Pankaj A. Dhakate Department of Computer Engineering, Dr. D. Y. Patil College of Engineering and Innovation, Varale, Talegaon, India

Nitin Dhawas Information Technology (I.T.), Nutan Maharashtra Institute of Technology, Pune, Maharashtra, India

Vaishali Nitin Dhawas Department of Computer Engineering, Nutan Maharashtra Institute of Engineering & Technology, Pune, India

Bharti Dhote Department of Computer Engineering, Nutan Maharashtra Institute of Engineering & Technology, Pune, India

S. Ganesh Department of Computer Science and Engineering, Study World College of Engineering, Coimbatore, Tamil Nadu, India

Mayuri Gawade Department of Computer Science & Engineering (AI & ML), Vishwakarma Institute of Technology, Pune, India

P. Gomathi Department of Electrical and Electronics Engineering, Study World College of Engineering, Coimbatore, Tamil Nadu, India

V. Hemamalini Department of Networking and Communications, SRM Institute of Science and Technology, Kattankulathur; School of Law Forensic Justice & Policy Studies, National Forensic Sciences University, Gandhinagar, Gujarat, India

M. Jeyaselvi Department of Networking and Communications, SRM Institute of Science and Technology, Kattankulathur; School of Law Forensic Justice & Policy Studies, National Forensic Sciences University, Gandhinagar, Gujarat, India

Renuka Rajendra Kajale Department of Computer Engineering, Nutan Maharashtra Institute of Engineering & Technology, Pune, India

S. Kannadhasan Department of Electronics and Communication Engineering, Study World College of Engineering, Coimbatore, Tamil Nadu, India

Prabhakar Krishnan Department of Management, St.Joseph's University, Bengaluru, Karnataka, India

Sudesh Kumar Department of Computer Science, Indira Gandhi National Tribal University, Amarkantak, Madhya Pradesh, India

Shabnam Kumari Department of Computer Science, Faculty of Science and Humanities, SRM Institute of Science and Technology, Kattankulathur, Chennai, Tamil Nadu, India

Prasad Lahare Department of Information Technology, Pune Vidyarthi Griha's College of Engineering and Shrikrishna S. Dhamankar Institute of Management, Nashik, Maharashtra, India

Pravin C. Latane Department of Computer Engineering, Dr. D. Y. Patil College of Engineering and Innovation, Varale, Talegaon, India

Parikshit Mahalle Department of Computer Science & Engineering (AI & ML), Vishwakarma Institute of Technology, Pune, India

Edson Bernardo da Conceicao Mahangue Department of Computer Science & Engineering (CSE), Sharda School of Computing Science & Engineering (SSCSE), Sharda University, Greater Noida, India

Suresh N. Mali Department of Computer Engineering, Dr. D. Y. Patil College of Engineering and Innovation, Varale, Talegaon, India

Dnyaneshwar S. Mantri Department of Electronics and Telecommunication Engineering, Sinhgad Institute of Technology, Lonavala, Pune, India

T. Megala Department of Computing Technologies, SRM Institute of Science and Technology, Kattankulathur, Chennai, Tamil Nadu, India

Dariusz Mikołajewski Faculty of Computer Science, Kazimierz Wielki University, Bydgoszcz, Poland

Manali Mishrikotkar School of Computer Science and Engineering, Ramdeobaba University, Nagpur, Maharashtra, India

Prajakta Musale Department of Computer Science & Engineering (AI & ML), Vishwakarma Institute of Technology, Pune, India

R. Nagarajan Department of Electrical and Electronics Engineering, Gnanamani College of Technology, Namakkal, Tamil Nadu, India

Sakshi Paliye School of Computer Science and Engineering, Ramdeobaba University, Nagpur, Maharashtra, India

Anandkumar Pardeshi Department of Computer Science and Engineering, Fr. C. Rodrigues Institute of Technology, Vashi, Navi Mumbai, Maharashtra, India

Praful Pardhi School of Computer Science and Engineering, Ramdeobaba University, Nagpur, Maharashtra, India

Ashlesha Pathak School of Computer Science and Engineering, Ramdeobaba University, Nagpur, Maharashtra, India

Sheetal Phatangare Department of Artificial Intelligence & Data Science, Vishwakarma Institute of Technology, Pune, India

Sanika Pohare School of Computer Science and Engineering, Ramdeobaba University, Nagpur, Maharashtra, India

Abhijeet Raipurkar School of Computer Science and Engineering, Ramdeobaba University, Nagpur, Maharashtra, India

Vijaya G. Rajeshwarkar Department of Electronics and Telecommunication Engineering, Sinhgad Institute of Technology, Lonavala, Pune, India

Vaishali Rajput Department of Computer Science & Engineering (Artificial Intelligence), Vishwakarma Institute of Technology, Pune, India

Richa Department of Computer Science and Engineering, Birla Institute of Technology Mesra, Ranchi, India

Izabela Rojek Faculty of Computer Science, Kazimierz Wielki University, Bydgoszcz, Poland

Vaishali Sarbhukan Department of Computer Science and Engineering, Fr. C. Rodrigues Institute of Technology, Vashi, Navi Mumbai, Maharashtra, India

Avinash Kumar Sharma Department of Computer Science & Engineering (CSE), Sharda School of Computing Science & Engineering (SSCSE), Sharda University, Greater Noida, India

Deepali Shinde Department of Information Technology, Pune Vidyarthi Griha's College of Engineering and Shrikrishna S. Dhamankar Institute of Management, Nashik, Maharashtra, India

Megha Singh Department of Computer Science and Engineering, Oriental University, Indore, India

Richa Singh Department of Computer Science and Engineering, Birla Institute of Technology, Mesra, Ranchi, Jharkhand, India

Gulshan Soni Centre for Computer Science and Business Management, Madhav Institute of Technology & Science (MITS-DU), Gwalior, Madhya Pradesh, India

Tanuj Surve Department of Management, University of California, Berkeley, FL, United States

Smita Thakare Department of Information Technology, Pune Vidyarthi Griha's College of Engineering and Shrikrishna S. Dhamankar Institute of Management, Nashik, Maharashtra, India

Kaushalya Thopate Department of Computer Engineering, Vishwakarma Institute of Technology, Pune, India

Anshuman Tiwari Department of Computer Science, Indira Gandhi National Tribal University, Amarkantak, Madhya Pradesh, India

Shrikant Tiwari Department of Networking and Communications, SRM Institute of Science and Technology, Kattankulathur, Tamil Nadu, India

Khushboo Tripathi Department of Computer Applications, Sharda University, New Delhi, India

Department of Computer Applications, Sharda University, India

Bhawna Tunwal Department of Computer Science and Technology, Central University of Punjab, Bhatinda, India

Amit Kumar Tyagi School of Law Forensic Justice & Policy Studies, National Forensic Sciences University, Gandhinagar, Gujarat; School of Computing Science and Engineering, Galgotias University, Greater Noida, Uttar Pradesh; Department of Fashion Technology, National Institute of Fashion Technology, New Delhi, India

Vilas S. Ubale Department of Electronics and Communication Engineering, Amrutvahini College of Engineering, Lonavala, Pune, India

PART 1

Introduction

CHAPTER 1

Introduction to digital twin computing

Amit Kumar Tyagi[a], V. Hemamalini[b], M. Jeyaselvi[b], and Khushboo Tripathi[c]

[a]*School of Law Forensic Justice & Policy Studies, National Forensic Sciences University, Gandhinagar, Gujarat, India*

[b]*Department of Networking and Communications, SRM Institute of Science and Technology, Kattankulathur, India*

[c]*Department of Computer Applications, Sharda University, New Delhi, India*

1.1 Introduction

A Digital Twin is a virtual representation of a physical object, system, or process that accurately reflects it. By collecting real-world data via sensors and updating the virtual model on an ongoing basis, a digital twin allows us to observe, analyze, model, and forecast the behavior of the real-world counterpart. Digital twins are also distinct from static models or static simulations. Whereas static models are true representations, static simulations are not. It is the ongoing engagement that helps make a digital twin dynamic, enabling it to react to changes that occur in the real world. These digital twins can include multiple digital counterparts as a collective means to interact, work together, and address complex problems. The primary aspect of Digital Twin Computing (DTC) is that the focus is taken away from a direct replica of an object. DTC seeks to establish an ecosystem of virtual counterparts that work together to simulate complex situations, optimize networks, and collaboratively drive omnidirectional decision-making across interconnected systems. In this manner, through DTC, we see that it goes further than a digital representation. Now, the objects are able to interact and work collectively to have a transformative impact across various industry verticals (Sharma et al., 2022).

Digital twins have their roots in NASA's Apollo program in the 1960s. To support remote space vehicles, NASA engineers created exact physical duplicates on Earth to diagnose and fix problems with the spacecraft. These physical copies were not digital twins, as they were not digital representations, but they did provide the conceptual foundation for today's digital twin practices. The first identified use of the term "Digital Twin" was by Dr. Michael Grieves in 2002 while at the University of Michigan. Although Dr. Grieves applied the concept to product lifecycle management (PLM) specifically, the idea of having a digital equivalent for every physical product in the lifecycle is an earlier development. Since then,

Artificial Intelligence, Machine Learning and Blockchain in Digital Twin Computing.
https://doi.org/10.1016/B978-0-443-43914-8.00010-8

the triad of the development of Internet of Things (IoT), big data, artificial intelligence (AI), and simulation development has proven that the digital twin is a viable concept that can be put to practical use today. By the 2010s, major corporations like General Electric and Siemens had begun leveraging digital twin technologies at scale in areas like aviation and manufacturing. It was through further technological maturity, particularly the capability to orchestrate communication and interactions between multiple digital twins, that the emergence of DTC occurred—opening the door for optimization and decision-making across systems. Organizations such as the Digital Twin Consortium (established in 2020) have helped to establish standards and accelerate the global adoption of DTC frameworks (Semeraro et al., 2021).

DTC has the potential to disrupt industries by providing insights, predictions, and autonomous management opportunities in real-time. Industries such as manufacturing, health care, smart cities, energy, automotive, and aerospace will depend on the advanced predictive capabilities of DTC in order to thrive in the future. Digital twins enable smart factories and manufacturers to understand the factors leading to downtime, offer better product quality, and improve operational costs. In health care, digital twins have the potential to allow clinicians to simulate a patient's treatment options and predicted outcomes and perform remote monitoring of that patient—ultimately delivering simpler, better, more efficient, and safer health care. In smart cities, digital twins have the potential to allow city planners and leaders to use data from sensors around the city to integrate all complexities into a comprehensive view of urban ecosystems. In the energy industry, digital twins have the potential to provide an understanding of how to optimize sustainable harvesting of renewable energy sources, leverage transmission across the power grid to other stakeholders, and complete real-time simulations of grid stability. In the aerospace and automotive industries, digital twins allow designers, manufacturers, and maintainers of complex machinery to run simulations of environments with the machinery working under testing conditions—thus reducing time, costs, and potential safety and performance risks (Abayadeera, 2024). To conclude, DTC potentially provides a critical technology toward the digital transformation of many valuable activities—ultimately offering industries opportunities to improve efficiency, resilience, and innovation on an unprecedented scale. Fig. 1.1 illustrates an overview of DTC and its relationship with other technologies.

DTC is an emerging field that depends on many technologies. IoT devices are important sources of real-time information from the physical world, providing real-time insights that support accurate modeling and updating. AI and machine learning (ML) techniques can also assess this real-time data and provide insights on potential failures, performance optimization, and intelligent prescriptions. Cloud computing allows anytime, anywhere access to a vast amount of information. As the size of datasets expands, this scalability offers an opportunity to expand collaboration in real-time and draw data-driven conclusions on big data. Edge computing is also an application that may support use cases such as autonomous vehicles or health monitoring

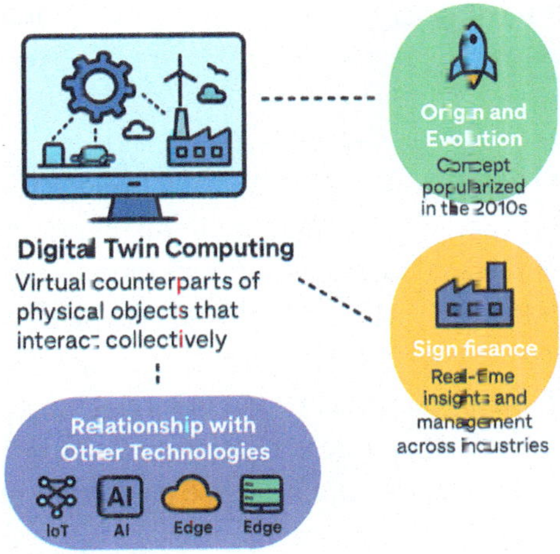

Fig. 1.1 An overview of DTC and its relationship with other technologies.

by bringing computation closer to the original data sources, allowing real-time analytics capabilities without needing to rely on centralized cloud resources. Finally, big data analytics is one of the newest technologies used to process, analyze, and visualize data on the scale of the information generated by DTC systems. By leveraging the interconnections of these technologies, DTC creates a robust framework that can mirror, understand, and optimize (create innovative solutions for) complex systems in the real world (Yao et al., 2023).

This paper is intended to serve as a valuable introductory resource for DTC, covering conceptual foundations, architectural aspects, technology enablers, and transformation across various applications. This paper will:

- Define and describe the fundamental concepts associated with DTC
- Describe different architectures and the fundamental technological components of implementing DTC
- Provide specific examples across industries that substantiate its transformative potential
- Explain high-level problems, constraints, and security and cyber-security issues related to DTC

The remainder of the paper is organized as follows: Section 1.2 discusses the related work in detail regarding DTC and related concepts; Section 1.3 presents a comprehensive background on the history of digital twins and the conceptual underpinnings of DTC; Section 1.4 provides an overview of the architecture and key constituents of DTC systems; Section 1.5 explores top-end applications of DTC across manufacturing, healthcare, smart city, and energy industries; Section 1.6 examines the challenges, limitations, and risks involved in the adoption of DTC; Section 1.7 presents real-world case studies to contextualize theoretical perspectives; Section 1.8 offers a comparative review of DTC and other pertinent concepts;

and Section 1.9 concludes the paper by summarizing essential findings and providing directions for future research.

1.2 Related work

In the last decade, DTC has gained momentum due to the ongoing evolution of IoT, AI, and cloud computing. The first research on digital twin models primarily investigated PLM and the modeling of industrial systems. However, the scope adapted and expanded into emerging domains, including healthcare, smart cities, energy systems, and logistics. The earlier work on digital twins focused on producing realistic and reliable virtual representations of physical assets. The research literature from industrial automation, for example, illustrated how a digital twin could improve predictive maintenance, operational efficiency, and asset management (Mishra and Tyagi, 2019). The initial investigations also demonstrated how network sensor data, coupled with 3D models, could be used to monitor and control manufacturing systems and eventually provided the foundation for DTC development.

Subsequent research reiterated the importance of real-time data integration in converting a digital twin from a static model to one that is actively evolving and dynamic. Architectural methods of integrating IoT devices in combination with ML algorithms were described to create digital twins that can adapt in response to changing operating contexts (Fuller et al., 2020; Barricelli et al., 2019). These advancements began to enable intelligent digital twins capable of self-diagnosing failures, optimizing functional states, and learning from real-world information with real-world feedback. The growing acceptance of edge computing has also led to a body of work exploring decentralized models for digital twins. Digital twins operating on edge with real-time processing close to the point of origin for data, which limits latency, throughput, and bandwidth, were conceptualized by researchers (Rasheed et al., 2020; Boschert and Rosen, 2016). Some of this work demonstrated the important role of distributed computing in scaling digital twin contexts into complex, large systems such as city infrastructure and industrial IoT networks.

Healthcare has been another notable focus area of DTC research. DTCs of human organs and full human physiological systems have been developed for personalized medicine and simulation-based diagnosis. The work by (Bruynseels et al., 2018) and (Corral-Acero et al., 2020) described patient-specific digital models based on the sequential progression of disease and the effects of treatment. The advantages of DTCs include patient-centered preventive healthcare, real-time predictions of clinical pathways, disease and intervention, and personalizing diagnostic and treatment methods for chronic illnesses. Smart cities research has also adopted a digital twin focus. Urban digital twins, used by the cities of Singapore and Helsinki, have been employed to manage infrastructure dependencies, optimize traffic flows, and monitor the environment (Wang et al., 2023; Lin et al., 2024). In this scenario, researchers developed complex urban systems models using multimodal sensor data and facilitated policy decisions through real-time simulation analysis.

The aerospace sector has utilized digital twins for mission planning, structural health monitoring, and predicting maintenance of spacecraft and aircraft systems over the years. As discussed in (Glaessgen and Stargel, 2012), methodologies have been proposed using multifidelity modeling and real-time simulations to make aerospace operations safer and more efficient. The authors of that work indicated that high-fidelity digital twins were important in high-risk industries. Other types of systems, in general, have adopted digital twin technology (DTC), such as energy systems. The authors of the study (Tan and Li, 2024) used a digital twin to determine how to optimize energy consumption in smart grids, while work on managing renewable energy sources using a digital twin was documented by (Do Amaral et al., 2023). Dynamic modeling of energy networks allowed practitioners to improve load forecasting, enhance fault detection, and create grid resilience.

In addition to the domain-specific contributions, there has been significant focus on the theoretical foundations and reference architectures of DTC. Wu et al. presented frameworks that emphasized the modularity, interoperability, and scalability of digital twin systems (Rosen et al., 2015; Wang et al., 2022). They identified issues such as data governance, model synchronization, and the need for standardization of digital twins in multiple industries They surveyed the evolution of digital twin research in recent reviews—developed a comprehensive classification scheme to represent the space of digital twins, described the challenges that are specific to applications, and pointed out the emergence of cognitive digital twins and hybrid physics-data-driven modeling (Kritzinger et al., 2018). Table 1.1 provides a summary of related works in the field of DTC.

Prior research in DTC has made notable strides across a vast array of fields, including manufacturing, healthcare, smart cities, and energy systems. The research has made headway in modeling, real-time integration, and simulation, alongside challenges in scalability, interoperability, and data security. This paper extends existing work to expand our understanding of the evolving space of DTC and offers suggestions related to new avenues for research and applications.

1.3 Background and conceptual foundations

The advent of the IoT, data explosion via exponential analytics cloud computing, and the evolution of ML technologies during the 2010s drove the idea of Digital Twins into practice. Major industries such as General Electric demonstrated the practical use of digital twins in managing and optimizing jet engines and powerplants. These uses achieved significant advances in predictive maintenance, cost reduction, and system resilience. Over the past few years, the development has progressed even further from standalone, asset-level digital twins

Table 1.1 Summary of related work on digital twin computing.

Reference	Focus area	Key contribution	Application domain
(Mishra and Tyagi, 2019)	Foundational concept	Introduced the foundational concept of the Digital Twin in the field of manufacturing excellence	Manufacturing
(Fuller et al., 2020)	Enabling technologies	Identified challenges and open research possibilities in Digital Twin development	Cross-domain
(Barricelli et al., 2019)	Survey study	Reviewed definitions, characteristics, and implications for the design of Digital Twins	Cross-domain
(Rasheed et al., 2020)	Modeling perspective	Discussed modeling challenges, including the value propositions of Digital Twins	Industrial systems
(Boschert and Rosen, 2016)	Simulation aspect	Explored the role of simulation in Digital Twin constructs	Mechatronics
(Bruynseels et al., 2018)	Healthcare ethics	Addressed some ethical considerations of digital twins in personalized health	Healthcare
(Corral-Acero et al., 2020)	Precision cardiology	Presented applications of digital twins in personalized cardiac health	Healthcare
(Wang et al., 2023)	Smart cities	Examined the practical challenges of using Digital Twins for urban management	Smart cities
(Lin et al., 2024)	Urban digital twins	Discussed opportunities for using digital twins in city planning, analytics, and environmental monitoring	Urban development
(Glaessgen and Stargel, 2012)	Aerospace applications	Proposed applying digital twins for mission assurance and system monitoring	Aerospace
(Tan and Li, 2024)	Energy management	Used digital twins to understand energy consumption and optimize smart cities	Smart grids
(Do Amaral et al., 2023)	Energy systems	Reviewed ideas and applications of digital twins for sustainable energy systems	Energy
(Rosen et al., 2015)	Autonomy in manufacturing	Emphasized the potential of digital twins and autonomy in future smart factories	Manufacturing
(Wang et al., 2022)	Key technologies	Summarized technological challenges and future research directions	Cross-domain
(Kritzinger et al., 2018)	Literature classification	Provided an organized review and typology of the research on digital twins	Manufacturing

to more sophisticated DTC ecosystems. In these systems, several digital twins communicate, exchange data, and simultaneously simulate large, interdependent systems like entire production lines, hospital networks, or smart city infrastructures. The evolution from passive digital echoes to dynamic computational environments heralds the entry of a new paradigm in which digital models are not merely descriptive but prescriptive and self-directed (Boje et al., 2020).

A good grasp of the evolution from simple digital models to sophisticated DTC systems calls for a study of several key conceptual differences. First, digital models were frequently reduced to static models, updated manually from intermittent observations or past data. Such models, though valuable for planning and design, were not responsive in real time. The second phase of this evolution came in the form of digital shadows, where modifications taking place in a physical object were naturally reflected in its digital counterpart. However, the information flow within digital shadows was only one way; while the digital model could update the physical state, it had no capability to command or drive the physical system. The actual coming of age of digital twin functionality occurred when two-way communication became possible. In a complete digital twin, physical world changes automatically replicate in the virtual equivalent, and operations or analysis on the digital twin can trigger real-world change. DTC is essentially based on this concept of fluid, dynamic synchronization between the physical and digital worlds. Supporting this interaction is the concept of virtual-physical convergence. DTC relies on the real-time, continuous integration of real-world data with virtual simulations. Continuous monitoring, predictive analytics, optimization of operations, and autonomous corrective actions in some instances can be achieved through this integration (Borangiu et al., 2019).

In addition, DTC inherits and broadens the underlying principles of Cyber-Physical Systems (CPS). CPS is used to denote the close integration between computational algorithms and physical processes, where embedded computers observe and regulate physical processes with feedback. DTC broadens this concept to not only connect digital and physical objects but also to allow networks of digital twins to cooperate, learn together, and coevolve with their physical analogues. Whereas CPS set the foundation for smart physical systems, DTC expands such capabilities to an extended, intricate ecosystem level. The achievement of DTC has been driven by the synergy of several seminal technological advancements. First and foremost among these is the IoT, which serves as the sensory system of DTC. Through the integration of sensors, actuators, and connectivity into physical products, IoT makes it possible to continuously gather real-time information about an asset's status, environment, and behavior. This information is the source of life for digital twins, making their virtual counterparts accurate and responsive. AI and ML provide the analytical and cognitive functions needed by DTC. ML software can detect patterns, forecast failures, optimize processes, and even suggest repairs based on historical and real-time data streams. Predictive maintenance models, for instance, analyze equipment operating history to predict when components will fail and allow interventions in advance to minimize downtime and cost Reinforcement learning, on the other hand, has proven to be a highly effective tool in DTC, allowing digital twins to learn through self-discovery of different operating strategies and converge to optimal solutions over time.

Its storage, processing, and scalability demands are addressed by the combined use of cloud computing, edge computing, and fog computing frameworks. Cloud computing provides immense, elastic capacity for big data storage and high-performance analytics and is well-suited for the hosting of large digital twin networks and the execution of advanced simulations. Edge computing, conversely, brings computation to the edge of the network near the sources of information, thereby reducing latency and enabling real-time responses that are critical for applications such as autonomous cars or medical monitoring devices. Fog computing offers a middle layer between cloud and edge that provides a distributed computing paradigm balancing speed, efficiency, and scalability, particularly in high-complexity industrial environments. Along with RPA, Big Data Analytics is one of the cornerstone technologies supporting DTC. This is mainly because of the volume or velocity at which data comes from IoT devices and operational systems, where normal data processing is insufficient. Hadoop and its successor, Spark, are analytic engines with the capability to ingest data in real time, store it, and process it so that it can be used for analysis, provided the volume is very large (Brenner and Hummel, 2017).

These technologies assist DTC systems in extracting pertinent information from streams of heterogeneous data, detecting anomalies, improving system performance, and forecasting upcoming trends. Modeling and simulation technologies also accompany DTC. Computational environments such as MATLAB, ANSYS, and Simulink, along with physics-based and data-based models specifically designed, offer support for detailed mechanical systems simulations, biological phenomena simulations, thermal systems simulations, fluid flows, and complex human behavior modeling. Increasingly, hybrid modeling approaches combining first-principles physical modeling and data-driven ML techniques are being adopted. Such approaches enhance the accuracy, adaptability, and predictability of digital twins for a wide range of applications. The combination of these enabling technologies has transformed the Digital Twin from a fixed notion into a living, knowledge-based computational construct. Contemporary DTC systems can fully automate real-world operation monitoring, diagnosis, prediction, and optimization at levels of complexity and scope previously unseen. As these technologies improve, the range of capabilities within DTC is set to grow even further, unlocking new areas of science, industry, medicine, urban development, and more (Cai et al., 2017).

1.4 Proposed conceptual architecture and components of digital twin computing

A DTC architecture is a highly complex amalgam of physical systems, data acquisition tools (sensors), computational models, and feedback control. Essentially, a DTC ecosystem perpetuates the constant, dynamic, bidirectional flow of information flow between physical and virtual domains. This architecture needs to not only facilitate the real-time mirroring of the physical system but also allow us to predictively simulate, assist in decision-making, take autonomous actions, and update our virtual models based on that analysis. This is typically represented in the architectural design as being multilayered, starting with the physical layer, which represents a real-world asset, system, or environment that requires mirroring. In this regard, it ties directly to the sensing and actuation pipeline, which collects data relevant for operational decisions. Above this sits the data management layer, which is responsible for ingesting, preprocessing, storing, and performing quality assurance (QA) on massive, continuous streams of information at scale. On top of this data layer is the modeling and simulation tier, which consists of computational models that embody the behaviors, states, and dynamics of a given physical system. Some of these models are purely mathematical and data-driven, based on empirical observations; others are physical (first-principle) models or hybrids (publication pending). Above this is the analytics and decision-making layer, driven by AI and ML, to interpret data, identify patterns, predict outcomes, and recommend or initiate actions. The third and final level is the application and interaction layer, where human users or automated systems interact with the digital twin. Stakeholders engage with user interfaces, visualization dashboards, or automated API integrations to assess performance, receive alerts for failures, and identify potential efficiency improvements through the platform's predictive models. They can also validate projected trajectories of key metrics over time periods based on configurable prediction scenarios and trends at play. Crucially, this underpinning architecture is capable of bi-directional command proxying, enabling a digital twin not only to reflect reality but also to directly act on it by issuing commands in order to carry out actions in the real world—thus closing an operational loop.

The physical layer comprises the basics of a DTC system, which includes physical assets like engines, cars, medical equipment, buildings, or even cities; biological systems like the human body; or environmental systems like forests and oceans. The nature and complexity of the physical object have a significant impact on the design of its digital twin, dictating parameters such as the level of sensing accuracy, model complexity, and computational needs. Sensing and data acquisition are crucial to ensuring that the physical system is accurately and timely represented. Contemporary DTC exploits a broad range of sensors, such as temperature sensors, accelerometers, gyroscopes, Global Positioning System (GPS) units, Radio-Frequency Identification (RFID) tags, optical cameras, Light Detection and Ranging (LiDAR) systems, and biosensors, among others. Besides real-time sensing, information can also be obtained from historical data, maintenance logs, social media streams, environmental databases, or third-party data providers. The fidelity and completeness of sensing are key to the performance of the digital twin, as noisy or missing data can critically degrade model accuracy and predictive ability.

The virtual representation, or the virtual equivalent of the physical object, is built by integrating a mixture of simulation models, ML techniques, and real-time data fusion. Physics-based modeling methods, including finite element analysis, computational fluid dynamics, and multibody system simulations, provide high-fidelity views of system behaviors governed by physical laws. Parallel to this, ML models offer flexibility and predictive capabilities, particularly in areas where physical phenomena are too intricate to model accurately using equations alone. Regression analysis, neural networks, decision trees, support vector machines, and reinforcement learning are commonly applied to enhance the intelligence of digital twins. Storage and processing facilities for data are the backbone of the real-time functioning of DTC. Due to the massive amount of data being created in real time, scalable and fault-tolerant storage technologies like distributed cloud databases, data lakes, and edge storage nodes are utilized. Processing engines need to handle both batch and streaming data to support historical analysis and real-time monitoring, respectively. Emerging technologies like in-memory computing, real-time event processing, and container orchestration through platforms like Kubernetes are increasingly incorporated into DTC architectures.

Analytics engines are the intelligence core of DTC, which integrate diagnostic, predictive, and prescriptive analytics. Diagnostic analytics focus on establishing the root causes of anomalies, predictive analytics forecast future actions and activities, and prescriptive analytics prescribe or automatically apply measures to ensure maximum performance. ML models are constantly retrained with fresh data so that the twin continues to be a dynamic, self-optimizing entity and not a fixed image. The communication infrastructure supports robust and secure data exchange between the physical system, digital twin, and end-users. Low-latency, high-reliability machine-to-machine communication protocols like Message Queue Telemetry Transport (MQTT), Constrained Application Protocol (CoAP), and Data Distribution Service (DDS) are widely employed in DTC environments. Emerging 5G and 6G networks further enhance the capability for ultra-reliable low-latency communications, enabling new applications like real-time digital twins for autonomous vehicles or telesurgery. Finally, the user interaction and visualization layer transforms the complex data environment of the digital twin into actionable, intuitive insights for human operators. Advanced visualization techniques, such as 3D modeling, virtual reality (VR), and augmented reality (AR), allow users to interact with digital twin environments to gain insights into system status, operational risks, and optimization potential. Human-centric interface design is essential to enable stakeholders with varying degrees of experience to interact with, comprehend, and use the digital twin effectively.

In DTC, synchronization of data streams between components is critical for providing timely, consistent, and meaningful operation. Data flow generally begins in the physical layer, where raw observations are generated by sensors. The raw streams of data are communicated through communication networks to preprocessing units, where initial filtering, normalization, aggregation, and error correction are applied. Preprocessed data are then input into the modeling and analytics layers, where they are utilized to update the digital twin's state, re-calibrate predictive models, and initiate alerts or optimization routines. Data flows can be set up in real-time, near real-time, or batch modes based on application needs. Real-time applications, like self-driving vehicle control or remote surgery, require millisecond-level or submillisecond latencies, which necessitate edge computing. Other use cases, like fleet tracking or farm monitoring, can handle minute-level or hour-level updates, allowing

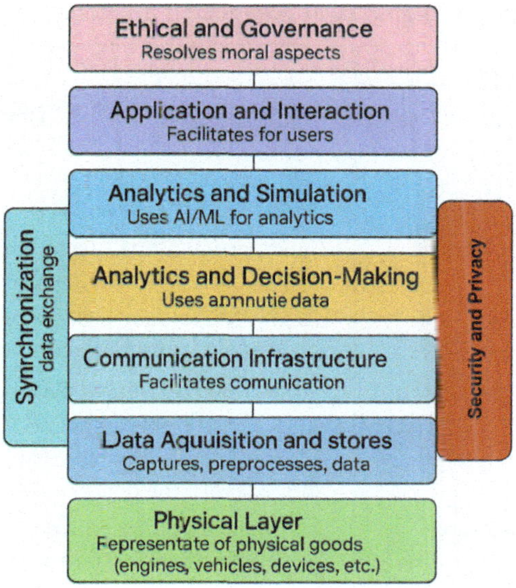

Fig. 1.2 Proposed DTC architecture.

for greater reliance on centralized cloud computing. Fig. 1.2 illustrates the proposed architecture of DTC along with its various components.

Bi-directional communication flows are also crucial. Decisions or actions created within the digital twin need to be fed back to the physical system so that they can be implemented. Reliable command channels are required to ensure the integrity, authenticity, and nonrepudiation of control messages. Blockchain technology is under investigation to make these feedback loops more reliable, particularly in high-risk sectors like energy and healthcare. Communication models also need to address scalability and resilience. As DTC shifts to systems-of-systems, in which there are thousands or millions of twins that communicate with one another, the old-fashioned centralized communication models do not suffice. Distributed messaging systems, peer-to-peer networks, and mesh communication architectures are being touted as solutions to the scalability problem. Fault tolerance is another major concern. DTC needs to be immune to network interruptions, data loss, sensor failures, and cyberattacks. Redundant communication channels, failover mechanisms, data replication policies, and end-to-end encryption are all key components of a secure DTC communication infrastructure. Table 1.2 provides a summary of the proposed DTC architecture and its various components.

The growing deployment of DTC in critical infrastructures requires utmost attention to security and privacy issues. The sensitivity of real-time operational information and the capacity of digital twins to drive physical-world effects create opportunities for attackers, making DTC systems tempting targets. Data protection controls should include data encryption at rest and

Table 1.2 Summary of digital twin computing architecture and components.

Layer/component	Description
Physical layer	Represents physical goods such as engines, vehicles, medical devices, cities, and biological or ecological systems
Data acquisition and management layer	Captures, preprocesses, stores, and performs quality-checks on live data streams
Modeling and simulation layer	Builds virtual models using a combination of real-time data and simulations of AI models
Analytics and decision-making layer	Uses AI/ML to deliver prescriptive, predictive, and diagnostic analytics for decision-making and self-execution
Communication infrastructure	Facilitates secure, reliable, low-latency communication between physical and virtual systems
Application and interaction layer	Interfaces for human users and automated systems to interact with the digital twin through dashboards and APIs
Synchronization and feedback	Manages bidirectional real-time data exchange and command-sending between virtual and physical systems
Security and privacy	Maintains data integrity, confidentiality, and regulatory compliance
Ethical and governance layer	Resolves moral aspects of autonomy and AI decision-making in DTC systems

in transit, authenticated protection mechanisms for all devices and users, and sound access control policies that support the principle of least privilege. Ongoing intrusion, anomaly, and vulnerability monitoring must be implemented to detect and respond to evolving threats in a timely and effective manner. Privacy concerns are particularly relevant in domains such as healthcare, where patient digital twins contain individual medical data. Compliance with the Health Insurance Portability and Accountability Act and the General Data Protection Regulation is highly required to be achieved. Differential privacy, federated learning, and anonymization are some of the suggested methods that can be used to safeguard sensitive data while still allowing meaningful insights to be derived from digital twin systems. Lastly, the moral implications of digital twin autonomy, bias in predictive algorithms, and the impacts on human life from twin-driven decision-making need to be addressed upfront. Ethical frameworks, transparency mandates, and human-in-the-loop governance paradigms need to be in place to ensure that DTC emerges as a positive and reliable technology.

1.4.1 Key characteristics and features of DTC

DTC is an advanced technology compared to conventional simulation models and fixed digital representations in terms of its distinct combination of defining features and attributes. All these features, when combined, facilitate dynamic interaction between the virtual and physical realms, allowing for real-time monitoring, predictive analysis, and self-governing decision-making. It is crucial to comprehend these features to fully understand the revolutionary potential of DTC in various industrial, scientific, and societal domains. One of the core features of DTC is the synchronization between the physical entity and its digital representation in real time. In contrast to traditional models run in separate simulation environments, digital twins are dynamically updated with current data from the physical world. This real-time coupling enables the digital twin to replicate the up-to-date state of the asset, system, or environment with high accuracy, thereby enabling real-time diagnostics, performance measurement, and event detection. Sustaining such ongoing synchronization requires robust sensing technologies, fast communication infrastructures, and significant data processing capabilities (Cheng et al., 2020).

A second essential characteristic is the two-way interaction between the physical and cyber realms. In DTC, the information flow is not one way; the digital twin does not simply sit and receive information but can also send commands, suggestions, and autonomous actions in return to the physical object. The ability to provide feedback allows the digital twin to not just observe but actually control operations, refine processes, and act in real time. Such two-way interaction is important in applications ranging from industrial automation and grid management to autonomous transport and telemedicine. Through the use of advanced modeling techniques, ML programs, and historical datasets, digital twins have the ability to predict the future state of the physical system under various conditions, and this predictive analysis and simulation capability further define DTC. This predictive feature allows stakeholders to examine possible risks, predict maintenance needs, optimize resource usage, and improve overall decision-making. For instance, a jet engine that is able to predict the failures of its components at the earliest can minimize downtime and maximize operational efficiency. Predictive modeling added to digital twins transforms them into forward-looking instruments beyond the scope of descriptive analytics (Cimino et al., 2019). Fig. 1.3 provides a visual presentation of the key features and attributes of DTC.

Autonomous behavior is a new capability becoming more prevalent with advanced DTC systems. With the use of AI and reinforcement learning, digital twins are shifting away from advisory software to autonomous agents that can independently make decisions. In mission-critical applications such as autonomous mobility or personalized medicine, digital twins are able to adjust system parameters in real time, determine optimal routes, or prescribe optimized treatments without ongoing human oversight. This transition to autonomy offers new promise but also requires strong protection, ethical operation, and human-in-the-loop features to enable safe deployment. Scalability and interoperability are key features that allow DTC to function across complex, highly interconnected ecosystems. Contemporary applications increasingly involve not one twin but constellations of digital twins within systems-of-systems. For example, in a smart city scenario, individual digital twins of buildings, transportation, utilities, and citizens must interact with one another seamlessly to enable city-wide optimization. Such integration at the system level is

Fig. 1.3 Key features of DTC.

facilitated by adhering to common data formats, communication protocols, and semantic models so that digital twins from various vendors and domains can seamlessly interact with each other. Scalability is also important to ensure that the digital twin architecture can accommodate growth in data volumes, device counts, and system complexity over time. Adaptivity and self-learning are two defining characteristics of DTC, similar to but distinct from rigid digital models. Digital twins must adapt in response to the same issues facing physical systems, such as operational shifts, degradation, and weather impacts. Digital twins leverage ML approaches that allow them to refresh their forecasting models, reset parameters as needed, and improve their simulations based on observations from previous iterations. This self-evolving ability keeps digital twins relevant and valid during their operational lifetime, ultimately providing a higher degree of trust and usefulness. Resilience and security are two intrinsic characteristics that must be included in DTC frameworks. Digital twins are vulnerable to being targeted by cyber-attacks, as they are essentially tied to critical physical systems. Security measures must include standard features such as end-to-end encryption, authentication, anomaly detection, and secure updates to protect the integrity and confidentiality of a digital twin's operations. With DTC, security needs to extend to fault tolerance, network obstacles, and attack incursions by malicious actors, which must be designed into the system with the intention of maintaining operations under worst-case scenarios.

Transparency and explainability increasingly reflect important considerations, especially as digital twins take on more autonomous and decision-making roles. There must be an understanding of how decisions or recommendations are made by a digital twin, as stakeholders must understand why a twin makes a recommendation or takes an action. Transparency is especially important in regulated environments such as healthcare, finance, and aerospace. Explainable AI (XAI), model visualization, and traceability mechanisms can increase the transparency of DTC systems, which will build trust and facilitate compliance. Personalization is another specific feature used in domains like healthcare, education, consumer services, etc. Digital twins designed for individual users can offer personalized recommendations, adaptive or personalized services, and individualized interventions. For example, a patient-specific digital twin can model a disease's trajectory based on genetic information, lifestyle factors, and treatment response, allowing for hyperpersonalized medical treatment. However, personalization involves more complex integration of data, user modeling, and privacy-preserving analytics in order to maintain efficacy and responsibility (Greif et al., 2020).

Another notable feature is support for multifidelity and multiscale modeling. Many DTC systems need to represent complex systems in various degrees of detail and abstraction. For example, in the aerospace sector, an aircraft digital twin would model the system simultaneously, looking at the level of components (engines, wings, avionics) as well as the level of systems-of-systems (aircraft behavior in an air traffic network). Multifidelity modeling contributes to the efficiency of simulations by allowing for dynamic fidelity changes depending on the application context, resources available, or user preferences, ensuring digital twins align with the purpose of the digital twin. Immersive interaction is the next capability expected to be included in DTC environments, associated with recent technological developments in visualization. Through AR, VR, and mixed reality (MR) platforms, individuals can interact with digital twin systems more intuitively and immersively than before. An engineer can walk completely around a virtual twin of a machine, a surgeon can perform an interactive rehearsal of carrying out complex operations using a patient-specific digital model, and a city planner can interact with 3D simulations of urban development scenarios. Immersive interaction signifies a shift toward increasing situational awareness, collaborative decision-making, and user engagement. Lifecycle management is a key and overarching aspect of DTC. Digital twins are not simply snapshots but rather dynamic entities that evolve with their physical counterparts throughout the entire lifecycle of their existence (i.e., design, manufacture, sustain, maintain, and retire). A well-designed digital twin will far surpass data point snapshots and capture historical information spanning the cycle of usage (e.g., dates of use, operational context or states, maintenance actions, upgrades, etc.), helping to develop a digital history that will inform future design, optimize operational performance, or enhance knowledge transfer (Haag and Anderl, 2018). Table 1.3 provides key features and attributes of DTC.

Table 1.3 Key features and attributes of digital twin computing.

Feature	Description
Real-time synchronization	Real-time streaming data ensures continuous and fluid updates between physical models and digital twins for the real-time and efficient monitoring and diagnostics of the digital twins
Two-way interaction	The level of two-way communication allows digital twins not only to receive information but also to send commands and make autonomous choices
Predictive analysis	Capabilities to encourage simulation and forecasting of impending states enable better risk prediction in advance of failures, allow maintenance to be scheduled at optimal times, and enhance overall performance levels
Autonomous behavior	Digital twins can be delivered in an autonomous operation mode using AI and reinforcement learning for rational decision-making, optimizing time, and eliminating the need for human oversight
Scalability and interoperability	Digital twins have the capacity to work simultaneously in an interconnected system with recognized, standardized approaches to data formats and data protocols, while effectively enhancing growth through the use of models, concurrently increasing both complexity and data
Adaptivity and self-learning	Updates implemented by machine learning allow for reasonable assurance that digital twins will adapt to operational changes as their number of observations changes, ultimately maintaining accuracy and contemporary relevance
Resilience and security	Our systems address cybersecurity risks even when operating over the internet or on a remote operations or cloud-based platform by encompassing reliable safeguard protocols, including encryption, authentication dependencies, anomaly detection, and fault-tolerance system assessments
Transparency and explainability	Utilization of XAI mechanisms and/or XAI visualizations provides the required transparency so that any principal decision-makers understand the basis of the decisions and actions taken regarding the twin and the level of assumptions made
Personalization	Provide customized digital twins tailored to individuals, enabling personalized service offerings, recommendations, actions, and interventions, all while maintaining acceptable privacy levels
Multifidelity and multiscale modeling	Different levels of representation can convey the most detailed complexity versus simpler abstraction for enhanced simulation process effectiveness
Immersive interaction	With access to AR, VR, and MR as necessary or relevant, interactions allow for enhanced intuitive experiences with acceptable interactions around the digital twins, improving the level of situational awareness
Lifecycle management	Current tracking and the initiation of a digital history from the physical system allow the ongoing tracking and evolution of the digital twin throughout the full lifecycle of the physical system

1.5 Application and use cases of DTC

The real-world uses of DTC have accelerated in almost all sectors, distinctly changing the way we design operations, models of service, and how we approach innovation. DTC is leading the drivers of efficiency, personalization, resilience, and sustainability in sectors as varied as energy, transport, healthcare, and smart city development, bringing with it an approach truly beyond what is possible with mere concepts of design.

In manufacturing, DTC has emerged as a central part of the Industry 4.0 revolution. With digital twins of machines, production lines, and factories being prepared, manufacturers are able to access real-time data on parameters, predictive maintenance, and adaptive production, while simultaneously simulating their workflows and machine behavior in real-time. This allows them to anticipate faults before they cause expensive breakdowns, adapt schedules to changing shifts in the market, and better manage their energy consumption. Digital twins extend not only to the shop floor of factories but also to products and their lifecycles, with the ability to model product behavior based on multiple uses. This enables manufacturers to adjust their designs, test scenarios, and offer better after-sales service (Lee et al., 2015). Overall, this results in manufacturing processes being intrinsically linked in such a way that the outcome is much more resilient, adaptable, and customized systems. In healthcare, DTC is creating new horizons for personalized medicine, clinical decision support, and operational optimization. Patient-specific digital twins, built from medical imaging, genetics, electronic health records, and real-time biometric monitoring, enable clinicians to model disease progression, forecast treatment outcomes, and tailor therapeutic interventions. For example, a digital twin of a patient's cardiovascular system can model the impact of various surgical approaches, allowing surgeons to choose the most suitable tactic with reduced risk. In hospital operations, digital twins of healthcare facilities streamline patient flow, resource utilization, and emergency response plans, thereby improving the quality of care while eliminating operational bottlenecks. In addition, digital twins enable remote monitoring and telemedicine through virtual models that bridge the gap between healthcare professionals and patients.

The energy sector is undergoing a dramatic transformation with the influence of DTC. In renewable energy facilities such as wind farms and solar panels, digital twins monitor turbine and panel performance in real time, forecast maintenance needs, and maximize energy production based on weather conditions. In grid operations, digital twins allow grid operators to replicate load-balancing scenarios, identify anomalies, and control distributed energy resources like microgrids and batteries. Real-time analysis and predictive optimization features significantly enhance grid resilience, lower carbon footprints, and facilitate the integration of intermittent renewable power sources into the baseline power supply. At scale, digital twins of entire energy systems are now becoming the centerpiece of planning for smart energy transitions, predicting demand, and optimizing sustainable energy infrastructures.

Smart cities are another area in which DTC is making significant inroads. City digital twins combine data from diverse sources, including traffic sensors, weather stations, surveillance networks, and devices operated by citizens, with the aim of building a dynamic, holistic image of city functions. Digital twins are used by city planners to simulate patterns of urban growth, analyze the resilience of infrastructure, optimize public transport networks, and facilitate emergency response planning. For instance, in the case of natural disasters, a city's digital twin may provide real-time situational awareness, simulate evacuation paths, and predict infrastructure vulnerabilities, enabling authorities to respond proactively and save lives. Furthermore, digital twins facilitate citizen-oriented services by enabling participatory city planning, mobility adapted to individuals, and context-based public services, making cities more habitable, inclusive, and sustainable (Macchi et al., 2018).

In the transportation industry, DTC is transforming vehicle design, maintenance, and operation. Automotive manufacturers employ digital twins to test vehicle performance across different environmental and operating conditions virtually, making it easier to prototype and minimizing dependency on expensive physical testing. In aviation, aircraft engine digital twins monitor wear and tear, predict component failure, and plan the most efficient maintenance, thereby enhancing safety, reducing operating costs, and prolonging asset life. For railways, digital twins of tracks, signaling systems, and rolling stock support real-time infrastructure management and predictive maintenance. In addition, the development of autonomous vehicles depends largely on digital twin simulations to test navigation algorithms, sensor integrations, and traffic behavior models prior to real-world deployment, thereby ensuring safety and robustness. The construction and real estate industries are maximizing their gains through DTC. Building Information Modeling has developed into full digital twin applications that now stretch through the operational lifecycle of buildings and beyond design and construction. Smart buildings with digital twins optimize energy use, enhance occupant comfort, enable predictive maintenance on essential assets (e.g., Heating, Ventilation, and Air Conditioning (HVAC) systems and elevators), and help with regulatory compliance. In the case of large construction projects, digital twins allow construction sequences to be simulated, which are then used to anticipate and modify possible delays and optimize resource stewardship, thus reducing risks and costs in the project. In the real estate space, digital twins provide clients with virtual property tours, dynamic occupancy management, and offer facility management strategies based on analytics that maximize sustainability goals (Panetto et al., 2019).

The defense and aerospace sectors have long been early adopters of digital twin concepts, and their engagement with DTC is expanding. Military organizations utilize digital twins of weapons systems, vehicles, and even entire operational battlefields to simulate scenarios, train personnel, and improve mission planning. Digital twins are also being applied to space exploration in the form of digital twins of spacecraft, satellites, and planetary environments to help design missions, detect anomalies, and provide autonomous decision options during missions. For long-duration missions like the Mars Rovers and the International Space Station, digital twins have been invaluable in dealing with lessons learned and responding to unforeseen incidents, allowing engineers to simulate potential solutions from Earth. As more and more studies in environmental management utilize DTC, it is becoming clear that DTC has the potential to significantly change our management of ecosystems, our management of natural resources, and how we respond to the effects of climate change. Digital twins of forests, river basins, and coastal management areas rely on satellite imagery and remote sensing, sensor/spatial data, and simulation models to facilitate monitoring of biodiversity, predicting shifts in the environment, and planning for conservation efforts. Climate scientists use digital twins and coupled computer models to build representations of the complex interactions between meteorological elements driving the Earth's climate system, increasing the accuracy of climate projections and decreasing the risk of influences beyond our control. Furthermore, digital twins can be applied to agriculture. Digital twins specifically designed for a farm produce recommendations for irrigation scheduling, fertilizer application, plant selection, and other management decisions supported by real-time sensor, soil, weather, and market data to increase yield, minimize resource use, and better incorporate sustainable management practices.

Financial services organizations are also starting to explore the possibilities of bringing DTC to life. For example, many institutions have begun to develop digital twins of portfolios, markets, and customer profiles to better model market interactions, examine systemic risks, and customize financial products. In education and training, DTC is changing how pedagogy is employed, as it provides learners with an immersive, interactive learning environment. Digital twins of laboratories, machinery, and ecosystems allow students to carry out virtual experiments, develop skills, and map the interactions of complex systems in a risk-free and cost-free learning environment. DTC can also be extremely useful in developing professional training for high-risk situations, such as flight simulation for pilots, surgical training for surgeons, emergency response team training, and engineering training. The benefit of using DTC for professional training is that it minimizes risk, maximizes preparedness, and reduces the time it takes for individuals to gain competency (Platenius-Mohr et al., 2020).

As more universities and companies adopt both remote and hybrid approaches to learning, the value of using digital twins to provide high-fidelity experiential learning will only grow. DTC is another exciting area that has the potential to innovate entertainment and gaming experiences. Game creators are using digital twins of real-world environments to create exciting, hyperrealistic gaming experiences, while the cinema and film industries are using digital twins of actors, sets, and objects to assist in virtual production workflows. Entertainment and sports events are using digital twins to facilitate engaged virtual audiences, create performance simulations, and enable real-time interaction between fans and performers across both physical and digital environments. Ultimately, with DTC being integrated with AR, VR, and metaverses, it defines the future of storytelling, entertainment, and social engagement.

1.6 Challenges, limitations and research opportunities in DTC

Even though DTC can transform the industry as a whole, it will face significant challenges and limitations to large-scale adoption. Below, we outline the significant challenges and limitations, which range from technical, data management, ethical, and organizational challenges that present interesting research opportunities and will shape the next generation of digital twin systems.

1.6.1 Technical challenges

Among the major hurdles of DTC is the accurate representation of complex, dynamic, and often nonlinear physical systems. Creating a digital twin that properly replicates the physical system's behavior relies upon the establishment of very high-fidelity models, sophisticated simulations, and a rich contextual domain knowledge of the phenomena involved. The complexity increases exponentially when we expand from individual assets to systems of systems, such as integrating an entire manufacturing ecosystem or sets of interconnected urban infrastructure. In addition, the requirement for real-time synchronization with the physical world is a significant challenge. Delays in data acquisition, communication, processing, and actuation can render synchronizing the states of the twins unproductive if they become stale or incorrect, especially in mission-critical operations. Achieving ultra-low latencies while maintaining acceptable system robustness will require further advances in edge computing, 5G/6G networking, and distributed AI. Interoperability is also a technical hurdle. In heterogeneous ecosystems, digital twins must retrieve data and processes from multiple sources, formats, and standards. Continuing collaborative research on universally accepted protocols and ontologies for data transfer, model representation, and process orchestration is still required before practical implementations can emerge.

1.6.2 Data management complexities

DTC systems process and can produce massive amounts of data, which makes data accuracy, data integration, data governance, data lifecycle management, and more a daunting challenge. Data inconsistency, inaccuracies, and missing values can significantly degrade the performance of twins. Real-world systems operate in environments where many factors of normal corruption and uncertainty, such as sensor failure, network interruptions, and human error (due to manual entry), occur. However, big data, when handled well, involves enhanced data cleansing and data fusion, accompanied by metadata management and real-time processing analytics. Figuring out which data to keep, aggregate, or delete over time (while not losing some of the historical data) adds to the complexity of correctly representing the digital twin. Because many industry sectors, such as healthcare, aerospace, and finance, are highly regulated, tracking or tracing the lineage of data over the life of the digital twin is paramount. A further step is the possible use of automated ways to assure data quality, such as using blockchain technologies to track data, and, most recently, applications of intelligent summarization in data systems where rapid summary characterizations are needed.

1.6.3 Model fidelity and scalability

While the early applications of digital twins usually involve an individual component or subsystem, larger systems introduce a myriad of challenges related to model fidelity and computational efficiency. This is especially true for models that are high fidelity; for instance, physics-based interactions and models that encompass interactions between multidomains tend to be expensive from a computational perspective. Therefore, the key design challenge is managing the trade-off between model accuracy and computational tractability, and there are new approaches involving surrogate modeling, reduced-order modeling, and multiresolution modeling attempting to address this challenge. Still, these approaches are not developed enough for use in a significant number of complex contexts. Scalability is not just a computational challenge; it is also a challenge of maintaining coherent relationships between interacting twins, their states being updated consistently on all digital twins in a federation, and the potential for compound errors across related hierarchically connected systems. Areas such as hierarchical modeling architectures, federated digital twins, and autonomous model orchestration frameworks have the potential to address these research problems.

1.6.4 Security and privacy issues

There will be security and privacy issues as digital twins are used in critical infrastructure, healthcare, defense, and finance. Unauthorized access to digital twins may lead to the disclosure of sensitive operational data, enable industrial espionage, and permit malicious interference in physical systems. Ensuring appropriate security throughout the entire lifecycle of a digital twin (data collection, communication, data storage, data simulation, and actuation) requires effective encryption technologies, access control, and intrusion detection systems. Unfortunately, conventional cybersecurity methods struggle with the scale, heterogeneity, and real-time needs in DTC environments. Privacy issues are more pronounced in personal digital twins, such as individual health profiles, behaviors, or financial transactions. Protecting personally identifiable information and ensuring compliance with global data protection regulations require privacy-preserving computation methods like differential privacy, federated learning, and homomorphic encryption. Establishing all-purpose security frameworks for digital twin ecosystems that can autonomously selfheal and dynamically detect threats remains a significant research endeavor.

1.6.5 Ethical and societal challenges

Beyond technical and operational issues, DTC raises important ethical and societal questions. The generation of highly detailed digital twin representations of people, communities, and organizations raises questions regarding issues related to surveillance, profiling, and who retains autonomy. Ethical questions include informed consent around the uses of data, the transparency of AI-based decision-making that digital twins perform, the potential for discrimination to be embedded in twin models, and accountability for the actions that autonomous twins initiate. If not well-monitored, the applications of digital twins can amplify social inequities, perpetuate discrimination, or covertly alter behaviors. To address these issues, ethically informed design principles, transparent governance structures, explainable AI models within twins, and participatory approaches need to be developed that include all stakeholders in the digital twin process throughout the entire lifecycle of a digital twin project.

1.6.6 Standardization and regulatory gaps

With no universally accepted definitions for DTC, there is neither interoperability, collaboration, nor trust among stakeholders. Right now, there are proprietary methods in different industries and even within organizations, which result in numerous fragmented and difficult-to-port digital twin solutions. Existing standards are needed for model description languages, data exchange protocols, performance metrics, lifecycle management, and ethics. A few standards organizations, like International Organization for Standardization (ISO), Institute of Electrical and Electronics Engineers (IEEE), and consortiums, are starting to address these gaps, but standards, as a whole or across domains, are very much in the nascent stages. The same can be said of regulatory structures for rights, responsibilities, and liability in the creation and operation of digital twins. Defining legal issues such as ownership of the data, fidelity claims about the model, or blame for damages caused by an error from the twin is key to establishing trust and moving forward with digital twins.

1.6.7 Research opportunities

The issues outlined above also present a number of exciting research opportunities in the area of DTC. When considering real-time simulation tools and techniques, there will be substantial advances from developing and demonstrating closed-loop twin models that draw upon self-consistent physics-based and AI approaches for on-the-fly improvements in twin fidelity. Research into distributed twin architectures, and the capability for future twinning infrastructures to cognitively operate millions of twins in a coherent, decentralized fashion, will be critical if we wish to scale up DTC ecosystems. There is also considerable scope for future research in the exploration of new communication paradigms, such as the tactile internet based on 6G and the quantum internet, which would provide ultra-low latency, high-reliability communication channels that would enable real-time twin synchronization. The potential of quantum computing, if able to scale-up, would considerably advance research focused on large-scale twin simulations. In the direction of security, adaptive autonomous cybersecurity models may see researchers exploring the development of systems that leverage AI to detect, predict, and counteract cyber-attacks autonomously and in real time. Integral to personal and social acceptance will be the extent to which privacy-enhancing technologies are encapsulated within the architecture of the twin rather than as an adjunct to it. Furthermore, we anticipate an increased need for interdisciplinary research that brings together technology, ethics, law, and public policy in order to form holistic digital twin frameworks that are not only technologically sound but also socially responsible. Collaboration between technologists, ethicists, legal scholars, sociologists, and end-users will be critical when shaping responsible futures for DTC.

1.7 Case studies and applications of DTC

DTC is rapidly being recognized for its transformative potential across many industries. Whether it is faster manufacturing and improved health care, smart cities, or changing aerospace, the use of digital twins has great power to provide efficiency, predictiveness, and automation.

1.7.1 General electric and predictive maintenance

General Electric (GE) has led the way in DTC for manufacturing, especially with respect to predictive maintenance. Digital twins allow GE to virtualize turbines, engines, and other industrial equipment. Data is collected in real time from built-in sensors, both embedded and installed in physical assets, and this data is used in predictive models to simulate the wear-and-tear of parts of equipment. The digital twins have given GE the ability to predict failures before they happen, which helps to reduce downtime and prevent costly unplanned maintenance. This is especially important in the aviation sector, where turbine failures create life-or-death consequences. The digital twin approach to predictive maintenance has significantly reduced maintenance spending and improved the longevity of their machinery by identifying specific parts of machinery that require attention, leading to better overall performance in GE's manufacturing business (Siddiqui et al., 2024). Fig. 1.4 illustrates the discussed case study.

1.7.2 Philips and personalized medicine

In the healthcare field, DTC is being used to facilitate the process of personalized medicine to improve patient outcomes. An example of this is Philips Healthcare, which is developing digital twins for individual patients that replicate their medical history, health parameters,

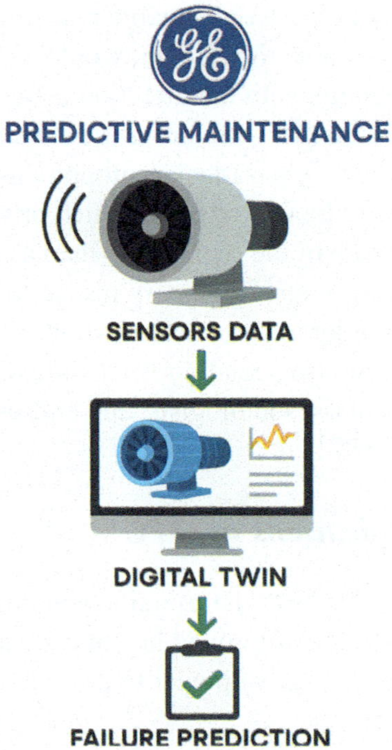

Fig. 1.4 Case study illustration: General electric (GE) and predictive maintenance.

and treatment responses. These digital models enable doctors of the same patient to simulate the effects of a range of treatment plans related to the patient's health and illness, supporting more sensible diagnoses and recommendations for treatment. Digital twins in healthcare can also be used to monitor the condition of a patient in real time, where treatment protocols might change dynamically based on the patient's current state. In the example of cardiac care, we can use digital twins to simulate the effect of drugs, surgical procedures, or lifestyle changes on a patient's heart health, making individual interventions possible depending on patient responses (Heluany and Gkioulos, 2023). Fig. 1.5 illustrates the discussed case study.

1.7.3 Singapore's smart nation initiative

Singapore is a world leader in the provision of smart city technology, and digital twins are included in the Smart Nation initiative. Singapore's GIS program has created an extensive digital twin of its vast urban landscape. Sources of data come from various areas, including traffic management, environmental monitoring, and public safety. The twin model is used to optimize traffic flows, reduce energy consumption, and enrich the overall living experience. For example, real-time traffic sensor data is fed into the digital twin, which simulates traffic

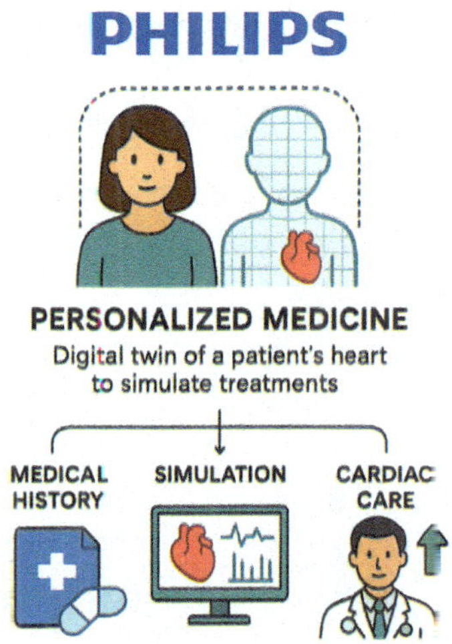

Fig. 1.5 Case study illustration: Phillips and personalized medicine.

patterns and optimizes traffic signals to reduce congestion and improve traffic flow. The digital twin can also be used to monitor air quality, identify the sources of pollution, and use that information to reduce pollution in real-time. Fig. 1.6 illustrates the discussed case study.

1.7.4 NASA and aircraft design

In aerospace, NASA implemented digital twins to design and simulate aircraft systems, or more specifically, flight conditions. By creating a digital replica of aircraft components, NASA engineers can simulate how various components will function when subjected to varied conditions, such as extreme temperatures, high speeds, and turbulence. These simulations make it possible to streamline aircraft design and identify potential structural issues prior to the actual construction of prototypes. Digital twins also facilitate real-time monitoring of aircraft in flight, predictive maintenance, and improved flight safety. Sensors on aircraft send data back to the digital twin, where predictive models evaluate possible wear and damage, enabling maintenance teams to make repairs before a catastrophic failure (Argolini et al., 2023).

1.8 BP and oil rig optimization

In the oil sector, British Petroleum (BP) uses digital twins to maximize efficiency on offshore rigs. With the rigs' digital twins, BP can model the operation of several systems on the rigs, such as drilling machinery, generators, and protection systems. Digital twins receive live data from the rigs, including weather conditions, machine performance, and power consumption,

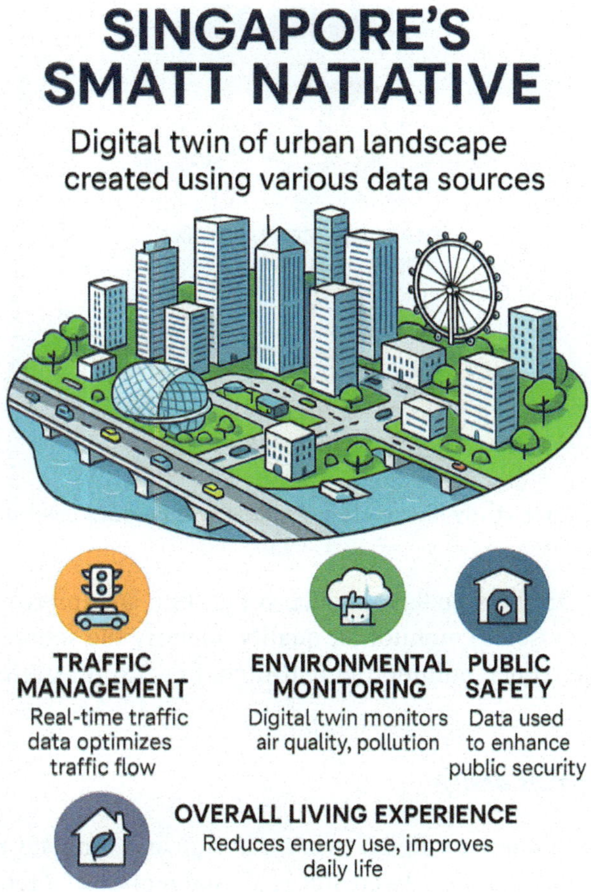

Fig. 1.6 Case study illustration: Singapore smart initiative.

enabling BP to predict faults and optimize processes (Barricelli et al., 2019). For instance, BP employs digital twins to simulate fluid flow in drilling operations, forecast where clogs may occur, and adapt operations to avoid risks. The digital twin also facilitates real-time tracking of energy usage, enabling BP to reduce waste and enhance efficiency throughout its operations.

1.9 Conclusion

DTC offers an innovative way to model, monitor, and optimize physical systems in near real-time using dynamic virtual representations of physical manifestations. While traditional simulations have much in common with DTC, they rely on a system that replicates in time and shifts from synchronous to continuous synchronization with independent yet dependent bidirectional interaction. DTC encompasses predictive intelligence that relies on observations from connected ecosystems derived from IoT, AI, cloud computing, edge computing, big data analytics, and other enabling technologies. The convergence of all these enabling technologies in DTC has brought us from simply a conceptual model toward something much more tangible across a variety of sectors (healthcare, manufacturing, smart cities, energy, aerospace, etc.). This paper defines the conceptual foundations and architecture of DTC, its shared architecture and enabling technologies, and its main application areas while raising the challenges of scale, interoperability, data privacy, and ethical issues. The study demonstrates, through detailed case studies, how DTC is transforming application areas, allowing for predictive maintenance, personalized medicine, intelligent cities and urban planning, and energy management. As DTC matures, it is postulated to become the cornerstone of overall digital transformation, enabling efficiency, resilience, and innovation opportunities that have not yet been fully realized. DTC will also grow with research, identifying the standards and ethical frameworks needed to enable the industry to realize the full potential of the DTC era.

References

Abayadeera, M.R., 2024. Digital twin technology: a comprehensive review. Int. J. Sci. Res. Eng. Trends. 2395-566X. 10 (4), 1485–1504. doi:10.61137/ijsret.vol.10.issue4.199.

Argolini, R., Bonalumi, F., Deichmann, J., Pellegrinelli, S., 2023. Digital Twins: The Key to Smart Product Development. McKinsey & Company.

Barricelli, B.R., Casiraghi, E., Fogli, D., 2019. A survey on digital twin: definitions, characteristics, applications, and design implications. IEEE Access. 2169-3536. 7, 167653–167671. doi:10.1109/access.2019.2953499.

Boje, C., Guerriero, A., Kubicki, S., Rezgui, Y., 2020. Towards a semantic construction digital twin: directions for future research. Autom. Constr. 09265805. 114, 103179. doi:10.1016/j.autcon.2020.103179.

Borangiu, T., Trentesaux, D., Thomas, A., Leitão, P., Barata, J., 2019. Digital transformation of manufacturing through cloud services and resource virtualization. Comput. Ind. 01663615. 108, 150–162. doi:10.1016/j.compind.2019.01.006.

Boschert, S., Rosen, R., 2016. Digital Twin-the Simulation Aspect Mechatronic Futures: Challenges and Solutions for Mechatronic Systems and Their Designers. Springer International Publishing, Germany, pp. 59–74. Available from: http://dx.doi.org/10.1007/978-3-319-32156-1.

Brenner, B., Hummel, V., 2017. Digital twin as enabler for an innovative digital shopfloor management system in the ESB logistics learning factory at Reutlingen—University. Proc. Manuf. 23519789. 9, 198–205. http://www.journals.elsevier.com/procedia-manufacturing. doi:10.1016/j.promfg.2017.04.039.

Bruynseels, K., de Sio, F.S., van den Hoven, J., 2018. Digital twins in health care: ethical implications of an emerging engineering paradigm. Front. Genet. 16648021. 9. Available from: https://www.frontiersin.org/articles/10.3389/fgene.2018.00031/full. doi:10.3389/fgene.2018.00031.

Cai, Y., Starly, B., Cohen, P., Lee, Y.S., 2017. Sensor data and information fusion to construct digital-twins virtual machine tools for cyber-physical manufacturing. Proc. Manuf. 23519789. 10, 1031–1042. http://www.journals.elsevier.com/procedia-manufacturing. doi:10.1016/j.promfg.2017.07.094.

Cheng, J., Zhang, H., Tao, F., Juang, C.-F., 2020. DT-II: digital twin enhanced industrial Internet reference framework towards smart manufacturing. Robot. Comput.-Integr. Manuf. 07365845. 62, 101881. doi:10.1016/j.rcim.2019.101881.

Cimino, C., Negri, E., Fumagalli, L., 2019. Review of digital twin applications in manufacturing. Comput. Ind. 01663615. 113, 103130. doi:10.1016/j.compind.2019.103130.

Corral-Acero, J., Margara, F., Marciniak, M., Rodero, C., Loncaric, F., Feng, Y., Gilbert, A., Fernandes, J.F., Bukhari, H.A., Wajdan, A., Martinez, M.V., Santos, M.S., Shamohammdi, M., Luo, H., Westphal, P., Leeson, P., DiAchille, P., Gurev, V., Mayr, M., Geris, L., Pathmanathan, P., Morrison, T., Cornelussen, R., Prinzen, F., Delhaas, T., Doltra, A., Sitges, M., Vigmond, E.J., Zacur, E., Grau, V., Rodriguez, B., Remme, E.W., Niederer, S., Mortier, P., McLeod, K., Potse, M., Pueyo, E., Bueno-Orovio, A., Lamata, P., 2020. The 'Digital Twin' to enable the vision of precision cardiology. Eur. Heart J. 15229645. 41 (48), 4556–4564. Available from: http://eurheartj.oxfordjournals.org/. doi:10.1093/eurheartj/ehaa159.

Do Amaral, J.V.S., Dos Santos, C.H., Montevechi, J.A.B., de Queiroz, A.R., 2023. Energy digital twin applications: a review. Renew. Sustain. Energy Rev. 13640321. 188, 113891. doi:10.1016/j.rser.2023.113891.

Fuller, A., Fan, Z., Day, C., Barlow, C., 2020. Digital twin: enabling technologies, challenges and open research. IEEE Access. 21693536. 8, 108952–108971. Available from: http://ieeexplore.ieee.org/xpl/RecentIssue.jsp?punumber=6287639. doi:10.1109/ACCESS.2020.2998358.

Glaessgen, E.H., Stargel, D.S., 2012. The digital twin paradigm for future NASA and U.S. air force vehicles. In: 53rd AIAA/ASME/ASCE/AHS/ASC Structures, Structural Dynamics and Materials Conference, United States.

Greif, T., Stein, N., Flath, C.M., 2020. Peeking into the void: digital twins for construction site logistics. Comput. Ind. 01663615. 121, 103264. doi:10.1016/j.compind.2020.103264.

Haag, S., Anderl, R., 2018. Digital twin—proof of concept. Manuf. Lett. 22138463. 15, 64–66. Available from: http://www.journals.elsevier.com/manufacturing-letters/. doi:10.1016/j.mfglet.2018.02.006.

Heluany, J.B., Gkioulos, V., 2023. Survey on digital twins: from concepts to applications. In: ACM International Conference Proceeding Series. Association for Computing Machinery, Norway. 9798400707728. http://portal.acm.org/. doi:10.1145/3600160.3605070.

Kritzinger, W., Karner, M., Traar, G., Henjes, J., Sihn, W., 2018. Digital twin in manufacturing: a categorical literature review and classification. IFAC-PapersOnLine. 24058963. 51 (11), 1016–1022. http://www.journals.elsevier.com/ifac-papersonline/. doi:10.1016/j.ifacol.2018.08.474.

Lee, J., Bagheri, B., Kao, H.A., 2015. A cyber-physical systems architecture for industry 4.0-based manufacturing systems. Manuf. Lett. 22138463. 3, 18–23. Available from: http://www.journals.elsevier.com/manufacturing-letters/. doi:10.1016/j.mfglet.2014.12.001.

Lin, Y., Chen, L., Ali, A., Nugent, C., Cleland, I., Li, R., Ding, J., Ning, H., 2024. Human digital twin: a survey. J. Cloud Comput. 2192113X. 13 (1). Available from: https://journalofcloudcomputing.springeropen.com. doi:10.1186/s13677-024-00691-z.

Macchi, M., Roda, I., Negri, E., Fumagalli, L., 2018. Exploring the role of digital twin for asset lifecycle management. IFAC-PapersOnLine. 24058963. 51 (11), 790–795. http://www.journals.elsevier.com/ifac-papersonline/. doi:10.1016/j.ifacol.2018.08.415.

Mishra, S., Tyagi, A.K., LLC, 2019. Intrusion Detection in Internet of Things (IoTs) Based Applications using Blockchain Technology, 2019 Third International Conference on I-SMAC (IoT in Social, Mobile, Analytics and Cloud) (I-SMAC), pp. 123–128. doi:10.1109/I-SMAC47947.2019.9032557.

Panetto, H., Iung, B., Ivanov, D., Weichhart, G., Wang, X., 2019. Challenges for the cyber-physical manufacturing enterprises of the future. Annu. Rev. Control. 13675788. 47, 200–213. doi:10.1016/j.arcontrol.2019.02.002.

Platenius-Mohr, M., Malakuti, S., Grüner, S., Schmitt, J., Goldschmidt, T., 2020. File- and API-based interoperability of digital twins by model transformation: an IIoT case study using asset administration shell. Future Gener. Comput. Syst. 0167739X. 113, 94–105. Available from: https://www.journals.elsevier.com/future-generation-computer-systems. doi:10.1016/j.future.2020.07.004.

Rasheed, A., San, O., Kvamsdal, T., 2020. Digital twin: values, challenges and enablers from a modeling perspective. IEEE Access. 21693536. 8, 21980–22012. Available from: http://ieeexplore.ieee.org/xpl/RecentIssue.jsp?punumber=6287639. doi:10.1109/ACCESS.2020.2970143.

Rosen, R., Von Wichert, G., Lo, G., Bettenhausen, K.D., 2015. About the importance of autonomy and digital twins for the future of manufacturing. IFAC-PapersOnLine. 24058963. 28 (3), 567–572. http://www.journals.elsevier.com/ifac-papersonline/. doi:10.1016/j.ifacol.2015.06.141.

Semeraro, C., Lezoche, M., Panetto, H., Dassisti, M., 2021. Digital twin paradigm: a systematic literature review. Comput. Ind. 01663615. 130, 103469. doi:10.1016/j.compind.2021.103469.

Sharma, A., Kosasih, E., Zhang, J., Brintrup, A., Calinescu, A., 2022. Digital twins: state of the art theory and practice, challenges, and open research questions. J. Ind. Inf. Integr 2452414X. 30, 100383. doi:10.1016/j.jii.2022.100383.

Siddiqui, E.F., Ahmed, T., Nayak, S.K., 2024. A decision tree approach for enhancing real-time response in exigent healthcare unit using edge computing. Meas. Sensors. 26659174. 32, 100979. doi:10.1016/j.measen.2023.100979.

Tan, Z., Li, Z., 2024. Digital twins for sustainable design and management of smart city buildings and municipal infrastructure. Sustain. Energy Technol. Assess. 22131388. 64, 103682. doi:10.1016/j.seta.2024.103682.

Wang, H., Chen, X., Jia, F., Cheng, X., 2023. Digital twin-supported smart city: status, challenges and future research directions. Expert Syst. Appl. 09574174. 217, 119531. doi:10.1016/j.eswa.2023.119531.

Wang, Y., Kang, X., Chen, Z., 2022. A survey of digital twin techniques in smart manufacturing and management of energy applications. Green Energy Intell. Transp. 27731537. 1 (2), 100014. doi:10.1016/j.geits.2022.100014.

Yao, J.F., Yang, Y., Wang, X.C., Zhang, X.P., 2023. Systematic review of digital twin technology and applications. Vis. Comput. Indust. Biomed. Art. 25244442. 6 (1). Available from: https://www.springer.com/journal/42492. doi:10.1186/s42492-023-00137-4.

CHAPTER 2

Introduction to artificial intelligence and machine learning

Megha Singh
Department of Computer Science and Engineering, Oriental University, Indore, India

2.1 Introduction

Digital Twin Computing (DTC) is transforming sectors by assimilating live information from various sources with sophisticated models to perform simulations, forecasting, as well as decision-making. The primary drivers behind this shift are artificial intelligence (AI) and machine learning (ML), which improve the DT's capabilities through unsupervised learning, real-time adaptive control, and optimization in the physical world. DTs powered by AI apply deep learning (DL), reinforcement learning (RL), and generative learning models to increase the effectiveness of detecting anomalies, system optimization, and predictive maintenance.

Specific ML algorithms, including supervised learning, unsupervised learning, and RL, enable real-time adaptation and selfgenerating DTs. The integration of AI/ML with Internet of Things (IoT) sensors and edge computing technology takes DTs one step further by enabling intelligence at the edge, as well as decreasing latency in agile environments. The edification of blockchain over IoT augments the sense of integrity, security, and transparency within a digital twin (DT) ecosystem, thus giving more trust and confidence to ecosystems powered by DT technologies (DTTs).

This chapter explores the foundational principles of AI and ML in DTC, emphasizing their role in enhancing simulation accuracy, decision intelligence, and automation. Research advancements in federated learning, transfer learning, and explainable AI (XAI) are also discussed, highlighting their potential in real-time cyber-physical system modeling. The discussion extends to industrial applications, future research directions, and challenges in achieving scalable, trustworthy, and ethically aligned DT frameworks.

2.1.1 Defining artificial intelligence and machine learning

AI is a multidisciplinary field of computer science that focuses on developing systems capable of performing tasks that typically require human intelligence, such as reasoning,

Artificial Intelligence, Machine Learning and Blockchain in Digital Twin Computing.
https://doi.org/10.1016/B978-0-443-43914-8.00014-5

learning, perception, and decision-making. AI encompasses various subfields, including expert systems, natural language processing (NLP), robotics, and computer vision, with the goal of creating intelligent agents that can interact with their environment autonomously (Russell and Norvig, 2020). AI can be broadly categorized into narrow AI (task-specific intelligence) and general AI (human-like cognitive abilities), with current advancements primarily focused on narrow AI applications in healthcare, finance, and industrial automation.

ML is a subset of AI that enables systems to learn patterns from data and improve performance without explicit programming. ML algorithms are broadly classified into supervised learning, unsupervised learning, semisupervised learning, and RL (Goodfellow et al., 2016). Supervised learning relies on labeled datasets to train models, while unsupervised learning identifies hidden patterns in unlabeled data. RL, inspired by behavioral psychology, enables agents to learn optimal actions through reward-based feedback mechanisms. The evolution of DL, a subset of ML using artificial neural networks (ANNs), has significantly advanced AI applications, including image recognition, natural language understanding, and predictive analytics (LeCun et al., 2015).

AI and ML are increasingly being integrated with emerging technologies such as blockchain, the IoT, and edge computing to enhance automation, decision-making, and efficiency across various domains. Ongoing research focuses on improving model interpretability, scalability, and ethical considerations in AI-driven systems. As AI and ML continue to evolve, their applications will redefine industries and human-computer interactions, making them indispensable for the future of intelligent computing.

2.1.2 Relationship between AI and ML

AI and ML are closely intertwined fields that have revolutionized computational intelligence and decision-making across various industries. AI is an umbrella term that refers to the development of intelligent agents capable of reasoning, learning, and performing tasks typically requiring human cognitive abilities. ML, a subset of AI, focuses on developing algorithms that enable systems to learn from data and improve their performance over time without explicit programming (Hagendorff, 2020). The synergy between AI and ML has led to significant advancements in automation, predictive analytics, and adaptive decision-making.

2.1.2.1 AI as a superset of ML

AI encompasses a broader spectrum of technologies, including symbolic reasoning, expert systems, robotics, and NLP. ML, on the other hand, is data-driven and relies on statistical methods to identify patterns and make decisions. While early AI systems relied on rule-based expert systems, modern AI implementations increasingly leverage ML techniques to enhance adaptability and scalability (Jordan and Mitchell, 2022) (Fig. 2.1).

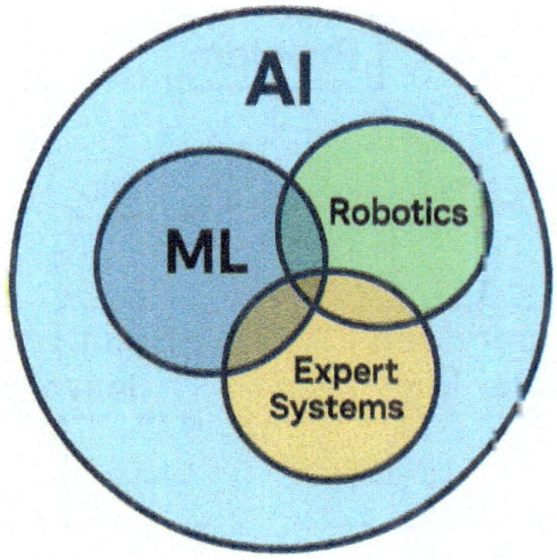

Fig. 2.1 AI as a superset.

2.1.2.2 ML as the driving force behind AI evolution

ML has become the dominant approach for achieving AI capabilities, primarily due to its ability to process large datasets efficiently. The rapid growth of DL, a subset of ML utilizing ANNs, has propelled AI into new domains, including autonomous systems, healthcare diagnostics, and personalized recommendations (Zhang et al., 2021). The availability of big data and advances in computational power have enabled ML algorithms to outperform traditional AI approaches in complex pattern recognition and decision-making tasks (Fig. 2.2).

2.1.2.3 Types of ML driving AI progress

ML can be broadly classified into:

- **Supervised learning**—Requires labeled data for training models in applications such as speech recognition and fraud detection
- **Unsupervised learning**—Identifies hidden patterns in unlabeled data, playing a crucial role in anomaly detection and clustering
- **Reinforcement learning**—Enables AI agents to learn optimal strategies through reward-based mechanisms, essential for robotics and gaming (Silver et al., 2021)

2.1.2.4 Interplay between AI and ML in real-world applications

The interplay between AI and ML is pivotal across real-world domains. In healthcare, AI-driven ML models significantly enhance diagnostics and treatment planning by analyzing complex datasets such as medical imaging and genomics (Esteva et al., 2021). Autonomous systems, like self-driving cars, utilize ML algorithms for real-time object detection and decision-making, showcasing seamless AI–ML integration. Similarly, in financial services, AI-powered ML systems detect fraud and guide algorithmic trading by evaluating transaction

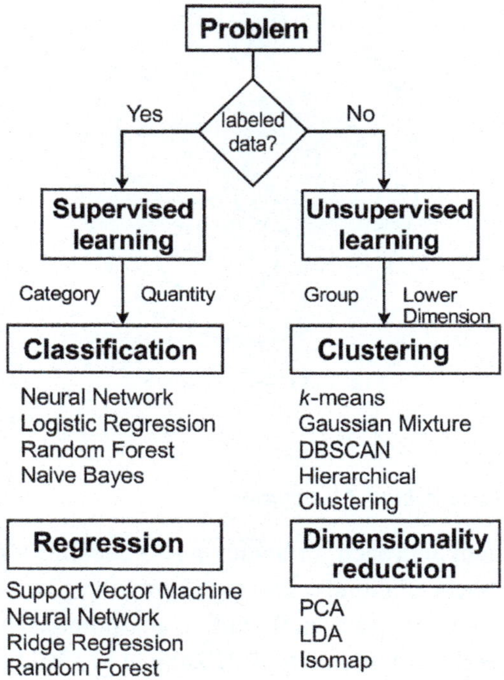

Fig. 2.2 Types of machine learning algorithms.

patterns instantaneously. This convergence enables intelligent, adaptive, and data-driven decision-making across sectors.

Despite its potential, the integration of AI and ML faces challenges such as explainability, bias mitigation, and data privacy concerns. The emergence of federated learning and neuromorphic computing aims to address these limitations by enabling distributed AI models and brain-inspired architectures (Wu et al., 2022). Ensuring ethical AI deployment remains a critical area of ongoing research.

2.1.3 The convergence of AI/ML with digital twin computing

The convergence of AI and ML with DTC has transformed the way complex systems are monitored, analyzed, and optimized. A DT is a virtual representation of a physical system that continuously updates itself with real-time data, enabling predictive analytics and intelligent decision-making (Tao et al., 2022). The integration of AI and ML into DTC enhances the ability of DTs to learn from past data, adapt to changing conditions, and autonomously optimize system performance.

2.1.3.1 AI and ML enhancing DT capabilities

Traditional DTs relied on rule-based models and physics-based simulations, which had limitations in handling dynamic and large-scale environments. AI/ML-powered DTs leverage data-driven approaches, allowing real-time adaptation and self-learning capabilities. ML algorithms, particularly DL and RL, facilitate anomaly detection, predictive maintenance, and intelligent process automation within DT frameworks (Kapteyn et al., 2021).

1. **Predictive maintenance and fault diagnosis**—AI-driven DTs use ML models to detect anomalies and predict equipment failures before they occur. This proactive approach reduces downtime and optimizes resource utilization in industries such as aerospace, manufacturing, and energy (Zheng et al., 2023).
2. **Autonomous decision-making**—RL enables DTs to simulate multiple scenarios and identify optimal decision pathways, making them valuable in urban planning, autonomous vehicles, and smart grids.
3. **Real-time optimization**—AI-driven optimization models enhance DTs by continuously adjusting parameters in response to real-time data, improving operational efficiency in dynamic environments.

2.1.3.2 Integration with Internet of Thingsand edge computing

The synergy of AI/ML with DTs is further strengthened by the integration of the IoT and edge computing. IoT sensors provide continuous data streams, which are processed by ML algorithms at the edge, reducing latency and enabling real-time decision-making. This decentralized approach enhances scalability and efficiency in applications such as smart cities and Industry 4.0 (Shahzad et al., 2023).

2.1.3.3 Blockchain for secure DT transactions

Blockchain technology plays a crucial role in securing AI/ML-powered DTs by ensuring data integrity and preventing unauthorized modifications. According to Wang et al. (2023), blockchain-based frameworks enable transparent and verifiable interactions, making them particularly valuable in supply chain management, healthcare, and financial services. However, key challenges remain—ensuring data privacy, managing the high computational demands of large-scale ML models, and improving model explainability for trust and regulatory compliance. Advancements in federated learning, neuromorphic computing, and hybrid AI models are expected to enhance DT capabilities, making them more secure, efficient, and autonomous in real-time decision-making (Fig. 2.3).

2.1.4 AI/ML as the foundation for intelligent decision-making

AI and ML have emerged as fundamental enablers of intelligent decision-making across multiple domains, including healthcare, finance, manufacturing, and autonomous systems.

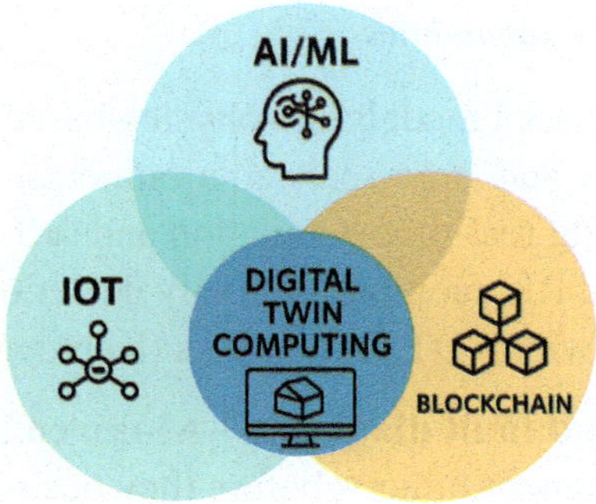

Fig. 2.3 Conceptual diagram illustrating the convergence of Artificial Intelligence/Machine Learning (AI/ML), the Internet of Things (IoT), and Blockchain with Digital Twin Computing (DTC).

Intelligent decision-making involves the ability to process complex data, identify patterns, and make accurate predictions or recommendations. AI/ML enhances decision-making processes by leveraging vast datasets, extracting meaningful insights, and automating adaptive responses in real-time (Jordan and Mitchell, 2022).

2.1.4.1 AI/ML and decision-making frameworks

Decision-making traditionally relied on rule-based systems, expert knowledge, and heuristic models, which often struggled with dynamic, high-dimensional data. AI/ML revolutionizes this approach by introducing data-driven methodologies that allow for continuous learning and improvement. The integration of AI/ML in decision-making frameworks follows a structured process:

1. **Data collection and preprocessing**—Large-scale datasets from diverse sources, including IoT devices, sensors, and digital platforms, are gathered and cleaned to ensure quality input
2. **Feature extraction and learning**—ML models extract relevant patterns and correlations from the data, enabling predictive and prescriptive analytics
3. **Model training and evaluation**—Algorithms are trained using supervised, unsupervised, or RL techniques to optimize performance
4. **Automated decision execution**—AI-driven decision engines automate responses, recommendations, and real-time adjustments

This AI-driven paradigm reduces human bias, enhances decision accuracy, and enables scalability across complex systems (Goodfellow et al., 2016).

2.1.4.2 Key AI/ML techniques for intelligent decision-making

Supervised learning for predictive analytics

Supervised learning models, such as decision trees, support vector machines (SVMs), and deep neural networks (DNNs), are extensively used for forecasting and classification tasks.

For instance, AI-driven decision support systems in healthcare analyze patient histories to predict disease progression and suggest personalized treatments (Esteva et al., 2021).

Unsupervised learning for pattern recognition

Unsupervised learning, including clustering and dimensionality reduction techniques, is vital for detecting hidden structures in large datasets. In financial markets, AI-powered anomaly detection identifies fraudulent transactions, minimizing risks and improving compliance (Zhang et al., 2023).

RL for adaptive decision-making

RL enables AI agents to learn optimal strategies by interacting with environments and receiving feedback. RL is particularly effective in robotics, gaming, and autonomous systems, where decisions must be continuously adjusted based on real-time conditions (Silver et al., 2021).

Deep learning for complex decision scenarios

DL models, including convolutional neural networks (CNNs) and recurrent neural networks (RNNs), process high-dimensional data such as images, speech, and time-series data. AI-powered diagnostic tools in radiology, for instance, analyze medical images to detect abnormalities with higher accuracy than traditional methods (Shen et al., 2022)

AI-driven decision-making in real-world applications

Healthcare: AI for precision medicine AI-driven decision support systems are revolutionizing precision medicine by analyzing genomic data, predicting disease risks, and optimizing treatment plans. ML models improve early cancer detection and assist in drug discovery by simulating molecular interactions (Krittanawong et al., 2022).

Finance: Risk assessment and fraud detection Financial institutions leverage AI/ML for credit risk assessment, fraud detection, and algorithmic trading. AI-powered models analyze transaction patterns, detect anomalies, and optimize investment strategies to minimize financial losses (Wang et al., 2023).

Manufacturing: AI for predictive maintenance Smart manufacturing integrates AI/ML to monitor equipment performance, detect faults, and prevent unexpected breakdowns. Predictive maintenance using AI reduces operational downtime and enhances productivity in industries such as aerospace and automotive (Zheng et al., 2023).

Autonomous systems: AI in self-driving cars AI/ML enables intelligent decision-making in autonomous vehicles by processing real-time sensor data, recognizing road conditions, and making split-second decisions to ensure safety. RL models optimize driving strategies, reducing accident risks (Shahzad et al., 2023).

Challenges in AI-based decision-making

Despite its advantages, AI-driven decision-making presents challenges:

- **Bias and fairness**—AI models can inherit biases from training data, leading to ethical concerns and unfair outcomes. Developing bias-mitigation techniques remains a critical research area.
- **Explainability and transparency**—Black-box AI models often lack interpretability, making it difficult for stakeholders to trust AI decisions. XAI techniques are being developed to address this issue (Li et al., 2022).
- **Security and privacy**—The reliance on large datasets raises concerns regarding data security and privacy. Blockchain integration with AI offers potential solutions by enhancing data integrity and transparency (Wang et al., 2023).

Future directions

The future of AI-driven decision-making is shaped by emerging technologies such as federated learning, which enables decentralized model training while preserving data privacy, and neuromorphic computing, offering brain-inspired, energy-efficient architectures. In addition, hybrid AI models combine symbolic reasoning with DL, enhancing interpretability and advancing intelligent, transparent, and adaptive systems (Fig. 2.4).

AI/ML serves as the foundation for intelligent decision-making by enabling data-driven insights, predictive analytics, and adaptive automation. The convergence of AI with real-world applications enhances efficiency, accuracy, and scalability across diverse sectors.

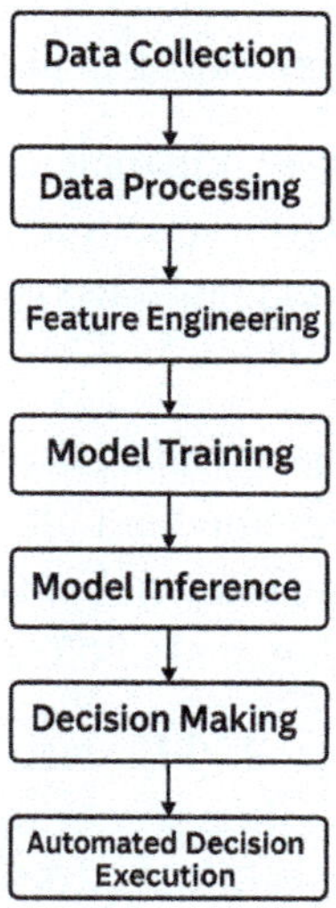

Fig. 2.4 A flowchart illustrating AI-driven decision-making.

As AI research advances, addressing challenges related to bias, interpretability, and security will be essential to building trustworthy and ethically responsible AI-driven decision systems.

2.2 Evolution and theoretical foundations of AI/ML

AI and ML have evolved significantly over the past several decades, rooted in theoretical advancements in mathematics, statistics, and computer science. The foundations of AI date back to the 1950s, when Alan Turing proposed the concept of machine intelligence and introduced the Turing Test. The term "Artificial Intelligence" was officially coined at the 1956 Dartmouth Conference, marking the beginning of AI as a formal discipline.

Early AI research focused on rule-based systems and symbolic reasoning, leading to expert systems in the 1970s and 1980s. However, these systems lacked adaptability, which led to a shift toward data-driven approaches. The rise of ML in the 1990s and 2000s was fueled by developments in statistical learning theory, pioneered by Vapnik and Chervonenkis, and the increased availability of computational power.

ML, a subset of AI, is based on algorithms that learn patterns from data rather than relying on explicit programming. Key theoretical foundations include probability theory, optimization, neural networks, and Bayesian inference. The breakthrough in DL, driven by multilayered neural networks, transformed AI capabilities, enabling advancements in computer vision, NLP, and robotics. Today, AI and ML continue to evolve, integrating ethical considerations and interdisciplinary research.

2.2.1 Historical milestones in AI and ML

The evolution of AI and ML has been a remarkable journey, driven by interdisciplinary advances in mathematics, neuroscience, computer science, and data analytics. While AI's roots can be traced back to early philosophical inquiries into intelligence, its practical implementation began in the 20th century. ML, a subset of AI, has evolved through statistical modeling, probabilistic reasoning, and neural network innovations, transforming industries and scientific research alike.

2.2.1.1 The birth of AI: 1940s–1950s

The conceptual foundation of AI began with Alan Turing, who, in 1950, proposed the Turing Test, a criterion for determining whether a machine can exhibit intelligent behavior indistinguishable from that of a human (Turing, 1950). This era also witnessed the emergence of cybernetics, as Norbert Wiener's work laid the foundation for control systems and self-regulating mechanisms (Johnson and Wiener, 1949). The Dartmouth Conference (1956), organized by John McCarthy and colleagues, officially marked the birth of AI as a field of study, introducing key concepts like heuristic search and symbolic reasoning (McCarthy et al., 1956).

2.2.1.2 The rise and fall of symbolic AI: 1960s–1970s

In the 1960s and 1970s, AI research was dominated by symbolic AI, also known as Good Old-Fashioned AI (GOFAI), which focused on expert systems and rule-based logic. Notable milestones include Weizenbaum's ELIZA (1966), an early NLP program that simulated human-like conversation (Weizenbaum, 1966). The era also saw the development of the Shakey robot (1972) by SRI International, one of the first mobile robots with decision-making capabilities (Nilsson, 1984).

However, the limitations of rule-based systems, particularly their inability to handle uncertainty and learn from data, led to the first AI Winter in the late 1970s. Funding cuts and skepticism slowed progress, highlighting the need for more adaptive AI models.

2.2.1.3 The emergence of ML: 1980s–1990s

A shift toward data-driven AI began in the 1980s, with renewed interest in ML. This period saw the revival of neural networks, inspired by Frank Rosenblatt's Perceptron (1958), but significantly improved with the introduction of backpropagation by Rumelhart et al. (1986). The 1990s further propelled ML with developments in SVMs and Bayesian networks, enabling probabilistic reasoning in AI (Vapnik, 1995).

Another significant milestone was IBM's Deep Blue (1997), which defeated world chess champion Garry Kasparov, showcasing AI's ability to process large-scale computations and strategic decision-making (Campbell et al., 2002).

2.2.1.4 The rise of data-driven AI: 2000s–2010s

The 21st century witnessed an explosion in AI capabilities, primarily due to the increasing availability of big data and improvements in computing power. Google introduced the PageRank algorithm in 1998, a foundational AI-driven search technology that revolutionized the internet (Brin and Page, 1998). The early 2000s saw the rise of RL, with Deep Q-Networks (DQN) developed by DeepMind (Mnih et al., 2013), later leading to AI systems mastering games like Go and Dota 2.

DL became a game-changer with AlexNet (2012), a deep CNN that dramatically improved image classification tasks, leading to AI breakthroughs in computer vision (Krizhevsky et al., 2012). The launch of Google's AlphaGo (2016), which defeated human Go champions using deep RL, further solidified AI's dominance in strategic problem-solving (Silver et al., 2016).

2.2.1.5 AI in the era of automation and explainability: 2020s–present

The 2020s have been defined by advancements in AI-driven automation and the increasing need for explainability and ethical AI. AI has become an integral part of industries such as healthcare, finance, manufacturing, and autonomous systems, where **AI-powered automation** has significantly enhanced efficiency and productivity. Technologies like

Robotic Process Automation (RPA) and **AI-driven decision support systems** are streamlining workflows and optimizing resource management (Brynjolfsson and McAfee, 2021).

Explainability has emerged as a crucial area of AI research, addressing the "black box" problem in DL models. Researchers and policymakers are focusing on **XAI** techniques that provide transparency in AI-driven decisions (Doshi-Velez and Kim, 2017). Regulatory bodies worldwide are pushing for ethical AI frameworks to ensure fairness, accountability, and bias mitigation in AI applications (Floridi, 2020).

The rise of **generative AI models**, such as OpenAI's Generative Pretrained Transformer-4 (**GPT-4)** and Google's **Bard**, has transformed content generation, programming, and creative industries, showcasing AI's capabilities in text, image, and video synthesis (Brown et al., 2020). AI-powered **autonomous vehicles** and **robotic systems** are nearing widespread adoption, further emphasizing the need for robust AI safety protocols (Amodei et al., 2016).

AI's integration with other emerging technologies like **blockchain and IoT** is paving the way for more secure and efficient digital ecosystems. As AI continues to evolve, its impact on society, the economy, and scientific advancements will remain a focal point of global research and governance efforts.

AI and ML have evolved through theoretical advancements and technological breakthroughs, each milestone shaping their trajectory. While early AI struggled with symbolic reasoning, the shift to ML and DL has made AI more robust and scalable. As AI enters an era of ethical considerations and interdisciplinary applications, its future remains a dynamic and evolving landscape.

2.2.2 Key theoretical advancements: Turing test, neural networks, and DL

The foundations of AI and ML rest on several key theoretical advancements, among which the **Turing test**, **neural networks**, and **DL** play a pivotal role. The Turing Test, proposed by Alan Turing in 1950, provides an early philosophical and practical framework for assessing machine intelligence. Neural Networks, inspired by the structure of the human brain, enable pattern recognition and self-learning capabilities in AI systems. Finally, DL, an advanced subset of neural networks, has revolutionized AI by leveraging vast datasets and computational power to achieve human-like performance in various domains. These advancements have propelled AI from theoretical constructs to real-world applications, transforming industries and scientific research.

2.2.2.1 The turing test

The **Turing test**, introduced by Alan Turing in his seminal paper Turing (1950), was designed to assess a machine's ability to exhibit human-like intelligence. Turing proposed a simple yet profound question: *Can machines think?* To evaluate this, he devised an imitation game where a human judge interacts with a machine and a human via text-based communication. If the machine can generate responses indistinguishable from those of a human, it is said to have passed the Turing Test (Turing, 1950).

This test laid the theoretical groundwork for modern AI, influencing research in **NLP**, **chatbots**, and **machine–human interactions** (Shieber, 1994). Early AI models, such as ELIZA (1966) by Joseph Weizenbaum, attempted to simulate human conversations, highlighting both the potential and limitations of AI in linguistic tasks (Weizenbaum, 1966). However, critics like John Searle, 1980 challenged the Turing Test with arguments such as the **Chinese Room Argument**, which suggests that syntactic processing does not equate to true understanding (Searle, 1980).

Despite its criticisms, the Turing Test remains an essential benchmark in AI, evolving with advances in DL and large language models (LLMs) such as **GPT-4** (Brown et al., 2020). Modern AI systems increasingly blur the lines between human and machine communication, reigniting debates on machine consciousness and ethical considerations in AI (Floridi, 2020) Fig. 2.5).

2.2.2.2 Neural networks

Neural networks are computational models inspired by the structure and functionality of biological neural networks found in the human brain. These networks consist of interconnected processing units called neurons, organized in multiple layers—input, hidden, and output layers. Each neuron processes inputs, applies weights, and passes the information through an activation function to determine the output.

ANNs are foundational to modern ML and DL, allowing systems to recognize complex patterns, make predictions, and improve performance over time through learning algorithms such as backpropagation. These networks have revolutionized fields such as computer vision,

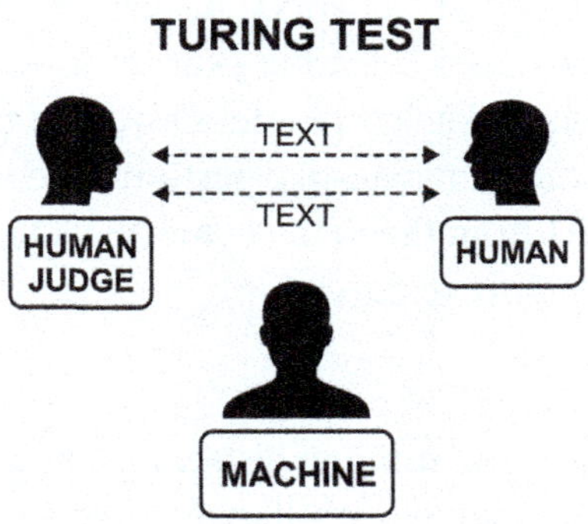

Fig. 2.5 Turing test setup.

speech recognition, NLP, and robotics by enabling AI systems to process vast amounts of data with high accuracy.

Neural networks represent a fundamental breakthrough in AI, inspired by the structure and functioning of biological neurons in the human brain. The concept dates back to Warren McCulloch and Walter Pitts (1943), who introduced artificial neurons as mathematical models of human cognition (McCulloch and Pitts, 1943). However, practical implementations were limited until Frank Rosenblatt (1958) developed the **Perceptron**, an early single-layer neural network capable of learning patterns (Rosenblatt, 1958).

Neural networks gained significant traction in the 1980s with the introduction of the **backpropagation algorithm** by Rumelhart et al. (1986), allowing multilayer networks to efficiently adjust their weights and improve learning capabilities (Rumelhart et al., 1986). This advancement led to the emergence of **DL**, where neural networks with multiple hidden layers enabled AI systems to learn intricate patterns in large datasets.

Modern neural networks, particularly **DNNs** and **CNNs**, have revolutionized AI applications, powering advancements in **image recognition, speech processing, and autonomous systems** (LeCun et al., 2015). Architectures such as **RNNs** and **Transformer models** have further enhanced AI's ability to process sequential data and generate human-like text (Vaswani et al., 2017).

Despite their success, neural networks pose challenges such as computational intensity, **black-box decision-making**, and ethical concerns in AI deployment. Addressing these limitations remains a focus of contemporary AI research.

A **figure illustrating the structure of a neural network**, highlighting layers, nodes, and connections, would be beneficial for visualizing this concept.

2.2.3 Foundational models: Symbolic AI vs. connectionist AI

The development of AI has been driven by two primary paradigms: Symbolic AI (logic-based) and Connectionist AI (neural networks). These approaches have distinct methodologies, advantages, and limitations, shaping the evolution of AI research.

2.2.3.1 Symbolic AI

Symbolic AI, also known as GOFAI, is based on formal logic, rules, and symbolic representations (Newell and Simon, 1976). Early AI systems, such as expert systems and knowledge-based systems, relied on hand-coded rules to mimic human reasoning. Notable examples include MYCIN (Buchanan and Shortliffe, 1984) for medical diagnosis and DENDRAL for chemical analysis.

However, Symbolic AI struggled with scalability and adaptability, particularly in handling ambiguous or noisy data. The reliance on explicit rules made it challenging to model real-world learning processes.

2.2.3.2 Connectionist AI

Connectionist AI, in contrast, is inspired by the biological neural networks of the brain. It relies on artificial neurons and learning algorithms to discover patterns in data. Unlike Symbolic AI, which follows predefined logic, Connectionist AI learns from examples, making it suitable for perception-based tasks like image recognition and NLP (LeCun et al., 2015).

The success of DL has positioned Connectionist AI as the dominant paradigm in AI research. Modern neural network architectures, including CNNs and Transformers, have surpassed Symbolic AI in many domains, particularly those requiring flexibility and adaptability (Vaswani et al., 2017).

2.2.3.3 Hybrid AI: The future

Given the strengths and weaknesses of both approaches, recent research has explored hybrid models that combine Symbolic AI's reasoning abilities with Connectionist AI's learning capabilities (Marcus, 2018). This approach aims to create XAI systems capable of both robust reasoning and adaptive learning (Table 2.1).

Table 2.1 Comparison: Symbolic AI vs. connectionist AI.

Feature	Symbolic AI	Connectionist AI (Neural Networks)
Definition	Uses explicit rules and logic to represent knowledge and perform reasoning	Uses artificial neural networks (ANNs) that learn from data through pattern recognition
Knowledge representation	Based on symbols, rules, and structured logic (e.g., knowledge graphs, ontologies)	Based on distributed representations in neural network weights
Learning approach	Relies on human-defined rules and expert systems (top-down approach)	Uses machine learning and deep learning to automatically learn from data (bottom-up approach)
Explainability	Highly interpretable and provides clear reasoning for decisions	Often seen as a "black box" with limited interpretability
Handling of uncertainty	Struggles with noisy, ambiguous, or incomplete data	Handles uncertainty well through probabilistic models and adaptive learning
Applications	Used in expert systems, rule-based reasoning, theorem proving, and symbolic NLP (e.g., Wolfram Alpha and IBM Watson)	Used in deep learning applications like image recognition, speech processing, and autonomous systems (e.g., GPT models, AlphaGo)
Limitations	Difficult to scale, requires extensive manual rule creation and lacks adaptability	Requires large amounts of data and computing power and lacks inherent reasoning abilities
Future trends	Integration with neural models (neuro-symbolic AI) for hybrid intelligence, and advancements in explainable AI (XAI)	More efficient architectures, self-learning AI, better interpretability, and improved energy efficiency

2.3 Core concepts in AI and ML

Core concepts in AI and ML include Neural Networks, DL, NLP, Computer Vision (CV), and XAI. They form the foundation for developing intelligent systems and enabling machines to perform complex tasks. These technologies power applications such as autonomous systems, healthcare diagnostics, and predictive analytics. The future of AI lies in hybrid models, ethical AI, and self-learning systems, driving advancements in multiple industries. These concepts drive the ability of AI to learn, reason, perceive, and interact with the world. They form the building blocks of intelligent systems, enabling AI to process structured and unstructured data, make data-driven decisions, and solve real-world problems efficiently. As AI evolves, these core areas continue to expand, leading to more ethical, reliable, and autonomous AI solutions.

2.3.1 Distinguishing AI, ML, and DL

Within AI, ML and DL represent distinct yet interconnected disciplines that drive intelligent decision-making. Understanding the nuances between these fields is essential for researchers and practitioners alike. AI is the overarching field that enables machines to simulate human intelligence, encompassing rule-based systems, expert systems, and learning algorithms (Russell and Norvig, 2020). ML, a subset of AI, focuses on algorithms that improve with experience (Mitchell, 1997). DL, a specialized branch of ML, employs ANNs to model complex patterns and representations (LeCun et al., 2015).

2.3.1.1 Artificial intelligence: The broad spectrum

AI encompasses a wide range of techniques, including knowledge representation, logical reasoning, search algorithms, and statistical learning. Early AI systems were largely symbolic, relying on predefined rules and logic. The expert systems of the 1980s, such as MYCIN in medical diagnosis, exemplify rule-based AI (Shortliffe, 1976).

2.3.1.2 Core characteristics of AI

AI is a multidisciplinary field that aims to create systems capable of reasoning, learning, and decision-making. At its core, AI is built on fundamental characteristics that enable machines to simulate human cognitive abilities. Four essential aspects define AI's capability to function effectively in diverse applications: **Symbolic reasoning**, **knowledge representation**, **automated learning**, and **problem-solving**. These characteristics provide the foundation for AI's ability to handle complex tasks, make informed decisions, and continuously improve over time.

2.3.1.3 Symbolic reasoning: Using logic and rules to infer decisions

Symbolic reasoning, also known as rule-based reasoning, is a fundamental approach in AI where logic and explicitly defined rules guide decision-making. This approach represents knowledge using symbols and logical relationships, allowing AI systems to perform structured reasoning tasks. Some key aspects of symbolic reasoning are: it makes decisions using predetermined logic and if-then principles; uses ontologies, predicate calculus, and mathematical logic to explicitly represent knowledge; and provides explainability and transparency, making it easy to trace how AI reaches conclusions.

The challenges of symbolic reasoning are that it struggles with **handling uncertainty** and ambiguous information. It requires manual **rule creation**, which is labor-intensive and lacks scalability when dealing with large datasets or dynamic environments.

Despite its limitations, symbolic reasoning remains crucial for applications where explainability and formal decision-making are essential, such as legal AI, financial auditing, and regulatory compliance systems.

Example applications:

- **Expert systems:** AI-based expert systems, such as MYCIN (used in medical diagnosis), rely on symbolic reasoning to infer decisions based on rules provided by human experts.
- **Automated theorem proving:** AI systems can use logic to solve mathematical proofs.
- **Natural language understanding:** Early AI-driven chatbots and question-answering systems used symbolic reasoning to interpret queries and respond accurately.

2.3.1.4 ML: Data-driven intelligence

ML shifts from rule-based AI to data-driven learning, where models extract patterns from large datasets. Samuel, 1959 self-learning checkers program is an early example of ML in action. The practical applications of ML are numerous and varied. By evaluating enormous volumes of data in real time with a speed and precision that humans cannot match, ML algorithms assist banks in identifying fraudulent transactions. Using predictive models of patient outcomes, ML helps physicians diagnose illnesses based on medical imaging and guides therapy regimens. In addition, many businesses in the retail industry employ ML to forecast inventory demands, improve supply chains, and personalize shopping experiences. Moreover, ML handles manual activities that humans cannot complete at scale, such as processing the massive amounts of data produced every day by digital devices. This capacity to draw conclusions and patterns from large data sets has emerged as a differentiator in industries such as scientific research and finance.

To make better decisions and increase productivity, a number of today's top businesses, such as Uber, Google, and Meta, incorporate ML into their operations. To make sense of the ever-increasing amount of data produced by contemporary civilizations, ML is essential. ML improvements can be accelerated by using the vast amount of data generated by humans to further train and refine ML models. The most sophisticated AI systems of today are based on this ongoing learning loop, which has significant implications.

2.3.1.5 Types of ML

1. **Supervised learning**: Models learn from labeled data (e.g., SVMs, random forests).
2. **Unsupervised learning**: Discovers patterns in unlabeled data (e.g., clustering, dimensionality reduction).
3. **RL**: Models learn via rewards and penalties (e.g., AlphaGo, autonomous agents).

2.3.1.6 DL: A breakthrough in AI

DL is a subset of ML that utilizes ANNs, particularly DNNs, to model and solve complex problems. Inspired by the structure and function of the human brain, DL algorithms process large datasets through multiple layers of neurons, enabling them to extract hierarchical features and learn patterns without explicit programming.

At the core of DL are **multilayer perceptrons, CNNs, and RNNs**. CNNs excel in computer vision tasks such as image classification and object detection, while RNNs and transformer models, like Bidirectional Encoder Representations from Transformers **(BERT) and GPT**, have revolutionized NLP.

DL thrives on **big data** and **high computational power**, with GPUs and TPUs significantly accelerating training processes. Backpropagation and optimization techniques, like **stochastic gradient descent (SGD) and the Adam optimizer,** refine neural network parameters for improved accuracy.

DL applications span diverse fields, from **autonomous vehicles and healthcare diagnostics to financial forecasting and personalized recommendations**. Despite its successes, challenges such as **data dependency, model interpretability, and computational costs** remain areas of active research. With advancements in **quantum computing, federated learning, and neuromorphic engineering**, DL is poised to redefine the future of AI-driven innovation.

2.3.1.7 Distinguishing AI, ML, and DL

AI, ML, and DL are interconnected yet distinct fields within computational intelligence. AI is a broad discipline that encompasses **the simulation of human intelligence** in machines, allowing them to **perceive, reason, learn, and make decisions** (Russell and Norvig, 2020). It includes rule-based systems, expert systems, robotics, and intelligent automation.

ML is a **subset of AI** that focuses on **data-driven learning from experience**. ML algorithms use statistical techniques to identify patterns and make predictions or decisions without explicit programming (Mitchell, 1997). Traditional ML approaches include **supervised learning, unsupervised learning, and RL**, with algorithms such as decision trees, SVMs, and k-means clustering.

DL is an **advanced subset of ML**, leveraging **ANNs** with multiple layers (deep architectures) to process and extract hierarchical features from complex data (LeCun et al., 2015). Unlike traditional ML, DL models, such as **CNNs for image processing and Transformer models for NLP**, automatically learn high-level abstractions from raw data. However, DL is computationally intensive and requires **large-scale datasets and high-performance computing resources** (Table 2.2).

2.3.2 The AI hierarchy: Narrow AI, general AI, and superintelligence

AI has evolved significantly, progressing from simple rule-based systems to complex self-learning models. The AI hierarchy is categorized into narrow AI (weak AI), general AI (strong AI), and superintelligence, each representing different levels of machine intelligence and capabilities. Understanding this hierarchy is essential in assessing AI's potential, limitations, and implications for humanity (Russell and Norvig, 2020).

2.3.2.1 Narrow AI (weak AI): Specialized problem-solving

Narrow AI, also known as weak AI, refers to AI systems designed to perform specific tasks without possessing human-like intelligence or consciousness. These systems rely on pattern recognition, statistical models, and preprogrammed algorithms to execute predefined operations efficiently (Goodfellow et al., 2016).

Table 2.2 Comparison of AI, ML, and deep learning.

Key aspect	Artificial intelligence (AI)	Machine learning (ML)	Deep learning (DL)
Definition	The broad concept of machines mimicking human intelligence	A subset of AI that enables machines to learn from data	A subset of ML, using deep neural networks for feature learning
Approach	Rule-based, heuristic, symbolic reasoning, and statistical learning	Algorithm-driven data learning	Neural network-based hierarchical learning
Examples	Expert systems, robotics, chatbots, self-driving cars	Regression, decision trees, SVMs, k-means clustering.	CNNs for image recognition, RNNs for sequential data, and Transformers for NLP
Data requirement	Can work with structured data and predefined rules	Requires labeled or unlabeled data for training	Requires large amounts of data for optimal performance
Computational power	Moderate to high, depending on the application	Moderate, depending on the complexity of the algorithms	High, requiring GPUs/TPUs for efficient processing
Interpretability	Generally interpretable	More interpretable than DL models	Often considered a "black box" due to its complex feature extraction
Application areas	Healthcare, automation, robotics, decision support systems	Fraud detection, recommendation systems, predictive analytics	Autonomous vehicles, speech recognition, medical image analysis

Examples of narrow AI include virtual assistants (Siri, Alexa), recommendation systems (Netflix, Spotify), fraud detection systems, and self-driving technologies. These AI models outperform humans in specialized domains, such as diagnosing diseases through medical imaging or playing chess at superhuman levels (Silver et al., 2017). However, they lack cognitive flexibility and cannot transfer knowledge beyond their trained scope.

Despite its limitations, narrow AI dominates modern AI applications and continues to transform industries through automation and efficiency improvements. However, ethical concerns, such as bias, fairness, and transparency, remain critical challenges in deploying Narrow AI at scale (Binns, 2018).

2.3.2.2 General AI (strong AI): The human-level intelligence frontier

General AI, or strong AI, represents machines that can understand, learn, and apply intelligence across diverse domains, similar to human cognitive abilities (Goertzel and Pennachin, 2007). Unlike narrow AI, general AI would possess self-awareness, reasoning skills, and adaptability, enabling it to perform any intellectual task that a human can do.

The development of general AI remains theoretical, as no AI system has yet achieved human-like cognition, problem-solving, or creativity. Researchers aim to build adaptive learning frameworks, neuro-symbolic AI, and hybrid intelligence systems that could pave the way for general AI (Lake et al., 2017). The key challenges include:

- Causal reasoning: Machines currently lack the ability to understand cause-and-effect relationships.
- Common sense reasoning: AI struggles with tasks that require contextual understanding beyond data-driven learning.
- Ethical and moral decision-making: Unlike humans, AI does not inherently possess moral reasoning.

While general AI remains an ambitious goal, progress in RL, neuro-evolution, and self-supervised learning could eventually lead to more autonomous and intelligent AI systems.

2.3.2.3 Superintelligence: Beyond human capabilities

Superintelligence represents an AI system that surpasses human intelligence across all cognitive domains, including creativity, problem-solving, and social intelligence (Bostrom, 2014). Such AI could outperform humans in scientific discovery, strategic thinking, and innovation, potentially leading to profound societal transformations.

Theoretical discussions on superintelligence often focus on the existential risks associated with uncontrollable AI autonomy. Scholars argue that, without proper safeguards, superintelligent AI could prioritize goals misaligned with human values, leading to unintended consequences (Russell, 2019). Concepts like AI alignment, ethical constraints, and explainability are being explored to mitigate these risks.

Although superintelligence remains speculative, the rapid advancements in DL, neuromorphic computing, and AI-human symbiosis suggest that machines with superior cognitive capabilities may emerge in the future. Ensuring that AI aligns with human interests will be crucial in determining the role of superintelligent systems in society.

The AI hierarchy—narrow AI, general AI, and superintelligence—illustrates the evolution of machine intelligence from task-specific automation to hypothetical human-level and beyond-human capabilities. While Narrow AI is ubiquitous today, researchers continue to explore pathways toward general AI, with caution surrounding superintelligence. The ethical and societal implications of AI's progression demand careful consideration, ensuring AI remains a tool that enhances human potential rather than replaces it.

2.3.3 Key learning paradigms: Supervised, unsupervised, and RL

ML enables computers to learn from data and improve their performance without explicit programming. The three primary learning paradigms—Supervised learning, unsupervised learning, and RL—each have distinct approaches, applications, and challenges (Mitchell, 1997). Understanding these paradigms is essential in developing intelligent, adaptable, and data-driven AI systems (Russell and Norvig, 2020).

2.3.3.1 Supervised learning: Learning from labeled data

Supervised learning is a task-driven learning paradigm where the algorithm learns from input-output mappings provided in labeled datasets. The goal is to discover the underlying relationship between features (inputs) and their corresponding labels (outputs), enabling the model to make accurate predictions for unseen data (Goodfellow et al., 2016).

Supervised learning is broadly categorized into:

- **Classification**: Predicting discrete labels (e.g., email spam detection, disease diagnosis)
- **Regression**: Predicting continuous values (e.g., stock price forecasting, house price estimation)

Popular algorithms include SVMs, decision trees, random forests, and neural networks. While supervised learning excels in accuracy, it requires large labeled datasets, making it time-consuming and expensive to implement in some domains (LeCun et al., 2015).

2.3.3.2 Unsupervised learning: Discovering hidden patterns

Unlike supervised learning, unsupervised learning operates without labeled data, focusing on pattern discovery and data structure extraction. This paradigm is useful when manual labeling is impractical or impossible, allowing AI systems to learn autonomously (Murphy, 2012).

Key techniques include:

- **Clustering**: Grouping similar data points (e.g., customer segmentation in marketing)
- **Dimensionality reduction**: Reducing data complexity while retaining essential information (e.g., Principal Component Analysis in bioinformatics)
- **Anomaly detection**: Identifying unusual patterns (e.g., fraud detection in financial transactions)

Common algorithms include K-means clustering, hierarchical clustering, autoencoders, and generative adversarial networks (GANs). Unsupervised learning is highly flexible but lacks explicit ground truth, making evaluation and interpretability challenging (Hastie et al., 2009).

2.3.3.3 RL: Learning through trial and error

RL is inspired by behavioral psychology, where an agent learns to take actions in an environment by maximizing cumulative rewards. Unlike supervised learning, RL does not rely on labeled data but instead interacts with an environment, receiving rewards or penalties based on its decisions (Sutton and Barto, 2018).

Key concepts in RL include:

- **Agent**: The decision-maker (e.g., a self-driving car)
- **Environment**: The world in which the agent operates
- **State**: The current situation of the agent
- **Action**: The choice the agent makes
- **Reward**: Feedback received for actions taken

Breakthroughs in RL, such as DQN, Policy Gradient Methods, and Actor-Critic Models, have led to superhuman performance in games like AlphaGo, autonomous robotics, and real-time decision-making (Silver et al., 2017). However, RL requires extensive computational resources and can be unstable due to delayed rewards.

2.3.4 Fundamental AI/ML algorithms and their theoretical underpinnings

AI and ML rely on fundamental algorithms that drive decision-making, pattern recognition, and predictive analytics. These algorithms, inspired by mathematical and statistical principles, have revolutionized industries such as healthcare, finance, robotics, and cybersecurity (Russell and Norvig, 2020). Understanding their theoretical foundations is essential for advancing AI-driven solutions and enhancing their interpretability and efficiency.

2.3.4.1 Linear regression: The foundation of predictive modeling

One of the earliest ML techniques, Linear Regression, models the relationship between a dependent variable (Y) and one or more independent variables (X) using a linear equation (Montgomery et al., 2021). The equation:

$$Y = \beta_0 + \beta_1 X + \epsilon$$

where β_0 is the intercept, β_1 is the coefficient (slope), and ε represents the error term. The model is optimized using the least squares method, minimizing the sum of squared residuals. Linear regression remains widely used in econometrics, risk assessment, and medical diagnostics (Hastie et al., 2009).

2.3.4.2 Logistic regression: A statistical approach to classification

Logistic Regression is an extension of linear regression designed for binary classification problems. Instead of predicting continuous values, it estimates the probability of an event occurring using the sigmoid activation function (Hosmer et al., 2013):

$$P(Y=1) = \frac{1}{1+e^{-(\beta 0+\beta 1X)}}$$

This method is extensively applied in spam detection, disease prediction, and fraud detection, where outcomes are binary (e.g., spam/nonspam, healthy/diseased).

2.3.4.3 Decision trees: Rule-based learning

Decision Trees create a hierarchical structure where data is split based on entropy reduction or Gini impurity (Quinlan, 1986). They provide a simple yet powerful framework for classification and regression problems. The most common tree-learning algorithm, CART (classification and regression trees), recursively partitions the dataset to maximize information gain.

Although easy to interpret, decision trees are prone to overfitting—a challenge mitigated by ensemble techniques like Random Forests and Gradient Boosting (Breiman, 2001).

2.3.4.4 Support vector machines: Maximizing decision boundaries

SVM rely on the concept of hyperplanes to classify data by maximizing the margin between different classes (Cortes and Vapnik, 1995). The optimization is solved using Lagrange multipliers and kernel functions (e.g., polynomial, radial basis function) for handling nonlinear classification problems.

SVM is widely used in image recognition, bioinformatics, and text classification, where high-dimensional data requires robust separation.

2.3.4.5 Neural networks and DL: The brain-inspired model

ANNs mimic the human brain, consisting of neurons (nodes) interconnected by weighted edges. The fundamental principle involves forward propagation, backpropagation, and gradient descent optimization (LeCun et al., 2015).

DL, a subset of neural networks, utilizes multiple hidden layers to extract complex patterns. Key architectures include:

- CNNs—used in computer vision tasks like facial recognition.
- RNNs and long short-term memories (LSTMs)—applied in speech recognition and time-series forecasting.
- Transformers (e.g., BERT, GPT) have revolutionized NLP (Vaswani et al., 2017).

2.3.4.6 RL: Learning through rewards

RL is based on the Markov decision process, where an agent interacts with an environment to maximize cumulative rewards (Sutton and Barto, 2018). Algorithms such as Q-Learning and DQN have led to breakthroughs in robotics, autonomous driving, and game playing (e.g., AlphaGo) (Silver et al., 2017).

2.4 Mathematical and statistical foundations

Mathematical and statistical foundations form the core framework of AI, enabling algorithms to learn, optimize, and make data-driven decisions. Key areas include linear algebra (for neural networks), probability theory (for uncertainty modeling), optimization techniques (for training models), and information theory (for data compression and entropy). These principles ensure AI systems are efficient, interpretable, and generalizable across diverse applications (Goodfellow et al., 2016).

2.4.1 Probability theory and Bayesian reasoning in AI

Probability theory serves as the mathematical foundation for decision-making under uncertainty, a crucial aspect of AI and ML. It provides a structured way to quantify uncertainty, enabling AI systems to make informed predictions, handle missing data, and adapt to dynamic environments (Murphy, 2012). Bayesian reasoning, a powerful extension of probability theory, allows AI models to continuously update their beliefs as new data becomes available, making it particularly valuable in real-world applications like medical diagnosis, autonomous systems, and NLP (Bishop, 2006).

2.4.1.1 Probability theory: The language of uncertainty

Probability theory is based on the fundamental concept of measuring the likelihood of an event occurring. It is defined by a probability space (Ω, F, P), where Ω represents the sample space, F is the set of events, and P is a probability function satisfying:

$$0 \leq P(A) \leq 1, P(\Omega) = 1$$

Key principles include:

- Law of Total Probability: Helps in handling multiple possible outcomes
- Conditional Probability: Expresses the probability of an event given another event; crucial for AI systems handling dependencies in data (Russell and Norvig, 2020)
- Bayes' Theorem: The foundation of Bayesian reasoning

2.4.1.2 Bayesian reasoning: Learning from data

Bayesian reasoning allows AI systems to dynamically update their beliefs based on prior knowledge and new evidence. This is represented by Bayes' Theorem:

$$P(H \mid E) = \frac{P(E \mid H)P(H)}{P(E)}$$

where:

- P(H|E) is the posterior probability (updated belief after seeing the evidence)
- P(E|H) is the likelihood (the probability of the evidence given the hypothesis)
- P(H) is the prior probability (initial belief)
- P(E) is the marginal likelihood (the overall probability of evidence)

Bayesian models are widely used in AI, particularly in:

- Spam detection: Naïve Bayes classifiers categorize emails based on word probabilities (Metsis et al., 2006)
- Medical diagnosis: Bayesian networks assess disease risks based on symptoms and prior cases (Lucas et al., 2004)
- Autonomous systems: Self-driving cars use Bayesian filtering (e.g., Kalman filters) to track objects and make navigation decisions (Thrun et al., 2005)

Probability theory and Bayesian reasoning form the backbone of AI's ability to handle uncertainty, learn from data, and make probabilistic predictions. As AI systems become more complex, Bayesian methods continue to enhance robustness, interpretability, and adaptability, making them essential tools for the next generation of intelligent systems.

2.4.2 Optimization techniques in ML

Optimization techniques in ML are mathematical methods used to minimize errors and improve model performance by adjusting parameters efficiently. Key techniques include gradient descent (SGD, Adam, RMSprop) for neural network training, convex optimization for loss minimization, and Bayesian optimization for hyperparameter tuning. These techniques ensure faster convergence, better generalization, and improved computational efficiency in AI models (Bishop, 2006; Goodfellow et al., 2016).

2.4.2.1 Optimization techniques in ML

In the realm of ML, optimization techniques are pivotal for enhancing model performance by fine-tuning parameters and minimizing errors. Key methodologies include **gradient descent** variants for neural network training, **convex optimization** for loss minimization, and **Bayesian optimization** for hyperparameter tuning.

2.4.2.2 Gradient descent and its variants

Gradient Descent is a foundational algorithm used to minimize the loss function in neural networks by iteratively adjusting parameters in the direction of the steepest descent. However, standard Gradient Descent can be inefficient, especially with large datasets, leading to the development of variants such as **SGD**, **RMSprop**, and **Adam**.

- **SGD:** Unlike batch gradient descent, which computes gradients using the entire dataset, SGD updates parameters using a single data point per iteration. This approach introduces noise into the updates, which can help escape local minima but may lead to oscillations around the optimum.
- **RMSprop:** Proposed by Geoffrey Hinton, RMSprop addresses the diminishing learning rates in AdaGrad by maintaining a moving average of the squared gradients. This adaptive learning rate ensures efficient training, even in the presence of nonstationary objectives, making it suitable for online and nonconvex optimization problems.
- **Adam (adaptive moment estimation):** Combining the benefits of RMSprop and momentum, Adam computes adaptive learning rates for each parameter by estimating the first and second moments of the gradients. This results in faster convergence and is particularly effective for problems with sparse gradients or noisy objectives.

Recent studies have highlighted the efficacy of these optimizers. For instance, research indicates that the utilization of optimizers such as SGD and Adam improves accuracy in the training, testing, and validation stages.

2.4.2.3 Convex optimization for loss minimization

Convex optimization plays a crucial role in ML, especially when dealing with convex loss functions, where any local minimum is also a global minimum. Techniques such as **Newton's method** leverage second-order derivatives (Hessian matrices) to find the optimal parameters efficiently. While powerful, these methods can be computationally intensive for large-scale problems due to the need to compute and invert the Hessian. To mitigate this, quasi-Newton methods like **L-BFGS** approximate the Hessian, offering a balance between computational efficiency and convergence speed.

2.4.2.4 Bayesian optimization for hyperparameter tuning

Hyperparameters, unlike model parameters, are set prior to training and significantly influence model performance. **Bayesian optimization** offers a probabilistic framework to find the optimal hyperparameters by constructing a surrogate model, typically a Gaussian Process, to model the objective function. By iteratively selecting hyperparameters that balance exploration and exploitation, Bayesian optimization efficiently converges to optimal configurations. This approach is particularly advantageous when training models is expensive, as it reduces the number of required evaluations.

Optimization techniques are the backbone of effective ML models. Gradient Descent variants enhance neural network training efficiency, convex optimization ensures effective loss minimization, and Bayesian optimization streamlines hyperparameter tuning. A deep understanding of these methods enables practitioners to select and tailor algorithms that best suit their specific applications, leading to robust and high-performing AI systems.

2.4.3 Information theory and its role in AI

Information theory, established by Claude Shannon in the mid-20th century, is the mathematical study of data transmission, compression, and processing. It provides a framework for quantifying information, measuring uncertainty, and analyzing communication systems. In the realm of AI, information theory offers essential tools and concepts that enhance the efficiency and effectiveness of learning algorithms, data representation, and decision-making processes.

2.4.3.1 Quantifying uncertainty and entropy

At the heart of information theory lies the concept of **entropy**, which measures the uncertainty or unpredictability in a set of possible outcomes. In AI, entropy is utilized to assess the amount of information gained when making decisions or predictions. For instance, in decision tree algorithms, entropy guides the selection of attributes that best split the data, aiming to reduce uncertainty and improve classification accuracy. By quantifying uncertainty, AI systems can prioritize information that maximizes learning efficiency.

2.4.3.2 Mutual information and feature selection

Mutual information quantifies the amount of information shared between variables, indicating how the knowledge of one variable reduces uncertainty about another. In AI, mutual information is employed in feature selection processes to identify which input variables are most informative about the output. By selecting features with high mutual information relative to the target variable, models can achieve better performance with reduced complexity, leading to more interpretable and efficient systems.

2.4.3.3 Data compression and efficient representation

Information theory introduces principles of data compression, such as Huffman coding and Shannon-Fano coding, which aim to represent data in the most efficient manner by reducing redundancy. In AI, these principles are applied to develop compact representations of data, enabling models to process and store information more effectively. Efficient data representation is crucial in scenarios with limited storage or bandwidth, as it allows AI systems to maintain performance while operating under constraints.

2.4.3.4 Error detection and correction in communication

Reliable data transmission is vital for AI systems, especially in distributed networks and real-time applications. Information theory provides the foundation for error detection and correction techniques, such as parity checks and error-correcting codes, ensuring that data received is accurate and intact. Implementing these techniques allows AI systems to function robustly even in noisy environments, maintaining the integrity of information processing and decision-making.

2.4.3.5 DL and information bottleneck

In DL, the information bottleneck method applies information-theoretic principles to optimize neural networks. This approach involves compressing input data while preserving relevant information for the task, effectively balancing complexity and performance. By focusing on the most informative aspects of the data, models can generalize better to unseen examples, enhancing their predictive capabilities.

2.4.3.6 RL and reward optimization

Information theory also plays a role in RL, where agents learn to make decisions by interacting with an environment. Kullback-Leibler divergence, a measure from information theory, is often used to ensure that the updated policy remains close to the previous policy, promoting stable learning. This balance between exploration and exploitation is critical for optimizing long-term rewards in dynamic settings.

The integration of information theory into AI provides a robust mathematical framework for addressing challenges related to uncertainty, data representation, and learning efficiency. By leveraging concepts such as entropy, mutual information, and error correction, AI systems can achieve more reliable and interpretable outcomes. As AI continues to evolve, the principles of information theory will remain integral to developing intelligent systems capable of processing information in a manner that is both efficient and effective.

2.4.4 Complexity theory and computational constraints in artificial intelligence

Complexity theory, a cornerstone of theoretical computer science, delves into classifying computational problems based on the resources required for their resolution, such as time and space. In the realm of AI, understanding these complexities is paramount, as it directly influences the feasibility and efficiency of algorithmic solutions. Computational constraints, encompassing limitations in processing power, memory, and energy, further dictate the practical deployment of AI systems.

2.4.4.1 Foundations of complexity theory

At its core, complexity theory seeks to determine the inherent difficulty of computational problems by analyzing the resources needed to solve them. Problems are categorized into complexity classes, with **P** representing those solvable in polynomial time and **NP** encompassing problems verifiable in polynomial time. The enigmatic **P** vs. **NP** question probes whether every problem whose solution can be quickly verified can also be quickly solved—a query that remains unresolved and is pivotal to both theoretical and applied computer science.

2.4.4.2 Implications for artificial intelligence

AI algorithms often grapple with problems that reside in higher complexity classes, making them computationally intensive. For instance, exact inference in Bayesian networks has been proven to be NP-hard, indicating that as the size of the network grows, the resources required for precise computation escalate exponentially. This necessitates the development of approximate methods or heuristics to render problem-solving tractable in real-world applications.

2.4.4.3 Navigating computational constraints

The deployment of AI systems is invariably influenced by computational constraints. Processing power, memory capacity, and energy consumption are critical factors, especially in environments like mobile devices or embedded systems, where resources are limited. To address these challenges, AI practitioners employ strategies such as model compression, which reduces the size of neural networks without significant loss of performance, and algorithmic optimizations that enhance efficiency. Moreover, distributed computing frameworks allow for the partitioning of complex tasks across multiple processors, thereby mitigating individual resource burdens.

2.4.4.4 Balancing complexity and practicality

A profound understanding of complexity theory enables AI researchers to anticipate potential computational hurdles and devise algorithms that balance optimality with feasibility. For example, while certain ML models may offer high accuracy, their training and inference times might be prohibitive. In such scenarios, selecting models with a favorable trade-off between complexity and performance becomes essential. In addition, awareness of computational constraints guides the design of AI systems that are both effective and efficient, ensuring their applicability across diverse platforms and use cases.

2.5 Key AI/ML techniques and frameworks

AI and ML encompass diverse techniques and frameworks that power intelligent systems. Neural networks, particularly DL architectures, drive breakthroughs in image recognition, speech processing, and decision-making. NLP enables human-like text comprehension, with transformer models like GPT and BERT revolutionizing language understanding. Computer vision techniques enhance image analysis for applications in healthcare, security, and automation. XAI ensures model transparency and interpretability, addressing ethical concerns. Widely used frameworks such as TensorFlow, PyTorch, and Scikit-learn facilitate AI/ML development, providing scalable solutions for predictive modeling, simulation, and real-time optimization in DTC.

2.5.1 Neural networks and DL architectures

2.5.1.1 Introduction to neural networks

Neural networks are computational models inspired by the structure and functionality of biological neurons. These networks form the foundation of modern AI and ML, enabling systems to recognize patterns, make decisions, and perform complex tasks with minimal human intervention (LeCun et al., 2015).

A neural network consists of multiple layers of interconnected artificial neurons, each processing information and passing it to the next layer. The core components include:

- **Input layer**—Receives raw data inputs
- **Hidden layers**—Perform feature extraction and transformation
- **Output layer**—Produces predictions or classifications

2.5.1.2 DL and its evolution

DL is a subset of ML that involves training DNNs with multiple hidden layers, enabling superior learning from large datasets (Goodfellow et al., 2016). Traditional ML techniques rely on feature engineering, whereas DL models automatically extract relevant features, making them particularly effective for image recognition, speech processing, and natural language understanding.

Advancements in computational power, the availability of big data, and optimized training algorithms like **backpropagation** and **SGD** have contributed to the rapid evolution of DL. State-of-the-art architectures include **CNNs** for image tasks and **transformer networks** for NLP.

2.5.1.3 Types of neural network architectures

Feedforward neural networks

Feedforward neural networks represent the simplest form of neural networks, where information moves in a single direction—from input to output. They are primarily used in classification and regression tasks (Schmidhuber, 2015).

Convolutional neural networks

CNNs are widely used for image and video processing. They leverage spatial hierarchies and convolutional layers to automatically detect features such as edges, textures, and shapes (Krizhevsky et al., 2012). A standard CNN consists of:

- **Convolutional layers**—Extract spatial features using filters
- **Pooling layers**—Reduce dimensionality while preserving important information
- **Fully connected layers**—Interpret extracted features for final classification (Fig. 2.6)

Recurrent neural networks and long short-term memory

RNNs process sequential data by maintaining memory across time steps. They are used in speech recognition, text generation, and financial forecasting. However, traditional RNNs suffer from the vanishing gradient problem, which LSTMs and gated recurrent units address by introducing memory cells with gated mechanisms (Hochreiter and Schmidhuber, 1997).

Transformer networks

Transformers, introduced by Vaswani et al., 2017, have revolutionized NLP by replacing sequential processing with self-attention mechanisms. They power advanced models like BERT (Devlin et al., 2019) and GPT (Brown et al., 2020), which have significantly improved natural language understanding and text generation (Fig. 2.7).

Generative adversarial networks

GANs consist of a **generator** and a **discriminator,** competing against each other to generate realistic synthetic data. They have applications in image generation, style transfer, and drug discovery (Goodfellow et al., 2014).

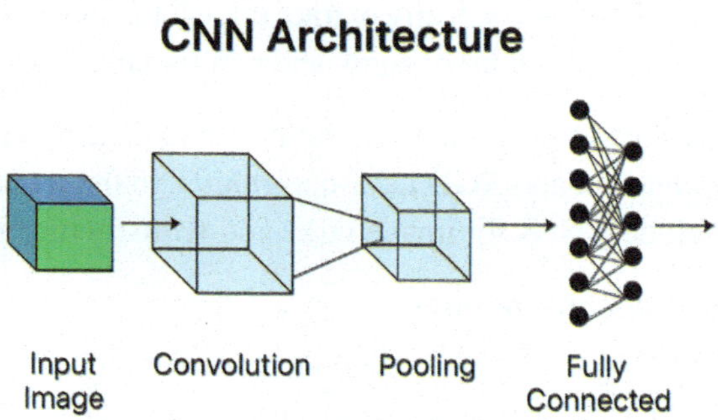

Fig. 2.6 CNN architecture.

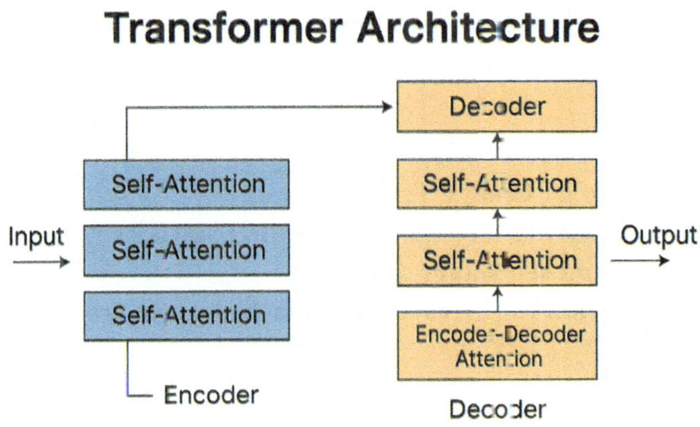

Fig. 2.7 Transformer architecture.

2.5.1.4 Challenges and future directions

Despite their success, DNNs face challenges such as high computational costs, interpretability, and vulnerability to adversarial attacks. Researchers are exploring XAI, neuromorphic computing, and quantum AI to address these issues (Lipton, 2018).

Neural networks and DL architectures have transformed AI, driving progress in fields like computer vision, NLP, and robotics. Future advancements will focus on improving efficiency, interpretability, and integration with emerging technologies like quantum computing and DTC.

2.5.2 Natural language processing and transformer models

2.5.2.1 Introduction to NLP

NLP is a branch of AI that enables computers to understand, interpret, and generate human language. NLP combines computational linguistics with ML and DL to facilitate tasks such as machine translation, sentiment analysis, and text summarization (Jurafsky and Martin, 2021).

Traditional NLP approaches relied on rule-based systems and statistical methods, but recent advancements in DL, particularly Transformer models, have revolutionized the field, enabling more sophisticated language comprehension and generation (Young et al., 2018).

2.5.2.2 Core NLP techniques and applications

NLP techniques can be broadly categorized into syntactic and semantic processing:

- **Syntactic analysis**: Focuses on grammar, structure, and parsing techniques, such as Part-of-Speech (POS) tagging and dependency parsing.

- **Semantic analysis**: Involves meaning representation using methods such as word embeddings and attention mechanisms.

Key applications of NLP include:

- **Machine translation** (e.g., **Google Translate)**
- **Chatbots and virtual assistants** (e.g., **Siri, Alexa, ChatGPT)**
- **Text summarization and sentiment analysis**
- **Named entity recognition for extracting key information from text**

2.5.2.3 Evolution of NLP models

NLP has evolved from basic rule-based systems to DL-based models:

1. **Rule-based NLP**—Early systems relied on manually crafted linguistic rules.
2. **Statistical NLP**—ML-based models use probabilities to process language, such as Hidden Markov Models and Conditional Random Fields (Manning and Schütze, 1999).
3. **Neural network-based NLP**—The introduction of DL enabled more efficient NLP models, including RNNs and LSTM networks (Hochreiter and Schmidhuber, 1997).
4. **Transformer models**—Introduced in 2017, transformers replaced sequential models with self-attention mechanisms, leading to major advancements in NLP (Vaswani et al., 2017).

2.5.2.4 Transformer models: A breakthrough in NLP

Transformer models represent the most significant advancement in NLP, enabling state-of-the-art performance across various language tasks. The **Transformer architecture,** introduced by Vaswani et al. (2017), utilizes a self-attention mechanism that allows models to process entire sequences efficiently.

2.5.2.5 Key components of transformer architecture

A Transformer model consists of an **encoder-decoder** structure, where:

- **Encoders** extract key representations from input text
- **Decoders** generate meaningful responses or translations
- **Self-attention mechanisms** enable the model to focus on different parts of the input text dynamically

2.5.2.6 Popular transformer-based NLP models

1. **BERT**—A deep bidirectional model that improves contextual understanding in NLP tasks (Devlin et al., 2019).
2. **GPT**—A unidirectional model designed for text generation, powering applications like ChatGPT (Brown et al., 2020).

3. **Text-to-Text Transfer Transformer**—A model that treats all NLP tasks as a text-to-text problem (Raffel et al., 2020).

2.5.2.7 Challenges and future directions

Despite their success, Transformer models face challenges such as:

- **High computational cost and energy consumption** (Strubell et al., 2019)
- **Bias in training data, leading to ethical concerns** (Bender et al., 2021)
- **Lack of interpretability in deep NLP models** (Lipton, 2018)

Future research focuses on efficient transformers, multimodal AI (combining text, image, and speech processing), and quantum-enhanced NLP for faster computations (Preskill, 2018).

NLP has transformed significantly with DL, particularly through Transformer models. These models power cutting-edge applications in AI, from automated translation to conversational AI. Future advancements will focus on improving efficiency, reducing bias, and integrating NLP with emerging technologies like blockchain and DTC.

2.5.3 Computer vision and image processing

CV and Image Processing (IP) are interconnected fields that enable machines to interpret and manipulate visual data. These domains have witnessed rapid advancements due to the evolution of AI and DL. CV focuses on enabling machines to understand and analyze images and videos, whereas IP involves enhancing, manipulating, and transforming visual data before analysis. Together, these technologies drive innovations in autonomous systems, healthcare, security, and industrial automation (Goodfellow et al., 2016).

2.5.3.1 Fundamentals and techniques

Image processing is primarily concerned with operations such as filtering, noise reduction, segmentation, edge detection, and feature extraction. It involves the use of mathematical and statistical models to improve image quality or extract essential features (Gonzalez and Woods, 2018). Techniques like histogram equalization, Gaussian filtering, and Fourier transforms play a crucial role in preprocessing images before they are analyzed by computer vision models.

On the other hand, CV extends beyond basic image processing by integrating AI and ML algorithms to interpret and understand images. This includes object detection, facial recognition, scene understanding, and motion tracking. DL models, particularly CNNs, have revolutionized computer vision by achieving state-of-the-art performance in tasks like image classification and segmentation (Krizhevsky et al., 2012).

2.5.3.2 Applications in modern technology

The integration of CV and IP has transformed multiple industries. In **healthcare**, medical imaging technologies such as MRI and CT scan analysis rely on image processing for enhanced visualization and AI-driven diagnostics for disease detection (Litjens et al., 2017). Automated tumor detection and retinal disease screening are among the significant breakthroughs in this field.

In **autonomous vehicles**, computer vision enables real-time object detection, lane tracking, and obstacle recognition, ensuring safe navigation (Redmon and Farhadi, 2018). Tesla and Waymo leverage sophisticated DL models to enhance the perception abilities of self-driving cars.

Security and surveillance have also benefited significantly from these advancements. Facial recognition systems, powered by DL, assist in identity verification and crime prevention. Governments and private sectors employ biometric authentication for security applications, although ethical concerns related to privacy and bias remain (Buolamwini and Gebru, 2018).

In **industrial automation**, manufacturing processes use computer vision for quality control, defect detection, and robotic guidance. Smart factories employ automated visual inspection to ensure precision and efficiency (Li et al., 2020).

2.5.3.3 Challenges and future directions

Despite its vast potential, computer vision and image processing face challenges such as data privacy, bias in AI models, and computational complexity. The accuracy of vision-based AI systems depends heavily on high-quality annotated data, and bias in datasets can lead to discriminatory outcomes (Mitchell et al., 2019). Furthermore, real-time image processing requires significant computational power, necessitating advances in hardware acceleration and efficient algorithms.

The future of computer vision lies in integrating **XAI**, **neuromorphic computing**, and **edge computing** to develop robust, interpretable, and real-time vision systems. With continuous advancements, these technologies will further revolutionize domains such as smart cities, augmented reality, and space exploration, making machines more perceptive and intelligent.

2.5.4 Explainable AI and model interpretability

AI has made significant advancements in complex decision-making tasks, yet the **"black box"** nature of many AI models, especially DL systems, raises concerns regarding transparency, trust, and accountability. **XAI** aims to bridge this gap by making AI models more interpretable, understandable, and trustworthy for users, regulators, and stakeholders (Doshi-Velez and Kim, 2017).

2.5.4.1 Understanding XAI

XAI refers to techniques and frameworks that provide human-interpretable explanations of AI model decisions. It is crucial in high-stakes applications such as healthcare, finance, and criminal justice, where understanding why a model made a specific prediction is as important as the prediction itself (Adadi and Berrada, 2018). XAI enhances user confidence, regulatory compliance, and fairness in AI-driven decision-making.

XAI techniques can be categorized into:

1. **Intrinsic interpretability**: Models that are inherently interpretable due to their simpler structures, such as decision trees and logistic regression.
2. **Post hoc explainability**: Methods applied after model training to explain complex models, such as feature importance analysis, Local Interpretable Model-agnostic Explanations (LIME), and SHapley Additive exPlanations (SHAP) (Ribeiro et al., 2016).

2.5.4.2 Importance of model interpretability

Model interpretability ensures that AI systems are transparent, accountable, and fair. It helps detect bias, ensures compliance with regulations like the EU's General Data Protection Regulation (GDPR), and allows end-users to trust AI-driven decisions (Lipton, 2018). In addition, interpretability aids in debugging AI models, improving their robustness and reliability.

2.5.4.3 Challenges and future directions

Despite its importance, achieving interpretability in complex AI models is challenging. Trade-offs exist between model accuracy and explainability, as simpler models are easier to interpret but may lack predictive power compared to DL models (Gunning et al., 2019). Moreover, biases in training data can lead to misleading explanations, necessitating ethical considerations in AI model development.

Future research in XAI focuses on causal explanations, human-in-the-loop AI, and hybrid models that balance complexity with interpretability. The integration of XAI into AI governance frameworks will be essential in ensuring responsible AI deployment in society.

2.6 DTC: The role of AI/ML

DTC creates virtual replicas of physical systems to simulate, analyze, and optimize real-world processes. AI and ML enhance DTC by enabling predictive analytics, anomaly detection, and real-time decision-making. AI-driven DTs improve efficiency in industries such as manufacturing, healthcare, and smart cities by continuously learning from sensor data and adapting to environmental changes (Tao et al., 2019). ML algorithms optimize system performance, forecast failures, and facilitate autonomous decision-making, making DTs a powerful tool for innovation and operational efficiency (Grieves and Vickers, 2017).

2.6.1 Overview of DT technology

DTT is a revolutionary concept that creates virtual representations of physical systems, enabling real-time monitoring, analysis, and optimization. A DT is a dynamic, data-driven replica of a physical entity that evolves with real-world changes through continuous data exchange. This technology is transforming industries such as manufacturing, healthcare, smart cities, and aerospace by improving operational efficiency and decision-making (Tao et al., 2019).

2.6.1.1 Core components of DT technology

A DT typically comprises the following components:

1. **Physical system**—The real-world entity (e.g., a machine, the human body, or urban infrastructure).
2. **Virtual model**—A digital counterpart created using simulations, 3D modeling, and AI-driven analytics.
3. **Data flow and connectivity**—IoT sensors, cloud computing, and edge devices enable real-time data exchange.
4. **AI and ML**—advanced algorithms analyze data patterns, predict outcomes, and optimize system performance (Grieves and Vickers, 2017).

2.6.1.2 Applications of DTT

1. **Manufacturing and Industry 4.0** DTs enhance predictive maintenance, optimize production processes, and improve product design. Smart factories use DTs to simulate **supply chain dynamics, detect equipment failures, and reduce downtime** (Kritzinger et al., 2018).
2. **Healthcare and personalized medicine** DTs of human organs and biological systems help in personalized treatment, surgical planning, and drug development. Virtual simulations of patient conditions allow **real-time monitoring and proactive medical interventions** (Bruynseels et al., 2018).
3. **Smart cities and urban planning** Governments leverage DTs for **traffic management, energy optimization, and disaster response planning**. AI-powered simulations assist in infrastructure development and policy decision-making (Batty, 2018).
4. **Aerospace and automotive industry** DTs in aviation and automotive industries improve safety, optimize fuel efficiency, and enhance vehicle design. Boeing and Airbus use **DTs for aircraft lifecycle management** (Glaessgen and Stargel, 2012).

2.6.1.3 Future prospects and challenges

Despite its potential, DT adoption faces challenges such as high implementation costs, cybersecurity risks, and data integration complexities. The future of DTT lies in edge computing, blockchain for secure data exchange, and integration with AI-driven autonomous systems (Fuller et al., 2020).

2.6.2 AI-driven predictive modeling in DTs

DTT has revolutionized how industries monitor, analyze, and optimize physical systems in real time. The integration of AI and ML into DTs enhances their capabilities, enabling predictive modeling to forecast system behavior, detect anomalies, and optimize performance. AI-driven predictive modeling allows DTs to anticipate future events, reduce risks, minimize downtime, and improve decision-making (Tao et al., 2019). This approach is widely applied in manufacturing, healthcare, smart cities, and aerospace, making operations more data-driven and intelligent.

2.6.2.1 Fundamentals of AI-driven predictive modeling

Predictive modeling in DTs leverages AI and ML algorithms to analyze vast amounts of real-time data collected from IoT sensors, industrial machines, and cloud platforms. The core processes involved in AI-driven predictive modeling include:

1. Data collection and preprocessing
    - IoT sensors capture real-time operational data from physical assets
    - Data is cleaned, normalized, and structured for AI processing
    - Advanced data fusion techniques combine multiple data sources for accuracy (Grieves and Vickers, 2017)
2. AI and ML algorithm integration
    - Supervised Learning (e.g., decision trees, random forests) predicts outcomes based on historical, labeled data
    - Unsupervised learning (e.g., k-means clustering, autoencoders) identifies patterns and anomalies in unlabeled data
    - DL models (e.g., neural networks, LSTMs) analyze complex temporal data and predict future trends (Glaessgen and Stargel, 2012)
3. Simulation and real-time predictions
    - AI models continuously simulate multiple operational scenarios
    - Predictive analytics forecasts equipment failures, energy consumption, production efficiency, and system anomalies
    - Adaptive learning mechanisms refine predictions based on feedback loops
4. Decision support and automation
    - AI-generated insights support human decision-makers

- Automated decision-making systems adjust maintenance schedules, resource allocation, and workflow optimizations
- Edge computing and cloud-based AI enable decentralized intelligence (Fuller et al., 2020)

2.6.2.2 Applications of AI-driven predictive modeling in DTs

Smart manufacturing and industry 4.0

Predictive maintenance in DTs helps factories anticipate machine breakdowns before they occur, minimizing downtime and improving efficiency. AI-driven models analyze vibration patterns, thermal readings, and operational data to optimize maintenance cycles (Kritzinger et al., 2018).

Healthcare and personalized medicine

AI-powered DTs in healthcare simulate human organs, medical conditions, and treatment responses. Predictive models help doctors anticipate disease progression, drug reactions, and surgery outcomes in personalized medicine (Bruynseels et al., 2018).

Smart cities and infrastructure

DTs in smart cities use AI to predict traffic congestion, energy consumption, and environmental changes. Predictive analytics enhance urban planning, disaster response, and resource management (Batty, 2018).

Aerospace and automotive industry

AI-driven DTs in aerospace monitor aircraft engines, predicting component failures before they happen. Automotive companies use DTs to optimize vehicle fuel efficiency, safety mechanisms, and autonomous driving performance (Glaessgen and Stargel, 2012).

2.6.2.3 Challenges and future directions

Despite the advantages of AI-driven predictive modeling, challenges remain:

- Data privacy and security: Handling vast amounts of sensitive data raises cybersecurity concerns.
- Computational complexity: Training large-scale AI models requires high-performance computing resources.
- Model interpretability: AI models must be transparent to ensure trust and regulatory compliance (Lipton, 2018).

Future advancements in quantum computing, XAI, and self-learning AI will further enhance DTs, making them more autonomous and adaptive. AI-driven DTs will play a crucial role in shaping next-generation industrial automation, precision healthcare, and intelligent urban systems.

2.6.3 ML for real-time simulation and optimization

ML has emerged as a transformative force in real-time simulation and optimization, particularly in fields that rely on high-speed decision-making, predictive modeling, and process automation. The integration of ML with DTT allows for the creation of intelligent, self-adaptive systems capable of learning from real-world data, predicting future states, and optimizing operations dynamically (Tao et al., 2019). From manufacturing and healthcare to smart cities and financial markets, real-time ML-driven simulation enables organizations to improve efficiency, reduce risks, and enhance decision-making accuracy.

2.6.3.1 The role of ML in real-time simulation

Real-time simulation refers to the ability to model and replicate complex systems instantly, incorporating real-world data streams and computational algorithms to provide actionable insights. Traditional simulation methods often rely on static models and predefined rules, making them less effective at handling dynamic and uncertain environments. ML enhances real-time simulation by:

- **Predicting system behavior**: Using historical and live data, ML algorithms forecast future trends, system failures, and operational inefficiencies.
- **Reducing computational load**: Instead of processing extensive simulations from scratch, ML enables approximate models that deliver near-instant results with high accuracy (Glaessgen and Stargel, 2012).
- **Enhancing adaptability**: Self-learning models evolve over time, refining their predictions and recommendations based on real-world feedback (Fuller et al., 2020).

A key example of ML in real-time simulation is in autonomous vehicles, where DL models predict road conditions, vehicle dynamics, and potential hazards to enable real-time decision-making for navigation and safety. Similarly, smart grids leverage ML-based simulations to balance energy distribution, predict power outages, and optimize resource allocation dynamically (Batty, 2018).

2.6.3.2 ML for real-time optimization

Optimization involves making systems more efficient, cost-effective, and performance-driven. ML-driven optimization techniques include RL, DL, and neural network-based evolutionary algorithms. These methods continuously refine decision-making by analyzing vast datasets, learning from outcomes, and adjusting control parameters to achieve optimal performance.

One of the most impactful applications is in Industry 4.0 and smart manufacturing, where ML algorithms:

- **Optimize production lines:** AI-driven models predict machine failures and schedule maintenance proactively, reducing downtime (Kritzinger et al., 2018).
- **Enhance supply chain management**: Predictive models anticipate demand fluctuations, enabling inventory adjustments in real-time.
- **Improve quality control:** Vision-based ML systems detect defects during production, ensuring zero-error manufacturing.

Beyond manufacturing, ML-powered real-time optimization plays a critical role in financial trading, where AI algorithms process millions of transactions per second to identify trading opportunities, minimize risks, and maximize profits (Lipton, 2018).

2.6.3.3 Challenges and future prospects

While ML-based real-time simulation and optimization offer unprecedented efficiency and accuracy, several challenges remain. Data quality and availability significantly impact model performance, as unreliable data can lead to biased or incorrect predictions. Furthermore, computational complexity and the demand for high-processing power remain barriers to widespread adoption (Grieves and Vickers, 2017).

To overcome these challenges, advancements in quantum computing, federated learning, and edge AI are being explored. Future ML models will not only predict and optimize but also explain their decision-making processes using XAI, increasing transparency and trust.

ML is redefining real-time simulation and optimization, transforming industries by enabling data-driven intelligence, automation, and adaptability. Whether predicting machine failures in manufacturing, optimizing energy consumption in smart cities, or enhancing precision medicine in healthcare, ML is making systems more resilient, efficient, and proactive. The future holds immense potential for self-learning, AI-driven ecosystems that operate in real time, continuously improving outcomes across diverse domains.

2.6.4 Case studies: AI/ML-powered DTs in healthcare, manufacturing, and smart cities

2.6.4.1 Healthcare: AI-driven DTs for personalized medicine

One of the most groundbreaking applications of DTs in healthcare is in personalized medicine. AI-powered DTs simulate an individual's physiology, genetic makeup, and disease progression, enabling customized treatment plans and drug testing without human trials (Bruynseels et al., 2018).

For instance, Siemens Healthineers developed a cardiac DT that replicates a patient's heart function based on real-time data from imaging and wearable sensors. This allows doctors to predict the impact of interventions like stent placement or drug therapy, reducing the risks of invasive procedures (Fuller et al., 2020). Similarly, General Electric (GE) Healthcare employs AI-driven DTs to simulate the behavior of organs, helping clinicians detect early-stage diseases such as cancer and neurological disorders with higher accuracy.

2.6.4.2 Manufacturing: AI-powered DTs in smart factories

In Industry 4.0, AI and ML-powered DTs enhance predictive maintenance, process optimization, and quality control. A notable case is GE, which uses AI-driven DTs in gas turbines and jet engines. These DTs process real-time operational data, predict failures before they happen, and optimize fuel efficiency, reducing maintenance costs by up to 30% (Kritzinger et al., 2018).

Another example is BMW's smart factory, where AI-driven DTs simulate entire production lines, material flow, and worker interactions. This enables real-time detection of inefficiencies and ensures seamless coordination between human workers and autonomous robots (Tao et al., 2019). By leveraging ML algorithms, BMW has reduced production defects by 25% and improved overall factory efficiency.

2.6.4.3 Smart cities: AI-enhanced DTs for urban planning

DTs powered by AI are transforming smart city development by optimizing traffic management, energy distribution, and disaster preparedness. Singapore's Virtual Singapore project is an AI-driven urban DT that simulates real-time population movement, infrastructure development, and energy usage (Batty, 2018). The system helps policymakers predict traffic congestion, plan sustainable infrastructure, and respond to natural disasters more efficiently.

Similarly, the city of Las Vegas uses an AI-powered DT to monitor air pollution, water supply, and energy consumption. ML models analyze real-time environmental data to optimize waste management and reduce carbon emissions, contributing to a more sustainable and resilient urban ecosystem.

AI-powered DTs are transforming healthcare, manufacturing, and urban planning by enabling real-time simulations, predictive analytics, and adaptive decision-making. As technology advances, these intelligent systems will play a crucial role in shaping the future of industries and societies worldwide.

2.7 Challenges and ethical considerations

The rapid advancement of AI and ML has brought transformative benefits across various sectors, yet it also introduces significant challenges and ethical concerns. AI-driven systems, including DTs, influence high-stakes domains like healthcare, finance, and security, where decisions directly impact human lives. Issues such as bias in AI models, lack of transparency, inadequate regulatory frameworks, and safety risks in critical applications have raised concerns about fairness, accountability, and ethical AI deployment (Jobin et al., 2019). Addressing these challenges requires a multidisciplinary approach, combining technical innovations, governance policies, and ethical AI principles to ensure responsible AI development and deployment.

2.7.1 Bias, fairness, and AI ethics

Bias in AI models is a pressing ethical concern, as it can lead to discriminatory outcomes, reinforce societal inequalities, and erode trust in AI-driven decision-making. Bias often originates from historical data imbalances, flawed feature selection, or algorithmic design choices that disproportionately affect marginalized communities. A notable example is biased facial recognition software, which has exhibited higher error rates for people of color, leading to concerns over racial discrimination in law enforcement and hiring processes.

Fairness in AI demands equitable model training, inclusive dataset curation, and continuous bias detection mechanisms. Techniques such as Fairness-Aware Learning and Adversarial Debiasing aim to mitigate disparities by adjusting model predictions based on fairness constraints (Mehrabi et al., 2021). However, ensuring fairness is context-dependent, as different applications require tailored fairness metrics that balance trade-offs between accuracy and equity.

Ethical AI frameworks emphasize the principles of accountability, beneficence, and human-centric design. Organizations like the Institute of Electrical and Electronics Engineers (IEEE) and Organisation for Economic Co-operation and Development (OECD) advocate for ethical AI guidelines, urging developers to prioritize human welfare, respect privacy, and promote responsible AI governance. Addressing bias and fairness challenges requires interdisciplinary collaboration among AI researchers, ethicists, policymakers, and industry leaders to build equitable and ethical AI systems.

2.7.2 Trust, transparency, and explainability in AI systems

Trust in AI systems is fundamental to their widespread adoption, yet many models operate as "black boxes", where decision-making processes are opaque. This lack of transparency raises concerns, particularly in critical areas such as healthcare diagnostics, financial lending, and criminal justice, where AI-driven recommendations must be explainable and interpretable (Lipton, 2018).

Transparency involves making AI operations understandable to both technical and nontechnical stakeholders. Techniques such as model visualizations, rule-based decision trees, and case-based reasoning enhance interpretability, allowing users to understand how and why AI reaches specific conclusions. Post hoc explainability methods, like LIME and

SHAP, offer insights into individual AI decisions without altering the underlying model (Ribeiro et al., 2016).

XAI is critical in regulatory compliance, particularly under frameworks like the EU GDPR, which mandates "meaningful explanations" for automated decisions. Without explainability, AI models risk legal challenges, user distrust, and unintended harmful consequences. The future of XAI lies in causality-driven models, interactive AI explanations, and human-in-the-loop systems that integrate user feedback to enhance trust and transparency in AI applications.

2.7.3 AI governance and regulatory frameworks

The rapid deployment of AI across industries necessitates robust governance and regulatory frameworks to ensure responsible development and deployment. AI governance refers to the policies, guidelines, and oversight mechanisms that regulate AI systems, addressing concerns related to bias, privacy, accountability, and security (Floridi et al., 2018).

Governments and international organizations have introduced various AI regulatory frameworks. The European Union's AI Act proposes a risk-based classification system that categorizes AI applications into unacceptable, high-risk, and low-risk levels, imposing stricter compliance requirements for high-risk AI (European Commission, 2021). Similarly, the U.S. National Institute of Standards and Technology (NIST) advocates for an AI Risk Management Framework, promoting best practices for safe and ethical AI use.

Corporate governance in AI is also evolving, with tech companies establishing AI ethics boards, transparency reports, and impact assessments to ensure compliance with ethical AI principles. However, regulatory challenges persist, including cross-border AI policies, enforcement complexities, and balancing innovation with risk mitigation. The future of AI governance requires global cooperation, adaptive regulations, and industry-wide commitment to ethical AI practices.

2.7.4 AI safety and robustness in critical applications

AI safety and robustness are crucial in mission-critical applications such as autonomous driving, healthcare, financial systems, and defense. Ensuring that AI models operate reliably under diverse conditions, adversarial attacks, and unexpected inputs is essential for preventing catastrophic failures (Amodei et al., 2016).

One of the primary concerns in AI safety is adversarial attacks, where slight modifications in input data can manipulate AI predictions, leading to misclassifications. In autonomous vehicles, adversarial perturbations in traffic signs have been shown to trick AI systems into making dangerous driving decisions (Kurakin et al., 2017). Robust AI models employ defensive training, uncertainty quantification, and anomaly detection to resist adversarial manipulations.

In healthcare AI, robustness ensures that diagnostic models generalize across diverse populations and are not skewed by biased training data. AI-driven medical imaging tools must be rigorously tested on multisource datasets to confirm reliability across demographics (Litjens et al., 2017).

Regulatory bodies emphasize safe AI deployment, with frameworks like the Food and Drug Administration (FDA)'s AI/ML-Based Software as a Medical Device outlining safety and efficacy requirements for medical AI systems. The future of AI safety involves self-learning models, real-time error detection, and AI auditing mechanisms, ensuring trustworthy AI in high-stakes domains.

2.8 Future directions and research challenges

The evolution of AI and ML in DTC continues to open new frontiers, enabling smarter, more adaptive, and autonomous systems. However, as AI-driven DTs become more complex, new challenges emerge in terms of scalability, real-time decision-making, security, and interoperability. Future research must focus on advancing AI/ML models, integrating Blockchain and IoT, leveraging quantum AI, and overcoming current limitations in AI for highly dynamic and mission-critical applications. Addressing these challenges will unlock next-generation AI-powered DTs that enhance efficiency, safety, and predictive capabilities across multiple industries.

2.8.1 AI/ML innovations for next-generation DTs

AI and ML are at the core of next-generation DTs, transforming them into self-learning, self-adaptive, and highly responsive systems. Future innovations in AI/ML will focus on enhancing real-time decision-making, improving model accuracy, and reducing computational complexity.

One key area of development is self-supervised and few-shot learning, which will enable DTs to function with minimal labeled data. Unlike traditional supervised learning, self-supervised models can extract patterns from raw data without explicit annotations, reducing the dependency on large datasets (Zhang et al., 2021). This is particularly beneficial for industrial and medical applications, where collecting labeled data is expensive and time-consuming.

Another breakthrough is cognitive AI-powered DTs, where RL and DNNs help these systems predict, adapt, and optimize operations autonomously. In aerospace and autonomous vehicle applications, AI-driven DTs can simulate thousands of operational scenarios in real-time, optimizing control systems for maximum efficiency and safety (Tao et al., 2019).

Furthermore, AI innovations will focus on explainability and trustworthiness, ensuring that XAI methods are integrated into DTs. Trustworthy AI models will not only predict outcomes but also justify their decision-making processes, which is a crucial requirement in high-stakes domains such as healthcare and finance. Future research in AI/ML for DTs will prioritize transparency, real-time analytics, and resilience in mission-critical applications.

2.8.2 The integration of AI with blockchain and IoT in DTC

The convergence of AI, Blockchain, and the IoT is shaping the next phase of secure, decentralized, and intelligent DTs. AI-powered DTs generate and process vast amounts of sensor data, but ensuring data integrity, security, and interoperability remains a challenge.

Blockchain technology provides tamper-proof data records, ensuring that DTs operate on verifiable and immutable information. Smart contracts can automate transactions and enforce data access permissions, preventing unauthorized manipulation of real-time DT models (Casino et al., 2019). For example, in smart cities, blockchain-backed DTs enhance energy distribution and urban infrastructure security by securely sharing real-time data across multiple stakeholders.

IoT integration further enhances DT functionality by enabling real-time data exchange from physical entities. AI models analyze this data stream to optimize predictive maintenance, process automation, and decision-making. In manufacturing, AI + IoT-enabled DTs can detect anomalies in machine performance, while blockchain ensures the authenticity and traceability of sensor data (Khan, 2021).

One of the key challenges is scalability, as AI-driven DTs require enormous computational resources to process high-frequency IoT data streams. Researchers are exploring edge computing and federated AI to distribute computational loads, reducing latency and improving efficiency. Future research will focus on developing scalable architectures that integrate AI, blockchain, and IoT for next-generation DTs in critical sectors like healthcare, transportation, and energy systems.

2.8.3 Emerging trends: Quantum AI, federated learning, and neuromorphic computing

As DTs become more complex, emerging technologies such as quantum AI, federated learning, and neuromorphic computing are set to redefine the landscape of AI-powered DT applications.

Quantum AI has the potential to exponentially accelerate AI computations, allowing DTs to process massive datasets and solve optimization problems that classical AI struggles with (Preskill, 2018). In high-stakes fields like drug discovery and climate modeling, quantum-enhanced DTs could revolutionize real-time simulations and decision-making.

Federated learning (FL) addresses privacy concerns by allowing AI models to be trained across decentralized data sources without sharing raw data. This is particularly valuable in healthcare and finance, where sensitive data must remain confidential while still contributing to AI-driven insights (Yang et al., 2019). By integrating FL, DTs can learn from distributed datasets while maintaining compliance with privacy regulations such as General Data Protection Regulation (GDPR) and Health Insurance Portability and Accountability Act (HIPAA).

Neuromorphic Computing, inspired by the human brain, aims to create energy-efficient AI models that can perform low-power, real-time learning and inference (Indiveri and Liu, 2015). Future DTs could leverage neuromorphic chips to process real-world sensor data efficiently, making them ideal for autonomous robots, edge AI, and real-time industrial applications.

These emerging trends are set to redefine AI-driven DT architectures, enabling high-speed, privacy-preserving, and ultra-efficient simulations across multiple industries.

2.8.4 Open research challenges in AI/ML for DT applications

Despite rapid progress, several challenges remain in developing AI-powered DTs that are scalable, interpretable, and secure. One of the primary concerns is data quality and consistency, as AI models require high-quality labeled data to make reliable predictions. Inconsistencies in sensor data streams can lead to biased or incorrect DT simulations, affecting decision-making accuracy.

Another major challenge is AI model generalizability, as current AI-driven DTs are often domain-specific and struggle to adapt across multiple environments. Researchers are exploring transfer learning and metalearning to build AI models that can generalize across different DT applications (Tao et al., 2019).

Furthermore, AI model explainability and ethical considerations remain unresolved issues. Many AI-powered DTs operate as black-box models, making it difficult for users to understand and trust predictions. Future research will need to focus on integrating XAI techniques to ensure transparent and interpretable AI decision-making.

Addressing these challenges will require collaboration across AI, IoT, blockchain, and computational sciences, driving the next generation of intelligent, secure, and adaptive DT systems.

2.9 Conclusion

AI and ML have become foundational pillars in modern computing, transforming industries through intelligent automation, predictive modeling, and real-time decision-making. AI encompasses a broad spectrum of technologies, including symbolic reasoning, expert systems, and neural networks, while ML enables systems to learn from data and improve over time. The convergence of AI and ML with DTC has created dynamic systems capable of real-time simulation, anomaly detection, and adaptive optimization. ML models, including supervised, unsupervised, and RL, enable DTs to adapt to changing conditions and autonomously enhance performance.

The evolution of AI, from symbolic reasoning to connectionist models—including neural networks and DL—has driven advancements in computer vision, NLP, and autonomous systems. DL, in particular, has enabled the development of transformer-based models, which have revolutionized language understanding and image processing. The integration of AI and ML with emerging technologies, such as the IoT, blockchain, and edge computing, further enhances the scalability and security of DT ecosystems.

Key challenges in AI and ML include bias, explainability, data privacy, and computational complexity. XAI techniques are critical for increasing transparency and trust in AI-driven decisions. Federated learning and neuromorphic computing represent promising solutions for improving data privacy and reducing computational demands. Despite these challenges, AI and ML continue to redefine decision-making frameworks, enabling more efficient and accurate outcomes across diverse sectors, including healthcare, finance, manufacturing, and autonomous systems. As AI research advances, addressing ethical concerns and improving model transparency will be essential for building trust and ensuring equitable AI deployment.

2.9.1 Research implications and future outlook

The integration of AI and ML with DTC presents significant research opportunities for enhancing predictive accuracy, real-time decision-making, and system adaptability. The rise of federated learning and neuromorphic computing could enable more secure, efficient, and scalable AI models, reducing reliance on centralized data processing. In addition, improving model interpretability through XAI will be critical for regulatory compliance and user trust.

Future research should focus on hybrid AI models that combine symbolic reasoning with neural networks, creating systems that are both adaptable and explainable. Addressing data privacy and ethical concerns through blockchain-based security frameworks and bias-mitigation techniques will be essential for responsible AI deployment. Furthermore, exploring the potential of Quantum AI and edge-based ML could unlock new frontiers in AI-driven automation and intelligent decision-making. The continuous evolution of AI and ML promises to transform industries, enhance human–machine collaboration, and redefine the boundaries of technological innovation.

References

Adadi, A., Berrada, M., 2018. Peeking inside the black-box: A survey on explainable artificial intelligence (XAI). IEEE Access 6, 52138–52160. doi:10.1109/ACCESS.2018.2870052.

Amodei, D., Olah, C., Steinhardt, J., Christiano, P., Schulman, J., Mané D., 2016. Concrete problems in AI safety, arXiv preprint arXiv:1606.06565. https://arxiv.org/abs/1606.06565.

Batty, M., 2018. Digital twins. Environ. Plan. B Urban Anal. City Sci. 45 (5), 817–820. doi:10.1177/2399808318796416.

Bender, E.M., Gebru, T., McMillan-Major, A., Shmitchell, S., 2021. On the dangers of stochastic parrots: Can language models be too big?, in: Proc. 2021 ACM Conf. Fairness, Accountability, and Transparency (FAccT), pp. 610–623. doi:10.1145/3442188.3445922.

Binns, R., 2018. Fairness in machine learning: lessons from political philosophy. In: Proceedings of Machine Learning Research, vol. 81. ML Research Press, United Kingdom, pp. 149–159. 26403498. https://proceedings.mlr.press/.

Bishop, C.M., 2006. Pattern Recognition and Machine Learning, Springer.

Bostrom, N., 2014. Superintelligence: Paths, Dangers, Strategies, Oxford University Press.

Breiman, L., 2001. Random forests. Mach. Learn. 08856125. 45 (1), 5–32. doi:10.1023/A:1010933404324.

Brin, S., Page, L., 1998. The anatomy of a large-scale hypertextual Web search engine. Comput. Netw. ISDN Syst. 01697552. 30 (1–7), 107–117. doi:10.1016/s0169-7552(98)00110-x.

Brown, T.B., Mann, B., Ryder, N., Subbiah, M., Kaplan, J., Dhariwal, P., Neelakantan, A., Shyam, P., Sastry, G., Askell, A., Agarwal, S., Herbert-Voss, A., Krueger, G., Henighan, T., Child, R., Ramesh, A., Ziegler, D.M., Wu, J., Winter, C., Hesse, C., Chen, M., Sigler, E., Litwin, M., Gray, S., Chess, B., Clark, J., Berner, C., McCandlish, S., Radford, A., Sutskever, I., Amodei, D., 2020. Language models are few-shot learners. In: Advances in Neural Information Processing Systems. Neural Information Processing Systems Foundation, United States. 10495258. https://papers.nips.cc/.

Bruynseels, K., Santoni de Sio, F., van den Hoven, J., 2018. Digital twins in health care: Ethical implications of an emerging engineering paradigm. Front. Genet. 9, p. 31. doi:10.3389/fgene.2018.00031.

Brynjolfsson, E., McAfee, A., 2021. The Business of Artificial Intelligence, Harvard Business Review.

Buchanan, B.G., Shortliffe, E.H., 1984. Rule-based Expert Systems: The MYCIN Experiments of the Stanford Heuristic Programming Project, Addison-Wesley.

Buolamwini, J., Gebru, T., 2018. Gender shades: Intersectional accuracy disparities in commercial gender classification. In: Proc. Conf. Fairness, Accountability and Transparency (FAT*), pp. 77–91. doi:10.1145/3287560.3287596.

Campbell, M., Hoane, A.J., Hsu, F.H., 2002. Deep blue. Artif. Intell. 00043702. 134 (1–2), 57–83. doi:10.1016/S0004-3702(01)00129-1.

Casino, F., Dasaklis, T.K., Patsakis, C., 2019. A systematic literature review of blockchain-based applications: Current status, classification and open issues. Telemat. Inform. 36, 55–81. doi:10.1016/j.tele.2018.11.006.

Cortes, C., Vapnik, V., 1995. Support-vector networks. Mach. Learn. 0885-6125. 20 (3), 273–297. doi:10.1007/bf00994018.

Devlin, J., Chang, M.W., Lee, K., Toutanova, K., 2019. BERT: Pre-training of deep bidirectional transformers for language understanding. In: Proc. NAACL-HLT, pp. 4171–4186. doi:10.18653/v1/N19-1423.

Doshi-Velez, F., Kim, B., 2017. Towards a rigorous science of interpretable machine learning, arXiv preprint arXiv:1702.08608. https://arxiv.org/abs/1702.08608.

Esteva, A., Robicquet, A., Ramsundar, B., et al., 2021. A guide to deep learning in healthcare. Nat. Med. 27 (1), 9–21.

European Commission, 2021. Proposal for a Regulation of the European Parliament and of the Council Laying Down Harmonised Rules on Artificial Intelligence (Artificial Intelligence Act) and Amending Certain Union Legislative Acts, COM 206 final. Brussels, 21 April 2021.

Floridi, L., 2020. Establishing an ethical framework for AI. Nat. Mach. Intell. 2 (5), 261–263.

Floridi, L., Cowls, J., Beltrametti, M., Chatila, R., Chazerand, P., Dignum, V., Luetge, C., Madelin, R., Pagallo, U., Rossi, F., Schafer, B., Valcke, P., Vayena, E., 2018. AI4People—An ethical framework for a good AI society: Opportunities, risks, principles, and recommendations. Minds Mach. 28 (4), 689–707.

Fuller, A., Fan, Z., Day, C., Barlow, C., 2020. Digital twin: Enabling technologies, challenges and open research. IEEE Access 8, 108952–108971. doi:10.1109/ACCESS.2020.2998358.

Glaessgen, E., Stargel, D., 2012. The digital twin paradigm for future NASA and U.S. Air Force vehicles In: 53rd AIAA/ASME/ASCE/AHS/ASC Structures, Structural Dynamics and Materials Conf., Honolulu, HI, pp. 1–14. doi:10.2514/6.2012-1818.

Goertzel, B., Pennachin, C., 2007. Cognitive Technologies series, 8, (Springer, Berlin, Heidelberg).

Gonzalez, R.C., Woods, R.E., 2018. Digital Image Processing. 4th ed. Pearson, New York.

Goodfellow, I., Bengio, Y., Courville, A., 2016. Deep Learning. MIT Press, Cambridge, MA. https://www.deeplearningbook.org/.

Goodfellow, I., Pouget-Abadie, J., Mirza, M., Xu, B., Warde-Farley, D., Ozair, S., Courville, A., Bengio, Y., 2014. Generative adversarial nets, in: Adv. Neural Inf. Process. Syst. 27, 2672–2680.

Grieves, M., Vickers, J., 2017. Digital twin: Mitigating unpredictable, undesirable emergent behavior in complex systems. In: Kahlen, F.-J., Flumerfelt, S., Alves, A. (Eds.), Transdisciplinary Perspectives on Complex Systems: New Findings and Approaches. Springer, Cham 85–113. doi:10.1007/978-3-319-38756-7_4.

Gunning, D., Stefik, M., Choi, J., Miller, T., Stumpf, S., Yang, G.Z., 2019. XAI—Explainable artificial intelligence Sci. Robot. 4 (37), eaay7120. doi:10.1126/scirobotics.aay7120.

Hagendorff, T., 2020. The ethics of AI ethics: an evaluation of guidelines. Minds Mach. 0924-6495. 30 (1), 99–120. doi:10.1007/s11023-020-09517-8.

Hastie, T., Tibshirani, R., Friedman, J., 2009. The Elements of Statistical Learning, Springer.

Hochreiter, S., Schmidhuber, J., 1997. Long short-term memory. Neural Comput. 9 (8), 1735–1780. doi:10.1162/neco.1997.9.8.1735.

Hosmer, D.W., Lemeshow, S., Sturdivant, R.X., 2013. Applied Logistic Regression Wiley Series in Probability and Statistics. Wiley. doi:10.1002/9781118548387.

Indiveri, G., Liu, S.-C., 2015. Memory and information processing in neuromorphic systems. Proc. IEEE 103 (8), 1379–1397. doi:10.1109/JPROC.2015.2444094.

Jobin, A., Ienca, M., Vayena, E., 2019. The global landscape of AI ethics guidelines. Nat. Mach. Intell. 1 (9), 389–399. doi:10.1038/s42256-019-0088-2.

Johnson, H.G., Wiener, N., 1949. Cybernetics: control and communication in the animal and the machine. Econ. J. 00130133. 59 (236), 573. doi:10.2307/2226579.

Jordan, M.I., Mitchell, T.M., 2022. Machine learning: trends, perspectives, and prospects. Science 377 (6604), 1163–1171.

Jurafsky, D., Martin, J.H., 2021. Speech and language processing: An introduction to natural language processing, computational linguistics, and speech recognition. 3rd ed. Pearson.

Kapteyn, M.G., Knezevic, D.J., Willcox, K.E., 2021. Toward predictive digital twins via Bayesian inference. AIAA J. 59 (2), 739–755.

Khan, M.A., et al., 2021. Industrial IoT and digital twin technologies for smart manufacturing systems: A review. IEEE Access 9, 155051–155072.

Krittanawong, C., Virani, S.S., Kitai, T., et al., 2022. Machine learning in precision medicine. JACC Adv. 1 (2), 100017.

Kritzinger, W., Karner, M., Traar, G., Henjes, J., Sihn, W., 2018. Digital twin in manufacturing: A categorical literature review and classification. IFAC-PapersOnLine 51 (11), 1016–1022. doi:10.1016/j.ifacol.2018.08.474.

Krizhevsky, A., Sutskever, I., Hinton, G.E., 2012. ImageNet classification with deep convolutional neural networks. Adv. Neural Inf. Process. Syst. 2, 1097–1105 10495258.

Kurakin, A., Goodfellow, I., Bengio, S., 2017. Adversarial examples in the physical world. In: Proc. Int. Conf. Learning Representations (ICLR) Workshop.

Lake, B.M., Ullman, T.D., Tenenbaum, J.B., Gershman, S.J., 2017. Building machines that learn and think like people. Behav. Brain Sci. 14691825. 40. Available from: https://www.cambridge.org/core/journals/behavioral-and-brain-sciences/all-issues. doi:10.1017/S0140525X16001837.

LeCun, Y., Bengio, Y., Hinton, G., 2015. Deep learning. Nature. 0028-0836. 521 (7553), 436–444. doi:10.1038/nature14539.

Li, T., Sahu, A.K., Talwalkar, A., Smith, V., 2020. Federated learning: challenges, methods, and future directions. IEEE Signal Process. Mag. 15580792. 37 (3), 50–60. Available from: http://ieeexplore.ieee.org/xpl/RecentIssue.jsp?punumber=79&year=2008. doi:10.1109/MSP.2020.2975749.

Lipton, Z.C., 2018. The mythos of model interpretability: In machine learning, the concept of interpretability is both important and slippery. Queue 16 (3), 31–57. doi:10.1145/3236386.3241340.

Litjens, G., Kooi, T., Bejnordi, B.E., Setio, A.A.A., Ciompi, F., Ghafoorian, M., van der Laak, J.A.W.M., van Ginneken, B., Sánchez, C.I., 2017. A survey on deep learning in medical image analysis. Med. Image Anal. 42, 60–88. doi:10.1016/j.media.2017.07.005.

Lucas, P.J., van der Gaag, L.C., Abu-Hanna, A., 2004. Bayesian networks in biomedical engineering. Artif. Intell. Med. 30 (3), 201–214.

Manning, C.D., Schütze, H., 1999. Foundations of Statistical Natural Language Processing, MIT Press, Cambridge, MA.

Marcus, G., 2018. Deep learning: a critical appraisal. arXiv. 23318422. Available from: https://arxiv.org. doi:10.48550/arxiv.1801.00631.

McCarthy, J., Minsky, M.L., Rochester, N., Shannon, C.E., 1956. A proposal for the Dartmouth summer research project on artificial intelligence. Dartmouth College, Hanover, NH. http://jmc.stanford.edu/articles/dartmouth/dartmouth.pdf .

McCulloch, W.S., Pitts, W., 1943. A logical calculus of the ideas immanent in nervous activity. Bull. Math. Biophys. pp. 115–133. doi:10.1007/BF02478259.

Mehrabi, N., Morstatter, F., Saxena, N., Lerman, K., Galstyan, A., 2021. A survey on bias and fairness in machine learning. ACM Comput. Surv. 54 (6), 1–35. doi:10.1145/3457607.

Metsis, V., Androutsopoulos, I., Paliouras, G., 2006. Spam filtering with Naive Bayes—Which Naive Bayes? In: 3rd Conference on Email and Anti-Spam—Proceedings, CEAS 2006 Conference on Email and Anti-Spam. CEAS, Greece.

Mitchell, M., Wu, S., Zaldivar, A., Barnes, P., Vasserman, L., Hutchinson, B., Spitzer, E., Raji, I.D., Gebru, T., 2019. Model cards for model reporting. In: Proc. Conf. Fairness, Accountability, and Transparency (FAT*), pp. 220–229. doi:10.1145/3287560.3287596.

Mitchell, T.M., 1997. Machine Learning, McGraw-Hill.

Mnih, V., Kavukcuoglu, K., Silver, D., Rusu, A.A., Veness, J., Bellemare, M.G., Graves, A., Riedmiller, M., Fidjeland, A.K., Ostrovski, G., Petersen, S., Beattie, C., Sadik, A., Antonoglou, I., King, H., Kumaran, D., Wierstra, D., Legg, S., Hassabis, D., 2013. Playing Atari with deep reinforcement learning, arXiv preprint arXiv:1312.5602. https://arxiv.org/abs/1312.5602.

Montgomery, D.C., Peck, E.A., Vining, G.G., 2021. Introduction to Linear Regression Analysis. 6th ed. Wiley, Hoboken, NJ. doi:10.1002/9781119578727.

Murphy, K.P., 2012. Machine Learning: A Probabilistic Perspective, MIT Press.

Newell, A., Simon, H.A., 1976. Computer science as empirical inquiry: symbols and search. Commun. ACM. 15577317. 19 (3), 113–126. doi:10.1145/360018.360022.

Nilsson, N.J., 1984. Shakey the Robot. AI Center, SRI International.

Preskill, J., 2018. Quantum computing in the NISQ era and beyond. Quantum 2, 79. doi:10.22331/q-2018-08-06-79.

Quinlan, J.R., 1986. Induction of decision trees. Mach. Learn. 0885-6125. 1 (1), 81–106. doi:10.1007/bf00116251.

Raffel, C., Shazeer, N., Roberts, A., Lee, K., Narang, S., Matena, M., Zhou, Y., Li, W., Liu, P.J., 2020. Exploring the limits of transfer learning with a unified text-to-text transformer. J. Mach. Learn. Res. 21 (140), 1–67.

Redmon, J., Farhadi, A., 2018. YOLOv3: An incremental improvement, arXiv preprint arXiv:1804.02767.

Ribeiro, M.T., Singh, S., Guestrin, C., 2016. Why should I trust you?: Explaining the predictions of any classifier. In: Proc. 22nd ACM SIGKDD Int. Conf. Knowledge Discovery and Data Mining (KDD), 1135–1144. doi:10.1145/2939672.2939778.

Rosenblatt, F., 1958. The perceptron: A probabilistic model for information storage and organization in the brain. Psychol. Rev. 65 (6), 386–408. doi:10.1037/h0042519.

Rumelhart, D.E., Hinton, G.E., Williams, R.J., 1986. Learning representations by back-propagating errors. Nature 323 (6088), 533–536.

Russell, S., 2019. Human Compatible: Artificial Intelligence and the Problem of Control, Penguin Books.

Russell, S., Norvig, P., 2020. Artificial intelligence: a modern approach. 4th ed. Pearson, Harlow, UK.

Samuel, A.L., 1959. Some studies in machine learning using the game of checkers, IBM. J. Res. Dev. 3 (3), 210–229. doi:10.1147/rd.33.0210.

Schmidhuber, J., 2015. Deep learning in neural networks: An overview. Neural Netw. 61, 85–117. doi:10.1016/j.neunet.2014.09.003.

Searle, J.R., 1980. Minds, brains, and programs. Behav. Brain Sci. 3 (3), 417–424. doi:10.1017/S0140525X00005756.

Shahzad, A., Ullah, Z., Kim, K., 2023. Digital twin-enabled industrial IoT for real-time optimization. Sensors 23 (2), 276–289.

Shen, D., Wu, G., Suk, H.I., 2022. Deep learning in medical imaging: a review. Med. Image Anal. 68, 101794.

Shieber, S.M., 1994. Lessons from a Restricted Turing Test, arXiv preprint arXiv:cmp-lg/9404002. doi:10.48550/arXiv.cmp-lg/9404002.

Shortliffe, E.H., 1976. Computer-Based Medical Consultations: MYCIN (Doctoral dissertation, Stanford University).

Silver, D., Huang, A., Maddison, C.J., Guez, A., Sifre, L., van den Driessche, G., Schrittwieser, J., Antonoglou, I., Panneershelvam, V., Lanctot, M., Dieleman, S., Grewe, D., Nham, J., Kalchbrenner, N., Sutskever, I., Lillicrap, T., Leach, M., Kavukcuoglu, K., Graepel, T., Hassabis, D., 2016. Mastering the game of Go with deep neural networks and tree search. Nature. 0028-0836. 529 (7587), 484–489. doi:10.1038/nature16961.

Silver, D., Hubert, T., Schrittwieser, J., et al., 2021. Mastering chess and shogi by self-play with a general reinforcement learning algorithm. Nature 588 (7839), 120–126.

Silver, D., Schrittwieser, J., Simonyan, K., Antonoglou, I., Huang, A., Guez, A., Hubert, T., Baker, L., Lai, M., Bolton, A., Chen, Y., Lillicrap, T., Hui, F., Sifre, L., van den Driessche, G., Graepel, T., Hassabis, D., 2017. Mastering the game of Go without human knowledge. Nature 550, 354–359. doi:10.1038/nature24270.

Strubell, E., Ganesh, A., McCallum, A., 2019. Energy and policy considerations for deep learning in NLP. In: Proc. 57th Annu. Meet. Assoc. Comput. Linguist. (ACL), pp. 3645–3650.

Sutton, R.S., Barto, A.G., 2018. Reinforcement Learning: An Introduction, MIT Press.

Tao, F., Zhang, H., Liu, A., Nee, A.Y.C., 2019. Digital twin in industry: State-of-the-art. IEEE Trans. Ind. Inform. 15 (4), 2405–2415. doi:10.1109/TII.2018.2873186.

Tao, F., Zhang, M., Liu, Y., Nee, A.Y.C., 2022. Digital twin in industry: state-of-the-art. IEEE Trans. Ind. Inform. 18 (5), 3153–3168.

Thrun, S., Burgard, W., Fox, D., 2005. Probabilistic Robotics, MIT Press.

Turing, A.M., 1950. I.—Computing machinery and intelligence. Mind. 1460-2113. LIX (236), 433–460. doi:10.1093/mind/lix.236.433.

Vapnik, V.N., 1995. The Nature of Statistical Learning Theory. Springer, New York. doi:10.1007/978-1-4757-2440-0.

Vaswani, A., Shazeer, N., Parmar, N., Uszkoreit, J., Jones, L., Gomez, A.N., Kaiser, Ł., Polosukhin, I., 2017. Attention is all you need. Adv. Neural Inf. Process. Syst. 30, 5998–6008.

Wang, S., Zhang, L., Guo, Y., et al., 2023. Blockchain-enabled secure digital twin framework for industrial applications. Comput. Ind. 145, 103793.

Weizenbaum, J., 1966. ELIZA—a computer program for the study of natural language communication between man and machine. Commun. ACM. 0001-0782. 9 (1), 36–45. doi:10.1145/365153.365168.

Wu, Y., Zhao, R., Zhu, J., Chen, F., Xu, M., Li, G., et al., 2022. Brain-inspired global-local learning incorporated with neuromorphic computing. Nat. Commun. 13, 65. doi:10.1038/s41467-021-27653-2.
Yang, Q., Liu, Y., Chen, T., Tong, Y., 2019. Federated machine learning: Concept and applications, ACM Trans. Intell. Syst. Technol. 10 (2), 1–19.
Young, T., Hazarika, D., Poria, S., Cambria, E., 2018. Recent trends in deep learning based natural language processing. IEEE Comput. Intell. Mag. 13 (3), 55–75. doi:10.1109/MCI.2018.2840738.
Zhang, A., Lipton, Z.C., Li, M., Smola, A.J., 2021. Dive into deep learning. arXiv. 23318422. Available from: https://arxiv.org. doi:10.48550/arXiv.2106.11342.
Zhang, A., Lipton, Z.C., Li, M., Smola, A.J., 2023. AI-powered anomaly detection in financial systems. JMLR 24 (1), 1–22.
Zheng, Y., Cai, J., Zhao, J., et al., 2023. AI-driven predictive maintenance using digital twin technology. IEEE Internet Things J. 10 (1), 1123–1135.

CHAPTER 3

Basics of blockchain technology

Prabhakar Krishnan[a], **Amit Kumar Tyagi**[b], **Tanuj Surve**[c], **and Shabnam Kumari**[d]

[a]*Department of Management, St.Joseph's University, Bengaluru, Karnataka, India*
[b]*School of Law Forensic Justice & Policy Studies, National Forensic Sciences University, Gandhinagar, Gujarat, India*
[c]*Department of Management, University of California, Berkeley, FL, United States*
[d]*Department of Computer Science, Faculty of Science and Humanities, SRM Institute of Science and Technology, Kattankulathur, Chennai, Tamil Nadu, India*

3.1 Introduction

3.1.1 Background

One significant advance in the digital sphere is blockchain technology. It became the basis for Bitcoin, the first decentralized cryptocurrency developed by the anonymous Satoshi Nakamoto in 2008 and initially presented in the well-known Bitcoin whitepaper. Fundamentally, blockchain functions as a distributed ledger technology, enabling the safe, unambiguous, and unchangeable logging of transactions across a network of computers. Unlike conventional centralized systems, which operate on a decentralized model, one institution or authority does not control and confirm the data (Aggarwal and Kumar, 2021). The consensus approach, like Bitcoin's proof-of-work (PoW), makes decentralization feasible by preventing any party from altering the data. Decentralization is significant in that it eliminates intermediaries, reduces fraud risks, and fosters network members' trust-building abilities. This is somewhat unlike conventional centralized arrangements, in which reliance on a central authority could result in inefficiencies, security flaws, and single points of failure. Blockchain's journey began with Bitcoin's release, but its applications swiftly expanded beyond that (Makridakis et al., 2018). These built-right-into-code agreements automatically carry out their provisions. Smart contracts automate complex tasks and transactions, leaving room for programmed blockchain ecosystems and decentralized applications (dApps). Ethereum's fresh concept revealed that blockchain technology may be applied for numerous purposes besides transactions, including supply chain management, online personification of identity, and decentralized finance (DeFi). This shift from Bitcoin to Ethereum and beyond demonstrated the adaptability of blockchain technology and how it may transform established industries.

Artificial Intelligence, Machine Learning and Blockchain in Digital Twin Computing.
https://doi.org/10.1016/B978-0-443-43914-8.00004-2

For many more reasons than just technical ones, blockchain technology is vital. Blockchain might reduce costs, simplify processes, and enhance security, transforming financial institutions' payment systems, cross-border trades, and asset management practices. Blockchain-based systems can, for example, provide real-time settlement of trades; therefore, clearinghouses and banks are not required (Macharia, 2023). In supply chain management, blockchain can provide end-to-end visibility and traceability, allowing companies and consumers to verify that items are authentic and originate from the correct source. This capability is incredibly beneficial in sectors like food safety, medications, and high-end products, where fraud and counterfeit goods are significant issues. Blockchain technology is also drastically altering the management of digital identities on a large scale. By making personal data secure, distributed, and decentralized for storage and verification, blockchain can enable individuals to take control of their data and reduce their risk of identity theft.

Blockchain technology is acknowledged by several of the most significant organizations and establishments worldwide. Reports from Deloitte and the World Economic Forum (WEF) highlight how blockchain might revolutionize various spheres of industry (Dhanekulla, 2024). The WEF has discussed how blockchain might enable fresh business models and foster confidence in digital ecosystems. Conversely, Deloitte claims that blockchain is the primary catalyst for innovation in business applications. According to this research, blockchain is increasingly viewed as a fundamental technology that can tackle some of the most critical issues in the digital economy today, including data security, transparency, and efficient working practices.

3.1.2 Objectives

This chapter's primary objective is to provide a comprehensive overview of blockchain technology, its applications, and how it could impact various types of companies. Blockchain, sometimes referred to as a distributed and decentralized ledger system, is a revolutionary concept that has the potential to transform data storage, sharing, and verification. By the end of this chapter, readers will have a solid understanding of blockchain's fundamental concepts, including how it operates and the security and transparency measures in place. With a focus on decentralized governance, the chapter also examines the various forms of governance that enable blockchain systems. This is a significant aspect, as it differentiates blockchain from traditional centralized systems and introduces a novel approach to trust, accountability, and decision-making. Highlighting how blockchain has revolutionized industries such as payments, asset management, and DeFi, this section will also explore its potential applications in the financial sector. These use cases illustrate that blockchain is not only practical but also capable of transforming established banking institutions.

This chapter's primary objective is to clarify the reasons behind the great relevance of decentralized government to blockchain technology. Unlike other systems in which a small number of central leaders have authority and control, blockchain does not operate in this manner. Rather, decisions are made by a network of unrelated players. Consensus systems enable these decentralizations by ensuring that everyone agrees on the state of the ledger without the need for central authority (Walch, 2019). Decentralized government is crucial because it enhances transparency, reduces the possibility of corruption, and fosters user confidence. Centralized control and data breaches have generated numerous scandals and inefficiencies across various sectors. The distributed approach of blockchain is a better, safer, and fairer substitute. By eliminating single points of failure, blockchain technology maintains the system's robustness and immutability. This holds true even in cases of technical issues or threats.

3.1.3 Methodology

The study began with a thorough review of scholarly publications to establish a theoretical foundation for blockchain technology. Priority was given to peer-reviewed publications to ensure the inclusion of carefully vetted, scientifically validated material. Journals focused on computer science, cryptography, and financial technology were particularly helpful in understanding the scientific principles of blockchain, including cryptographic algorithms, consensus mechanisms, and distributed ledger designs. Publications from Institute of Electrical and Electronics Engineers (IEEE) and The Association for Computing Machinery (ACM) also provided valuable insights into emerging trends, challenges, and advancements specific to the field. These resources were instrumental in identifying topics for future research and highlighting gaps in existing studies.

Technical reports and industry whitepapers provided valuable viewpoints on blockchain deployment, complementing the academic assessment. Leading blockchain platforms, financial institutions, and technology companies' whitepapers offered insightful analyses of industry best practices, scaling solutions, and practical applications. Since they provide standards and frameworks for developing safe and effective systems, The National Institute of Standards and Technology (NIST) studies were constructive for understanding blockchain technology's security and standardization issues. Moreover, legal and compliance aspects of blockchain adoption were evaluated by employing regulatory systems from both national and international entities. These models highlighted the challenges and opportunities of integrating blockchain into current financial and legal institutions.

3.2 Fundamentals of blockchain technology

3.2.1 Definition and core concepts

Blockchain: Essentially, a blockchain is a distributed ledger technology that saves transactions on numerous computers in such a way as to ensure data security and integrity. Every block features a list of events vetted by every network member (Souncararajan and Tyagi, 2024).

Once a block full of transactions passes through a process known as consensus, every network node agrees that the transactions are authentic. A block in the chain contains a list of transactions, a timestamp, and a hash of the last block, linking them in sequential order. The setup makes it very hard to alter anything without the network's consensus, hence fostering trust among players. There are four key segments of blockchain: decentralization, consensus mechanism, smart contract, and cryptography (Fig. 3.1).

3.2.1.1 Dencentralization in blockchain

Blockchain decentralization distributes control, authority, and decision-making from a single central party to a distributed participant network. The system eliminates intermediaries in such a way that there is no single party with supreme control over the system. In a decentralized blockchain, every participant possesses a copy of the distributed ledger, which is updated through consensus mechanisms (Nakamoto, 2008). This approach encourages a state of trustlessness, where the participants don't need to trust or rely on each other since the system itself ensures data integrity and security. Decentralization encourages transparency, reduces vulnerabilities such as single points of failure, and enhances resource allocation for better performance and consistency (e.g., in finance (DeFi), governance [Decentralized Autonomous Organizations (DAOs), and supply chain management, it also introduces challenges such as scalability and governance disputes (Buterin et al., 2020). It primarily involves trade-offs, such as lower transaction throughput compared to centralized systems.

3.2.1.2 Consensus mechanisms

Conversely, everyone bears this responsibility with decentralized blockchain systems. Using consensus approaches, these participants can agree on which transactions are legitimate and the sequence in which they should be included in the blockchain. Using cryptography, financial incentives, and the concept of games helps achieve this. Consensus algorithms reward individuals for being honest and help everyone obey a set of guidelines, thereby maintaining the safety and dependability of the network.

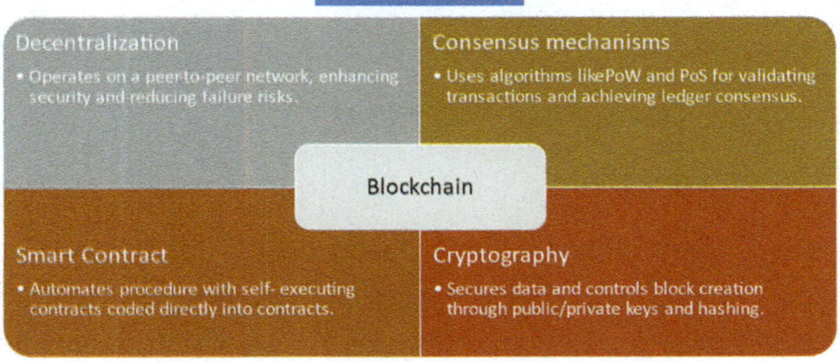

Fig. 3.1 Key segments of blockchain technology.

Maintaining the security of the blockchain depends greatly on this consensus approach. Different blockchain systems apply various consensus techniques, such as PoW, proof-of-stake (PoS), or delegated PoS (DPoS), thereby enabling everyone to agree on everything. The block is included in the blockchain once confirmed (Perwej et al., 2018). This records all immutable transactions in order and ensures alignment. The comparison of these pillars is shown in Table 3.1.

An examination of several consensus systems

Reaching an agreement can be done in several ways, each with its advantages and drawbacks. PoW is the most well-known and is employed by Bitcoin; it was the first consensus mechanism included in blockchain architecture (Jung et al., 2024). In participating in PoW, individuals compete to solve challenging math problems, verify transactions, and add fresh blocks to the blockchain. PoW is relatively safe but also highly energy-intensive, as this process consumes a significant amount of computational power and energy. Meanwhile, PoW is criticized for its inability to scale and for its negative impact on the environment.

Another approach to establishing an agreement aimed at solving the issue of PoS using excessive energy is PoS. Validators selected in PoS, based on token count, are ready to "stake" tokens as collateral to create new blocks (Lundin and Rahm, 2018). This speeds up transaction processing and reduces the need for computations that require a lot of energy. PoS also offers financial incentives to discourage dishonesty, as validators may lose their staked tokens should they misbehave (Ren et al., 2020). One of Ethereum's largest blockchain systems is converting from PoW to PoS with its Ethereum 2.0 update. This transition is aimed at enabling less energy consumption and more straightforward scaling.

Since only a few delegates have the authority to approve deals, this approach reduces decentralization even while it increases efficiency and scalability. It relies on a small group of reliable validators, typically companies or individuals with a strong reputation. PoA loses decentralization even though it is quite scalable and quick. Usually found in private or consortium blockchains, where everyone trusts one another, Byzantine Fault Tolerance (BFT) is a means of consensus whereby everyone may agree on something, allowing flawed individuals to be part of the system. Using BFT-based systems such as Hyperledger and Tendermint, all nodes agree, even if some engage in unethical behavior or fail (Fan, 2023). Though it is only used in permissioned blockchains, where only a limited number of users can join, BFT is relatively safe and quick.[1]

[1]Delegated Proof of Stake (DPoS) is a form of PoS that provides a voting mechanism to select a limited number of delegates entrusted with transaction validation. In DPoS, token holders vote for a limited number of delegates (also called witnesses or block producers), who are responsible for validating transactions and securing the network. EOS, TRON (TRX), Steem, and Lisk are examples.

Table 3.1 Comparison of proof-of-work (PoW), proof-of-stake (PoS), and delegated proof-of-stake (DPoS).

Aspect	Proof of work (PoW)	Proof of stake (PoS)	Delegated proof of stake (DPoS)
Definition	Miners solve complicated mathematical problems (hashing) to validate transactions and generate blocks	Validators are elected based on the volume of coins they "stake" (or lock up as collateral)	To validate transactions, token holders elect a fixed number of delegates
Energy Efficiency	High energy consumption owing to mathematical power required for mining	Energy-efficient, as it eradicates the demand for intensive calculations	Energy-efficient, as only a small group of delegates perform validation
Decentralization	It is highly decentralized, but mining power is often concentrated	It is more decentralized than PoW, but wealth-based selection can lead to centralization	Less decentralized as fewer delegates control the network
Transaction Speed	Slower due to the time required to solve puzzles (e.g., Bitcoin ~ 10 min per block)	Faster than PoW, as no computational puzzles are involved (Ethereum ~ 12 s per block)	Fastest, as only a few delegates are responsible for block creation
Security & its mechanism	Very secure but susceptible to 51% attacks. Relying on computational work for network security	Secure but possibly vulnerable to staking centralization. Founded on economic stakes to secure the network	Secure but depending on the integrity of the voting system. Founded on voting mechanisms and democratically elected delegates for security
Scalability	Low scalability (having computational restrictions)	More scalable than PoW	Highly scalable with fast block confirmations
Incentive Mechanism	Block rewards and fees for transactions are given to miners	Validators earn transaction fees and occasionally block rewards according to their stake	Delegates are rewarded for transaction validation, which is shared with the voters
Examples	Bitcoin (BTC), Ethereum (premerge, now PoS), Litecoin (LTC)	Ethereum (postmerge), Cardano (ADA), Tezos (XTZ)	EOS, TRON, BitShares
Key Advantage	Proven security and robustness over time	Energy efficiency and reduced hardware requirements	High scalability and faster transaction processing
Key Disadvantage	High energy consumption and environmental impact	Potential for wealth concentration and "rich get richer" dynamics	Centralization risk due to reliance on a small group of delegates

Author comprehended from several sources: Buterin, V., Reijsbergen, D., Leonardos, S., Piliouras, G., 2020. Incentives in ethereum's hybrid casper protocol. Int. J. Netw. Manag. 30 (5). doi:10.1002/nem.2098; Antonopoulos, A.M., 2014. Mastering Bitcoin: Unlocking Digital Cryptocurrencies, O'Reilly Media, Inc.; Nakamoto, S., 2008. Bitcoin: a peer-to-peer electronic cash system. Available from: https://assets.pubpub.org/d8wct41f/31611263538139.pdf.

Consensus mechanisms: Meaning for governance

The operation of a blockchain network depends heavily on the type of consensus mechanism applied. PoW and PoS allow many people to participate in the process of verification, so they are often associated with decentralized governance. PoW, however, favors participants with substantial computational power, whereas PoS favors those with significant token holdings. As wealthier individuals gain more influence over time, this can lead to power becoming increasingly concentrated. Conversely, DPoS and PoA operate from a more centralized perspective. In DPoS, a small team of elected delegates can verify transactions, while in PoA, such authority rests with a select group of trusted validators. These approaches may compromise the principle that blockchain technology is decentralized, even though they can enhance scalability and efficiency (Zanfino, 2024). A group of companies may choose to operate BFT-based systems, which often function in environments accessible only to specific individuals. While this architecture is not as transparent and open as public blockchains, it is well-suited for commercial purposes.

Ethereum (ETH) changed from PoW to PoS with its Ethereum 2.0 release. In the realm of blockchain, this is a significant transformation. While maintaining security and decentralization, this shift aims to solve issues with PoW's scalability and energy use. To participate in the consensus process, validators of Ethereum 2.0 have to lock up at least 32 ETH. Ethereum is a more ecologically friendly platform since this modification is expected to reduce energy consumption by over 99% (Islam et al., 2022). Renowned blockchain Cardano also employs the Ouroboros PoS system, designed to be both secure and energy-efficient. Ouroboros slices time into epochs and slots. During every slot, a leader is selected to begin a fresh block. This approach guarantees equity and progress with the minimum energy required. Ouroboros has evolved as a case study in creating secure and functional consensus systems, as Cardano emphasizes academic research and peer-reviewed development.

Savings in energy security

Designing consensus techniques calls for much consideration of security and the energy economy. PoW consumes a lot of energy, so people sometimes criticize it for its negative effects. People have searched for more ecologically friendly substitutes, including DPoS and PoS. Strong security is therefore also essential for these systems to prevent attacks, double spending, and 51% attacks. Researchers are still investigating hybrid techniques, including BFT, to improve security or a combination of PoW and PoS (Heilman et al., 2015).

3.2.1.3 Smart contracts

A smart contract is an autonomous digital agreement with preprogrammed rules in code, saved on a blockchain, and executed automatically when certain conditions are fulfilled. Smart contracts differ from conventional contracts in that they eliminate intermediaries.

thereby lowering transaction costs and enhancing efficiency. Designed directly into code, smart contracts are agreements that automatically carry out their terms. In 1996, Nick Szabo developed the concept for them. He envisioned them as digital guidelines that simplify, protect, or increase the likelihood of a contract being complied with, free from mediators (Parenti and Billi, 2023). Szabo's concept was novel since it offered a means to automate dependability and reduce reliance on external sources (Szabo, 1996). Although smart contracts were theoretically feasible before blockchain technology—especially Ethereum—made them viable in practice (Giancaspro, 2017). Initially, Ethereum served as a decentralized platform where developers could create and operate smart contracts using Solidity, Ethereum's programming language (Tikhomirov, 2018). These contracts run on decentralized blockchain networks like Ethereum, providing security, transparency, and immutability. Smart contracts are widely used in DeFi, supply chain management, real estate, and digital identity. Since they are immutable after deployment, they reduce fraud and ensure trust between parties. However, coding vulnerabilities can lead to security breaches, as demonstrated by past incidents such as the DAO attack in 2016. Their functionality is visualized in Fig. 3.2.

One of the most well-known instruments for this is Ethereum. Smart contracts are written using programming languages such as Solidity. Solidity is designed to enable Ethereum's dApps. These contracts are executed by the Ethereum Virtual Machine (EVM). The EVM manages transactions and guarantees adherence to contract terms by providing a decentralized operating environment. A JavaScript library known as Web3.js is commonly used to interface with the Ethereum blockchain. This library allows developers to create user interfaces that interact seamlessly with smart contracts. Once a smart contract is executed, it becomes open and immutable. This means that everyone on the network can see how it operates, and no one can modify its code.

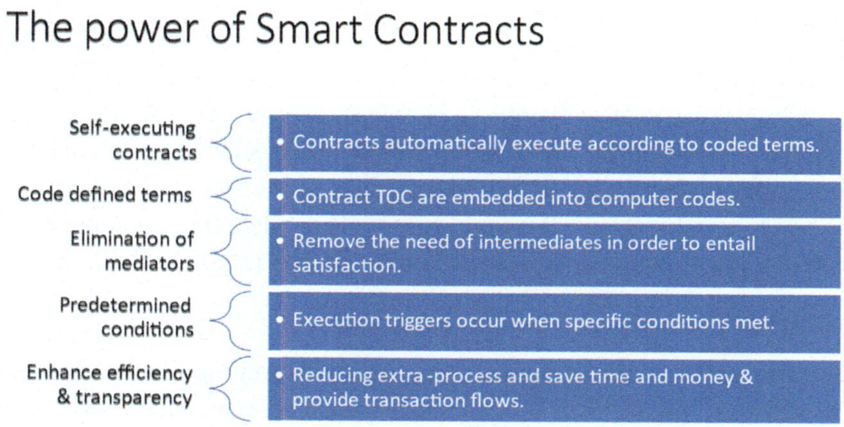

Fig. 3.2 Power of smart contracts.

Though primarily employed in the corporate sector, smart contracts have several uses Standard banks are no longer required since smart contracts can automatically grant and repay loans. For example, DeFi systems use smart contracts to enable peer-to-peer lending, facilitating direct communication between borrowers and lenders, free from middleman involvement. Smart contracts can streamline insurance claims by paying out when specific criteria are satisfied, such as a delayed trip or a natural disaster. Smart contracts are also being utilized for automatic compliance, guaranteeing that trades meet the regulations in real time, reducing the danger of fraud and human error.

An integral component of blockchain architecture, blocks are connected using hashes. Unique to every block, a cryptographic hash is a fixed-length string of characters created by a mathematical algorithm. This hash includes the block's hash prior to it in the chain in addition to the data within the block. This creates a strong, secure relationship between blocks that is unbroken. It is not feasible for someone to try to alter a transaction in an earlier block since they would have to change every block that followed it. Thanks to this cryptographic linking structure, blockchain is relatively secure and cannot be altered. Blockchain technology's decentralized nature is among its most salient features (de Filippi, 2016). In a decentralized system, the record is distributed among several nodes, each retaining a copy of the complete blockchain. This eliminates the need for a middleman or central authority, reducing the possibility of a single point of failure. Under traditional centralized systems, a hacked or failing central server might cause the entire system to crash (Cai et al., 2018). Conversely, in a decentralized blockchain network, the network as a whole continues functioning even if some nodes are attacked or go offline. Blockchain is ideal for applications where trust, transparency, and security are highly valued due to its robustness.

Blockchain is distributed; hence, no entity can alter the data. This helps individuals trust one another more easily. Everyone on the network can view and review transactions, ensuring accountability and reducing the possibility of fraud. Blockchain is ideal for sectors such as healthcare, voting systems, finance, and supply chain management since the ledger cannot be altered, and thus, what is happening is transparent.

3.2.1.4 Crypotgraphy

Cryptography is the science and art of securing information with mathematical algorithms, offering confidentiality, integrity, and authenticity of data. In other words, it is the method of encrypting information so that only intended people can read or decrypt it, not others. Cryptography employs algorithms and keys—public keys for encryption and private keys for decryption—to protect data in transit or storage. Blockchain technology uses cryptography to secure transactions, create digital signatures, and render the ledger tamper-proof. Bitcoin, for example, uses cryptographic hashing (SHA-256) to link blocks in the blockchain and digital signatures for verifying ownership of funds. The foundational principles of modern cryptography have origins in research such as Whitfield Diffie and Martin Hellman's introduction of public-key cryptography (Diffie and Hellman, 1976), which formalized the concept of asymmetric encryption. Bruce Schneier's book Applied Cryptography (1996) also provides an in-depth overview of cryptographic protocols and their application. As Nakamoto's (2008) Bitcoin white paper identifies, cryptography is the solution to achieving decentralized security. Similarly, Stallings and Brown (2015), in Cryptography and Network Security, discuss modern encryption methods and their application in digital security. Research by Katz and Lindell (2020) explored cryptographic concepts and their role in secure computing. However, with advancements in quantum computing, traditional encryption techniques could be exposed to new vulnerabilities, and hence, postquantum cryptography is being developed to protect the future.

3.2.2 Applications of blockchain

The evolution of blockchain technology has introduced a new age of digital transformation that overturns traditional centralized systems through cryptographic innovation and converts their activities into distributed ledgers. Like a modern *Gutenberg Press*, blockchain ensures transparency and accountability to each person, enabling peer-to-peer interactions in the absence of intermediaries (Tapscott and Tapscott, 2016). This technological giant has come a long way since it started, expanding beyond cryptocurrencies to other financial, health, supply chain, and government spheres, among countless others. This academic critique synthesizes literature, whitepapers, and empirical studies to explain blockchain's numerous applications alongside the philosophical underpinnings behind it.

3.2.2.1 Cryptocurrencies and financial services

Blockchain originally emerged in the financial sector through Bitcoin, as described by Nakamoto (2008) in *Bitcoin: A Peer-to-Peer Electronic Cash System*. Bitcoin's blockchain introduced a network of decentralized ledgers, which eliminated central authorities in financial dealings. This concept further evolved with the rise of Ethereum, which introduced smart contracts to enable self-executing agreements (Schneider, 2019). According to Schär (2021), DeFi applications such as MakerDAO, Uniswap, and Aave have utilized blockchain technology to facilitate lending, borrowing, and market-making in environments free of intermediaries. Central Bank Digital Currencies (CBDCs) also demonstrate the application of blockchain in finance, with research by Auer et al. (2022) highlighting their potential to serve as enablers for cross-border payments and monetary policy. Satoshi Nakamoto's first whitepaper (Nakamoto, 2008) positioned Bitcoin not only as a currency but also as a trustless protocol, where consensus replaces institutional endorsement. This is analogous to Habermas' (1985) communicative action theory, in which decentralized agents coordinate through shared rules rather than hierarchical control.

3.2.2.2 Supply chain management

Blockchain demonstrated to consumers its potential, realism, trustworthiness, and real-time applications in supply chain traceability and logistics. Tian (2016) projected the use of a Chinese food blockchain mechanism for traceability in supply chains and emphasized how blockchains address food safety by preventing fraud and contamination. In previous years, various researchers investigated how blockchain enables real-time monitoring and reduces inefficiencies within logistics networks. IBM's Food Trust, in partnership with companies like Walmart, leverages blockchain to trace product origins and conduct authenticity tests (Kshetri, 2017). Among the major challenges of blockchain supply chain systems are energy consumption and scalability, as Wang et al. (2018) pointed out, citing trade-offs between private and public blockchains in supply chain networks.

3.2.2.3 Healthcare and record administration

Blockchain technology-based industries in the health sector have ensured secure medical data management. Zhang et al. (2018) proposed a blockchain-based EHR system to enable the protected sharing of patient information between healthcare providers while sustaining data privacy. Similarly, Mettler (2016) discusses how blockchain is implemented to avoid counterfeit medicines by tracing pharmaceutical supply chains. One of the major advantages of blockchain in healthcare is data integrity. Azaria et al. (2016) have suggested MedRec, a blockchain-based patient data-sharing system that ensures tamper-proof medical records and offers control of data to the patients. Concerns such as data storage limitations and compliance with regulations (e.g., General Data Protection Regulation (GDPR), Health Insurance Portability and Accountability Act (HIPAA)) are yet to be addressed (Agbo et al., 2019).

3.2.2.4 Intellectual property and digital rights management

Blockchain has been applied to copyright protection and digital rights management (DRM). Tyagi et al. (2024) and Tyagi (2023) draw attention to how KodakOne and Spotify's blockchain royalty system protect artists' intellectual property. Another study presented a blockchain-based DRM model with ownership verification and fair revenue sharing (Naz et al., 2019). However, scalability and enforceability issues persist (Kouhizadeh and Sarkis, 2018). Moreover, additional applications are available, and these are elucidated below.

3.3 Decentralized governance in blockchain

3.3.1 Concept and importance

Rather than being possessed by one, power and control are distributed among several people or companies. This approach eliminates intermediaries like governments or banks, which typically act as the primary authorities in government systems and banking. Blockchain technology allows individuals and companies to communicate directly without using a third party to monitor events. This fosters confidence and facilitates cooperation among people. Along with improving the flow of events, this shift reduces the dangers associated with centralized systems, including corruption, single points of failure, and data theft (Atzori, 2015; Tyagi, 2025a; Tyagi 2025b; Wright and de Filippi, 2015).

Among the most crucial concepts guiding blockchain technology is transparency. Every person connected to the network can view every activity on the blockchain. This feature guarantees that the information is readily available and open. It helps consumers trust the material more, as they can verify that it is accurate and authentic (Zwitter and Hazenberg, 2020). Moreover, blockchain is immutable once a transaction is recorded, meaning it cannot be undone or altered. This further increases the system's dependability. This quality is vital in healthcare, banking, and supply chain management, where data integrity and accountability are highly valued. Enabling blockchain through decentralized collaboration and governance entails building systems where decision-making power and control are distributed among participants in a network, establishing transparency, inclusiveness, and robustness. Decentralized governance allows stakeholders such as token holders, developers, and end-users to collectively influence a blockchain network's direction and policies. This is often accomplished through on-chain voting, where participants propose and vote on amendments directly on the blockchain, and off-chain governance, in which decisions are made and debated in forum environments before implementation. Collaboration is essential to ensure that multiple perspectives are considered to achieve innovation and flexibility.

DAOs are a great example of this practice since they operate through smart contracts and community voting, eliminating centralized control. On-chain governance usually conducts protocol decision-making through voting mechanisms enforced by smart contracts (e.g., Tezos, Polkadot). Off-chain governance performs decision-making through discussions among communities, development teams, and governing bodies (e.g., Ethereum Improvement Proposals—EIPs). DAOs function like fully autonomous governance frameworks wherein token holders vote on proposals (e.g., MakerDAO, Uniswap). Initiatives such as Ethereum and Tezos have adopted decentralized governance, enabling stakeholders to suggest and enforce upgrades (e.g., Ethereum's switch to PoS). Voshmgir and Zargham (2019) research highlights decentralized governance as a key factor in developing sustainable and fair blockchain communities. All these activities are summarized in Fig. 3.3.

3.3.2 Governance models

Under on-chain governance, the decision-making process is ingrained into the blockchain architecture. Usually, token owners and stakeholders can participate in governance by voting directly on ideas on the blockchain. The prompt handling of the votes by the protocol

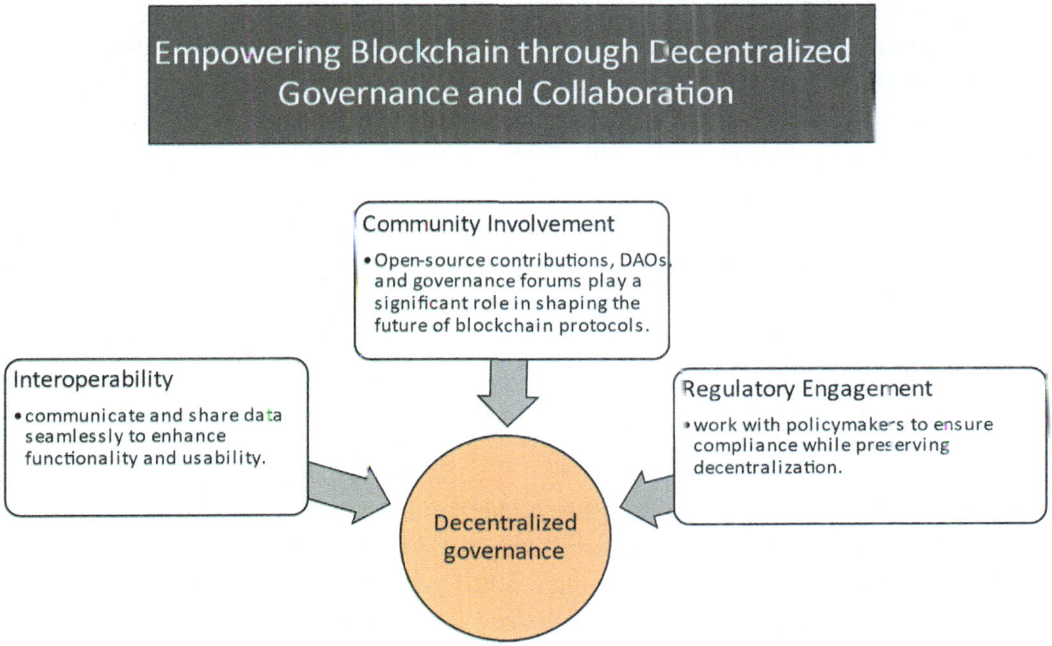

Fig. 3.3 Empowering blockchain through decentralized governance.

guarantees their openness and free will from influence by a small number of individuals. Two blockchain systems employing on-chain control are Tezos and Polkadot. Tezos, for instance, includes an on-chain amendment system whereby users may propose and vote on protocol modifications (Kiayias and Lazos, 2022; Goodman, 2014; Wood, 2016). Enough agreement with a plan automatically results in its implementation without a hard fork. This strategy reduces the possibility of unpleasant societal divisions and promotes ongoing transformation. Polkadot has a sophisticated on-chain governance structure includes a council and technical committee to simplify choices and ensure the network meets evolving needs (Wood, 2016).

Conversely, off-chain governance is predicated on dialogues and choices outside the blockchain. Usually less formal, this model incorporates collaborative attempts to reach consensus, including community meetings, debates, and other activities. One well-known instance of off-chain governance is the development approach for Bitcoin Core. Running Bitcoin is primarily the responsibility of the group of currency developers. They propose protocol modifications using Bitcoin Improvement Proposals (Ekblaw et al., 2016; Filippi and Loveluck, 2016). People discuss and advance off-chain concepts only implemented when a consensus exists. Though it can also slow things down and increase the likelihood of core developers having a lot of influence, this methodology allows individuals to deliberate for a lengthy period. It reduces the danger of making hurried decisions. Among the most often used blockchain systems are Ethereum. It employs a governance style combining off-chain and on-chain management. The EIP approach defines much of Ethereum's operation. Ideas for EIPs come from off-chain developers, consultants, community members, and experts; they are discussed and improved upon. Once everyone approves the changes, they are implemented by network upgrading (Fracassi et al., 2024). This approach balances the orderly execution of on-chain upgrades with the openness of talks occurring off-chain. Though it can be challenging to set up and may have issues with voters who don't care or who are manipulated, on-chain governance provides openness, automation, and involvement. Conversely, off-chain government allows individuals to have more nuanced dialogues and is more adaptable, but it may not be as transparent and might slow down change adaptation. A comparison view is elucidated in Table 3.2.

3.3.3 Challenges

In PoS-based blockchains, stakeholders with higher holdings of the native cryptocurrency have a more substantial say in network decisions, such as transaction validation or protocol updates. This concentration of power among wealthy participants has the potential to centralize, undermining blockchain's decentralized spirit. Critics claim that this dynamic results in a society where the "rich get richer," since those with more resources can gain even

Table 3.2 Comparison of on-chain governance and off-chain governance.

Aspect	On-chain governance	Off-chain governance
Decision-making process	Formal, automated, and executed through smart contracts	Informal, community-driven, and manually implemented
Transparency	High as all decisions are recorded on the blockchain	Moderate as decisions are made via discussions
Speed	Faster as decisions are automatically enforced	Slower due to the rising demand for consensus-building and manual implementation
Flexibility	Low due to strict rules encoded in smart contracts	High due to informal discussions allows adaptability
Participators	Open access for all token holders	Limited to developers, miners, and stakeholders
Examples	Tezos, Decred, Polkadot	Bitcoin, Ethereum, Litecoin
Challenges	Low voter participation, potential dominance by large stakeholders	Risk of disagreements, forks, and lack of transparency

Author comprehended and gathered information from Goodman, L.M., 2014. A self-amending crypto-ledger. Tezos white paper; Kappos, G., Yousaf, H., Piotrowska, A., Kanjalkar, S., Delgado-Segura, S., Miller, A., Meiklejohn, S., 2021. An empirical analysis of privacy in the lightning network. Lect. Notes Comput. Sci. 167–186. doi:10.1007/978-3-662-64322-8_8; Filippi, D., Loveluck, B., 2016. The invisible politics of bitcoin: governance crisis of a decentralized infrastructure. Ssrn.com. Available from: https://papers.ssrn.com/sol3/papers.cfm?abstract_id=2852691; Wood, G., 2016. Polkadot: vision for a heterogeneous multichain framework. White Paper. 21 (2327), 4662.

more authority, thus leading to unjust governance and decision-making processes (Reiman, 1999). This difficulty is significant as many blockchain networks shift from energy-intensive PoW systems to more energy-efficient PoS models, raising concerns about combining efficiency with equal participation.

Another main difficulty is the scalability vs. decentralization trade-off, often referred to as the blockchain trilemma. According to the trilemma, a blockchain cannot achieve scalability, decentralization, and security simultaneously without sacrificing at least one of these aspects. For example, boosting transaction throughput (scalability) necessitates sacrificing decentralization, as evidenced by some high-throughput networks that use fewer validators or more centralized infrastructure (Halim, 2022). This trade-off has sparked ongoing debates within the blockchain community about creating systems capable of handling large-scale adoption while adhering to the key principles of decentralization and security. Solutions, including sharding, layer-2 protocols, and alternative consensus techniques, are being explored, but each comes with its own set of drawbacks and limitations.

Furthermore, coordination issues in decentralized decision-making present substantial challenges for blockchain ecosystems. Unlike traditional centralized systems, where a single authority makes decisions, decentralized networks rely on the agreement of a distributed set of members. This can result in inefficiencies, delays, and disputes, particularly when parties have competing interests (Yoo, 2023). For example, adopting protocol changes or settling conflicts frequently necessitates broad consensus, which can be difficult to achieve in a decentralized setting. These coordination challenges are especially visible in DAOs, where governance issues such as voter apathy, low participation rates, and the power of significant stakeholders can stymie effective decision-making.

The research into these concerns has focused on understanding and addressing governance issues in DAOs and examining real-world examples of coordination failures and achievements. For example, hard forks—situations in which a blockchain separates into two different chains due to participant disagreements—provide useful case studies. The Bitcoin Cash hard fork, caused by arguments over block size restrictions, and Ethereum's DAO split, implemented to undo a massive hack, demonstrate the complexity of decentralized governance (Kappos et al., 2021). These instances highlight the significance of developing strong governance frameworks that balance stakeholders' interests while ensuring the network's integrity and security.

3.4 Applications in financial services

3.4.1 Decentralized finance

DeFi operates somewhat differently from traditional financial systems. It creates transparent, open, and permissionless financial systems using blockchain technology. Built on decentralized networks primarily composed of smart contract platforms like Ethereum,

DeFi functions without the need for centralized intermediaries. Unlike conventional finance, which relies on entities such as banks, traders, and clearinghouses, DeFi eliminates these intermediaries (Friesendorf and Blütener, 2023; Werner et al., 2022; Daian et al., 2019). This section not only illustrates how DeFi differs from conventional financial systems but also covers its fundamental elements, primary building blocks, and working mechanisms. Among these are cryptocurrencies like DAI, decentralized lending platforms such as Aave, and decentralized exchanges (DEXs) like Uniswap (Cedra, 2024). For instance, Aave automates the lending and borrowing process by using smart contracts, enabling individuals to lend and borrow cryptocurrency without relying on central banks (Schär, 2021). Conversely, Uniswap allows users to trade tokens directly with one another via an automated market-making (AMM) system that replaces conventional order books with liquidity pools. Stablecoins such as DAI, which are linked to fiat currencies, serve as safe havens for value retention. However, unlike centralized stablecoins, DAI maintains its stability through distributed governance and overcollateralization. Some common key features of DeFi are illustrated below (Fig. 3.4).

These liquidity pools are among the most original concepts of DeFiare. DEXs, including Uniswap, cannot function without these pools. Individuals create a liquidity pool by putting pairs of tokens into a smart contract. This builds a stockpile of assets fit for trading that traders can use. Deals occurring in the pool pay fees to liquidity providers. If the loan is taken out and paid back in the same transaction block, flash loans—another creative concept from DeFi—let anyone borrow assets without providing collateral (Arslanian, 2022). This makes complex financial strategies like collateral swapping and arbitrage—that most individuals couldn't employ prior—available. Conversely, staking locks down coins in a smart contract to support network operations—akin to PoS blockchains confirming transactions in exchange for rewards.[2]

The DeFi community, which is vast and fast-evolving, consists of various apps and services (Harvey et al., 2021). The DeFi ecosystem comprises three components: the blockchain infrastructure, the protocol layer (which includes loans, DEXs, and derivatives), and the application layer (which encompasses wallets and dashboards). Compared to conventional finance, this ecosystem differs significantly. Traditional finance, usually characterized by higher costs and lengthier transaction times, is centered on centralized companies and follows strict guidelines. Conversely, DeFi offers faster, less expensive, and more inclusive banking services; it is decentralized and operates internationally without boundaries. However, it also carries risks, including unsafe smart contracts, ambiguous rules, and the possibility of market manipulation.

[2]Decentralized Finance (DeFi) is a blockchain-based financial system that eliminates middlemen, such as banks, and enables peer-to-peer transactions through the application of smart contracts. DeFi is founded on fundamental components such as decentralized exchanges (DEXs), lending and borrowing protocols, stablecoins, and yield farming, and it provides a range of financial services such as trading, lending, and asset management.

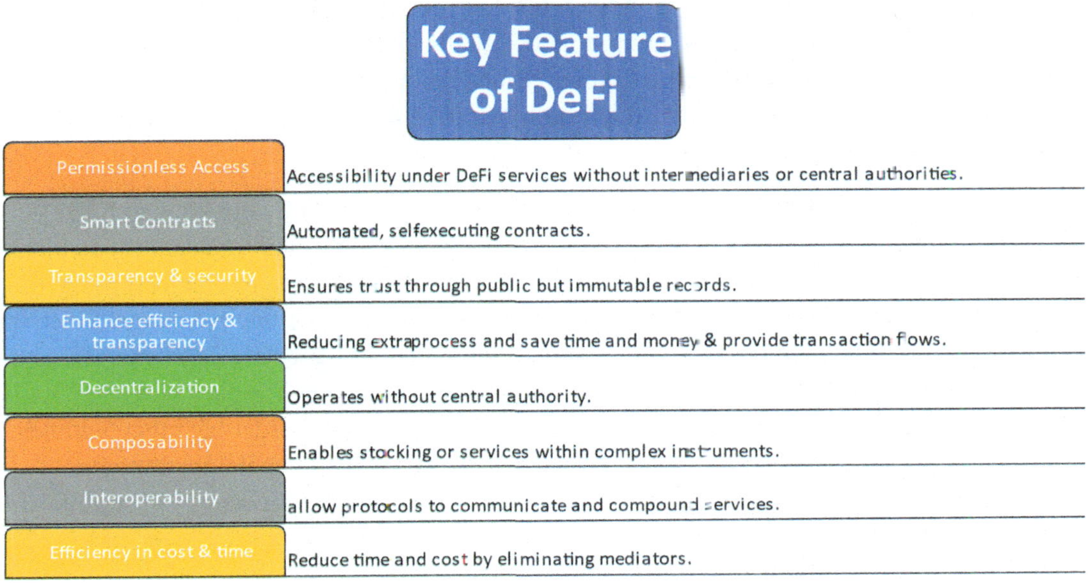

Fig. 3.4 Key features of decentralized finance (DeFi).

Some common DeFi tools are addressed as follows:

DEXs—Uniswap, SushiSwap, and Curve Finance—are exchanges that facilitate users in swapping cryptocurrencies without the involvement of intermediaries (Makarov and Schoar, 2022).

Transaction—Aave, Compound, and MakerDAO are systems that offer decentralized loans through collateralized lending (Qin et al., 2021; Wieandt and Heppding, 2023).

Stablecoins—fiat currency-pegged cryptocurrencies (DAI, USDC, and USDT)—minimize volatility.

Agriculture and staking—The user is rewarded for providing liquidity to DeFi protocols (Harvey et al., 2021).

Insurance—Smart contract failure risk protection is offered through decentralized platforms like Nexus Mutual (Howell and Potgieter, 2021).

3.4.2 Cross-border transactions

Cross-border trading has long been challenging due to poor speed, a high frequency of intermediaries, and its costly nature. This is mostly attributed to outdated financial infrastructure and complex policies. Standard systems like SWIFT incur hefty fees and sometimes take days to process foreign payments (Chang et al., 2020). Sending money overseas becomes expensive for both individuals and companies. Blockchain technology has emerged as a game-changing solution to these challenges by providing a decentralized, open, and fast business method across borders. Blockchain eliminates intermediaries and uses encryption for security, reducing the time and cost of sending money overseas. It also enhances transparency and trust.

Blockchain makes this feasible primarily through distributed ledger technology, or DLT. It allows transactions across national boundaries. Blockchain enables individuals to send money to one another under a network of nodes that verify exchanges. This is not the case with conventional systems based on central authorities handling and verifying payments. Since the transaction doesn't have to pass through several middlemen, this accelerates the process and drastically reduces transaction fees. Built on blockchain technology, Ripple (XRP) and Stellar (XLM), for example, have been the front-runners in altering cross-border payment methods. RippleNet, the payment system developed by the company, helps financial institutions settle transactions in real-time with low fees, using XRP as a bridge currency to simplify transactions (Coutinho et al., 2023). Similarly, Stellar's network focuses on connecting people, financial institutions, and payment systems to deliver money rapidly and cheaply, particularly to underdeveloped areas that aren't well served.

Case studies of Stellar and Ripple demonstrate how blockchain technology might support international trade. Ripple has partnered with numerous banks and payment companies worldwide to facilitate international money transfers, including MoneyGram and Santander (Armknecht et al., 2015). Its technology has made a significant difference in places like the U.S. and Mexico, where substantial money flows exist. It has reduced expenditures by up to 60% and shortened process times from days to seconds. Conversely, Stellar has concentrated on financial inclusion, allowing people from underdeveloped nations to send money back to their families inexpensively (Bracciali et al., 2021). For international payments, Stellar's partnership with IBM and Circle, for instance, has made using USDC—a stablecoin—simpler (Vasselin, 2024; García-Pérez and Schett, 2019). This provides individuals with an affordable and safe alternative to conventional remittance methods. Another significant advancement in blockchain technology that could further transform cross-border activities is CBDCs. CBDCs are digital variants of fiat money, issued and controlled by central banks. They aim to combine the security of government-backed money with the advantages of blockchain technologies. China's digital yuan (e-CNY) and the Sand Dollar from the Bahamas are progressing well in their development (Caudevilla and Kim, 2022). On the m-CBDC Bridge, a project using blockchain technology to enable low-cost, real-time international payments, the central banks of Hong Kong, Thailand, China, and the UAE are collaborating. These initiatives demonstrate how blockchain can comply with regulations and maintain a stable economy while enabling faster and safer international trade. While Stellar has focused on financial inclusion and decentralization for individuals and small businesses, Ripple was established to serve financial institutions by facilitating high-speed international transactions.

Despite similarities in transaction speed and cost, Ripple has faced more regulatory scrutiny, whereas Stellar has maintained a non-profit, open-source approach (Singh and Singh, 2016). Both studies are summarized in Table 3.3.

3.4.3 Asset tokenization

Through a process known as "asset tokenization," real-world assets such as bonds, equities, and real estate are transformed into digital bits on a blockchain. These tokens represent ownership or a share in the underlying asset. This permits fractional ownership, improved liquidity, and more straightforward access to otherwise illiquid markets. Tokenization makes commercial opportunities more accessible to everyone through blockchain technology By reducing substantial entry barriers, it allows individuals to own modest portions of valuable assets that were previously beyond reach (Incutti, 2023). For instance, a one-million-dollar piece of real estate can be divided into thousands of tokens so that numerous investors may own a portion of the property. Along with increasing the pool of investors, this process clarifies asset management and negotiations, making them more efficient.

Table 3.3 Comparison study of stellar (XLM) & ripple (XRP).

Aspect	Stellar (XLM)	Ripple (XRP)
Evolution & goal	Founded in 2014 by Jed McCaleb and Joyce Kim, the organization aims to facilitate low-cost cross-border transactions for individuals and developing economies	Founded in 2012 by Chris Larsen and Jed McCaleb, the company was established to enable efficient cross-border payments for financial institutions
Target consumers	Focuses on unbanked populations and small businesses, promoting financial inclusion	Primarily serves banks, payment providers, and financial institutions for fast and cost-effective remittances
Consensus mechanism	Uses the Stellar Consensus Protocol (SCP), a Federated Byzantine Agreement (FBA) model, allowing faster decentralized consensus	Uses the XRP Ledger Consensus Protocol, which does not rely on mining but instead on trusted validators
Decentralization	More decentralized, as anyone can become a validator and participate in the consensus	Less decentralized, as Ripple selects trusted validators, though it aims to increase decentralization
Transaction Speed & fees	Approximately 3–5 seconds per transaction. Fees are extremely low (~0.00001 XLM per transaction)	3–5 seconds per transaction, similar to Stellar. Low fees (~0.00001 XRP per transaction), but Ripple retains control over its supply
Partnerships & adoption	Used by IBM's World Wire, NGO projects, and cross-border payment services	Adopted by Santander, American Express, and SBI Holdings for remittances
Regulatory challenges	Fewer legal issues arise, as it is structured as a non-profit organization promoting open-source finance	SEC has faced lawsuits regarding whether XRP is a security

Real-world assets, which have been difficult to divide or sell in the past, notably benefit from tokenization. For tokenization, real estate is an excellent sector since it is difficult to sell and requires a significant amount of capital to launch. Platforms like RealT, which allow consumers to purchase tokens representing a portion of real estate ownership, first pioneered real estate tokenization. These tokens can be sold on secondary marketplaces, augmenting asset-class liquidity. Tokenizing bonds and equities in the same manner can simplify transactions, reduce intermediaries, and ease handling. This innovative concept could make regular financial markets more transparent and efficient for everyone, fundamentally altering their operation.

In the realm of tokenization, one extremely significant difference is between Initial Coin Offerings (ICOs) and Security Token Offerings (STOs). STOs produce tokens issued under rules where real-world assets underlie them and must comply with regulations. They are, thereby, a safer and more open approach to trading. Since these tokens are regarded as assets, the U.S. Securities and Exchange Commission (SEC) and other regulatory agencies have policies that these tokens must abide by. Conversely, ICOs sell utility tokens, granting access to a specific good or service but not conferring asset ownership. ICOs grew common when cryptocurrencies were popular. However, they have been vigorously attacked since they are not controlled and are easy targets for fraud. Conversely, STOs operate with the concept of asset tokenization and are safer and more regulated.

3.5 Case studies

3.5.1 Decentralized autonomous organizations

The emergence of DAOs has fundamentally altered the way companies are set up and governed. Operating on blockchain technologies, DAOs employ smart contracts to govern and make decisions automatically. This is not the case in conventional companies, which apply levels-based centralized leadership and decision-making. The concept of decentralization is the foundation of a DAO (Napieralska and Kępczyński, 2023). Power and control are distributed among the members rather than being vested in a small number of individuals. Token-based voting systems enable this. Tokens awarded to members based on their level of ownership in the organization grant them voting rights. These tokens are connected to the DAO's own cryptocurrency or control token, which facilitates a democratic and transparent decision-making approach.

MakerDAO is primarily associated with the DAI platform, which is also referred to as a stablecoin platform operating on the Ethereum blockchain. MakerDAO uses smart contracts to regulate the production of DAI, a decentralized stablecoin pegged to the US dollar (Feng et al., 2024; Kjäer et al., 2021). Governance in MakerDAO is achieved through its token, MKR. It also enables token holders to make decisions such as adjusting interest rates, introducing new types of collateral, and managing risk. MakerDAO is decentralized; thus, no single group owns the stablecoin. This structure modifies and makes censorship difficult (Angeris and Chitra, 2020). MakerDAO emphasizes decentralized lending and stablecoin issuance through DAI, ensuring stability and financial accessibility (Sun et al., 2024).

Another significant example is the well-known DEX Uniswap DAO, which operates a prominent network. The Uniswap (UNI) governance token allows the Uniswap community to propose and vote on modifications to the protocol, including how fees are set, new features are added, and how the treasury is managed. By letting users worldwide determine what the protocol should do, the Uniswap DAO demonstrates how distributed control can be applied to a financial platform (Furnari and Villani, 2024). This approach clarifies processes, provides consumers with control, and motivates them to participate. Not all aspects of DAOs are straightforward, however. Issues such as voter apathy, low participation rates, and the "whale dominance" effect—resulting from major token holders making all the decisions—have frequently been raised. Furthermore, uncertainty in many countries regarding the legal and regulatory standing of DAOs could compromise their long-term viability. Despite these challenges, DAOs are becoming increasingly popular as a fresh and innovative approach to managing groups, initiatives, and entire ecosystems. This comparison is illustrated in the chart below (Fig. 3.5).

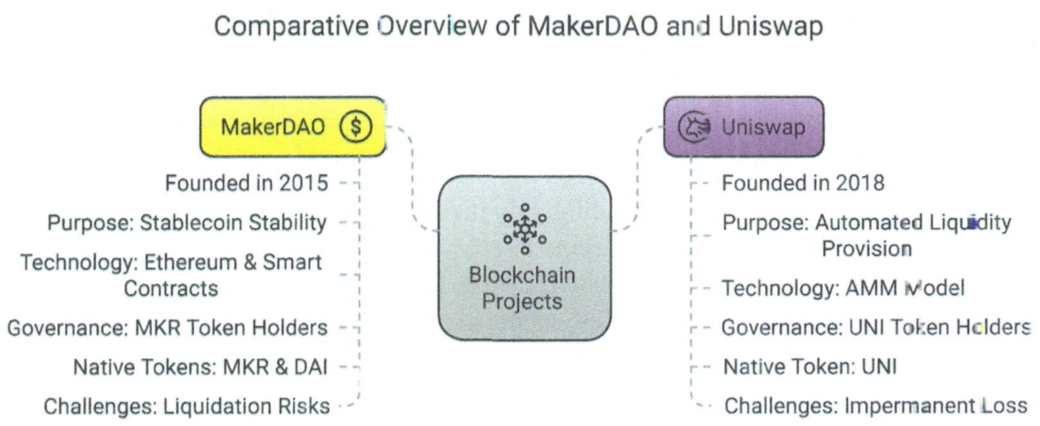

Fig. 3.5 Comparative overview of maker DAO and uniswap. *Author demonstrated and collected materials from Angeris, G., Chitra, T., 2020. Improved price oracles. ArXiv (Cornell University). doi:10.1145/3419614.3423251; Kjäer, M., Di Angelo, M., Salzer, G., 2021. Empirical evaluation of MakerDAO's resilience. In: 3rd Conference on Blockchain Research & Applications for Innovative Networks and Services (BRAINS). IEEE, pp. 193–200. doi:10.1109/brains52497.2021.9569811; Fan, Z., Marmolejo-Cossío, F., Moroz, D.J., Neuder, M., Rao, R., Parkes, D.C., 2021. Strategic liquidity provision in uniswap v3. arXiv.org. Available from: https://arxiv.org/abs/2106.12033; Sun, X., Stasinakis, C., Sermpinis, G., 2024. Decentralization illusion in decentralized finance: evidence from tokenized voting in MakerDAO polls. J. Financ. Stab. 73, 101286. doi:10.1016/j.jfs.2024.101286.*

3.5.2 Central bank digital currencies

As central banks investigate how blockchain technology might be applied to create more modern financial institutions, CBDCs have taken center stage for central banks worldwide. Digital replicas of a nation's fiat money, produced and controlled by its central bank, are known as CBDCs (Belke and Beretta, 2020). Unlike cryptocurrencies like Bitcoin and Ethereum, which are decentralized and free from central authority control, this is not the case for CBDCs (Kappos et al., 2021; Filippi and Loveluck, 2016). Primarily used to make payment systems more efficient, reduce transaction costs, enable more people to access money, and facilitate customized money creation via smart contracts, CBDCs stand out due to their programmability. This feature allows central banks to embed specific guidelines and requirements into the currency. For example, a CBDC might be designed to expire after a specific period to encourage spending during a recession or to restrict its use for particular purposes, such as aid payments. CBDCs—which can be programmed—are a valuable tool for central banks in the digital era. They pave the way for financial innovation and new approaches to monetary policy.

Among the most sophisticated CBDC initiatives ever developed is the Digital Yuan (e-CNY) in China. Launched by the People's Bank of China in line with its digitalization strategy, the e-CNY is designed to interact with existing payment systems and reduce reliance on cash and private payment apps like Alipay and WeChat Pay (Bhattacharya, 2022). Within the European Union, the European Central Bank (ECB) is considering the digital euro. The Digital Euro seeks to maintain the euro's worldwide reserve value while providing businesses and individuals with a simple and safe online payment method. When developing the euro, the ECB emphasized the importance of privacy and security to ensure it meets consumer needs and complies with government policies. The project is still in the research and development phase, so decisions on when to unveil it are expected to be made in the next few years.

The United States Federal Reserve has diligently investigated the benefits and drawbacks of establishing a US CBDC. Essential concerns like financial security, privacy, and the impact on the banking system have been raised by the Federal Reserve for careful consideration. The Fed has been cautious, seeking to fully understand the consequences of a CBDC before initiating its deployment. On the other hand, China has been introducing the e-CNY more rapidly, indicating that its objectives and legal systems differ.

3.6 Benefits and challenges

3.6.1 Advantages

Blockchain technology offers one of its most important benefits: security. Blockchain's security of transactions depends on cryptographic principles. Each encrypted transaction connects with its predecessor, forming a tamper-proof blockchain. Blockchain is quite resistant to fraud and hacking because its cryptographic security provides a strong foundation for safe financial transactions. Furthermore, the distributed nature of blockchain eliminates the necessity of a central authority, reducing the risk of single points of failure and improving overall system resilience (Jiang and Lucero, 2023).

Transparency on the blockchain is another major advantage. Operating on an unchangeable ledger, the technology cannot be undone or altered once a transaction is recorded. Since all participants have access to the same validated data, this openness fosters confidence among them. In financial services, this capability can simplify procedures, including compliance and auditing, as stakeholders can quickly track transactions and verify their legitimacy. Because the blockchain provides a single source of truth, its unchangeable nature also reduces the potential for conflicts (Wang, 2023). In addition, by "banking the unbanked," blockchain promises to support financial inclusion. Particularly in underdeveloped regions, traditional financial systems often overlook those without access to banking facilities. Blockchain technology's distributed and accessible nature enables the provision of financial services to underserved populations. For example, blockchain-based systems can facilitate remittances, microloans, and peer-to-peer lending without the need for intermediaries. This democratization of peer-to-peer financial development could empower millions of individuals and drive economic growth in underprivileged areas.

3.6.2 Challenges

Blockchain technology presents significant difficulties that prevent its general acceptance, even though it offers many benefits (Tyagi et al., 2024a, 2024b; Tyagi, 2025b; Surve and Khandelwal, 2023; Nair and Tyagi, 2024). Scalability is among the most urgent problems. The growing transaction volume brought on by blockchain networks causes congestion and higher transaction fees. One of the most often-used blockchain systems, Ethereum, has had significant scalability problems, whereby users pay hefty gas fees during network congestion. These scalability issues must be resolved so that blockchain can meet the needs of global financial systems. Regulatory issues represent yet another major obstacle. Blockchain's distributed and pseudonymous nature raises concerns regarding knowledge-of-customer compliance and antimoney laundering (AML). Particularly concerning DeFi, authorities worldwide are struggling to implement current financial regulations for blockchain-based platforms. Operating without intermediaries, DeFi networks create unique challenges for authorities trying to stop illegal activity while encouraging innovation. The sustainable development of blockchain technology depends on finding a balance between control and creativity.

3.7 Future outlook

3.7.1 Emerging trends

Zero-knowledge proofs (ZKPs) and the incorporation of artificial intelligence (AI) stand out as transformative ideas. ZKP systems are cryptographic techniques that allow one party to validate a statement to another party without disclosing any underlying facts. One of the most time-sensitive issues in the digital era is being addressed by this technology, which is being embraced to improve privacy in blockchain systems. Particularly in industries like finance, healthcare, and identity management, ZKPs are paving the way for more private blockchain uses by enabling transactions to be confirmed without disclosing private information (Ajayi et al., 2024). ZKPs can, for example, guarantee privacy compliance by enabling anonymous voting systems or confidential financial transactions; therefore, they preserve transparency and trust even as privacy laws are being followed.

AI and blockchain convergence is another significant trend opening up fresh automation and efficiency possibilities. Often known as smart contracts, AI can be combined with blockchain to produce better, self-executing agreements. These agreements minimize human error by automatically triggering activities based on established criteria, reducing the necessity for middlemen (Dua and Kumar, 2024). For instance, smart contracts driven by AI might independently verify product authenticity or instantly optimize logistics, streamlining supply chain management. AI can also enhance blockchain scalability and security by analyzing data to identify abnormalities or predict potential weaknesses. AI and blockchain are generating a synergy that could transform sectors by enabling more intelligent, autonomous, and secure systems.

3.7.2 Regulatory developments

The regulatory terrain surrounding blockchain technology changes over time and also flourishes in its activities. Governments and international organizations are contributing by establishing worldwide legal frameworks to address the complexity of distributed autonomous organizations (DAOs), DeFi, and CBDCs. Operating without established intermediaries like banks, DeFi has raised questions about consumer protection, financial stability, and AML compliance (Benson et al., 2023). Similarly, DAOs, which are controlled by smart contracts and community voting, challenge accepted corporate governance frameworks and legal definitions. Regulators are exploring ways to strike a balance between innovation and control so that these decentralized networks operate within legal boundaries while fostering development and inclusion simultaneously.

Conversely, CBDCs dramatically change how central banks view digital payments and monetary policy. To modernize national financial institutions, improve payment efficiency, and combat the spread of private cryptocurrencies, many nations are aggressively investigating or launching CBDCs. However, the evolution of CBDCs also raises issues about cybersecurity, privacy, and the possible influence on commercial banks. Regulators are thus trying to design systems that address these problems while advancing the advantages of CBDCs. Apart from these advancements, the Financial Action Task Force (FATF) has been crucial in developing global norms for Bitcoin compliance. The FATF's recommendations underline the need to apply AML and counter-terrorism financing policies in cryptocurrency.

These rules motivate nations to impose more rigorous regulations for wallet providers, crypto exchanges, and other virtual asset service providers. The FATF seeks to reduce risks related to illegal activity by encouraging a consistent approach to crypto compliance and, therefore, supporting the responsible expansion of the blockchain sector.

3.8 Conclusion

One pillar of blockchain technology is decentralized governance, which is changing traditional financial systems. Blockchain allows people to engage in governance processes without depending on central institutions through DAOs and consensus-driven decision-making. As demonstrated by the emergence of DeFi platforms that provide lending, borrowing, and trading services free from intermediaries, this democratization of money is encouraging innovation; moreover, more open and inclusive financial institutions are being made possible by blockchain's capacity to create a trustless environment, whereby transactions are confirmed by the network instead of a central authority.

Blockchain technology has enormous promise to transform financial systems. Blockchain solves several inefficiencies and inequalities in conventional finance by allowing trustless, open, and quick transactions. Powered by cryptographic algorithms and consensus procedures, trustless systems eliminate the need for intermediaries, lowering expenses and accelerating transaction times. This is especially significant in cross-border payments, where blockchain might simplify typically lengthy and costly procedures. Moreover, the openness of blockchain guarantees that all players have access to the same information, thereby promoting trust and responsibility in financial contracts.

Furthermore, blockchain's open nature promises greater financial inclusivity. Blockchain can empower millions of people worldwide by providing those barred from conventional banking systems access to financial services. This benefit is especially relevant in developing regions, where access to banking infrastructure is limited. The efficiency of blockchain systems, characterized by automated procedures and reduced operational overhead, could result in significant cost reductions for consumers and companies.

References

Agbo, C.C., Mahmoud, Q.H., Eklund, J.M., 2019. Blockchain technology in healthcare: a systematic review. Healthcare. 7 (2), 56. doi:10.3390/healthcare7020056.

Aggarwal, S., Kumar, N., 2021. Basics of blockchain. In: Aggarwal, S., Kumar, N., Raj, P. (Eds.), ScienceDirect, vol. 121. Elsevier, pp. 129–146. doi:10.1016/bs.adcom.2020.08.007. https://www.sciencedirect.com/science/article/pii/S0065245820300620. Chapter 7.

Ajayi, A.A., Emmanuel, E., Soyele, A.D., Enyejo, J.O., 2024. Enhancing digital identity and financial security in decentralized finance (Defi) through zero-knowledge proofs (ZKPs) and blockchain solutions for regulatory compliance and privacy. Iconic Res. Eng. J. 8 (4). https://www.irejournals.com/paper-details/1706417.

Angeris, G., Chitra, T., 2020. Improved price oracles. ArXiv (Cornell University). doi:10.1145/3419614.3423251.

Armknecht, F., Karame, G.O., Mandal, A., Youssef, F., Zenner, E., 2015. Ripple: overview and outlook. Lect. Notes Comput. Sci. 163–180. doi:10.1007/978-3-319-22846-4_10.

Arslanian, H., 2022. Decentralized finance (DeFi). In: Friesendorf, C., Blütener, A. (Eds.), The Book of Crypto. Springer International Publishing, pp. 291–313. doi:10.1007/978-3-030-97951-5_16.

Atzori, M., 2015. Blockchain technology and decentralized governance: is the state still necessary? SSRN Electron. J. doi:10.2139/ssrn.2709713.

Auer, R., Frost, J., Gambacorta, L., Monnet, C., Rice, T., Shin, H.S., 2022. Central bank digital currencies: motives, economic implications, and the research frontier. Annu. Rev. Econ. 14 (1), 697–721. doi:10.1146/annurev-economics-051420-020324.

Azaria, A., Ekblaw, A., Vieira, T., Lippman, A., 2016. MedRec: using blockchain for medical data access and permission management. In: 2nd International Conference on Open and Big Data (OBD). IEEE, pp. 25–30. doi:10.1109/obd.2016.11.

Belke, A., Beretta, E., 2020. From cash to central bank digital currencies and cryptocurrencies: a balancing act between modernity and monetary stability. J. Econ. Stud. 47 (4), 911–938. doi:10.1108/jes-07-2019-0311.

Benson, V., Türkşen, U., Adamyk, B., 2023. Dark side of decentralized finance: a call for enhanced AML regulation based on use cases of illicit activities. J. Financ. Regul. Compl. 32 (1). doi:10.1108/jfrc-04-2023-0065.

Bhattacharya, D., 2022. Digital yuan (e-CNY): china's official digital currency. Strateg. Anal. 46 (1), 1–7. doi:10.1080/09700161.2022.2039582.

Bracciali, A., Grossi, D., Haan, R.D., 2021. Decentralization in open quorum systems: limitative results for ripple and stellar. In: Anceaume, E., Bisière, C., Bouvard, M., Bramas, Q., Casamatta, C. (Eds.), OASIcs, vol. 82. Schloss Dagstuhl—Leibniz-Zentrum für Informatik. p. 20. doi:10.4230/oasics.tokenomics.2020.5.

Buterin, V., Reijsbergen, D., Leonardos, S., Piliouras, G., 2020. Incentives in ethereum's hybrid casper protocol. Int. J. Netw. Manag. 30 (5). doi:10.1002/nem.2098.

Cai, W., Wang, Z., Ernst, J.B., Hong, Z., Feng, C., Leung, V.C., 2018. Decentralized applications: the blockchain-empowered software system. IEEE Access. 6, 53019–53033.

Caudevilla, O., Kim, H.M., 2022. The digital yuan and cross-border payments: china's rollout of its central bank digital currency. Papers.ssrn.com. Available from: https://papers.ssrn.com/sol3/papers.cfm?abstract_id=4371414.

Cedra, A., 2024. Mitigating risks in decentralized finance: a systematic review of challenges and solutions. Int. J. Econ. Perspect. 18 (1), 104–125. Available from: https://ijeponline.lingcure.org/index.php/journal/article/view/549.

Chang, Y., Iakovou, E., Shi, W., 2020. Blockchain in global supply chains and cross border trade: a critical synthesis of the state-of-the-art, challenges and opportunities. Int. J. Prod. Res. 58 (7), 1–18. doi:10.1080/00207543.2019.1651946.

Coutinho, K., Khairwal, N., Wongthongtham, P., 2023. Towards a truly decentralized blockchain framework for remittance. J. Risk Financ. Manag. 16 (4), 240. doi:10.3390/jrfm16040240.

Daian, P., Goldfeder, S., Kell, T., Li, Y., Zhao, X., Bentov, I., Breidenbach, L., Juels, A., 2019. Flash boys 2.0: frontrunning, transaction reordering, and consensus instability in decentralized exchanges. ArXiv.org. Available from: https://arxiv.org/abs/1904.05234.

de Filippi, P., 2016. The interplay between decentralization and privacy: the case of blockchain technologies. J. Peer Prod. 7. https://hal.science/hal-01382006.

Dhanekulla, P., 2024. Blockchain and distributed ledger technology in modernizing insurance systems: enhancing transparency and reducing fraud. Int. J. Comput. Eng. Technol. 15 (6), 275–290. Available from: https://lib-index.com/index.php/IJCET/article/view/IJCET_15_06_023.

Diffie, W., Hellman, M.E., 1976. New directions in cryptography. IEEE Trans. Inf. Theory IT-22 (6), 644–654. https://ee.stanford.edu/~hellman/publications/24.pdf.

Dua, A., Kumar, G., 2024. Mastering Zero-Knowledge Proofs: Practical Study of Security, Scalability, and Privacy in Blockchain and Modern Systems, English ed. BPB Publications.

Ekblaw, A., Barabas, C., Harvey-Buschel, J., Lippman, A. (2016). Bitcoin and the Myth of decentralization: socio-technical proposals for restoring network integrity. In: IEEE 1st International Workshops on Foundations and Applications of Self* Systems (FAS*W). doi:10.1109/fas-w.2016.18.

Fan, C., 2023. Blockchain-based Design for Performant Peer-to-Peer Energy Trading Systems. ERA. doi:10.7939/r3-han7-jj81.

Feng, Z., Mohanty, H., Krishnamachari, B., 2024. Modeling and analysis of crypto-backed over-collateralized stable derivatives in DeFi. Front. Blockchain. 7. doi:10.3389/fbloc.2024.1392812.

Filippi, D., Loveluck, B., 2016. The invisible politics of bitcoin: governance crisis of a decentralized infrastructure. Ssrn.com. Available from: https://papers.ssrn.com/sol3/papers.cfm?abstract_id=2852691.

Fracassi, C., Khoja, M., Schär, F., 2024. Decentralized crypto governance? transparency and concentration in ethereum decision-making. Soc. Sci. Res. Netw. doi:10.2139/ssrn.4691000.

Friesendorf, C., Blütener, A. (Eds.), 2023. Decentralized finance (DeFi) In: Business Guides on the Go. Springer International Publishing. doi:10.1007/978-3-031-37488-3.

Furnari, S., Villani, C., 2024. Regulation of Financial Protocol DAOs. Addressing the Problems of Decentralization and AI Governance. Elsevier BV. doi:10.2139/ssrn.5023440.

García-Pérez, Á., Schett, M.A., 2019. Deconstructing stellar consensus (extended version). arXiv.org. Available from: https://arxiv.org/abs/1911.05145.

Giancaspro, M., 2017. Is a 'smart contract'really a smart idea? Insights from a legal perspective. Comput. Law Secur. Rev. 33 (6), 825–835.

Goodman, L.M., 2014. A self-amending crypto-ledger. Tezos white paper.

Habermas, J., 1985. The Theory of Communicative Action: Volume 1: Reason and the Rationalization of Society. Beacon Press.

Halim, R., 2022. Decentralization, scalability, and security trade-off in blockchain system: comparison on different approaches. Essay.utwente.nl. Available from: http://essay.utwente.nl/91994/.

Harvey, C.R., Ramachandran, A., Santoro, J., 2021. DeFi and the Future of Finance, John Wiley & Sons.

Heilman, E., Kendler, A., Zohar, A., Goldberg, S., 2015. Eclipse attacks on {Bitcoin's} {peer-to-peer} network. In: 24th USENIX Security Symposium (USENIX Security 15). pp. 129–144.

Howell, B.E., Potgieter, P.H., 2021. Uncertainty and dispute resolution for blockchain and smart contract institutions. J. Inst. Econ. 17 (4), 545–559. doi:10.1017/s1744137421000138.

Incutti, V., 2023. Streamlining Derivative Trading: Enhanced Liquidity and Risk Mitigation with Blockchain-Based Tokenised Collateral Management. University College London. Available from: https://christopherclack.com/images/Documents/Vincenzo-Incutti-Dissertation2023.pdf.

Islam, M.R., Rashid, M.M., Rahman, M.A., Mohamad, M.H.S.B., Embong, A.H.B., 2022. A comprehensive analysis of blockchain-based cryptocurrency mining impact on energy consumption. Int. J. Adv. Comput. Sci. Appl. 13 (4), 590–598.

Jiang, J., Lucero, K., 2023. Background and implications of China's Central Bank digital currency: e-CNY. UF Law Scholarship Repository. Available from: https://scholarship.law.ufl.edu/facultypub/1221/.

Jung, J.W., Islam, M.M., In, H.P., 2024. Proof of work with random selection (PoWR): an energy saving consensus algorithm with proof of work and the random selection function. Sustainability. 15 (21), 9342–9342. doi:10.3390/su16219342.

Kappos, G., Yousaf, H., Piotrowska, A., Kanjalkar, S., Delgado-Segura, S., Miller, A., Meiklejohn, S., 2021. An empirical analysis of privacy in the lightning network. Lect. Notes Comput. Sci. 167–186. doi:10.1007/978-3-662-64322-8_8.

Katz, J., Lindell, Y., 2020. Introduction to Modern Cryptography Crc Press, vol. 10. Taylor & Francis.

Kiayias, A., Lazos, P., 2022. SoK: blockchain governance. In: Proceedings of the 4th ACM Conference on Advances in Financial Technologies. pp. 61–73.

Kjäer, M., Di Angelo, M., Salzer, G., 2021. Empirical evaluation of MakerDAO's resilience. In: 3rd Conference on Blockchain Research & Applications for Innovative Networks and Services (BRAINS). IEEE, pp. 193–200. doi:10.1109/brains52497.2021.9569811.

Kouhizadeh, M., Sarkis, J., 2018. Blockchain practices, potentials, and perspectives in greening supply chains. Sustainability. 10 (10), 3652. doi:10.3390/su10103652.

Kshetri, N., 2017. Will blockchain emerge as a tool to break the poverty chain in the Global South? Third World Q. 38 (8), 1710–1732. doi:10.1080/01436597.2017.1298438.

Lundin, F., Rahm, F., 2018. Evaluating risk and reward for validators in a cryptocurrency proof-of-stake network. DIVA. Available from: https://www.diva-portal.org/smash/record.jsf?pid=diva2:1214786.

Macharia, D.N., 2023. Distributed Ledger Technology (DLT) Applications in Payment, Clearing, and Settlement Systems: A Study of Blockchain-Based Payment Barriers and Potential Solutions, and DLT Application in Central Bank Payment System Functions, University of Huddersfield.

Makarov, I., Schoar, A., 2022. Cryptocurrencies and decentralized finance (DeFi). Brook. Pap. Econ. Act. 2022 (1), 141–215. doi:10.1353/eca.2022.0014.

Makridakis, S., Polemitis, A., Giaglis, G., Louca, S., 2018. Blockchain: the next breakthrough in the rapid progress of AI. Artif. Intell.-Emerg. Trends Appl. 10. https://www.intechopen.com/chapters/60772.

Mettler, M., 2016. Blockchain technology in healthcare: the revolution starts here. In: IEEE 18th International Conference on e-Health Networking, Applications and Services (Healthcom). IEEE, pp.1–3. doi:10.1109/healthcom.2016.7749510.

Nair, M.M., Tyagi, A.K., 2024. Blockchain technology for next-generation society: current trends and future opportunities for smart era. In: Blockchain Technology for Secure Social Media Computing. IET. doi:10.1049/PBSE019E_ch11.

Nakamoto, S., 2008. Bitcoin: a peer-to-peer electronic cash system. Available from: https://assets.pubpub.org/d8wct41f/31611263538139.pdf.

Napieralska, A., Kępczyński, P., 2023. Smart contracts and web 3: from automated transactions to DAOs. Www.igi-Global.com; IGI Global. https://www.igi-global.com/chapter/smart-contracts-and-web-3/329860.

Naz, M., Al-zahrani, F.A., Khalid, R., Javaid, N., Qamar, A.M., Afzal, M.K., Shafiq, M., 2019. A secure data sharing platform using blockchain and interplanetary file system. Sustainability. 11 (24), 7054–7054. doi:10.3390/su11247054.

Parenti, A., Billi, M., 2023. Building trust in smart legal contracts. In: Transparency or Opacity. Nomos Verlagsgesellschaft MbH & Co. KG EBooks, pp. 95–114. https://cris.unibo.it/handle/11585/908148. doi:10.5771/9783748936060-95.

Perwej, Y., Akhtar, N., Parwej, F., 2018. A technological perspective of blockchain security. Int. J. Recent Sci. Res. 9 (11), 29472–29493.

Qin, K., Zhou, L., Gamito, P., Jovanovic, P., Gervais, A., 2021. An empirical study of DeFi liquidations. ArXiv (Cornell University). 336–350. doi:10.1145/3487552.3487811.

Reiman, J., 1999. The critical criminologist 1 volume 9 #2 newsletter of ASC's division on critical criminology the rich (Still) get richer … understanding ideology, outrage and economic bias. Available from: https://divisiononcriticalcriminology.com/wp-content/uploads/Critical-Criminology-09-2.pdf.

Ren, W., Hu, J., Zhu, T., Ren, Y., Choo, K.-K.R., 2020. A flexible method to defend against computationally resourceful miners in blockchain proof of work. Inf. Sci. 507, 161–171. doi:10.1016/j.ins.2019.08.031.

Saberi, S., Kouhizadeh, M., Sarkis, J., Shen, L., 2018. Blockchain technology and its relationships to sustainable supply chain management. Int. J. Prod. Res. 57 (7), 2117–2135. doi:10.1080/00207543.2018.1533261.

Schär, F., 2021. Decentralized finance: on blockchain and smart contract-based financial markets—edoc. Unibas.ch. Available from: https://edoc.unibas.ch/86500/1/decentralized-finance-on-blockchain-and-smart-contract-based-financial-markets.pdf.

Schneider, N., 2019. Decentralization: an incomplete ambition. J. Cult. Econ. 12 (4), 265–285. doi:10.1080/17530350.2019.1589553.

Singh, S., Singh, N., 2016. Blockchain: future of financial and cyber security. In: 2016 2nd International Conference on Contemporary Computing and Informatics (IC3I). IEEE. doi:10.1109/ic3i.2016.7918009.

Soundararajan, G., Tyagi, A.K. 2024. Blockchain technology: an introduction. In: Blockchain Technology in the Automotive Industry. CRC Press. doi:10.1201/9781003450306-2.

Stallings, W., Brown, L., 2015. Computer Security: Principles and Practice, Pearson.

Sun, X., Stasinakis, C., Sermpinis, G., 2024. Decentralization illusion in decentralized finance: evidence from tokenized voting in MakerDAO polls. J. Financ. Stab. 73, 101286. doi:10.1016/j.jfs.2024.101286.

Surve, T., Khandelwal, R., 2023. The emergence of cryptography in blockchain technology. In: Lekhi, P., Kaur, G. (Eds.), Concepts, Technologies, Challenges, and the Future of Web 3. IGI Global Scientific Publishing, pp. 47–63. doi:10.4018/978-1-6684-9919-1.ch004.

Szabo, N., 1996. Smart contracts: building blocks for digital markets. EXTROPY. 18 (2), 28.
Tapscott, D., Tapscott, A., 2016. Blockchain Revolution: How the Technology behind Bitcoin Is Changing Money, Business, and the World, Penguin.
Tian, F., 2016. An agri-food supply chain traceability system for China based on RFID & blockchain technology. In: 2016 13th International Conference on Service Systems and Service Management (ICSSSM). pp. 1–6. doi:10.1109/icsssm.2016.7538424.
Tikhomirov, S., 2018. Ethereum: state of knowledge and research perspectives. Found. Pract. Secur. 10723, 206–221. doi:10.1007/978-3-319-75650-9_14.
Tyagi, A.K., 2023. Decentralized everything: a practical use of blockchain technology in future applications. In: Distributed Computing to Blockchain: Architecture, Technology, and Applications. Elsevier, pp. 19–38. doi:10.1016/B978-0-323-96146-2.00010-3.
Tyagi, A.K., 2025a. Blockchain for smart hospital in Healthcare 5.0: modeling structure, challenges, and future emerging trends. In: Human- Centric Integration of Next-Generation Data Science and Blockchain Technology. Elsevier. doi:10.1016/B978-0-443-33498-6.00026-1.
Tyagi, A.K., 2025b. Blockchain technology: values, challenges, and possible applications from an industry perspective. In: Human- Centric Integration of Next-Generation Data Science and Blockchain Technology. Elsevier. doi:10.1016/B978-0-443-33498-6.00027-3.
Tyagi, A.K., Kumari, S., Surve, T., 2024. Advanced topics for blockchain-based applications: open issues, technical, legal, and research challenges. In: Artificial Intelligence-Enabled Digital Twin for Smart Manufacturing. doi:10.1002/9781394303601.ch15.
Tyagi, A.K., Kumari, S., Surve, T., 2024a. Blockchain technology. In: Tyagi, A.K. (Ed.), Digital Twin and Blockchain for Smart Cities. Wiley, pp. 27–45. doi:10.1002/9781394303564.ch2.
Tyagi, A.K., Kumari, S., Surve, T., 2024b. Advanced topics for blockchain-based applications. In: Tyagi, A.K., Tiwari, S., Arumugam, S.K., Sharma, A.K. (Eds.), Artificial Intelligence-Enabled Digital Twin for Smart Manufacturing. Wiley, pp. 325–339. doi:10.1002/9781394303601.ch15
Vasselin, F., 2024. Blockchain for migrants: promoting self-sovereign identity and financial inclusion. Hal.science. Available from: https://hal.science/hal-04815373.
Voshmgir, S., Zargham, M., 2019. Foundations of cryptoeconomic systems. In: Research Institute for Cryptoeconomics, Vienna, Working Paper Series/Institute for Cryptoeconomics/Interdisciplinary Research, vol. 1.
Walch, A., 2019. Deconstructing "decentralization": exploring the core claim of crypto systems. Papers.ssrn.com. Available from: https://papers.ssrn.com/sol3/papers.cfm?abstract_id=3326244.
Wang, H., 2023. How to understand China's approach to Central Bank Digital Currency? Comput. Law Secur. Rev. 50, 105788–105788. doi:10.1016/j.clsr.2022.105788.
Wang, Y., Han, J.H., Beynon-Davies, P., 2018. Understanding blockchain technology for future supply chains: a systematic literature review and research agenda. Supply Chain Manag. Int. J. 24 (1), 62–84. doi:10.1108/scm-03-2018-0148.
Werner, S., Perez, D., Gudgeon, L., Klages-Mundt, A., Harz, D., Knottenbelt, W., 2022. SoK: decentralized finance (DeFi). ArXiv (Cornell University). 30–46. doi:10.1145/3558535.3559780.
Wieandt, A., Heppding, L., 2023. Centralized and decentralized finance: coexistence or convergence? Palgrave Stud. Financ. Serv. Technol. 11–51. doi:10.1007/978-3-031-23069-1_2.
Wood, G., 2016. Polkadot: vision for a heterogeneous multi-chain framework. White Paper. 21 (2327), 4662.
Wright, A., De Filippi, P., 2015. Decentralized blockchain technology and the rise of lex cryptographia. SSRN Electron. J. doi:10.2139/ssrn.2580664.
Yoo, S., 2023. Comparative analysis of blockchain trilemma. Int. J. Adv. Smart Converg. 12 (1), 41–52. doi:10.7236/IJASC.2023.12.1.41.
Zanfino, G., 2024. Enhancing privacy and scalability of permissioned blockchain—ePrints soton. Soton.ac.uk. Available from: https://eprints.soton.ac.uk/491205/1/Gilberto-Zanfino-PhD-thesis.pdf.
Zhang, P., Schmidt, D.C., White, J., Lenz, G., 2018. Blockchain technology use cases in healthcare. In: Advances in Computers. Elsevier, pp. 1–41. doi:10.1016/bs.adcom.2018.03.006.
Zwitter, A., Hazenberg, J., 2020. Decentralized network governance: blockchain technology and the future of regulation. Front. Blockchain 3. doi:10.3389/fbloc.2020.00012.

CHAPTER 4

Convergence of intelligence: Exploring the integration of artificial intelligence, machine learning and blockchain

Praful Pardhi, Ashlesha Pathak, Abhijeet Raipurkar, Sanika Pohare, Sakshi Paliye, and Manali Mishrikotkar
School of Computer Science and Engineering, Ramdeobaba University, Nagpur, Maharashtra, India

4.1 Overview of AI, ML, and blockchain

4.1.1 Blockchain

It is a groundbreaking way to store and manage blockchain data, designed to ensure basic openness, security, and decentralization. At its core, a blockchain is a distributed ledger system, which means it does not reside in the same place or server. Instead, it operates within a large network of computers, or "nodes," that maintain synchronized copies of all data entries. Although blockchain technology received global recognition through its role in enabling cryptocurrency, such as Bitcoin, its utility goes far beyond digital currencies. It provides a safe and irreversible structure to record any form of information, making it valuable in industries ranging from finance and health services to logistics and identity management.

The peculiar feature of a blockchain is how it processes data. Unlike a traditional database, which stores records in tables or rows, a blockchain stores information in small parts called blocks. Each block is securely connected to the previous one through a cryptographic hash, forming an unbreakable chain. When a block is filled with data and sealed, it becomes a permanent part of the blockchain and cannot be altered without affecting all subsequent blocks. This design eliminates the need for intermediaries, such as accountants or centralized officers, thereby reducing both costs and human error.

Since the arrival of Bitcoin in 2009, blockchain applications have expanded rapidly. It has enabled digital assets and programmable agreements such as decentralized finance (DeFi), non-fungible tokens (NFTs), and smart contracts. These innovations are possible because of the main principles of blockchain: decentralization, transparency, and irreversibility.

Artificial Intelligence, Machine Learning and Blockchain in Digital Twin Computing.
https://doi.org/10.1016/B978-0-443-43914-8.00005-4

4.1.2 How blockchain works

To understand blockchain, imagine a digital ledger that behaves truly like a shared spreadsheet. Users can enter new statistics; however, as soon as entered and proven, it becomes read-only. Every block within the chain consists of a list of new transactions or information, a timestamp, and a unique hash. When the block reaches capacity, the records are compressed into a hash and linked to the next block, securing the relationship and maintaining the integrity of the data.

This entire system is governed by a decentralized network where consensus is key. For instance, in the Bitcoin network, each transaction is first sent to a memory pool and then selected by miners—specialized individuals who validate and verify blocks. Miners solve complex cryptographic puzzles, often by adjusting a variable known as a nonce, until they discover a valid block hash. The winner of this computational race adds the block to the chain and receives a reward. However, the transaction is not considered fully confirmed until several additional blocks are added, reinforcing its authenticity and preventing fraud.

Not all blockchains use mining. Ethereum, for instance, has moved to a proof-of-stake (PoS) mechanism. Instead of competing via computation, validators are randomly selected primarily based on the amount of cryptocurrency they have staked. This approach is more electricity-efficient and quicker, allowing for faster transaction confirmations while still maintaining high security.

4.1.2.1 Decentralization and trust

One of the important strengths of blockchain technology is decentralization. Rather than relying on a central authority, the blockchain network operates through a consensus protocol in which each node has a copy of the entire chain. If a person tries to tamper with a record on one device, it would immediately be flagged as invalid by different nodes because of hash mismatches. This peer-to-peer verification ensures that no single person can unilaterally alter data, protecting the network from corruption and manipulation.

Because of this distributed structure, blockchains are resistant to data loss and cyber-assaults. Even if one or more nodes are compromised, the data remains safe and accessible on others. This redundancy makes blockchain particularly suitable for essential data storage, from legal documents and medical records to supply chain logs and personal identity.

4.1.2.2 Transparency and anonymity

Public blockchains, including Bitcoin, offer a remarkable level of transparency. Every transaction is visible to everyone with access to the network, and blockchain explorers provide tools to track and verify the records of each coin or contract. Despite this openness, users maintain anonymity. Wallet addresses, rather than personal identities, are displayed, ensuring privacy while allowing anyone to audit the system's activity.

This combination of transparency and pseudonymity makes blockchain both secure and consumer-friendly. Even in instances of cyberattacks, where hackers may remain anonymous, the stolen property can still be traced across the network, thanks to blockchain's permanent, timestamped records.

4.1.2.3 Security and immutability

The protection of a blockchain is tightly bound to its structure. Each block consists of the hash of the previous block, creating a chain in which any modification to a single record disrupts the whole sequence. To alter existing data, one would need to recompute all subsequent blocks and gain control of the majority of the community's computing power—an incredibly difficult feat known as a 51% attack.

On smaller blockchains, such an assault is theoretically possible. But for major networks like Bitcoin or Ethereum, this becomes practically impossible because of the sheer scale and velocity of operations. For example, as of late 2024, the Bitcoin network processes over 640 Exa hashes second, which means any malicious attempt would require inconceivable resources and coordination. Similarly, Ethereum now relies on more than 33 million staked ETH from over 1,000,000 validators, making unauthorized access both computationally and economically infeasible.

Blockchain isn't just a technological breakthrough—it represents a paradigm shift in how we manage trust, data, and value exchange within the digital world. Its capability to combine security, transparency, and decentralization opens the door to innovations that can redefine industries and empower users. As the technology evolves, its potential applications—from decentralized voting systems to cross-border payments—will continue to grow, promising a future where transparency and trust are no longer optional but built into the fabric of our digital lives.

4.1.3 Overview of artificial intelligence and machine learning

Artificial intelligence (AI) and machine learning (ML) are two closely associated branches of computer technology that concentrate on building systems capable of performing tasks that usually require human intelligence. These technologies are reshaping industries, driving innovation, and playing an important role in our digital world.

4.1.3.1 AI

AI refers to the broader idea of machines being able to carry out responsibilities in a manner that we'd consider "intelligent." It aims to create systems that can simulate human thinking, learn from experience, make decisions, and even understand natural language. AI spans an extensive spectrum, from simple rule-based systems to highly advanced neural networks.

Some usual applications of AI consist of:

- Voice assistants like Siri, Alexa, and Google Assistant
- Recommendation structures utilized by Netflix, Amazon, and YouTube
- Autonomous cars navigate using AI-powered vision and decision-making
- Healthcare diagnostics that help in early sickness detection through the use of medical imaging statistics

4.1.3.2 ML

ML is a subset of AI that specializes in specialty algorithms that enable computers to learn from and make predictions based on data. Instead of being explicitly programmed to perform a task, ML systems learn patterns from historical data and improve over time.

ML can be widely categorized into three types:

- Supervised learning: Algorithms are trained using labeled data (e.g., predicting house prices based on features like location, size, and so on.).
- Unsupervised learning: Algorithms find hidden patterns in data without labeled outputs (e.g., client segmentation).
- Reinforcement learning: Systems discover ways to make selections by interacting with an environment and receiving feedback (e.g., training a robot to walk or play a game).

Relationship between AI and ML

AI is the broader aim of sensible behavior, while ML is the method used to attain this. In other words, all ML is AI; however, not all AI is ML. ML provides the foundation for most of today's practical AI systems.

Importance and impact

The integration of AI and ML is reworking fields, which include finance, healthcare, education, agriculture, cybersecurity, and beyond. These technologies help automate repetitive responsibilities, provide data-driven insights, and make complex decision-making processes more efficient.

With the development of computing power, the availability of vast amounts of data, and the improvement of effective algorithms, the future of AI and ML promises even more transformative advancements—leading toward the era of explainable AI (XAI), moral AI, and human-AI collaboration.

4.1.4 Need and logic for AI/ML and blockchain convergence

4.1.4.1 Data security and integrity

The integration of AI and ML is transforming fields including finance, healthcare, education, agriculture, cybersecurity, and beyond. These technologies help automate repetitive tasks, provide data-driven insights, and make complex decision-making processes more efficient.

With the development of computing power, the provision of big data, and the improvement of effective algorithms, the future of AI and ML promises even more innovative changes—primarily in the direction of the generation of XAI, ethical AI, and human-AI collaboration.

The decentralized and tamper-proof architecture of blockchain drastically enhances the security of records used in AI systems. Since information is distributed across multiple nodes and cannot be easily altered, it becomes more reliable for AI to process. When AI learns from decentralized data sources as opposed to centralized, potentially biased datasets, the outcomes become more accurate and fairer. This shift helps reduce the chances of producing skewed results, inaccuracies, or unfair decisions. A biased dataset can result in low model accuracy, poor predictions, and even unjustified discrimination in automated systems. Building intelligent systems, especially agent-based AI, on unreliable or partial datasets may inadvertently amplify bias or favoritism. However, when blockchain ensures that the input data is decentralized and validated from multiple sources, it helps maintain a level playing field and builds trust in the AI outputs.

In addition, AI plays a crucial role in reinforcing the safety of blockchain networks themselves. By continuously tracking transaction data, AI can discover uncommon patterns or behaviors that indicate malicious activity. This real-time surveillance supports fraud detection and access control. For instance, AI can analyze how transactions are conducted—considering parameters such as time of transfer, geolocation, amount transferred, and transaction frequency—to detect inconsistencies or anomalies. An unexpected transfer from a brand-new location or an unusually high number of transactions within a short period may be immediately flagged as suspicious, helping prevent fraud before it escalates.

Moreover, analyzing behavioral behavioral information, which includes login frequency, device types used, or the pattern of interaction with the device, AI can detect unauthorized access attempts or account takeovers. AI also has the potential to recognize known fraud patterns from historical cases, allowing it to predict and block future threats before any damage is done. What makes this system even more effective is its ability to analyze continuously. As AI encounters new data and threats, it adapts, fine-tunes its predictions, and becomes more accurate over time—building a proactive defense mechanism within the blockchain ecosystem.

4.1.4.2 Transparency and accountability

Blockchain's largest strength lies in its transparency. Every transaction, once recorded, becomes immutable and is visible to all approved participants. This creates a single source of truth, reducing the need for each enterprise to maintain its own information and minimizing errors and discrepancies. With blockchain, all stakeholders can see the same versions of transaction data at the same time, helping build mutual trust. Every transaction is timestamped and documented, providing an unchangeable history of interactions that can be referenced at any point. This ensures complete accountability across the system.

This transparency can also revolutionize supply chains, finance, healthcare, and other sectors in which traceability is critical. Consumers or auditors can trace a merchandise or asset's complete journey—from its origin to its current state—ensuring ethical practices, compliance, and authenticity. For example, in industries where ethical sourcing or anticounterfeit measures are important, blockchain-backed traceability can verify the legitimacy of claims. Customers can scan a product and immediately see where it came from, who handled it, and how it reached them. AI can enhance this by interpreting large volumes of traceability data, flagging inconsistencies, or suggesting optimization routes for supply chain efficiency. It also helps identify vulnerable spots in operational flows, such as delays or bottlenecks, by analyzing data trends and raising alerts based on predictive insights.

4.1.4.3 Enhanced decision-making and automation

AI's power to process and extract insights from large datasets will become appreciably more impactful when paired with blockchain's reliable records storage. By mining blockchain data, AI can uncover trends, relationships, and hidden patterns that inform smarter business strategies. These insights would be difficult or time-consuming for humans to discover manually. Whether it is predicting customer behavior, identifying investment opportunities, or streamlining internal operations, the AI-blockchain combination enables organizations to act faster and with greater confidence.

Smart contracts—a vital characteristic of blockchain—additionally gain substantially from AI integration. These contracts are programmed to execute automatically once specific conditions are met. With AI in the loop, these conditions can become more dynamic and intelligent. Instead of relying on static regulations, smart contracts could evaluate a variety of real-time factors, including market conditions, consumer reputations, or shipping delays, before executing actions. This transforms them into "smart contracts," reducing human involvement while increasing adaptability and precision.

Beyond automation, AI can fast-track how blockchain networks function. By analyzing network load, transaction quantity, and performance metrics, AI can adjust resources and scale the infrastructure as needed. This improves machine performance, reduces transaction delays, and cuts operational expenses. It also contributes to long-term scalability by predicting usage spikes and reallocating computing power intelligently. As blockchain applications develop in size and complexity, this type of smart optimization becomes essential to maintaining pace, affordability, and usefulness.

4.1.5 Objective

The primary goal of this paper is to explore and provide a comprehensive understanding of the evolving relationship among advanced digital technologies—in particular, AI, ML, and Blockchain. It aims to examine how these technologies function independently and in combination, with a focus on their practical applications, advantages, limitations, and the emerging synergies created through their integration.

This observation seeks to provide readers with:

- A clear conceptual basis of AI, ML, and blockchain technology
- An evaluation of their individual and combined talents
- Real-world use cases illustrating their mutual enhancemen
- Insight into potential destiny traits, challenges, and study guidelines

By addressing these regions, the paper endeavors to make contributions to a more informed perspective for technologists, researchers, and decision-makers who are engaged in designing or deploying intelligent and reliable digital systems.

4.1.6 Scope

This paper covers the core ideas, technological frameworks, and operational models of AI, ML, and Blockchain systems. The scope includes—but is not limited to—the following key aspects:

- A breakdown of foundational concepts associated with AI and ML, including types of learning, model training, and statistical analysis
- An evaluation of blockchain structure, consensus mechanisms, and decentralized ledger structures
- A deep dive into the practical intersections where AI and blockchain enhance each other's functionality—along with secure data sharing, smart contracts, decentralized AI (DAI) models, and transparent automation
- Critical analysis of demanding situations, which includes scalability, security, computational value, and moral concerns
- Evaluation of real-world global case studies and industry packages across finance, healthcare, logistics, and governance

4.2 AI and ML integrated in blockchain systems

In recent years, AI and blockchain have emerged as two of the most disruptive technological breakthroughs. Individually, each of these offers great strengths—AI with its cognitive computing power, and blockchain through its decentralized, safe, and transparent nature. However, when these two technologies converge, they represent a whole new field that enables autonomous decision-making with minimal human intervention, making them highly reliable as well. Their combination represents not only greater efficiency and security for online environments but also paves the way for agile, decentralized applications (dApps) that can learn and adjust over time.

4.2.1 Technical frameworks for the integration of AI and blockchain

Integrating AI and Blockchain is a tough but rewarding process. Nonetheless, it is clear that for this to operate seamlessly, both parties must have considerable knowledge of data support. AI and Blockchain are usually globe-spanning communities that produce favorable environments for mutual trust among peers. In contemporary terminology, except for large-scale supercomputers, AI and Blockchain can operate fully autonomously within the global community of developers; from a single platform or device, they could build their mutually contributable computer systems. Blockchain is a decentralized ledger technology that stores data in blocks that are immutable, ensuring transparency and trust throughout a peer network. In contrast, AI focuses on enabling machines to analyze data, recognize patterns, and make informed decisions without needing step-by-step instructions.

4.2.1.1 Smart contracts empowered with AI logic

Smart contracts are blockchain-encoded, self-executing agreements. Infusing AI capabilities into smart contracts makes them more dynamic and responsive. Notably, while the complexity of on-chain logic is limited by computational resources and gas costs, low-complexity AI models—such as simple rule-based approaches or decision trees—can be integrated to achieve autonomous decision-making for industries like transportation, finance, and insurance.

4.2.1.2 Decentralized learning and model training

Traditional AI systems store and process data in centralized servers, which usually generate controversy about data privacy and errors. Blockchain facilitates a distributed approach where AI models can be trained in a decentralized manner across multiple nodes. This idea—called decentralized or federated learning—allows you to train a model without having to bring all the data to a central server. Blockchain's immutable characteristic guarantees that updates to models are verifiable, timestamped, and traceable, further enhancing trust and accountability in the AI lifecycle.

4.2.1.3 Role of oracles and data feeds

AI systems require real-time data inputs to make accurate decisions. Blockchains, by design, operate independently of external systems. To bridge this gap, oracles are employed. Oracles act as trusted intermediaries that feed external data (like stock prices, weather conditions, or sensor readings) to smart contracts. This allows AI models operating in blockchain ecosystems to analyze real-world data and respond accordingly. Oracles are crucial for enabling dynamic contracts that adapt based on external events.

4.2.1.4 Securing federated learning with blockchain

The core idea behind federated ML is that a number of participants can jointly train a ML model without the need to share their raw data. Models are trained locally, and only the updates are exchanged. Blockchain is the technology that can securely and immutably log these updates. This makes the training process auditable and preserves the privacy of every participant, which is especially beneficial in healthcare, finance, and educational use cases.

4.2.2 Execution methods: On-chain and off-chain AI processing

A key decision in AI-blockchain integration is where AI computation will be performed. This decision influences system performance, cost, and scalability.

On-chain AI execution

It is very limited because of the special hardware requirements of the on-chain system, which has very limited processing power and high operating costs. Blockchain environments, like Ethereum, have been designed for security and consensus, not necessarily for computational power. Blockchain platforms currently support only basic AI tasks, such as checking conditions or running simple classification rules, due to processing limitations. As a result of these limitations, on-chain AI is better suited for deterministic applications where complete transparency and traceability are required.

Off-chain AI processing

This makes off-chain the ideal choice for most practical applications. In this context, traditional computing infrastructure is leveraged to build and deploy AI models, while only the final outcomes (predictions, alerts, or recommendations) are represented on-chain. This hybrid model provides a blend of efficiency and transparency. For instance, it could flag suspicious blockchain transactions using an off-chain fraud detection system powered by a deep learning model. Then, the transactions or alerts are noted on-chain for auditing.

Model versions, hashes of the training dataset, and decision logs are stored on the blockchain (in some cases) to create immutable, reproducible, and auditable AI-driven processes.

4.2.3 Appropriate algorithms for ML in blockchain solutions

Not all ML models suit blockchain use-cases, as the efficiency, speed, and explainability of the model are deemed prerequisites. Certain models fit more naturally with the constraints and goals of blockchain systems:

4.2.3.1 Decision trees and random forests

They are rule-based and interpretable models. Smart contract logic is simply conditional code that humans can present variables to, or contract wallets can use to automate contract enforcement and/or decision-making logic within Dapps.

4.2.3.2 Anomaly detection models

Together, models used for outlier detection and identifying fraudulent behaviors are very vital in financial blockchain applications, such as crypto trading sites, NFT markets, or decentralized trade.

4.2.3.3 Clustering algorithms

Behavioral or attribute-based clustering models segment blockchain users or transactions into groups. Clustering is used for analyzing markets, scoring risks, and coordinating attack patterns.

4.2.3.4 Reinforcement learning

For example, RL models could be utilized within blockchain-backed gaming platforms or for independent agent planning. They gain knowledge through interactions and improve over time, which aligns well with dynamic environments.

4.2.3.5 Deep learning neural networks

These models are too large to run on-chain, but they are commonly found off-chain for use cases such as image recognition, sentiment analysis, and fraud prediction, among others. On-chain storage of outputs or inference results ensures transparency and auditability.

4.3 Use cases of AI/ML in blockchain

AI and ML are revolutionizing a variety of industries, and their integration into blockchain technology pushes the boundaries of new innovation. While blockchain provides a decentralized, secure, transparent, and immutable framework, AI and ML bring intelligence, adaptability, and predictive capabilities to the table. This section delves into five key areas where AI and ML are being used in blockchain environments to enable smarter, safer, and more self-sufficient systems.

4.3.1 Smart contracts with AI

Smart contracts are digital contracts that can be programmed to execute once conditions are met. Once within a blockchain platform, AI and ML remove intermediaries by creating a transparent and automatically operational implementation of predefined rules. Traditionally, smart contracts have deterministic execution based solely on static inputs and on-chain events to drive the required actions. This deterministic nature is intended to create consistency and dependability, but it also introduces rigidity, which limits the overall capability of the contract in scenarios that require flexible or context-dependent recognition.

By leveraging the immutability of blockchain and the flexible modeling nature of ML models, smart contracts can adapt or develop beyond the original static contracts. These smart contracts can become reactive and proactive systems, allowing the interpretation of actual real-world trends and the adjustment of supervisory actions.

These types of contracts can process factual and historical data and can adapt how they execute throughout their durations. Let's take the example of decentralized insurance. Rather than using only fixed values for whether you offer coverage or how you set premium costs, adaptive smart contracts can continuously evaluate streams of related data—such as forecasts or historical claims—and behaviors. Contracts can continuously assess insurance conditions and provide guidance on policies that are more personalized and data-driven through ML techniques such as regression-based models or clustering models. This can help provide operational efficiencies and build trust with clients by offering contracts that respond to actual conditions.

One of the most relevant applications is found in data-oriented logic, where smart contracts can be combined with predictive models or classification techniques to leverage and make more nuanced decisions. This is especially pertinent in DeFi, lending itself to more agile systems in fluid environments. For example, ML algorithms can be built, underpinned by credit scores, asset volatility, and broad market trends, to smartly determine interest rates, approve loan permissions, and reduce collateral thresholds. These artificially intelligent augmented contracts, better than a single credit valuation or a rule-based system, could provide some level of personalization and accuracy.

Moreover, the utilization of ML allows smart contracts to operate under uncertainty within the underlying mechanisms and constraints of traditional logic-based systems. Because ML can interpret probabilistic results and learn from patterns, smart contracts can easily adjust to edge cases and anomalies that static codes cannot foresee. The capacity of smart contracts to make decisions in uncertain contexts is extremely valuable within complex systems like decentralized markets, autonomous supply chains, and governance frameworks, where the variables are always in flux and not all finality can be preempted. The potential of this transition is remarkable, from designing economic systems that are more resistant to shocks to automating complex, uncertain interactions in multiple domains.

4.3.2 AI techniques for fraud detection in blockchain networks

Despite blockchain technology being much praised for its transparency, immutability, and trackability, these features are not foolproof in suppressing fraud of every kind. Even after remediation and vulnerabilities are patched, bad actors still locate opportunities to find weaknesses and exploit them for phishing, laundering money, or more complex schemes such as double-spending in less secure blockchain installations. In order to combat these activities, AI—particularly ML—has become an important component of defense.

AI, on the other hand, provides proactive support for fraud detection by learning routines based on transaction behaviors and patterns. Many of these methods involve the use of classification models, which detect whether the transaction is real or fraudulent. These classification models are trained on a number of features that might include transaction size, frequency, time of day, geographical location/origin, wallet reputation, and consistency of behavior over time. Given the features of each transaction, supervised learning methods (such as logistic regression, decision trees, or random forests) can create a model to classify transactions as fraudulent or legitimate and typically provide a risk score. The more data the model can process, the more adept it becomes at reliably assessing fraudulent behavior and adjusting its methods when new approaches prove effective, even if those approaches were unanticipated.

In addition to supervised learning, anomaly detection algorithms can identify atypical behavior when certain parameters differ from typical behavior. This type of analysis is unsupervised (the model is not trained on labels; rather, it learns to identify what is defined as "normal"). Anomaly detection (or outlier detection) is based on unsupervised learning, in which we train our models to detect unusual behavior or patterns based on some input dataset, whether that is k-means, isolation forests, or deep learning-based auto encoders. For example, a sudden spike in transactions from a dormant wallet or an unusual pattern of behavior associated with a smart contract may raise the alarm for further investigation. AI is the perfect solution to this issue, as it works in near real-time and learns continuously. It's a perfect alternative to traditional rule-based systems that need constant tuning and ultimately fail to keep up due to the rapidly changing behavior of fraudsters. Whereas human moderation may be limited in the number of posts they can review or the variety of transaction behaviors they can recognize, AI models adaptively learn and provide a dynamic and scalable approach to security. These techniques can be a great supplement to blockchain systems' decentralized properties by functioning as off-chain analytics or analytics-based smart contract triggers that communicate with AI engines.

Organizations can develop a stronger defense mechanism around blockchain networks by combining classification and anomaly detection approaches. Throughout the process of using this approach, the multilayered method not only protects against unauthorized access, market manipulation, or fraudulent financial activity but also increases trust and accountability in decentralized systems without central authority, which is, of course, the premise of decentralized systems.

4.3.3 Decentralized AI marketplaces: A new paradigm for intelligent sharing

A great use case for blockchain technology is the creation of decentralized market places for AI. In contrast to traditional AI ecosystems that are usually dominated by a few centralized entities, DAI marketplaces aim to foster a fair competition ecosystem by removing roadblocks related to ownership, access, and control. These kinds of platforms are designed to promote open collaboration among the provided AI models and datasets on a trustless basis, where developers, researchers, and organizations can share, access, and monetize their work.

The core idea is to use blockchain technology to manage transactions, ownership records, and licensing agreements. Tokenization offers models and data resources the power to be represented as digital assets, making it easy to transfer and access them. Users can pay for these services using cryptocurrency, which allows for fast, transparent, tamper-proof, and verifiable transactions, with no reliance on intermediaries. This method provides a trusted way for creators to monetize their intangible assets while retaining control over how their assets are used. A handful of innovative projects have begun to work toward making this vision a reality. For example, Ocean Protocol offers an innovative decentralized method for individuals and companies to sell and share datasets and AI models. Ocean Protocol gives users data sovereignty, which means that major asset holders have complete ownership and custodianship of their assets, while others are authorized to use them under mutually agreed conditions. This raises challenges related to compromising data privacy and intellectual property rights, particularly in proprietary data-driven spaces.

The vision of DAI marketplaces is much more than just technical developments; it also encompasses ethical and social concerns. One of the key steps to preventing monopolies and providing various models for collaboration between nations and organizations is equalizing access to AI. Moreover, this will play an important role in providing strong guarantees with the help of immutable records on the blockchain regarding the tracking of usage, licensing, and intellectual property rights.

4.3.4 Exploiting AI for forecasting in cryptocurrency networks

AI-based predictive analytics has been a strategic asset for blockchain ecosystems, and incorporating it is growing in importance very rapidly. AI stakeholders can forecast future developments across various aspects of a blockchain network by examining past trends and current signals. This is more than just unique data gathering; it reveals trending analytics that you would otherwise miss.

Predictive models have shown considerable potential in the cryptocurrency trading sector. Through the use of ML algorithms trained on large datasets such as historical price charts, social media sentiment, and wider economic indicators, the short- and long-term behavior of the asset can be predicted. Artificial neural networks, support vector machines, and autoregressive integrated moving average models, among others, are frequently employed to capture nonlinearity and predict stock market volatility. AI solutions have the potential to analyze multiple complex inputs and assist investors and traders with timely, data-driven decisions.

Nonetheless, the possibilities for AI in blockchain technology extend beyond simply forecasting financial predictions. Another significant application involves forecasting the behavior of the overall network. Public blockchain systems, especially those that are open to the public, experience varying transaction volumes from time to time, which ultimately results in congestion and increased transaction costs. AI can be used to monitor transaction frequency, variance in block size, and changes in gas prices to provide an indication of when the network will be experiencing the greatest volume of transactions. Oftentimes, by being able to predict future transaction demand, the developers or providers of that technology can prepare for peak usage, implement scalable solutions, and reduce latency. This can be particularly advantageous in an environment with layer-2 scaling solutions processing multiple transactions or a blockchain platform routed across chains, relying on effective routing in order to achieve optimized performance.

Predictive analytics can also provide insights into miner behavior, including how miners propagate blocks or when their hash rates change. Understanding these parameters can aid researchers in anticipating potential threats when hash rates might be concentrated and also when potential weaknesses might exist in the consensus protocol. These insights are essential in maintaining the principles of security and decentralization upon which blockchain technologies must be founded.

4.3.5 Decentralized blockchain networks: Toward self-regulating digital ecosystems

The emergence of fully autonomous blockchain systems is one of the most fascinating developments, representing a convergence of AI and blockchain. These types of systems function, adapt, and evolve with very little human intervention and are designed to be self-governing, self-optimizing, and self-maintaining systems enabled by highly sophisticated algorithms, thus shifting from static protocols to active systems of dynamic yet self-sustainable digital infrastructure.

In standard blockchain networks, the basic principle of governance operates as a strict consensus mechanism based on a group's agreement to either deploy protocols or sign off on code changes or updates through proof-of-work (PoW), PoS, or community voting systems. While these models often lead to decentralization, they are inherently limited in their agility to modify, may be subject to system manipulation, or are not necessarily effective at responding to rapid shifts in technology. The incorporation of AI in the context of governance models can maintain the rules of a consensus mechanism but may shift to a process of creating more fluid and contextual decision-making frameworks. To illustrate, intelligent agents may model the effects of a proposed protocol upgrade and its downstream effects on network security, economic incentives, and user acceptance. In turn, intelligent agents may offer suggested priority actions based on objective performance metrics and stakeholder objectives.

Beyond governance, AI can enhance a network's ability to maintain its own availability. Industrial applications have long been making use of predictive maintenance algorithms, and the same is now being done with digital networks. These services can look for patterns in transaction-processing, nodes' responsiveness, or anomalies to predict failures before they occur. For example, an AI could detect subtle signs of a distributed denial-of-service (DDoS) attack or a memory leak in a node client, and take defensive or remedial action without the need for human involvement.

Among the most engaging futures is the notion of self-healing blockchains, which can open the possibility for entirely new modes of functioning for blockchain technology. In these systems, AI could continuously assess conditions, such as monitoring the state inside the blockchain and the environment outside it. If a problem is detected—whether it be a vulnerability, a congestion issue, or a performance drop—such a blockchain could autonomously act to change parameters, redistribute work, or begin to self-patch. All of this demonstrates an entirely new level of independence, flexibility, and adaptability not previously observed in distributed systems.

The larger vision is very consistent with the concept of a digital organism—a self-governing system that can adapt and evolve based on feedback loops and cues from its environment. Like other living ecosystems, these decentralized networks would learn from their previous behaviors, modify their actions over the course of their existence, and even adjust aspects of their governing structures based on emerging behaviors. These systems disrupt our thinking about how networks are governed today and open up completely new design and governance possibilities in a decentralized infrastructure.

4.4 Challenges of integrating AI and blockchain

4.4.1 Computational power and scalability

The integration of AI and Blockchain technology promises transformative improvements across industries. However, one of the primary hurdles in merging these domains lies in their conflicting computational necessities. AI, particularly in its present-day form using deep learning strategies, demands massive computational resources, while blockchain networks, specifically those using traditional consensus mechanisms like PoW, are inherently resource-restricted and operate under strict scalability boundaries.

4.4.1.1 AI's high computational demands

Modern AI systems are predominantly powered by deep learning, a complex subset of machine learning. The exponential rise of AI in the past decade is largely attributed to two factors: the availability of vast datasets and the advent of high-performance computing hardware, including Graphics Processing Units (GPUs) and Tensor Processing Units. These advancements have enabled AI models to perform complex tasks such as image recognition, natural language understanding, and predictive analytics with remarkable accuracy.

Training deep learning models is computationally intensive for numerous reasons:

Large datasets: Deep mastering models thrive on facts. To attain high accuracy and generalizability, they should be trained on massive datasets that frequently include millions of labeled examples. This scale of records processing needs not only sizable memory but also high processing speed.

Complex model structures: Neural networks, particularly those with more than one layer (deep neural networks), contain tens of millions—even billions—of parameters. These include weights and biases that need to be updated iteratively through optimization algorithms like stochastic gradient descent. The deeper and more intricate the model, the higher the number of operations per training step.

Iterative learning and optimization: Training involves more than one forward and backward pass through the network. During each new iteration (or epoch), the model computes predictions, compares them toward actual outcomes, calculates loss, and updates its internal parameters to reduce errors. This repetitive process continues until the model achieves acceptable performance levels. For large datasets and complex networks, this training can take several hours to weeks, even on high-end GPUs.

Preventing overfitting and improving generalization: To ensure that AI models do not simply memorize the training data but instead learn patterns that generalize to new inputs, extensive data and computation are critical. Regularization techniques, cross-validation, and dropout mechanisms further increase computational overhead.

Parallel and distributed processing: To speed up processing, many AI systems leverage parallel computing, where tasks are distributed across multiple GPUs or even distinct nodes in a computing cluster. While this improves efficiency, it also demands specialized hardware infrastructure and increased energy consumption.

Real-time inference: Deploying trained models in real-time systems—including autonomous vehicles, smart surveillance, or fraud detection—also requires fast, low-latency processing. Achieving real-time predictions without compromising accuracy frequently entails complex trade-offs between model size and inference speed.

4.4.1.2 Blockchain's resource constraints

On the other hand, blockchain networks are designed to be decentralized, stable, and tamper-resistant; however, these qualities come at a price. The underlying consensus mechanisms and the need for data replication across all participating nodes introduce significant constraints in terms of storage, processing power, and scalability.

PoW and high energy consumption: Traditional blockchain systems like Bitcoin depend on PoW, a consensus algorithm that requires individuals (miners) to solve cryptographic puzzles. This process, while ensuring security and immutability, is extremely resource-intensive. It consumes sizable amounts of energy and demands high-performance hardware, making it impractical for integration with AI systems that already require substantial computational resources.

Alternative consensus mechanisms: Newer consensus methods, including PoS, Delegated PoS, and Practical Byzantine Fault Tolerance, provide more efficient alternatives. However, even these mechanisms require nodes to perform validation, preserve partial or complete copies of the ledger, and remain constantly on line—all of which introduce resource demands incompatible with lightweight or embedded AI programs.

Storage and bandwidth bottlenecks

Full nodes: Full blockchain nodes store the entire transaction records of the blockchain. As the ledger grows over the years, so does the demand for nonvolatile storage space. This is particularly challenging when deploying blockchain-AI hybrids in resource-constrained environments, including mobile devices or edge networks.

Light nodes: While mild or "thin" clients mitigate a number of these problems by storing only the most crucial transaction statistics, they nonetheless require constant internet connectivity and computational resources to verify blocks and maintain participation in the network.

Bandwidth requirements: Blockchain structures, especially those with excessive transaction throughput or smart contract capability (e.g., Ethereum), generate vast network traffic. Synchronizing nodes and validating transactions in near real-time necessitate high bandwidth, further complicating AI integration in environments with restricted connectivity.

Scalability conflicts between AI and blockchain

Both AI and blockchain technology face their own scalability challenges, and integrating them tends to exacerbate the problem. While AI scalability is essentially related to data size, model complexity, and inference latency, blockchain scalability pertains to transaction throughput, block size, and consensus latency.

Throughput limitations: Most blockchain networks can process only a limited number of transactions per second (e.g., Bitcoin's ~ 7 TPS, Ethereum's ~ 30 TPS). In contrast, AI programs like autonomous vehicles or financial fraud detection require real-time processing and high-frequency data exchange, far exceeding blockchain's native capabilities.

Latency and real-time constraints: Blockchain's consensus mechanisms, even optimized ones, introduce delays. Finality (the time it takes for a transaction to be considered permanent) is not immediate. When paired with AI systems that rely on low-latency inputs for decision-making, this becomes a critical bottleneck.

Energy efficiency: Deploying AI models on blockchain nodes is also intricate from an energy viewpoint. Running inference models or constantly updating them in a decentralized environment can significantly increase energy consumption, especially if combined with power-intensive consensus protocols.

4.4.2 Transparency versus immutability—The challenge of updating opaque AI models on immutable blockchains

The integration of AI with blockchain technology brings together powerful yet fundamentally distinct paradigms—intelligent automation and decentralized trust. However, one of the most pressing challenges in this fusion lies in addressing the tension between transparency and immutability, particularly when attempting to update or refine AI models that are inherently opaque in nature and deployed on blockchain networks that resist change.

4.4.2.1 AI model opacity and its consequences

Most modern-day AI structures, especially the ones primarily based on deep learning, function as "black boxes." These models are capable of identifying complex patterns and making highly accurate predictions; however, they do so through a vast network of interconnected layers and parameters that are not easily interpretable. In many cases, even the developers of such models can't fully explain why a model arrived at a particular decision. This opacity poses a problem when transparency and accountability are required, particularly in sectors like healthcare, finance, or criminal systems, where explainability is essential for trust and compliance.

4.4.2.2 Blockchain's inherent immutability

In comparison, blockchain is designed around the principle of immutability. Once a piece of data is recorded on the blockchain, it becomes a permanent part of the ledger. This feature guarantees trust, data integrity, and resistance to tampering. It is one of the key reasons blockchain is seen as a reliable medium for recording transactions, verifying identities, and ensuring auditability.

However, this very strength becomes a problem when AI models are involved. Unlike conventional software that can be patched or updated regularly, deploying an AI model on a blockchain means that any iteration of the model becomes "frozen" once recorded. If problems are later discovered—such as biased outputs, flawed logic, or performance degradation—the process of updating or correcting the model becomes extraordinarily complex, especially in public, decentralized networks where consensus is required to make even minor modifications.

4.4.2.3 The tension between change and permanence

This creates a fundamental tension: AI systems want to adapt, enhance, and adjust to new facts, while blockchain resists change to preserve trust and protection. In environments where

AI is used to automate decision-making and blockchain is used to ensure data integrity, this contradiction can cause significant challenges:

Lack of flexibility: Any attempt to update a model requires either bypassing the blockchain or developing complex workarounds, such as off-chain computation or sidechains.

Risk of obsolescence: AI models that cannot be updated in real-time or near real-time may become outdated, ineffective, or even dangerous over time.

Auditability versus explainability: Blockchain can show that a version has not been tampered with, but if the version itself isn't interpretable, auditability does little to enhance knowledge or trust.

Regulatory conflicts: In sectors governed by strict compliance standards, the inability to modify or explain AI behavior can lead to legal and ethical complications, especially when decisions impact human lives or financial outcomes.

4.4.3 Data privacy and security concerns—Safeguarding user privacy in DAI systems

As AI and blockchain technology continue to converge, one of the most urgent issues that emerges is how to maintain user data privacy in decentralized environments. While both AI and blockchain provide transformative capabilities, their combination also raises unique and complex challenges—especially with regard to gathering, processing, and sharing personal data across distributed networks.

4.4.3.1 The nature of AI and its dependence on data

AI structures thrive on statistics. From healthcare diagnostics to personalized guidelines, modern-day AI models require enormous amounts of information to learn, adapt, and enhance. This regularly involves processing sensitive user information, including clinical records, monetary transactions, browsing history, or biometric identifiers. The effectiveness of AI algorithms largely relies upon the depth and type of this data.

However, centralizing such facts—even for the sake of training a sensible model—introduces significant privacy dangers. Central statistics repositories become attractive targets for cyberattacks, data breaches, and unauthorized surveillance. The issue intensifies when individual consent and information transparency are overlooked or poorly managed.

4.4.3.2 Blockchain's decentralization: A double-edged sword

Blockchain, through its design, distributes data throughout a peer-to-peer network to eliminate the need for centralized control. This decentralized approach enhances transparency, trust, and resilience. Yet, when applied to AI systems, it creates a paradox: How can we maintain privacy when data is inherently distributed and immutable?

In DAI frameworks, wherein device learning models can be trained across multiple nodes (often owned by distinct entities), ensuring that individual data remains private becomes increasingly challenging. Since data cannot easily be modified or deleted once recorded on a blockchain, any inadvertent exposure of sensitive information can lead to long-term privacy violations.

4.4.3.3 Key challenges in maintaining privacy

Data exposure in training

In traditional AI schooling pipelines, data is amassed and saved centrally. In DAI, training may occur regionally across numerous nodes. While this protects against centralized breaches, it additionally raises the question of how to coordinate learning without exposing individual data points.

Lack of data control

Users can also lose visibility into where their statistics are stored, who has access to it, and how it is used or reused. The very openness of decentralized structures can become a hazard if data access rules are not strictly enforced.

Immutable records

The immutability of blockchain data poses a challenge when customers wish to exercise their "right to be forgotten," as outlined in data protection policies like the General Data Protection Regulation (GDPR). Once personal data is written to a blockchain, removing or modifying it is almost impossible.

Re-identity risks

Even anonymized records can, every now and then, be re-identified when combined with other datasets. In a decentralized setting, where datasets are more accessible, the risk of inadvertently disclosing a person's identity increases.

4.5 Solutions to key challenges within the integration of AI and blockchain

4.5.1 Computational power and scalability

The fusion of AI with blockchain introduces a sizable computational burden. Blockchain networks, by design, require consensus mechanisms that can be highly resource-intensive, while AI models—specifically deep learning architectures—demand considerable processing power and memory for training and inference. This dual requirement creates a scalability bottleneck, limiting the widespread deployment of DAI structures.

4.5.1.1 Proposed solutions

Off-chain computation with on-chain validation

One promising answer is to offload the heavy computation tasks (like version evaluation and inference) to off-chain environments, consisting of edge gadgets or cloud infrastructure, while recording the results or version hashes on the blockchain. This hybrid model ensures computational performance without compromising auditability.

Layer-2 scaling solutions

Layer-2 technologies such as rollups or sidechains can manage AI-associated transactions or model interactions off the primary blockchain, drastically reducing network congestion and latency. These mechanisms provide high throughput and decrease costs while preserving linkage to the security of the underlying chain.

Distributed AI model execution

Utilizing decentralized computing networks like Golem or Akash, which permit customers to lease idle computing resources, can offer scalable environments for AI execution. These structures democratize access to computation and decrease reliance on centralized infrastructure.

4.5.2 Potential paths forward: Ensuring updatability without compromising integrity

As AI models evolve swiftly, keeping them relevant and accurate often requires continuous fine-tuning or retraining. However, blockchain's immutability presents a challenge—once information is recorded, it cannot be modified. Updating opaque AI models in such environments can conflict with the core principles of decentralized ledgers.

4.5.2.1 Proposed solutions

Model versioning and governance mechanisms

Instead of storing whole AI models on-chain, only cryptographic hashes or metadata summaries can be logged. The actual models are stored off-chain (e.g., IPFS, cloud). This method permits new versions to be linked immutably while preserving a transparent audit trail of modifications and version updates.

Federated learning with blockchain coordination

Models may be trained collaboratively across decentralized nodes, wherein records never leave their origin. The blockchain acts as a ledger for recording version updates, player contributions, and trust metrics. This strategy ensures that models evolve continuously while respecting immutability.

Explainable AI for trust and interpretability

By incorporating XAI strategies, developers could make AI models more transparent without having to replace them regularly. Interpretable models foster trust among stakeholders, reducing the need for model revisions solely for clarity.

Smart contract wrappers for controlled mutability

Embedding AI models into clever contracts through modular "wrappers" permits regulations-based control over when and how models can be updated. These contracts can check for proper authorization, confirm digital signatures, or even use community consensus to trigger model revisions in a verifiable and automated way.

4.5.3 Data privacy and security concerns: Protecting personal data in DAI

When AI structures depend on sensitive statistics and blockchain thrives on transparency, ensuring consumer privacy becomes a delicate balancing act. Storing or processing personal information in decentralized networks can cause accidental exposure or long-term privacy violations, especially when data is immutable.

4.5.3.1 Proposed solutions

Federated learning for data locality

Training models regionally on personal devices without shifting data to significant servers ensures privacy. Only the updates or version parameters are shared, not the raw data. Blockchain can track the origin of updates, verify authenticity, and preserve transparency.

Homomorphic encryption for confidential computation

This method allows computations to be carried out directly on encrypted records. AI systems can learn or generate inferences without accessing the underlying data, making it suitable for privacy-critical applications like finance or healthcare.

Zero-knowledge proofs for data validation

Zero-knowledge proofs (ZKPs) enable entities to show compliance or data possession without exposing the real data. In DAI, ZKPs may be used to validate information inputs, enforce access control, and verify computation outcomes, all while keeping data hidden.

Private or permissioned blockchain architectures

Unlike public blockchains, permissioned systems restrict participation and visibility. These managed environments are ideal for use in instances requiring confidentiality and compliance with data safety guidelines like GDPR: General Data Protection Regulation.

4.5.3.2 Differential privacy for individual anonymity

Adding statistical noise to datasets or outputs allows models to derive insights without compromising the privacy of individuals. This approach is particularly effective when constructing composite AI models from decentralized data sources.

4.6 Emerging trends and innovations

As AI and blockchain technology continue to evolve, their convergence is unlocking completely new paradigms of computation, governance, privacy, and interactivity. From eliminating centralized bottlenecks to constructing intelligent agents in digital environments, the fusion of these domains is fueling a wave of innovation with significant implications for how data is used, managed, and monetized in decentralized systems. This phase delves into some of the most promising and rapidly growing trends reshaping the AI-blockchain landscape.

4.6.1 DAI

The idea behind DAI is to shift management away from centralized entities that historically own and operate AI infrastructure. Instead of relying on large businesses or cloud providers to train, host, and execute models, DAI leverages distributed computing resources and blockchain-based coordination to democratize AI deployment.

This version enhances transparency and accessibility by allowing any member of the community to contribute computing power, data, or model improvements. Ownership and contributions can be tracked through blockchain ledgers, enabling fair compensation and accountability. DAI not only reduces single points of failure but also creates an open marketplace for intelligent services, making AI more inclusive and community-driven.

Examples of DAI encompass decentralized compute networks and AI marketplaces, in which algorithms are traded, collaboratively trained, or rented on demand without intermediaries.

4.6.2 Federated learning on blockchain

Federated learning is a groundbreaking approach that permits multiple contributors to train a shared AI model without exchanging raw data. When integrated with blockchain, this model becomes even more stable and reliable. Each participant trains the model locally on their device and shares only the model updates (such as gradients or weights), which are then aggregated into a global model.

Blockchain plays an essential role in recording these updates immutably, verifying player contributions, and managing trust through consensus mechanisms. This integration is particularly useful in scenarios where privacy is paramount—such as healthcare, finance, and

IoT systems—as it ensures that personal records remain localized while still contributing to the broader learning process.

In this version, AI becomes not only collaborative but also privacy-preserving and verifiably fair, paving the way for responsible innovation across decentralized networks.

4.6.3 Web3 and AI-powered dapps

Web3 marks the transition from static, centralized internet programs to dynamic, decentralized platforms that provide users control over their identity, data, and digital assets. When powered by AI, dApps within the Web3 environment gain the potential to offer smarter, more personalized services with out compromising user autonomy.

For instance, AI algorithms embedded inside dApps can tailor content material, propose movements, or automate obligations primarily based on user behavior—all while maintaining data ownership in the hands of the consumer. With blockchain serving as the underlying trust and coordination layer, these intelligent dApps eliminate the need for intermediaries and enable peer-to-peer services in domains like finance, education, gaming, and social media.

This fusion of AI and Web3 is driving a new class of programs where intelligence is embedded at the edge, controlled by users, and governed through transparent protocols rather than centralized algorithms.

4.6.4 AI in the metaverse

The metaverse—a persistent, shared, and immersive virtual environment—is poised to be a chief beneficiary of AI-blockchain synergy. Within these environments, AI can play numerous roles: from powering nonparticipant characters with human-like behavior, to producing dynamic content on the fly, to personalizing experiences for every individual.

When combined with decentralized architectures, these smart dealers are not managed by any single entity. Instead, their movements, choices, and evolution may be governed by the network, recorded on-chain, or even influenced by virtual asset ownership.

Generative AI models can be used to design digital real estate, outfits, and even complete landscapes. Meanwhile, AI-driven recommendation systems can guide users through vast metaverse areas based on their interactions and preferences. Blockchain ensures that all contributions, interactions, and virtual possessions within the metaverse are verifiable, secure, and user-owned.

4.6.5 Quantum computing and blockchain

Quantum computing is rapidly approaching a point where it could undermine many of the cryptographic foundations on which current blockchain systems rely. At the same time,

AI models may benefit from quantum acceleration for certain optimization and pattern recognition tasks.

To future-proof DAI ecosystems, researchers are now exploring quantum-resistant cryptographic algorithms that can withstand the power of quantum machines. These include lattice-based, hash-based, and multivariate polynomial cryptosystems designed to secure blockchain transactions and model ownership against quantum attacks.

In addition, quantum-enhanced AI could someday revolutionize decentralized intelligence, making it faster and more capable. Integrating quantum-safe protocols into the design of AI-blockchain platforms ensures long-term security, enabling these technologies to evolve safely together.

4.6.6 AI in decentralized autonomous organizations and governance

Decentralized Autonomous Organizations (DAOs) constitute a unique form of governance where decisions are made by smart contracts and network consensus, as opposed to centralized leadership. Incorporating AI into DAOs introduces new capabilities such as automated policy analysis, risk evaluation, and dispute resolution.

For example, AI models can analyze voting patterns, simulate consequences, or detect potential governance assaults in real time. They can also help optimize aid allocation or suggest improvements to smart contract logic based on evolving consumer behavior.

By combining the strategic foresight of AI with the democratic principles of DAOs, governance becomes more adaptive, information-driven, and resilient. This hybrid approach holds immense potential for managing complex systems without centralized control.

4.6.7 ZKPs and AI

ZKPs, in particular Zero-Knowledge Succinct Non-Interactive Arguments of Knowledge (zk-SNARKs), are emerging as effective tools for preserving privacy in decentralized systems. In the context of AI, ZKPs allow for the verification of machine learning computations without revealing the underlying data or model parameters.

This method allows an AI version to make predictions, validate compliance, or demonstrate that it has adhered to a particular rule set—without exposing any sensitive records. This is especially applicable in domains such as healthcare, law, and identity management, where confidentiality is crucial.

With ZKPs, AI can function in notably regulated or trust-sensitive environments, preserving both practical transparency and data secrecy. As zk-tech matures, we can expect to see its significant adoption in exclusive AI inference structures that operate seamlessly within blockchain ecosystems.

Further reading

Buterin, V., 2014. Ethereum White Paper: a next-generation smart contract and decentralized application platform. White Paper.

Crosby, M., Pattanayak, P., Verma, S., Kalyanaraman, V., 2016. Blockchain technology: beyond bitcoin. Appl. Innov. Rev. 2, 6–10.

Goodfellow, I., Bengio, Y., Courville, A., 2016. Deep Learning, MIT Press.

Kshetri, N., 2018. Blockchain's roles in strengthening cybersecurity and protecting privacy. Telecommun. Policy. 42 (4), 313–327.

Nakamoto, S., 2008. Bitcoin: a peer-to-peer electronic cash system. [Online]. Available: https://bitcoin.org/bitcoin.pdf.

Nguyen, G., Kim, K., 2018. A survey about consensus algorithms used in blockchain. J. Inf. Process. Syst. 14 (1), 101–128.

Russell, S., Norvig, P., 2021. Artificial Intelligence: A Modern Approach, fourth ed. Pearson Education.

Tapscott, D., Tapscott, A., 2016. Blockchain Revolution: How the Technology behind Bitcoin and Other Cryptocurrencies Is Changing the World, Penguin.

Yang, Q., Liu, Y., Chen, T., Tong, Y., 2019. Federated machine learning: concept and applications. ACM Trans. Intell. Syst. Technol. 10 (2), 1–19.

Zyskind, G., Nathan, O., Pentland, A., 2015. Decentralizing privacy: using blockchain to protect personal data. In: 2015 IEEE Security and Privacy Workshops.

PART 2

Integration of artificial intelligence/machine learning and blockchain in digital

CHAPTER 5

Synergizing artificial intelligence/machine learning and digital twin computing

Amit Kumar Tyagi[a], **Shabnam Kumari**[b], **and Richa**[c]

[a]*School of Law Forensic Justice & Policy Studies, National Forensic Sciences University, India, Gandhinagar, Gujarat, India*

[b]*Department of Computer Science, Faculty of Science and Humanities, SRM Institute of Science and Technology, Kattankulathur, Chennai, Tamil Nadu, India*

[c]*Department of Computer Science and Engineering, Birla Institute of Technology, Mesra, Ranchi, India*

5.1 Introduction

Digital Twin Computing (DTC) is a powerful tool for constructing dynamic, data-driven virtual representations of physical assets, systems, and processes as Industry 4.0 advances. Real-time Internet of Things (IoT) data updates these digital replicas, allowing organizations to simulate, monitor, and optimize operations remotely. Traditional digital twins (DTs) cannot adjust to changing situations or learn from experience due to their predefined models and deterministic behavior. Integrating artificial intelligence (AI) and machine learning (ML) enables DTs to become intelligent systems capable of predictive analytics, real-time optimization, and autonomous decision-making. The growing need for self-adaptive, resilient, and context-aware systems in manufacturing, energy, transportation, and healthcare drives this synergy. AI/ML technologies enable DTs to detect abnormalities, learn from historical and real-time data, optimize complex processes, and adapt to changing inputs and environments (Grieves and Vickers, 2017; Tao et al., 2019). This fusion enhances system efficiency, reduces operational risk, and supports proactive maintenance and decision-making. AI/ML and DTC are crucial for next-generation intelligent cyber-physical systems as companies automate and respond in real time. It can be summarized as follows:

- **Emergence of DT technology**: DTs are virtual replicas of physical systems that mirror real-time data from IoT devices to simulate performance and operations.
- **Limitations of traditional DTs**: Conventional DTs rely on static models and rules, making them less responsive to dynamic and uncertain environments.
- **Need for intelligence and adaptability**: To address complex, real-time decision-making scenarios, DTs require learning capabilities that go beyond preprogrammed behavior

Artificial Intelligence, Machine Learning and Blockchain in Digital Twin Computing.
https://doi.org/10.1016/B978-0-443-43914-8.00002-9

- **Role of AI/ML in enhancing capabilities**: AI/ML enables DTs to analyze data patterns, predict failures, detect anomalies, and optimize processes autonomously.
- **Industry demand for smart, self-optimizing systems**: Sectors such as manufacturing, energy, healthcare, and urban infrastructure are increasingly adopting AI-enabled DTs for predictive maintenance, energy optimization, and process automation.
- **Toward intelligent cyber-physical systems**: The synergy between AI/ML and DTs is key to building resilient, self-learning, and efficient systems that align with the vision of Industry 4.0 and smart ecosystems.

5.2 Foundations and concepts

5.2.1 Digital twin: Definition and evolution

DTC is a powerful tool for constructing dynamic, data-driven virtual representations of physical assets, systems, and processes as Industry 4.0 advances. Real-time IoT data updates these digital replicas, allowing organizations to simulate, monitor, and optimize operations remotely. Traditional DTs cannot adapt to changing situations or learn from experience due to their predefined models and deterministic behavior. Integrating AI and ML enables DTs to become intelligent systems capable of predictive analytics, real-time optimization, and autonomous decision-making. The growing need for self-adaptive, resilient, and context-aware systems in manufacturing, energy, transportation, and healthcare drives this synergy. AI/ML technologies enable DTs to detect abnormalities, learn from historical and real-time data, optimize complex processes, and adapt to changing inputs and environments. This fusion enhances system efficiency, reduces operational risk, and supports proactive maintenance and decision-making. AI/ML and DTC are crucial for next-generation intelligent cyber-physical systems as companies automate and respond in real time (Boschert and Rosen, 2016).

5.2.2 Core concepts of artificial intelligence and machine learning

AI is a broad discipline of computer science dedicated to the development of systems that can replicate human intelligence in order to perform tasks such as language comprehension, problem-solving, learning, and reasoning. Knowledge representation, natural language processing (NLP), robotics, computer vision, and decision-making comprise the fundamental domains of AI. These systems are designed to operate intelligently in intricate environments, rendering them applicable in a diverse array of disciplines, including industrial automation, smart assistants, and healthcare diagnostics. ML is a subset of AI that focuses on the ability of computers to learn from data and make predictions or decisions without being explicitly programmed. The three primary types of ML are as follows: supervised learning, which involves the model learning from labeled data; unsupervised learning, which identifies hidden patterns in unlabeled data; and reinforcement learning, in which an agent learns optimal behavior by interacting with an environment and receiving feedback in the form of rewards or penalties. These learning paradigms are implemented in practical applications, including robotics, fraud detection, and consumer segmentation. Other critical concepts in ML include loss functions, training and testing, and evaluation metrics such as F1 score and accuracy, which are essential for evaluating model performance. Deep learning, a more sophisticated form of ML that employs neural networks with numerous layers, has facilitated advancements in fields such as NLP, image classification, and speech recognition. Model deployment, data preprocessing, feature engineering, and model development are essential stages that must be completed in conjunction with model development to guarantee reliable and precise results. AI and ML technologies are becoming more integrated into everyday systems, which is why ethics, fairness, and explainability are becoming increasingly vital. Building trust and reliability in intelligent systems is facilitated by ensuring that models are transparent, accountable, and unbiased. The future of automation, analytics, and intelligent decision-making in various sectors is still being influenced by the convergence of AI and ML (Wu et al., 2021).

5.2.3 DT computing: An emerging paradigm

By incorporating computational intelligence, coordination, and collaboration among numerous DTs, DTC builds upon the basic idea of DTs, which are dynamic digital representations of real-world objects or systems. By integrating and computing interactions between numerous DTs, DTC aspires to model entire ecosystems, predict complex system behaviors, and support real-time decision-making across interconnected domains. This is in contrast to traditional DTs, which mainly concentrate on real-time monitoring, simulation, and performance optimization of individual physical entities. DTs in DTC not only reflect their physical analogues but also take part in a collaborative computer environment. Complex features like autonomous coordination, group problem-solving, multi-agent interaction, and cross-domain simulation are made possible by this. To illustrate the point, conventional DTs operating independently cannot accomplish the kind of coordinated optimization of energy consumption, traffic flow, and emergency response that can be achieved when public infrastructure, transportation networks, and power grids are considered as part of a smart city. With the use of cloud/edge computing, AI, ML, the IoT, and other advancements, DTC may adapt to changing circumstances, learn from data, and evolve over time (Lee et al., 2015). It heralds the arrival of digital ecosystems that are proactive, smart, and federated rather than reactive and isolated.Personalized healthcare, intelligent manufacturing, disaster resilience, and national infrastructure planning are all use cases that can be supported by this paradigm. While DTC is a promising new area of study, it also poses various challenges related to data interoperability, cybersecurity, model standardization, scalability, and ethical governance. There needs to be continuous effort made into creating uniform frameworks, robust computing architectures, and regulatory standards to guarantee accountability, fairness, and transparency across massive DT networks if it is to reach its full potential. With this advancement, DTC is well-positioned to play a pivotal role in the intelligent cyber-physical systems of the future.

5.2.4 Synergistic potential: AI/ML in DTC

The incorporation of AI and ML into DTC creates a potent synergy that evolves DTs from reactive, data-driven models into intelligent, adaptable, and autonomous systems. AI and ML augment DTs by enabling them to learn from historical and real-time data, identify trends, discover abnormalities, and formulate predictive or prescriptive choices. This integration enables DTs to perpetually advance, enhancing their functionality over time without requiring manual oversight.

AI/ML algorithms empower DTs to transcend simulation by facilitating autonomous control, scenario analysis, and real-time decision-making in intricate contexts. In smart manufacturing, an AI-driven DT can adapt production parameters in real-time using sensor data to enhance productivity and reduce downtime. In healthcare, ML can facilitate the creation of a patient-specific DT to forecast health risks and recommend tailored interventions. In a DTC ecosystem, the interaction of several intelligent twins fosters collaborative intelligence, facilitated by federated learning (FL) or distributed AI, which aids in the administration of extensive, interconnected systems like smart cities, energy grids, and transportation networks. The integration of AI/ML with DTC not only improves the performance of individual systems but also facilitates large-scale system-of-systems intelligence (Madni et al., 2019).

5.3 AI/ML integration with DTC

The amalgamation of AI and ML with DTC facilitates the development of intelligent, self-adaptive systems that go beyond mere monitoring and simulation. Traditional DTs reproduce the physical attributes and behaviors of assets using real-time sensor data, whereas the integration of AI/ML enables these twins to analyze trends, identify anomalies, and predict future states with enhanced precision. This leads to improved functionalities, including predictive maintenance, process optimization, real-time diagnostics, and autonomous control, which are essential for enhancing efficiency, minimizing downtime, and facilitating proactive decision-making. As DT ecosystems become increasingly intricate and interlinked, AI/ML is essential for facilitating collaborative intelligence among various digital entities. Through the utilization of deep learning, reinforcement learning, and FL models, DTs can adjust to changing situations, acquire knowledge from decentralized data sources, and synchronize actions with minimal human oversight. This synergy is particularly beneficial in domains such as smart manufacturing, healthcare, energy systems, and urban infrastructure, where intelligent coordination among many systems is crucial. The incorporation of AI/ML with DTC signifies a substantial advancement from static data representations to self-sufficient, adaptive digital ecosystems that facilitate scalable and robust cyber-physical systems.

5.3.1 AI-driven modeling and simulation

AI-driven modeling and simulation constitute a revolutionary method for comprehending and enhancing intricate systems by integrating data-driven intelligence with conventional simulation methodologies. In contrast to traditional models that depend on static mathematical formulas or rule-based reasoning, AI methodologies, especially ML and deep learning, can discern inherent patterns and system dynamics directly from data. This facilitates the development of adaptive, high-fidelity models capable of managing nonlinear dynamics, uncertain inputs, and changing situations with greater efficacy. These AI-augmented models are particularly advantageous when the physical processes are excessively intricate or inadequately comprehended to be represented solely by first-principle models. In the realm of DTC, AI-enhanced simulations facilitate predictive functionalities and instantaneous decision-making by perpetually refreshing digital models in accordance with incoming sensor inputs. In smart manufacturing, AI can model the impacts of modifying process parameters, anticipate equipment malfunctions, and suggest enhancements. In urban systems, AI models can replicate traffic flow, energy consumption, or disaster scenarios to inform preemptive measures. The outcome is a more responsive and intelligent simulation environment that not only replicates reality but also forecasts future conditions, facilitating expedited, data-driven, and autonomous decision-making across several sectors (Mohammadi et al., 2018).

5.3.2 Real-time decision making using ML

Real-time decision-making utilizing ML entails the application of predictive and prescriptive algorithms to evaluate streaming data and produce immediate, data-informed responses. In contrast to conventional decision-making systems that depend on established rules or user input, ML models derive insights from historical and real-time data to generate precise predictions or classifications in dynamic contexts. By persistently analyzing incoming data such as sensor readings, user behavior, or market conditions, ML systems can modify judgments according to context, patterns, and anomalies. This functionality is especially advantageous in time-critical applications such as autonomous vehicles, intelligent manufacturing, healthcare surveillance, and financial trading. In DTC, ML is essential for facilitating real-time responsiveness by improving the decision-making process across the physical and digital domains. The DT, utilizing real-time data from its physical equivalent, employs ML algorithms to simulate scenarios, assess results, and suggest or implement best actions, occasionally within milliseconds. For example, an intelligent energy grid can autonomously equilibrate supply and demand, while a linked manufacturing facility can adaptively modify machine operations to avert downtime. Integrating ML into direct-to-consumer systems enhances their autonomy, resilience, and ability to function in intricate, real-world settings with limited human oversight.

5.3.3 Predictive analytics and forecasting

Predictive analytics and forecasting utilize statistical methods, data mining, and ML algorithms to examine current and historical data to anticipate future events, behaviors, or trends. These strategies reveal patterns and linkages in data that can be utilized to predict probable events, allowing organizations to make proactive, data-informed decisions. Prevalent predictive techniques encompass regression analysis, time series modeling, decision trees, and neural networks. These instruments are extensively utilized in domains including finance (risk evaluation), retail (demand forecasting), healthcare (disease prognosis), and manufacturing (equipment failure prediction). In the realm of DTC, predictive analytics augments the intelligence of DTs by enabling them to foresee future conditions of their physical counterparts (Zhang et al., 2019). In predictive maintenance, DTs can anticipate the failure of a machine component by analyzing sensor data and usage patterns, facilitating prompt repairs and preventing expensive downtime. In energy systems, predicting energy demand enhances grid operations and resource distribution. Through the use of predictive analytics, DTs transcend mere real-time depiction, evolving into proactive systems that facilitate strategic planning, enhance operational efficiency, and enable real-time risk mitigation (Zhang et al., 2019).

5.4 System architecture and design

5.4.1 Reference architecture for AI-enhanced DTC

Predictive analytics and forecasting utilize statistical methods, data mining, and ML algorithms to examine current and historical data to anticipate future events, behaviors, or trends. These strategies reveal patterns and linkages in data that can be utilized to predict probable events, allowing organizations to make proactive, data-informed decisions. Prevalent predictive techniques encompass regression analysis, time series modeling, decision trees, and neural networks. These instruments are extensively utilized in domains including finance (risk evaluation), retail (demand forecasting), healthcare (disease prognosis), and manufacturing (equipment failure prediction). In the realm of DTC, predictive analytics augments the intelligence of DTs by enabling them to foresee future conditions of their physical counterparts. In predictive maintenance, DTs can anticipate the failure of a machine component by analyzing sensor data and usage patterns, facilitating

Fig. 5.1 Architecture of AI-enhanced DTC.

prompt repairs and preventing expensive downtime. In energy systems, predicting energy demand enhances grid operations and resource distribution. Through the use of predictive analytics, DTs transcend mere real-time depiction, evolving into proactive systems that facilitate strategic planning, enhance operational efficiency, and enable real-time risk mitigation (Fig. 5.1).

5.4.2 Data acquisition and fusion

Data acquisition is the fundamental phase of DTC, wherein real-time data is gathered from diverse physical sources using IoT sensors, actuators, and embedded devices. These devices assess several characteristics, including temperature, pressure, vibration, humidity, location, and energy usage. The gathered data is conveyed via communication protocols such as MQTT (Message Queuing Telemetry Transport), OPC-UA (Open Platform Communications Unified Architecture), 5G, or Zigbee, contingent upon the application and connectivity specifications. Preprocessing methods, including noise filtration, normalization, and formatting, are employed to guarantee that the data is clean, consistent, and prepared for subsequent processing.

Data fusion is the act of integrating data from several heterogeneous sources, such as sensor readings, historical logs, external APIs (Application Programming Interface), and corporate systems, to provide a cohesive, contextual, and more precise dataset for decision-making. Fusion improves the comprehensiveness, dependability, and precision of the DT model. It can manifest at multiple tiers: low-level fusion (raw data), feature-level fusion (extracted features), and decision-level fusion (inferred outputs). Efficient data fusion allows the DT to accurately represent intricate system states, facilitates predictive analytics through AI/ML, and enhances real-time responses and coordination in multi-system contexts, such as smart factories, energy grids, and autonomous mobility.

5.4.3 Scalability, interoperability, and edge-AI integration

Scalability is an essential criterion in DTC, particularly as the quantity of connected devices, data sources, and modeled systems grows exponentially. An adaptable DTC architecture must effectively manage increasing volumes of real-time sensor data, simultaneous simulations, and AI-driven analytics without sacrificing speed. Cloud-native technologies, containerization (e.g., Docker, Kubernetes), and microservices design are essential facilitators of scalability, enabling dynamic resource allocation and management of computational loads across diverse contexts. Scalability guarantees that DTC can progress from overseeing a solitary machine to coordinating comprehensive industrial processes or city-wide infrastructures.

Interoperability denotes the seamless exchange and integration of data, models, and control methods among diverse systems and platforms. Within the DTC ecosystem, DTs frequently require interaction with historical industrial systems, contemporary IoT platforms, external APIs, and diverse corporate applications. Interoperability necessitates compliance with open standards and protocols, including OPC-UA, MQTT, REST (Representational State Transfer), and new frameworks such as DT Definition Language. Middleware solutions and standardized APIs enable communication among many components, fostering a federated and collaborative DT environment. In the absence of interoperability, data silos emerge, constraining the precision and usability of the system.

Edge-AI integration entails the implementation of AI and ML models at the edge, in proximity to data generation sources such as IoT devices, gateways, or local servers. This diminishes latency, conserves bandwidth, and facilitates real-time decision-making, essential for mission-critical applications like autonomous vehicles, robotics, and industrial automation. In DTC, edge-AI enables DTs to function autonomously and execute local optimizations when offline from the cloud. Edge computing improves privacy and data security by retaining sensitive information locally. The integration of edge intelligence with centralized cloud resources creates a hybrid architecture that is responsive and scalable, facilitating resilient and dispersed DT systems (Shi et al., 2016).

5.5 Applications and use cases

5.5.1 Smart manufacturing and industry 4.0

Smart Manufacturing employs sophisticated technologies, including IoT, AI, ML, robotics, cloud computing, and DTs, to establish highly flexible, efficient, and data-driven manufacturing environments. It allows manufacturers to automate decision-making, monitor equipment in real time, forecast maintenance requirements, and adjust flexibly to fluctuating client demands. Smart Manufacturing converts conventional production lines into intelligent ecosystems by integrating cyber-physical systems with real-time data, thereby optimizing resource utilization, minimizing waste, enhancing product quality, and improving operational agility. Industry 4.0, or the Fourth Industrial Revolution, denotes the extensive industrial transformation propelled by digitalization and intelligent automation. It amalgamates physical production with digital technology, facilitating comprehensive visibility, decentralized decision-making, and self-optimizing systems. Essential facilitators of Industry 4.0 comprise DTC, Edge-AI, blockchain for traceability, and interoperable platforms that integrate machines, systems, and individuals throughout the value chain. Smart production and Industry 4.0 signify a transformative move toward autonomous, interconnected, and sustainable production, which is essential for future-oriented industrial organizations (Lin et al., 2017).

5.5.2 Smart cities and infrastructure monitoring

Smart Cities utilize digital technologies such as IoT, AI, DTs, and data analytics to elevate urban living standards, improve governance, and promote sustainable resource management. In a smart city, real-time data is gathered from various sources, including traffic signals, surveillance systems, public transport, utility grids, weather stations, and mobile applications, to enhance urban operations such as transportation, energy consumption, waste management, and emergency response. DTC is essential for generating virtual duplicates of urban infrastructure (e.g., roads, bridges, water systems) to simulate, monitor, and forecast urban dynamics, facilitating proactive planning and enhancing the responsiveness of public services.

Infrastructure monitoring in smart cities emphasizes the safety, dependability, and efficiency of essential assets such as bridges, tunnels, pipelines, and buildings. Utilizing embedded IoT sensors and edge-AI, these systems can perpetually evaluate structural integrity, identify anomalies, and anticipate maintenance requirements prior to failures. This predictive methodology minimizes downtime, averts catastrophes, and prolongs asset longevity. When combined with DTs, infrastructure monitoring systems may replicate stress reactions, traffic loads, and environmental effects in real time, facilitating enhanced urban planning, disaster resilience, and effective lifetime management of public infrastructure.

5.5.3 Healthcare and personalized medicine

The integration of technologies such as AI, ML, IoT, and DTC is transforming healthcare and personalized medicine. A DT of a patient can be generated utilizing real-time physiological data (e.g., from wearable devices), medical history, genetic information, and clinical records. This digital depiction enables physicians to model therapy reactions, continuously evaluate health states, and forecast illness risks, resulting in more accurate and personalized care. AI and ML augment this process by detecting patterns in extensive health data to facilitate early diagnosis, prognosis, and the determination of appropriate treatment strategies. The objective of personalized medicine is to transition from a universal approach to targeted therapies customized to an individual's genetic composition, lifestyle, and environmental factors. DTs enable the simulation of pharmacological effects or therapies on a virtual model prior to real-world application, thereby minimizing trial-and-error approaches and enhancing outcomes. This integration holds significant potential for controlling chronic diseases, enhancing surgical planning, and facilitating real-time monitoring in postoperative care. Ultimately, personalized healthcare utilizing DT technology improves predictive, preventative, and participative medicine, signifying a significant transformation in the delivery and management of health services.

5.5.4 Energy and utilities

The Energy and Utilities sector is experiencing a digital transformation propelled by the integration of AI, IoT, and DTC, facilitating more intelligent, efficient, and resilient energy systems. DTs of power plants, transmission lines, substations, and grid components provide real-time monitoring, predictive maintenance, and simulation functionalities that assist operators in optimizing performance and minimizing downtime. By amalgamating sensor data with AI-driven analytics, utilities can identify defects, predict energy demand, equilibrate loads, and proactively oversee asset health, ensuring a dependable and economical energy supply.

Moreover, the integration of renewable energy, decentralized energy production, and dynamic grid management is becoming progressively intricate and reliant on data. AI-augmented DTs facilitate energy forecasting, battery storage optimization, and grid stability assessment amid variable conditions induced by solar and wind fluctuations. This signifies enhanced energy dispatch planning, expedited outage response, and superior customer service for utilities. Within the realms of smart grids, water systems, and waste management, DT technology facilitates comprehensive visibility and data-informed decision-making, hence fostering sustainable, secure, and intelligent utility infrastructures.

5.6 Challenges and limitations

Despite its transformational promise, AI-enhanced DTC encounters numerous technological and operational hurdles. A significant restriction is the necessity for high-quality, real-time data from physical systems, which can be challenging to guarantee due to sensor malfunctions, data noise, or insufficient datasets. Furthermore, the integration of varied data sources, spanning from older systems to contemporary IoT platforms, presents considerable challenges in interoperability and standardization. Developing precise and dependable DT models necessitates considerable computational resources, particularly when simulating intricate systems or executing AI/ML algorithms continually. Furthermore, scalability emerges as an issue when shifting from individual asset twins to city-scale or enterprise-wide DT ecosystems.

From a comprehensive viewpoint, security, privacy, and ethical considerations pose significant obstacles. DTs frequently depend on sensitive personal, operational, or infrastructural data, rendering them appealing targets for hackers. Ensuring data protection, secure access management, and adherence to rules such as GDPR is crucial. The opacity

Table 5.1 Challenges and limitations of AI-enhanced digital twin computing.

Technical Challenges	Data quality and availability	Inaccurate, noisy or missing sensor data can compromise the accuracy of digital twin simulations and AI predictions.
	Real-time data processing	High-frequency data streams require fast processing and low-latency infrastructure, which can be difficult to scale efficiently.
	Computational complexity	Running AI models and high-fidelity simulations in real-time requires significant processing power, especially in large systems.
	Integration with legacy systems	Many industrial systems still rely on outdated infrastructure, making integration with modern digital twins challenging.
	Scalability issues	Moving from single-asset digital twins to full-scale systems (e.g., factories, cities) demands robust, scalable architectures.
Security and Privacy Challenges	Cybersecurity risks	The interconnected nature of digital twins and IoT devices makes them vulnerable to cyberattacks and data breaches.
	Data privacy concerns	Handling personal or sensitive operational data requires strict compliance with privacy regulations (e.g., GDPR (General Data Protection Regulation), HIPAA (Health Insurance Portability and Accountability Act)).
	Access control and identity management	Ensuring secure access to digital twin data across distributed stakeholders is complex and requires robust authentication frameworks.
AI-Specific Limitations	Black box nature of AI models	Many AI/ML models lack explainability, making it difficult to justify or audit decisions in high-stakes applications.
	Data dependency of AI	ML algorithms require large, diverse, and labeled datasets, which are often unavailable or expensive to collect in real-world settings.
Economic and Organizational Barriers	High initial costs	Implementation of DTC involves costs related to sensors, data infrastructure, cloud/edge computing, and AI development.
	Lack of skilled workforce	Successful deployment requires cross-disciplinary expertise in AI, systems engineering, cybersecurity, and domain knowledge.
	Governance and policy gaps	Absence of clear frameworks for data ownership, twin-to-twin communication, and automated decision governance.

of AI models complicates the interpretation and auditing of decision-making, hence posing questions of trust and accountability. Additional restrictions encompass substantial initial deployment expenses, a deficiency of skilled personnel, and the absence of clearly delineated governance frameworks for overseeing twin-to-twin interactions and automated decision-making. Surmounting these obstacles necessitates technological advancements, intersectoral collaboration, and unequivocal policy endorsement (Radanliev et al., 2021) (Table 5.1).

5.7 Security and privacy issues

Security and privacy are crucial issues in AI-augmented DTC, as these systems depend significantly on real-time data from IoT devices, cloud infrastructures, and AI models. Safeguarding the security, integrity, and availability of data is crucial for ensuring the veracity of DT simulations and averting unauthorized access or manipulation. Employing stringent encryption, secure communication protocols, and identity management systems effectively protects data both in transit and at rest. Moreover, access control measures like role-based access and multifactor authentication inhibit unauthorized individuals from modifying or accessing critical information. DTC systems frequently manage personal, operational, or critical infrastructure data, necessitating rigorous compliance with standards such as GDPR and HIPAA. Data anonymization, minimization, and consent-driven collection are crucial for ensuring compliance. Furthermore, AI models employed in DTs are susceptible to adversarial attacks and privacy violations, hence requiring the implementation of secure training methodologies and explainable AI (XAI) frameworks. In intricate contexts where numerous DTs interact, secure intertwin communication, logging, and auditability are essential for maintaining system trust, accountability, and resilience against cyber threats (Lu et al., 2020) (Table 5.2).

5.7.1 AI bias and explainability in DTs

As AI becomes essential to DTC, apprehensions regarding AI bias intensify. Bias in ML models may arise from uneven, incomplete, or historically biased training data, resulting in inequitable or erroneous predictions. Integrating biased AI into DTs utilized for healthcare diagnoses, predictive maintenance, or infrastructure planning can lead to systemic errors or discriminatory results, particularly in high-stakes scenarios. A DT of a smart city traffic system may disproportionately enhance routing for some locations while disregarding underdeveloped regions, thus perpetuating inequality.

The necessity for explainability in AI-driven DTs is equally significant. As DTs become more integral to automated decision-making, stakeholders, including engineers and regulators, must comprehend the rationale behind specific predictions or actions. The absence of transparency in intricate AI models, commonly referred to as "black boxes," can impede confidence, restrict adoption, and complicate regulatory compliance. To tackle this issue, methodologies, including model interpretability, visualizations, and XAI frameworks, are being devised to elucidate model behavior. Guaranteeing justice, accountability, and transparency in AI-augmented DTs is essential for establishing ethical and reliable systems across several areas (Shokri et al., 2017).

5.7.2 Secure data sharing and federated learning

Secure data sharing is an essential prerequisite in DTC, particularly when several stakeholders, such as hospitals, manufacturers, energy utilities, or governments, must work without jeopardizing data ownership or privacy. Conventional centralized data-sharing

Table 5.2 Security and privacy issues with challenges and solutions.

Security and privacy considerations	Challenge	Solution
Data Confidentiality	Sensitive data (e.g., personal health info, critical infrastructure metrics) collected from IoT sensors must be protected from unauthorized access.	Implement encryption (both at rest and in transit) and use secure communication protocols (e.g., TLS, HTTPS).
Data Integrity	Tampered or falsified data can lead to inaccurate digital twin simulations and incorrect AI-based decisions.	Use blockchain, digital signatures, and hash-based validation to ensure data authenticity and traceability.
Access Control and Authentication	Unauthorized access to the digital twin environment could allow manipulation or theft of critical data.	Deploy role-based access control (RBAC), multi-factor authentication (MFA), and secure identity management systems.
Cybersecurity of Connected Devices	IoT sensors and edge devices are often vulnerable to malware, DoS attacks, and spoofing.	Use device-level firewalls, intrusion detection/prevention systems (IDS/IPS), and regular firmware updates.
AI Model Security	AI models used in DTC are vulnerable to adversarial attacks and model inversion techniques.	Apply secure model training techniques, adversarial robustness testing, and differential privacy in ML pipelines
User Privacy and Data Regulations	Personal data collected and processed must comply with privacy laws like GDPR, HIPAA, etc.	Implement data minimization, anonymization/pseudonymization, and consent-based data collection practices.
Secure Twin-to-Twin Communication	In multi-twin environments, interactions between digital twins must be secure to prevent cross-system breaches.	Use end-to-end encryption, secure APIs, and trust-based protocols for inter-twin communication.
Auditability and Logging	Lack of transparency in AI decisions and system behavior can hinder incident response and accountability.	Maintain secure logs of data access, system changes, and AI decision trails for audit and compliance purposes.

approaches present risks associated with data breaches, unauthorized access, and regulatory noncompliance. To address these problems, methods such as end-to-end encryption, access control mechanisms, blockchain-based audit trails, and privacy-preserving protocols are being implemented. These mechanisms guarantee the secure sharing of sensitive data between DTs while preserving data sovereignty, traceability, and integrity. Note that FL enhances secure collaboration by enabling the training of AI models on decentralized datasets without transferring the data itself. In a FL framework, each DT locally trains the model utilizing its own data and exclusively transmits model parameters (not raw data) to a central aggregator. This method mitigates the danger of data exposure, facilitates real-time learning across decentralized systems, and complies with rules such as GDPR. FL is especially advantageous in sectors such as healthcare, finance, and smart cities, where data is both immensely valuable and sensitive. In DTC ecosystems, the integration of FL with secure data sharing facilitates collaborative intelligence while safeguarding privacy and preserving trust among members.

5.7.3 Privacy-preserving techniques

As DTs increasingly depend on sensitive personal, operational, or environmental data, the implementation of privacy-preserving strategies has become crucial for ensuring ethical and secure deployment. These methodologies seek to safeguard data confidentiality while facilitating data analytics, AI training, and collaborative decision-making. Common methodologies include data anonymization (eliminating or concealing identifiable information), pseudonymization (substituting IDs with arbitrary tokens), and differential privacy, which introduces stochastic noise to datasets to prevent the tracing of individual data points. These methods facilitate adherence to data protection rules, including GDPR, HIPAA, and sector-specific standards, especially in healthcare, banking, and intelligent infrastructure. Advanced privacy-preserving techniques include homomorphic encryption, enabling computations on encrypted data without decryption, and secure multiparty computing (SMPC), wherein many participants collaboratively compute a function over their inputs while maintaining confidentiality. Furthermore, FL facilitates decentralized model training, wherein data remains local and only model updates are transmitted, thereby substantially mitigating the risk of data leakage. In the realm of DTC, the integration of these methodologies ensures that real-time analytics and AI-driven simulations can occur without compromising sensitive data, thus enhancing trust, compliance, and scalability across multi-entity ecosystems (Lin et al., 2017).

5.7.4 Threats and risk management

As DTs increasingly depend on sensitive personal, operational, or environmental data, the implementation of privacy-preserving strategies has become crucial for ensuring ethical and secure deployment. These methodologies seek to safeguard data confidentiality while facilitating data analytics, AI training, and collaborative decision-making. Common methodologies encompass data anonymization (eliminating or concealing identifiable information), pseudonymization (substituting IDs with arbitrary tokens), and differential privacy, which introduces stochastic noise to datasets to inhibit the tracing of individual data points. These methods facilitate adherence to data protection rules, including GDPR, HIPAA, and sector-specific standards, especially in healthcare, banking, and intelligent infrastructure. Advanced privacy-preserving techniques encompass homomorphic encryption, enabling computations on encrypted data without decryption, and SMPC, wherein many participants collaboratively compute a function over their inputs while maintaining confidentiality. Furthermore, FL facilitates decentralized model training, wherein data remains local and only model updates are transmitted, thereby substantially mitigating the risk of data leakage. In the realm of DTC, the integration of these methodologies guarantees that real-time analytics and AI-driven simulations can occur without compromising sensitive data, thus enhancing trust, compliance, and scalability across multi-entity ecosystems.

5.8 Future directions

The future of AI-enhanced DTC is predicated on the advancement of more intelligent, autonomous, and collaborative ecosystems. Advancements in edge AI, FL, and 5G/6G connectivity will enable DTs to transform into self-learning systems that can make real-time decisions with minimal human involvement. Future DTC platforms will facilitate multi-agent collaboration, wherein numerous DTs representing interconnected systems such as factories, smart grids, and cities cooperate to enhance performance at a network or ecosystem level. Integration with technologies like blockchain will guarantee secure, verifiable interactions among stakeholders, thereby augmenting confidence in collaborative contexts. Moreover, forthcoming research will focus on enhancing the contextual awareness, ethical alignment, and

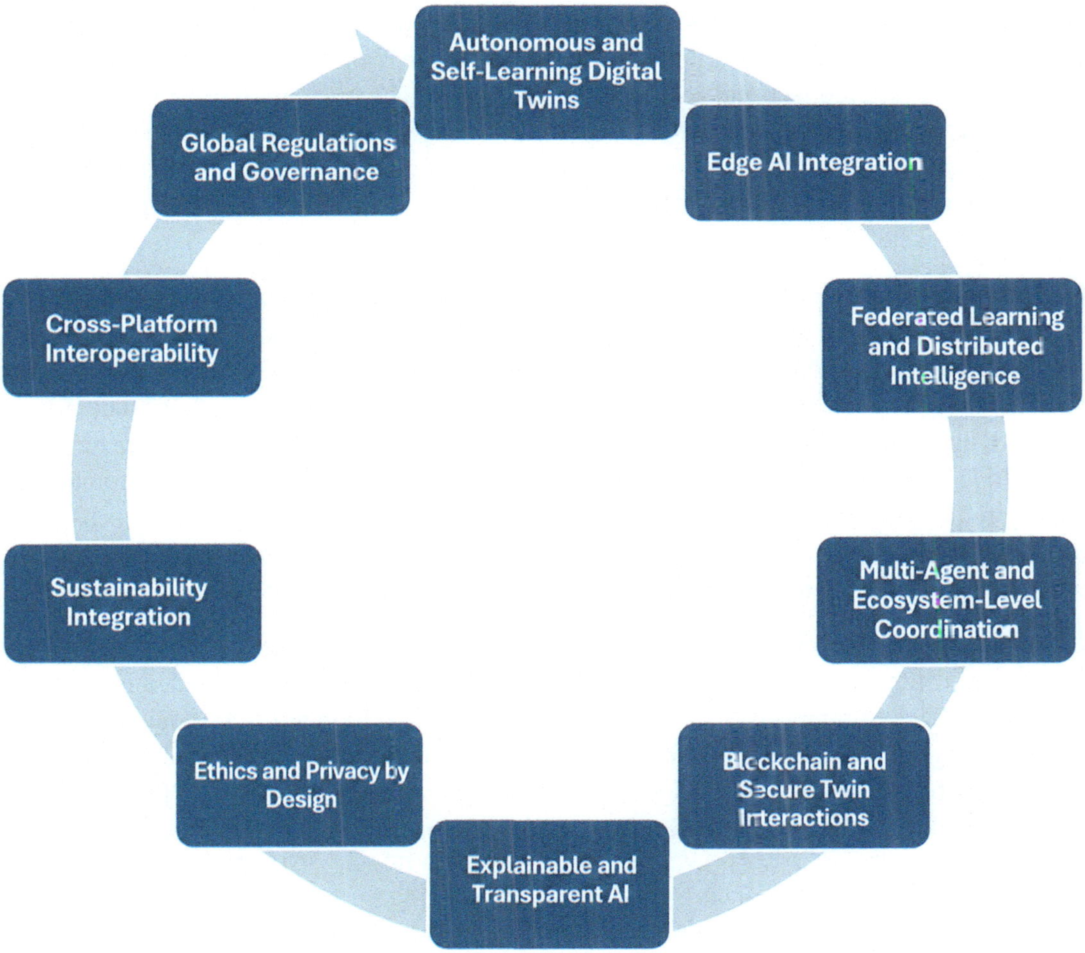

Fig. 5.2 Future direction.

explicability of DTs. This includes the creation of transparent AI models, the enhancement of privacy-preserving computation, and the integration of sustainability measures into simulations. Standardization initiatives will aim to ensure interoperability across industries and systems, underpinned by global regulatory frameworks. The next generation of DTs will function as cognitive agents, imitating reality while also comprehending, forecasting, and enhancing it in areas such as healthcare, climate resilience, transportation, and national infrastructure planning (Radanliev et al., 2021; Chen et al., 2017) (Fig. 5.2).

5.9 Emerging trends of AI-enhanced DT computing towards integration of futuristic emerging technology

In the era of digital transformation, DTC has emerged as a pivotal paradigm, driving the evolution of how physical systems are modeled, monitored, and optimized in cyberspace. DTs are virtual representations of physical entities that use real-time data to simulate behavior, predict outcomes, and enable decision-making. The integration of AI into DTC systems has significantly enhanced their capabilities, enabling more accurate modeling, predictive analytics, and autonomous control. As industries adopt increasingly sophisticated technologies, AI-enhanced DTs are becoming a cornerstone for futuristic innovations across sectors such as healthcare, manufacturing, urban planning, and energy.

One of the most significant trends is the fusion of AI and DTs to create intelligent, adaptive systems, often referred to as "Cognitive DTs." These twins not only replicate real-world processes but also use AI techniques such as ML, deep learning, and NLP to learn from past data, identify patterns, and make autonomous decisions. This intelligence allows them to optimize operations without human intervention. For instance, in smart manufacturing, AI-powered DTs continuously monitor machinery, predict maintenance needs, and automatically adjust production parameters to maximize efficiency and reduce downtime. These self-learning systems are also instrumental in high-stakes sectors like aerospace and defense, where real-time decision support and predictive maintenance can prevent costly failures.

In parallel, the convergence of AI-enhanced DTs with the IoT and Edge Computing is enabling real-time data flow and instant decision-making. IoT devices embedded in physical assets collect vast amounts of sensor data, which is streamed to their digital counterparts for analysis. Edge computing ensures that data processing occurs closer to the source, reducing latency and bandwidth issues. AI algorithms deployed at the edge empower DTs to operate with minimal delay, crucial for applications such as autonomous vehicles, smart grids, and remote surgery. This triad—AI, IoT, and edge computing (Tyagi, 2016, 2020, 2021, 2022, 2023, Tyagi, 2024a, Tyagi, 2024b, Tyagi, 2024c, Tyagi, 2024d, Tyagi, 2024e, Tyagi, 2025a, Tyagi, 2025b; Tyagi and Aghila, 2011) forms the backbone of real-time responsive systems, ushering in a new era of hyperconnectivity and operational agility.

Another emerging trend is the integration of DTs with Blockchain technology to enhance security, trust, and transparency in digital interactions. In a world where DTs interact with one another autonomously, such as in supply chains or smart infrastructure, the authenticity and integrity of shared data become paramount. Blockchain offers decentralized ledgers and smart contracts that ensure immutable data records, verifiable transactions, and self-executing rules. For instance, in logistics, DTs of cargo containers can autonomously negotiate and confirm handovers using smart contracts, ensuring traceability and reducing human errors. This integration paves the way for trusted, autonomous ecosystems where digital and physical assets interact securely and seamlessly.

The rise of immersive technologies, such as augmented reality virtual reality, and mixed reality (MR) has expanded the application space of AI-enhanced DTs into the realm of extended reality (XR). These technologies provide intuitive and interactive visual interfaces, enabling stakeholders to engage with DTs in 3D environments. Engineers can now walk through virtual power plants, interact with machinery DTs, or simulate emergency scenarios in real-time, all from remote locations. AI adds another layer of intelligence by analyzing user behavior, interpreting context, and dynamically adapting the visualization to provide meaningful insights. The combination of XR and AI-enhanced DTC is particularly transformative in training, design prototyping, and remote collaboration.

Further, quantum computing promises to further revolutionize the capabilities of DTC. While still in its infancy, quantum computing can exponentially speed up complex simulations and optimizations, making it suitable for industries requiring high-dimensional data modeling. For example, AI-enhanced DTs of urban infrastructure can use quantum algorithms to simulate city-wide traffic flows, energy consumption, or climate scenarios with unprecedented speed and accuracy. Additionally, DTs in pharmaceuticals could simulate protein folding and drug interactions far faster than classical methods, opening doors for real-time drug development and personalized medicine. As quantum computing matures, its convergence with AI and DTs could define a new computational frontier.

Another essential trend is the emergence of AI-driven Bio-DTs in the healthcare sector. These are hyper-personalized virtual replicas of human organs, body systems, or even entire patients. AI models, trained on an individual's medical history, genetics, and real-time health data, simulate how the patient's body responds to treatments, lifestyle changes, or disease progression. Physicians can use these digital replicas to test interventions before applying them to the patient, thereby reducing trial-and-error treatments. Additionally, hospital-level DTs, powered by AI, can model and optimize workflows, manage resources, and simulate disaster response scenarios, significantly improving care delivery and operational efficiency.

The application of AI-enhanced DTs in smart cities and infrastructure is another area seeing rapid development. Urban planners are leveraging real-time DTs of entire cities to simulate traffic flow, pollution levels, public service demand, and infrastructure wear. AI algorithms analyze data streams from thousands of sensors across the city, allowing administrators to make proactive decisions like rerouting traffic, managing power consumption, or responding to emergencies. Moreover, DTs help cities achieve sustainability goals by simulating environmental impact scenarios and guiding green infrastructure development. The result is more resilient, efficient, and livable urban environments driven by intelligent digital models.

Meanwhile, autonomous systems and robotics are undergoing significant enhancements through AI-powered DTs. Robots and drones often operate in uncertain or dynamic environments where simulation is crucial. A DT can simulate a robot's operations, predict its failures, and optimize its tasks before actual deployment. AI enhances these twins by enabling adaptive behaviors, path planning, and decision-making. In swarm robotics, for instance, AI-enhanced DTs can simulate the collective behavior of drones and adjust their algorithms for better coordination. This leads to more efficient operations in agriculture, mining, surveillance, and disaster response.

A critical enabler of many of these advancements is FL, which allows AI models to be trained across decentralized data sources without sharing raw data. In the context of DTs, FL ensures that models embedded in different twins, such as those representing smart appliances, buildings, or vehicles, can collaboratively improve their learning without violating privacy. This is particularly beneficial in sectors like finance, defense, and healthcare, where data sensitivity is paramount. As privacy-preserving AI becomes more essential, FL will be a vital component of large-scale, intelligent DTC ecosystems.

In summary, AI-enhanced DTC is rapidly evolving from a static, simulation-based concept to a dynamic, intelligent, and interconnected system capable of reshaping how we design, monitor, and control complex physical systems. As it integrates with futuristic technologies such as IoT, edge computing, blockchain, XR, quantum computing, and FL, its applications are expanding exponentially across industries. These trends are not isolated; they are interdependent and synergistic, forming a robust technological ecosystem that will define the future of digital-physical convergence. The result is a transformative shift toward self-optimizing, resilient, and intelligent environments that blur the lines between the real and the virtual, enabling more responsive, efficient, and personalized solutions for tomorrow's challenges.

5.10 Conclusion

AI-enhanced DTC signifies a transformative change in the monitoring, simulation, and optimization of physical systems. Through the integration of real-time data capture, sophisticated simulation models, and ML algorithms, DTs are transforming into intelligent agents that can replicate reality, anticipate future outcomes, and make autonomous decisions. This shift is allowing organizations in several sectors, such as manufacturing, energy, healthcare, and smart cities, to attain enhanced efficiency, resilience, and agility in overseeing intricate processes. The integration of AI, IoT, edge computing, and FL within DT frameworks establishes a basis for developing interconnected and adaptable systems capable of collaborative operation in decentralized environments. These systems can assess and react to dynamic alterations, manage uncertainties, and perpetually learn from data, all while safeguarding data privacy and system security. The increasing integration of blockchain and privacy-preserving technology is augmenting trust and transparency in multi-party DTC marketplaces. Nonetheless, actualizing the complete potential of DTC necessitates surmounting critical obstacles associated with scale, data integrity, interoperability, cybersecurity, AI bias, and governance. As these systems gain autonomy and become integral to vital infrastructure, ethical considerations and regulatory compliance will be paramount for assuring safe and responsible implementation. Future research and development should prioritize XAI, secure data exchange, standardization, and sustainability-focused design. In conclusion, AI-augmented DTC is at the forefront of digital transformation. With appropriate technological, organizational, and policy frameworks, it has the capacity to initiate a new era of intelligent, efficient, and human-centric systems that transform innovation and resilience in the physical realm.

References

Boschert, S., Rosen, R., 2016. Digital twin—the simulation aspect. In: Hehenberger, P., Bradley, D. (eds.) Mechatronic Futures. Springer, Cham, pp. 59–74. doi: 10.1007/978-3-319-32156-1_5.

Chen, M., Ma, Y., Li, Y., Wu, D., Zhang, Y., Youn, C.H., 2017. Wearable 2.0: enabling human-cloud integration in next generation healthcare systems. IEEE Commun. Mag. 55 (1), 54–61. doi:10.1109/MCOM.2017.1600397CM.

Grieves, M., Vickers, J., 2017. Digital twin: mitigating unpredictable, undesirable emergent behavior in complex systems. In: Kahlen, J., Flumerfelt, S., Alves, A. (eds.) Transdisciplinary Perspectives on Complex Systems. Springer, Cham. doi:10.1007/978-3-319-38756-7_4.

Kairouz, P., McMahan, H.B., Avent, B., et al., 2019. Advances and open problems in federated learning. arXiv arXiv:1912.04977. https://arxiv.org/abs/1912.04977.

Lee, J., Bagheri, B., Kao, H.A., 2015. A cyber-physical systems architecture for industry 4.0-based manufacturing systems. Manuf. Lett. 3, 18–23. doi:10.1016/j.mfglet.2014.12.001.

Lin, D., Yu, W., Zhang, N., Yang, X., Zhang, W., Zhao, W., 2017. Survey on internet of things: a review of enabling technologies, security and privacy, and applications. IEEE Internet Things J. 4 (5), 1125–1142. doi:10.1109/JIOT.2017.2683200.

Lu, Y., Liu, C., Wang, K.I.K., Huang, H., Xu, X., 2020. Digital twin-driven smart manufacturing: connotation, reference model, applications and research issues. Robot. Comput. Integr. Manuf. 61, 101837. doi:10.1016/j.rcim.2019.101837.

Madni, A.M., Madni, C.C., Lucero, S.D., 2019. Leveraging digital twin technology in model-based systems engineering. Systems. 7 (1), 7. doi:10.3390/systems7010007.

Mohammadi, M., Al-Fuqaha, A., Guizani, M., Oh, J.S., 2018. Semisupervised deep reinforcement learning in support of IoT and smart city services. IEEE Internet Things J. 5 (2), 624–635. doi:10.1109/JIOT.2017.2748798.

Radanliev, P., De Roure, D., Walton, R., Burnap, P., 2021. Digital twins: applications, challenges, and opportunities. Technol. Soc. 67, 101728. doi:10.1016/j.techsoc.2021.101728.

Shi, W., Cao, J., Zhang, Q., Li, Y., Xu, L., 2016. Edge computing: vision and challenges. IEEE Internet Things J. 3 (5), 637–646. doi:10.1109/JIOT.2016.2579198.

Shokri, R., Stronati, M., Song, C., Shmatikov, V. (2017). Membership inference attacks against machine learning models. In: Proceedings of the 2017 IEEE Symposium on Security and Privacy. pp. 3–18. doi:10.1109/SP.2017.41.

Tao, F., Sui, F., Liu, A., Qi, Q., Zhang, M., Song, B., Nee, A.Y.C., 2019. Digital twin-driven product design, manufacturing and service with big data. Int. J. Adv. Manuf. Technol. 94 (9), 3563–3576. doi:10.1007/s00170-017-0233-1.

Tyagi, A.K., 2016. Cyber physical systems (CPSs)—opportunities and challenges for improving cyber security. Int. J. Comput. Appl. 0975-8887. 137 (14), 19–27. doi:10.5120/ijca2016908877.

Tyagi, A.K., 2022. SecVT: securing the vehicles of tomorrow using blockchain technology. In: In the proceeding of Springer/ ISAI 2022, 17–19 February 2022, Kolkata. doi:10.1007/978-3-031-22485-0_11. ISBN: 978-3-031-22485-0.

Tyagi, A.K. (ed.). 2024b. Dew computing: state of the art, opportunities, and research challenges. In: Machine Learning Algorithms Using Scikit and TensorFlow Environments. IGI Global, USA, pp. 332–345. doi:10.4018/978-1-6684-8531-6.ch017.

Tyagi, A.K. (ed.). 2024c. Blockchain-enabled internet of things (IoTs) platforms for IoT-based healthcare and biomedical sectors. In: Artificial Intelligence-Enabled Blockchain Technology and Digital Twin for Smart Hospitals. Wiley, pp. 201–217. doi:10.1002/9781394287420.ch10. ISBN: 978-1-394-28739-0.

Tyagi, A.K. (ed.). 2024d. Sensors and digital twin application in healthcare facilities management. In: Artificial Intelligence-Enabled Blockchain Technology and Digital Twin for Smart Hospitals . Wiley, pp. 369–390. doi:10.1002/9781394287420.ch19. ISBN: 978-1-394-28739-0.

Tyagi, A.K. (ed.). 2024e. Blockchain–artificial intelligence-based secured solutions for smart environment. In: Digital Twin and Blockchain for Smart Cities. Wiley, pp. 547–577. doi:10.1002/9781394303564.ch23. ISBN: 9781394303533.

Tyagi, A.K. (ed.). 2025a. Blockchain for smart hospital in Healthcare 5.0: modeling structure, challenges, and future emerging trends. In: Human- Centric Integration of Next-Generation Data Science and Blockchain Technology. Elsevier, pp. 333–347. doi:10.1016/B978-0-443-33498-6.00026-1. ISBN: 978-0-443-33498-6.

Tyagi, A.K., Aghila, G., 2011. A wide scale survey on botnet. Int. J. Comput. Appl. 0975-8887. 34 (9), 9–22. doi:10.1016/j.iotcps.2021.12.002.

Tyagi, A.K., 2024a. Transformative Effects of ChatGPT on modern era of education and society: from society and industry's perspective. In: Maruthi, P.B., Prasad, S., Tyagi, A.K. (eds.) Machine Learning Algorithms Using Scikit and TensorFlow Environments. IGI Global, USA, pp. 374–387. doi:10.4018/978-1-6684-8531-6.ch019

Tyagi, A.K., 2023. Decentralized everything: a practical use of blockchain technology in future applications. In: Maruthi, P.B., Prasad, S., Tyagi, A.K. (eds.) Distributed Computing to Blockchain: Architecture, Technology, and Applications. Elsevier, pp. 19–38. ISBN: 978-0-323-96146-210.1016/B978-0-323-96146-2.00010-3.

Tyagi, A.K., 2020. Prediction models. In: Rani, G., Tiwari, P.K. (eds.) Handbook of Research on Disease Prediction through Data Analytics and Machine Learning. IGI Global, USA, pp. 50–69. ISBN 13:978179982742910.4018/978-1-7998-2742-9

Tyagi, A.K., 2021. Analysis of security and privacy aspects of blockchain technologies from smart era' perspective: the challenges and a way forward. In: Tyagi, A.K., Abraham, A. (eds.) CRC- Recent Trends in Blockchain for Information Systems Security and Privacy. CRC Press, pp. 1–17. eBook-ISBN: 97810031397 3710.1201/9781003139737.

Tyagi, A.K., 2025b. Blockchain technology: values, challenges, and possible applications from an industry perspective. In: Tyagi, A.K., Tiwari, S. (eds.) Human- Centric Integration of Next-Generation Data Science and Blockchain Technology. Elsevier, pp. 349–367. ISBN: 978-0-443-33498-6. doi:10.1016/B978-0-443-33498-6.00027-3.

Wu, M., Lu, T.J., Ling, F.Y.Y., Sun, J., 2021. Explainable AI applications in digital twins: a systematic review. J. Intell. Manuf. doi:10.1007/s10845-021-01787-8.

Zhang, Y., Kasahara, S., Shen, Y., Jiang, X., Wan, J., 2019. Smart contract-based access control for the internet of things. IEEE Internet Things J. 6 (2), 1594–1605. doi:10.1109/JIOT.2018.2847705.

CHAPTER 6

Leveraging blockchain in digital twin systems

Gulshan Soni[a], V. Hemamalini[b], M. Jeyaselvi[b], and Amit Kumar Tyagi[c]

[a]Centre for Computer Science and Business Management, Madhav Institute of Technology & Science (MITS-DU), Gwalior, Madhya Pradesh, India

[b]Department of Networking and Communications, SRM Institute of Science and Technology, Kattankulathur, India

[c]School of Law, Forensic Justice and Policy Studies, National Forensic Sciences University, Gandhinagar, Gujarat, India

6.1 Introduction

Technological advancements in digital technologies have enabled innovations that are creating intelligent systems capable of replicating physical environments, processes, and entities in virtual spaces (Semeraro et al., 2021). Digital twins (DTs) represent a revolutionary shift in producing a digital representation of a physical asset, process, or system by creating a dynamically updating digital replica of the physical counterpart. DTs can create a digital version of reality by assimilating data in real-time from sensors, actuators, or Internet of Things (IoT) devices and then using that data to support analysis, forecasting, and optimization. The coupling of a physical and digital counter part allows DTs to leverage critical applications across many sectors, such as aerospace, manufacturing, healthcare, urban planning, and energy systems (Jones et al., 2020).

Nevertheless, as demand for DT systems to integrate and influence decision-making expands in mission-critical infrastructures, expectations for data accuracy, synchronization, and communication security have also increased. In fact, the ability of a DT to truly deliver on its potential relies on having timely and credible data in its calculations and methods. In aerospace and healthcare, for example, an inconsequential difference in the synchronization of a physical entity with its digital counterpart can result in catastrophe. Current operational architectures for developing DTs tend to rely on centralized or semicentralized databases or communication channels (Yao et al., 2023). In many cases, centralized designs have led to security breaches, data and/or operational manipulation, single-point failures, and a lack of transparency.

Artificial Intelligence, Machine Learning and Blockchain in Digital Twin Computing.
https://doi.org/10.1016/B978-0-443-43914-8.00018-2

Blockchain technology can improve the potential of DT systems by providing a decentralized and immutable ledger system that ensures data integrity, attributes provenance, and enhances transparency. Smart contracts (SC), deployed on blockchains, can provide automation and enforceable rules in the interactions and conditions of DTs. Nonetheless, the current DT infrastructure struggles with data security, interoperability, latency, standardization, and limited resources. DT platforms apply a centralized data storage approach, making them susceptible to cyberattacks. Blockchain use cases leverage immutability as a security characteristic. Interoperability and scalability are significant concerns that impact DT's future capabilities (Boschert and Rosen, 2016). In addition, latency and transaction throughput limitations can impair real-time integration. There are no established, universal standards defining DT-blockchain integration, leading to challenges in scaling or generalizing. Fig. 6.1 illustrates the conceptual integration of DT with blockchain.

This research paper aims to overcome these obstacles by analyzing the strategic incorporation of blockchain technology into DT systems. The primary aim of such a framework is to develop an architectural and functional framework to enhance the trustworthiness, efficiency, and transparency of DT applications by leveraging the decentralization, security, and SC capabilities of blockchain. This paper will contribute to the body of research in the following ways:

- It defines a modular, scalable architecture for blockchain-enabled DT systems, which enables secure data synchronization and auditing across a distributed environment.

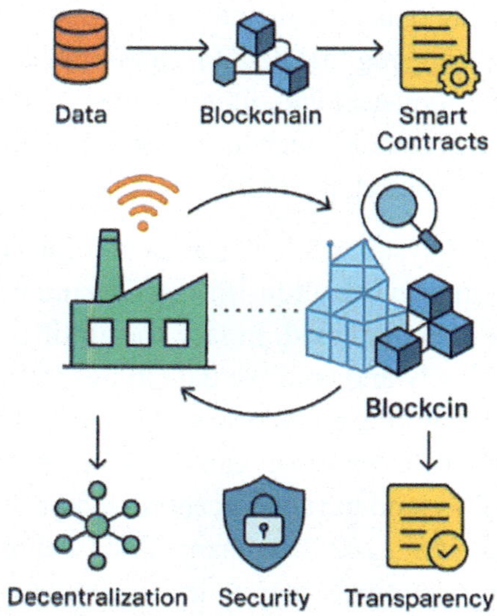

Fig. 6.1 Conceptual integration of DT-Blockchain.

- It identifies a series of principles of design, including data offloading, the use of permissioned blockchains, and hybrid on-chain/off-chain storage of data for specific DT use cases.
- It offers practical application scenarios associated with current trends in smart manufacturing, healthcare monitoring, and smart city structures to present the feasibility of the model.
- It assesses the performance of the integration system using simulations through a benchmark scenario by observing and measuring performance factors related to latency, throughput, scalability, and security resilience.

The remainder of the paper is organized as follows: In Section 2, a comprehensive overview of the fundamental concepts surrounding DTs and blockchain is provided, followed by a discussion of synergies and a review of the relevant work in Section 3. In Section 4, the paper discusses the system requirements, focusing on on-chain and off-chain data storage and the interoperability aspects of blockchain-enabled DT systems. In Section 5, the paper showcases applied concepts within the proposed framework in the smart manufacturing, health care, smart cities, aerospace, and agriculture sectors. In Section 6, a multilayered architecture is presented, encapsulating the layers of the DT model, blockchain, storage layer, integration layer, and analytics layer. In Section 7, quantitative and qualitative assessments of performance, scalability, security, and latency improvements are presented as features of the framework. In Section 8, the challenges regarding blockchain-enabled DT systems, including data privacy risks, scalability, interoperability, and risks associated with SCs, are discussed, along with potential solutions. In Section 9, the authors conclude the paper by reviewing the work, providing a wrap-up discussion, and outlining areas for future research.

6.2 Background and theoretical foundations

The growth of digital systems has experienced two major paradigm shifts over the past few years: DT technology and Blockchain. The first adds a dimension to modeling, simulation, and real-time monitoring, while the second establishes a decentralized, permanent, and secure infrastructure for establishing trust and exchanging digital transactions. In order to effectively understand the potential of integrating blockchain with DT systems, it is important to understand the fundamental principles that guide each domain.

6.2.1 DT systems

A DT is a digital representation that mirrors a physical object or process, including all internal and external structures and properties, which continually updates itself through software-connected sensors and devices that are attached to the object. Originating largely in the aerospace engineering sector, the DT concept has made inroads into many areas such as manufacturing, healthcare, municipal planning, and energy systems. It is a modeling system enabled with mathematical algorithms, artificial intelligence techniques, and computational analytics to view the state of the physical object in real-time and also forecast state changes. The accuracy of the DT relies heavily on the fidelity and frequency with which the attributes are derived from IoT sensors (Lo et al., 2021). DTs have many uses in various industries by providing real-time monitoring, predictive maintainability, virtual testing, and process optimization. They can identify failures in products, alter operations autonomously, predict patient-level physiological systems, and manage all forms of infrastructure in smart cities. However, as indicated above, despite these advantages, DTs can face trust issues in the form of data manipulation, exploitation of systemic vulnerabilities due to centralized control, implicit distrust, and lack of end-to-end trust. There are inherent risks and difficulties in establishing critical trust in systems, and blockchain solutions provide the infrastructure for trusted, secure, and transparent DTs (Nielsen et al., 2020). Fig. 6.2 illustrates the concept of the DT.

6.2.2 Blockchain technology

Blockchain technology is a decentralized and distributed ledger system that provides a way for multiple nodes to share data and keep it in sync without relying on a central authority. The primary principles of blockchain technology are outlined below, and these principles must be considered when deciding how to use blockchain technology in DT contexts. These primary principles include Decentralization, Immutability, Transparency, and Security. Decentralization lowers the risk of a single point of failure. Immutability implies that data can no longer be altered retroactively. Transparency fosters trust in collaborative settings. Blockchain employs various cryptographic techniques, such as hashing and digital signatures, to ensure security against unauthorized access and data breaches. Blockchain

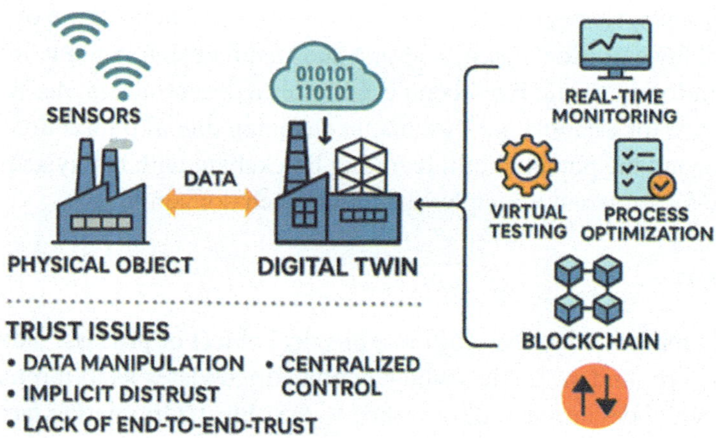

Fig. 6.2 Overview of the digital twin concept.

platforms can be classified based on how they allow access (Raj, 2021). Public blockchains, like Ethereum, allow participation by all users but face scalability and latency challenges. Private blockchains restrict access to a single organization; they perform better but sacrifice decentralization. Consortium blockchains enable shared use and management of the network by multiple organizations. Each type of blockchain has its pros and cons. The type you choose for your DT must closely align with the requirements of its DT context. Bitcoin popularized the use of blockchain for financial transactions, but now the capabilities of blockchain technology are being applied in areas such as supply chains, healthcare, identity systems, and implantable cyber-physical systems (Negri et al., 2017). One of the key innovations in blockchain is the SC—self-executing code that resides on the blockchain and automatically enforces transaction rules once certain conditions are met. In cases where SCs automatically enforce rules, there are no intermediaries, latency is reduced, and workflows can be executed autonomously and verified. This is especially important in developmental DT systems, where the need for autonomous responses to changing conditions (which can be programmed with great granularity) can be met without human intervention. While blockchain provides a strong foundation of security and trust in systems, the key architectural design required for integrating DTs with blockchain should be carefully scoped, particularly with regard to performance demands and near real-time expectations in DT applications (Grieves and Vickers, 2016). Fig. 6.3 provides an overview of blockchain technology.

6.2.3 Synergy between blockchain and DTs

The combination of blockchain with DT systems overcomes several limitations of classic DT architectures. One of the most important barriers faced by DT environments is the trustworthiness and integrity of real-time data. As data from physical systems move through possibly multiple layers and organizations before being consumed by the DT model, it

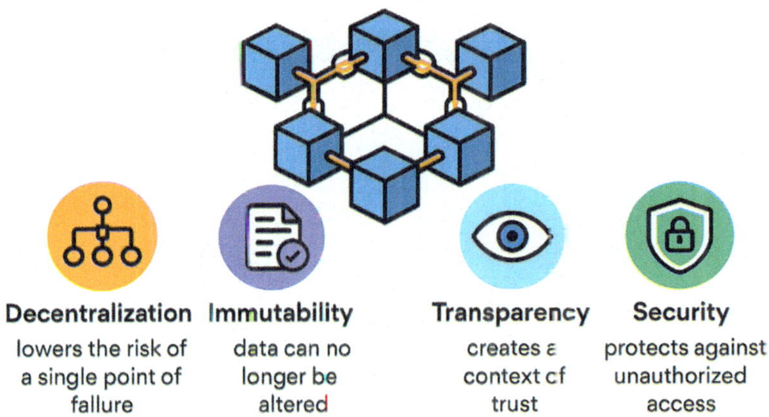

Fig. 6.3 Blockchain concept overview.

becomes vulnerable to malicious tampering, interception, and even loss. Recording every data transaction through a blockchain leads to an end-to-end database-level trustworthiness and integrity model. Blockchain enables timestamping, hashing, and linking to the original source, which allows the DT model to operate using authenticated and verifiable inputs. Another distinct advantage of blockchain integration is the ability to securely share credentials through permissions (Ma et al., 2024). Many instances of DT implementations, particularly in industrial or healthcare environments, rely on trusted data being exchanged between multiple parties. Entrusted data transactions often depend on a centralized third-party authority or server, which creates a data-sharing bottleneck and introduces potential vulnerabilities at the three different levels of data sharing described earlier. Blockchain provides a de-centralized method for access control with permission-based access, allowing multiple parties or stakeholders to share data based on predefined criteria by assessing roles, policies, and SCs—all without jeopardizing personal data privacy or requiring intermediaries. Fig. 6.4 illustrates the synergy between blockchain and DT.

SCs in DT systems offer improved efficiency and even the mitigation of downtime through automated responses and decisions. SCs can trigger a chain of actions such as maintenance, reordering parts, or notifying technicians in response to real-time sensor data. These actions would be recorded on the blockchain in an immutable, verifiable, and auditable way. This reliance on automation and trust can reduce or eliminate disputes about who made a decision. Furthermore, blockchain brings its own methods of verifiability and accountability, creating a uniform trust record for data interaction, decisions, and actions, as well as transparency with regulatory reporting. This is especially vital in industries like aerospace, aviation, energy, and pharmaceuticals, where deviation from established protocols could cause fatalities. Using decentralized architecture, blockchain introduces a new type of resiliency for DT systems. Traditional or centralized architectures for DT systems are subject to failure or attacks on the

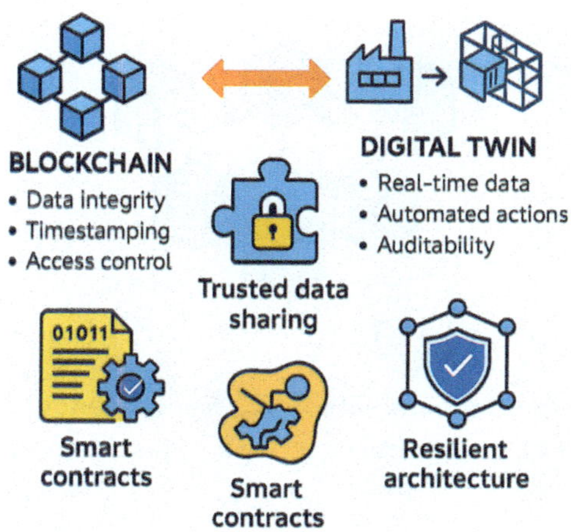

Fig. 6.4 Synergy between DT and Blockchain Technology.

control server (rather than the devices), whereas blockchain/DT architectures would continue to function and report even if some of the nodes go offline, making the DT system more robust and resilient in a challenging working environment.

6.2.4 Related work

In the Fourth Industrial Revolution, DT systems offer innovative technology that enables continuous monitoring, simulation, diagnosis, and optimization of complex systems. DTs first emerged in aerospace and manufacturing industries, and their applications now also include healthcare, smart cities, energy, and logistics (Tao et al., 2018). DTs monitor the conditions of physical systems and leverage IoT data to reproduce the state and behavior of the physical system using virtual tools, providing stakeholders with actionable insights. However, the quality and usefulness of outputs are directly tied to the quality and timeliness of the input data; inaccurate, stale, or corrupted data inputs will produce simulations inconsistent with reality in terms of state and/or dynamic behavior, leading to poor strategic decisions (Fuller et al., 2020). Real-time feedback loops, or the immediate reconstruction of physical states to their logical state that rivals human cognition, are essential for maintaining an unbroken relationship and ensuring accurate, secure transmission of invariants and variations between the physical and virtual realms (Gehrmann and Gunnarsson, 2020). However, the increased complexity of modern systems, especially those involving interactions across multiple stakeholders, scales, and/or locations, fosters the introduction of challenges such as data inconsistency, cyber vulnerability, and transparency within high-stakes environments, such as autonomous transportation or smart grids—all while operating under a constant fear of threats or attacks (Tyagi, 2025). The integrity of data is crucial for reliable operation within a DT's functional environment; it ensures that data has not been affected by malicious intent or inadvertent error. Even relatively minor breaches or unwanted alterations to data integrity can result in erroneous decision-making, which may negatively impact operators or stakeholders. Consequently, the top priority of mission-critical systems is to develop and maintain trust through an unbroken chain of trusted data (Wang et al., 2023). Real-time updates are critical in industrial machinery and healthcare monitoring systems, as failure to provide them can introduce delays that may result in equipment breakdowns, financial losses, and risks to patient safety if a fault goes undetected (Nakamoto, no date). Secure communication channels are paramount for improving data integrity and confidentiality. Since DT implementations are typically built on wireless and distributed networks, they are susceptible to man-in-the-middle attacks and unauthorized access. Traditional security solutions often lack the scalability and resilience needed to effectively prevent these attacks (Underwood, 2016; Padmapriya et al., 2022).

Blockchain is a type of distributed ledger technology (DLT) that records and verifies transactions in a tamper-proof and transparent manner. Originally developed for cryptocurrency, blockchain is now being applied in finance, logistics, healthcare, and supply chain management. The main characteristic of a blockchain is that the data is immutable, meaning that it cannot be altered retroactively without the consensus of every other participant in the network (Li et al., 2023). Unlike traditional methods of recording and managing DTs, blockchain provides decentralized infrastructure for DTs without the need for a trusted third party and also reduces reliance on centralized cloud-based approaches (Li et al., 2018). Blockchain also uses a combination of technologies, including consensus, to apply uniform views of the state of the entire system, which is critical for collaborative environments, particularly ones that include multiple organizations (Zheng et al., 2017). SCs are programmatic logic, often written in blockchain, that can allow for additional automation of DTs, specifically of the rules governing data-sharing, alerts, and intended maintenance actions. Blockchain also provides traceability and auditability, enabling the examination of historical data from the raw input source to the end application, which is highly valuable from a corporate governance perspective and for regulatory compliance and accountability purposes. In addition, blockchain supports identity management and access control so that only authorized users (or actors) can control and/or modify some portion of the DT as appropriate, which could have numerous applications in supply chains or healthcare scenarios.

Leading current systems for DT often suffer from performance and scalability issues because they rely on centralized architectures that lack scalability and resiliency. These architectures are a source of latency, security vulnerabilities, and single points of failure (Fernandez-Carames and Fraga-Lamas, 2018) Interoperability also remains a significant issue for DT due to the diversity of infrastructure in DT implementations, which stems from the heterogeneity of devices and platforms. This diversity necessitates some form of coordinated but standardized architecture to enable seamless interoperability and facilitate data sharing, which ultimately limits the usability of the digital system in environments involving multiple stakeholders (Khan et al., 2024). It is now well known that DT environments require constant attention to security, and making DT systems more connected and autonomous increases the attack surface. Standard frameworks for security are not yet prepared for a proactive approach to security within such environments, sometimes leading to real-world consequences (Mettler, 2016). Using trust frameworks for collaborative environments within ecosystems such as smart cities will be fundamental to ensuring the integrity of shared and planned digital environments. The challenge of establishing and maintaining trust is where blockchain demonstrates its potential as a trust-based consensus backbone for collaborative ecosystems. However, there is a concurrent challenge of ensuring transparency while addressing data privacy concerns through trust and trust frameworks. While blockchain provides immutability and openness for transparency, privacy issues become a challenge that may limit the overall usability of digital TS systems. Advanced security mechanisms, such as zero-knowledge proofs, can be adopted to address these challenges (Adu-Amankwa et al., 2023). Table 6.1 provides a summary of key components, issues, and the discussion on Blockchain-DT integration.

Table 6.1 Summary of key components, issues, and blockchain integration in digital twin systems.

Aspect	Description	Supporting Citations
Definition of Digital Twins	Digital replicas of physical assets are used for real-time monitoring, simulation, diagnostics, and optimization	(Tao et al., 2018; Fuller et al., 2020)
Real-time synchronization	DTs ingest data from IoT devices to show the current status and understand the future status	(Tyagi 2025)
Data integrity	Ensures data is always accurate and unaltered throughout its lifetime, keeping everything highly reliable for dependable operations	(Wang et al., 2023)
Real-time updates	Essential to be responsive and accurate for timely decision-making in disciplines such as predictive maintenance or healthcare monitoring	(Nakamoto, n.d.)
Secure communication	It is important to counter attacks such as data spoofing. Conventional systems often struggle to scale and remain resilient	(Underwood 2016)
Blockchain as a Solution	Provides a decentralized, immutable, and transparent infrastructure for building DT ecosystems	(Padmapriya et al., 2022; Li et al., 2023)
Smart Contracts in dts	Support automated actions based on embedded sensor data and determine data-sharing privileges	(Li et al., 2018)
Identity and Access Control	Trust through blockchain is ensured with the limited interaction of authorized actors with DT components, which builds privacy and trust	(Underwood, 2016)
Centralization challenges	Cloud-based DT systems suffer from bottlenecks, data silos, and a single point of failure	(Zheng et al., 2017)
Data interoperability	Integrating devices is difficult when dealing with multisourced data devices without standardized protocols or uniform models	
Cybersecurity threats	DTs face increased attack surfaces as they become interconnected; legacy systems are insufficient	(Fernandez-Carames and Fraga-Lamas, 2018)
Trust framework deficiencies	Multiparty DT systems need blockchain-based consensus approaches to develop trust in an increasingly complex digital environment	(Khan et al., 2024)
Transparency vs Privacy	Blockchain's openness requires balancing privacy through sophisticated modern techniques, such as using zero-knowledge proofs	(Mettler, 2016; Adu-Amankwa et al., 2023)

Blockchain technology's integration is a viable solution for the ongoing limitations of current DT systems, including ensuring data integrity, securing enhanced layers of security, and establishing trust in decentralized contexts. This convergence lays the foundation for more robust, scalable, and intelligent digital ecosystems.

6.3 Design principles and architecture

The design of a robust and efficient DT system integrated with blockchain technology requires careful consideration of system requirements, data storage strategies, and interoperability aspects, which have been discussed in detail.

6.3.1 System requirements

DTs play a vital role in protecting sensitive data flowing back and forth between physical and digital entities from cyber threats, as well as unauthorized access and tampering. One of the benefits of blockchain's decentralized structure is that no single person can modify or falsify records of data of any kind without the consensus of the network, making it very difficult for someone to engage in malicious activity. This is particularly critical when applied in industries such as healthcare, transportation, and energy, where a breach in security could easily lead to catastrophic scenarios (TAO et al., 2024). Blockchain provides full traceability of transactions capable of being recorded from the DT system through its time-stamped ledger, recording every transaction, change, or update to the DT. By providing a visible history of all transactions, stakeholders are allowed to track the provenance and lineage of data all the way from its inception to its final disposition. Transparency fosters trust, ensuring all stakeholders can rely on the data provided by the digital replica of a physical entity (Sadri et al., 2023). Blockchain's public ledger system promotes transparency in this way and gives all parties access to a verifiable, immutable record so that no party has the ability to manipulate the data or alter it without the other parties being able to verify. Scalability is an important consideration, especially as DT systems scale in complexity, connectivity, and functionality. Centralized/relational databases typically struggle with increased data storage, tracking, and updating new data due to the need for rapid changes to distributed nodes (Yaqoob et al., 2020). Blockchain systems can scale through a distributed network of nodes that process data independently, enhancing the system's ability to manage complex, widespread, large-scale, geographically distributed, and digitally interconnected DTs. Latency is certainly a point of consideration, especially for real-time data projects in crucial applications such as autonomous vehicles, equipment monitoring, or automated maintenance systems (Tao et al., 2019). The decision-making processes in these environments require fast data, and latency can significantly hinder data requirements. Regardless, blockchain consensus can add latency to how data is processed since consensus groups require a degree of validation on each piece of information and some form of block propagation. By using an optimized consensus algorithm such as Proof of Stake (PoS) or Delegated PoS, latency could be reduced, and the consensus process could be optimized without compromising security.

6.3.2 Data storage strategies

Data storage needs to be a serious concern in digital twin (DT) ecosystems, as IoT devices can generate enough data to fill a warehouse and often generate data in real time. Some key features to bear in mind when deciding how to store the data in a data storage (DS)-Blockchain combo can be summarized as follows.

- **On-chain storage:** the data is stored on a blockchain, allowing you to take advantage of immutability and transparency. These on-chain-based products have limited data storage, and the on-chain transactions most likely won't be free, so on-chain data products only make sense for the most important data that you can prove is secure and traceable (i.e., when you need to store transaction records, device states, information regarding system integrity, and compliance) (Xie et al., 2019).
- **Off-chain storage:** To manage the volume of data being generated by DTs, it is common to employ off-chain data storage solutions. In this use case, off-chain storage is generally understood as storing the bulk of data (potentially in external systems such as cloud storage or distributed file systems) while referencing that data on the blockchain. This can allow for scalability and help avoid data costs while not compromising data integrity and while allowing blockchain data verification when authenticating the off-chain data.

6.3.3 Interoperability considerations

DT systems are key in creating interoperability among the equipment, devices, and platforms that make up an ecosystem. APIs (Application Programming Interfaces) are required to transmit information between the various systems and play an important role in establishing secure and transparent data transfer (Liu et al., 2019). The decentralized nature of blockchain may also integrate well with these APIs, as it enhances security and authenticity in data transfer. Following standard communication protocols, such as Message Queuing Telemetry Transport (MQTT), Constrained Application Protocol (CoAP), and Hyper Text Transfer Protocol, is vital for ensuring interoperability across the frameworks of the systems (Gehrmann and Gunnarsson, 2020). The decentralized nature of blockchain could improve the interoperability of IoT by providing a universal framework for validating and recording data from various sources, thereby creating uniformity across multiple platforms while enabling interoperability between many IoT components of different technologies. This is achieved while utilizing and accessing DT and IoT actualization. Finally, the integration of blockchain-based systems with old legacy infrastructure can be challenging due to differences in networks, technology, data formats, and communication protocols (Salah et al., 2019). However, blockchain could support new and legacy systems working within a secure framework standardized between the two, providing a trusted framework for interaction between old and new systems. In addition, blockchain can facilitate connections to legacy systems via SCs, APIs, and adapters that link old systems to the blockchain, resulting in secure data transfer and enhanced security and transparency.

6.4 Use cases and application scenarios

The integration of blockchain into DT systems offers significant advantages across various sectors by enhancing transparency, security, and real-time data processing. The following use cases demonstrate the practical relevance and utility of blockchain-enabled DT systems in diverse domains, including smart manufacturing, healthcare, smart cities, and aerospace and defense. These applications show how blockchain can improve operational efficiency, optimize decision-making, and ensure secure data handling in real-world scenarios.

6.4.1 Smart manufacturing

Smart manufacturing employs DTs to monitor a product's lifecycle from design to production, usage, and, ultimately, when the product reaches the end-of its life. DTs of products represent physical attributes and operational conditions of items to gain real-time insights about performance and maintenance needs. Blockchain can take things to the next level by providing a secure, immutable way to log and record each stage of the lifecycle. Blockchain allows for recording lifecycle events for each product in a decentralized, transparent ledger; all stakeholders will have access to a verifiable record of the product's information. Blockchain provides ways for stakeholders to trace the product during product recalls or in the name of quality assurance. The data generated throughout the lifecycle can be tamper-proof, help ensure compliance with regulatory standards, and maintain stakeholder confidence. By using DT systems that are Blockchain-enabled, supply chain management can be ushered into the 21st century with fully visible, transparent, multisector supply chain orchestration capabilities. Implementing DTs with Blockchain enables the real-time verification and recording of all transactions and movements in the supply chain. DTs will provide stochastic situation assessments, and the application of Blockchain will give visibility and verifiability. This will allow stakeholders to verify product authenticity, reduce fraud, and comply with ethical sourcing and environmental standards. Blockchain provides a significant advantage for industries like pharmaceuticals that utilize digital DTs, as it can provide secure provenance records. The capability for real-time analysis of data can be critical in detecting any disruptions in the supply chain, or even a slight inefficiency, and provide swift actions to intervene before further downstream impact occurs. The potential for automating supply chain processes using SCs is substantial with DT models working in conjunction with Blockchain's decentralized ledger. SCs can automatically release payment to suppliers as soon as goods are delivered or arrive at their location. This can reduce administrative costs and disputes while also speeding up the supply chain cycle.

6.4.2 Healthcare systems

DTs in healthcare represent real-time data variations of the physical body of a patient based on data derived from IoT applications like wearables, medical sensors, and medical imaging systems. This data can be used to enable medical professionals to engage in continuous monitoring and diagnosis and optimize treatment for patients. Blockchain technology enhances the privacy, integrity, and security of patient data and enables easy access and sharing among various healthcare providers. A DT of a patient, established in a namespace on the blockchain, creates a comprehensive health record that is immutable, where only authorized healthcare entities are able to view it. For each interaction with the healthcare system, such as a medical consultation, diagnosis, medical treatment, or prescribed medication for an ailment, the system creates a reference in the blockchain, generating information and evidence that helps mitigate the risks of error, duplication, and miscommunication. Blockchain itself provides transparency and traceability of operations in compliance with systems like HIPAA in the United States and the General Data Protection Regulation (GDPR) in Europe, which protect patient data. Patients will also have firm control over their health data in a blockchain system, being able to determine who has access to their records and their associated reliability, along with any conditions. Furthermore, in the event of trauma, instantaneous access to a patient's latest, reliable health record can be provided, allowing for more efficient and quality care. Blockchain also facilitates telemedicine use, enabling patients to seek remote consultation and care from medical professionals, providing convenient access to health services through secure methods that protect data security and private information.

6.4.3 Smart cities

More smart cities are using DTs to collect, monitor, and manage critical infrastructure like transportation systems, utilities, and public services. Blockchain technology can improve the security, scalability, and transparency of DT deployments in various regions. By tracking and managing data from sensors along with DTs through blockchain, management systems can keep data secure, verifiable, and transparent. For example, if a region had a DT for every neighborhood or transportation asset, it could monitor real-time traffic flow, predict when traffic might come to a standstill, and assist with urban planning. Moreover, they can ensure that data, especially critical data, cannot be tampered with or manipulated by unauthorized individuals. In smart energy grids, they can enable peer-to-peer energy trading, allowing consumers to sell excess energy to others in their community. Blockchain technology could monitor the transactions made between participants, while DTs can monitor energy usage and predict future demand—identifying where the need arises and what developments will occur in the sector over time. Energy grid management can be enhanced through a combination of blockchain technology and DT technology, enabling accurate monitoring of energy generation, distribution, and consumer consumption in real-time. With blockchain, energy consumption data from smart meters can be stored on a decentralized ledger that cannot be tampered with, providing a reliable source of information trusted by utilities and consumers alike. SCs can also support automated energy transactions, such as changes in electricity tariffs based on current energy consumption, toggling the backup energy supply, and implementing emergency response controls during peak demand. All of this can happen through simulation and be immutably and transparently recorded using blockchain technology, ensuring that both energy providers and consumers have greater certainty to inform their decision-making.

6.4.4 Aerospace and defense

DTs in aerospace and defense help to model the health and performance of aircraft and military equipment. This allows engineers to predict potential failures and optimize maintenance schedules. Blockchain can enhance DTs by securing the records of maintenance and allowing trusted data sharing between manufacturers, service providers, and regulatory bodies. Integrating blockchain with DTs can record all of a system's maintenance activities, including inspections, repairs, or component replacements, on a secure and trusted ledger, verifying compliance with maintenance standards or regulations. SCs could be used to schedule maintenance activities to ensure optimal service of equipment, avoiding failures or costly downtime. Blockchain added to DTs can measure and verify the performance of aerospace and defense systems. Sensor readings could be validated with blockchain to confirm the system meets specifications and operational standards. For example, once an aircraft completes a flying mission, its fuel consumption and engine status data could be recorded on a blockchain and used to create a transparent record for the manufacturer and the governing body.

6.5 Conceptual framework for blockchain-enabled DT systems

A DT Framework on blockchain can be viewed as a multilayered system, in which every layer performs a certain function contributing to the preservation of integrity, security, and performance of the system. The major components of the conceptual system include the DT model layer, blockchain layer, data storage and retrieval layer, integration and communication layer, and decision-making and analytics layer. These components have all been explained in detail. The DT Model Layer is the layer that creates the digital representations of real-world elements, actions, or structures (physical machines, assets, or even whole infrastructures). The DT Model is constantly updated with real-world data from physical, embedded sensors, providing a real-time depiction of the physical asset's current state, and it represents the functionality that the physical entity is modeled to perform. IoT devices will be embedded in the physical assets and are able to download data on temperature, pressure, humidity, etc., which will then be integrated into the DT for Intelligence Analysis and Decision Making. Blockchain technology provides an immutable ledger and can be used to document any changes made to the DT and confirm the integrity of the data used to model simulations and predictions.

Next, the blockchain layer constitutes the basic layer that enables the common functionality of the system and records and verifies transactions in a decentralized, transparent way. Blockchain also provides confidence that all data, from physical components to that data's transactions, are stored securely and cannot be changed. SCs can also be established on blockchain DLT platforms such as Ethereum or Hyperledger. The main advantage of SCs is that they are capable of autonomously and programmatically automating a process or process cycle (e.g., data verification, decision, execution of an action) in all aspects of an IoT-based workspace. An important use of SCs is for automating maintenance cycles, verification/compliance functions, or executing predefined responses to real-time streaming data from sensors. As the foundational layer, the blockchain provides trust for every stakeholder within the system to share information transparently and verify the data provenance and history of all transaction events. The data storage layer could enable effective management of the vast quantities of data generated by IoT sensors and DTs. This layer could utilize the Interplanetary File System (IPFS) to take advantage of decentralized storage, a secure and distributed way of storing long-term data for other types of datasets. On-chain storage on the blockchain may be used in a manner consistent with the use of DLT to record critical transaction data (e.g., maintenance history, system updates, sensor data), while off-chain storage in IPFS could be reserved for large datasets (e.g., video footage, complex simulations) that would not be suitable to store directly on the blocks created by the blockchain. This hybrid technology solution provides scalability and reduced cost while ensuring the integrity and availability of critical data.

The integration layer ensures the compatibility of the blockchain-enabled DT system, allowing it to properly communicate with the physical world and other systems. Real-time communication protocols, such as MQTT and CoAP, are used to transfer data from IoT devices to the DTs, integrating with them and each other in real-time. This layer provides communication with the blockchain to merge the physical world with the DT ecosystem and other external systems or legacy platforms through the use of APIs or middleware solutions. These integrations provide the DT system with the ability to communicate with multiple devices, software, and databases. Fig. 6.5 illustrates the proposed framework.

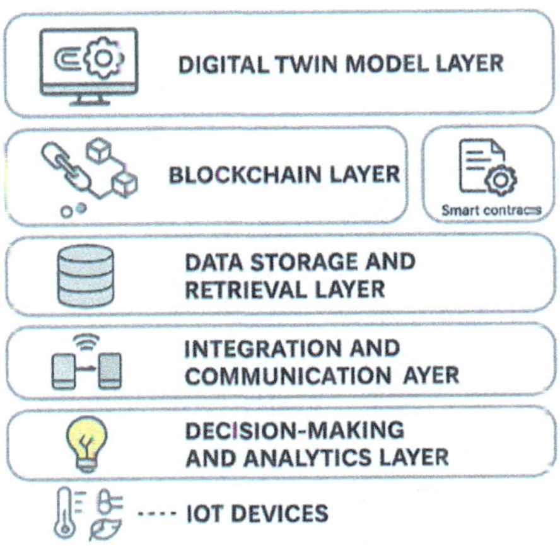

Fig. 6.5 Proposed conceptual integrated framework.

6.6 Evaluation of the using multiple case studies

In order to demonstrate the real-world effectiveness of the proposed blockchain-integrated DT system, various case studies and their implications have been considered to measure the effectiveness.

6.6.1 Case study 1: Smart manufacturing—assembly line optimization

A manufacturer of high-precision components for the electronics sector depended on operational efficiency. The organization employed DTs in conjunction with blockchain to increase efficiency in a robotic assembly line. Each component, including robots, sensors, and conveyor belts, was mapped to DTs that provided real-time data on temperature, vibrations, alignment, and speed. A permissioned blockchain (hyperledger fabric) was used to preserve a system-wide record of immutable system logs, events, and maintenance processes. SCs were used to facilitate predictive maintenance and automatically invoke maintenance requests to the blockchain when sensor thresholds exceeded the specified limits. The overall architecture could process over 15,000 events each day while maintaining a latency of 5 seconds from the presentation of an event to an action by a proposed DT or contract. As a result, ordinary machine downtime due to failure was reduced by approximately 20%. Furthermore, transparent operations with immutable audit trails increased efficiency in preventive maintenance by 25%. The measured improvements delivered not only a more reliable and consistent operation but also reduced the burden and costs of manual inspections, as well as unplanned and unanticipated downtimes.

6.6.2 Case study 2: Healthcare—secure patient DTs

A large hospital in an urban area faced the challenges of monitoring intensive care unit (ICU) patients while adhering to strict data privacy restrictions. With the goal of improving monitoring and reducing the information overload and stress common in ICU environments, DTs were designed to replicate the patient's physiological state and merge it with real-world data from medical IoT devices such as heart monitors, ventilators, and IV pumps. The real-time data was transmitted to Ethereum-based SCs. The patient data was hashed and encrypted with zk-SNARKs to ensure confidentiality, while only metadata and access logs were pushed to the blockchain. The SCs also included the consent of various specialists, external laboratories, and even insurance companies to share data. The latency for real-time alerts from the encrypted data to the SCs creating alerts was less than three seconds. During the six-month pilot, there were no data breaches, and it was observed that decisions were made 19% faster due to the security and availability of constant data recording. The relationship with standards for HIPAA compliance was strengthened as the blockchain technology provided an audit record based on accessibility, which could be relied upon to enhance trust in the patient data.

6.6.3 Case study 3: Smart cities—urban water infrastructure monitoring

In order to oversee its extensive urban water supply, a municipal government has incorporated blockchain-supported DTs into its pipeline inspection system. Sensors placed at strategic points provided data on pressure, flow rate, and chemical makeup, which were fed into the DTs. A Quorum blockchain network was used to register all flow anomalies and maintenance actions. SCs were coded to automatically dispatch maintenance crews if a threshold for leaks or contamination was met. The platform's integration with GIS allowed for precise mapping of each occurrence. The platform monitored 1000 + segments of the system and thereby allowed for almost instantaneous alerts and actions when measured. Leakage losses as a result of leaks were reduced by 28%, and incident response time was cut by 30%. Public trust was established through the immutable record of events, and maintenance histories were easily accessed to comply with regulatory requirements.

6.6.4 Case study 4: Aerospace and defense—aircraft component validation

A digital maintenance operation used DTs for managing the lifecycle and validation of aircraft engine components. These twins received data from telemetry sensors on flights and simulated flights. Blockchain (Corda) stored usage logs, environmental conditions, and compiled reports. SCs verified the components used against flight hours and environmental stress or abuse to inform users when to inspect or replace a part. The framework allowed for multiple stakeholders, such as original equipment manufacturers (OEMs), airlines, and regulators, to be involved. The blockchain eliminated paperwork and helped validate compliance 40% faster. Engine down time was reduced by 15% due to better prediction of part failures. The audit process was fast and tamper-proof, making regulatory approvals faster and more reliable.

6.6.5 Case study 5: Agriculture—crop supply chain transparency

A cooperative for organic crops implemented a blockchain-enabled DT process to authenticate end-to-end traceability. Environmental sensors measured soil quality, pesticide usage, and environmental effects, and this data provided updates to crop-specific

Table 6.2 Summary of Implications of the Proposed Framework Across various Case Studies.

Case Study	Blockchain Platform	Use Case Focus	Smart Contract Role	Key Benefits	Measured Improvements
Smart manufacturing	Hyperledger Fabric	Continuous oversight of automations, such as robots and conveyor systems, is essential	Request predictive maintenance based on sensor thresholds	Decreased downtime, streamlined maintenance, and immutable logging	20% less downtime, 25% better preventive maintenance efficiency, latency ~ 5 seconds
Healthcare	Ethereum + zk-SNARKs	Encrypted patient data twin for integrated real-time health status	Automate alerts and enforce patient data access based on consent	Privacy-preserving real-time alerts, HIPAA-aligned audit trail	0 breaches, 19% faster decisions, latency < 3 s
Smart cities	Quorum	Leak detection, contamination monitoring	Dispatch maintenance teams based on detected anomalies	Enhanced responsiveness, regulatory compliance, and public trust	28% leak reduction, 30% faster response time
Aerospace & defense	Corda	Basic lifecycle monitoring and validation of engine parts	Automate inspections based on flight logs and stress factors	Faster audits, reduced paperwork, proactive replacement	40% faster compliance checks, 15% reduction in engine downtime
Agriculture	Hyperledger Sawtooth	Farm-to-fork traceability of crops	Verify organic compliance and enable product lifecycle access via QR	Trust-building, faster export certification	40% less certification time and improved consumer transparency

DTs. Harvest documentation, transport details, and packaging records were stored in Hyperledger Sawtooth. SCs evaluated whether all organic growing requirements were fulfilled, and Quick Response (QR) codes allowed consumers full access to every stage of the product's lifecycle. The process was monitored in real-time across 50 + farms, with no downtimes in the system. Certification time for exports was reduced by 40%, and consumer trust surged with growing transparency. Retailers chose the cooperative due to its verifiable blockchain records, which proved to consumers the safety and provenance of the products. Table 6.2 provides a detailed summary of the practical implications of the proposed integrated framework.

6.7 Challenges and mitigation strategies

The incorporation of blockchain technology into DT systems offers a number of benefits, including improved data integrity, transparency, and traceability. However, there are significant challenges to overcome in achieving an effective integration of blockchain into DT systems. These challenges include data integrity and privacy issues, scalability, interoperability of blockchain systems, and issues related to SCs.

6.7.1 Data integrity and privacy

The integration of blockchain into DT ecosystems is incredibly important for data integrity and privacy, especially in industries regulated by national mandates, such as healthcare. Data integrity is paramount to ensuring the DT's virtualized model is effective for decision-making. If data is identified as inaccurate, blockchain's immutability and transparency could then magnify the consequences of such inaccuracies. In highly sensitive industries, such as manufacturing or healthcare sectors, inaccurate sensor readings could lead to poor decision-making (e.g., decisions that could be harmful to certain individuals). With that said, data integrity feeds into privacy. Data that may be immutable and visible to all participants in the network raises concerns regarding privacy in regulated industries that maintain legal privacy obligations. The GDPR, for example, provides individuals the right to erase their data, yet there is a conflict with blockchain's immutability. There are numerous methods to mitigate data integrity and privacy risks in a blockchain setting. These include the use of data validation mechanisms, ZKPs, permissioned blockchains, and off-chain data storage. Firstly, in a data validation mechanism, IoT sensors are capable of running checks on themselves prior to posting their data to a chain or attaching it to the DT model. An IoT sensor may identify outliers or incorrect readings and flag this data to a human for review prior to transfer to the chain. ZKPs enable verification of data without revealing the actual data, balancing privacy and trust with data integrity. Permissioned blockchains restrict access to data on the blockchain, ensuring that only participants who are authorized can view or change it. Off-chain storage of data stores sensitive data off-chain and retains only the necessary metadata or a hash value on-chain, allowing for privacy while still using blockchains for data integrity and traceability.

6.7.2 System scalability

DT systems that have been integrated with blockchain face additional challenges to their scalability due to the tremendous amount of data transferred from IoT devices. These systems must be able to constantly process the data with speed and ease. However, in large-scale implementations, blockchain hinders scalability due to transaction throughput limitations and the time required for consensus mechanisms. The criticality of transaction throughput is vital since delays in transaction completion lead to system performance degradation, especially when there are delays in updating the system in real-time or near real-time. Network congestion can result in excessive transaction costs and insufficient or delayed processing time at substantially higher frequencies. low latency applications, such as healthcare monitoring and smart cities, are often impacted by this. Layer 2 solutions may help overcome scalability issues and bottlenecks that can occur. Layer 2 solutions, like sidechains or state channels, allow participants to transact off-chain and eventually settle back to the main-chain. This is useful because it not only alleviates congestion during transactions but also expedites transaction completion, as the underlying chains are separate. The system can also utilize sharding, which involves delegating pieces of a blockchain into smaller, manageable segments that can process transactions without delays in a more scalable way at high speeds while maintaining decentralization. Using consensus mechanisms such as Proof of Authority or Practical Byzantine Fault Tolerance can significantly reduce transaction validation durations compared to Proof of Work-based systems.

6.7.3 Interoperability

Interoperability presents a critical challenge for integrating blockchain with existing systems, particularly across heterogeneous and legacy technology environments. IoT devices, platforms, and applications are also heterogeneous and usually operate using different protocols, data formats, or communication standards. Blockchain, as a technology, is new compared to existing legacy systems, and it will be difficult to integrate with legacy systems without modifying those systems or using additional middleware. It may be difficult for legacy systems, which are usually centralized, to operate in a decentralized environment such as a blockchain. Also, typically, nonstandardized IoT devices will operate using nonstandardized protocols for the purpose of transmitting data, which makes integrating them into a blockchain-based DT system more complex. In addition to the challenge of IoT devices, the heterogeneity of IoT standards across industries makes communicating between different devices and systems difficult and interoperability challenging. Interoperability challenges can be mitigated through the standardization of IoT protocols, the use of middleware solutions, and blockchain gateways as intermediaries between an IoT device and a blockchain. These intermediaries can ensure that data is transmitted securely and correctly formatted, and all of these solutions should improve interoperability.

6.7.4 Smart contract risks

SC are simply programs that self-execute on the blockchain and automatically enforce rules and conditions for their operation. They can increase the automation and efficiency of systems integrating DT technology with blockchain but also raise concerns related to bugs, vulnerabilities, and exploits. One of the concerns specific to SCs is the fact that transactions on a blockchain are decentralized and cannot usually be modified or reverted. This means that organizations deploying SCs must ensure the code is thoroughly reviewed and error-free before deployment. There are already several SCs deployed with bugs and vulnerabilities that can be exploited by adversarial actors, compromising the system. Blockchain-enabled SCs are heavily reliant on sound logic being written into the SC, which means that unintended actions can occur, especially in systems dealing with critical operating conditions, such as in a healthcare facility. Strategies for mitigating the risks associated with SCs include formal verification using tools such as Solidity Static Analysis, Ada, Myco, and, more recently, bug bounty programs; regular third-party oversight audits by security firms; and upgradable contracts. These strategies aim to mitigate risks associated with SCs and support the efficiency and security requirements of the blockchain network.

6.7.5 Mitigation strategies

To effectively combat the issues of blockchain integration into DT ecosystems, there are multiple approaches to improve performance, security, and scalability, which consist of permissioned blockchains, ZKP, and hybrid storage, respectively. The use of permissioned blockchains will enhance data privacy, protection, and scalability to good effect. Since participants in permissioned networks will be preapproved, it reduces the possibility of having malicious participants in the network. Permissioned blockchains can provide better transaction throughput and an improved consensus mechanism (Nair and Tyagi, 2024; Tyagi 2023, 2025), which can alleviate some scalability problems. ZKPs can improve data security while still maintaining the integrity of the data being recorded on the blockchain. This could enable privacy-sensitive industries, such as healthcare, to leverage blockchain technology without violating their data protection policies. A mix of on-chain and off-chain storage can help improve performance. For example, critical metadata and transaction hashes could be stored on-chain while storing other large data sets, such as sensor logs or high-resolution images, off-chain. This will reduce the bloat of the blockchain and transaction fees for using the blockchain, providing improved and better scalability.

Table 6.3 summarizes the challenges and their corresponding mitigation strategies toward implementing an integrated framework.

Table 6.3 Summary of challenges and mitigation strategies for integrating blockchain into digital twin systems.

Challenge	Description	Mitigation Strategies
Data Integrity and Privacy	It is vital to substantiate the accuracy of data being entered into the blockchain, particularly in regulated industries such as healthcare, due to the permanent immutability of inaccurate data, while also understanding that blockchain's transparency may conflict with privacy regulations such as the GDPR.	**Data Verification Methods:** Data Validation—assurance from additional IoT sensor prechecks to avoid any erroneous readings, **ZKPs:** allows verification of the validity of data without revealing the data, **Permissioned blockchains**: limiting access to data visibility and updating rights only to relevant parties, **Off-Chain Storage:** data is stored off the chain, but metadata/hashes are on the chain.
System Scalability	High volumes of IoT data will cause a number of performance problems, since blockchain has low throughput and typically features high latency, which makes real-time operational applications difficult, such as continuous health monitoring or the utilization of smart cities.	**Layer 2 solutions:** Leverage sidechains/state channels to address high-volume transactions off-chain. **Sharding:** Disaggregate the blockchain into smaller pieces to allow for concurrent processing. **Efficient consensus:** Implement an alternative to Proof of Work that will significantly improve the validation duration (e.g., use Proof of Authority or PBFT).
Interoperability	The integration of distributed ledger technologies (DLT) and blockchain with a variety of heterogeneous IoT devices or legacy systems is not easy because they operate using different protocols, data formats, and architectures.	**Standardized protocols:** Help synthesize uniformity in communicating IoT instrumentation. **Middleware:** Commonly referred to as a "bridge" that enables communication and information exchange between systems not designed to share data. **Blockchain gateways:** can provide a level of translation and security between an IoT device's data transport and the blockchain in a manner that permits access control and security.
Smart Contract Risks	The care and caution taken with smart contract coding should not be underestimated, as vulnerable smart contract code may pose a risk of irreversible losses resulting from unintended operations or applications, especially in highly regulated sectors such as healthcare and defense.	**Formal verification:** employ tools for ensuring the correctness of your code (e.g., using Solidity analyzers). **Third-party audits:** invite cybersecurity experts to assess and audit your system. **Bug bounty programs:** offer rewards/incentives for discovering vulnerabilities. **Upgradable contracts:** allow for deploying patches to deployed contracts using a proxy/module framework.
General Mitigation Approaches	General strategies for improving the ability to integrate DLTs and blockchain technologies within the dimensions of scalability, privacy, and performance.	**Permissioned blockchains:** you have clear access control built into the design, increasing throughput. **Use of zero-knowledge proofs:** Supports privacy while ensuring the validity of data integrity. **Hybrid storage (On/Off-chain):** This is a trade-off. Storing less exhaustive full datasets on-chain could be limited to the key materials, while the off-chain capabilities will use the peer-to-peer model to share data, allowing for large, abundant, and immensely pervasive datasets to be represented on-chain.

6.8 Conclusion

Incorporating blockchain technology into DT networks is revolutionary in developing safe, transparent, and reliable cyber-physical infrastructures. This research has clearly examined how blockchain can solve pressing problems in existing DT systems, including data integrity, data traceability, privacy, and trust. Blockchain uses decentralized consensus, immutability, and SCs to allow DTs to function autonomously and verifiably in complex multistakeholder environments. Through various detailed case studies—including manufacturing, healthcare, smart cities, aerospace, and agriculture—it is evident that the operational efficiency, decision-making responsiveness, regulatory compliance, and transparency of the system are improved. However, while blockchain-enabled DT systems show significant potential, there are still various technical limitations, including the scalability of blockchain networks, interoperability across heterogeneous IoT and legacy systems, and the vulnerability of SCs due to flaws in coding. The research recommends the following options to overcome these limitations: permissioned blockchains, ZKPs, hybrid on-chain/off-chain data storage, and formal verification for SCs. Overall, this research establishes a conceptual and architectural platform for the implementation of real-world blockchain-enabled DT systems. The proposed framework offers a basis for the development of resilient, data-driven ecosystems that support autonomous operations, build trust, and provide secure operations at scale, as industries advance toward more complex and connected systems.

References

A.K. Tyagi., 2025. Blockchain for smart hospital in Healthcare 5.0: Modeling structure, challenges, and future emerging trends. In: Human-Centric Integration of Next-Generation Data Science and Blockchain Technology. Elsevier, pp. 431–444. doi:10.1016/B978-0-443-33498-6.00026-1.

Adu-Amankwa, N.A.N., Rahimian, F.P., Dawood, N., Park, C., 2023. Digital twins and blockchain technologies for building lifecycle management. Autom. Constr. 09265805. 155. Available from: https://www.journals.elsevier.com/automation-in-construction. doi:10.1016/j.autcon.2023.105064.

Boschert, S., Rosen, R., 2016. Digital Twin-the Simulation Aspect Mechatronic Futures: Challenges and Solutions for Mechatronic Systems and Their Designers. Springer International Publishing, Germany, pp. 59–74. Available from http://dx.doi.org/10.1007/978-3-319-32156-1. doi:10.1007/978-3-319-32156-1_5.

Diamantopoulos, G., Tziritas, N., Bahsoon, R., Theodoropoulos, G., 2024. Dynamic Data-Driven Digital Twins for Blockchain Systems. In: Lecture Notes in Computer Science (Including Subseries Lecture Notes in Artificial Intelligence and Lecture Notes in Bioinformatics), Vol. 13984. Springer Science and Business Media Deutschland GmbH, United Kingdom, 283–292. 16113349. https://www.springer.com/series/558. doi:10.1007/978-3-031-52670-1_28.

Fernandez-Carames, T.M., Fraga-Lamas, P., 2018. A review on the use of blockchain for the internet of things. IEEE Access. 2169-3536. 6, 32979–33001. doi:10.1109/access.2018.2842685.

Fuller, A., Fan, Z., Day, C., Barlow, C., 2020. Digital twin: enabling technologies, challenges and open research. IEEE Access. 21693536. 8, 108952–108971. Available from: http://ieeexplore.ieee.org/xpl/RecentIssue.jsp?punumber=6287639. doi:10.1109/ACCESS.2020.2998358.

Gehrmann, C., Gunnarsson, M., 2020. A digital twin based industrial automation and control system security architecture. IEEE Computer Society, Sweden IEEE Transactions on Industrial Informatics. 19410050. 16

(1), 669–680. Available from: http://ieeexplore.ieee.org/xpl/RecentIssue.jsp?punumber=9424. doi:10.1109/TII.2019.2938885.

Gehrmann, C., Gunnarsson, M., 2020. A Digital Twin Based Industrial Automation and Control System Security Architecture. IEEE Transactions on Industrial Informatics 16 (1), 669–680. doi:10.1109/TII.2019.2938885.

Grieves, M., Vickers, J., 2016. Digital Twin: Mitigating Unpredictable, Undesirable Emergent Behavior in Complex Systems. Springer Science and Business Media LLC, pp. 85–113. doi:10.1007/978-3-319-38756-7_4.

Jones, D., Snider, C., Nassehi, A., Yon, J., Hicks, B., 2020. Characterising the digital twin: a systematic literature review. CIRP J. Manuf. Sci. Technol. 17555817. 29, 36–52. Available from: http://www.elsevier.com/wps/find/journaldescription.cws_home/714185/description#description. doi:10.1016/j.cirpj.2020.02.002.

Khan, I., Majib, Y., Ullah, R., Rana, O., 2024. Blockchain applications for internet of things — a survey. Internet Things. 25426605. 27 (101254). doi:10.1016/j.iot.2024.101254.

Li, S., Xu, L.D., Zhao, S., 2018. 5G Internet of things: a survey. J. Ind. Inf. Integr. 2452414X. 10, 1–9. Available from: http://www.journals.elsevier.com/journal-of-industrial-information-integration. doi:10.1016/j.jii.2018.01.005.

Li, Y., Su, D.A., Mardani, A., 2023. Digital twins and blockchain technology in the industrial Internet of Things (IIoT) using an extended decision support system model: industry 4.0 barriers perspective. Technol. Forecast. Soc. Change. 00401625. 195. Available from: https://www.journals.elsevier.com/technological-forecasting-and-social-change. doi:10.1016/j.techfore.2023.122794.

Liu, J., Zhou, H., Liu, X., Tian, G., Wu, M., Cao, L., Wang, W., 2019. Dynamic evaluation method of machining process planning based on digital twin. IEEE Access. 21693536. 7, 19312–19323. Available from: http://ieeexplore.ieee.org/xpl/RecentIssue.jsp?punumber=6287639. doi:10.1109/ACCESS.2019.2893309.

Lo, C.K., Chen, C.H., Zhong, R.Y., 2021. A review of digital twin in product design and development. Adv. Eng. Inform. 14740346. 48 (101297). doi:10.1016/j.aei.2021.101297.

Ma, X., Du, W., Li, L., Liu, J., Yuan, H., 2024. Examining the nexus of blockchain technology and digital twins: bibliometric evidence and research trends. Higher Education Press Limited Company. China Front. Eng. Manag. 20960255. 11 (3), 481–500. Available from: https://www.springer.com/journal/42524. doi:10.1007/s42524-024-0306-4.

Mettler, M., 2016. Blockchain technology in healthcare: the revolution starts here. 2016 IEEE 18th International Conference on e-Health Networking, Applications and Services, Healthcom 10.1109/HealthCom.2016.7749510 9781509033706 Institute of Electrical and Electronics Engineers Inc. Switzerland

Nair M.M., A.K. Tyagi., 2024. Blockchain technology for next-generation society: Current trends and future opportunities for smart era. In: Blockchain Technology for Secure Social Media Computing. IET, pp. 215–236. doi:10.1049/PBSE019E_ch11.

Nakamoto, S., n.d. Bitcoin: a Peer-to-Peer electronic cash system.

Negri, E., Fumagalli, L., Macchi, M., 2017. A review of the roles of digital twin in CPS-based production systems. Elsevier B.V., Italy Procedia Manufacturing. 23519789. 11, 939–948. Available from: http://www.journals.elsevier.com/procedia-manufacturing. doi:10.1016/j.promfg.2017.07.198.

Nielsen, C.P., Da Silva, E.R., Yu, F., 2020. Digital twins and blockchain - Proof of concept. Procedia CIRP. 22128271, 93, 251–255. doi:10.1016/j.procir.2020.04.104. http://www.sciencedirect.com/science/journal/22128271

Padmapriya, N., Kumar, T.A., Rajmohan, R., Pavithra, M., Kanimozhi, P., 2022. Secure Vehicular Communication Using Blockchain Technology EAI/Springer Innovations in Communication and Computing. Springer Science and Business Media Deutschland GmbH, India, pp. 141–162. Available from https://springer.com/series/15427. doi:10.1007/978-3-030-77637-4_8.

Raj, P., 2021. Empowering digital twins with blockchain. Adv. Comput. 121, 267–283. Available from http://www.elsevier.com/wps/find/bookdescription.cws_home/705045/description#description. doi:10.1016/bs.adcom.2020.08.013.

Sadri, H., Yitmen, I., Tagliabue, L.C., Westphal, F., Tezel, A., Taheri, A., Sibenik, G., 2023. Integration of blockchain and digital twins in the smart built environment adopting disruptive technologies—a systematic review. Sustainability. 2071-1050. 15 (4), 3713. doi:10.3390/su15043713.

Salah, K., Rehman, M.H.U., Nizamuddin, N., Al-Fuqaha, A., 2019. Blockchain for AI: review and open research challenges. IEEE Access. 21693536. 7, 10127–10149. Available from: http://ieeexplore.ieee.org/xpl/RecentIssue.jsp?punumber=6287639. doi:10.1109/ACCESS.2018.2890507.

Semeraro, C., Lezoche, M., Panetto, H., Dassisti, M., 2021. Digital twin paradigm: a systematic literature review. Comput. Ind. 01663615. 130, 103469. doi:10.1016/j.compind.2021.103469.

Tao, F., Cheng, J., Qi, Q., Zhang, M., Zhang, H., Sui, F., 2018. Digital twin-driven product design, manufacturing and service with big data. Int. J. Adv. Manuf. Technol. 14333015. 94 (9-12), 3563–3576. Available from: http://www.springerlink.com/content/0268-3768. doi:10.1007/s00170-017-0233-1.

TAO, F., SUN, X., CHENG, J., ZHU, Y., LIU, W., WANG, Y., XU, H., HU, T., LIU, X., LIU, T., SUN, Z., XU, J., BAO, J., XIANG, F., JIN, X., 2024. makeTwin: a reference architecture for digital twin software platform. Chin. J. Aeronaut. 10009361. 37 (1), 1–18. Available from: https://www.sciencedirect.com/science/journal/10009361. doi:10.1016/j.cja.2023.05.002.

Tao, F., Zhang, H., Liu, A., Nee, A.Y.C., 2019. Digital twin in industry: state-of-the-Art. IEEE Trans. Ind. Inform. 15513203. 15 (4), 2405–2415. Available from: http://ieeexplore.ieee.org/xpl/RecentIssue.jsp?punumber=9424. doi:10.1109/TII.2018.2873186.

Tyagi A.K., 2023. Decentralized everything: A practical use of blockchain technology in future applications. In: Distributed Computing to Blockchain: Architecture, Technology, and Applications. Elsevier, pp. 19–38 doi:10.1016/B978-0-323-96146-2.00010-3.

Tyagi, A.K., 2025. Blockchain technology: values, challenges, and possible applications from an industry perspective. In Human-Centric Integration of Next-Generation Data Science and Blockchain Technology. Elsevier, pp. 445–460. doi:10.1016/B978-0-443-33498-6.00027-3.

Underwood, S., 2016. Blockchain beyond bitcoin. Commun. ACM. 0001-0782. 59 (11), 15–17. doi:10.1145/2994581.

Wang, Y., Su, Z., Guo, S., Dai, M., Luan, T.H., Liu, Y., 2023. A survey on digital twins: architecture, enabling technologies, security and privacy, and future prospects. IEEE Internet Things J. 23274662. 10 (17), 14965–14987. Available from: http://ieeexplore.ieee.org/servlet/opac?punumber=6488907. doi:10.1109/JIOT.2023.3263909.

Xie, J., Tang, H., Huang, T., Yu, F.R., Xie, R., Liu, J., Liu, Y., 2019. A survey of blockchain technology applied to smart cities: research issues and challenges. IEEE Commun. Surv. Tutor. 1553877X. 21 (3), 2794–2830. Available from: http://ieeexplore.ieee.org/xpl/RecentIssue.jsp?punumber=9739. doi:10.1109/COMST.2019.2899617.

Yao, J.F., Yang, Y., Wang, X.C., Zhang, X.P., 2023. Systematic review of digital twin technology and applications. Visual Computing for Industry, Biomedicine, and Art. 25244442. 6 (1). Available from: https://www.springer.com/journal/42492. doi:10.1186/s42492-023-00137-4.

Yaqoob, I., Salah, K., Uddin, M., Jayaraman, R., Omar, M., Imran, M., 2020. Blockchain for digital twins: recent advances and future research challenges. IEEE Netw. 1558156X. 34 (5) 290–298. Available from: https://ieeexplore.ieee.org/xpl/mostRecentIssue.jsp?punumber=65. doi:10.1109/MNET.001.1900661.

Zheng, Z., Xie, S., Dai, H., Chen, X., Wang, H., 2017. Proceedings - An Overview of Blockchain Technology: Architecture, Consensus, and Future Trends. 2017 IEEE 6th International Congress on Big Data (BigData Congress), Institute of Electrical and Electronics Engineers Inc., 2017, 557–564. doi: 10.1109/BigDataCongress.2017.85. ISBN: 9781509033706.

CHAPTER 7

Blockchain for collaborative artificial intelligence/machine learning in digital twin computing

T. Megala[a], Shabnam Kumari[b], and Khushboo Tripathi[c]

[a]*Department of Computing Technologies, SRM Institute of Science and Technology, Kattankulathur, Chennai, Tamil Nadu, India*

[b]*Department of Computer Science, Faculty of Science and Humanities, SRM Institute of Science and Technology, Kattankulathur, Chennai, Tamil Nadu, India*

[c]*Department of Computer Applications, Sharda University, India*

7.1 Introduction to digital twin computing

Digital twin (DT) computing is a revolutionary concept that bridges the physical and digital worlds, enabling real-time simulation, monitoring, and optimization of physical systems through their virtual counterparts. A DT is essentially a dynamic, data-driven model that replicates the behavior and state of a real-world asset, system, or process. It continuously receives data from sensors, Internet of Things (IoT) devices and operational systems to reflect the current condition of the physical counterpart, allowing for advanced analytics, predictive maintenance, and intelligent decision-making (Tyagi, 2024a; Tyagi (2024b)).

The concept of the DT originated in aerospace and manufacturing, where engineers needed real-time models of aircraft, engines, and production systems to optimize performance and reduce downtime. Today, DTs are applied across various industries, including healthcare, smart cities, transportation, energy, agriculture, and logistics. With the rise of Industry 4.0 and now Industry 5.0, DTs have evolved beyond static simulations to intelligent, self-learning systems driven by artificial intelligence (AI), machine learning (ML), and real-time data analytics.

At the core of DT computing lies the ability to mirror physical systems through digital models that evolve and update based on a continuous data flow. This real-time synchronization allows users to simulate scenarios, detect anomalies, predict failures, and test new strategies without affecting the actual system. For example, a DT of a smart building can monitor energy consumption, occupancy, and temperature patterns to optimize energy efficiency and user comfort.

Artificial Intelligence, Machine Learning and Blockchain in Digital Twin Computing.
https://doi.org/10.1016/B978-0-443-43914-8.00015-7

The architecture of a typical DT system includes four main components: the physical asset, a digital model or replica, data communication interfaces (usually through IoT), and analytics or decision-making modules. Sensors embedded in the physical asset collect data, which is transmitted to the DT in real-time (Tyagi, 2024b). The digital model processes this data using AI/ML algorithms to provide insights, predictions, and actionable recommendations. These insights are then fed back to optimize or control the physical system, creating a continuous feedback loop.

One of the key enablers of DT computing is the advancement in connectivity technologies, such as 5G, edge computing, and cloud infrastructure, which ensure seamless data transfer and computational scalability. In addition, AI and ML enhance the analytical capabilities of DTs, making them more adaptive and capable of learning from new patterns. As a result, DTs are becoming more autonomous, context-aware, and capable of proactive decision-making.

Despite its transformative potential, DT computing also presents challenges such as high implementation costs, data privacy concerns, integration complexity, and the need for standardized frameworks. Moreover, the increasing interconnectivity of DTs with other intelligent systems requires robust cybersecurity and governance mechanisms.

In summary, DT computing represents a paradigm shift in how we model, manage, and interact with complex systems. It provides a foundation for smarter, more resilient, and efficient operations across diverse sectors. As technologies like AI, blockchain, and IoT continue to mature, the capabilities of DTs will expand, paving the way for autonomous, collaborative, and decentralized digital ecosystems aligned with the vision of Industry 5.0.

7.1.1 Overview of DT importance, and evolution in cyber-physical systems

DT technology has emerged as a foundational component in the advancement of cyber-physical systems (CPS), providing a powerful means to bridge the gap between physical entities and their digital representations. A DT is a dynamic virtual model of a physical system, process, or object that is continuously updated with real-time data through sensors and connectivity. It allows for simulation, monitoring, prediction, and optimization of real-world operations, enabling smarter, safer, and more efficient system management.

The importance of DTs lies in their ability to replicate and simulate the behavior and state of complex systems, offering deep insights into performance, faults, and future outcomes. By combining the physical and digital worlds, DTs empower decision-makers to visualize operations, predict failures, enhance efficiency, and implement changes virtually before applying them to physical systems. This predictive capability is especially important in industries like aerospace, automotive, manufacturing, healthcare, and energy, where unplanned downtime or system failures can result in significant losses.

The evolution of DT technology is closely tied to the development of CPS—systems where physical components are tightly integrated with computation, networking, and control functions. In the early stages, digital models were limited to static computer-aided design or simulation tools used in design and engineering. With the growth of the IoT and real-time data streaming, these static models evolved into intelligent, responsive systems capable of interacting with live data from sensors and actuators.

The second generation of DTs introduced real-time analytics, ML, and cloud computing to enhance the decision-making process. These digital models began learning from operational data, allowing them to adapt, predict failures, and recommend improvements autonomously (Tyagi, 2024c; Tyagi and Kumari, 2024; Tao et al., 2019). Today, modern DTs incorporate AI, blockchain, edge computing, and advanced visualization technologies to build fully integrated, context-aware CPS ecosystems.

In smart manufacturing (Industry 4.0), DTs play a critical role in monitoring factory floors, optimizing production lines, and reducing downtime (refer to Fig. 7.1). In healthcare, they enable personalized treatment planning and real-time patient monitoring. In infrastructure and urban planning, DTs support the creation of smart cities by modeling traffic flows, energy

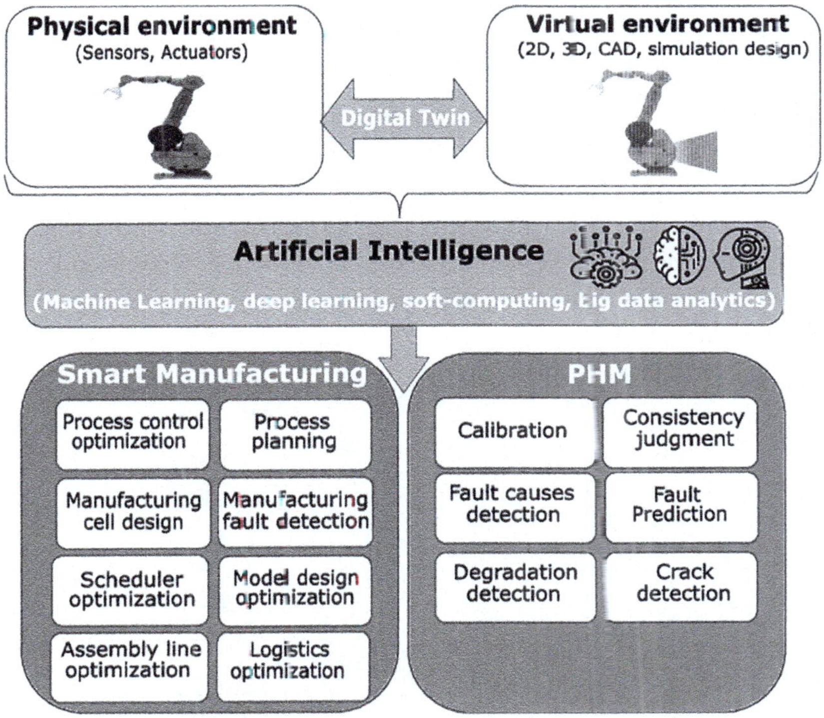

Fig. 7.1 DT-based smart manufacturing.

usage, and public safety systems. Across all these domains, DTs contribute to improved operational reliability, better resource management, cost savings, and sustainability.

As we move toward Industry 5.0, which emphasizes human-centricity, resilience, and sustainability, DTs are becoming more collaborative and autonomous. They enable not only interaction between humans and machines but also among machines themselves, driven by decentralized intelligence. Blockchain and AI technologies are being integrated with DTs to support secure, traceable, and decentralized collaboration between multiple stakeholders.

In summary, the DT is no longer just a digital representation—it is an intelligent, evolving entity central to the functioning of modern CPS. Its evolution marks a significant leap in how we design, operate, and interact with complex physical systems. As industries increasingly adopt DTs, they pave the way for transformative innovations in smart, interconnected, and autonomous systems that define the future of human-machine collaboration.

7.2 Role of AI/ML in DTs

AI and ML play a transformative role in enhancing the capabilities of DTs, enabling them to move beyond static digital replicas to intelligent, predictive, and autonomous systems (Tao et al., 2019; Boschert and Rosen, 2016). DTs, which serve as dynamic virtual models of physical assets or systems, become significantly more powerful when infused with AI/ML, as these technologies allow for real-time analysis, continuous learning, and data-driven decision-making.

One of the core functions AI/ML brings to DTs is predictive analytics (refer to Fig. 7.2). By analyzing historical and real-time sensor data, ML algorithms can identify patterns and trends that may not be visible through traditional monitoring methods. For example, in a manufacturing environment, an AI-enhanced DT of a machine can predict when parts are likely to fail, allowing for predictive maintenance that reduces downtime and prevents costly breakdowns. This shift from reactive to proactive maintenance is a major benefit of integrating ML into DT systems.

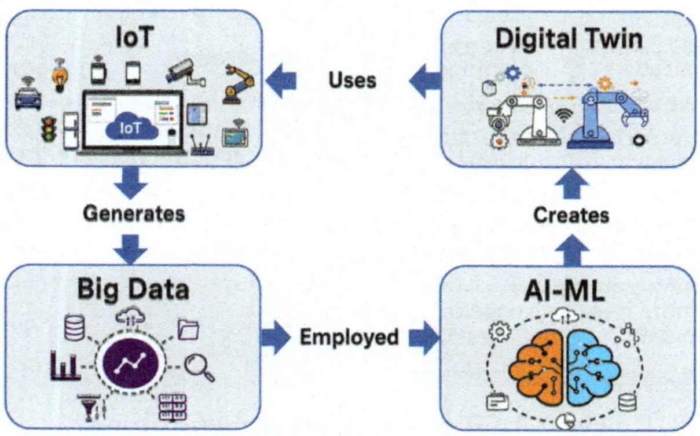

Fig. 7.2 Relationship between IoT, AI, and DT with Big Data.

Another major role of AI/ML in DTs is optimization. Whether it's optimizing energy usage in a smart building, logistics in a supply chain, or performance parameters in a wind turbine, ML models can process vast amounts of data to find the most efficient configurations and operating conditions. Reinforcement learning, a type of ML, is particularly useful for continuously optimizing dynamic systems in real time.

AI also enables anomaly detection and diagnostics in DTs. Using classification or clustering algorithms, a DT can flag abnormal behavior in machinery, processes, or environments, and even diagnose the likely root causes. This helps in early issue identification and ensures system stability and safety.

In addition, AI/ML enhances the autonomy of DTs (Madni et al., 2019). With intelligent agents and self-learning algorithms, DTs can make decisions with minimal human intervention. For example, an AI-powered DT in an autonomous vehicle system can evaluate real-time traffic and weather conditions to adjust routes or driving behavior without driver input.

Moreover, natural language processing allows DTs to interact with human users more intuitively. For example, users can query or command a DT through voice or text, receiving intelligent responses that aid in system management or decision support.

Another area where AI/ML is impactful is personalization. In healthcare, AI-integrated DTs of patients can simulate treatment responses based on individual health data, enabling doctors to tailor therapies more effectively. In customer-focused industries, personalized product or service experiences can be designed and tested through consumer-specific DTs.

As the volume and complexity of data in DT environments grow, the role of AI/ML becomes even more critical. Techniques like deep learning, neural networks, and federated learning (FL) allow DTs to continuously evolve, adapt to changing conditions, and learn from distributed data sources without compromising privacy.

In conclusion, AI and ML are essential for unlocking the full potential of DTs. They enable smarter, faster, and more accurate decision-making, leading to enhanced efficiency, reduced costs, and increased innovation across sectors. The fusion of AI/ML with DTs is not just an enhancement—it's a necessity for building the intelligent, autonomous, and adaptive systems of the future.

7.2.1 How AI/ML enhances real-time prediction, simulation, and optimization in dts?

AI and ML significantly enhance the capabilities of DTs by enabling them to predict future states, simulate various scenarios, and optimize performance in real-time. Here's how AI/ML contributes to each of these key areas:

7.2.1.1 Real-time prediction

AI/ML algorithms allow DTs to forecast future behavior and conditions of physical systems based on historical and live data inputs (Lee et al., 2015). This is critical in applications like predictive maintenance, risk management, and operational forecasting.

- **Predictive maintenance:** ML models trained on sensor data can predict failures before they occur, enabling timely intervention and reducing downtime.
- **Demand forecasting:** In energy or supply chain DTs, AI predicts future consumption or demand patterns to ensure better resource allocation.
- **Behavioral forecasting:** In smart mobility, AI-enabled DTs of vehicles or traffic systems can anticipate congestion and dynamically reroute traffic.

7.2.1.2 Simulation of scenarios

AI enhances DT simulations by introducing learning-based models that go beyond physics-based approaches. These simulations help stakeholders explore "what-if" scenarios to evaluate performance under different conditions.

- **Data-driven modeling:** ML can create accurate surrogate models of complex systems that are difficult to describe mathematically, allowing for faster simulations.
- **Scenario testing:** AI allows DTs to test how systems behave under hypothetical scenarios, such as equipment failures, environmental changes, or usage fluctuations.
- **Virtual prototyping:** AI-driven DTs can simulate the impact of design changes or operational adjustments before implementing them in the real world.

7.2.1.3 Optimization of operations

ML algorithms, such as reinforcement learning, genetic algorithms, and deep learning, enable DTs to continuously learn and improve system performance autonomously.

- **Process optimization:** In manufacturing, AI optimizes machine parameters for quality, speed, and energy use by learning from production data.
- **Energy efficiency:** In smart buildings or grids, AI-powered DTs analyze usage patterns to optimize heating, cooling, and electricity distribution.
- **Autonomous decision-making:** Reinforcement learning enables DTs to make and refine decisions (e.g., in autonomous vehicles or robotic systems) without human intervention.

7.3 Open challenges in collaborative AI/ML for DTs

While the integration of collaborative AI/ML with DT systems offers immense potential, it also brings several open challenges that must be addressed to ensure secure, scalable, and effective deployment (Lee et al., 2015; Wu et al., 2021; Mohammadi et al., 2018). These challenges span data sharing, model coordination, infrastructure limitations, and ethical concerns.

- **Data privacy and security:** Collaborative AI/ML models often require data sharing across organizations or devices, raising serious concerns about data leakage, unauthorized access, and compliance with privacy laws like General Data Protection Regulation (GDPR). Ensuring secure, privacy-preserving learning without exposing sensitive data is a major challenge.
- **Interoperability and standardization:** DTs are deployed in diverse domains with different data formats, communication protocols, and platforms. The lack of common standards and interoperability makes it difficult to integrate and collaborate across heterogeneous DT systems.
- **Trust and model validation:** In collaborative AI/ML, multiple stakeholders may contribute data or models. In this context, ensuring trust in shared models, verifying their validity, and preventing malicious contributions are open research areas. Note that a lack of transparency in ML algorithms also reduces user confidence.
- **Scalability and resource constraints:** As the number of participating devices or DTs increases, so does the complexity of model coordination and data management. Note that scaling collaborative learning frameworks while maintaining performance and minimizing communication overhead is a significant challenge, especially for edge or IoT devices.
- **Real-time responsiveness:** Collaborative AI/ML must often operate in real-time environments (e.g., smart factories, healthcare monitoring). Note that ensuring low-latency communication and decision-making across distributed systems, while maintaining accuracy, is complex.
- **Model ownership and intellectual property (IP):** Collaboratively trained models may involve contributions from multiple parties. Note that determining ownership rights, usage permissions, and IP policies is legally and ethically challenging.
- **Incentivization and participation:** In decentralized collaborative environments, participants may lack the motivation to contribute data or computing power. Note that designing fair and transparent incentive mechanisms is essential to sustaining collaboration, especially in federated or peer-to-peer learning.
- **Model drift and lifelong learning:** DT environments are dynamic, and models need continuous adaptation. Note that managing model drift, updating shared models without conflict, and enabling lifelong learning in a distributed setup remain an open challenge.
- **Network reliability and bandwidth constraints:** Here, collaborative learning relies on reliable communication networks. In edge or remote scenarios, limited bandwidth or intermittent connectivity can disrupt synchronization and model sharing.
- **Ethical and bias concerns:** Bias in data or algorithms can be amplified in collaborative AI/ML systems. Note that ensuring fairness, accountability, and ethical use of AI within

and across DT systems is a growing concern, especially when decisions affect human safety or well-being.

Hence, while collaborative AI/ML brings intelligence and adaptability to DT ecosystems, addressing these open challenges is essential for its trustworthy, ethical, and scalable adoption. Multidisciplinary research across AI, cybersecurity, legal frameworks, and system design will be key to overcoming these barriers.

7.4 Blockchain fundamentals for secure collaboration with DT

Blockchain technology provides a robust foundation for secure, transparent, and decentralized collaboration in DT ecosystems (Lin et al., 2017; Lu et al., 2020; Tyagi, 2016, Tyagi (2020), Tyagi (2021), 2022, Tyagi (2023), Tyagi (2024d), Tyagi (2024e), Tyagi (2025a), Tyagi (2025b); Tyagi and Aghila, 2011). Its core features—decentralization, immutability, and consensus—address many challenges in data sharing, trust, and security that arise when multiple stakeholders interact within DT environments.

- **Decentralization:** Unlike traditional centralized databases, blockchain operates as a distributed ledger maintained across multiple nodes. This eliminates single points of failure and reduces reliance on centralized authorities, enabling trustless collaboration among participants in a DT network.
- **Immutability and data integrity:** Blockchain stores transaction records in blocks linked cryptographically, making past data tamper-proof. For DTs, this ensures that sensor data, model updates, or operational logs remain unaltered and verifiable, providing a reliable audit trail for system monitoring and compliance.
- **Consensus mechanisms:** To add data or model changes to the blockchain, participants follow consensus protocols (e.g., Proof-of-Work, Proof-of-Stake). These mechanisms ensure agreement on the validity of transactions without requiring trust among parties, which is critical for multientity collaboration in DTs.
- **Smart contracts:** Smart contracts are self-executing code stored on the blockchain that automate workflows based on predefined rules. In DT collaborations, smart contracts can enforce data-sharing agreements, trigger alerts on anomalies, or automate payments and access control without intermediaries.
- **Security and privacy:** Blockchain uses cryptographic techniques like hashing and digital signatures to secure transactions and authenticate participants. Combined with privacy-enhancing solutions such as zero-knowledge proofs (ZKPs) or permissioned blockchains, this allows DT ecosystems to protect sensitive data while enabling controlled transparency.
- **Traceability and auditability:** Every transaction recorded on the blockchain is time-stamped and traceable. This end-to-end visibility supports accountability, provenance tracking, and regulatory compliance within DT collaborations.

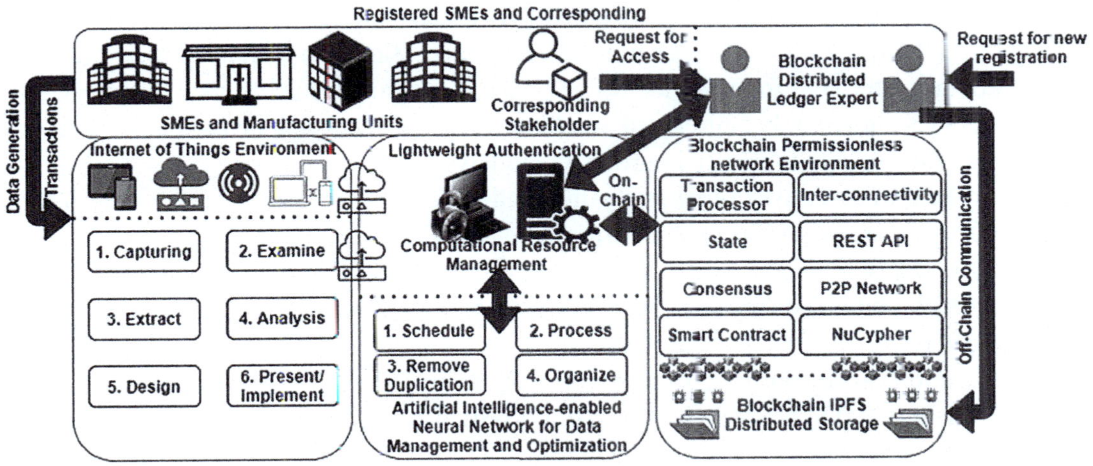

Fig. 7.3 The collaborative role of blockchain, AI, and other emerging technologies.

- **Interoperability and integration:** Blockchain platforms can integrate with IoT devices and AI/ML models within DTs, facilitating seamless, secure data exchange and collaborative analytics across heterogeneous systems.

Note that blockchain fundamentals—decentralization, immutability, consensus, and smart contracts—create a secure, transparent, and automated environment for collaborative DT computing (also, a collaborative framework with blockchain can be found in Fig. 7.3). By using these features, stakeholders can build trusted, resilient, and efficient DT ecosystems that ensure data integrity, privacy, and coordinated decision-making across distributed networks.

7.5 Integrating blockchain with AI/ML in DT systems

Integrating blockchain technology with AI and ML within DT systems offers a powerful synergy that enhances security, trust, transparency, and intelligence across complex cyber-physical environments (Zhang et al., 2019; Shi et al., 2016). This fusion addresses critical challenges related to data integrity, collaboration, and decentralized intelligence, driving more robust and autonomous DT ecosystems.

- **Ensuring data integrity and trustworthiness:** Blockchain's immutable ledger guarantees that data fed into AI/ML models within DTs is tamper-proof and verifiable. This is vital because the quality and trustworthiness of training data directly impact AI/ML model accuracy. By recording sensor data, model updates, and transaction logs on a blockchain, stakeholders can confidently rely on shared data without fearing manipulation or fraud.

- **Decentralized collaborative learning:** AI/ML models in DT systems often require data from multiple sources for training and inference. Blockchain enables decentralized collaboration through frameworks like FL, where local models are trained independently, and updates are securely aggregated on-chain. This preserves data privacy while allowing diverse stakeholders to jointly improve AI models.
- **Automated model governance with smart contracts:** Smart contracts automate and enforce rules around AI/ML model usage, updates, and access rights in DT systems. For example, they can manage licensing agreements, track model provenance, or trigger retraining based on performance metrics, ensuring transparent and auditable AI lifecycle management.
- **Secure and transparent decision-making:** By recording AI/ML inference results and decisions on the blockchain, DT systems provide an auditable trail that enhances accountability, especially in critical applications like healthcare, manufacturing, or autonomous vehicles (refer to Fig. 7.4). This transparency helps verify that AI decisions comply with regulatory or ethical standards.
- **Incentivizing data and model sharing:** Blockchain-based tokens or rewards can incentivize participants to share high-quality data or contribute computational resources for AI/ML model training within DT ecosystems. This encourages active

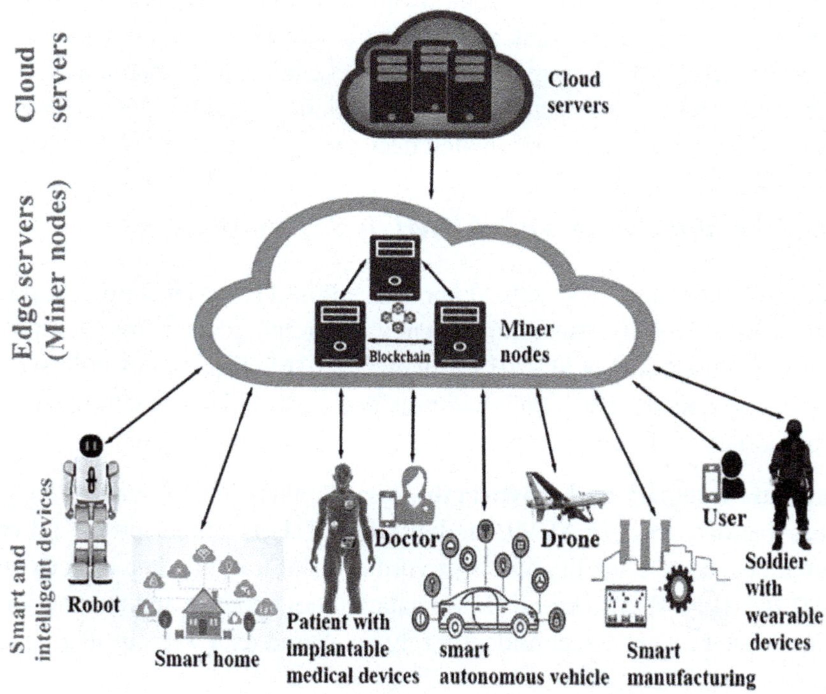

Fig. 7.4 Architecture of blockchain-based internet of things.

participation and resource pooling, which are important for large-scale collaborative intelligence.

- **Enhancing privacy through cryptographic techniques:** Combining blockchain with privacy-preserving AI methods (e.g., differential privacy, secure multiparty computation, ZKPs) allows DT systems to perform collaborative AI/ML tasks without exposing sensitive data, thereby balancing transparency with confidentiality.
- **Improving resilience and fault tolerance:** Decentralized storage and distributed consensus reduce single points of failure, making integrated DT systems more robust against attacks or outages. AI-driven anomaly detection, combined with blockchain's auditability, further strengthens system security.

Hence, the integration of blockchain with AI/ML in DT systems creates a secure, transparent, and collaborative environment that enhances data integrity, privacy, governance, and decision-making. This convergence unlocks new possibilities for decentralized, trustworthy, and intelligent DT ecosystems, accelerating innovation and adoption across industries.

7.6 Federated learning and blockchain synergy for collaborative AI/ML in DT computing

The convergence of FL and blockchain technologies creates a robust framework for collaborative AI/ML in DT computing, enabling decentralized, privacy-preserving, and secure model training across distributed entities. A few useful points here are:

i. **FL: Privacy-preserving collaboration:** FL allows multiple participants—such as IoT devices or organizations—to collaboratively train a shared AI/ML model without exchanging raw data. Each participant trains the model locally on their own data, and only model updates (gradients or weights) are shared. This approach safeguards sensitive information, making FL ideal for DT managing confidential or proprietary data.

ii. **Blockchain: Decentralized trust and integrity:** Blockchain provides a decentralized ledger to securely record and validate transactions, including model updates in FL. Its immutable nature ensures data integrity and prevents tampering or malicious manipulation of model parameters during transmission and aggregation. Blockchain consensus mechanisms guarantee that only legitimate updates are accepted, increasing trust among collaborators.

iii. **Synergistic benefits: A few benefits include:**

   - **Enhanced security:** Blockchain's cryptographic protocols secure FL model updates from unauthorized alterations and replay attacks, protecting the collaborative learning process in DT networks.

- **Auditability and transparency:** Every model update and aggregation step is logged on the blockchain, enabling traceability and accountability, which are important for compliance and debugging.
- **Incentive mechanisms:** Blockchain-based tokens can reward participants for contributing quality data and computational resources, encouraging active engagement in the FL process.
- **Decentralized aggregation:** Blockchain smart contracts can automate the aggregation of model updates without reliance on a central server, reducing single points of failure and improving system resilience.

iv. **Applications in DT computing:** In DT ecosystems, combining FL and blockchain supports cross-organizational collaboration, such as multiple factories sharing equipment health data to improve predictive maintenance models, or healthcare providers jointly training patient outcome models without exposing private data. This synergy provides scalable, secure, and privacy-conscious AI/ML solutions (Zhang et al., 2019; Shi et al., 2016; Kairouz et al., 2019; Radanliev et al., 2021).

A few key challenges include managing communication overhead, ensuring scalability with many participants, handling heterogeneous data and models, and developing robust incentive and governance frameworks. Research continues into optimizing blockchain consensus for FL, privacy-enhancing techniques, and integrating edge computing for real-time DT applications. FL and blockchain integration offer a powerful paradigm for collaborative AI/ML in DT computing, balancing data privacy, trust, and decentralization. Their synergy enables secure, transparent, and scalable model training across distributed stakeholders, driving smarter and more resilient DT ecosystems.

7.7 Data integrity and trust in DT environments

7.7.1 Ensuring tamper-proof data sharing and validation using blockchain in a DT environment

In DT environments, where real-time, accurate data sharing among multiple stakeholders is essential, blockchain technology offers an effective solution to ensure data integrity, tamper-proofing, and trustworthy validation.

a. **Immutable ledger for data integrity:** Blockchain stores data in cryptographically linked blocks, forming a ledger that is immutable—once recorded, data cannot be altered or deleted without consensus from the network. This ensures that sensor data, operational logs, or model updates shared within a DT ecosystem remain unchanged and trustworthy.
b. **Decentralized data validation:** Instead of relying on a central authority, blockchain uses decentralized consensus mechanisms (e.g., Proof-of-Work, Proof-of-Stake),

where multiple nodes validate transactions. This collective validation ensures that only legitimate, verified data entries are added to the blockchain's shared record, preventing malicious tampering or fraud.

c. **Cryptographic hashing for verification:** Each data block in the blockchain contains a cryptographic hash of the previous block and the current data. Any unauthorized modification changes the hash, immediately alerting participants to tampering attempts. This continuous chain of hashes guarantees end-to-end data integrity in DT collaborations.
d. **Smart contracts for automated validation and access control:** Smart contracts—self-executing code on the blockchain—can automate data validation rules, access permissions, and compliance checks. For example, they can ensure that only authorized devices upload data to the DT or trigger alerts when anomalous or inconsistent data is detected.
e. **Traceability and auditability:** Blockchain records every data transaction with a timestamp and participant identity, creating a transparent and auditable history of all interactions. This traceability is critical for debugging, compliance with regulations, and building trust among DT stakeholders.
f. **Integration with IoT and edge devices:** Blockchain can be integrated with IoT sensors and edge devices in DT systems to securely capture and timestamp data at the source. This prevents data spoofing and ensures authenticity from the point of collection.

Hence, by using blockchain's immutable ledger, decentralized consensus, cryptographic verification, and smart contracts, DT environments can achieve tamper-proof data sharing and reliable validation. This ensures data integrity, transparency, and trustworthiness, which are essential for accurate simulations, analytics, and decision-making in complex CPS.

7.7.2 Smart contracts for collaborative ML automation in DT environments

Smart contracts are self-executing programs stored on a blockchain that automatically enforce rules and agreements without intermediaries (Lin et al., 2017; Lu et al., 2020; Tyagi, 2021, Tyagi (2023), Tyagi (2024d), Tyagi (2024e)). In DT environments, smart contracts play an essential role in automating collaborative ML workflows, enhancing efficiency, trust, and transparency among multiple stakeholders.

a. Automated data sharing and access control: Smart contracts can define and enforce permissions for data sharing within DT ecosystems. They ensure that only authorized participants and devices can upload, access, or modify data used for ML model training, thereby maintaining privacy and compliance.
b. Model training coordination: In collaborative ML scenarios, smart contracts automate the coordination of training tasks—such as aggregating model updates from multiple DT

nodes in FL. They verify contributions, trigger aggregation once conditions are met, and ensure fairness in the process.

c. Incentivization and rewards: Smart contracts can manage incentive mechanisms by automatically distributing tokens or payments to participants based on their data quality, computational resources, or model improvements. This encourages active and honest participation in collaborative ML.
d. Model versioning and provenance tracking: By recording every ML model update and retraining event on the blockchain, smart contracts maintain an immutable history of model versions and contributors. This provenance enhances accountability and enables rollback to previous states if needed.
e. Performance monitoring and automated retraining: Smart contracts can monitor ML model performance metrics stored on-chain and trigger automated retraining or alerts when accuracy drops below thresholds, ensuring continuous model relevance and robustness in DT systems.
f. Dispute resolution and compliance enforcement: In multistakeholder environments, smart contracts provide transparent and tamper-proof records that help resolve disputes regarding data use, model ownership, or results. They also enforce compliance with regulatory policies encoded in contract logic.

Smart contracts enable automated, transparent, and secure management of collaborative ML workflows within DT environments. By orchestrating data sharing, training coordination, incentives, and governance, they provide trust and efficiency, accelerating the deployment of intelligent, decentralized DT systems.

7.8 Use cases and applications

7.8.1 Blockchain for collaborative AI/ML in DT computing in smart manufacturing, smart healthcare, and smart cities

Blockchain-integrated collaborative AI/ML in DT systems is revolutionizing key sectors by enabling decentralized, secure, and intelligent operations. In smart manufacturing, smart healthcare, and smart cities, this synergy enhances data-driven decision-making, interoperability, and trust across distributed systems.

7.8.1.1 Smart manufacturing

In smart factories, DTs model the real-time state of machines, production lines, and supply chains. Collaborative AI/ML enhances predictive maintenance, quality control, and production optimization. Blockchain supports this by:

- Securing machine-to-machine data shared for FL without exposing proprietary information.

- Ensuring traceability of parts, operations, and models, enabling full audit trails for quality assurance.
- Automating workflows with smart contracts for predictive maintenance alerts, resource allocation, or inventory updates.
- Incentivizing collaboration among suppliers or manufacturers contributing to shared AI/ML models.

For example, a consortium of manufacturers collaboratively trains a predictive failure model across different plants while maintaining privacy using blockchain and FL.

7.8.1.2 Smart healthcare

In healthcare, DTs represent patients, equipment, or hospital operations. Collaborative AI/ML can power diagnosis, treatment personalization, and operational efficiency. Blockchain enhances trust and compliance by:

- Preserving patient data privacy during AI/ML model training across hospitals using decentralized data validation.
- Recording model performance and usage history for regulatory compliance and ethical transparency.
- Enforcing consent management via smart contracts, giving patients control over their digital health data.
- Enabling multihospital collaboration in training models for rare disease detection or outbreak prediction.

For example, hospitals collaborate using blockchain-based FL to train AI models for disease prediction without sharing patient records.

7.8.1.3 Smart cities

DTs in smart cities model urban infrastructure, transportation systems, and utilities. AI/ML drives traffic optimization, energy management, and environmental monitoring. Blockchain supports this by:

- Securing real-time sensor data streams from traffic lights, energy grids, or pollution monitors.
- Coordinating AI model updates from different city departments using tamper-proof smart contracts.
- Enabling transparent public service through audit logs of decisions made by AI systems.
- Encouraging citizen participation via blockchain-enabled data-sharing incentives.

For example, city transport and energy departments collaboratively use AI to optimize traffic flow and energy load balancing, with blockchain ensuring model integrity and operational transparency.

Hence, blockchain empowers collaborative AI/ML in DT computing by providing decentralized trust, transparency, and security. Whether it's optimizing production in factories, advancing diagnostics in hospitals, or enhancing sustainability in cities, this integration is key to building resilient, intelligent, and collaborative ecosystems for the smart era.

7.9 Performance, scalability, and limitations toward blockchain for collaborative AI/ML in DT computing

The integration of blockchain with collaborative AI/ML in DT environments offers significant advantages in terms of security, data integrity, and decentralized collaboration. However, real-world deployment also involves challenges in performance, scalability, and architectural limitations.

7.9.1 Performance challenges

- **Transaction latency**: Traditional blockchains, like Ethereum or Bitcoin, suffer from high transaction latency due to their consensus mechanisms (e.g., Proof-of-Work). In real-time DT systems requiring fast data exchange and model updates, such delays can hinder system responsiveness.
- **Computational overhead**: Blockchain operations involve cryptographic processes and consensus algorithms that are computationally expensive, especially in resource-constrained DT environments like IoT-enabled factories or smart healthcare devices.
- **Smart contract execution time**: Complex smart contracts for coordinating ML training or access control can further slow down system performance if not optimized.

7.9.2 Scalability issues

- **Limited throughput**: Most public blockchains can handle only a limited number of transactions per second (e.g., Bitcoin ~ 7 transactions per second (TPS), Ethereum ~ 30 TPS). DT systems generating high-frequency data streams may quickly overwhelm this capacity.
- **Data storage constraints**: Storing large volumes of AI/ML model parameters or sensor data on-chain is impractical due to storage costs and chain bloat. Off-chain solutions are often necessary, adding architectural complexity.
- **Node synchronization**: In large-scale DT ecosystems (e.g., smart cities), synchronizing multiple blockchain nodes can introduce delays and inconsistencies, especially during network strain or outages.

7.9.3 Limitations and bottlenecks

- **Energy consumption**: Consensus mechanisms like Proof-of-Work consume vast energy resources, making them unsuitable for green or low-power DT systems. Alternatives like Proof-of-Stake or hybrid models are more efficient but are still evolving.

- **Data privacy risks**: Although blockchain offers transparency, publicly storing even metadata can raise privacy concerns. Additional cryptographic methods (e.g., zk-SNARKs, homomorphic encryption) must be layered on, complicating implementation.
- **Complexity of integration**: Merging blockchain with FL, smart contracts, and real-time DT data streams requires advanced architectural design and interoperability standards, which are still under development.
- **Lack of standards and regulation**: The absence of universal protocols for blockchain integration in AI/ML and DT contexts creates fragmentation and hampers large-scale adoption, especially in sensitive domains like healthcare.

Note that while blockchain offers strong security and trust mechanisms for collaborative AI/ML in DT computing, its performance and scalability limitations must be addressed to meet the demands of real-time, large-scale applications. Ongoing research into lightweight consensus mechanisms, off-chain computation, Layer-2 scaling, and standardization is vital to unlocking its full potential. A hybrid approach—combining blockchain with edge computing and privacy-preserving AI—may provide a practical path forward.

7.10 Future trends and research directions toward blockchain for collaborative AI/ML in DT computing

The convergence of blockchain, AI/ML, and DT technologies has emerged as a transformative approach for secure, collaborative, and intelligent systems. As industries increasingly adopt CPS across sectors like smart manufacturing, smart healthcare, smart cities, and autonomous vehicles, the demand for decentralized, trustworthy data exchange and collaborative intelligence is growing. Blockchain, with its inherent capabilities for decentralization, immutability, and transparency, provides an ideal foundation for trustworthy collaboration in AI/ML-powered DT environments. Looking ahead, several trends and research directions are poised to shape the future of this interdisciplinary ecosystem.

7.10.1 Next-generation blockchain protocols for DT integration

Traditional blockchain systems face inherent limitations in terms of throughput, latency, and energy consumption, which are bottlenecks for real-time DT environments. Future research is moving toward lightweight consensus algorithms such as proof-of-authority, delegated proof-of-stake, and Byzantine fault tolerance-based consensus. These algorithms are more suitable for real-time, high-frequency data interactions required in DTs.

In addition, sharding and Layer-2 solutions, like state channels and rollups, are gaining attention to enhance scalability. These approaches allow the blockchain layer to process more AI/ML-related operations without compromising speed or integrity, thus enabling broader integration across large-scale DT ecosystems.

7.10.2 Quantum-resistant and postquantum cryptography

With the evolution of quantum computing, current cryptographic methods used in blockchain could be rendered obsolete. DT systems, especially in critical domains such as defense, healthcare, and finance, require long-term data integrity and security. Future research will focus on integrating quantum-resistant algorithms (e.g., lattice-based cryptography) into blockchain infrastructures that support AI/ML-enabled DTs.

In a futuristic DT ecosystem, postquantum blockchain will ensure that model transactions, decision logs, and data provenance records remain secure for decades—even in the face of quantum threats.

7.10.3 FL on blockchain with enhanced privacy

FL enables distributed AI/ML model training without sharing raw data, making it ideal for data-sensitive environments. However, FL still requires secure aggregation and incentive mechanisms. Integrating blockchain with FL will allow the secure coordination of model updates and the recording of contributions from different participants in a decentralized, tamper-proof ledger.

Emerging techniques like ZKPs, secure multiparty computation (SMPC), and homomorphic encryption will enhance privacy during model aggregation and validation. Smart contracts can be used to govern the FL lifecycle, from the registration of nodes to model convergence and reward distribution.

7.10.4 DT interoperability using blockchain standards

For blockchain-enabled DTs to scale, interoperability between different DT platforms and blockchains is critical. Future directions include the development of universal data exchange protocols and semantic ontologies to standardize interactions across heterogeneous systems. Projects like Interledger Protocol, Polkadot, and Cosmos are early steps toward enabling blockchain interoperability.

Research will likely focus on creating standardized smart contract libraries and open APIs for managing cross-domain AI/ML workflows in DT environments, allowing seamless integration across sectors and geographies.

7.10.5 Autonomous decision-making with blockchain and AI in DTs

The combination of AI agents and smart contracts in DT systems will lead to autonomous decision-making mechanisms that are transparent, verifiable, and trustworthy. For instance, AI models embedded within a DT can make operational decisions (e.g., rescheduling manufacturing or routing traffic), while smart contracts automatically validate these decisions and log them on the blockchain.

This trend aligns with the rise of Agentic AI, where AI agents independently negotiate and collaborate. Research will focus on defining governance frameworks, ethical boundaries, and accountability models for such systems, especially when they interact with real-world physical processes.

7.10.6 Edge-blockchain-ai convergence for real-time DT computing

As DT systems are increasingly deployed at the edge (e.g., in vehicles, factories, or hospitals), future architectures will combine edge computing, blockchain, and AI/ML. These hybrid architectures will:

- Reduce latency by processing data closer to the source
- Use blockchain for secure coordination and traceability
- Apply AI for local inference and optimization

Innovations like fog computing, lightweight blockchains (e.g., Internet of Things (IoT) applications (IOTA), Nano), and federated edge intelligence will play a critical role. Future research will explore energy-efficient consensus for edge nodes and dynamic smart contracts that adjust behavior based on edge-context awareness.

7.10.7 Trustworthy AI and auditable ML models on blockchain

One of the biggest future concerns in collaborative AI/ML is model trustworthiness. Blockchain offers a means to track model lineage, from training data origin to algorithm updates, thus enabling transparent and auditable AI/ML pipelines. This is especially important in critical sectors like healthcare and finance, where decisions must be explainable and verifiable. Here, future research will explore:

- Model watermarking and fingerprinting stored on-chain
- Token-curated registries for AI models with verified performance
- Smart contract-based governance for AI retraining and validation
- Decentralized Autonomous Organizations managing AI models in DTs

7.10.8 Tokenized incentive systems for data and knowledge sharing

A critical aspect of collaborative ML in DTs is motivating data owners and model contributors. Token-based incentive systems built on blockchain can reward users for:

- Sharing quality data
- Contributing compute power

- Validating models
- Detecting anomalies

Hence, future work will focus on reputation systems, adaptive reward mechanisms, and tokenomics models that align with long-term ecosystem goals. Game-theoretic models and reinforcement learning can be combined with smart contracts to optimize these incentive strategies in real-time.

7.10.9 Regulatory, ethical, and sustainability issues

As blockchain-based DT–AI systems grow, regulatory compliance and ethical AI frameworks must evolve. Researchers will explore how to encode legal and ethical rules directly into smart contracts (e.g., GDPR compliance, Health Insurance Portability and Accountability (HIPAA), explainability, fairness). In addition, sustainability in blockchain design—especially in energy use and e-waste—will become a growing research priority. Green blockchains using Proof-of-Space, Proof-of-Reputation, or Proof-of-Collaboration will gain traction. Regulatory sandboxes will be vital for testing these systems in controlled real-world environments before mass deployment.

7.10.10 Human-DT interaction and cognitive integration

The future will see deeper integration between humans and their DTs, facilitated by wearable sensors, neuro-interfaces, and immersive extended reality (XR) technologies. Blockchain will be essential to secure personal data streams and AI models that adapt to individual behavior.

Here, further research will explore:

- Digital identity management on blockchain
- Consent and preference learning through smart contracts
- Ethical boundaries in cognitive augmentation
- Collaborative AI for group-level DTs (e.g., community health or collective productivity)

These advances will shift DTs from being passive replicas to active, learning companions.

The convergence of blockchain, AI/ML, and DT computing is poised to transform future industries, infrastructures, and societies. Emerging technologies like quantum-resistant cryptography, edge-AI, FL, and decentralized autonomous agents will make DTs more intelligent, secure, and collaborative. Future research must focus on improving scalability, interoperability, ethical governance, and user trust. With these innovations, blockchain-enabled collaborative AI/ML in DT computing will become the backbone of resilient, adaptive, and intelligent systems in the era of Industry 5.0 and beyond.

7.11 Conclusion

The convergence of blockchain with collaborative AI/ML in DT computing represents a transformative step toward realizing decentralized, intelligent, and secure digital ecosystems. As DTs become integral to sectors like manufacturing, healthcare, smart cities, and logistics, they require robust infrastructures that support secure data sharing, trust, and accountability across stakeholders. Blockchain technology addresses these needs by providing a decentralized ledger system that ensures transparency, immutability, and trustless collaboration. Note that integrating blockchain with AI/ML enables distributed learning paradigms such as FL, where multiple entities can collaboratively train models without exposing sensitive data. This not only preserves privacy but also promotes inclusivity by allowing participation from edge devices and resource-constrained environments. Smart contracts further automate governance, enforce rules, and incentivize cooperation without relying on central authorities, creating self-regulating AI ecosystems. However, a few challenges, such as scalability, latency, energy consumption, and interoperability, must be carefully addressed to ensure practical deployment. Advances in lightweight blockchain protocols, consensus mechanisms, and off-chain computation can help overcome these barriers. For the future, the synergy of blockchain and AI/ML in DT computing holds immense potential to drive the next wave of Industry 5.0—making sustainable, human-centric, and resilient systems. It encourages the development of autonomous, trustworthy DTs capable of learning, evolving, and collaborating securely.

References

A.K., Tyagi, 2025b. Blockchain technology: values, challenges, and possible applications from an industry perspective. In: Tyagi, A.K., Tiwari, S. (Eds.), Human- Centric Integration of Next-Generation Data Science and Blockchain Technology. Elsevier. doi:10.1016/B978-0-443-33498-6.00027-3. ISBN: 978-0-443-33498-6.

Boschert, S., Rosen, R., 2016. Digital twin—the simulation aspect. In: Hehenberger, P., Bradley, D. (Eds.), Mechatronic Futures. Springer, pp. 59–74. doi:10.1007/978-3-319-32156-1_5.

Kairouz, P., McMahan, H.B., Avent, B., et al., 2019. Advances and open problems in federated learning arXiv arXiv:1912.04977. Available from: https://arxiv.org/abs/1912.04977.

Lee, J., Bagheri, B., Kao, H.A., 2015. A cyber-physical systems architecture for industry 4.0-based manufacturing systems. Manuf. Lett. 3, 18–23. doi:10.1016/j.mfglet.2014.12.001.

Lin, D., Yu, W., Zhang, N., Yang, X., Zhang, W., Zhao, W., 2017. Survey on internet of things: a review of enabling technologies, security and privacy, and applications. IEEE Internet Things J. 4 (5), 1125–1142. doi:10.1109/JIOT.2017.2683200.

Lu, Y., Liu, C., Wang, K.I.K., Huang, H., Xu, X., 2020. Digital twin-driven smart manufacturing: connotation, reference model, applications and research issues. Robot. Comput.-Integr. Manuf. 61, 101837. doi:10.1016/j.rcim.2019.101837.

Madni, A.M., Madni, C.C., Lucero, S.D., 2019. Leveraging digital twin technology in model-based systems engineering. Systems. 7 (1), 7. doi:10.3390/systems7010007.

Mohammadi, M., Al-Fuqaha, A., Guizani, M., Oh, J.S., 2018. Semisupervised deep reinforcement learning in support of IoT and smart city services. IEEE Internet Things J. 5 (2), 624–635. doi:10.1109/JIOT.2017.2748798.

Radanliev, P., De Roure, D., Walton, R., Burnap, P., 2021. Digital twins: applications, challenges, and opportunities. Technol. Soc. 67, 101728. doi:10.1016/j.techsoc.2021.101728.

Shi, W., Cao, J., Zhang, Q., Li, Y., Xu, L., 2016. Edge computing: vision and challenges. IEEE Internet Things J. 3 (5), 637–646. doi:10.1109/JIOT.2016.2579198.

Tao, F., Sui, F., Liu, A., Qi, Q., Zhang, M., Song, B., Nee, A.Y.C., 2019. Digital twin-driven product design, manufacturing and service with big data. Int. J. Adv. Manuf. Technol. 94 (9), 3563–3576. doi:10.1007/s00170-017-0233-1.

Tyagi, A.K., 2016. Cyber physical systems (CPSs)—opportunities and challenges for improving cyber security. Int. J. Comput. Appl. 0975-8887. 137 (14), 19–27. doi:10.5120/ijca2016908877.

Tyagi, A.K., 2022. SecVT: securing the vehicles of tomorrow using blockchain technology. In: In the Proceeding of Springer/ ISAI 2022, 17–19 February 2022, Kolkata. doi:10.1007/978-3-031-22485-0_11. ISBN: 978-3-031-22485-0.

Tyagi, A.K. (Ed.), 2024b. Blockchain-enabled internet of things (IoTs) platforms for IoT-based healthcare and biomedical sectors. In: Artificial Intelligence-Enabled Blockchain Technology and Digital Twin for Smart Hospitals.Wiley, pp. 201–217. doi:10.1002/9781394287420.ch10. ISBN: 978-1-394-28739-0.

Tyagi, A.K. (Ed.), 2024c. Sensors and digital twin application in healthcare facilities management. In: Artificial Intelligence-Enabled Blockchain Technology and Digital Twin for Smart Hospitals.Wiley, pp. 369–390. doi:10.1002/9781394287420.ch19. ISBN: 978-1-394-28739-0.

Tyagi, A.K. (Ed.), 2024d. Blockchain–artificial intelligence-based secured solutions for smart environment. In: Digital Twin and Blockchain for Smart Cities.Wiley, pp. 547–577. doi:10.1002/9781394303564.ch23. ISBN: 9781394303533.

Tyagi, A.K., Aghila, G., 2011. A wide scale survey on botnet. Int. J. Comput. Appl. 0975-8887. 34 (9), 9–22. doi:10.1016/j.iotcps.2021.12.002.

Tyagi, A.K., Kumari, S., 2024. Blockchain and digital twin for smart grid. In: Tyagi, A.K, Kumari, S (Eds.), Blockchain and digital twin for smart grid. Wiley-Scrivener. doi:10.1002/9781394303564. ISBN: 9781394303533.

Tyagi, A.K., 2024a. Transformative effects of ChatGPT on modern era of education and society: from society and industry's perspective. In: Maruthi, P.B., Smirti, P., Tyagi, A.K. (Eds.), Machine Learning Algorithms Using Scikit and TensorFlow Environments. IGI Global, USA. doi:10.4018/978-1-6684-8531-6.ch019.

Tyagi, A.K., 2024e. Dew computing: state of the art, opportunities, and research challenges. In: Maruthi, P.B., Smirti, P., Tyagi, A.k (Eds.), Machine Learning Algorithms Using Scikit and TensorFlow Environments. IGI Global, USA. doi:10.4018/978-1-6684-8531-6.ch017.

Tyagi, A.K., 2023. Decentralized everything: a practical use of blockchain technology in future applications. In: Pandey, R., Goundar, S., Fatima, S. (Eds.), Distributed Computing to Blockchain: Architecture, Technology, and Applications. Elsevier, pp. 19–38. doi:10.1016/B978-0-323-96146-2.00010-3. ISBN: 978-0-323-96146-2

Tyagi, A.K., 2020. Prediction models. In: Rani, G., Tiwari, P.K. (Eds.), Handbook of Research on Disease Prediction through Data Analytics and Machine Learning. IGI Global, USA, pp. 50–69. doi:10.4018/978-1-7998-2742-9.ch004. ISBN 13:9781799827429

Tyagi, A.K., 2021. Analysis of security and privacy aspects of blockchain technologies from smart era' perspective: the challenges and a way forward. In: Tyagi, A.K., Abraham, A. (Eds.), Recent Trends in Blockchain for Information Systems Security and Privacy. CRC Press, pp. 1–17. doi:10.1201/9781003139737. eBook-ISBN: 9781003139737.

Tyagi, A.K., 2025a. Blockchain for smart hospital in Healthcare 5.0: modeling structure, challenges, and future emerging trends. In: Tyagi, A.K, Tiwari, S. (Eds.), Human- Centric Integration of Next-Generation Data Science and Blockchain Technology, Elsevier. doi:10.1016/B978-0-443-33498-6.00026-1. ISBN: 978-0-443-33498-6.

Wu, M., Lu, T.J., Ling, F.Y.Y., Sun, J., 2021. Explainable AI applications in digital twins: a systematic review. J. Intell. Manuf. doi:10.1007/s10845-021-01787-8.

Zhang, Y., Kasahara, S., Shen, Y., Jiang, X., Wan, J., 2019. Smart contract-based access control for the internet of things. IEEE Internet Things J. 6 (2), 1594–1605. doi:10.1109/JIOT.2018.2847705.

CHAPTER 8

Blockchain for decentralized and secure artificial intelligence/machine learning in DT computing

Avinash Kumar Sharma and Edson Bernardo da Conceicao Mahangue

[a]*Department of Computer Science & Engineering (CSE), Sharda School of Computing Science & Engineering (SSCSE), Sharda University, Greater Noida, India*

8.1 Introduction

With the need for a reduction in human intervention in daily operations through the transformation of more effective processes, technology has been advancing and creating new subfields. Digital twin (DT) computing has been described as a digital transformation technology that aims to reduce cost effects in the maintenance of buildings and systems, including those in the healthcare environment.

DT computing has been increasingly used due to its capabilities to mimic the functions of real-world scenarios through the creation of virtual entities in industrial machines, smart cities, or human health systems. These virtual representations offer multiple advantages, from the creation of real-time monitoring windows to the analysis of the data collected, which helps in proposing the optimization of processes (Oulefki et al., 2025). At the same time, these technologies provide valuable data that enrich decision-making and enhance the understanding of the procedures of the scenarios they represent, allowing for optimized identification, efficiency improvement, and cost reduction. The use of machine learning (ML), a subset of artificial intelligence (AI) known for its ability to learn through data, has been identified as a key factor that supports the goals of DT computing when the two are combined. Through the analysis and predictions made by ML algorithms, DT computing enables accurate simulations and optimizations. The implementation of AI/ML has been recognized as the element that facilitates the introduction of innovative features and functions in DT processes (Adnan et al., 2024), thereby being regarded as the driving force behind the effective utilization of DT computing features.

Artificial Intelligence, Machine Learning and Blockchain in Digital Twin Computing.
https://doi.org/10.1016/B978-0-443-43914-8.00013-3

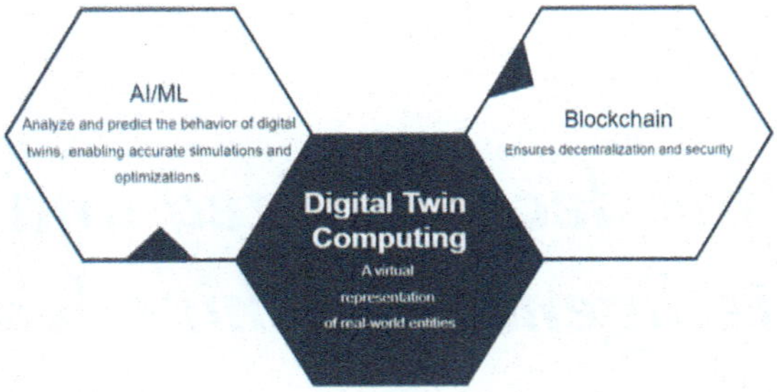

Fig. 8.1 Blockchain, AI/ML, and DT integration.

Security has been described as a critical element in every technology, and due to this, the secure implementation of such technology relies on the use of blockchain. The use of blockchain has been highlighted due to its capability to create a decentralized infrastructure that enables the secure sharing of records across multiple nodes in the network, allowing the continued availability of data. When combined with AI/ML in DT computing, it enables the ML models to learn in an environment resilient to data tampering, making it possible to validate data transactions and increasing the trustworthiness of the data provided by the DT in the decision-making process, as the data across this technology cannot be altered (Liu et al., 2024). The integration of these technologies with decentralized and secure AI/ML in DT computing produces a robust framework for trust, transparency, and security. While blockchain guarantees data integrity, AI/ML enhances analytical capabilities, and DTs offer real-time insights into physical systems, as briefly shown in Fig. 8.1. Together, these technologies facilitate innovative solutions across numerous industries, from healthcare and smart cities to manufacturing and autonomous systems.

With the appearance of Industry 4.0, the need for secure, scalable, and autonomous DT has become critical. Traditional centralized DT, however, face challenges including single points of failure, data breaches, and scalability issues. Recent research has proposed DT twin frameworks that integrate blockchain and ML. Blockchain's decentralized ledger provides tamper-proof, transparent data sharing and consensus mechanisms that mitigate security risks. On the other hand, ML algorithms process the massive data streams that DTs produce, enabling predictive maintenance, anomaly detection, and real-time optimization.

8.2 Literature review

DT has emerged as a transformative innovation that provides a real-time virtual representation of physical systems, directly applied in sectors such as manufacturing, energy, and healthcare, where it facilitates process monitoring, performance optimization, and predictive maintenance. Traditional implementations, however, are usually managed centrally, making them vulnerable to cybersecurity threats and issues related to data integrity.

Decentralizing DT involves distributing the data and control logic across multiple nodes. This paradigm arises from the need for greater resiliency, enhanced security, and the ability to manage distributed systems in an era where edge computing is prevalent.

8.2.1 's role in DT computing

Blockchain technology, traditionally developed for cryptocurrencies, offers a decentralized record that is inherently secure and transparent. It has since been applied to various domains, including supply chain management, healthcare, and Internet of Things (IoT). In the context of DT, blockchain facilitates secure data exchange between distributed nodes, ensures data immutability, and provides traceability of actions. This is particularly useful for decentralized DT, where ensuring consistency and trust among nodes is vital.

Due to reduced reliance on technologies used without proper security measures, the use of blockchain has been widely recognized as the solution to guarantee the safeguard and availability of data in emerging technologies. Blockchain has been described as the technology that allows data to be transported in a decentralized and encrypted manner (Janani et al., 2023).

Being able to create prototypes of products through the use of DT computing, the application of blockchain makes it possible to fingerprint each transaction of the digital representation, securing the records in the chains for further analysis and consequent decision-making (Chatterjee et al., 2024).

Each block in a blockchain contains a collection of transactions that are cryptographically linked to the previous block, creating a chain that is resistant to tampering. Consensus algorithms are used to ensure that all participants agree on the validity of transactions, making blockchain an ideal technology for environments where trust is vital.

Blockchain's decentralized nature means that no single node or centralized authority is responsible for maintaining the data integrity. Instead, an agreement among multiple nodes ensures that data is correctly updated and verified through the use of built-in algorithms. With the use of this approach, system robustness is enhanced, particularly in environments such as Industrial IoT (IIoT), where large volumes of data are generated continuously and require real-time processing.

As a solution for centralized architectures in DT, the use of blockchain has been proposed, where by leveraging a blockchain register, DT data can be distributed across multiple nodes, each responsible for storing, validating, and sharing data in a trusted environment. This ensures that even if one node fails or is compromised, the overall system continues to operate reliably.

The data created by the digital representations/prototypes enables the analysis of the behavior of the real-world represented element and predicts the optimizations required in the process, which makes this data sensitive to the decision-making process. Blockchain can be defined as a chain of blocks, each containing a list of transactions made in the network. These characteristics enable data integrity while, at the same time, through various blocks, it implements decentralization, and the redundancy of data guarantees that data cannot be tampered with (Alharbi et al., 2024).

Security concerns in DT computing, such as Denial-of-Service attacks and malware like botnets, have been identified as the most common methods used by attackers to gain unauthorized access to data and render data unavailable in this type of technology. The use of blockchain has been highlighted as a key solution due to its reliance on decentralization technologies and cryptography to safeguard data (Lv et al., 2023).

The blockchain has been highlighted as a defense tool against Man-in-the-Middle attacks, Distributed Denial-of-Service, malware, and code injection attacks (Kumar et al., 2023) through the use of cryptography and decentralized blocks, which safeguard the sharing of data.

When DT is implemented in the Internet of Vehicles (IoVs), DT computing is responsible for creating and analyzing data that will be used for network traffic prediction in the environment through the calculation of time fluctuations versus the features of traffic flow. In these technologies, the use of blockchain not only guarantees the efficient operation of all infrastructure but also safeguards the data produced by the devices, making it critical that the digital representation of this technology be equipped with similar technology (Iqbal et al., 2025). This justifies the transparency in data handling found in blockchain use (Qu et al., 2023) safeguarding the efficiency of the technology.

8.2.2 Artificial intelligence/machine learning role in DT computing

ML algorithms empower DT by analyzing large volumes of data and predicting system behavior. They are essential for tasks such as anomaly detection, failure prediction, and system optimization. ML models integrated with DT can continuously learn from sensor data and fine-tune simulation parameters in real time. When combined with blockchain, ML models benefit from improved data integrity and secure access to distributed data, thereby enhancing the overall decision-making process.

The deployment of ML models in DT Computing aims to achieve effectiveness in operations facilitated by DT Computing technology, enhancing the accuracy of optimization predictions. This is due to the capability of ML algorithms to learn from data, reducing the necessity for human intervention. The key advancements in this effort are attributed to AI/ML in the following areas:

- Predictive maintenance (e.g., predicting equipment failure before it occurs)
- Anomaly detection (e.g., identifying drift away from expected performance)
- Control optimization (e.g., automating control adjustments in real-time). In sectors such as manufacturing, aerospace, and healthcare, AI/ML-trained DTs enable reduced downtime, improved safety, and faster design iteration cycles.

The transformation of the way in which physical entities are monitored and managed has been described as the key element in the integration of AI/ML with DT computing, making it possible to achieve predictive maintenance with data and accurate decision-making driven by data produced by the model, which has been integrated into DT (Khalaj et al., 2024; Oulefki et al., 2025).

The working functionality of DT computing has key components:

- A physical entity: This is the basis of this technology from which the digital representation is derived.
- The digital model: This is the digitally created replica of the physical entity
- Connectivity: This component enables the communication of the model with sensors that collect data, which is used to predict the optimization of the physical entity
- Sensors: Have the role of collecting data for digital models.
- ML model: Based on an algorithm, this model plays a role in making the functioning of the digital model more effective

This last component has variations depending on the physical entity to replicate. It can be unsupervised, which has been described as more effective in the use of building optimization and energy efficiency improvement in projects related to smart cities (Kobayashi and Alam, 2024). In addition, it can be supervised, which has been described as more effective for projects involving forecasting, classification, regression, and anomaly detection tasks. These tasks assist in the maintenance and management of projects. Fig. 8.2 illustrates the integration of the components discussed above.

8.2.3 Security and technical challenges in AI/ML combined with DT computing

The use of these technologies in DT computing raises issues concerning the security and integrity of data created and analyzed by the ML model. The common issues known are:

- The risk of real-time data flowing into the twin being tampered with, therefore making it unreliable for creating analytics, is significant.
- Adversarial attacks: Threat actors may also input generated data into an ML model to affect its prediction.
- Privacy: Interacting in real-time with sensitive sensor or user data may result in the disclosure of confidential information.

8.2.4 Securing AI/ML models in DT computing using blockchain

The use of the architecture shown in Fig. 8.2, combined with blockchain, safeguards that AI models are trained on truthful data, decreasing risks associated with biased or manipulated

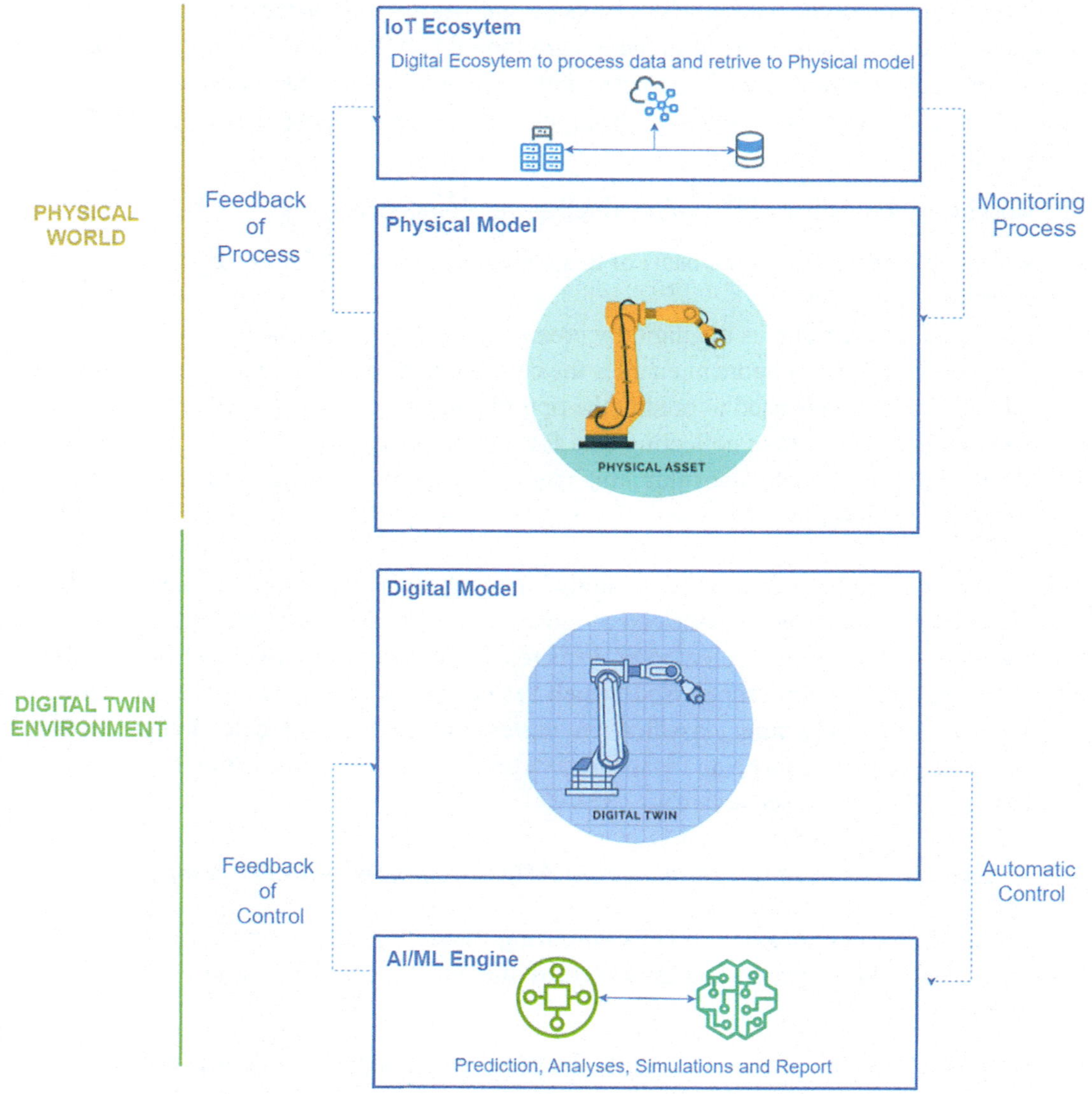

Fig. 8.2 DT components.

datasets, which may influence the functioning of the model when deployed in the environment, ultimately affecting the digital representation of the real-world entity.

The use of blockchain has been selected since traditional security measures may not be sufficient to protect AI models against threats such as model poisoning, adversarial attacks, or unauthorized access. Blockchain, on the other hand, has capabilities that help mitigate these risks by ensuring cryptographic security, which guarantees that data produced by models remains tamper-proof. The security layer provided by blockchain can be enumerated as follows:

- Data immutability: By design, blockchain records sensor logs and ML training data in a way that is unalterable after the fact and can facilitate auditability.
- Decentralized trust: Blockchain displaces central authorities, thereby decreasing single points of failure and ensuring cooperative trust between many stakeholders.
- Model verification and provenance: Blockchain can store cryptographic hashes of AI models, and the hash provides a way to verify updates and conduct version control.
- Access control: Smart contracts can be used to automate permissions, ensuring that only authorized "actors" can access the twin or interact with the ML pipeline. Once blockchain is introduced into the architecture of the DT (edge, cloud, or device layer),

Knowing that AI/ML plays a vital role in analyzing and predicting the behavior of DT Computing, as well as enabling accurate simulations and optimizations, it is crucial to apply these security measures to safeguard the ultimate role of DT Computing.

The secure data exchange process between DTs and their real-world counterparts is essential. Due to this, the implementation of blockchain, which ensures the integrity and confidentiality of these data exchanges by proposing a decentralized framework for recording and verifying interactions, is an indispensable task. This helps prevent data from being tampered with and unauthorized access, making DT computing more reliable and trustworthy. In Table 8.1, a comparative analysis is made among the different implementations of DT.

Table 8.1 provides a detailed analysis of different approaches used to implement the DT, focusing on improvements in data interaction as well as data privacy and security concerns.

The analyzed studies consistently highlight challenges such as data privacy and security issues, high computational costs, and a lack of real-time adaptability across various applications of DT from IoV and healthcare to the Metaverse and human-robot interfaces.

Key gaps include insufficient integration proofs between AI models and DT layers, difficulties in managing diverse data streams, and inadequate threat detection capabilities. The research underscores how the continuous exchange of sensitive data and high resource demands can impede system efficiency and security, particularly in environments where emerging threats are evolving rapidly.

To address these challenges, the studies propose a range of potential solutions. These include enhancing cybersecurity through advanced encryption, blockchain-based verification, and dynamic, AI-driven threat detection systems. Other suggested improvements are the adoption of cost-effective, modular, and scalable system designs, along with edge computing and hardware acceleration to manage computational burdens. Furthermore, establishing standardized integration frameworks and conducting rigorous proof-of-concept studies can

Table 8.1 Comparative analyses.

Reference	Methodology	Gap analyses
Oulefki et al. (2025)	CNN, RNN, and reinforcement learning in DT computing	Data privacy and security issues due to the continuous exchange of data between AI models and the physical layer without proper cybersecurity countermeasures. High computational cost of implementation and adaptability
Iqbal et al. (2025)	Blockchain in DT for IoV	Adaptability to emerging threats, lack of real-time threat detection
Adnan et al. (2024)	Blockchain integration with multiverse and DT computing	Lack of proof of integration of the AI model with DT layers
Liu et al. (2024)	Human robot digital twin	High cost of implementation; issues in data management and integration with reality; lack of proof of effectiveness of the model
Janani et al. (2023)	Blockchain as a security feature in healthcare systems	High cost of implementation, combined with a lack of adaptability due to the high computational cost
Chatterjee et al. (2024)	Blockchain as a security feature in the metaverse in combination with DT	Adaptability to emerging threats, lack of real-time threat detection
Alharbi et al. (2024)	Blockchain integration with AI and DT for IDS improvement	Lack of proof of integration of technologies and data flow between the layers of DT
Lv et al. (2023)	Blockchain in DT	Adaptability to emerging threats, lack of real-time threat detection
Kumar et al. (2023)	Blockchain and deep learning (LSTM) in DT	High cost of implementation due to the high computational requirements
Qu et al. (2023)	AI combined with Blockchain in DT	High energy consumption, along with high computational requirements and lack of real-time responsiveness; lack of proof of adaptability

validate system interoperability, ensuring that DT technologies remain both adaptable and secure in the face of evolving demands.

To address issues highlighted by the implementation of AI models in DT without security countermeasures, the use of advanced encryption protocols and blockchain-based verification has been pointed out as a suitable solution. Moreover, integrating edge computing strategies and optimizing hardware operation may be used as solutions to help mitigate the computational problem, while adaptive algorithms could be implemented to dynamically adjust to resource availability and emerging threats.

The use of the above-mentioned solutions aligns with the need for the transformation of DT technology into an adaptable technology, while at the same time ensuring that security countermeasures are taken. On the other hand, issues related to real-time responsiveness can be addressed by integrating AI-driven real-time monitoring systems, which could provide rapid threat detection, while the incorporation of adaptive blockchain protocols or modular blockchain architectures could enable quicker responses to new security risks. The combination of these technologies, creating a hybrid security framework, can be used to strengthen proactive threat management.

8.3 The role of blockchain in AI-enabled digital twins

The integration of blockchain with AI in DT computing has been described as key for security, trust, and reliability. DT, which in their definition have been described as technologies that create virtual representations of physical assets, rely heavily on real-time data and AI-driven analytics to work as a primordial element to optimize operations, predict maintenance needs, and detect anomalies. Nevertheless, these capabilities brought by AI/ML models introduce security and data integrity concerns.

Blockchain technology has been introduced to address these challenges by providing a decentralized, immutable, and transparent framework for handling DT data, ensuring secure and verifiable AI/ML operations.

8.3.1 Enhancing data integrity and security

As the primary benefit of blockchain use in DT is its ability to secure data integrity, it is crucial to address this aspect. Since DTs continuously generate large volumes of data from sensors embedded in physical assets that interact with the real-world, the unauthorized manipulation or corruption of this data could lead to incorrect AI-driven decisions, potentially resulting in significant operational failures, thereby making it strictly important to secure this operation.

As a solution in blockchain, the technology has been used to record all operations on a decentralized ledger, ensuring that data remains tamper-proof and verifiable.

On the other hand, blockchain has been equipped with cryptographic security mechanisms, which prevent unauthorized access to data and are used to secure sensitive DT data. Compared with traditional centralized databases, which are vulnerable to cyberattacks and where a single breach can compromise the entire system, blockchain distributes data across multiple nodes, thereby reducing single points of failure and making unauthorized alterations virtually impossible. With this, AI models operate on trusted data, thereby improving the reliability of predictions and decision-making processes.

8.3.2 AI model verification and trustworthiness

Another role of blockchain in combination with AI/ML in DT has been defined as the verification of the authenticity and reliability of AI models deployed in DT. Since AI models are dependent on vast datasets for training and inference, the use of compromised data can affect integrity and lead to biased or malicious outputs. The use of blockchain, which provides a transparent method to register, authenticate, and track changes, when applied to AI models, enables accountability and trust in their decision-making capabilities.

In this way, each AI model can be assigned a unique digital fingerprint on the blockchain, which records all updates and modifications. This capability of blockchain prevents unauthorized tampering, model poisoning, or adversarial attacks, which can affect AI performance. On the other hand, AI model verifications stored on the blockchain allow stakeholders to audit and validate the model's decision-making process, fostering greater confidence in AI-driven DT operations.

8.3.3 Securing data exchange and collaboration

DT often require continuous data exchange across multiple entities and layers of their structure, including manufacturers, operators, and maintenance teams. The reliance on traditional data-sharing mechanisms may introduce security risks, including unauthorized data access and loss of control over shared information. Through the use of blockchain, which enables secure and transparent data sharing via decentralized access control and cryptographic verification, not only is unauthorized access prevented, but predefined access control rules, which automatically execute permissions without requiring a centralized authority, are introduced. This decentralized approach eliminates the need for intermediaries and reduces the risk of data breaches while maintaining transparency in all transactions.

Furthermore, blockchain-based merged learning allows AI models to be trained collaboratively across multiple DTs without directly sharing raw data. This improves privacy while still enabling robust AI-driven insights across interconnected systems, making it particularly valuable in industries such as healthcare, smart cities, and industrial automation.

8.3.4 Resilience against cyber threats

Being a major concern in DT ecosystems, cybersecurity threats, given their reliance on interconnected IoT devices, cloud services, and AI-driven automation, can be mitigated by the use of blockchain, which provides an added layer of resilience by safeguarding against cyber threats such as data breaches, insider attacks, and ransomware incidents.

By the use of immutable records, any attempt to alter data can be detected immediately, preventing attackers from manipulating DT operations. On the other hand, the decentralized nature of blockchain ensures that even if a single node is successfully compromised, the integrity of the entire system remains intact, since the data is replicated in every other node. This significantly reduces the risk of AI-driven decisions being manipulated by malicious actors, enhancing overall cybersecurity in DT environments.

8.3.5 Challenges and considerations

Although blockchain provides robust security advantages for AI-enabled DT, its implementation comes with challenges. Scalability remains a key concern, as traditional blockchain networks struggle to process high volumes of real-time DT data efficiently. As a mitigation for this, hybrid approaches incorporating off-chain storage solutions and layer-2 scaling mechanisms have been widely proposed as solutions.

High computational requirements have been described as another factor to consider, since blockchain validation processes can introduce delays, potentially affecting real-time AI inference in DT systems. High computational resources are required, along with significant energy consumption by the entire system.

The transparent nature of blockchain has been recognized as a point of privacy concern since certain sensitive information may require additional privacy-preserving techniques, such as zero-knowledge proofs or homomorphic encryption, to balance security with confidentiality.

8.3.6 Strengths gained from blockchain integration in AI-enabled DTs

The integration of blockchain into AI-driven DT significantly strengthens operational security, efficiency, and transparency. The following are the key strengths gained from this combination:

- **Enhanced security:** Blockchain has proven to fortify AI-driven DT against cyber threats, ensuring the integrity of data and AI model security.
- **Decentralization and availability:** Blockchain uses its decentralized nature to ensure that DT are resilient to system failures and unauthorized data manipulations.
- **Trust and transparency:** The unauthorized changes brought by blockchain provide AI model decisions with a trustworthy and verifiable audit trail.
- **Improved collaboration:** By leveraging secure data exchange mechanisms of blockchain, multistakeholder participation in DT ecosystems is achieved.
- **Reliable AI predictions:** Ensuring that AI operates on tamper-proof data leads to more accurate predictions and decision-making.
- **Operational efficiency:** Blockchain automation via smart contracts enhances process automation in DT operations, reducing the need for manual oversight.
- **Sustainability and energy efficiency:** The integration of blockchain optimizes the energy usage of DT infrastructures, ensuring sustainable and responsible computing.

8.4 Applications of decentralized DTs

Decentralized DT enhanced by blockchain and ML are finding applications in several domains. Below, we discuss some prominent applications:

8.4.1 Industrial IoT and smart manufacturing

In the IIoT domain, decentralized DT offer significant advantages over traditional centralized systems, since, in manufacturing environments, machines and production lines generate large volumes of data containing operational information (Mikhailov et al., 2022). A decentralized framework ensures that this data is stored securely and is available whenever required. By using blockchain, this aim is easily achieved, while the integrated ML models analyze the data to optimize production schedules, predict maintenance needs, and detect anomalies.

DTs in this field serve as real-time digital replicas of physical assets, processes, or entire production systems. These clones continuously receive data from IIoT sensors implanted in machinery, such as temperature, vibration, torque, and cycle time readings. This data is streamed into the DT, allowing it to emulate the exact state of the physical system at any given time. As a result, machinists and engineers gain full visibility into the condition and performance of machines without needing to be physically present at the manufacturing facility (Dong et al., 2022).

This real-time monitoring, which is achieved by the use of DT, not only improves situational awareness of the machines and the entire replicated environment but also enables faster responses to anomalies or inefficiencies (Wang et al., 2022).

The adoption of decentralized DT using blockchain takes this concept a step further by removing dependence on centralized infrastructure, which sometimes may expose the vulnerability of a single point of failure. By using blockchain, DT can operate across distributed networks, which allows the interaction of all levels of the company, such as manufacturers, suppliers, and service providers, through tamper-proof records of asset performance and status, since each and every update made to the DT, including sensor readings, maintenance logs, or configuration changes, is cryptographically secured and recorded on the blockchain.

The decentralized structure brought by the use of blockchain improves transparency, safeguards data integrity, and supports compliance and traceability in multiparty industrial environments.

With the aim of unlocking the full potential of DT, ML has been integrated, playing a role when applied in IIoT to analyze both historical and real-time IIoT data, identify hidden patterns, forecast future conditions, and ultimately support autonomous decision-making. These insights are fed into the DT, allowing proactive maintenance scheduling, and when combined with blockchain, the entire maintenance history and predictions can be securely shared among authorized partners, ensuring accountability and auditability.

For the optimization of processes, DT uses ML-determined models to test various production parameters and find optimal configurations. For example, reinforcement learning algorithms can be used to train DT to minimize energy consumption or reduce cycle time by continuously learning from operating feedback. On the other hand, blockchain in smart contracts is applied to implement these optimizations automatically. This combination generates a closed-loop system where the ML model provides intelligence, blockchain safeguards trust, and the DT executes and simulates changes across the physical environment.

For quality assurance, ML helps DT detect real-time anomalies during production. Through the use of image recognition, statistical analysis, or deep learning models, it can flag defects as they occur, permitting the DT to immediately alert human operators or initiate corrective actions. These quality actions and responses are logged immutably on the blockchain, providing producers with a verified record of compliance, quality control, and root cause tracing. This reduces recalls, ensures consistent output, and increases confidence in automated quality systems. ML can assess long-term performance trends to suggest system improvements, while blockchain guarantees that the data used is accurate and unaltered. Decentralized DTs, therefore, serve not only as operating tools but also as intellectual, independent entities that learn from their environment and interact securely across a network of stakeholders.

8.4.2 Energy systems and smart grids

The energy sector is increasingly adopting DT to manage and optimize grid operations. The enhancement of decentralized DT can simulate grid behavior, predict load variations, and prevent outages. In this field, blockchain technology is used to secure data exchanges between various grid components, while ML models predict energy consumption patterns and suggest load-balancing strategies (Jafari et al., 2023).

In smart grids, DT simplifies progressive monitoring and control by integrating data from distributed energy resources, sensors, smart meters, and control devices. This technology can simulate the effect of the addition of renewable energy sources, such as solar and wind, to the grid, helping grid operators maintain stability and reliability. Moreover, DT can be used to predict energy demand and generation patterns, enabling more efficient energy delivery and reducing energy losses.

Fault detection and resilience have been described as other applications of DT in smart grids, where, by continuously analyzing real-time data, it can detect anomalies and measure the potential impact of errors before they occur. This ability permits faster response times and better grid reliability. Furthermore, during risky weather events or cyber-attacks, DT can mimic different rescue scenarios, guiding operators in choosing the best response strategies (Das et al., 2024).

The concern brought about by the complexity and modern energy system decentralization highlights that the centralized form of DT architecture is no longer suitable, necessitating the adoption of a decentralized form of DT architecture. By integrating blockchain technology into DT frameworks, the decentralized and tamper-proof approach to data sharing and asset management is significantly enhanced. In traditional DT systems, where data is typically centralized, this centralization may lead to single points of failure and security vulnerabilities. On the other hand, the use of blockchain, with its distributed ledger and consensus mechanisms, ensures that data generated by energy assets, sensors, and user devices is stored securely and transparently across a peer-to-peer network.

Decentralized DT driven by blockchain are predominantly valuable in peer-to-peer energy trading environments, where energy producers and consumers can interact without depending on a central authority (Mourtzis et al., 2022). Each prosumer's energy data is securely recorded on the blockchain and accessed by the DT, which ensures an accurate real-time illustration of their energy production and consumption. Smart contracts can automate transactions, ensuring fair and transparent energy exchanges. This approach not only improves trust among participants but also empowers scalable and self-regulating energy markets.

ML further more improves the capabilities of DT in energy systems and smart grids by allowing intelligent data analysis and predictive modeling. In this, ML helps in predictive maintenance by analyzing sensor data to detect early signs of equipment degradation, reducing downtime and maintenance costs. In load forecasting, ML models can be applied to predict energy consumption patterns with high precision, allowing for better resource distribution and grid balancing.

8.4.3 Healthcare and personalized medicine

The healthcare applications of DT are emerging rapidly, with potential uses in personalized medicine and remote patient monitoring. A decentralized DT framework in healthcare can securely aggregate patient data from multiple sources through the use of blockchain, ensuring data privacy and integrity (Vallée, 2024). ML models can then analyze this data to predict disease progression or modify treatment plans to adjust to individual patients. Although still an emerging area, this combination promises to revolutionize patient care by enabling proactive and personalized healthcare solutions.

A DT in healthcare refers to a virtual replica of a physical entity, such as a patient, medical device, or even an entire hospital, created using data from sensors, medical records, and other digital sources. This digital model can mimic physical functions, disease progression, and treatment outcomes, allowing healthcare professionals to make informed and accurate decisions, predict health risks, and improve clinical workflows. For illustration, in hospital administration, a DT helps optimize resource allocation, reduce wait times, and enhance patient care by modeling patient flow and equipment usage.

In personalized medicine, DTs play a vital role by allowing custom-made treatment plans based on a person's unique physiological and genetic makeup. These models integrate data from wearables, genomic sequencing, and electronic health records to simulate how a precise patient might react to various treatments or lifestyle changes (Garg, 2020). By using virtual experiments on a patient's DT, doctors can select the most effective treatment with minimal side effects, decreasing the trial-and-error method often associated with treatment planning. However, the sensitive and highly personal nature of health data increases concerns about security, privacy, and centralized data control, which require robust solutions to ensure the ethical and secure use of this technology.

To address these challenges and enhance DT intelligence, blockchain and ML technologies are progressively combined into healthcare systems. Blockchain offers a decentralized and tamper-proof framework for managing DT data, ensuring transparency, security, and patient ownership of health records. Through this integration, patients can have access control to their data, allowing secure collaboration between stakeholders without compromising privacy. Concurrently, ML algorithms analyze the vast and complex datasets within DT to detect patterns, predict disease routes, and recommend personalized interventions.

8.4.4 Smart cities and urban infrastructure

Smart cities rely on the incorporation of various subsystems, including traffic management, energy, water, and waste management, to improve urban living. DT provide a virtual model of the city infrastructure, which can be managed in a decentralized fashion using blockchain to ensure data security and availability. On the other hand, ML algorithms analyze real-time data to optimize traffic flow, manage public utilities, and enhance emergency responses. Through the use of DT, urban planning decisions and predictions of the impacts of infrastructural changes can be simulated, allowing the effects to be observed, thereby making cities more adaptive and resilient.

City organizers and policymakers can use DT to monitor traffic patterns, energy usage, waste management, and public transportation systems, allowing for more efficient and approachable urban operations (Sharifi et al., 2024). For example, by modeling traffic congestion or utility usage, cities can optimize traffic light timings, reduce energy waste, and anticipate maintenance requirements before disturbances occur. In addition, DT supports premeditated planning by allowing simulations of infrastructure projects and environmental scenarios, helping to build more sustainable, safe, and livable urban areas.

To improve the reliability, intelligence, and security of DT in smart cities, blockchain and ML have been progressively integrated into their frameworks. Blockchain introduces decentralization, ensuring that urban data collected across various entities such as utility companies, transport agencies, and environmental monitors is securely stored, traceable, and transparently accessible without reliance on a central authority (Weil et al., 2023). This brings about trust and continuous collaboration between public and private stakeholders. In the meantime, ML enables DT to learn from historical and real-time data, refining their predictive capabilities in areas like traffic forecasting, energy optimization, and disaster management. Together, DT, blockchain, and ML form a powerful ecosystem for building intelligent, decentralized, and adaptive smart cities that prioritize efficiency, resilience, and citizen-centric services.

8.4.5 Transportation and autonomous vehicles

Transportation systems and autonomous vehicles require real-time decision-making and continuous learning from operational data. Due to this, the use of ML, which can analyze data to improve navigation, optimize routes, and enhance safety protocols, is mandatory. A decentralized DT framework for transportation systems ensures that data from vehicles, roads, and traffic systems are securely recorded on blockchain, where rapid data processing brought by ML models and secure, decentralized communication are essential for safety and efficiency (Ali et al., 2023).

The integration of DT technology, ML, and blockchain in e-transportation and autonomous vehicles is driving a new era of intelligent and secure mobility solutions. DTs act as real-time virtual complements of physical vehicles and infrastructure, continually updated through data streams from sensors and IoT devices built into vehicles. In electric transportation, the use of DTs helps to monitor parameters such as battery efficiency, motor performance, and route optimization. On the other hand, ML algorithms analyze the data captured by the sensors to identify patterns, predict maintenance needs, and optimize energy usage (Kušić et al., 2023). When combined with blockchain, all data transactions and updates of DTs are securely logged and shared across decentralized networks, ensuring transparency and trust among users.

In the domain of autonomous vehicles, ML improves the decision-making capabilities of both the physical and DT systems. The DT replicates these processes virtually, mimicking numerous scenarios to test and train the vehicle's AI in a risk-free environment and enhance efficiency. On the other hand, blockchain adds an important layer of security by decentralizing data ownership and permitting secure, peer-to-peer data exchange (Chen and Lv, 2022).

The combination of these technologies—DT, ML, and blockchain—has been described as the core of a robust and scalable foundation for future flexibility systems. ML enhances the predictive power of DT, enabling real-time modifications to routes, driving behavior, and energy consumption and efficiency. Blockchain ensures that these insights are securely recorded and shared across a decentralized network, eliminating data silos and enabling collaborative intelligence.

8.4.6 Agriculture and supply chain management

Agriculture benefits significantly from DT technology, where monitoring soil conditions, crop health, and weather patterns can drive precision farming. Blockchain is used in the field to secure the data collected from distributed sensors in agricultural fields; on the other hand, ML models are used to forecast crop yields and optimize irrigation and fertilization processes. Moreover, in supply chain management, DT twins ensure transparency and traceability of products from production to delivery, improving overall efficiency and reducing waste.

The decentralized DT enhanced by the combination of blockchain and ML is key to transforming multiple domains by addressing critical challenges in data security, real-time analytics, and decision-making. In IIoT and smart manufacturing environments, these systems secure large volumes of operational data via blockchain, guaranteeing that the data is tamper-proof and always available. Combined with ML models, which analyze this data to optimize production schedules, predict maintenance needs, and detect anomalies, the efficacy of DT is significantly enhanced.

In the energy sector, such frameworks have been used to simulate grid behavior, predict load variations, help prevent outages, and smooth secure data exchanges between various grid components through blockchain, while ML forecasts energy consumption patterns and updates load balancing strategies.

Likewise, in healthcare, decentralized DT frameworks securely accumulate patient data from multiple sources using blockchain to maintain privacy and integrity, with ML models analyzing the data to predict disease progression and modify treatment plans for proactive, personalized care.

Moreover, in the context of smart cities and urban infrastructure, DT offers a virtual model of city systems that, when managed on a decentralized network, allows ML algorithms to process real-time data to optimize traffic flow, manage services, and enhance emergency responses, thereby assisting adaptive urban planning.

In the same way, in transportation, the use of these systems ensures that data from vehicles, roads, and traffic networks is securely recorded on blockchain, ensuring that this data cannot be accessed by an attacker who could cause accidents by changing the behavior of traffic lights or cars. It also enables ML to continuously analyze the data to improve navigation, optimize routes, and enhance safety protocols, which is an essential requirement for autonomous vehicles.

Lastly, in agriculture and supply chain management, digital twins monitor soil conditions, crop health, and weather patterns. Through the use of blockchain, the data from sensors is secured, producing accurate information that is utilized by ML to forecast crop yields and optimize irrigation and fertilization processes. In addition, transparency and traceability of products from production to delivery are ensured, thereby enhancing overall efficiency and reducing waste.

8.5 Conclusion

The integration of blockchain with AI in DT computing strengthens security, trust, and transparency. The capabilities of blockchain, such as its decentralized nature, which safeguards data integrity and prevents unauthorized access, have been identified as factors that enhance the trustworthiness of AI-driven DT. By securing AI models, which act as the brain of the entire system, enabling transparent data exchange, and fortifying resilience against cyber threats, blockchain provides a solid foundation for the responsible adoption of DT technology across various industries.

Regardless of challenges such as scalability and high computational requirements, ongoing advancements in blockchain and AI integration continue to improve efficiency and security.

8.5.1 Future direction

Future research should focus on optimizing blockchain performance for real-time DT applications and exploring innovative solutions to enhance privacy and interoperability due to the huge quantity of data generated by these technologies, which require continued control. By addressing these challenges, blockchain and AI-driven DT can unlock new levels of efficiency, security, and innovation in the digital economy.

References

Adnan, M., Ahmed, I., Iqbal, S., Fazal, M.R., Siddiqi, S.J., Tariq, M., 2024. Exploring the convergence of Metaverse, Blockchain, Artificial Intelligence, and digital twin for pioneering the digitization in the envision smart grid 3.0. Comput. Electr. Eng. 0045-7906. 120. Available from: https://www.sciencedirect.com/science/journal/00457906. doi:10.1016/j.compeleceng.2024.109709.

Alharbi, O., Shaikh, R.A., Asif, R. 2024. Data-aided intrusion detection systems: leveraging AI, blockchain and digital twin technology. In: Proceedings—2024 IEEE International Conference on Big Data, BigData 2024. Institute of Electrical and Electronics Engineers Inc., United Kingdom, pp. 8214–8215. 9798350362480. Available from: http://ieeexplore.ieee.org/xpl/mostRecentIssue.jsp?punumber=10824975. doi:10.1109/BigData62323.2024.10825899.

Ali, W.A., Fanti, M.P., Roccotelli, M., Ranieri, L., 2023. A review of digital twin technology for electric and autonomous vehicles. Appl. Sci. 2076-3417. 13 (10). Available from: www.mdpi.com/journal/applsci/. doi:10.3390/app13105871.

Chatterjee, P., Das, D., Rawat, D.B., Ghosh, U., Banerjee, S., Al-Numay, M.S., 2024. Digital twins and blockchain fusion for security in metaverse-driven consumer supply chains. IEEE Trans. Consum. Electron. 1558-4127. 70 (3), 5688–5697. Available from: https://ieeexplore.ieee.org/servlet/opac?punumber=30. doi:10.1109/TCE.2024.3477297.

Chen, D., Lv, Z., 2022. Artificial intelligence enabled digital twins for training autonomous cars. Internet Things Cyber-Phys. Syst. 2667-3452. 2, 31–41. Available from: https://www.sciencedirect.com/science/journal/26673452. doi:10.1016/j.iotcps.2022.05.001.

Das, O., Zafar, M.H., Sanfilippo, F., Rudra, S., Kolhe, M.L., 2024. Advancements in digital twin technology and machine learning for energy systems: a comprehensive review of applications in smart grids, renewable energy, and electric vehicle optimisation. Energy Convers. Manag. X 2590-1745. (24). Available from: https://www.sciencedirect.com/science/journal/25901745. doi:10.1016/j.ecmx.2024.100715.

Dong, Y., Li, Y., Ke, H. 2022. Enhancing production scheduling provisioning in IIoT systems with digital twin. In: 4th International Academic Exchange Conference on Science and Technology Innovation, IAECST 2022. Institute of Electrical and Electronics Engineers Inc., China, pp. 1188–1191. 9798350320008. Available from: http://ieeexplore.ieee.org/xpl/mostRecentIssue.jsp?punumber=10061847. doi:10.1109/IAECST57965.2022.10061886.

Garg, H., 2020. Digital twin technology: revolutionary to improve personalized healthcare. Sci. Prog. Res. 2635-0955. 1 (1). doi:10.52152/spr.2020.01.104.

Iqbal, M., Suhail, S., Matulevičius, R., Shah, F.A., Malik, S.U.R., McLaughlin, K., 2025. IoV-TwinChain: predictive maintenance of vehicles in internet of vehicles through digital twin and blockchain. Internet Things. 2542-6605. 30. Available from: https://www.sciencedirect.com/science/journal/25426605. doi:10.1016/j.iot.2025.101514.

Jafari, M., Kavousi-Fard, A., Chen, T., Karimi, M., 2023. A review on digital twin technology in smart grid, transportation system and smart city: challenges and future. IEEE Access 2169-3536. 11, 17471–17484. Available from: http://ieeexplore.ieee.org/xpl/RecentIssue.jsp?punumber=6287639. doi:10.1109/ACCESS.2023.3241588.

Janani, S.R., Mukesh Kumar, A., Nigilesh, R., Karunya, G., Nitheesh, C., 2023. Securing the confidential data using blockchain and DT framework. In: 9th International Conference on Advanced Computing and Communication Systems, ICACCS 2023. Institute of Electrical and Electronics Engineers Inc., India, pp. 933–936. 9798350397376. Available from: http://ieeexplore.ieee.org/xpl/mostRecentIssue.jsp?punumber=10112659. doi:10.1109/ICACCS57279.2023.10112904.

Khalaj, O., Hassas, P., Mašek, B., Štadler, C., Svoboda, J., 2024. Optimization of cooling rate of Q-P treated 42SiCr steel using AI digital twinning. Heliyon. 2405-8440. 10 (11). Available from: https://www.sciencedirect.com/science/journal/24058440. doi:10.1016/j.heliyon.2024.e32101.

Kobayashi, K., Alam, S.B., 2024. Explainable, interpretable, and trustworthy AI for an intelligent digital twin: a case study on remaining useful life. Eng. Appl. Artif. Intell. 0952-1976. 129. Available from: https://www.sciencedirect.com/science/journal/09521976. doi:10.1016/j.engappai.2023.107620.

Kumar, P., Kumar, R., Kumar, A., Franklin, A.A., Garg, S., Singh, S., 2023. Blockchain and deep learning for secure communication in digital twin empowered industrial IoT network. IEEE Trans. Netw. Sci. Eng. 2327-4697. 10 (5), 2802–2813. Available from: http://www.computer.org/portal/web/tnse. doi:10.1109/TNSE.2022.3191601.

Kušić, K., Schumann, R., Ivanjko, E., 2023. A digital twin in transportation: real-time synergy of traffic data streams and simulation for virtualizing motorway dynamics. Adv. Eng. Inform. 1474-0346. 55, 101858. doi:10.1016/j.aei.2022.101858.

Liu, X., Li, G., Xiang, F., Tao, B., Jiang, G., 2024. Blockchain-based cloud-edge collaborative data management for human-robot collaboration digital twin system. J. Manuf. Syst. 0278-6125. 77, 228–245. Available from: https://www.sciencedirect.com/science/journal/02786125. doi:10.1016/j.jmsy.2024.09.006.

Lv, Z., Cheng, C., Lv, H., 2023. Blockchain-based decentralized learning for security in digital twins. IEEE Internet Things J. 2327-4662. 10 (24), 21479–21488. Available from: http://ieeexplore.ieee.org/servlet/opac?punumber=6488907. doi:10.1109/JIOT.2023.3295499.

Mikhailov, A., Tretyakov, S., Andreev, Y. 2022. A new approach to build industrial internet of things (IIoT) systems based on digital twin's technologies. In: Proceedings—2022 International Conference on Industrial Engineering, Applications and Manufacturing, ICIEAM 2022. Institute of Electrical and Electronics Engineers Inc., Russian Federation, pp. 1091–1095. 9781665483698. Available from: http://ieeexplore.ieee.org/xpl/mostRecentIssue.jsp?punumber=9786772. doi:10.1109/ICIEAM54945.2022.9787171.

Mourtzis, D., Angelopoulos, J., Panopoulos, N., 2022. Development of a PSS for smart grid energy distribution optimization based on digital twin. Procedia CIRP. 107, 1138–1143. 22128271. Available from: http://www.sciencedirect.com/science/journal/22128271. doi:10.1016/j.procir.2022.05.121.

Oulefki, A., Kheddar, H., Amira, A., Kurugollu, F., Himeur, Y., Bounceur, A., 2025. Innovative AI strategies for enhancing smart building operations through digital twins: a survey. Emirates Energy Build. 0378-7788. 335. Available from: https://www.sciencedirect.com/science/journal/03787788. doi:10.1016/j.enbuild.2025.115567.

Qu, B., Zhu, C., Liu, M., Cheng, W., Zhou, R., Wang, 2023. Urna l Pref. J. Lumin. 2. doi:10.1016/j.jobe.2025.112439.

Sharifi, A., Tarlani Beris, A., Sharifzadeh Javidi, A., Nouri, M., Gholizadeh Lonbar, A., Ahmadi, M., 2024. Application of artificial intelligence in digital twin models for stormwater infrastructure systems in smart cities. Adv. Eng. Inform. 1474-0346. 61, 102485. doi:10.1016/j.aei.2024.102485.

Vallée, A., 2024. Envisioning the future of personalized medicine: role and realities of digital twins. J. Med. Internet Res. 1438-8871. 26, e50204. doi:10.2196/50204.

Wang, P.T., Lu, C.J., Chang, C.L. 2022. GRAFCET virtual machine enables digital twin and implements PLCopen systems. In: 10th International Conference on Orange Technology, ICOT 2022. Institute of Electrical and Electronics Engineers Inc., Taiwan. 9781665454193. Available from: http://ieeexplore.ieee.org/xpl/mostRecentIssue.jsp?punumber=10008107. doi:10.1109/ICOT56925.2022.10008133.

Weil, C., Bibri, S.E., Longchamp, R., Golay, F., Alahi, A., 2023. Urban digital twin challenges: a systematic review and perspectives for sustainable smart cities. Sustain. Cities Soc. 2210-6707. 99, 104862. doi:10.1016/j.scs.2023.104862.

CHAPTER 9

Blockchain for IoT-enabled digital twin

Amit Kumar Tyagi[a], Shabnam Kumari[b], and Richa[c]

[a]*Department of Fashion Technology, National Institute of Fashion Technology, New Delhi, India*
[b]*Department of Computer Science, Faculty of Science and Humanities, SRM Institute of Science and Technology, Kattankulathur, Chennai, Tamil Nadu, India*
[c]*Department of Computer Science and Engineering, Birla Institute of Technology, Mesra, Ranchi, India*

9.1 Introduction

Decentralized technology represents a paradigm shift from traditional centralized systems by distributing control, data, and decision-making across multiple nodes or participants. Unlike centralized architectures, where a single authority governs the system and data flows through a central hub, decentralized systems rely on peer-to-peer networks, consensus mechanisms, and cryptographic protocols to ensure trust, transparency, and resilience. This fundamental change empowers individuals and organizations by reducing dependency on intermediaries, enhancing data privacy, and enabling more democratic forms of governance.

At the core of decentralized technology is blockchain, a distributed ledger system where information is securely recorded across a network of computers. Each block of data is cryptographically linked to the previous one, making the entire chain tamper-resistant and transparent. Blockchain forms the foundation for cryptocurrencies like Bitcoin and Ethereum but has far broader applications in areas such as finance, supply chain, healthcare, and digital identity. Smart contracts—self-executing programs on the blockchain—further automate and decentralize agreements, reducing the need for manual intervention or third-party enforcement.

The rise of decentralized applications, Decentralized Autonomous Organizations (DAOs), and Web3 technologies is redefining how people interact with digital services, own digital assets, and participate in online communities. In parallel, decentralized networks like Interplanetary File System (IPFS) and mesh networks are changing how data is stored and transmitted, reducing reliance on centralized servers and improving data sovereignty. Note that decentralization also complements emerging technologies like artificial intelligence (AI) and the Internet of Things (IoT) by enabling secure, scalable, and interoperable ecosystems. As concerns about privacy, censorship, and centralized control grow, decentralized

Artificial Intelligence, Machine Learning and Blockchain in Digital Twin Computing.
https://doi.org/10.1016/B978-0-443-43914-8.00020-0

technology offers a promising pathway to build systems that are not only more transparent and trustworthy but also more resilient and inclusive in the digital age.

9.1.1 Background and motivation

In the era of Industry 4.0, the integration of physical and digital systems is transforming the design, operation, and maintenance of industrial and cyber-physical systems. A digital twin (DT) is a dynamic virtual representation of a physical entity, process, or system that is perpetually updated via real-time data from IoT devices (Alam and El Saddik, 2017; Lee et al., 2015; Ferrari et al., 2020). These virtual entities facilitate predictive maintenance, optimization, and modeling of real-world systems. The dependence on IoT data raises issues related to data security, privacy, traceability, and integrity. IoT ecosystems frequently experience centralized data structures, rendering them susceptible to cyberattacks, data manipulation, and single points of failure. Furthermore, in critical sectors such as smart grids, manufacturing, healthcare, or transportation, the veracity and permanence of sensor data are of utmost importance when employing DTs. To mitigate these issues, Blockchain Technology—a decentralized and immutable digital ledger—can be coupled with IoT-enabled DTs. Blockchain guarantees transparent, immutable, and verifiable data transfers between physical systems and their digital equivalents. This interface fosters confidence, enhances data provenance, and facilitates secure automation through the utilization of smart contracts.

9.1.2 Objectives of the study

This research is motivated by the increasing necessity to guarantee reliable and secure data transmission in IoT-centric digital environments. As systems become more networked and autonomous, decision-making increasingly depends on data-driven insights produced by DTs. Inaccurate, corrupted, or delayed data feeding these twins can lead to erroneous forecasts, safety hazards, or financial detriment. Conventional centralized data architectures are inadequate for fulfilling the scalability, decentralization, and resilience requirements of extensive IoT–DT applications. Blockchain offers a persuasive option due to its capacity to:

- Authenticate data using cryptographic methods
- Mitigate tampering with immutable transaction records
- Facilitate trust through the utilization of smart contracts
- Improve the auditability of modifications and occurrences in DTs

This chapter explores the utilisation utilize blockchain to establish a resilient digital infrastructure that guarantees data openness, operational robustness, and security in essential DT systems. This convergence has transformational possibilities across industries, including smart manufacturing and renewable energy systems, thus signifying a crucial advancement toward realizing a genuinely autonomous and reliable cyber-physical world.

9.2 Fundamentals of Internet of things, DT, and blockchain technology

9.2.1 Overview of IoT

The IoT denotes a network of interconnected physical devices—such as sensors, machinery, automobiles, and household appliances—that gather and transmit data via the internet. These devices incorporate sensors, software, and communication technologies, allowing them to monitor environments, interpret real-time data, and engage with other systems or users autonomously. The IoT is revolutionizing our engagement with the physical environment in various industries, including healthcare, manufacturing, energy, agriculture, and smart cities, through the facilitation of automation, remote monitoring, and data-driven insights. The rapid deployment of IoT yields substantial advantages in efficiency, cost reduction, and ease. Nonetheless, difficulties including data security, interoperability, and scalability remain. Facilitating safe communication among billions of devices, overseeing substantial quantities of real-time data, and standardizing protocols are persistent research domains. Advancements in AI, blockchain, and edge computing indicate that the future of IoT involves the development of intelligent, autonomous, and reliable systems that facilitate breakthroughs such as DTs, smart infrastructure, and real-time decision-making in essential applications.

9.2.2 Digital twins—An introduction

A DT is a virtual representation of a physical product, system, or process that accurately reflects its real-world counterpart in real time, utilizing data from embedded sensors and IoT devices. DTs continuously receive and process data to replicate the behavior, performance, and condition of a physical entity, enabling organizations to monitor, analyze, and optimize operations. Originally popularized in manufacturing and aerospace, DTs are now extensively utilized in sectors such as healthcare, energy, urban planning, and transportation to improve decision-making and predictive maintenance. The primary benefit of DTs is their ability to provide a dynamic, data-informed model that adapts alongside the physical system it represents. This allows stakeholders to evaluate scenarios, predict outcomes, and identify anomalies before difficulties arise, thereby minimizing downtime and enhancing operational efficiency. As DT technology evolves—bolstered by advancements in AI, machine learning (ML), and rapid data processing—it is essential for fostering more intelligent and robust cyber-physical systems and is integral to the concept of Industry 4.0 and intelligent infrastructure.

9.2.3 Fundamentals of blockchain technology

Blockchain technology is a decentralized and distributed ledger system that securely, transparently, and immutably records transactions over a network of computers. Each record or transaction is consolidated into a "block" and connected to the preceding block, creating a chronological "chain" of blocks. This framework guarantees that once data is documented, it cannot be modified retroactively without changing all subsequent blocks, necessitating consensus from the network. Blockchain is especially advantageous for applications necessitating trust, transparency, and data integrity, including cryptocurrency, digital identities, and smart contracts. Blockchain fundamentally relies on three essential principles: decentralization, immutability, and consensus. Decentralization signifies the absence of a singular authority governing the network; transactions are authenticated and approved by numerous participants (nodes) (Christidis and Devetsikiotis, 2016). Immutability guarantees that data, once recorded, is unalterable. Consensus mechanisms such as Proof-of-Work (PoW) and Proof-of-Stake facilitate the validation of transactions without the necessity of a central authority. These attributes render blockchain a formidable instrument not only for financial systems but also for supply chains, healthcare, IoT, and digital governance, where secure, verifiable, and traceable data transmission is essential.

9.3 Benefits and limitations, of blockchain, IoT, and DT—In general

As discussed in Tyagi (2024a, Tyagi, 2024, 2024c, 2024d, 2024b, 2023, 2021, 2020, 2022, 2016); Tyagi and Aghila (2011); and Tyagi (2025a, 2025b), blockchain is widely recognized for its ability to provide a secure, decentralized, and transparent framework for data management. Its key benefits include enhanced data integrity, immutability, and the elimination of intermediaries through the use of smart contracts. These features make blockchain especially useful in applications requiring trust, such as finance, supply chain management, and healthcare data sharing. However, blockchain also comes with certain limitations. Its scalability remains a challenge, particularly in public blockchain networks where transaction processing can be slow and energy-intensive. Moreover, integrating blockchain with existing legacy systems can be complex, and regulatory uncertainties still pose adoption hurdles in many regions.

The IoT has transformed the way physical devices interact with the digital world by enabling real-time data collection, remote monitoring, and automation. IoT offers numerous benefits, including improved operational efficiency, predictive maintenance, enhanced user experiences, and better decision-making through continuous data insights. These capabilities have made IoT critical in sectors such as smart homes, healthcare, agriculture, and industrial automation. Despite these advantages, IoT also presents several limitations. Security and privacy are major concerns, as the vast number of interconnected devices increases the potential attack surface. In addition, IoT systems often suffer from interoperability issues, especially when devices from different vendors need to work together seamlessly. Ensuring reliable connectivity and managing massive data volumes are also significant technical challenges.

DT technology enables the creation of virtual models of physical systems, allowing real-time monitoring, simulation, and optimization of assets. The main benefits of DTs include improved predictive maintenance, enhanced decision-making, reduced operational costs, and the ability to simulate various scenarios without physical risk. In industries like aerospace, manufacturing, and healthcare, DTs are revolutionizing system design, diagnostics, and performance analysis. However, implementing DTs is not without limitations. They require accurate, real-time data from sensors and systems, which can be expensive and technically complex to maintain. Moreover, creating high-fidelity models demands significant computational power and domain-specific expertise. There is also the risk of data overload if information from multiple systems is not effectively integrated and analyzed (see Tables 9.1 and 9 2).

Table 9.1 Comparison of blockchain, IoT, and digital twin.

Technology	Key features	Benefits	Limitations
Blockchain	• Decentralization • Immutable ledger • Smart contracts • Peer-to-peer transactions	• Enhanced data integrity and trust • Transparent transactions • Improved cybersecurity • Reduced need for intermediaries	• Scalability issues (especially public blockchains) • High energy consumption (PoW-based) • Regulatory and legal challenges • Complex integration with legacy systems
IoT	• Real-time sensing • Device interconnectivity • Remote monitoring • Edge computing support	• Real-time data collection and control • Improved operational efficiency • Predictive maintenance • Enhanced user experience	• Security vulnerabilities • Data privacy issues • Interoperability challenges • Requires robust network infrastructure
Digital twin	• Virtual replication of physical systems • Real-time synchronization • Simulation and prediction • AI/ML integration	• Enhanced decision-making • Predictive analytics and optimization • Reduced downtime and testing costs • Supports remote diagnostics	• High implementation cost • Requires accurate real-time data • Complexity in modeling and integration • Data overload, if not managed well

Table 9.2 Security and privacy issues and challenges.

Security issues	Challenges	Description
Vulnerability of IoT devices	IoT sensors often operate in unsecured or remote environments	Limited computational resources make them easy targets for cyberattacks such as spoofing, denial of service, or device hijacking
False data injection	Malicious or compromised IoT devices can feed inaccurate data into the digital twin	This leads to flawed simulations, incorrect decision-making, or unsafe automated actions
Smart contract vulnerabilities	Poorly written or untested smart contracts can be exploited	Once deployed, these contracts are immutable, so bugs can lead to irreversible security breaches or unintended behavior
End-to-end data security	Ensuring secure data transmission from physical devices to the DT and blockchain is complex	Requires encryption, secure communication protocols, and intrusion detection systems
Privacy issues	**Challenges**	**Description**
Data exposure on blockchain	Public blockchains make all stored data visible to all participants	Sensitive operational or personal data from IoT devices risk exposure
Data ownership and access control	Difficulty in defining and enforcing ownership of data in distributed systems	Fine-grained access control mechanisms are needed to manage permission levels
User and device identity management	Secure and scalable identity verification for billions of IoT devices is a major challenge	Without proper authentication, unauthorized access can compromise the system
Compliance with regulations	Regulations like the **GDPR** demand user consent and the ability to erase personal data	Blockchain's immutability conflicts with the "right to be forgotten"

In summary, while blockchain, IoT, and DT technologies offer transformative capabilities, each comes with its own challenges.

9.4 Integration of blockchain, IoT, and DT

The convergence of Blockchain, IoT, and DT technologies provides a robust framework for constructing safe, intelligent, and autonomous cyber-physical systems. IoT devices incessantly gather real-time data from physical assets, which is subsequently integrated into DTs—virtual representations that emulate the behavior and condition of those assets. This facilitates predictive maintenance, performance enhancement, and instantaneous decision-making. The integrity and security of data transmitted from IoT to the DT are essential for ensuring precise simulations and reliable operations. Blockchain technology fortifies this ecosystem by offering a decentralized and immutable ledger for documenting all IoT-generated data and DT transactions. Integrating blockchain ensures that each data point or operational change is securely timestamped and verified, thereby guaranteeing transparency, immutability, and traceability throughout the system. Smart contracts can automate responses to specified situations within the DT, facilitating autonomous operations without centralized supervision. This convergence provides confidence, mitigates risks, and facilitates the implementation of resilient, scalable solutions across sectors including manufacturing, energy, transportation, and healthcare (Reyna et al., 2018; Kumar and Tripathi, 2021).

9.4.1 Trust and security in integrated systems

As integrated systems that amalgamate IoT, DTs, and blockchain gain prominence, trust and security become essential foundations for their effective implementation. IoT devices frequently function in unprotected settings and are susceptible to cyberattacks, data tampering, and unauthorized access. When data is integrated into DTs—employed for real-time monitoring, modeling, and decision-making—any minor mistakes or malicious modifications might result in substantial operational hazards or system breakdowns. Ensuring the authenticity, confidentiality, and integrity of data is crucial for sustaining trust in DT outputs and automated activities. Blockchain technology mitigates these difficulties by providing a decentralized and immutable ledger, wherein all transactions and data transfers are cryptographically secured and transparently documented. This eliminates the necessity for a central authority and guarantees that all data—regardless of whether it originates from IoT sensors or system updates to the DT—can be autonomously verified and traced. Moreover, smart contracts provide automated, rule-governed processes with inherent security and audit capabilities. Utilizing blockchain's consensus mechanisms and tamper-resistance, integrated systems achieve improved resilience against data breaches, tampering, and insider threats, thereby cultivating more trust among stakeholders, users, and machines.

9.4.2 Smart contracts for DTs

Smart contracts are self-executing programs recorded on a blockchain that autonomously enforce stipulations and perform actions upon the fulfillment of predetermined criteria. When combined with DTs, smart contracts provide autonomous and secure interactions among the physical asset, its digital counterpart, and external systems. For instance, if a DT identifies that a machine's temperature has surpassed a safe limit, a smart contract can autonomously initiate a maintenance request, deactivate the device, or notify pertinent personnel—without human involvement. This enhances efficiency and guarantees prompt, rule-based reactions to real-world occurrences. Integrating smart contracts into DT ecosystems enables organizations to attain automated governance, real-time compliance, and reliable execution of operational processes. These contracts guarantee that actions performed by the DT—such as updates, notifications, or reconfigurations—are transparent, traceable, and immutable, as all executions are documented on the blockchain. This integration improves reliability, decreases manual labor, and alleviates dangers linked to centralized control and data manipulation in industries such as manufacturing, energy, and supply chain. Consequently, smart contracts are essential for rendering DTs intelligent, autonomous, and safe in blockchain-based systems.

9.5 Challenges and research issues

The promise of merging blockchain, IoT, and DT technologies is compelling; however, various technological and operational difficulties impede widespread adoption. A significant concern is the scalability and latency of blockchain networks, particularly in the context of high-frequency, real-time IoT data streams. Public blockchains, specifically, frequently experience constrained transaction throughput and elevated energy consumption. Moreover, on-chain data storage is inefficient and expensive, rendering it unfeasible to directly store substantial quantities of sensor data on the blockchain. The interoperability of various IoT protocols, DT systems, and blockchain frameworks continues to be a significant issue. Research necessitates the development of lightweight consensus mechanisms tailored for resource-constrained IoT contexts, alongside hybrid storage models (e.g., off-chain/on-chain architectures) that maintain data integrity without excessively taxing the blockchain. Security continues to be a critical focus, especially in relation to end-to-end encryption, identity management, and the secure execution of smart contracts. Additional unresolved concerns encompass the standardization of frameworks, real-time synchronization between the physical and DT, and the ethical utilization of autonomous smart contracts. Confronting these difficulties necessitates interdisciplinary research encompassing computer science, cybersecurity, systems engineering, and specialized applications (Reyna et al., 2018; Samaniego and Deters, 2017).

- **Scalability and performance**
  - **Challenge**: Traditional blockchains (like Bitcoin and Ethereum) have limited transaction throughput and high latency, which are unsuitable for real-time IoT data.
  - **Research focus**: Development of scalable blockchain architectures (e.g., sharding, DAG, Layer-2 solutions) optimized for high-frequency data environments.
  - **Resource constraints in IoT devices**
- **Challenge**: IoT devices often have limited processing power, memory, and energy, making it difficult to run blockchain nodes or validate blocks.
- **Research focus**: Design of lightweight consensus mechanisms (e.g., Proof-of-Authority, Practical Byzantine Fault Tolerance (PBFT)) and blockchain clients suitable for edge/IoT environments.
- **Data storage and management**
- **Challenge**: Storing large volumes of real-time IoT data on-chain is impractical due to storage limitations and costs.

- **Research focus**: Hybrid models that combine **off-chain storage** (e.g., IPFS, cloud) with **on-chain hash verification** for data integrity and traceability.
- **Privacy and data confidentiality**
- **Challenge**: Public blockchains expose transaction data to all participants, which may violate privacy regulations or compromise business confidentiality.
- **Research focus**: The use of **zero-knowledge proofs**, **homomorphic encryption**, and **private/permissioned blockchains** to ensure privacy in DT ecosystems.
- **Smart contract security**
- **Challenge**: Bugs or vulnerabilities in smart contracts can lead to data leaks or system manipulation.
- **Research focus**: Formal verification methods, secure contract templates, and runtime monitoring to improve smart contract reliability and trustworthiness.
- **Interoperability and standardization**
- **Challenge**: Integration of diverse IoT platforms, DT models, and blockchain frameworks is complex and lacks common standards.
- **Research focus**: Development of middleware, APIs, and open interoperability standards (e.g., Institute of Electrical and Electronics Engineers (IEEE), International Organization for Standardization (ISO)) for seamless integration.
- **Identity management and authentication**
- **Challenge**: Securing the identities of billions of IoT devices and ensuring trusted interactions are major hurdles.
- **Research focus**: Blockchain-based **decentralized identity (DID)** systems for secure, scalable, and privacy-preserving device and user authentication.
- **Regulatory and legal uncertainty**
- **Challenge**: Lack of clear regulatory frameworks for blockchain, especially in cross-border data transactions involving DTs.
- **Research focus**: Policy research to align blockchain usage with **General Data Protection Regulation (GDPR), Health Insurance Portability and Accountability Act (HIPAA), National Institute of Standards and Technology (NIST)**, and other domain-specific standards and legal norms.
- **Real-time synchronization and latency**
- **Challenge**: Achieving low-latency, real-time synchronization between the physical asset, IoT layer, and blockchain ledger is technically demanding.
- **Research focus**: Use of **edge computing** and **event-driven architectures** to reduce delays while maintaining data integrity.
- **High implementation and operational costs**
- **Challenge**: Initial costs for setting up a blockchain-enabled DT system can be high, especially with customized infrastructure.
- **Research focus**: Cost-benefit modeling and development of **blockchain-as–a-service** frameworks to lower entry barriers for adoption.

9.6 Security and privacy issues and challenges

Security and privacy are key challenges in the integration of Blockchain, IoT, and DT systems. IoT devices frequently possess constrained computational capabilities and operate within open, distributed environments, rendering them susceptible to threats such as spoofing, data interception, and unauthorized access (Dorri et al., 2017; Zhang et al., 2019). When these compromised devices transmit erroneous or harmful data to DTs, the ensuing actions or decisions—such as initiating a maintenance event or reconfiguring a system—can have significant real-world repercussions. Furthermore, DTs retain important operational data, and if inadequately safeguarded, they may jeopardize an organization's intellectual property or expose system vulnerabilities. Although blockchain provides attributes such as immutability, decentralization, and transparency, it also presents new challenges. Privacy issues arise when sensitive IoT data is stored on public or permissionless blockchains, rendering such data accessible to all network participants. Managing data ownership, access restrictions, and user anonymity is complex even in private blockchains. Furthermore, inadequately developed smart contracts may be susceptible to exploitation, resulting in unexpected actions or data breaches. Ensuring secure data exchange, precise access control, reliable identity management, and adherence to data protection regulations (such as GDPR) presents ongoing research and implementation challenges. Consequently, the creation of systems that are simultaneously secure and privacy-preserving is an urgent requirement in the advancement of reliable, large-scale blockchain-enabled DT ecosystems.

9.7 Future directions

The convergence of blockchain, IoT, and DT technologies is set to transform the framework of intelligent, secure, and autonomous systems across several industries. As these technologies converge, future advancements will concentrate on addressing existing restrictions, including scalability, interoperability, and security. Streamlined blockchain protocols designed for IoT, along with off-chain storage solutions and DID management, will facilitate the development of more efficient and reliable infrastructures. Moreover, real-time synchronization of DTs and standardized frameworks will be crucial for uninterrupted cross-platform communication and system-wide coherence. In the future, the implementation of AI-enhanced DTs and privacy-preserving cryptographic methods, such as zero-knowledge proofs, will provide sophisticated analytics while protecting sensitive information (Kumar and Tripathi, 2021; Kshetri, 2017; Singh et al., 2018; Conoscenti et al., 2016). Edge computing will be essential in minimizing latency and processing key data near the source. Furthermore, developments tailored to specific applications in fields such as healthcare, energy, and smart manufacturing, in conjunction with regulatory and ethical frameworks, will direct the appropriate implementation of these technologies. These directives will together

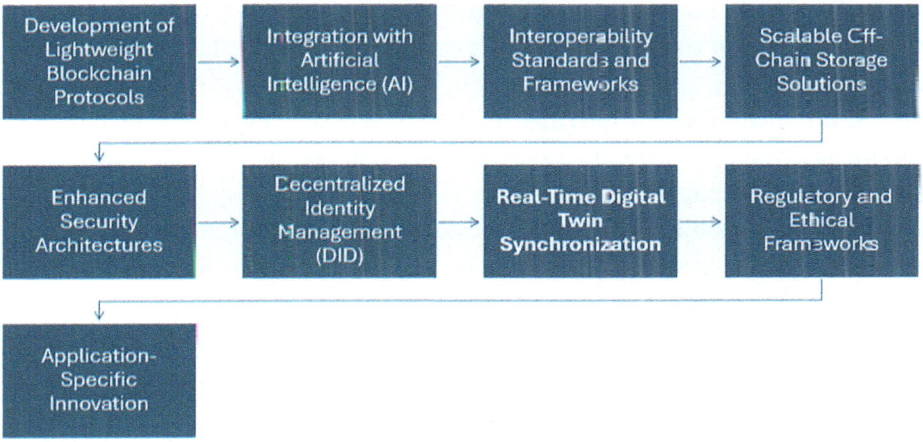

Fig. 9.1 Future direction.

foster the development of resilient, transparent, and intelligent cyber-physical ecosystems (Fig. 9.1).

9.8 Opportunities for AI and blockchain for IoT-enabled DT

The fusion of blockchain, IoT, and DT technologies is set to transform the framework of intelligent, secure, and autonomous systems across several industries. As these technologies converge, future advancements will focus on addressing existing limitations, including scalability, interoperability, and security. Streamlined blockchain protocols designed for IoT, along with off-chain storage solutions and DID management, will facilitate the development of more efficient and reliable infrastructures. Moreover, real-time synchronization of DTs and standardized frameworks will be crucial for uninterrupted cross-platform communication and system-wide coherence. In the future, the implementation of AI-enhanced DTs and privacy-preserving cryptographic methods, such as zero-knowledge proofs, will provide sophisticated analytics while protecting sensitive information. Edge computing will be essential in minimizing latency and processing key data near the source. Furthermore, developments tailored to specific applications in fields such as healthcare, energy, and smart manufacturing, in conjunction with regulatory and ethical frameworks, will guide the appropriate implementation of these technologies. These directives will collectively foster the development of resilient, transparent, and intelligent cyber-physical ecosystems (Ferrer, 2018; Lu and Xu, 2019; Huh et al., 2017).

- **Data integrity and immutability:** Blockchain ensures that all IoT-generated data recorded in the DT is tamper-proof and verifiable, enhancing the reliability of simulations and analytics.

- **Decentralized data management** Eliminates the need for centralized control systems, reducing the risk of a single point of failure and improving system resilience and availability.
- **Secure and transparent audit trails:** Every transaction, update, and data interaction within the DT system is logged on the blockchain, allowing full traceability and compliance with auditing requirements.
- **Smart contract automation:** Enables the automatic execution of predefined actions (e.g., alerts, repairs, or shutdowns) based on real-time IoT data changes captured by the DT.
- **Device authentication and access control:** Blockchain can securely manage the identities of IoT devices and users, ensuring that only authorized entities can access or control the DT.
- **Trustless multiparty collaboration:** Facilitates secure data sharing and collaboration among multiple stakeholders (manufacturers, operators, regulators) without the need for mutual trust.
- **Efficient dispute resolution:** Immutable records maintained on the blockchain can serve as credible evidence in cases of disputes regarding asset conditions, operations, or failures.
- **Data monetization and sharing models:** Enable new business models where IoT data from DTs can be securely and selectively shared or monetized via tokenized ecosystems.
- **Compliance with regulatory requirements:** Blockchain's traceability features help meet industry regulations related to data provenance, reporting, and transparency.
- **Enhancement of cybersecurity posture:** Adds a layer of protection against common cyber threats, such as data tampering, unauthorized access, and denial-of-service attacks.

9.9 Emerging trends toward emerging technologies

In the landscape of modern digital transformation, the fusion of AI, Blockchain, and the IoT with DT technology is driving a new wave of innovation. DTs, which are dynamic virtual representations of physical systems, processes, or objects, are gaining increasing relevance across industries. They are being empowered by IoT for real-time data acquisition and monitoring, enhanced by AI for predictive analytics and autonomous decision-making, and secured by Blockchain to ensure trust, transparency, and data integrity. As these technologies evolve independently, their convergence is shaping an intelligent, interconnected, and secure ecosystem that is expected to define the future of smart infrastructure, manufacturing, healthcare, logistics, and beyond. This integrated framework is pushing the boundaries of how we design, operate, and maintain complex systems.

At the heart of this transformation lies the concept of AI-enabled DTs. AI is being integrated into DTs to provide advanced capabilities such as real-time data analytics, anomaly detection, fault prediction, and autonomous decision support. Traditional DTs were primarily reactive, offering visual simulations and data monitoring. However, with AI algorithms—especially ML and deep learning—DTs can now analyze historical data patterns, learn from them, and predict future behavior. For instance, in predictive maintenance, AI-enhanced twins can monitor equipment wear and performance, identify signs of potential failure, and suggest preventive actions long before an issue escalates. This not only reduces downtime but also improves asset longevity and safety. In manufacturing, AI-driven DTs can optimize production schedules, simulate process modifications, and dynamically adapt to changes in resource availability or consumer demand.

Complementing AI, blockchain technology is emerging as a powerful enabler of data trust and secure interoperability in DT ecosystems. As DTs increasingly rely on data streams from distributed IoT devices, ensuring the authenticity, integrity, and nonrepudiation of this data becomes crucial. Blockchain, with its decentralized and tamper-proof ledger system, addresses this challenge effectively. It provides a verifiable record of transactions, events, and data exchanges between devices and their corresponding DTs. For example, in a supply chain network where DTs of goods and logistics systems interact, blockchain can ensure that the record of a shipment's temperature, location, or handling conditions remains unaltered and accessible to all stakeholders. Furthermore, smart contracts—self-executing scripts stored on the blockchain—can automate interactions between DTs, such as triggering maintenance protocols or payments upon fulfillment of certain conditions.

The role of IoT in this triad cannot be overstated. IoT forms the foundational layer that enables DTs to receive and transmit real-time data from physical entities. Sensors embedded in machines, vehicles, buildings, or even human bodies continuously collect information about operational conditions, environmental factors, or user behavior. This real-world data is transmitted to digital counterparts that mirror the physical state with high accuracy. The vast and growing network of IoT devices—projected to exceed 75 billion globally in the coming years—expands the coverage and resolution of DT models. With the support of edge computing, some processing tasks can be performed near the data source, reducing latency and enabling immediate feedback. This is especially useful in time-critical scenarios such as autonomous driving or smart grid management, where milliseconds matter.

The integration of AI and blockchain into IoT-enabled DT systems is leading to the emergence of what some researchers term "Smart Cognitive DTs." These advanced twins are not only reactive or predictive but also prescriptive and autonomous. They can learn from past behaviors, anticipate future states, and act on their own or in collaboration with other systems. For instance, in an intelligent building scenario, DTs of various subsystems (Heating, Ventilation, and Air Conditioning (HVAC), lighting, security) can communicate through blockchain-enabled protocols, while AI continuously optimizes comfort, energy efficiency, and security. The building learns from occupancy patterns, adapts its operations in real time, and ensures that all changes are recorded transparently for audit or compliance purposes.

An important emerging trend is the use of federated learning in AI-enabled DTs. In many sectors, especially healthcare and finance, data privacy is a critical concern. Federated learning allows machine learning models to be trained across multiple decentralized sources without exchanging raw data. In the context of IoT-enabled DTs, this means that individual twins (e.g., digital replicas of medical devices or vehicles) can collaboratively improve a global AI model while retaining sensitive data locally. Blockchain can facilitate this decentralized training process by providing verifiable records of data access and contribution, ensuring accountability, and managing access rights through smart contracts. This combination enables a scalable and privacy-respecting approach to training intelligent digital systems.

Another noteworthy trend is the application of DTs in sustainability and environmental monitoring, driven by AI and supported by blockchain for transparent reporting. DTs are increasingly used to simulate and monitor environmental impact in industries such as construction, energy, and transportation. For example, a smart city might use DTs to track emissions, simulate the impact of policy changes, or optimize energy consumption in real time. AI algorithms analyze massive sensor datasets to identify inefficiencies or violations, while blockchain ensures the integrity and transparency of this data for regulators and citizens. Such capabilities are vital in achieving climate goals and enabling responsible innovation.

In the healthcare sector, the convergence of AI, blockchain, and IoT within DTs is revolutionizing patient care and operational management. AI-enabled bio-DTs—virtual models of a patient's organs or physiological systems—can predict treatment outcomes, optimize drug dosing, and personalize therapy. IoT wearables provide continuous real-time health data, enabling accurate and dynamic modeling of the patient's condition. Blockchain ensures that sensitive health data is securely stored, accessed only by authorized parties, and remains immutable. This triad allows for a more proactive, data-driven approach to medicine, where decisions are informed by simulations rather than solely by symptoms or trial-and-error.

In industrial and manufacturing domains, the concept of "Industry 5.0" is being driven by human-centric, AI-augmented DTs. These twins collaborate with human operators to enhance productivity, safety, and innovation. For example, robotic arms in an assembly line may have their own DTs powered by AI that monitor performance and self-correct errors. IoT devices feed continuous sensor data, and blockchain records the production history for quality assurance and traceability. In this environment, DTs serve as intelligent collaborators—simulating potential improvements, coordinating with other assets, and adapting to changes in supply or demand dynamically.

Moreover, interoperability and standardization are emerging as key focus areas in the adoption of AI and blockchain for IoT-enabled DTs. As different vendors and sectors develop their own models and platforms, the lack of common standards can hinder integration and scalability. Organizations such as the DT Consortium, IEEE, and ISO are working toward standard frameworks that define data formats, communication protocols, and security measures. Blockchain is playing a vital role here by providing a neutral and auditable layer for cross-platform interactions, while AI helps bridge data gaps through semantic interpretation and machine learning.

One futuristic trend gaining traction is the convergence of the Metaverse and DTs, where physical environments and their digital replicas are experienced through immersive technologies like augmented reality and virtual reality. In such settings, AI-enhanced DTs can provide real-time feedback and simulations inside virtual environments, while blockchain can manage identity, ownership, and access rights. Imagine a virtual smart city where urban planners interact with the DTs of roads, buildings, and transportation systems in a fully immersive space. AI provides real-time predictions for traffic or energy demand, and blockchain ensures the security and traceability of every simulation or transaction. This integration is not only a technological marvel but also a new way to enhance human understanding and collaboration.

Despite the numerous advantages, this integration does face several challenges. AI models require large volumes of clean, labeled data to be effective, and such data may not always be available or interoperable across systems. Blockchain, while secure, can introduce latency and scalability concerns if not carefully designed, especially in high-frequency IoT environments. IoT devices themselves often have limitations in terms of computing power and battery life, which may not support heavy AI processing or constant blockchain interactions. Therefore, architectural decisions must balance efficiency, security, and usability. Solutions such as lightweight consensus mechanisms, edge AI processing, and hybrid blockchain models are being explored to mitigate these issues.

In summary, the emerging trends in integrating AI and Blockchain with IoT-enabled DTs are transforming industries into intelligent, autonomous, and secure ecosystems. This convergence is enabling real-time decision-making, predictive analytics, and automated trust in ways never seen before. From smart cities and precision healthcare to sustainable manufacturing and immersive virtual worlds, the fusion of these technologies is not just enhancing existing systems—it is redefining the very blueprint of how the physical world connects to the digital. As innovation continues and technical challenges are addressed, AI and Blockchain-powered DTs will become essential building blocks of a smarter, more connected, and more resilient future.

9.10 An open discussion towards betterment of society in this smart era towards AI and blockchain for IoT-enabled digital twin—from society and industry perspective

In today's rapidly evolving smart era, the convergence of AI, Blockchain, and IoT-enabled DT technologies is ushering in a transformative wave that has the potential to significantly improve both society and industry. From a societal perspective, these technologies are enabling smarter, safer, and more sustainable living environments. DTs, when fueled by real-time IoT data and governed by AI-driven insights, can model urban infrastructure, healthcare systems, and environmental processes to enhance the quality of life. Citizens can benefit from predictive healthcare systems, efficient traffic management, clean energy optimization, and personalized public services—all informed by intelligent, data-driven simulations. Furthermore, Blockchain ensures the privacy, transparency, and trust needed to secure sensitive personal and civic data in these complex systems. In public health, for example, DigitalDTs of patients or hospital networks can simulate disease progression and resource needs, while blockchain maintains the integrity of medical records, ensuring that data is shared only with authorized stakeholders.

From an industrial viewpoint, these integrated technologies are driving efficiency, innovation, and resilience. AI-powered DTs of machines, factories, or supply chains offer predictive maintenance, resource optimization, and adaptive production planning, helping industries minimize downtime, reduce waste, and respond agilely to market demands. Blockchain plays a crucial role in providing trusted, tamper-proof audit trails of transactions and processes, supporting transparency and accountability across the value chain. In sectors such as manufacturing, logistics, and energy, this leads to more efficient operations, enhanced compliance, and increased customer trust. Moreover, the real-time synchronization between physical assets and their digital counterparts enables dynamic modeling and continuous improvement—ushering in a new era of smart manufacturing and Industry 5.0, where human-centric design and collaborative AI systems become the norm.

Note that, as this digital transformation unfolds, it raises critical discussions about inclusivity, ethical design, data governance, and workforce readiness. While AI and blockchain offer immense potential, their impact must be equitably distributed across all sections of society. Ensuring digital literacy, protecting privacy rights, creating inclusive policies, and developing interoperable systems are key priorities. Collaborative efforts between governments, industries, academic institutions, and communities are essential to align these technologies with societal values and long-term sustainability goals. In this open dialog, the focus must not only be on technological excellence but also on how these innovations can be designed and deployed for the greater good—ensuring that smart systems truly serve humanity and create a more transparent, efficient, and equitable future.

9.11 Conclusion

The integration of blockchain in IoT-enabled DT systems offers immense potential for creating secure, transparent, and autonomous cyber-physical infrastructures. It addresses key challenges in data integrity, trust, decentralized control, and secure automation by leveraging features such as immutability, smart contracts, and distributed consensus. This integration enhances operational visibility, enables real-time decision-making, and fosters trust in collaborative environments across sectors like manufacturing, energy, logistics, and healthcare. However, deploying blockchain in such complex systems requires thoughtful adaptation to the unique requirements of IoT environments, such as high data volume, limited device capabilities, and low-latency communication. Despite the opportunities, several challenges and research gaps remain—ranging from scalability and energy efficiency to data privacy, interoperability, and regulatory compliance. Addressing these issues demands interdisciplinary research across computer science, engineering, and policy domains. Future work must focus on developing lightweight blockchain architectures, privacy-preserving mechanisms, and standardized frameworks that support real-time, secure integration of physical and digital environments. As these innovations mature, blockchain-enabled DTs will play a central role in driving the next generation of intelligent, resilient, and trusted systems.

References

Alam, K.M., El Saddik, A., 2017. C2PS: a digital twin architecture reference model for the cloud-based cyber-physical systems. IEEE Access 5, 2050–2062.

Christidis, K., Devetsikiotis, M., 2016. Blockchains and smart contracts for the internet of things. IEEE Access 4, 2292–2303.

Conoscenti, M., Vetro, A., De Martin, J.C., 2016. Blockchain for the internet of things: a systematic literature review. In: 2016 IEEE/ACS 13th International Conference of Computer Systems and Applications (AICCSA), pp. 1–6.

Dorri, A., Kanhere, S.S., Jurdak, R., 2017. Towards an optimized blockchain for IoT. In: Proceedings of the Second International Conference on Internet-of-Things Design and Implementation (IoTDI), pp. 173–178.

Ferrari, A., Rundo, F., Pirrone, R., Giudice, O., 2020. A deep learning approach for IoT-enabled digital twin for smart manufacturing. Procedia Comput. Sci. 170, 668–673.

Ferrer, E.C., 2018. The blockchain: a new framework for robotic swarm systems. In: Proceedings of the Future Technologies Conference (FTC), pp. 1037–1058.

Huh, S., Cho, S., Kim, S., 2017. Managing IoT devices using blockchain platform. In: 2017 19th International Conference on Advanced Communication Technology (ICACT), pp. 464–467.

Kshetri, N., 2017. Can blockchain strengthen the internet of things? IT Prof. 19 (4), 68–72.

Kumar, R., Tripathi, R., 2021. A review on blockchain and its integration with IoT for secure and scalable architecture. Comput. Commun. 162, 92–111.

Lee, J., Bagheri, B., Kao, H.A., 2015. A cyber-physical systems architecture for industry 4.0-based manufacturing systems. Manuf. Lett. 3, 18–23.

Lu, Y., Xu, X., 2019. Resource-aware scheduling and optimization for blockchain-enabled digital twin manufacturing in industry 4.0. Robot. Comput. Integr. Manuf. 61, 101845.

Reyna, A., Martín, C., Chen, J., Soler, E., Díaz, M., 2018. On blockchain and its integration with IoT: challenges and opportunities. Future Gener. Comput. Syst. 88, 173–190.

Samaniego, M., Deters, R., 2017. Blockchain as a service for IoT. In: Proceedings of the IEEE International Conference on Internet of Things (iThings), pp. 433–436.
Singh, S., Sharma, P.K., Moon, S.Y., Park, J.H., 2018. Blockchain-based intelligent IoT edge framework for secure public environments. IEEE Access 7, 24998–25010.
Tyagi, A.K., 2016. Cyber physical systems (CPSs)—opportunities and challenges for improving cyber security. Int. J. Comput. Appl. 0975-8887. 137 (14), 19–27.
Tyagi, A.K., 2020. Prediction models. In: Handbook of Research on Disease Prediction through Data Analytics and Machine Learning. IGI Global, USA.
Tyagi, A.K., 2021. Analysis of security and privacy aspects of blockchain technologies from smart era' perspective: the challenges and a way forward. In: CRC—Recent Trends in Blockchain for Information Systems Security and Privacy, CRC Press, pp. 1–17.
Tyagi, A.K., 2022. SecVT: securing the vehicles of tomorrow using blockchain technology. In: 17–19 February 2022, in the Proceeding of Springer/ISAI 2022, Kolkata. ISBN: 978-3-031-22485-0.
Tyagi, A.K., 2023. Decentralized everything: a practical use of blockchain technology in future applications. In: Distributed Computing to Blockchain: Architecture, Technology, and Applications, Elsevier, Academic Press, pp. 19–38.
Tyagi, A.K., 2024. Blockchain-enabled internet of things (IoTs) platforms for iot-based healthcare and biomedical sectors. In: Artificial Intelligence-Enabled Blockchain Technology and Digital Twin for Smart Hospitals, Wiley.
Tyagi, A.K., 2024a. Transformative effects of ChatGPT on modern era of education and society: from society and industry's perspective. In: Machine Learning Algorithms Using Scikit and TensorFlow Environments. IGI Global, USA.
Tyagi, A.K., 2024b. Dew computing: state of the art, opportunities, and research challenges. In: Machine Learning Algorithms Using Scikit and TensorFlow Environments. IGI Global, USA.
Tyagi, A.K., 2024c Sensors and digital twin application in healthcare facilities management. In: Artificial Intelligence-Enabled Blockchain Technology and Digital Twin for Smart Hospitals.
Tyagi, A.K., 2024d Blockchain–artificial intelligence-based secured solutions for smart environment. In: Digital Twin and Blockchain for Smart Cities. 9781394303533.
Tyagi, A.K., 2025a. Blockchain for smart hospital in Healthcare 5.0: modeling structure, challenges, and future emerging trends. In: Human-Centric Integration of Next-Generation Data Science and Blockchain Technology. Elsevier.
Tyagi, A.K., 2025b. Blockchain technology: values, challenges, and possible applications from an industry perspective. In: Human-Centric Integration of Next-Generation Data Science and Blockchain Technology. Elsevier.
Tyagi, A.K., Aghila, G., 2011. A wide scale survey on botnet. Int. J. Comput. Appl. 0975-8887. 34 (9), 9–22.
Zhang, Y., Kasahara, S., Shen, Y., Jiang, X., Wan, J., 2019. Smart contract-based access control for the internet of things. IEEE Internet Things J. 6 (2), 1594–1605.

CHAPTER 10

Converging technologies for innovation in digital twinning

Vaishali Nitin Dhawas, Renuka Rajendra Kajale, Neha Sharad Bhagwat, and Bharti Dhote

Department of Computer Engineering, Nutan Maharashtra Institute of Engineering & Technology, Pune, India

10.1 Introduction to digital twin technology

10.1.1 Definition and foundational concepts

Definition:

A digital twin is a virtual version of a real-world system, process, or physical object that is constantly updated with real-time data and sophisticated analytics. By gathering data from sensors or other sources and applying it to model, simulate, and enhance performance, it creates a bridge between the real and virtual worlds.

Key characteristics of digital twins:

- Data-driven models: To replicate real-world behavior, these models rely on Internet of Things (IoT) sensors and other data sources.
- Dynamic and evolving: Adapt in real-time to changes or shifts in the physical equivalent.
- Simulation and prediction: Enable predictive analytics and scenario testing to be possible.

Example:

By gathering information on temperature, vibration, and performance, an industrial machine's digital twin enables operators to anticipate malfunctions, optimize maintenance plans, and boost productivity.

Artificial Intelligence, Machine Learning and Blockchain in Digital Twin Computing.
https://doi.org/10.1016/B978-0-443-43914-8.00016-9

10.1.2 Historical evolution and significance

Origins of the concept:

- **National Aeronautics and Space Administration (NASA's) Apollo program (1960s):** The earliest concept of a digital twin emerged during NASA's Apollo program. Engineers created physical and digital replicas of spacecraft to monitor and address real-time issues during missions. This foundation laid the groundwork for modern digital twin technology.
- **Michael Grieves' formal definition (2002):** The term "digital twin" was formally introduced by Dr. Michael Grieves in his presentation on Product Lifecycle Management. He proposed the idea of integrating virtual models with real-world data throughout a product's lifecycle.

Technological advancements driving adoption:

- IoT expansion: Real-time data collection is now more accessible and reasonably priced, thanks to the growth of IoT devices.
- Cloud computing: To host and analyze intricate digital twin models, cloud systems offer the scalability and processing capacity required.
- Artificial intelligence (AI) and machine learning (ML) integration: Sophisticated algorithms improve automation, predictive power, and simulation accuracy.

Significance in the digital transformation era:

Digital twins play a pivotal role in transforming industries by enabling:

- **Enhanced operational efficiency:** Continuous monitoring and optimization
- **Predictive maintenance:** Reducing downtime and extending asset lifecycles
- **Data-driven decision-making:** Real-time insights for proactive management

10.1.3 Applications across industries

With its many uses in a variety of industries, digital twin technology helps businesses innovate successfully, reduce expenses, and enhance performance.

1. **Manufacturing:**

- **Smart factories:** Digital twins optimize production processes, monitor equipment performance, and predict maintenance needs.
- **Example:** General Electric uses digital twins in its industrial equipment to monitor health, predict failures, and improve efficiency.

1.2 **Healthcare:**

- **Personalized medicine:** Patient-specific digital twins model individual health conditions for personalized treatment plans.
- **Example:** Simulating the effects of a new drug on a patient's digital twin before administering it in real life.

1.3 **Aerospace and defense:**

- **Aircraft monitoring:** Digital twins of aircraft continuously monitor engine performance, structural integrity, and operational efficiency.
- **Example:** Boeing uses digital twins to optimize aircraft maintenance schedules and reduce downtime.

1.4 **Energy and utilities:**

- **Smart grids:** Digital twins monitor energy distribution systems, optimize power delivery, and predict faults.
- **Example:** Siemens manages electricity grids using digital twins to guarantee dependability and energy efficiency.

1.5 **Transportation and logistics:**

- **Autonomous vehicles:** Digital twins simulate road conditions, traffic, and vehicle dynamics for autonomous driving systems.
- **Example:** Tesla employs digital twin technology to update and optimize its self-driving algorithms.

1.6 **Urban planning and smart cities:**

- **City management:** Digital twins of cities model infrastructure, traffic, and resource usage to improve urban living conditions.
- **Example:** Singapore's Virtual Singapore project uses a digital twin to optimize urban planning and sustainability efforts.

1.7 **Retail and e-commerce:**

- **Customer experience optimization:** Digital twins of stores and supply chains help retailers optimize layouts, inventory, and customer engagement strategies.
- **Example:** Walmart employs digital twins to monitor and optimize store operations.

1.8 **Construction and real estate:**

- **Building information modeling:** Digital twins are used for the design, construction, and maintenance of buildings.
- Architects use digital twins to simulate energy efficiency and structural performance of buildings before construction.

Key takeaways

1. **Definition:** A digital twin is a real-time, data-driven virtual replica of a physical entity.
2. **Historical evolution:** From NASA's Apollo missions to modern IoT-driven systems, digital twins have evolved into critical tools for industries.
3. **Applications:** digital twin technology is transforming manufacturing, healthcare, energy, transportation, and more—driving efficiency, innovation, and sustainability.

10.2 The role of converging technologies

10.2.1 Overview of technological convergence

Definition of technological convergence:

The blending and integration of several technologies to produce new capabilities and solutions is referred to as technological convergence. In the context of digital twin technology, convergence combines developments in a number of domains, including cloud computing, edge computing, AI, ML, and the IoTs, to facilitate the development, management, and optimization of digital twins.

Historical perspective:

Rapid advancements in software development, computer power, and data collection have propelled the development of digital twin technologies. Physical systems were first modeled using discrete technologies like computer-aided design and simulation tools. However, the application of AI and the integration of real-time data via IoT have greatly increased the scope and usefulness of digital twins.

Importance of convergence:

The current digital twin is made possible by technological convergence, which enables adaptive systems, predictive analytics, and real-time monitoring. The full functionality of digital twins would not be feasible without the smooth integration of several technologies.

10.2.2 Synergies between technologies enabling digital twins

1. IoT: IoT acts as the backbone of digital twins by providing real-time data streams from sensors embedded in physical assets. These sensors capture information such as temperature, pressure, vibration, and operational metrics, enabling digital twins to mirror real-world conditions.

Synergy: IoT facilitates the dynamic connection between physical and virtual systems, allowing continuous data updates for simulations and analysis.

Example: In smart manufacturing, IoT sensors embedded in machines send real-time performance data to their digital twins, enabling predictive maintenance and process optimization.

2. AI and ML:

Digital twins can evaluate enormous volumes of data, spot trends, and make predictions thanks to AI and ML. Digital twins can gradually increase their accuracy and flexibility by learning from both historical and current data.

Synergy: The integration of AI allows digital twins to perform predictive analytics, automate decision-making, and recommend optimizations.

Example: In the energy sector, AI-powered digital twins of wind turbines predict equipment failures by analyzing vibration data, thereby reducing downtime and maintenance costs.

3. Cloud computing: Cloud platforms provide the scalability and computational power required for hosting and managing large-scale digital twin models. They enable seamless access to data and models from anywhere in the world, fostering collaboration among stakeholders.

Synergy: Cloud computing makes it possible for digital twins to manage enormous data volumes and provide worldwide accessibility, which improves their usefulness in sectors like logistics and smart cities.

Example: Virtual Singapore, a city-scale digital twin, relies on cloud infrastructure to store and process complex data related to traffic, infrastructure, and environmental conditions.

4. Edge computing: While edge computing addresses the requirement for low-latency data processing, cloud computing ensures scalability. Edge devices enhance digital twins' real-time capabilities and reduce delays by performing computations closer to the data source.

Synergy: Digital twins are able to strike a compromise between large-scale data analysis and real-time responsiveness by combining edge and cloud computing.

Example: In autonomous vehicles, edge computing enables digital twins to process sensor data locally, ensuring immediate decision-making for navigation and obstacle avoidance.

5. Big data analytics: In order to derive useful insights from the massive volumes of data produced by IoT devices, operational systems, and user interactions, digital twins rely on big data analytics. Predictive modeling and informed decision-making are fueled by these findings.

Synergy: The combination of big data analytics and digital twins facilitates a deeper understanding and optimization of complex systems.

Example: In the healthcare sector, patient-specific digital twins use big data analytics to simulate treatment outcomes, aiding in personalized medical care.

10.2.3 Key drivers of innovation

Several factors drive innovation in digital twin technology, encouraging its adoption across industries:

1. **Developments in sensor technology:** The widespread deployment of IoT devices that feed data into digital twin models is made possible by modern sensors' increasing capacity, affordability, and compact size.
2. **Development of ML and AI capabilities:** Digital twins can now carry out intricate simulations, identify inefficiencies, and provide more accurate suggestions for changes, thanks to the growing sophistication of AI and ML algorithms.
3. **Better communication (5G):** The deployment of 5G networks improves data transmission speed and dependability, enabling digital twins to function with almost-instantaneous updates.
4. **Predictive maintenance demand:** Reducing operational expenses and downtime is becoming more and more important to industries. Thanks to technological convergence, digital twins offer the instruments required to anticipate and prevent equipment problems.
5. **Sustainability goals:** As organizations strive to reduce their environmental footprint, digital twins play a critical role in optimizing energy use, reducing waste, and improving resource efficiency.

Key takeaways

1. Technological convergence: The operation of contemporary digital twins depends on the combination of IoT, AI, cloud computing, edge computing, and big data analytics.
2. Synergies across technologies: The full potential of digital twin systems is unlocked by combining the distinct capabilities that each enabling technology brings.
3. Innovation drivers: The development and use of digital twins across industries are mostly being driven by advancements in sensor technology, the expansion of AI, 5G connectivity, and the emphasis on sustainability.

10.3 Internet of things and digital twins

10.3.1 Iot sensors for real-time data collection

The role of IoT in digital twins:

The primary interface between the virtual and real worlds is provided by IoT sensors. They empower digital twins to accurately reproduce and mimic the habits of real-world entities by regularly gathering and transmitting data.

Key functions of IoT sensors:

- Real-time monitoring: Sensors collect vital operational data, such as temperature, pressure, vibration, and more, to mimic the real-world counterpart.
- Dynamic feedback loops: Real-time updates from IoT devices enable digital twin models to evolve and adapt in concert with physical changes.
- Data preprocessing at the edge: By filtering and processing raw data locally, advanced IoT devices with edge computing capabilities eliminate the need for high-bandwidth transfers.

Rolls-Royce aircraft engines case study:

In order to keep an eye on variables like temperature, pressure, and vibration while in flight, Rolls-Royce incorporates IoTs sensors into their jet engines. A digital twin of the engine gets data from these sensors and uses it to forecast maintenance requirements and enhance performance. This preventative measure lowers engine failure rates and enhances flight safety.

10.3.2 Iot applications in digital twins

1. Predictive maintenance:

IoT-enabled digital twins allow industries to anticipate failures and schedule maintenance proactively. This prolongs asset lifespans, lowers expenses, and minimizes downtime.

- **Example:** Siemens Energy uses digital twins to monitor turbines in power plants. IoT sensors collect data on vibration and temperature, which the digital twin analyzes to predict component wear and optimize maintenance schedules.

2. Asset monitoring and optimization:

Digital twins, powered by IoT, provide real-time visibility into asset performance and health. This helps organizations optimize resource utilization and improve operational efficiency.

- **Case study—Smart Buildings (IBM):** IBM's digital twin platform for smart buildings integrates IoT sensors to monitor energy consumption, occupancy patterns, and environmental conditions. By analyzing this data, the digital twin suggests energy-saving measures and improves space utilization.

3. Smart cities:

IoT sensors deployed across urban infrastructure gather data on traffic, energy consumption, and public services. Digital twins use this data to optimize city management and improve residents' quality of life.

- **Case study—Virtual Singapore:** The "Virtual Singapore" project employs IoT sensors across the city-state to create a digital twin of its infrastructure. This model helps urban planners simulate scenarios such as traffic flow, disaster response, and energy eficiency.

4. Healthcare:

IoT-enabled digital twins transform healthcare by enabling personalized medicine and remote patient monitoring.

- **Example:** In cardiology, digital twins of patients' hearts are created using IoT data from wearable devices. These Twins simulate the effects of treatments, helping doctors make informed decisions.

5. Supply chain and logistics:

IoT sensors in shipping containers and vehicles monitor location, temperature, and humidity. Digital twins analyze this data to optimize supply chain efficiency.

- **Case study—DHL:** DHL uses IoT-enabled digital twins to track shipments in real-time. Sensors provide updates on cargo conditions, enabling the Twin to recommend route adjustments or preventive actions.

10.3.3 Challenges and future prospects

Challenges:

1. **Data management and overload**:
   - Difficulty: Massive data generation from IoT devices can overwhelm processing and storage infrastructure.
   - Solution: This problem can be mitigated by implementing edge computing and AI-driven data prioritization.
2. **Interoperability:**
   - Difficulty: IoT networks are susceptible to cyberattacks, and security lapses may jeopardize the integrity of digital twin data.
   - Solution: Data security is ensured by implementing secure communication protocols and end-to-end encryption.
3. **High implementation costs:**
   - Difficulty: IoT deployment and integration with digital twins can be prohibitively expensive at first.
   - Solution: Government incentives for IoT adoption, combined with gradual installation.

Future Prospects

1. 5G-enabled IoT:

The deployment of 5G networks will greatly improve the reliability and speed of IoT data transfer, allowing digital twin systems to be updated almost instantly.

2. AI-driven automation:

AI integration will empower digital twins to analyze IoT data autonomously, driving smarter decision-making and reducing human intervention.

3. Sustainability and green initiatives:

By maximizing energy use, cutting waste, and encouraging resource efficiency, IoT-enabled digital twins will support sustainability initiatives.

4. Enhanced edge computing:

The proliferation of edge computing devices will enable faster, decentralized data processing, making digital twins more responsive.

Case study—Autonomous vehicles (Tesla):

Tesla's self-driving cars use IoT sensors to collect data on road conditions, vehicle performance, and surrounding traffic. This data is processed locally and sent to a central digital twin for broader analysis. The Twin uses this information to update navigation algorithms and improve vehicle autonomy.

Key takeaways

1. **IoT sensors as enablers:** IoT devices are integral to the functioning of digital twins, providing the real-time data needed for accurate simulations and analyses.
2. **Broad applications:** From predictive maintenance to smart cities, IoT-enabled digital twins are transforming industries globally.
3. **Challenges and solutions:** While data overload, security, and interoperability remain challenges, advancements in edge computing and standardization will address these concerns.
4. **Bright future:** The integration of 5G, AI, and edge computing promises a robust and efficient ecosystem for IoT-enabled digital twins.

10.4 Artificial intelligence and machine learning

AI and ML have emerged as transformative technologies, driving innovations across industries and unlocking unprecedented opportunities. This chapter explores the foundational concepts of AI and ML, their applications, and their potential to shape the future through insights, optimization, and autonomous decision-making.

10.4.1 AI-driven insights and predictions

Overview

AI excels at processing vast amounts of data, extracting meaningful insights, and making accurate predictions. AI offers useful information that improves decision-making by identifying patterns and trends in both structured and unstructured data.

Key concepts

- Data processing at scale: To produce insights, AI systems examine a variety of data formats, such as text, photos, audio, and video.
- Predictive analytics: AI algorithms may predict future patterns, such as consumer behavior, market changes, or possible hazards, by using historical data.
- Personalization: AI-driven insights allow for customized user experiences, including targeted marketing, individualized healthcare plans, and product recommendations.

Applications

- **Business intelligence:** AI-powered tools like Power BI and Google Analytics help businesses uncover patterns, optimize processes, and drive revenue growth.
- **Healthcare:** AI systems analyze patient data to predict disease outbreaks, improve diagnostics, and recommend preventive measures.
- **Finance:** Fraud detection, risk assessment, and predictive modeling streamline financial operations and enhance security.

Case study

A leading retailer used AI-powered analytics to predict customer purchasing trends. By leveraging these insights, the company optimized inventory management, reduced waste, and improved customer satisfaction.

10.4.2 ML models for continuous optimization

Overview

ML, a subset of AI, empowers systems to learn and improve over time. ML models adapt dynamically to new information, enabling continuous optimization of processes and performance.

Key concepts

- **Supervised learning:** Models are trained on labeled data to make predictions (e.g., spam detection or credit scoring).
- **Unsupervised learning:** Models uncover patterns in unlabeled data (e.g., customer segmentation or anomaly detection).

- **Reinforcement learning:** Systems learn through trial and error to optimize sequential decision-making (e.g., robotic control or game strategy).
- **Deep learning:** For tasks like image identification and natural language processing, sophisticated neural networks evaluate complex input.

Applications

- **Supply chain optimization:** ML models enhance logistics by predicting demand, optimizing routes, and improving inventory management.
- **Energy management:** Smart grids use ML to allocate energy efficiently and reduce waste.
- **Marketing:** Dynamic pricing, customer segmentation, and ad optimization rely on ML to maximize ROI.

Example in practice

Google DeepMind's reinforcement learning model optimized cooling systems in data centers, reducing energy consumption by 40% and saving millions in operational costs.

10.4.3 Autonomous decision-making

Overview

Autonomous decision-making represents the next frontier of AI, where systems move beyond providing recommendations to independently executing decisions. These systems use real-time data and predictive analytics to operate with minimal human intervention.

Key concepts

- **Real-time analytics:** AI systems process live data streams to make instantaneous decisions (e.g., autonomous vehicles avoiding collisions).
- **Risk analysis:** Advanced algorithms evaluate potential outcomes and select the best course of action.
- **Ethical considerations:** Ensuring fairness, transparency, and accountability in AI-driven decisions.

Applications

- **Autonomous vehicles (AVs):** Self-driving cars make split-second decisions to navigate traffic, ensure safety, and optimize routes.
- **Finance:** Algorithmic trading systems execute high-frequency trades based on market conditions.
- **Healthcare:** AI-powered surgical robots and diagnostic tools assist in critical decision-making during medical procedures.

Challenges

- **Bias in decision-making:** Ensuring unbiased outcomes in autonomous systems by addressing data and algorithmic biases.
- **Accountability:** Establishing clear lines of responsibility for decisions made by AI systems.
- **Ethics:** Balancing efficiency and fairness in high-stakes environments, such as healthcare and law enforcement.

10.4.4 Challenges and ethical considerations

While AI and ML offer immense potential, they also raise significant challenges:

- **Data privacy:** Protecting sensitive information while leveraging it for insights and predictions.
- **Bias and fairness:** Avoiding the reinforcement of societal biases through training data and algorithms.
- **Explainability:** Developing explainable AI to ensure human understanding of decision-making processes.
- **Job displacement:** Mitigating the impact of automation on the workforce and addressing the need for reskilling.
- **Security:** Protecting AI systems from adversarial attacks and ensuring robust cybersecurity measures.

10.4.5 The future of AI and ML

AI and ML are evolving rapidly, with groundbreaking advancements on the horizon:

- **Generative AI:** Creating art, music, and text using models like Generative Pre-trained Transformer (GPT) and DALL-E.
- **Edge AI:** Running AI models directly on devices, such as smartphones and IoT sensors, for real-time applications.
- **Quantum AI:** Combining quantum computing with AI to solve problems that are currently unsolvable by classical methods.
- **Human-AI collaboration:** Designing systems that enhance human capabilities rather than replacing them.

Conclusion

AI and ML are not just tools but transformative forces reshaping industries, societies, and the global economy. By harnessing their potential responsibly and ethically, we can unlock new possibilities, overcome challenges, and create a future driven by innovation and collaboration.

10.5 Cloud and edge computing

Introduction

The way businesses handle, analyze, and use data has been completely transformed by cloud and edge computing. While edge computing puts computation closer to the data source for real-time processing, cloud computing offers scalable, flexible, and affordable alternatives for data processing and storage. When combined, these technologies allow companies to function effectively, innovate quickly, and adjust to shifting needs.

10.5.1 Cloud-based scalability and collaboration

What is cloud computing?

Cloud computing refers to the delivery of computing services—including storage, processing power, and applications—over the internet ("the cloud"). It eliminates the need for physical hardware and allows users to access resources on-demand. The core principles of cloud computing involve resource pooling, scalability, and pay-as-you-go pricing models.

Cloud computing services are categorized into three primary models:

- **Infrastructure as a service:** Provides virtualized computing resources, such as servers, storage, and networking. Examples: Amazon Web Services (AWS) EC2, Microsoft Azure.
- **Product-as-a-service(PaaS):** Offers platforms for application development without requiring the management of the underlying infrastructure. Examples: Google App Engine, Azure App Service.
- **Software as a service (SaaS):** Delivers software applications over the internet, accessible via web browsers. Examples: Google Workspace, Salesforce.

Scalability in cloud computing

Scalability is a key advantage of cloud computing, enabling businesses to adjust resource usage according to demand. There are two types of scalability:

- **Vertical scaling:** Increasing the capacity of existing hardware, such as upgrading a server's RAM or CPU.
- **Horizontal scaling:** Adding more machines to handle increased workloads.

Cloud platforms offer auto-scaling and load-balancing features, which ensure optimal performance during peak loads. For instance, an e-commerce website can scale up during sales events and scale down afterward, optimizing costs.

Collaboration in cloud computing

Cloud computing fosters collaboration by providing tools and platforms that allow teams to work together seamlessly. Benefits include:

- **Real-time data sharing:** Teams can access and update files simultaneously from different locations.
- **Remote access:** Employees can work from anywhere, enhancing flexibility.
- **Version control:** Cloud platforms automatically save changes and maintain version histories, preventing data loss or conflicts.

Examples of collaborative tools include Google Workspace, Microsoft Teams, and Slack. These platforms enable organizations to coordinate projects, communicate effectively, and streamline workflows.

10.5.2 Edge computing for real-time data processing

What is edge computing?

Instead of depending on centralized cloud infrastructure, edge computing processes data closer to its source, such as IoT devices or local servers. This maximizes bandwidth use, lowers latency, and enhances reaction times. By managing time-sensitive processes at the edge and assigning less important duties to the cloud, edge computing enhances cloud computing.

Applications of edge computing

Edge computing is essential in scenarios requiring real-time data processing and low latency. Applications include:

- **AVs:** Processing data from sensors and cameras in real-time for navigation and decision-making.
- **Smart cities:** Managing traffic lights, surveillance systems, and utilities efficiently.
- **Industrial automation:** Monitoring and controlling machinery in factories to prevent downtime and improve efficiency.
- **Healthcare:** Enabling remote patient monitoring and real-time diagnostics through wearable devices.

Benefits of edge computing

The advantages of edge computing include:

- **Low latency:** Faster processing and response times for time-sensitive applications.
- **Reduced bandwidth usage:** Processing data locally reduces the amount of data sent to the cloud, thereby lowering costs.
- **Enhanced privacy and security:** Sensitive data can be processed locally, minimizing exposure to potential cyber threats.

Challenges in edge computing

Despite its advantages, edge computing presents challenges:

- **Device management:** Maintaining and updating distributed edge devices is complex.
- **Security risks:** Ensuring the security of edge devices and data is critical.
- **Integration issues:** Combining edge computing with existing IT infrastructure requires careful planning.

10.5.3 Hybrid computing models

What is hybrid computing?

The advantages of cloud and edge computing are combined in hybrid computing to produce an adaptable and effective IT environment. In this paradigm, more complex functions, like data analysis and storage, are managed in the cloud, while real-time data processing is handled at the edge.

Use cases for hybrid computing

Hybrid models are ideal for industries requiring a balance of real-time processing and centralized data management:

- **E-commerce:** Edge computing handles local order processing, while the cloud manages inventory and analytics.
- **Healthcare:** Medical devices process patient data locally for immediate use, while long-term records are stored in the cloud.
- **Manufacturing:** IoT sensors monitor equipment on-site, while cloud platforms analyze production data to optimize workflows.

Advantages of Hybrid Computing

- **Flexibility:** Organizations can tailor solutions to meet specific workload requirements.
- **Cost efficiency:** Edge computing reduces bandwidth costs, while the cloud provides scalable resources.
- **Enhanced performance:** Combines the speed of edge computing with the scalability of the cloud.

Challenges in hybrid computing

- **Complexity:** Managing hybrid environments requires advanced tools and expertise.
- **Data integration:** Ensuring seamless data flow between cloud and edge systems can be challenging.
- **Security and compliance:** Maintaining security and regulatory compliance across platforms is crucial.

Conclusion

By providing scalable, real-time, and adaptable data management solutions, cloud and edge computing are revolutionizing businesses. Hybrid models take advantage of both technologies' benefits to meet a variety of business requirements. Organizations can increase productivity, spur innovation, and maintain their competitiveness in a world that is becoming increasingly data-driven by implementing these advances.

Case studies and examples

- **Case study 1: Smart factories and hybrid models:** A manufacturing company implemented edge computing for real-time machine monitoring and cloud-based analytics for predictive maintenance, reducing downtime by 30%.
- **Case study 2: Edge computing in autonomous vehicles:** A leading automotive company utilized edge computing to process sensor data on-board vehicles, enabling split-second decision-making and enhancing safety.
- **Case study 3: Cloud collaboration in global organizations:** An international organization adopted cloud-based collaboration tools, improving team productivity and reducing operational costs by 20%.

10.6 Blockchain for trust and security

Introduction

In the digital age, blockchain technology has become a game-changing way to guarantee security, transparency, and trust. Blockchain provides unmatched data integrity and resilience by utilizing decentralized systems and cryptographic principles. This chapter examines how blockchain improves security and trust, how it may be used to create decentralized systems, and how it can be applied in delicate sectors.

10.6.1 Data Integrity and Security Through Blockchain

How blockchain ensures data integrity

Blockchain achieves data integrity by utilizing:

- **Immutable ledgers:** Data stored on a blockchain is immutable, meaning that once information is recorded, it cannot be altered without consensus from the network. This ensures the accuracy and reliability of records.
- **Cryptographic hashing:** Each block in the blockchain contains a unique cryptographic hash, linking it to the previous block. Any attempt to tamper with the data invalidates the entire chain.
- **Consensus mechanisms:** Blockchain uses consensus protocols, such as proof-of-work (PoW) or proof-of-stake (PoS), to validate transactions and ensure trust among participants.

For example, in a financial transaction system, blockchain guarantees that all recorded transactions are accurate and cannot be altered, which eliminates fraudulent activities.

Enhanced security with blockchain

Blockchain offers robust security through:

- **Decentralization:** Eliminating single points of failure reduces the risk of cyberattacks. Each node in the network has a copy of the ledger, making it difficult for hackers to compromise the system.
- **Encryption:** Transactions and data are encrypted, protecting them from unauthorized access. Public and private key cryptography ensure that only authorized parties can access or modify data.
- **Transparency:** All participants in the network can view and verify transactions, ensuring accountability and preventing fraud.
- **Smart contracts:** Self-executing contracts with predefined conditions increase security and reduce the risk of disputes by automating processes.

For instance, a smart contract in an insurance system can automatically release payments to customers after verifying predefined conditions, minimizing human error and fraud.

Challenges in blockchain security

While blockchain is inherently secure, it faces challenges such as:

- **51% attacks:** If a majority of the network's computational power is controlled by malicious actors, they can alter the blockchain.
- **Private key vulnerabilities:** Loss or theft of private keys compromises access to blockchain assets. Unlike traditional systems, lost keys cannot be recovered.
- **Scalability and speed:** Ensuring security while scaling up blockchain networks remains a challenge, as larger networks require more computational power.

For example, public blockchains like Bitcoin face challenges with transaction speed and scalability, which developers are actively working to address.

10.6.2 Decentralized and transparent systems

Decentralization in blockchain

Decentralization is a core feature of blockchain, where no single entity controls the network. Key aspects include:

- **Distributed ledger technology:** Data is distributed across multiple nodes, ensuring redundancy and eliminating central points of control.
- **Peer-to-peer networks:** Participants communicate and share data directly, fostering trust without intermediaries.

Benefits of decentralization include:

- **Reduced censorship:** No central authority can manipulate or censor data, ensuring fairness and transparency.
- **Enhanced fault tolerance:** The network remains operational even if some nodes fail, ensuring high availability.

For example, decentralized finance platforms allow users to perform financial transactions without relying on banks or intermediaries, giving individuals greater control over their assets.

Transparency and accountability

Blockchain provides unparalleled transparency by allowing:

- **Public visibility:** Transactions are recorded on a public ledger, accessible to all participants, promoting openness.
- **Traceability:** Every transaction is traceable, enabling audits and verifying data origins.

Transparency promotes:

- **Trust:** Participants have confidence in the system's fairness and accuracy.
- **Accountability:** Organizations and individuals are held accountable for their actions, as all data is recorded and visible.

For instance, blockchain is used in food supply chains to track products from farm to table, providing transparency to consumers about the origins of their food.

Challenges of decentralized systems

Despite its advantages, decentralization poses challenges:

- **Coordination issues:** Achieving consensus among distributed participants can be complex, especially in large networks.
- **Energy consumption:** Some consensus mechanisms, such as PoW, consume significant energy, raising environmental concerns.
- **Regulatory concerns:** A lack of centralized oversight may conflict with regulatory requirements, especially in sensitive industries like finance.

For example, blockchain-based cryptocurrencies often face scrutiny from regulators due to their decentralized nature.

10.6.3 Use cases in sensitive industries

Healthcare

Blockchain enhances healthcare by:

- **Secure patient records:** Storing medical records on a blockchain ensures data integrity and prevents unauthorized access.

- **Interoperability:** Blockchain facilitates seamless data sharing among healthcare providers while maintaining privacy through encryption.
- **Drug traceability:** Blockchain tracks pharmaceuticals from production to distribution, preventing counterfeit drugs from entering the market

Example: MediLedger, a blockchain-based platform, enables secure and transparent drug supply chains, ensuring that only authentic medications reach patients.

Finance

In the financial sector, blockchain provides:

- **Fraud prevention:** Immutable records reduce the risk of fraudulent transactions by ensuring data accuracy.
- **Efficient payments:** Blockchain enables faster and more cost-effective cross-border payments, bypassing traditional intermediaries.
- **Smart contracts:** Automating financial agreements reduces reliance on intermediaries, thereby increasing efficiency and reducing costs.

Ripple facilitates real-time, low-cost international payments using blockchain technology, providing an alternative to traditional banking systems.

Supply chain management

Blockchain optimizes supply chains by:

- **End-to-end visibility:** Providing transparency across all stages of the supply chain, from production to delivery.
- **Authenticity verification:** Ensuring products are genuine and ethically sourced through immutable records.
- **Streamlined operations:** Reducing inefficiencies and improving traceability to enhance productivity.

Example: IBM Food Trust uses blockchain to trace food from farm to table, ensuring quality and safety while minimizing waste.

Government and public services

Governments leverage blockchain for:

- **Transparent elections:** Blockchain enables secure and tamper-proof voting systems, ensuring the integrity of election results.
- **Identity management:** Digital identities stored on a blockchain reduce fraud and improve access to public services.
- **Land registries:** Immutable records of land ownership prevent disputes and corruption, ensuring fairness.

Example: Estonia uses blockchain to secure citizen data and provide efficient digital public services, setting a benchmark for e-governance.

Energy and Utilities

Blockchain transforms energy management by:

- **Peer-to-peer energy trading:** Enabling individuals to trade excess energy directly, thereby reducing reliance on centralized providers.
- **Renewable energy certificates:** Tracking and verifying renewable energy production and consumption to promote sustainability.
- **Grid optimization:** Enhancing efficiency and reducing waste in energy distribution through real-time data sharing.

Example: Power Ledger facilitates decentralized energy trading using blockchain, empowering consumers and promoting green energy.

Conclusion

In the digital age, blockchain technology has become a game-changing way to guarantee security, transparency, and trust. Blockchain provides unmatched data integrity and resilience by utilizing decentralized systems and cryptographic principles. This chapter examines how blockchain improves security and trust, how it may be used to create decentralized systems, and how it can be applied in sensitive sectors.

Case studies and examples

- **Case study 1: Blockchain in healthcare:** A hospital network implemented blockchain to securely store and share patient records, reducing errors and improving care coordination. This system ensured privacy and enabled seamless data sharing between different facilities.
- **Case study 2: Financial fraud prevention:** A leading bank used blockchain to create an immutable transaction ledger, significantly reducing instances of fraud and enhancing trust among customers.
- **Case study 3: Transparent supply chains:** A global retailer adopted blockchain to trace products from suppliers to consumers, ensuring ethical sourcing and reducing waste. This increased consumer trust and optimized operations across the supply chain.

10.7 Introduction to advanced simulation and modeling

- **Overview of simulation in engineering and science**:
  - **Historical perspective**: From basic analytical models to computational simulations. Early simulations were simple approximations (e.g., using hand calculations) but have evolved into complex multidisciplinary modeling frameworks.

- **Importance of simulations**: Simulations allow for virtual testing and validation of systems before physical prototypes are built. This leads to cost reduction, faster design cycles, and improved safety.
- **Types of simulations**:
- **Numerical simulations**: Using mathematical models solved computationally (e.g., finite difference and finite element methods).
- **Physics-based simulations**: Simulating physical phenomena such as fluid dynamics, heat transfer, or electromagnetic fields.
- **Agent-based simulations**: Modeling the behavior of individual agents (such as people, robots, or molecules) and how they interact within a system.

- **Role in industries**:
  - **Aerospace**: Flight simulations for aircraft design, airflow modeling, and heat resistance in high-speed environments.
  - **Automotive**: Crash simulations, fuel efficiency optimization, engine performance modeling, and autonomous vehicle testing.
  - **Energy**: Simulating power grid performance, wind turbine efficiency, solar energy optimization, and battery management systems.
  - **Medicine**: Organ modeling for surgical planning, simulating drug interactions at the molecular level, or personalized treatments based on simulations of the human body.
  - **Robotics**: Testing autonomous robots, multirobot systems' coordination, and task execution in dynamic environments.
- **Key objectives**:
  - Simulations aim to predict outcomes, optimize designs, reduce development time, and enhance understanding of complex systems that are otherwise too dangerous, expensive, or impractical to physically test.

10.7.1 Multiphysics simulations

- **Definition and importance**:

Multiphysics overview:

Simulations that simultaneously incorporate multiple forms of physics include simultaneous combinations of fluid dynamics, mechanical, thermal, and electrical interactions. For instance, modeling a heat exchanger requires the simultaneous analysis of fluid flow [computational fluid dynamics (CFD)] and heat transfer.

- **Applications**:
  - **Aerospace**: Modeling heat dissipation, airflow, and structural integrity of aircraft. Aircraft experience a range of physical phenomena, including aerodynamic forces, heat generation (from friction), and structural stress.

- **Automotive**: Vehicle crash testing often involves simulations that couple crash mechanics (structural) with fluid dynamics (airbag deployment) and thermal effects (fire hazards).
- **Renewable energy**: optimizing wind turbine designs that model the relationship between the mechanical characteristics of the structure, the electrical output, and the aerodynamics of the blades.
- **Biomedical engineering**: simulating the dynamics of blood flow in the cardiovascular system, where it may be necessary to connect fluid dynamics, tissue deformation, and electrical activity (such as ECG data).

- **Tools & Techniques**:
  - **Finite element analysis (FEA)**: Used for structural mechanics (stress/strain analysis). It can be coupled with other physics for more complex simulations.
  - **CFD**: Used to simulate the flow of fluids (liquids and gases) and their interactions with structures. When coupled with heat transfer and material properties, it provides a comprehensive model.
  - **Electromagnetic simulations**: Used in simulations for electric motors, antennas, and wireless devices, where electromagnetic fields and material properties interact.
  - **System dynamics models**: These help to model feedback loops in systems such as energy grids or ecological systems, where electrical, mechanical, and chemical interactions play a role.
- **Challenges**: Multiphysics simulations are computationally expensive, require specialized knowledge, and integrating different solvers (e.g., FEA and CFD) often requires custom scripting and high-level computational platforms.

10.7.2 Dynamic simulations

- **What are dynamic simulations?**:
  - **Dynamic systems**: These are systems where the state changes over time, influenced by varying conditions. The behavior is governed by time-dependent equations, which describe how the system evolves.
  - **Nonlinear dynamics**: Systems that do not follow linear equations and may display chaotic behavior, making predictions more challenging.
- **Applications**:
  - **Robotics**: Dynamic simulations help model robot movements and interactions with environments. These may include obstacle avoidance, path planning, and reactions to external forces (e.g., a human pushing a robot).
  - **Aerospace**: Flight simulations involve complex dynamics, accounting for changing forces (e.g., drag, lift) as the aircraft moves through various atmospheric conditions.
  - **Structural engineering**: Simulating the dynamic response of buildings, bridges, and dams to environmental forces, such as earthquakes or wind gusts.
  - **Energy**: Power grid simulations, where dynamic modeling is needed to handle fluctuations in energy demand, failure scenarios, and the variability of renewable energy sources.

- **Types of dynamic simulations**:
  - **Time domain simulations**: Track changes over a period, solving equations of motion or control. This is particularly important in control system design (e.g., feedback loops in industrial automation).
  - **Frequency domain simulations**: Often used for systems where oscillations and vibrations are important, such as in mechanical systems or electrical circuits.
  - **Stochastic simulations**: Dealing with systems that involve randomness, such as predicting weather patterns or market dynamics.

10.7.3 Tools and platforms driving innovation

- **ANSYS**:
  - Known for its powerful multiphysics capabilities, ANSYS integrates CFD, FEA, electromagnetics, and other physics into one platform. Engineers use it to perform simulations across industries such as aerospace, automotive, and energy.
  - **Key features**: High-fidelity simulations, parallel computing, and integration with optimization algorithms.
- **COMSOL multiphysics**:
  - COMSOL is renowned for its flexibility in coupling different types of physical simulations. It is widely used in academia and research for complex engineering and physical system simulations.
  - **Key features**: Multiphysics interface, easy-to-use graphical user interface, and a wide range of predefined modules (e.g., heat transfer, chemical reactions, acoustics, etc.).
- **Matrix Laboratory (MATLAB)/Simulink**:
  - Widely used for dynamic simulations, especially in control systems, robotics, and signal processing, Simulink's graphical interface makes it ideal for modeling, simulating, and analyzing dynamic systems.
  - **Key features**: Integration with Simscape for physical modeling, large libraries of pre-built components for control, system modeling, and optimization.
- **OpenFOAM**:
  - Open-source and highly versatile, OpenFOAM is used primarily for fluid dynamics simulations. It can simulate everything from simple pipe flow to complex turbulence, combustion, and multiphase flows.
  - **Key features**: Extensive solver libraries, community-driven development, and strong capabilities for CFD and multiphase simulations.
- **Cloud computing and high-performance computing**:
  - Cloud platforms like **SimScale** offer powerful computational resources for simulations without requiring in-house supercomputing capabilities. With the use of HPC, simulations can be run faster, even on massive multiphysics problems.

10.7.4 Real-time adaptability in models

- **What is real-time adaptability?**:
- The capacity for a simulation model to adjust to new, real-time data inputs while the simulation is running is especially useful in fields where the model must account for constantly changing conditions.
- **Applications**:
  - **Autonomous systems**: Self-driving cars must adapt to environmental changes (e.g., road conditions, traffic, pedestrians) in real-time, adjusting decisions and control based on sensory input.
  - **Smart manufacturing**: Real-time adaptive systems can modify production plans based on material shortages, equipment availability, or quality feedback.
  - **Smart grids**: In the energy sector, real-time simulations help manage the distribution of power, predicting and reacting to load changes or faults.
- **Real-time simulation methods**:
  - **Model predictive control**: A control strategy that uses real-time data to predict the future states of a system and optimizes control inputs accordingly.
  - **Digital twin technology**: Virtual representations of physical systems that are constantly updated with real-time data. This allows operators to simulate and optimize systems such as manufacturing lines, buildings, and urban infrastructures.
  - **Simulation-optimization**: Real-time data feeds into optimization algorithms to provide immediate adjustments, which are used in sectors like logistics, autonomous vehicles, and financial systems.

10.8 Integration with virtual and augmented reality

10.8.1 Immersive visualization of digital twins

- **What is a digital twin?**
  - A **digital twin** is a virtual representation or model of a physical object, process, or system that is used to simulate and analyze its real-world counterpart. This dynamic model updates in real-time with data from sensors on the physical object, enabling predictive analysis, performance optimization, and operational insights.
  - The integration of v**irtual reality/augmented reality** into digital twin technologies takes these virtual models to the next level, allowing users to interact with the models in immersive, spatially accurate environments.
- **How VR/AR enhances digital twin visualization**:
  - **VR**: With VR, users can fully immerse themselves in the digital twin model. Using VR headsets, operators, designers, and engineers can explore the digital replica in 3D, walk around it, and interact with it as if it were a physical object. This is especially useful in complex systems, such as:

  - **Aircraft design**: Engineers can virtually "walk through" an aircraft's interior, inspect components, and assess how changes to the design or layout might affect functionality or ergonomics.
  - **Buildings and infrastructure**: Architects can create virtual environments for urban planning, allowing them to simulate the impact of different building materials or designs before construction begins.
  - **Energy systems**: Simulating entire energy grids or power plants in VR, offering a comprehensive view of how power flows through systems and helping engineers to spot inefficiencies or potential points of failure.
- **AR**: Unlike VR, AR overlays virtual elements onto the real world. For example, an engineer could use AR glasses or a tablet to see a live feed of a factory floor with virtual overlays of a digital twin. This provides a real-time representation of the system's current status, highlighting components that need attention or optimization.
  - **Maintenance applications**: AR can be used to superimpose digital information (e.g., schematics, sensor data) on top of a physical asset, enabling technicians to perform maintenance tasks more efficiently. They can see where problems are occurring in real-time and access virtual manuals or repair instructions directly on the object.
  - **Real-time monitoring**: Using AR to visualize real-time data, such as airflow, temperature, or vibrations, as overlaid information on a physical system (e.g., an engine or a turbine). This allows for better situational awareness during operation.
- **Benefits of immersive digital twin visualization**:
  - **Improved decision-making**: Immersive VR and AR experiences help engineers, operators, and stakeholders make faster and better-informed decisions by interacting with 3D data-driven models in real time.
  - **Enhanced understanding of complex systems**: VR and AR allow users to view and interact with digital twins at various levels of detail, from high-level overviews down to microscopic details of individual components. This aids in understanding the behavior of complex systems that would otherwise be difficult to visualize.
  - **Risk reduction**: By using virtual models before making any physical changes, companies can simulate potential risks, failures, or safety issues, thereby preventing costly mistakes.

10.8.2 Applications in training and collaboration

- **Training applications**:
  - **Simulating dangerous or expensive scenarios**: VR allows trainees to interact with highly realistic simulations of dangerous or difficult-to-recreate situations. For example:
    - **Medical training**: VR is used to simulate surgeries or emergency response scenarios, offering a safe environment where trainees can practice without the risk of harming patients.

  - **Military training**: In defense sectors, VR-based simulations are used to train soldiers for combat scenarios or equipment handling, where physical replication might be too costly or dangerous.
  - **Industrial training**: VR provides a platform for training operators in hazardous environments (e.g., working in a chemical plant, oil rigs, or power plants), where they can practice operating machinery and respond to emergency situations without real-world consequences.
- **Advantages of VR in training**:
  - **Realistic and risk-free environment**: It enables users to engage in simulated, hands-on experiences where mistakes don't have real-world consequences.
  - **Standardization and scalability**: VR allows for uniform training programs that can be distributed across multiple locations and scaled easily, ensuring consistent quality and experience.
  - **Immersive learning**: VR engages more senses (sight, sound, and sometimes touch), leading to better retention and understanding of complex tasks.
- **Collaboration in AR/VR**:
- **Remote collaboration**: AR and VR can facilitate real-time collaboration, particularly in industries where experts and teams are geographically dispersed. With AR/VR platforms, individuals can "meet" in a virtual space and interact with 3D models, providing an effective way to work together on design or maintenance tasks.
- **Engineering and design**: Teams can collaborate on a virtual representation of a product or process, make real-time changes, discuss design alterations, and review different configurations in a shared virtual space.
- **Virtual prototyping and feedback**: During product development, teams can provide feedback on virtual prototypes in VR environments before physical prototyping, thereby reducing the development timeline and cost.
- **Shared AR/VR workspaces**:
  - **Virtual offices**: VR and AR enable remote teams to create shared virtual workspaces where they can interact as avatars, share 3D models, and brainstorm design ideas in a 3D collaborative environment.
  - **Maintenance collaboration**: For on-the-job assistance, AR can provide a "remote expert" feature, where a technician wearing AR glasses is guided by an expert in real time, who can annotate their view with instructions, diagrams, or solutions.
- **Benefits for collaboration**:
  - **Enhanced communication**: VR and AR enable the visual communication of complex information, making it easier for team members to understand each other's points or suggestions when working on intricate designs or problems.
  - **Increased efficiency**: By visualizing problems or solutions in 3D and in real-time, teams can make faster decisions, saving time and reducing the need for physical prototypes or trial-and-error testing.

- **Cross-disciplinary collaboration**: VR and AR support collaboration among different experts—engineers, designers, and operators—who can all interact with the same model, leading to more comprehensive solutions.

10.8.3 Enhancing design and maintenance processes

- **Enhancing the design process**:
  - **Virtual prototyping**: Using VR to create and interact with virtual prototypes can significantly reduce the number of physical prototypes needed, saving both time and money. For example, in automotive design, manufacturers can build a virtual prototype of a car and evaluate aerodynamics, passenger space, and material choices before physical testing.
  - **Design iteration and feedback**: VR facilitates the ability to quickly iterate on designs. Engineers and designers can virtually alter a product or structure, visualize changes instantly, and collaborate with others, ensuring the final design meets all necessary requirements before physical construction begins.
  - **Ergonomics and human factors**: VR allows designers to test the ergonomics of a product by simulating how it will be used in the real world. For example, it enables testing the interior layout of a car or the usability of a machine by allowing users to interact with it virtually, ensuring comfort and usability before finalizing the design.
- **Enhancing the maintenance process**:
  - **Real-time AR assistance**: With AR glasses or mobile devices, maintenance personnel can receive real-time data overlays about the equipment they are servicing, guiding them step-by-step through repairs, troubleshooting, and part replacements. AR also allows for visualizing the internal workings of machinery, enabling faster diagnostics.
  - **Remote maintenance support**: AR facilitates remote maintenance, where a technician on-site can connect with a remote expert for guidance. The expert can see what the technician sees and annotate the live feed with instructions, diagrams, and other helpful information.
  - **Predictive maintenance**: VR can be used to visualize trends and patterns in the health of machinery over time, making it easier to identify when components are likely to fail and plan maintenance accordingly. By integrating real-time sensor data into AR or VR environments, maintenance teams can anticipate problems and act proactively.

- **Benefits for design and maintenance**:
  - **Improved design quality**: By using immersive technologies to visualize designs from multiple perspectives and gather real-time feedback, teams can identify potential design flaws earlier in the process.

- **Faster, more accurate maintenance**: With AR tools that overlay critical data and schematics onto real-world components, maintenance becomes more accurate and can be performed faster, reducing downtime and operational costs.
- **Reduced operational downtime**: Predictive maintenance using AR and VR reduces the risk of unexpected breakdowns, helping ensure systems operate efficiently without costly, unplanned downtime.

10.9 5G connectivity for real-time applications

10.9.1 Low-latency communication and fast data transfer

- **What is 5G connectivity?**
  - **5G** refers to the fifth generation of mobile network technology, which is designed to provide faster speeds, lower latency, higher bandwidth, and better reliability than previous generations (4G, 3G, etc.). It leverages advanced technologies such as **millimeter-wave** bands, **MIMO (multiple input multiple output)** antennas, and **beamforming** to achieve ultra-fast communication speeds and near-instantaneous data transmission.
  - **Key features of 5G**:
  - **High speed**: 5G can offer data speeds of up to **10–100 Gbps**, enabling rapid data transfer, faster downloads, and seamless streaming.
  - **Ultra-low latency**: The most significant advantage of 5G over previous generations is its **latency**. 5G can achieve latencies as low as **1 ms** (millisecond), compared to 30–50 ms with 4G, which is essential for real-time communication and applications requiring immediate feedback.
  - **High capacity**: 5G supports a massive number of connected devices, making it ideal for IoT applications.
- **Impact of low-latency and fast data transfer**:
  - **Real-time decision-making**: Low latency allows for near-instantaneous communication between devices and systems, enabling real-time decision-making. For example, when autonomous vehicles communicate with traffic infrastructure, the minimal delay in data transmission ensures that vehicles can respond immediately to changes in the environment (such as road closures, obstacles, or speed limits).
  - **Fast data transfer**: Faster data transfer speeds ensure that large volumes of information (such as video feeds, sensor data, or real-time analytics) can be transmitted and processed quickly. This is crucial for applications like remote surgery, high-definition video surveillance, or industrial automation.
- **How 5G improves real-time applications**:
  - **Enhanced user experience**: Faster download/upload speeds, lower latency, and more reliable connections result in smoother user experiences in real-time applications such as gaming, video conferencing, or virtual meetings.

- **Enabling edge computing**: 5G reduces reliance on cloud servers by enabling **edge computing**, where data processing happens closer to the source (e.g., on the device or local servers), allowing for faster data analysis and response times.

10.9.2 Applications in autonomous systems

- **What are autonomous systems?**
  - Autonomous systems include technologies like **self-driving vehicles**, **drones**, and **robotics**, which operate without direct human intervention. These systems rely heavily on real-time data processing and communication with external environments (such as sensors, other vehicles, or infrastructure) to navigate and perform tasks.
- **How 5G supports autonomous systems**:
  - **AVs**:
    - **Real-time communication**: AVs require low-latency communication to interact with other vehicles, pedestrians, and traffic infrastructure in real time. For instance, when a vehicle detects a potential obstacle, it needs to send data to other nearby vehicles or a central traffic management system almost instantly to make decisions about speed or routing.
    - **Vehicle-to-everything (V2X) communication**: 5G enables **V2X** communication, where autonomous vehicles communicate not only with each other (vehicle-to-vehicle) but also with surrounding infrastructure (vehicle-to-infrastructure, V2I), pedestrians (vehicle-to-pedestrian), and networks (vehicle-to-network). This allows vehicles to make safer and more informed decisions, reducing accidents and improving traffic flow.
    - **Real-time data exchange**: With 5G, autonomous vehicles can share data (such as maps, sensor data, and location) in real time, allowing them to adjust to changing road conditions or traffic patterns without delays. Additionally, vehicles can download large amounts of data (such as high-definition maps or updates) quickly.
- **Drones**:
  - **Remote operation**: 5G's low latency and high-speed data transfer enable drones to be controlled remotely with high precision. This is particularly important for applications like search and rescue, aerial surveying, and delivery services, where quick responsiveness to the environment is crucial.
  - **Edge computing**: 5G facilitates **edge computing** for drones, where data is processed locally (onboard the drone or at nearby servers) instead of relying on distant cloud servers. This enables faster reaction times and reduces the chances of communication delays in critical situations, such as when avoiding obstacles or tracking moving targets.

- **Robotics**:
  - **Real-time coordination**: In industrial automation, robots that rely on 5G can communicate with other robots and machines in real time to synchronize tasks and operations. For example, in a warehouse, robots can communicate with each other to avoid collisions and coordinate pick-and-place tasks.
  - **Remote operation**: 5G enables the remote control of robots with minimal latency, allowing operators to control robots performing hazardous or complex tasks from a safe distance. This is useful in industries such as manufacturing, mining, or surgery, where robots might need to be operated in environments that are difficult or dangerous for humans.
- **Key benefits for autonomous systems**:
  - **Safety**: Low latency reduces response times and ensures that autonomous systems can react quickly to dynamic and unpredictable environments, improving overall safety.
  - **Efficiency**: Autonomous systems powered by 5G can operate more efficiently with faster data exchange, enhanced real-time decision-making, and better coordination with other systems.
  - **Scalability**: The ability to connect a large number of autonomous devices simultaneously makes 5G an ideal solution for scaling autonomous systems, such as fleets of self-driving cars or drones.

10.9.3 Scaling smart systems with 5G

- **What are smart systems?**
  - **Smart systems** refer to interconnected devices, sensors, and machines that use data and analytics to perform tasks autonomously or with minimal human intervention. These systems are part of the **IoT** ecosystem and range from smart homes to entire smart cities.
- **How 5G enables the scaling of smart systems**:
  - **Massive IoT connectivity**: 5G supports a much larger number of connected devices compared to previous generations of mobile networks. It is estimated that 5G can support up to **1 million devices per square kilometer**, which is crucial for deploying large-scale IoT networks such as smart cities or industrial automation environments.
  - **High bandwidth**: The bandwidth provided by 5G allows for the transmission of high volumes of data from multiple sensors, cameras, and devices without bottlenecks. This is essential for applications like **smart traffic management**, **healthcare monitoring**, and **environmental monitoring**, where large amounts of data need to be processed and analyzed in real-time.
  - **Smart cities**:
    - **Traffic management**: 5G enables smart traffic lights, road sensors, and real-time communication with vehicles to optimize traffic flow, reduce congestion, and

improve safety. Cities can monitor and manage traffic, air quality, and energy consumption more effectively.
- **Public safety**: Real-time surveillance cameras, gunshot detection systems, and emergency response systems can be seamlessly connected via 5G to ensure faster response times and improved public safety.
- **Energy efficiency**: 5G can support smart grids that enable real-time monitoring of energy usage and distribution. With 5G, utilities can efficiently manage energy production, distribution, and consumption across large cities or regions.

- **Industrial automation and smart factories**:
  - **Industrial IoT (IIoT)**: In manufacturing, 5G enables connected machines and robots to communicate in real time, optimizing production lines, facilitating predictive maintenance, and reducing downtime. The high bandwidth and low latency support high-definition video streams, real-time machine data, and remote control of equipment, all contributing to smarter and more efficient factories.
  - **Asset tracking and management**: Smart sensors connected via 5G can track the movement and status of assets in real-time across factories, warehouses, and supply chains, improving inventory management, reducing losses, and enhancing operational efficiency.
- **Key benefits of scaling smart systems with 5G**:
  - **Increased connectivity**: With the ability to support a large number of devices simultaneously, 5G facilitates the deployment of large-scale IoT systems across diverse industries, making smart cities, industries, and homes a reality.
  - **Improved efficiency**: 5G's high-speed and low-latency capabilities allow for real-time data processing and decision-making, enabling systems to operate more efficiently and autonomously.
  - **Better quality of service**: 5G's ability to handle high volumes of data traffic ensures uninterrupted connectivity, which is crucial for real-time applications like remote surgery, autonomous vehicles, and large-scale industrial operations.

10.10 Industry-specific innovations

10.10.1 Innovations in healthcare, manufacturing, and energy

- **Healthcare innovations**:
  - **Telemedicine and remote monitoring**:
    - Advances in **5G**, **IoT**, and **AI** have facilitated the rise of **telemedicine**, enabling doctors to consult with patients remotely via video calls, diagnostic tools, and real-time data exchange. With 5G's low latency, healthcare providers can perform real-time virtual consultations, monitor patients' vital signs remotely, and even provide remote surgeries or diagnostics with the assistance of robotic systems.

  - **Wearables**: Wearable devices, such as smartwatches, biosensors, and patches, now monitor health metrics like heart rate, glucose levels, and blood pressure. These devices continuously collect health data, which can be sent to healthcare professionals for analysis and immediate intervention, preventing emergencies.
  - **AI and ML**: AI-powered diagnostic tools are revolutionizing healthcare by analyzing medical imaging, predicting disease risks, and recommending treatment plans. ML algorithms are also used to analyze patient histories and medical records to identify early signs of chronic conditions, improving overall patient outcomes.
- **Robotic surgery**:
  - Robotic-assisted surgeries, supported by **AI** and **precision instruments**, allow surgeons to perform highly complex procedures with greater precision and minimal invasiveness. These innovations reduce recovery times and improve the overall success rates of surgeries.
- **Pharmaceuticals and drug discovery**:
  - AI and **big data analytics** are accelerating the drug discovery process. By analyzing massive datasets from clinical trials, genetic information, and disease patterns, AI systems can predict the effectiveness of drug compounds, reducing the time it takes to bring new drugs to market.
  - **3D printing** in healthcare has also made advances, enabling the creation of custom prosthetics, implants, and even bioprinted tissues for transplantation.
- **Manufacturing innovations**:
  - **Additive manufacturing (3D printing)**:
    - **3D printing** is transforming manufacturing by enabling on-demand production, creating complex, customized parts, and reducing material waste. Industries such as aerospace, automotive, and medical devices benefit greatly from this technology, as it accelerates prototyping and reduces production costs.
- **Automation and robotics**:
  - **Robotic process automation** and **collaborative robots (cobots)** are becoming widespread in factories, where robots work alongside humans to improve production efficiency and safety. Cobots can be programmed to handle repetitive tasks, leaving humans to focus on more complex and creative functions.
  - **AI and ML** are being integrated into production lines to predict maintenance needs (predictive maintenance), optimize production schedules, and even adjust the manufacturing process in real-time based on sensor data.
- **Smart factories**:
  - The **IoT** plays a crucial role in creating **smart factories**, where machines, devices, and robots communicate in real-time to optimize operations. Sensors and connected devices track inventory levels, machinery health, and even environmental factors, allowing managers to monitor and control production remotely.

    - Data-driven insights from connected systems allow manufacturers to improve quality control, reduce downtime, and enhance the overall efficiency of production lines.
- **Energy innovations**:
    - **Renewable energy**:
        - The integration of **AI** and **ML** is transforming the energy sector by optimizing the generation, distribution, and consumption of renewable energy. For example, AI can predict energy demand and adjust the output from solar, wind, or hydropower plants to match demand in real-time.
        - **Smart Grids**: Smart grids, powered by IoT sensors, allow for the efficient distribution of electricity from renewable sources and the optimization of energy consumption. These grids are also capable of integrating **energy storage** solutions, balancing supply and demand.
- **Energy storage**:
    - Advancements in **battery technology** and energy storage solutions are helping make renewable energy more viable by enabling excess energy to be stored and distributed when demand exceeds supply.
    - **Electric vehicles (EVs)** and **vehicle-to-grid** technologies are enabling bidirectional energy flows between electric vehicles and the grid, allowing EVs to serve as mobile energy storage units.
- **Grid optimization and demand response**:
    - Smart meters and demand response programs allow energy providers to monitor real-time consumption and adjust rates or manage energy distribution based on supply and demand. These innovations enhance energy efficiency and reduce waste.

10.10.2 Smart cities and urban development

- **What are smart cities?**
    - A **smart city** is an urban area that uses digital technology (IoT, 5G, big data, AI) to enhance the quality of life, reduce environmental impact, and optimize city operations. The goal is to create more sustainable, efficient, and livable urban environments.
- **Innovations in smart cities**:
    - **Smart infrastructure**:
        - **Smart grids**, **intelligent transportation systems**, and **smart buildings** form the backbone of a smart city. These systems use real-time data to manage energy usage, traffic flow, waste management, and environmental monitoring. For instance, smart traffic lights can adjust in real-time to reduce congestion, while buildings can optimize energy consumption based on occupancy patterns and external weather conditions.

- **Environmental monitoring**:
- Smart sensors placed throughout the city can monitor air quality, water quality, noise levels, and waste disposal in real-time. Cities can use this data to implement targeted interventions, such as adjusting traffic patterns to reduce pollution or improving waste collection in areas with high waste generation.
- **Public safety and security**:
  - **Smart surveillance systems** powered by AI and computer vision are used to monitor public spaces, identifying potential threats or accidents in real time and enabling quicker responses from law enforcement or emergency services.
  - **Gunshot detection systems** and **predictive policing,** powered by data analytics, help reduce crime rates by identifying patterns and deploying resources more effectively.
- **Urban mobility**:
  - **AVs, electric scooters**, and **ride-sharing services** are transforming urban mobility. With the help of 5G connectivity and AI, smart cities can integrate these modes of transport to create seamless and sustainable urban transport systems.
  - **Smart Parking**: Sensors and apps help drivers find available parking spots, reducing traffic congestion and improving the efficiency of parking space usage.
- **Smart healthcare**:
  - In smart cities, healthcare facilities are interconnected with real-time monitoring of patient data, allowing for more efficient care and resource allocation. **Telemedicine, smart clinics**, and **health monitoring systems** are integrated with urban infrastructure to improve overall public health.
- **Benefits of smart cities**:
  - **Sustainability**: Smart cities use resources more efficiently, reduce waste and emissions, and improve the quality of life for residents.
  - **Cost-Efficiency**: Real-time data and automation reduce operational costs in city management (e.g., traffic control, waste management, energy use).
  - **Citizen Engagement**: Citizens can actively participate in city governance through smart systems by providing feedback on urban issues, participating in smart voting, or reporting issues directly via digital platforms.

10.10.3 Industry 4.0 and digital twins

- **What is Industry 4.0?**
  - **Industry 4.0** represents the fourth industrial revolution, characterized by the integration of **IoT**, **AI**, **robotics**, **automation**, and **big data** to create smarter and more efficient manufacturing processes. This revolution focuses on connectivity, real-time data, and intelligent automation.

- **Digital twins in Industry 4.0**:
  - A **digital twin** is a virtual replica of a physical asset, system, or process powered by real-time data and simulations. By monitoring the actual system with sensors and feeding this data into a digital model, companies can optimize operations, predict failures, and improve product designs.
  - **Applications of digital twins in manufacturing**:
    - **Predictive maintenance**: Using real-time data from machines, digital twins can predict when maintenance will be required, reducing downtime and optimizing maintenance schedules.
    - **Design optimization**: Digital twins allow for the simulation of different design scenarios and operational conditions, helping manufacturers create more efficient processes and products before physical prototyping.
    - **Supply chain management**: Digital twins of entire supply chains can be used to track the movement of goods, optimize logistics, and predict bottlenecks or disruptions.
- **Applications of digital twins in energy**:
  - **Smart grid management**: Digital twins help model energy grids in real-time, optimizing energy distribution and identifying issues such as faults or imbalances.
  - **Asset management**: In the energy sector, digital twins of equipment like turbines, power plants, and solar panels allow for real-time monitoring, predictive maintenance, and operational efficiency improvements.
- **Benefits of Industry 4.0 and digital twins**:
  - **Increased efficiency**: Real-time monitoring and data-driven insights lead to more efficient production, optimized energy consumption, and improved product quality.
  - **Cost savings**: Predictive maintenance, optimized production schedules, and streamlined supply chains all contribute to significant cost savings in manufacturing and energy operations.
  - **Innovation**: Digital twins provide a platform for experimenting with new designs, processes, and products in a virtual environment before committing to physical changes.

10.11 Sustainability and green initiatives

10.11.1 Optimizing resource utilization and reducing waste

- **What is resource optimization?**
  - **Resource optimization** refers to the strategic use of natural, human, and capital resources to achieve maximum efficiency and minimize waste. This practice is crucial for **sustainable development**, ensuring that businesses and industries can meet their goals while reducing their environmental footprint.
  - In the context of sustainability, resource optimization focuses on using fewer resources (energy, water, raw materials, etc.) to produce more while reducing negative environmental impacts, such as pollution and habitat destruction.

- **Technologies driving resource optimization**:
  - **IoT**: IoT devices, such as sensors and smart meters, collect real-time data on resource consumption (water, energy, raw materials) across various sectors like manufacturing, agriculture, and construction. This data can be analyzed to identify inefficiencies, leading to optimized usage and waste reduction.
    - For example, **smart energy meters** in homes or factories monitor electricity consumption, helping identify energy waste and enabling users to adjust their behavior for more efficient use.
    - **Smart water management** systems, which use IoT-based sensors, allow for real-time monitoring of water use and leakage, helping to conserve this precious resource.
- **AI and ML**:
  - AI algorithms are increasingly used to predict demand, optimize production schedules, and reduce resource waste. In **manufacturing**, AI can fine-tune production lines to minimize the use of materials, energy, and labor while maintaining high levels of output.
  - In **agriculture**, AI models can predict water and fertilizer needs, ensuring that these resources are used only when necessary and in the right amounts.
- **Automation and robotics**:
  - Automation in industries such as **manufacturing** and **logistics** enables better resource planning by optimizing processes. Automated systems can reduce material waste by performing precise tasks that previously required more human input, which might have resulted in overuse or inefficiencies.
  - **Robotics** and **drones** are also being used for efficient monitoring of **agriculture** and **construction sites**, ensuring that resources like soil, water, and raw materials are used in the most efficient way possible.
- **Sustainable manufacturing and production**:
  - **Lean manufacturing** principles, which focus on reducing waste (e.g., material, time, labor), are now integrated with **smart technologies** to enhance sustainability. This includes advanced robotics, real-time production data analytics, and just-in-time inventory systems to prevent overproduction and reduce energy consumption.
  - **Green supply chain management** is also an emerging trend, where organizations ensure that the entire lifecycle of products—from raw material extraction to end-of-life disposal—uses sustainable methods and minimizes waste.
- **Examples of resource optimization**:
  - **Circular manufacturing**: Companies like **Patagonia** and **IKEA** focus on minimizing waste and maximizing resource efficiency by using recycled materials and designing products for long-lasting use, reusability, and recyclability.
  - **Zero-waste practices**: Organizations are adopting zero-waste strategies in production processes, where materials are reused, repurposed, or recycled to avoid landfill disposal.

10.11.2 Lifecycle analysis and circular economy

- **What is lifecycle analysis (LCA)?**
  - **LCA** is a comprehensive method of evaluating the environmental impact of a product or service over its entire lifecycle—from raw material extraction, manufacturing, distribution, use, and eventual disposal or recycling.
  - LCA assesses various environmental aspects, such as energy consumption, greenhouse gas emissions, water usage, and waste generation. This analysis helps businesses identify the most impactful stages of a product's lifecycle and implement sustainable practices to mitigate negative effects.
- **Importance of LCA in sustainability**:
  - By examining the full environmental impact of a product or process, businesses can identify areas where they can make improvements. For example, they might consider switching to energy-efficient technologies during the manufacturing phase, using renewable materials, or designing for easy disassembly and recycling at the product's end of life.
  - LCA also helps businesses understand **carbon footprints** and enables them to take proactive steps toward reducing emissions by optimizing processes or sourcing sustainable materials.
- **Circular economy concept**:
  - A **circular economy** is an economic system aimed at minimizing waste and making the most of resources. Unlike the traditional **linear economy**, where products are made, used, and disposed of, the circular economy promotes **reuse**, **repair**, **recycling**, and **refurbishing**.
  - The core principle of the circular economy is to create a closed-loop system in which products are continually repurposed, reducing the need for raw material extraction and cutting down on waste.
- **Key principles of the circular economy**:
  - **Design for longevity**: Products are designed to last longer, be easily repaired, and have upgradeable parts to extend their lifespan.
  - **Material recovery**: Products are made from materials that can be reused or recycled at the end of their lifecycle. This involves using biodegradable or recyclable materials and creating infrastructure to support efficient recycling processes.
  - **Product-as-a-service (PaaS)**: Instead of owning products, businesses or consumers can **rent** or **lease** them. For example, instead of buying products like lighting equipment or machinery, businesses pay for access or usage, and the manufacturer retains ownership to ensure they are reused or recycled at the end of the product's useful lives.
  - **Resource efficiency**: Manufacturers and consumers prioritize the efficient use of raw materials and energy in production and consumption.

- **Circular economy models in practice**:
  - **Upcycling and recycling**: Companies like **TerraCycle** and **Loop** are turning waste materials into new products. TerraCycle specializes in collecting and recycling nonrecyclable waste, while Loop has created a system for reusable packaging, allowing consumers to return empty containers for cleaning and reuse.
  - **Closed-loop manufacturing**: Companies like **Interface** in the carpet industry have adopted closed-loop systems, where used carpets are returned to the factory, recycled, and transformed into new products, thereby reducing the need for virgin materials.

10.11.3 Environmental monitoring and climate simulations

- **Environmental monitoring technologies**:
  - **Sensors and IoT**: The use of **IoT-based sensors** is expanding in environmental monitoring. These sensors measure parameters such as air quality, temperature, humidity, water quality, soil health, and energy consumption. Data from these sensors can be analyzed to track environmental changes in real time and identify pollution hotspots, resource consumption trends, or areas that need immediate action.
    - For instance, **air quality monitoring systems** powered by IoT sensors can detect pollutants like carbon dioxide, nitrogen dioxide, and particulate matter. This information can be used by cities to optimize traffic flow, reduce industrial emissions, and improve public health.
- **Remote sensing and satellites**:
  - Satellite-based remote sensing provides high-resolution imagery and data on large-scale environmental changes, such as deforestation, climate change, and water scarcity. This data is crucial for managing natural resources and implementing conservation efforts.
  - In **agriculture**, remote sensing helps farmers monitor crop health, soil conditions, and water usage, contributing to more efficient resource management and sustainable farming practices.
- **Climate simulations and predictive modeling**:

  a. **Climate simulation models** use complex algorithms and data to predict future climate changes and their potential impacts on the environment. These models take into account factors such as greenhouse gas emissions, deforestation, changes in land use, and renewable energy adoption.
    - Climate models are used by governments, organizations, and researchers to understand the long-term effects of different environmental policies, including the transition to **clean energy**, conservation efforts, and the global impact of climate change.
    - **AI and ML** are increasingly being used to enhance climate simulations by analyzing large datasets to make more accurate predictions about future climate scenarios, providing decision-makers with data-driven insights for sustainable development.

- **Environmental impact assessment**:
  - Before implementing large-scale infrastructure projects, businesses and governments use environmental impact assessments (EIAs) to predict the effects of the project on the environment. This includes analyzing air and water quality, biodiversity, and the overall ecosystem.
  - **Sustainability reports** often include data from environmental monitoring systems and climate simulations to demonstrate how organizations are reducing their ecological footprint and adhering to sustainability goals.
- **Green technology and innovations**:
  - **Carbon capture and storage** technologies capture carbon dioxide emissions produced by industrial processes and store them underground to prevent them from entering the atmosphere. This technology is viewed as a crucial method for mitigating climate change.
  - **Clean energy solutions**: The integration of renewable energy sources, such as wind, solar, and hydropower, into the energy grid is monitored in real time using smart grids, enabling efficient energy use and reducing reliance on fossil fuels.

10.12 Ethical and societal implications

10.12.1 Addressing data privacy and governance

- **The growing importance of data privacy**:
  - As technologies like **IoT**, **AI**, **big data**, and **cloud computing** generate vast amounts of data, concerns about **data privacy** have escalated. Personal data, including health information, financial details, and location data, is being collected, stored, and processed on an unprecedented scale. This raises serious concerns about how this data is used and whether individuals' rights are protected.
  - **Data privacy** refers to the protection of personal information from unauthorized access, misuse, or theft. Key considerations include how data is collected, who has access to it, and how it is shared or sold to third parties.
- **Regulations and governance models**:
  - **Data governance** refers to the policies, procedures, and standards that ensure data is used responsibly and ethically. Governments and organizations have implemented **data protection laws** and **regulations** to safeguard individuals' rights to privacy and ensure that data is handled responsibly.
    - The **General Data Protection Regulation**, implemented in the European Union, is one of the most robust data privacy laws, mandating that organizations obtain explicit consent from individuals to collect and process their data. It also gives individuals the right to access, correct, and delete their personal data.
    - The **California Consumer Privacy Act** in the U.S. offers similar protections, giving consumers control over their data, including the right to opt-out of data sales and request access to their personal information.

- **Challenges with Global Data Privacy**:
  - The global nature of digital services presents challenges in regulating data privacy, as data flows across borders. Different countries have varying standards and regulations, making it difficult for businesses to comply with all the rules.
  - Emerging technologies like **5G**, which can collect vast amounts of personal data, and the growing adoption of **biometrics** (e.g., facial recognition) raise questions about **how much data should be collected**, **who controls it**, and how it can be securely managed.
- **Ethical data collection and usage**:
  - Companies must be transparent about how they collect, store, and use data. **Informed consent** is critical; individuals should understand what data is being collected and how it will be used. **Anonymization** techniques can be used to remove personally identifiable information, thus reducing risks in case of data breaches.
  - There is also the issue of **data ownership**. Should the individual who generates the data retain ownership, or should companies and organizations control the data? This is a hotly debated issue with implications for business models and user rights.

10.12.2 Ethical use of converging technologies

- **Converging technologies**:
  - The convergence of technologies like **AI**, **robotics**, **nanotechnology**, **biotechnology**, and **neurotechnology** has the potential to drive significant advancements in fields such as healthcare, manufacturing, and environmental conservation. However, the fusion of these technologies raises new ethical questions that society must address to ensure their responsible use.
- **The Ethics of AI**:
  - **Bias and fairness**: AI systems are only as unbiased as the data used to train them. If the data reflect existing societal biases (e.g., racial, gender, or socioeconomic biases), the AI model will also perpetuate these biases. **Fairness** in AI decision-making, particularly in sensitive areas like hiring, law enforcement, and healthcare, is critical to ensuring that AI does not exacerbate existing inequalities.
  - **Transparency and accountability**: Many AI systems, especially those using deep learning algorithms, operate as "black boxes," meaning that their decision-making processes are not easily understandable by humans. This lack of transparency raises concerns about accountability when AI systems make incorrect or harmful decisions. For example, if an autonomous vehicle causes an accident, who is liable—the manufacturer, the software developer, or the owner?
  - **AI in surveillance**: AI-driven technologies, like **facial recognition**, are increasingly used for surveillance purposes by governments and corporations. While these technologies can enhance security, they also pose significant threats to privacy, civil liberties, and individual freedoms. There is ongoing debate about the ethical implications of mass surveillance and whether it infringes on people's rights to privacy and anonymity.

- **The ethics of biotechnology and human enhancement**:
    - **Gene editing**: Technologies like **Clustered Regularly Interspaced Short Palindromic Repeats (CRISPR)** allow for precise modifications of the human genome. While this offers the potential to eradicate genetic diseases and improve health outcomes, it also raises concerns about the possibility of "designer babies" and the ethical implications of modifying human traits.
    - **Human augmentation**: The use of technologies to enhance human capabilities (e.g., **neuroprosthetics**, **brain–computer interfaces**, and **exoskeletons**) opens up a new frontier of **human enhancement**. While these technologies can improve the quality of life, particularly for those with disabilities, they also raise questions about the ethics of enhancing human abilities beyond natural limits and the potential for inequality in access to such enhancements.
- **Ethical guidelines for emerging technologies**:
    - Developing clear **ethical frameworks** and guidelines for converging technologies is critical to ensuring they are used responsibly. This includes addressing issues such as safety, transparency, fairness, and human dignity.
    - **International collaboration** is essential in establishing common standards for emerging technologies to prevent misuse, ensure fairness, and protect human rights.

10.12.3 Impact on employment and skill development

- **Job displacement and the rise of automation**:
    - One of the most significant concerns associated with the adoption of emerging technologies is their impact on employment. **Automation**, powered by AI, robotics, and ML, is increasingly replacing human labor in sectors like manufacturing, transportation, and retail. Tasks that were once performed by workers are now being done by machines or software, leading to concerns about widespread job displacement.
    - **Examples of automation**:
        - In the **automotive industry**, robots have long been used to perform tasks like assembling parts, painting, and welding. The rise of **autonomous vehicles** threatens to displace millions of jobs in **transportation** and **logistics**.
        - The **retail sector** is experiencing a shift toward **self-checkout systems** and **automated warehouses**, where robots handle the packing and sorting of goods, reducing the need for human labor in traditional roles.
- **New job opportunities and emerging industries**:
    - While automation may displace some jobs, it also creates new job opportunities. For instance, the rise of **AI** and **robotics** requires workers in fields such as **data science**, **robotics engineering**, and **ML**. Additionally, as industries embrace **green technologies** and **sustainable practices**, new jobs in the renewable energy sector, waste management, and environmental conservation are being created.

- The **gig economy** and **remote work** are also on the rise, facilitated by digital platforms, allowing individuals to access flexible, short-term work opportunities in sectors ranging from technology to creative industries.
- **Skill development and lifelong learning**:
  - The rapid pace of technological change means that many workers will need to continually update their skills to remain competitive in the job market. This has led to an increasing emphasis on **reskilling** and **upskilling**.
  - **Technical skills**: Workers will need to acquire new technical skills to work alongside emerging technologies. This includes **coding**, **data analysis**, **AI literacy**, and **robotics operation**. Many industries are now offering **training programs** to help employees transition to new roles that require these skills.
  - **Soft skills**: As automation takes over routine tasks, human workers will be required to focus on roles that require **creativity**, **problem-solving**, and **emotional intelligence**—skills that machines cannot easily replicate. Emphasizing the importance of **critical thinking**, **collaboration**, and **adaptability** will help workers thrive in a technology-driven economy.
  - **Educational reform**: Governments and educational institutions are increasingly recognizing the need for **STEM education** (science, technology, engineering, and mathematics) and **vocational training** programs that prepare workers for the future job market. Lifelong learning initiatives will become essential, ensuring that workers have access to continuous education and training opportunities throughout their careers.
- **The role of governments and businesses**:
  - **Governments** play a crucial role in managing the transition to an economy that is increasingly dependent on technology. This includes developing **social safety nets**, implementing **universal basic income** programs, and investing in **retraining initiatives** for workers displaced by automation.
  - **Businesses** have a responsibility to ensure that their adoption of new technologies is carried out in a socially responsible manner. This includes implementing **fair labor practices**, supporting the retraining of workers, and ensuring that the benefits of technological advancements are shared equitably.

10.13 Future directions in digital twinning

10.13.1 Next-generation technologies and innovation

- **Advancements in sensor technology**:
  - **Sensors** are the foundation of the data that drives digital twins. The next generation of sensors will become more **accurate**, **smaller**, and **cost-effective**. Emerging technologies, such as **quantum sensors** and **nano-sensors,** could enable real-time, high-fidelity data collection from a wider variety of environments, ranging from human health monitoring to large-scale industrial operations.

- The integration of **IoT sensors** with **edge computing** will allow for faster data processing at the source, reducing dependency on centralized cloud systems and improving real-time responsiveness.
- **AI and ML**:
  - As digital twins evolve, **AI** and **ML** will continue to enhance their predictive capabilities, enabling more sophisticated simulations and optimizations. These technologies can **analyze large datasets** generated by digital twins to identify patterns, anomalies, and opportunities for improvement in real-time.
  - **AI-driven automation** could allow digital twins to not only simulate future scenarios but also make autonomous decisions based on those predictions. For example, an autonomous **smart city** system could adjust traffic flow or energy consumption based on the real-time data provided by digital twin models.
- **5G and beyond**:
  - The deployment of **5G** networks will be crucial for the future of digital twins, as it will provide the high-speed, low-latency communication needed for real-time data exchange between physical assets and their digital counterparts. **6G** and other next-generation wireless technologies will further enhance the capabilities of digital twins, enabling larger-scale deployments across entire industries and urban environments.
  - The high bandwidth and speed of 5G will allow for continuous streaming of data from sensors to digital twins in real-time, which is particularly important for applications in **autonomous vehicles**, **remote surgeries**, and **industrial automation**.
- **Blockchain for data integrity**:
  - As digital twins handle increasing amounts of sensitive data, ensuring the **integrity** and **security** of this data will be paramount. **Blockchain** technology can provide a decentralized, tamper-proof record of data exchanges, ensuring that the data feeding into digital twin systems remains authentic, secure, and traceable.
  - Blockchain can also facilitate **data sharing** between different organizations or sectors while maintaining trust and privacy. This is especially important in industries like **healthcare**, where data privacy is a significant concern.
- **Quantum computing and simulation**:
  - Quantum computing has the potential to revolutionize digital twin simulations by providing vastly increased processing power. This could enable the creation of highly detailed, large-scale digital twins for complex systems like **climate modeling**, **urban planning**, and **global supply chains**.
  - With the ability to model exponentially more data points and scenarios, quantum computers could simulate everything from individual molecules in **drug discovery** to the behavior of an entire city under various conditions, significantly advancing the capabilities of digital twins.

- **AR and VR**:
  - **AR** and **VR** technologies will provide immersive ways for users to interact with digital twins, transforming industries like **engineering**, **construction**, and **urban planning**.
    - Engineers or architects can visualize and manipulate a 3D model of a building or infrastructure project in real-time, providing better insight and improving decision-making processes.
    - **VR** could be used to create immersive training environments where employees can interact with virtual representations of complex systems (e.g., power plants, factories, or ships) to practice skills and troubleshoot issues in a safe virtual space.
- **Autonomous systems and digital twins**:
  - Autonomous systems—such as **drones**, **robots**, and **self-driving vehicles**—will become more tightly integrated with digital twin technology. These autonomous systems will feed real-time operational data into their corresponding digital twins to optimize performance, track maintenance needs, and enhance decision-making.
  - For example, a fleet of autonomous delivery drones could communicate with their digital twins, which would be constantly updated to reflect the drones' operational status, health, and environmental conditions. The digital twin would then be used to schedule maintenance, predict failure points, and improve routes in real-time.
- **Synthetic data generation**:
  - One challenge in deploying digital twins is the need for massive amounts of data for training and optimization. **Synthetic data generation**, powered by AI and simulation technologies, will play an increasingly important role. By creating realistic synthetic datasets, organizations can train their digital twins without needing to collect vast amounts of real-world data, which may not always be readily available, especially in nascent or experimental systems.

10.13.2 Global collaboration for digital twin ecosystems

- **Cross-sector collaboration**:
  - The development of robust **digital twin ecosystems** will require **cross-sector collaboration** between industries such as manufacturing, healthcare, transportation, and energy. digital twin models that span multiple industries will enable interconnected systems—such as smart cities, sustainable supply chains, and green energy grids.
  - For example, the transportation, energy, and urban planning sectors will need to collaborate to create **digital replicas** of entire cities, which could simulate and optimize traffic flow, energy consumption, waste management, and public services in real-time.
- **Standardization and interoperability**:
  - One of the major challenges in building global digital twin ecosystems is the lack of standardization across industries, platforms, and data formats. For digital twins to function seamlessly across various sectors and borders, there will need to be industry-wide **standardization** of protocols, data exchange formats, and communication methods.

- International bodies, such as the **International Organization for Standardization** and **Industry 4.0 consortiums**, are already working on creating these common standards for interoperability. These standards will allow organizations in different regions and sectors to integrate their digital twin technologies smoothly.

- **Public–private partnerships (PPP)**:
  - **PPP**will play a crucial role in creating a collaborative environment for developing and scaling digital twin technologies. Governments and industries will need to work together to create the infrastructure, regulatory frameworks, and funding mechanisms needed to support the large-scale adoption of digital twins.
  - For example, national governments could invest in **smart infrastructure** (such as digital roadways, urban planning projects, and transportation systems) that can support the integration of digital twin technology across cities and regions. Private companies can then leverage this infrastructure to build digital models of everything from traffic flows to healthcare systems.
- **Global knowledge sharing**:
  - Given that digital twin technology is still in its early stages, international collaboration is essential to accelerate innovation and knowledge-sharing. **Collaborative research** and **open-source development** initiatives will allow organizations, universities, and governments to share best practices, data models, and technological advances in real-time.
  - **Global consortia,** such as the **Digital Twin Consortium**, which bring together stakeholders from various sectors, will continue to be central in developing the ecosystems and frameworks that will guide digital twin evolution.

10.13.3 Vision for 2035 and beyond

- **Smart cities and integrated ecosystems**:
  - By **2035**, we can expect **smart cities** powered by digital twin technologies to be widespread. These cities will use digital twins to manage every aspect of urban life, from traffic and energy to waste management and public safety.
  - **Smart buildings** will be fully connected to their digital twins, allowing for real-time monitoring of everything from air quality to structural integrity. For example, if a building's digital twin detects a potential failure in its structural support, maintenance crews will be alerted immediately, potentially preventing costly damage or hazards.
- **Advanced healthcare systems**:
  - **Digital twins in healthcare** will revolutionize personalized medicine by creating digital replicas of individual patients. These patient-specific models will simulate responses to treatment, predict future health conditions, and guide medical decisions. By 2035, we may have **digital twins** of entire **human organs**, enabling doctors to test interventions and tailor treatments with unparalleled precision.

- **Telemedicine** will also benefit from digital twin technology, where doctors and patients can interact in immersive digital environments that closely replicate physical consultations.

- **Global supply chain optimization**:
  - **Digital twins** will play a pivotal role in the future of **global supply chains**, enabling real-time monitoring and optimization. Digital models will allow for seamless tracking of goods from raw material extraction to end consumers, optimizing production schedules, predicting inventory needs, and managing disruptions. This could lead to more efficient, sustainable, and resilient supply chains by 2035.
- **Sustainability and environmental protection**:
  - In terms of **sustainability**, Digital twins will be used to create **predictive models** of ecosystems and environmental systems to monitor climate change, biodiversity, and natural resource use. These models will help **governments**, **NGOs**, and **businesses** collaborate on mitigation strategies and ensure that actions taken today benefit future generations.
- **AI-driven decision-making**:
  - As **AI** and **ML** evolve, digital twins will become more autonomous, allowing systems not only to simulate and predict but also to make **real-time decisions** based on those predictions. This could range from managing the operations of **autonomous cities** to predicting energy demand on a global scale, creating a world where systems function with minimal human intervention, guided by continuous data from digital twins.

10.14 Conclusion

10.14.1 Recap of converging technologies' role in innovation

- **The convergence of technologies**:
  - Over the course of this book, we've explored how various **emerging technologies**, such as **AI**, **IoT**, **big data**, **5G**, **AR/VR**, and **blockchain**, are converging to transform industries, societies, and even our everyday lives. The combination of these technologies has created new possibilities for **automation**, **intelligent decision-making**, **predictive modeling**, and **real-time monitoring**.
  - **Digital twins** exemplify the power of this convergence. By merging physical systems with digital models, digital twins have become a cornerstone of innovation across sectors such as **healthcare**, **manufacturing**, **energy**, **smart cities**, and **sustainability**.
- **Innovation through integration**:
  - As we've seen, these technologies do not operate in isolation but rather complement one another. For instance, **AI and ML** improve the accuracy and predictive

capabilities of **digital twins**, while **5G connectivity** ensures real-time data transfer, and **blockchain** secures data integrity. The integration of these technologies is not only increasing operational efficiency but also driving **new business models**, **enhancing customer experiences**, and **transforming industries**.
  - These converging technologies are enabling **smarter products**, **connected environments**, and **data-driven decision-making**. Whether it's **smart manufacturing**, **personalized medicine**, or **autonomous vehicles**, these innovations are changing the way we interact with the world and opening up entirely new realms of possibility.
- **Acceleration of digital transformation**:
  - The speed at which these technologies are advancing is accelerating the pace of digital transformation across industries. Technologies that were once niche or experimental are now becoming mainstream, reshaping **business strategies**, **governance models**, and **societal frameworks**. As companies and governments adopt these tools, industries are witnessing radical shifts in how services are delivered, how assets are managed, and how problems are solved.

10.14.2 Call to action for responsible development

- **The need for ethical considerations**:
  - While the rapid development of converging technologies presents enormous opportunities, it also comes with significant **ethical challenges**. From **data privacy** concerns to **bias in AI** and the **impact on employment**, these technologies have the potential to disrupt societal norms and individual rights.
  - It is crucial for stakeholders—**governments**, **businesses**, **researchers**, and **technology developers**—to adopt frameworks for the **responsible development** of these technologies. This includes ensuring that these technologies are developed **ethically**, **transparently**, and with an eye toward the **long-term consequences** they may have on society.
- **Regulation, governance, and accountability**:
  - As digital twins and other technologies permeate every aspect of life, there must be strong **regulatory frameworks** in place to govern their use. This includes addressing issues related to **data ownership**, **security**, and **privacy**. For instance, how do we ensure that digital twins—especially those in **healthcare** or **public infrastructure**—are not misused or exploited for profit or surveillance?
  - It is also essential that **ethical guidelines** are established for technologies like **AI**, **biotechnology**, and **robotics**, ensuring that they are used for the greater good and do not perpetuate inequality or harm vulnerable populations. Collaboration across countries and industries will be vital to ensure that technology development is **inclusive**, **fair**, and **just**.

- **Social responsibility in innovation**:
  - Technology developers and companies must be mindful of the **societal impact** of their innovations. Beyond profit, there should be a strong focus on **social good**, with initiatives designed to ensure that the benefits of these technologies are **equitably distributed**. From ensuring that **underrepresented communities** have access to new technologies to minimizing the **digital divide**, the goal should be to create a more **inclusive and equitable** society.
  - **Sustainable development** is another crucial aspect of responsible innovation. As digital twins and other technologies are leveraged to address global challenges such as **climate change**, **resource scarcity**, and **social inequality**, it is essential to ensure that technological advancements do not come at the cost of future generations' ability to thrive.

10.14.3 Future potential of digital twins in society

- **Expansion of digital twins across industries**:
  - The future of **digital twin technology** is incredibly promising. As we continue to evolve the sophistication of **virtual models**, digital twins will play an increasingly pivotal role in a wide range of industries. The applications of digital twins are expected to expand beyond what we see today:
    - **Smart cities**: As cities grow and become more complex, digital twins will be at the center of managing everything from **traffic congestion** to **energy consumption** to **urban planning**. Entire city infrastructures will be mirrored digitally, allowing city planners and administrators to optimize services and predict future needs.
    - **Healthcare**: Personalized healthcare will be driven by **digital replicas** of individual patients, allowing for **tailored treatments**, **predictive diagnostics**, and better **patient outcomes**. Digital twins of **organs** or **whole bodies** will be used to simulate treatment effects, test interventions, and improve overall health management.
    - **Manufacturing and supply chains**: Digital twins will continue to revolutionize industries like **manufacturing** by enabling **predictive maintenance**, **process optimization**, and **quality control**. In **supply chains**, digital twins will be critical in managing logistics, reducing inefficiencies, and predicting disruptions.
- **Environmental and sustainability applications**:
  - As the world faces **climate change** and **resource depletion**, digital twins will be invaluable in creating **sustainable solutions**. For example, digital twins of **ecosystems** can simulate the effects of environmental changes or human interventions, allowing for more informed decision-making in conservation efforts and sustainable resource management.

    - **Circular economy models** will also benefit from digital twins. These digital models will allow businesses to track **product lifecycles**, understand the **environmental impact** of their processes, and implement **closed-loop systems** that reduce waste and maximize resource reuse.
- **The role of AI in digital twin evolution**:
    - The **integration of AI** and **ML** with digital twin models will enable more **autonomous decision-making**, where digital models can not only predict future conditions but also implement actions without human intervention. This will be particularly valuable in scenarios like **disaster management**, where AI-driven digital twins can automatically trigger emergency responses based on real-time data from the physical world.
    - AI can also help digital twins evolve and improve over time by learning from past performance, optimizing models, and suggesting improvements in real-time. This makes digital twins even more adaptable and dynamic in a world that is increasingly complex and interconnected.
- **Vision for a digital twin-driven future**:
    - Looking ahead, digital twins could shape a future where we live in an **intelligently connected world**, where everything from our homes to our cities to our healthcare is interconnected and optimized. These digital models will not just represent the physical world but will serve as a platform for real-time problem-solving and innovation.
    - **Interoperability** between different sectors and across national borders will be a key factor in the realization of this future. By 2035 and beyond, digital twins could allow for **global simulations**—for instance, modeling the combined effects of economic, environmental, and social changes on a global scale, helping humanity anticipate and address **global challenges** before they become critical.

Further reading

Awotunde, J.B., Muduli, K., Brahma, B., 2024. Computational Intelligence for Industry 4.0/5.0 Applications. doi:10.1201/9781003581963.

Bhattacharya, T., et al., 2025a. A survey on various security protocols of edge computing. J. Supercomput. 31 (1). doi:10.1007/s11227-024-06678-6.

Crespi, N., Drobot, A.T., Minerva, R., 2023. The Digital Twin. Springer International Publishing, France, pp. 1–1238. doi:10.1007/978-3-031-21343-4.

Gupta, P., Saini, D.K., Zia, K., 2024. Soft Computing Principles and Integration in Real-Time Service-Oriented Computing. doi:10.1201/9781032716718.

Harnal, S., Tiwari, R., Garg, L., Mathur, A., 2024. Cloud and Fog Optimization-Based Solutions for Sustainable Developments. doi:10.1201/9781003494430.

Kaiser, A.K., Meda, V., 2024. AI Integration in Software Development and Operations: Transformation through AI Infusion in DevOps, Testing, and SRE. Apress. doi:10.1007/979-8-8688-1044-2.

Kaswan, K.S., Dhatterwal, J.S., Nayyar, A., 2024. Digital Personality of Man Forever. doi:10.1201/9781032628431.

Kaur, M., Jain, V., Nitin, P.N., Rakesh, R., 2024. Software-Defined Network Frameworks. doi:10.1201/9781040018323.

Kavis, M., 2014. Architecting the Cloud: Design Decisions for Cloud Computing Service Models (Saas, PaaS, and IaaS). Wiley, pp. 1–199. doi:10.1002/9781118691779.

Khang, A., Shah, V., Abdullayev, V., Hahanov, V., 2024. Advanced IoT Technologies and Applications for Industry 4.0 and Digital Economy. doi:10.1201/9781003434269.

Krishnan, S., Anand, J., Sendhilkumar, S., 2024. Handbook of Industrial and Business Applications of Digital Twins. doi:10.1201/9781003465904.

Kumar, P., Kumari, A., 2024. Blockchain for Biomedical Research and Healthcare: Concept, Trends, and Future Implications. Springer Nature Singapore. doi:10.1007/978-981-97-4268-4.

Liu, L., Ramakrishna, S., 2020. An Introduction to Circular Economy. Springer Singapore, Thailand, pp. 1–631. doi:10.1007/978-981-15-8510-4.

Lloret Mauri, J., Gunjal, P., Jondhale, S., Agrawal, K., 2024. Internet of Things. doi:10.1201/9781003282945.

Mhlanga, D., 2024. FinTech, Financial Inclusion, and Sustainable Development. doi:10.4324/9781032657981.

Mishra, A., El Barachi, M., Kumar, M., 2024. Transforming Industry Using Digital Twin Technology. Springer Nature Switzerland. doi:10.1007/978-3-031-58523-4.

Mohanan, 2025. Artificial Intelligence in Biological Sciences. doi:10.1201/9781003492726.

Priyadharshini, A., et al., 2024. Intelligent patient monitoring through hybrid consensus algorithm based blockchain technology. Multimed. Tools Appl. doi:10.1007/s11042-024-19840-2.

Rani, S., Bhambri, P., Kumar, S., Pareek, P.K., Elngar, A., 2024. AI-Driven Digital Twin for Industry 4.0. doi:10.1201/9781003395416.

Rasheed, S.S.K., Amad, S., 2025. Applications of Digital Twins in Robotics and Construction Sector. doi:10.1201/9781003518747.

Sharma, S., Sharma, A., Chien, T.V., 2025. Intersection of 6G, AI, Machine Learning, and Embedded Systems. doi:10.1201/9781003540212.

Singh, T., 2024. Artificial Intelligence Ethics. doi:10.1201/9781003502708.

Singla, A., Tanwar, S., Hsiung, P.A., 2024. Artificial Intelligence and Internet of Things-Based Augmented Trends in Data-Driven Systems. doi:10.1201/9781003497318.

Whig, P., Sharma, P., Aneja, N., Elngar, A., Silva, N., 2024. Artificial Intelligence and Machine Learning for Sustainable Development. doi:10.1201/9781003497189.

PART 3

Emerging applications

Production optimization/lifecycle management in smart manufacturing (factory digital twin)

Pravin C. Latane[a], Pankaj A. Dhakate[a], Vijaya G. Rajeshwarkar[b], Vilas S. Ubale[c], Dnyaneshwar S. Mantri[b], and Suresh N. Mali[a]

[a]*Department of Computer Engineering, Dr. D. Y. Patil College of Engineering and Innovation, Varale, Talegaon, India*

[b]*Department of Electronics and Telecommunication Engineering, Sinhgad Institute of Technology, Lonavala, Pune, India*

[c]*Department of Electronics and Communication Engineering, Amrutvahini College of Engineering, Lonavala, Pune, India*

Nomenclature

CoAP constrained application protocol

DHT11 temperature and humidity sensor

FTP file transfer protocol

GE general electric

GlTF GL transmission format

HTTPS hyper text transfer protocol secure

JSON JavaScript Object Notation

IOT Internet of things

PHP Hypertext Preprocessor

LAMP Linux, Apache, MySQL, PHP

MQTT message queuing telemetry transport

PLM production lifecycle management

Artificial Intelligence, Machine Learning and Blockchain in Digital Twin Computing.
https://doi.org/10.1016/B978-0-443-43914-8.00001-7

REST API representational state transfer API

SQL structured query language

WiFi wireless fidelity

XAMPP apache, MySQL, PHP, and Perl stack

11.1 Introduction

In this decade, there has been a growing demand for self-service analysis tools and skills across various business domains. These tools enable organizations to maintain data records and perform data analysis tasks to make informed decisions and improve business operations. Particularly in the realm of the Internet of Things (IoT), gathering sensor data has become essential for measuring performance. To store IoT sensor records efficiently, many businesses rely on Excel sheets due to their speed and reliability. However, to gain deeper insights and flexibility in representing results, Real time analysis of these is crucial for corporations. Analyzing and visualizing this data is essential for identifying business trends, preventing diseases, forecasting future paradigms, combating crime, and more. Data visualization tools, like digital twin technology, provide accessible and insightful views of data patterns and outliers (Digital Twin Technologies in Transportation Infrastructure Management, 2023).

Digital Twins provide real-time data and insights about the physical system's performance and condition, helping to identify issues early. By using the digital twin's data, companies can anticipate equipment failures and perform maintenance before breakdowns occur. Digital twins can simulate changes and improvements to the physical entity, testing different scenarios and optimizing performance without physical interventions. Virtual models allow for simulations and testing without the need for costly physical prototypes or trials. Insights from digital twins help decision-makers improve operational efficiency and strategize more effectively.

Digital twins of factory machines help in monitoring wear and tear, improving maintenance schedules, and optimizing production lines. They can be created for human organs to assist in personalized treatment planning or surgical simulations. Cities use digital twins to optimize infrastructure, energy consumption, traffic flow, and urban planning. Digital twins simulate vehicle performance, allowing for safer designs, faster testing, and ongoing operational efficiency. They are used in power grids, wind farms, and oil rigs to monitor and manage energy production and consumption. General Electric (GE) uses digital twins for its industrial equipment (e.g., gas turbines) to monitor performance and predict maintenance needs. Tesla leverages digital twins for its cars, enabling them to improve vehicle performance through over-the-air updates based on real-world driving data.

11.2 Materials and methods

11.2.1 Data collection

The data utilized for visualization in this demonstration is secondary data originating from an IoT device, specifically the DHT11 sensor. The primary parameters measured by this device are temperature and humidity. The main goal was to measure and visualize industrial data using this IoT device. Due to the substantial amount of data, the preference is to view it on a cloud server. One practical application of this data is in digital agriculture, where temperature sensors can calculate growing degree days, or soil moisture sensors, in combination with relays and pumps, can monitor and water plants automatically when needed.

To achieve this, NodeMCU 8266 and DHT11 sensor are utilized. However, the challenge lies in transmitting data from these devices to the Apache, MySQL, PHP, and Perl stack (XAMPP) server. To address this, a relatively straightforward architecture can be employed. As long as the IoT device is equipped with wireless fidelity (WiFi) capabilities, it can expose a representational state transfer (REST) API over hyper text transfer protocol secure (HTTPS), as shown in Fig. 11.1. This API can then be accessed by an Apache server, allowing seamless communication with the device. Through this API, sensor data can be read, actuators controlled, and data visualized efficiently.

To achieve this, NodeMCU 8266 and DHT11 sensor are utilized. However, the challenge lies in transmitting data from these devices to the XAMPP server. To address this, a relatively straightforward architecture can be employed. As long as the IoT device is equipped with WiFi capabilities, it can expose a REST API over HTTPS. This API can then be accessed by an Apache server, allowing seamless communication with the device. Through this API, sensor data can be read, actuators controlled, and data visualized efficiently.

11.2.1.1 IoT device with a REST API

The Excel add-in JavaScript API has the capability to make calls to REST endpoints, including those running on your local network. To leverage this feature for IoT applications, you can expose a REST API on your IoT device, enabling data retrieval from sensors or control of actuators. For instance, let's consider a scenario where you have a Raspberry Pi

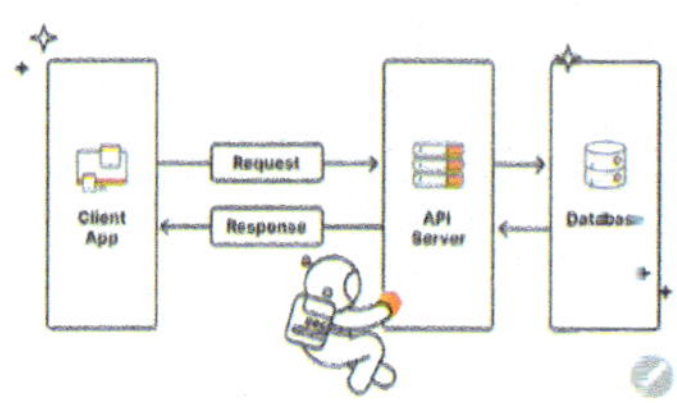

Fig. 11.1 An infographic diagram of client, API, and database showing data flow with requests and formats.

equipped with a soil moisture sensor and a relay. You can create a Python/Flask app on the Raspberry Pi and set up a REST API with two endpoints:

temperature/—Making a "GET" request to this endpoint will provide the current reading from the temperature sensor.

relay/—Making a "POST" request to this endpoint with a Boolean value in a JSON request body will allow you to turn the relay on or off, effectively controlling it.

The real-time data for temperature and humidity, measured using DHT11 is stored in a MySQL database in table form, and the intention was to visualize this data using digital twin technology. The interfacing of DHT11 with NodeMCU is as shown in Fig. 11.2, and the NodeMCU sketch is as shown in Table 11.1 to upload temperature and humidity data to the XAMPP server.

11.2.1.2 Environment setup in XAMPP

XAMPP is a free and open-source cross-platform web server solution stack package developed by Apache Friends, primarily for PHP-based applications. It provides a development environment for local web applications, especially for those that will be deployed on the LAMP stack (Linux, Apache, MySQL, PHP). Creating a REST API over HTTPS for real-time data collection using XAMPP involves several key architectural components and considerations. Below is an outline of the architecture.

- **Web Server:** XAMPP comes with Apache, which serves as the web server to handle incoming HTTP/HTTPS requests.

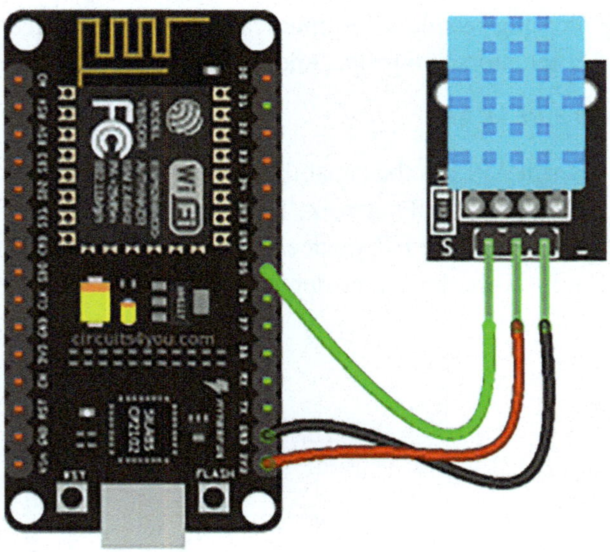

Fig. 11.2 A circuit diagram of the Node MCU board connected to the DHT 11 sensor showing signal, power, and ground wiring.

Table 11.1 DHT_XAMPP NodeMCU sketch.

```
#include <ESP8266WiFi.h>
#include <DHT.h> //DHT sensor library
#include "ESP8266HTTPClient.h"
#define WIFISSID "XXXX"
#define PASSWORD "XXXX"
#define DHTPIN 0 // For 0, Digital pin we're connected is D3 on
NodeMcu
#define DHTTYPE DHT11 // DHT 11
DHT dht(DHTPIN, DHTTYPE);
String URL = "http://Your IP Address/dht11_project/dht11.php";
int temperature =0;
int humidity =0;
void wifi()
{
WiFi.begin(WIFISSID, PASSWORD);
Serial.print("connecting");
while (WiFi.status() != WL_CONNECTED)
{
Serial.print(".");
delay(500);
}
Serial.println();
Serial.print("connected: ");
Serial.println(WiFi.localIP());
// client wifiConnect(WIFISSID, PASSWORD);
}
void Load_DHT11_Data()
{
temperature = dht.readTemperature();
humidity = dht.readHumidity();
Serial.print("Currnt Temperature = ");
Serial.print(temperature),
Serial.print("C ");
delay(1000);
Serial.print("Current Humidity = ");
Serial.print(humidity);
Serial.println("% ");
delay(1000);
}
```

```
void setup(){
Serial.begin(115200);
dht.begin();
wifi();
}
void loop()
{
Load_DHT11_Data();
String postData = "temperature=" +
String(temperature) + "&humidity=" +
String(humidity);
WiFiClient client;
HTTPClient http;
http.begin(client, URL);
http.addHeader("Content-Type",
"application/x-www-form-urlencoded");
// Send HTTP POST request
int httpCode = http.POST(postData);
// Get response payload
String payload = http.getString();
Serial.print("URL: ");
Serial.println(URL);
delay(10);
Serial.print("Data. "),
Serial.println(postData);
delay(10);
Serial.print("httpCode: ");
Serial.println(httpCode);
delay(10);
Serial.print("payload: ");
Serial.println(payload);
Serial.prin
tln("------------------------------");
// End the HTTP connection
http.end();
// Wait before next reading (e.g , 1
seconds)
delay(1000);
}
```

- **Database:** Use MySQL (or MariaDB) for storing collected data, with tables structured to store real-time data logs.
- **PHP for API Endpoints:** PHP scripts will handle the API logic, process incoming requests, and interact with the database.

XAMPP also includes other tools and utilities, such as phpMyAdmin for database management and FileZilla FTP Server for handling FTP connections, as shown in Fig. 11.3. This powerful feature enables users to interact with the Apache server using the database and also perform additional tasks using standard structured query language (SQL) queries to fetch table values.

11.2.1.3 Data visualization using digital twin technology

Data visualization with digital twin technology involves creating dynamic, interactive representations of physical objects or systems using real-time data. Digital twins are virtual replicas of physical entities, and they enable engineers, operators, and other stakeholders to monitor and simulate performance, detect issues, and optimize processes in real-time. Here's a breakdown of how digital twin technology is leveraged for data visualization:

1. **Physical entity:** The real-world object or system that is being represented digitally. This can be anything from a machine, vehicle, or building to entire ecosystems like factories or even cities.
2. **Digital model:** The digital twin itself—a virtual model that mimics the physical entity's characteristics, behavior, and performance in real-time or near real-time.

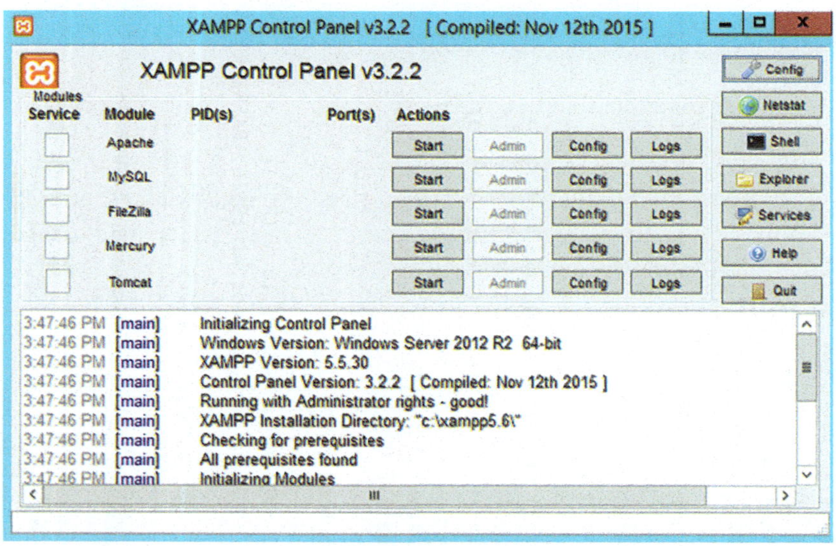

Fig. 11.3 XAMPP server dashboard.

3. **Data:** The continuous flow of data from sensors, IoT devices, and other sources that monitor the physical entity. This data is fed into the digital twin to ensure the virtual model remains synchronized with the real world.
4. **Analytics and algorithms:** The digital twin uses data analytics, artificial intelligence (AI), machine learning (ML), and simulations to understand, predict, and optimize the behavior of the physical entity.

11.2.1.4 Types of digital twins

Digital twin technology allows data visualization to be more interactive, predictive, and contextually aware by mirroring real-world systems in a virtual environment. This real-time, data-driven visualization empowers operators to make more informed decisions and optimize physical asset performance with a clear, comprehensive view of data insights (Stirling et al., 2020). The types of digital twins are as shown in Fig. 11.4.

1. **Component twins:** These are the most basic units and focus on individual parts of a larger system, such as the engine of a car.
2. **Asset twins:** Represent specific physical products or equipment, allowing companies to monitor and manage these products throughout their lifecycle.
3. **System twins:** Model an entire system of interconnected elements, such as a production line or supply chain, to ensure that the different parts work in harmony.
4. **Process twins:** Focus on replicating workflows or processes (such as manufacturing), helping to optimize efficiency and reduce bottlenecks.

11.2.2 Data preparation and connection

Data preparation and connection are critical steps in visualizing data using digital twin technology. Ensuring high-quality data and seamless data flow from physical assets to the digital twin model helps in creating accurate, real-time, and predictive insights. Here's a breakdown of the data preparation and connection process for visualizing a digital twin effectively.

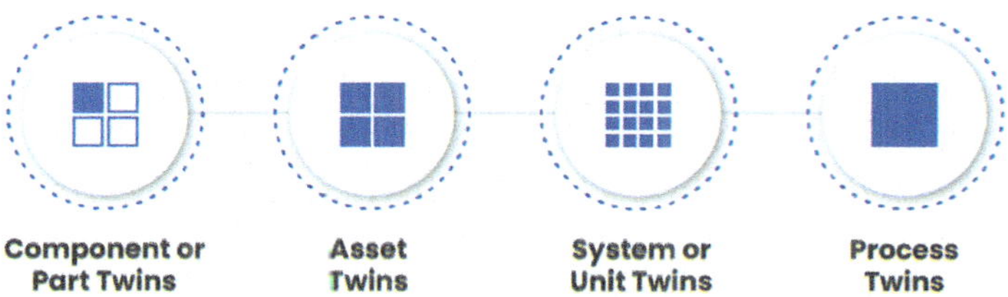

Fig. 11.4 Types of digital twins.

11.2.2.1 Data collection from physical assets

- **IoT sensors and devices**: Digital twins require data from physical assets, which is typically gathered through IoT sensors. These sensors measure relevant parameters like temperature, pressure, speed, and location, providing real-time data that updates the digital twin.
- **Connectivity**: Data is transmitted from sensors to a central system via connectivity protocols like message queuing telemetry transport (MQTT), HTTP, or constrained application protocol. The choice of protocol often depends on factors such as data transfer rate, energy consumption, and network reliability.
- **Time-series databases**: Store continuous sensor data streams in time-series databases. Use relational databases (e.g., MySQL, PostgreSQL) for structured data such as asset metadata, configurations, and transactional records using the XAMPP server.
- **APIs for data connections**: Use REST or MQTT APIs to connect real-time data feeds from IoT devices to the digital twin platform, ensuring the data flow between the physical system and the digital twin.
- **Real-time synchronization**: Synchronize data continuously between the physical system and the digital twin, especially for applications that require real-time visualization or predictive updates.

Following these steps ensures a robust data preparation and connection process for digital twins, leading to a reliable, dynamic visualization that accurately mirrors the physical asset. This setup enables organizations to gain deep insights, improve operations, and optimize performance based on the digital twin's visualized data insights (Wexler et al., 2017; Fireteanu, 2020; Boltaboyeva et al., 2024).

HTML script "digital_twin.html," shown in Table 11.2, calls the PHP script "dht11.php," shown in Table 11.3, and the JavaScript "data_temp.js," shown in Table 11.4, to generate the Digital Twins model. The HTML script sets up the scene, camera, and renderer. The PHP script connects with the database "sensor_dht11/dht11" and fetches the current temperature from the database using an SQL query, generating output in JSON format. The PHP script confirms the model is loaded and responds to its behavior along with real-time temperature. Here, the animation is designed such that the temperature threshold will determine the body color of the 3D motor model.

If logged into the XAMPP Server, users may also have access to saved data sources stored in the server's repository. Fig. 11.5 displays the phpMyAdmin window, with the data source being a table file that is being accessed using an SQL query such as: "SELECT Temperature FROM `dht11` ORDER BY `id` DESC LIMIT 1" (Aivaliotis et al., 2019; Nalepa and Najdek, 2024).

Table 11.2 Digital_twin.html script.

```
#<!DOCTYPE html>
<html lang="en">
<head>
<meta charset="UTF-8">
<title>Digital Twin Example</title>
<style>
body {margin: 0; overflow: hidden;}
</style>
</head>
<body>
<script     src="https://cdnjs.cloudflare.com/ajax/libs/three.js/r128/three.min.
js"></script>
<script   src="https://cdn.jsdelivr.net/npm/three/examples/js/loaders/GLTFLoader.
js"></script>
<script src="dht11.php"></script>
<script src="data_temp.js"></script>
<script>
// Set up the scene, camera, and renderer
renderer.setSize(window.innerWidth, window.innerHeight);
document.body.appendChild(renderer.domElement);
// Set camera position and add lighting
camera.position.z = 0.5;
const light = new THREE.DirectionalLight(0xffffff, 10);
light.position.set(5, 5, 15).normalize();
scene.add(light);
// Render the scene
function render() {
requestAnimationFrame(render);
renderer.render(scene, camera);
}
// Handle window resizing
window.addEventListener('resize', () => {
renderer.setSize(window.innerWidth, window.innerHeight);
camera.aspect = window.innerWidth / window.innerHeight;
camera.updateProjectionMatrix();
});
</script>
</body>
</html>
```

After selecting and customizing the data connection, users will be directed to the second data connection window (POP, 2024; Price et al., 2024). Here, they must decide whether to create a mirror of the data using the Motor.glb 3D model, which can enhance performance and improve data visualization efficiency, as shown in Fig. 11.6.

Table 11.3 Dht11.php script.

```
<?php
header("Content-Type: application/json");
header("Access-Control-Allow-Origin: *");
$hostname = "localhost";
$username = "root";
$password = "";
$database = "sensor_dht11";
$conn = mysqli_connect($hostname, $username, $password, $database);
if (!$conn){
die("Connection Failed: ". mysqli_connect_error());
}else{
// echo "Database Connection is OK";
}
if(isset($_POST["temperature"]) && isset($_POST["humidity"]))
{
$t = $_POST["temperature"];
$h = $_POST["humidity"];
$sql = "INSERT INTO dht11 (Temperature, Humidity) VALUES ($t, $h)";
}
// Fetch temperature from the database
$sql = "SELECT Temperature FROM `dht11` ORDER BY `id` DESC LIMIT 1"; // Adjust
this query as needed
$result = $conn->query($sql);
if ($result && $result->num_rows > 0) {
$row = $result->fetch_assoc();
echo json_encode([$row['Temperature']]);
} else {
echo json_encode(['temperature' => null]); // Or handle the empty result case
}
$conn->close();
?>
```

11.3 Formal analysis and investigation, validation, calculation, and expression of results

11.3.1 Visualization using digital twin technology

In this section, we will explore how the 3D model of the motor allows users to add trend lines, reference lines, and control data sorting and filtering to enhance their data analysis. Its primary mission is to facilitate self-service visual analytics, enabling nontechnical users to see and understand their data effectively (Kabir et al., 2024; Soula et al., 2024). The visualization of the 3D motor model is shown in Figs. 11.7 and 11.8. Near the 3D motor model on the console window, real-time readings of temperature are displayed, which are fetched from the XAMPP server database using an SQL query. Here, the threshold value is set to be 20°C. Fig. 11.7 shows the 3D motor model's color changing to red as the real-time

Table 11.4 Data_temp.js script.

```
let model = null; // Define model in the
   global scope
const raycaster = new THREE.Raycaster(); //
   Create a raycaster
const mouse = new THREE.Vector2(); // Vector
   to store mouse coordinates
const renderer = new THREE.WebGLRenderer({
   antialias: true });
renderer.setSize(window.innerWidth, window.
   innerHeight);
document.body.appendChild(renderer.
   domElement);-
const loader = new THREE.GLTFLoader();
const scene = new THREE.Scene();
const camera = new THREE.PerspectiveCamera(75,
   window.innerWidth / window.innerHeight,
   0.1, 1000);
camera.position.z = 5; // Set camera position
loader.load('motor.glb', (gltf) => {
console.log("Model loaded", gltf); // Confirm
   the model is loaded
model = gltf.scene; // Set model when loaded
scene.add(model); // Add model to the scene
}, undefined, (error) => {
console.error('An error occurred loading the
   model:', error);
});
```

```
// Temperature variable to store
   the latest temperature
let temperatureValue = 0;
// Function to fetch temperature
   from PHP server
async function fetchTemperature() {
try {
const response = await
   fetch("http://localhost/digital_
   twin_project/dht11.php");
if (!response.ok) throw new
   Error("Network response was not
   ok");
const data = await response.json();
// console.log("Raw response:",
   data); // Log response for
   debugging
// Update the global temperature
   variable
temperatureValue =
   parseFloat(data[0]) || 0;
console.log("Temperature:",
   temperatureValue) // Log
   temperature for debugging
} catch (error) {
console.error("Error fetching
   temperature:", error);
}}
```

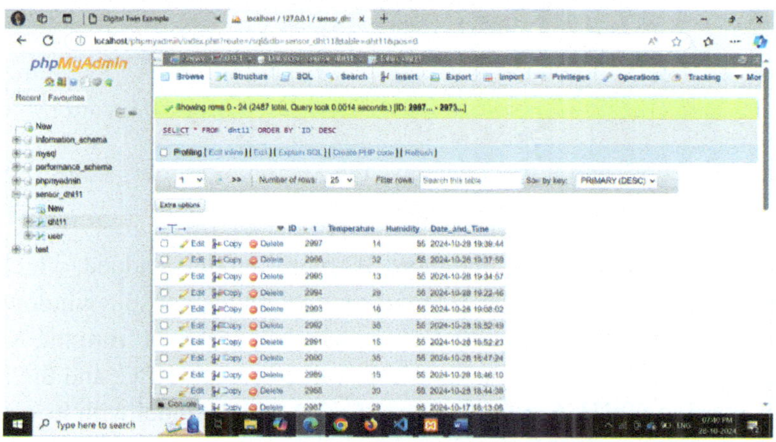

Fig. 11.5 phpMyAdmin dashboard of XAMPP server.

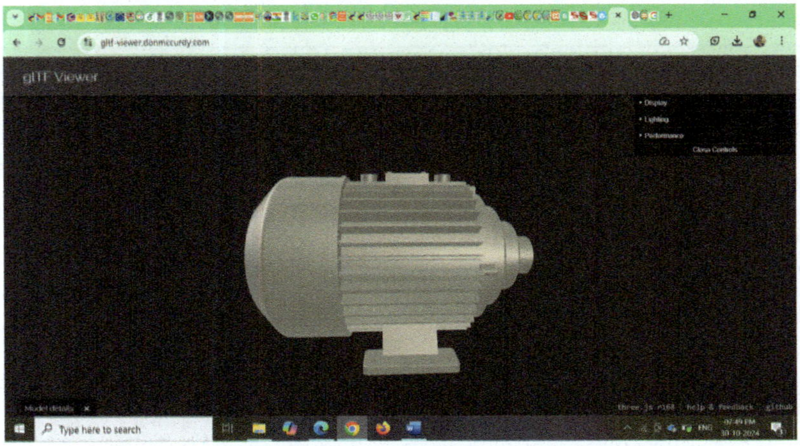

Fig. 11.6 Visualization of motor 3D model on glTF viewer.

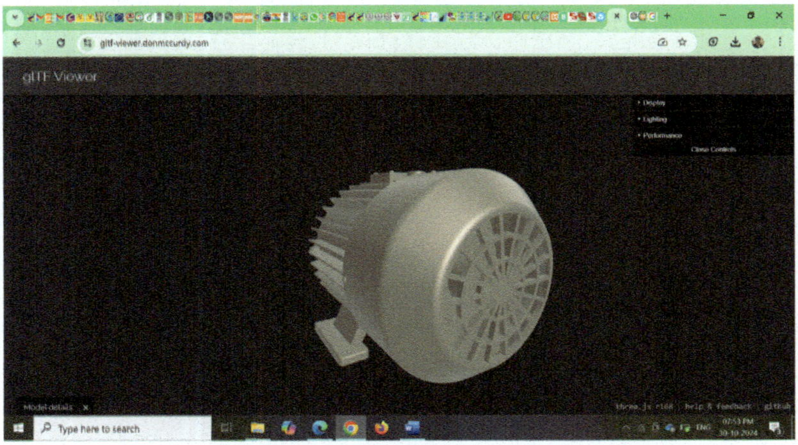

Fig. 11.7 Visualization of motor 3D model on glTF viewer.

temperature exceeds 20°C, and Fig. 11.8 shows the 3D motor model's color reverting to its original state as the real-time temperature falls below 20°C.

Now, to add more industrial devices, one more 3D motor model is added, which responds to real-time humidity as well. Near the 3D motor model on the console window, real-time readings of temperature and humidity are shown, which are fetched from the XAMPP server database using an SQL query. Here, the threshold value is set to 40°C, and the humidity threshold value is set to 50RH. Fig. 11.9 shows the 3D motor model with its original color.

The java script data_t.js is now modified for both temperature and humidity parameters.

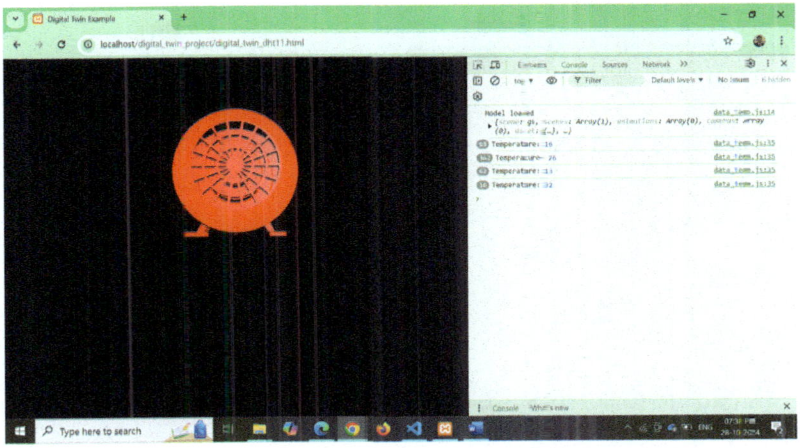

Fig. 11.8 Real-time visualization of a motor 3D model changing color below the threshold value of temperature.

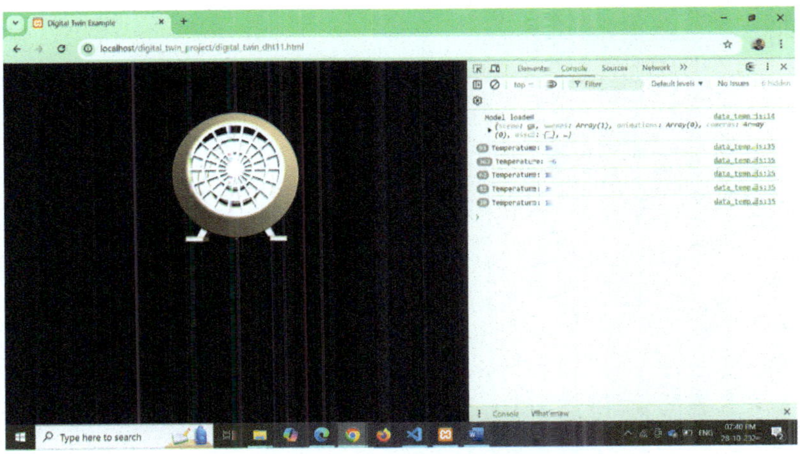

Fig. 11.9 Real time visualization of motor 3D models for temperature and humidity.

Now, the threshold value is set to 40°C, and the humidity threshold value is set to 40RH. So, the color of the 3D motor model 2 is changed to blue as the real-time humidity is greater than 40RH, as shown in Fig. 11.10. The 3D motor model 1 retains its original color as the real-time temperature is below the threshold value of 40°C. The visualization of the 3D motor model 2 is shown in Fig. 11.10.

Now, the threshold value is set to be 30°C, and the humidity threshold value is set to be 40RH. So, the color of the 3D motor model 1 is changed to red as the real-time temperature is greater than the threshold value of 40°C. The visualization of 3D motor models 1 and 2 is shown in Fig. 11.11.

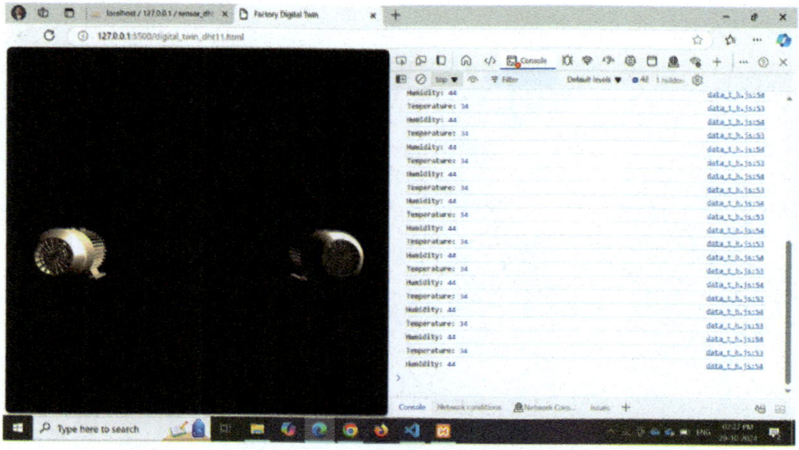

Fig. 11.10 Real-time visualization of a motor 3D model changing color to blue above the threshold value of humidity.

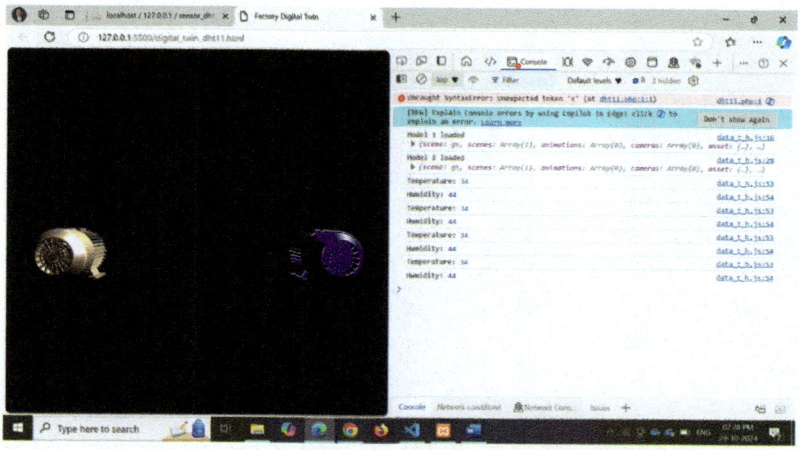

Fig. 11.11 Real-time visualization of a motor 3D model changing color to red above the threshold value of temperature.

11.4 Discussion and evaluation

11.4.1 Comparative study

A comparative study of digital twin technology focuses on evaluating how different industries and use cases implement and benefit from digital twins, along with comparing the technologies, platforms, and approaches that make these digital twins possible. Here's an outline of some key areas in a comparative study of digital twin technology:

11.4.1.1 Comparison of digital twin platforms

Several leading platforms support digital twin development, each with specific strengths and limitations. Here's a comparison of some popular digital twin platforms, as shown in Table 11.5.

The application of digital twin technology varies significantly across industries, each with tailored requirements, benefits, and challenges. The choice of platform, data management approach, and visualization capabilities depends on the specific goals and constraints of the industry. By continually evolving to integrate advanced analytics, ML, and enhanced 3D modeling, digital twins are rapidly expanding their role in optimizing operations, enhancing decision-making, and ensuring sustainable practices across sectors (Jameil Brunel and Al-Raweshidy, 2024; Satsuki et al., 2024; Narigina et al., 2024).

11.4.1.2 Future trends

Emerging trends in digital twin technology are pushing its boundaries:

- **Edge computing**: Processing data close to the physical asset (e.g., on-site) reduces latency and improves response times, which is beneficial for time-sensitive applications.

Table 11.5 Comparison of digital twin platforms.

Platform	Strengths	Weaknesses
Siemens MindSphere	Strong in manufacturing, powerful integration with Siemens' industrial IoT solutions and analytics tools	Steep learning curve; costs can be high
GE digital predix	Comprehensive IoT solutions for industries like energy and aviation, featuring strong asset monitoring and analytics	Limited integrations with non-GE products require advanced technical expertise
Azure digital twins	Supports a wide range of industries, is highly scalable, and integrates well with the Microsoft ecosystem (Power BI, Azure ML)	Dependency on the Microsoft ecosystem and licensing costs for high usage
IBM digital twin exchange	Strong in supply chain and logistics, AI and analytics-driven insights, good for predictive maintenance	Limited industry focus requires a complex setup
Dassault systemes 3DEXPERIENCE	Excellent 3D modeling capabilities, tailored for engineering-intensive industries such as aero-space and automotive	Higher costs, limited support for nonengineering applications
AWS IoT TwinMaker	Highly flexible, scalable, cloud-based solution with strong integrations (SageMaker, Lambda, Grafana)	Still emerging as a mature platform, it may require additional customization
Recent work	Powerful platform to make data-driven decisions; integrates well with the Microsoft ecosystem	Difficult to visualize by 360°

- **AI integration**: AI-powered digital twins are enabling predictive capabilities and adaptive learning, allowing systems to autonomously optimize performance.
- **Standardization efforts**: Industry standards for digital twins (such as ISO standards) are emerging to address interoperability and quality assurance.
- **Sustainability and energy efficiency**: Digital twins help track and optimize energy consumption and carbon footprint, especially relevant in manufacturing, smart cities, and energy sectors.

11.5 Conclusion

Digital twin technology allows us to connect with almost any database, visualize our data, and derive meaningful insights for better understanding. We can create interactive visualizations, enabling us to thoroughly analyze our data and construct compelling data-driven narratives. Digital twin technology proves to be an invaluable tool for generating data stories that are easily understandable by key decision-makers. Furthermore, digital twin technology facilitates the discovery of data patterns, complementing the results obtained through ML algorithms with its visualizations. One of the primary tasks is to efficiently connect with and extract information stored in diverse locations. It effortlessly collects data from XAMPP server databases. In essence, digital twin technology's capabilities extend to connecting and extracting information from multiple sources, thereby providing organizations with a powerful platform to make data-driven decisions and uncover valuable insights that contribute to their growth and success. A digital twin acts as a bridge between the physical and digital worlds, providing insights that allow for more effective management, optimization, and maintenance of physical systems. It's increasingly becoming a cornerstone of Industry 4.0, smart manufacturing, and IoT-enabled innovation. In smart manufacturing, production lifecycle management (PLM) with a factory digital twin revolutionizes how factories design, operate, maintain, and optimize production. A factory digital twin is a virtual replica of the entire manufacturing environment, from individual assets to the full production line, which enables manufacturers to visualize, simulate, and manage the production lifecycle in real-time. Factory digital twins facilitate PLM in smart manufacturing, enhancing efficiency, reducing downtime, and enabling data-driven decision-making.

References

Digital Twin Technologies in Transportation Infrastructure Management, 2023.

Aivaliotis, P., Georgoulias, K., Arkouli, Z., Makris, S., 2019. Methodology for enabling digital twin using advanced physics-based modelling in predictive maintenance. Proc. CIRP. 22128271. 81, 417–422. doi:10.1016/j.procir.2019.03.072.

Boltaboyeva, A., Baigarayeva, Z., Postolache, O., Mansurova, M., Karymssakova, N., Belgibayev, B., 2024. Smart sensors and IoT applied in digital twin for industry 4.0. In: International Symposium on Sensing and Instrumentation in 5G and IoT Era, ISSI 2024. Institute of Electrical and Electronics Engineers Inc.,

Kazakhstan. 9798350378689. http://ieeexplore.ieee.org/xpl/mostRecentIssue.jsp?punumber=10720444. doi:10.1109/ISSI63632.2024.10720505.

Fireteanu, V.V., 2020. Integrating Tableau with internet of things acquiring projects. In: Proceedings of the 12th International Conference on Electronics, Computers and Artificial Intelligence, ECAI 2020. Institute of Electrical and Electronics Engineers Inc., Romania. 9781728163432. http://ieeexplore.ieee.org/xpl/mostRecentIssue.jsp?punumber=9218228. doi:10.1109/ECAI50035.2020.9223228.

Jameil Brunel, A.K., Al-Raweshidy, H., 2024. Hybrid Cloud-Edge AI Framework for Real-Time Predictive Analytics in Digital Twin Healthcare Systems. Research Square, PREPRINT Version 1. doi:10.21203/rs.3.rs-5412158/v1.

Kabir, M.R., Halder, D., Ray, S., 2024. Digital twins for IoT-driven energy systems: a survey. IEEE Access. 2169-3536. 12, 177123–177143. doi:10.1109/access.2024.3506660.

Nalepa, R., Najdek, K., 2024. Data-driven NARX-based digital twin thread modelling of Boost converter inductance current under closed-loop output voltage control. In: IEEE 21st International Power Electronics and Motion Control Conference, PEMC. Institute of Electrical and Electronics Engineers Inc., Poland. 9798350385236. http://ieeexplore.ieee.org/xpl/mostRecentIssue.jsp?punumber=10726283. doi:10.1109/PEMC61721.2024.10726372.

Narigina, M., Romanovs, A., Merkuryev, Y., 2024. A review of AI-driven digital twin frameworks for cardiovascular disease diagnosis and management. In: ITMS—International Scientific Conference on Information Technology and Management Science of Riga Technical University. Institute of Electrical and Electronics Engineers Inc., Latvia. 27716937. https://ieeexplore.ieee.org/xpl/conhome/10741904/proceeding. doi:10.1109/ITMS64072.2024.10741948.

POP, F., 2024. Real-time monitoring software for CNC machine production using digital twin concepts. STAR 3, 1–11.

Price, J., Khatri, H., Gauthier, C., Coffey, B., Garza, J., 2024. Building a university digital twin. In: Proceedings—2024 IEEE International Symposium on Emerging Metaverse, ISEMV 2024. Institute of Electrical and Electronics Engineers Inc., United States, pp. 17–20. 9798350356052. http://ieeexplore.ieee.org/xpl/mostRecentIssue.jsp?punumber=10763946. doi:10.1109/ISEMV63338.2024.00018.

Satsuki, K., Yaginuma, H., Terabe, S., 2024. Improvement of traffic measurement AI by utilizing digital twin. In: GCCE 2024—2024 IEEE 13th Global Conference on Consumer Electronics. Institute of Electrical and Electronics Engineers Inc., Japan, pp. 582–583. 9798350355079. http://ieeexplore.ieee.org/xpl/mostRecentIssue.jsp?punumber=10759798. doi:10.1109/GCCE6237[illegible].2024.10760916.

Soula, M., Mbarek, B., Meddeb, A., 2024. A real-time trust management model using digital twin in IoT networks. IEEE Access. 2169-3536. 12, 183326–183343. doi:10.1109/access.2024.3506870.

Stirling, A., Tubb, T., Reiff, E.S., Grotegut, C.A., Gagnon, J., Weiyi, L., Bradley, G., Poon, E.G., Goldstein, B.A., 2020. Identified themes of interactive visualizations overlayed onto EHR data: an example of improving birth center operating room efficiency. J. Am. Med. Inform. Assoc. 1527-974X. 27 (5), 783–787. doi:10.1093/jamia/ocaa016.

Wexler, S., Shaffer, J., Cotgreave, A., 2017. The Big Book of Dashboards: Visualizing Your Data Using Real-World Business Scenarios, Wiley Online Library.

CHAPTER 12

Damage detection and predictive maintenance in smart infrastructures based on digital twining approach

Kaushalya Thopate[a], Parikshit Mahalle[b], Sheetal Phatangare[c], Vaishali Rajput[d], Mayuri Gawade[b], and Prajakta Musale[b]

[a]*Department of Computer Engineering, Vishwakarma Institute of Technology, Pune, India*
[b]*Department of Computer Science & Engineering (AI & ML), Vishwakarma Institute of Technology, Pune, India*
[c]*Department of Artificial Intelligence & Data Science, Vishwakarma Institute of Technology, Pune, India*
[d]*Department of Computer Science & Engineering (Artificial Intelligence), Vishwakarma Institute of Technology, Pune, India*

12.1 Introduction

This is a paradigm shift in how we approach the detection of damage and the predictive maintenance of road infrastructure. The traditional methods of maintaining roads usually cannot cope with modern infrastructure as cities expand and road systems become more congested and worn out. Digital twins are the essential solution here because they provide a very detailed framework for real-time monitoring and data-driven decision-making. Digital twins can be defined as virtual representations of physical assets, creating dynamic models that help in continuously monitoring infrastructure conditions. This should, therefore, result in the earliest possible identification of potential problems, long before they develop into costly repairs or safety issues.

Digital twins can make road infrastructure more resilient. Continuous data gathering from sensors installed in roads helps monitor the structural health constantly, meaning that vulnerabilities can be corrected promptly. This proactive approach not only makes the area safer but also extends the life of such assets, thereby lightening the burden of maintenance on municipal agencies. The use of digital twins also enhances the efficiency of maintenance work. With real-time traffic patterns, weather conditions, and pavement integrity data available, managers can target the repairs that are most important and have the greatest

Artificial Intelligence, Machine Learning and Blockchain in Digital Twin Computing.
https://doi.org/10.1016/B978-0-443-43914-8.00022-4

urgency and impact. Focused resource allocation reduces disruption to day-to-day traffic and decreases operational costs, ultimately achieving better service levels for users.

Sustainability is another advantage associated with the application of digital twin technology. The application of the digital twin can help support organizations in making decisions effectively in sync with environmental priorities by allowing the evaluation of materials and methodologies to be applied during road construction and subsequent maintenance. Less waste and fewer emissions are achieved through the prediction of maintenance needs as well as the maximization of available resource usage. It is an opportunity for pioneering innovation toward making the management of road infrastructure more resilient, efficient, and sustainable as the challenges of urbanization trends and system aging materialize. As such technologies advance, they will play an essential role in determining the course that road maintenance and urban mobility will follow in the future.

12.2 Key points on the role of digital twins in road infrastructure

This chapter delves into the concept of digital twins in road infrastructure and their use in damage detection and predictive maintenance, as well as their transformative role. The main points that underpin this technology include the following:

12.2.1 Understanding digital twins in road infrastructure

Digital twins are advanced, dynamic virtual models of physical assets. They facilitate real-time monitoring, analysis, and management since they bring together data from Internet of Things (IoT) sensors, environmental monitoring systems, and historical records to represent an extensive version of road conditions. Through this technology, road infrastructure acquires actionable insights into the health of its assets to inform data-driven decisions made by the authorities. These digital models accurately reproduce the physical road network. This allows stakeholders to observe minute changes and predict any potential issues before they affect the actual structure (Boschert and Rosen, 2016). In a road network, information is continuously refreshed with data by capturing characteristics like pavement condition, structural integrity, and environmental effects. It establishes direct interaction between the actual physical road asset and its digital counterpart, thus enabling data-driven management and more informed decisions. One of the most significant application areas for digital twins in the analysis of massive datasets is that complex networks of infrastructure may fail to remain adequate when older systems of monitoring and maintenance struggle to cope with growing cities and high traffic flow.

12.2.2 Damage detection and monitoring

The use of digital twins enhances proactive detection of damage since it enables continuous monitoring by advanced analytics. Digital twins that employ modern technologies, such as image recognition and other machine learning algorithms, use a remote-sensing method of observation to identify damage at different stages, including road cracks and potholes. Such road systems prevent severe problems by providing early signals and clearly specifying the focus areas; for example, computer recognition of defects such as road cracks can be identified by imaging technology (Grieves, 2014). Digital twins can also be integrated with sensor data to provide an overall assessment of the health of a structure. This preventive step helps avoid further degradation and costly repairs that may arise from damage going unchecked (Kritzinger et al., 2018).

Remote sensing technologies, including drones and autonomous vehicles, quickly cover vast spaces, map, and update the digital twin. By making proper use of these technologies, road authorities gain up-to-date infrastructure conditions with an accurate view. Using their real needs, therefore, helps establish maintenance plans instead of relying on maintenance based on fixed time limits. Real-time monitoring, therefore, truly helps bring about improvements in road safety to support effective asset management.

12.2.3 Predictive maintenance approaches

Predictive maintenance is a forward-thinking approach through digital twins. Based on the examination of historical and real-time data, road authorities can predict possible failures ahead of time and manage their maintenance work. Statistical as well as machine learning-based models analyze the trends developed in pavement degradation, and the impacts of weather conditions, along with traffic patterns, can be optimized to schedule necessary maintenance and prioritize repairs for better road infrastructure lifespan (Negri et al., 2017). Such models can also consider many intricate variables so that precise forecasts can be made. Therefore, the respective authorities can undertake measures for vulnerabilities well before they escalate into expensive failures and break-downs. Data on seasonal variations in weather, as well as the history of wear patterns, has helped these digital twins anticipate the emergence of possible faults within specific sections of roads.

This way, information gathered can lead to the high prioritization of maintaining areas where fault propensity is strong, hence ensuring adequate allocation of resources. This approach is in direct contrast to reactive maintenance, wherein repairs are only done when the damage is already visible and, therefore, the cost, as well as the disturbance to operations, is increased. The use of digital twins to perform predictive maintenance can be achieved at a lower cost and encourages resource savings while increasing the long-term resilience of infrastructure.

12.2.4 Technological integration to increase efficiency

The success of digital twins is based on a network of complementary technologies such as IoT, edge computing, cloud services, and artificial intelligence (AI). All these technologies work together to form a robust infrastructure for data synchronization, storage, and processing. Digital twins can work in real-time with this setup. There are sensors on the roads that continuously gather information on the flow of traffic, temperature, and structural integrity. This data is fed into the digital twin, where edge computing allows immediate analysis at the point of data collection with minimal latency, thus quickening the response. The large datasets that are generated are managed in the cloud, offering scalability and making it possible to share the data across departments (Tao et al., 2018a).

At the same time, AI analyzes the data to provide advanced analytics, predictive modeling, and decision support. It empowers digital twins to deal with the complexity around road networks, trends, and actionable insights. Thus, the integration of such a system provides cities with a chance to develop an adaptive infrastructure management ecosystem in order to ensure better safety and operational efficiency for the city.

12.2.5 Successful case studies of digital twins

Examples from countries such as the Netherlands, the United States, and Singapore show that digital twin technology has real benefits in the management of road infrastructure. The above countries have adopted the use of digital twin technology to improve resilience in infrastructure, streamline maintenance, and reduce environmental impact. For example, in the Netherlands, digital twins are applied in managing flood-prone areas and planning for proactive maintenance. The United States has utilized digital twins to improve safety and efficiency of transportation networks. It has achieved this by merging real-time monitoring systems with predictive models that limit congestion (Yang and Chen, 2017). Singapore's approach to the digital twin is holistic in strategy. The whole city itself becomes a digital twin through the optimization of traffic flow and the reduction of emissions while enhancing safety on roads. Such concrete applications show how digital twins can transform infrastructure management with significant gains in terms of efficiency, safety, and sustainability (Zheng and Li, 2020).

12.3 Benefits of digital twin technology

Digital twins for road infrastructure maintenance provide critical advantages that affect urban mobility, cost management, and social well-being.

12.3.1 Improving safety

Digital twins enhance safety on the roads by enabling proactive damage detection and taking interventions at the right time. Real-time monitoring allows for the identification of hazards that may not have been noticed before they manifest into accidents caused by pavement deterioration and structural weaknesses. This ensures that every road user, whether a commuter or a freight operator, is able to enjoy much safer trips, as the probability of accidents resulting from infrastructure failure decreases with early action (Bo¨hme and Spies, 2021).

12.3.2 Improved efficiency

Digital twins enable the scheduling of maintenance activities to be data-oriented and resource-efficient. Predictive maintenance strategies leveraging digital twins can avoid, or at least minimize, the amount of emergency repairs needed since focused efforts are directed toward critical areas, which can reduce general congestion. Therefore, this will result in less disruption of traffic and reduced operational costs, while more resources become available to address other emergencies or urgent infrastructure needs (Li and Wang, 2019).

12.3.3 Cost management

Digital twins have many financial benefits for the infrastructure to be maintained. Since unplanned repairs are minimized and the lifetimes of assets are increased, a road authority gains better budgetary control. Redeployment of saved sums of money due to emergency interventions can then be re-channeled toward addressing infrastructure deficits and other resource issues while also improving the infrastructure's long-term resource allocation capabilities (Wan and Yang, 2020).

12.3.4 Sustainability and environmental impact

Digital twins further contribute to sustainability in terms of resource usage through decreased waste and emissions. Through the accurate prediction of required maintenance, authorities can avoid unnecessary repairs, thereby reducing material consumption. Digital twins also enable the scheduling of maintenance, which alleviates traffic congestion, reduces emissions, and thus fosters a cleaner and more sustainable environment in urban cities (Alavi and H, 2019).

12.3.5 Infrastructure resilience

Digital twins significantly enhance the resilience of infrastructure by enabling authorities to monitor and manage conditions in real time. This allows infrastructure systems to adjust and cope with environmental changes, which may include heavy traffic and severe weather. Since the flexibility they offer to road networks ensures that such systems remain functional and safe in numerous circumstances, digital twins ensure functional and safe resilient urban mobility systems (Wang and Liu, 2021).

Fig. 12.1 represents the flow of data from virtual assets to their respective physical assets. It proceeds as follows: sensors, including IoT sensors, collect data from the

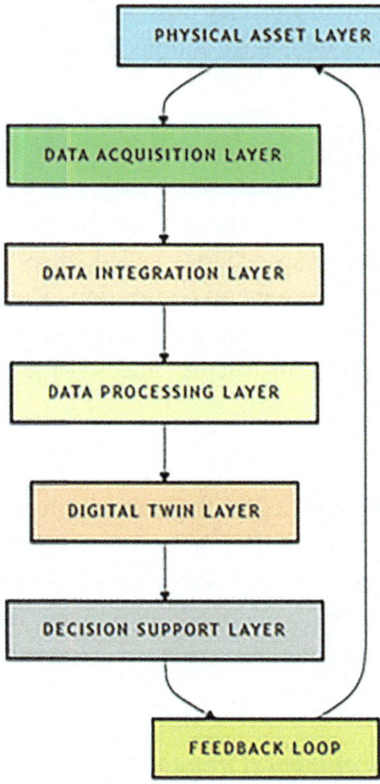

Fig. 12.1 Digital twin architecture.

physical layer, which then travels to the data acquisition layer for gathering and onward transit for further processing. The data is consolidated in the data integration layer within a centralized storehouse. Analytics and machine learning models at the data processing layer examine the data to develop the digital twin model, and insights are produced in the decision support layer in real time, with an incorporated feedback loop that allows continuous monitoring.

12.4 Long-term impact on infrastructure resilience, urban mobility, and cost management

The impacts of digital twin technology go beyond the momentary benefits and influence urban planning, the resilience of infrastructure, and resource management in the city (Fig. 12.2).

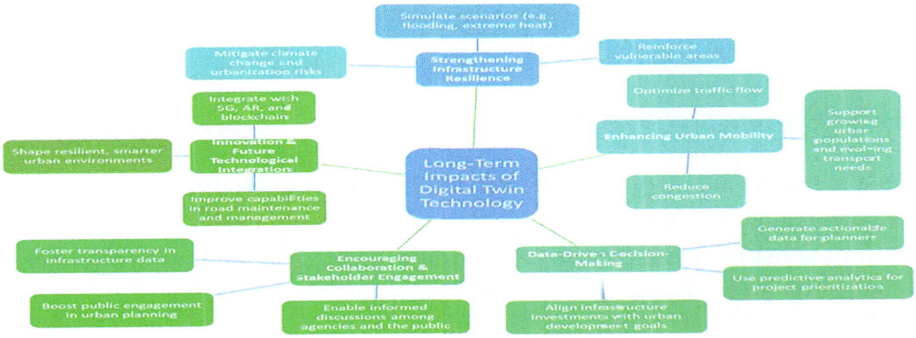

Fig. 12.2 Long-term impacts of digital twin technology.

12.4.1 *Infrastructure resilience*

One approach to the development of even stronger infrastructure systems is to deploy digital twins that can adapt to climate change and increasing urban growth. The process allows road authorities to evaluate different scenarios and be more responsive to floods or extreme heat. These insights are also useful for proactive reinforcement at vulnerable points, reducing further risks directly tied to environmental changes (Kim and Park, 2019).

12.4.2 *Smart urban mobility*

The use of digital twins can help enhance urban mobility by streamlining traffic flow, decreasing congestion, and making travel more enjoyable (Mura and Cuccuru, 2020). This can be achieved through real-time monitoring and analysis of traffic patterns to make informed decisions on infrastructure investments and improvements that will make roads better suited to the increasing population in cities and changing transportation demands (Chan and Wong, 2018).

12.4.3 *Data-driven decision making*

Digital twins deliver rich information that enables road authorities and city planners to make intelligent decisions. Predictive analytics and modeling enable stakeholders to focus projects on urgent current demands and future expectations, ensuring that the infrastructure aligns with long-term development goals in cities (Shakib and Pan, 2019).

12.4.4 *Enhancing collaboration and stakeholder engagement*

The use of digital twinning technology encourages interagency cooperation with the private sector and public collaboration by providing transparent information. The insights that digital twins provide serve to enable well-informed discussions and promote participation in urban planning (Zhang and Zhao, 2021).

12.4.5 Innovation and future technological integration

The new tech trends would merge into greater confluences with other emerging technologies, such as 5G, augmented reality (AR), and blockchain (Tao et al., 2018), in the context of the digital twin for the maintenance of roads and infrastructures, building toward greater, smarter urban resilience (Grieves, 2019).

The leading edge of managing road infrastructure is digital twin technology, which allows for earlier damage detection and predictive maintenance. Using real-time monitoring improves safety, efficiency, and sustainability, thus providing significant advantages to road authorities and urban communities. Effects in the long run concerning infrastructure resilience, urban mobility, and cost management through digital twins will influence infrastructure, thereby forming more sustainable and efficient transportation networks. The implementation of these new technologies will enhance the well-being of citizens and form a basis for robust, technologically sophisticated cities.

12.5 Introduction to smart infrastructure and road digital twins

Urbanization around the world and the evolving, dynamic nature of urban environments significantly increase the demand for smart infrastructure—most notably in transportation. Smart infrastructure refers to the integration of digital technology into traditional physical systems, aimed at optimizing efficiency, safety, and sustainability within urban environments. Among these, road digital twins represent one of the greatest leaps forward in urban infrastructure management, improving monitoring, maintenance, and capabilities in predictive analysis (Khatami et al., 2020). In the wave of the smart, sustainable city movement worldwide, road digital twins are rapidly emerging as essential tools that will revolutionize the optimization of road management while mitigating negative impacts on urban life (Khajavi and Parto, 2021).

12.5.1 What is smart infrastructure

In simple terms, smart infrastructure is the use of digital technologies in traditional physical infrastructure with real-time data gathering to optimize operations and facilitate adaptive decision-making. For road networks, smart infrastructure uses sensors and IoT devices along with data analytics to monitor conditions on an ongoing basis, enhancing safety and optimizing maintenance operations (Tao et al., 2018b). This represents a transformation from static systems to dynamic, self-monitoring networks that are sensitive enough to identify and respond to anomalies before they become problematic (Weng et al., 2020).

It has been developed on a unified system of sensors, actuators, and data-processing technologies, all contributing toward collecting information in real time. The technology continuously collects data from roads and highways with regard to the surface, vehicles crossing it, and other environmental conditions, and processes that data for adaptive and responsive management. For instance, in road networks, sensors and intelligent cameras can be embedded to capture data points related to vehicle flow, surface wear, and environmental conditions that provide critical insights to make proactive decisions for maintenance and planning. By moving from a reactive form of maintenance, where things are only addressed after a problem has manifested itself, to a proactive and data-centric approach, smart infrastructure systems would prevent problems from exacerbating, thus reducing interference and enhancing the socio-economic resilience of cities.

12.5.2 What is a digital twin for road networks?

Therefore, digital twins in the infrastructure management field provide real-time information about assets as well as their states through virtual replications of real physical entities. They first emerged during manufacturing and engineering, where such digital twins aided in simulation, testing, and assessment for analyzing machinery performance, and they have recently been applied to the urbanization of infrastructure. The integration of IoT, AI, and cloud computing enables digital twins to monitor large, complex systems—such as entire road networks—in a way that ensures efficient management and maintenance.

A road digital twin is a virtual model that depicts the physical features of road infrastructure. It comprises information on structural elements, environmental conditions, traffic loads, and pavement conditions for creating a nearly real-time digital replica of the road network. This virtual model is dynamically updated with information from sources like sensors embedded in the road, cameras, and environmental monitoring devices, thereby generating a dynamic depiction that changes with the actual infrastructure. The data collected provides an overview of the condition of the road network, which can be analyzed in detail and used for predictive modeling to effectively plan maintenance strategies. This model will enable designers and urban planners to simulate specific problems, forecast the impact of various environmental conditions, and test different maintenance strategies before applying them in the real world, thereby acting as a potent tool for infrastructure management.

Fig. 12.3 embodies the idea of digital twins in road networks. In the middle, a large node is labeled "Digital Twins for Road Networks" in dark blue, and five major branches emanate from it, each highlighting important components. These begin with definition and origins (light blue), which provide a background to the fundamental framework. Core components (teal) detail structural data, while technological integration (orange) emphasizes the relevance of IoT, AI, and cloud computing. Real-time data collection (green) indicates current updates

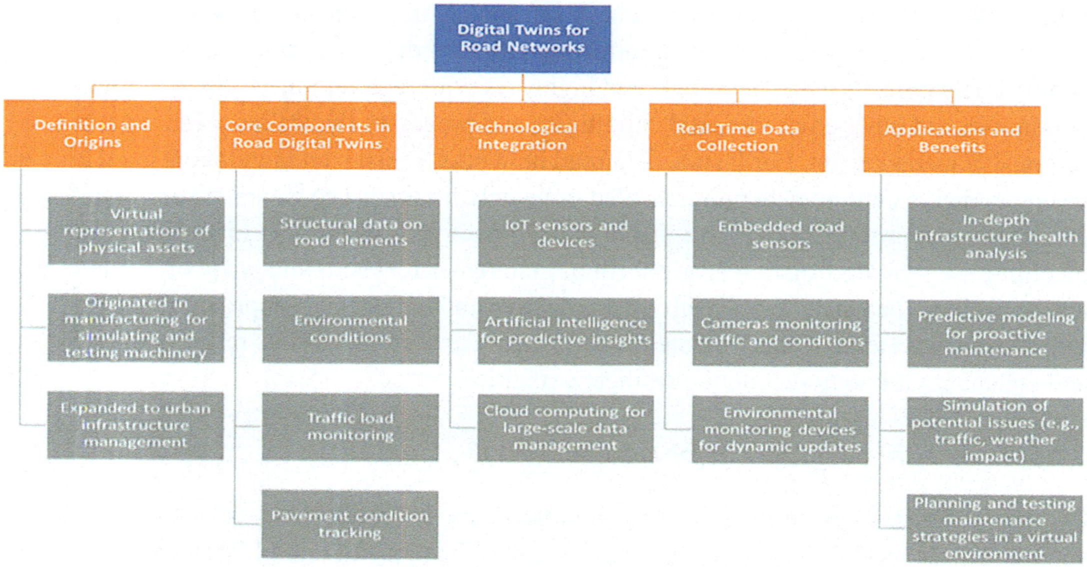

Fig. 12.3 Digital twins for road networks.

from sensors and cameras, and applications and benefits (purple) illustrate the added advantages in terms of predictive modeling and proactive maintenance planning. In other words, these components represent a holistic approach to managing infrastructure.

12.5.3 Relevance of digital twins in smart cities and smart infrastructure

In this regard, digital twins have been at the heart of the development of smart cities: they facilitate the creation of interconnected and data-driven urban systems where the quality of life improves for the population while simultaneously reducing resource consumption. In this respect, by employing digital twin technology, cities are able to enhance infrastructure management by fostering mobility, safety, and environmental sustainability.

Enhanced urban mobility: Traffic congestion and broken infrastructure characterize most world cities, an issue that worsens as the population rises and more people acquire cars. These issues can be addressed by monitoring continuous traffic patterns, wear and tear, and early signs of damage through digital twins. With predictive modeling, such digital twins enable timely interventions that prevent disturbances related to infrastructure, enhance the overall mobility of humans and freight, and even reduce congestion by operating in concert with other intelligent infrastructures, including intelligent traffic signals.

Safety infrastructure management is always concerned with safety. A digital twin improves safety by identifying potential dangers before they cause any accidents. For example, a digital twin may focus on potholes, structural weaknesses, or faded markings on the road, enabling road authorities to take immediate action to reduce the risks posed. When combined with other types of safety technologies, such as intelligent vehicles and smart traffic flow management systems, a digital twin enhances road safety for drivers, pedestrians, and cyclists.

Support environmental sustainability: Sustainability is one of the primary objectives of Smart Cities, and road digital twins help with this effort by optimizing schedules for maintenance, thereby preventing the need for avoidable repairs. Utilizing the digital twin to provide forecasts of potential problems before they develop into significant issues could reduce resource use, decrease waste, and minimize the environmental impact created by multiple construction cycles. Furthermore, reduced traffic improves air quality, as there is a decrease in emissions from vehicles, and reduced heat islands within the urban environment contribute to a healthier urban setting. This graphic (Fig. 12.4) illustrates how digital twins impact smart cities, particularly how they work to optimize urban infrastructure. There are three critical areas that highlight the value of digital twin technology for monitoring and optimization: improving urban mobility, enhance safety, and support environment sustainability, which includes reducing emissions, avoiding hazards through proactive detection, and improving safety in traffic flow. Some examples of improved management of urban infrastructure are as mentioned above.

12.5.4 Damage detection and predictive maintenance scope and objectives

Improving efficiency in operations, reducing costs on maintenance, and enhancing the lifespan of infrastructures are the primary objectives of digital twins in road networks. Road maintenance is traditionally reactive: visible damages are repaired when apparent. However, through digital twins, the authorities can shift from such reactive maintenance to a predictive approach, where they can anticipate problems before they cause disruptions significant enough to attract attention.

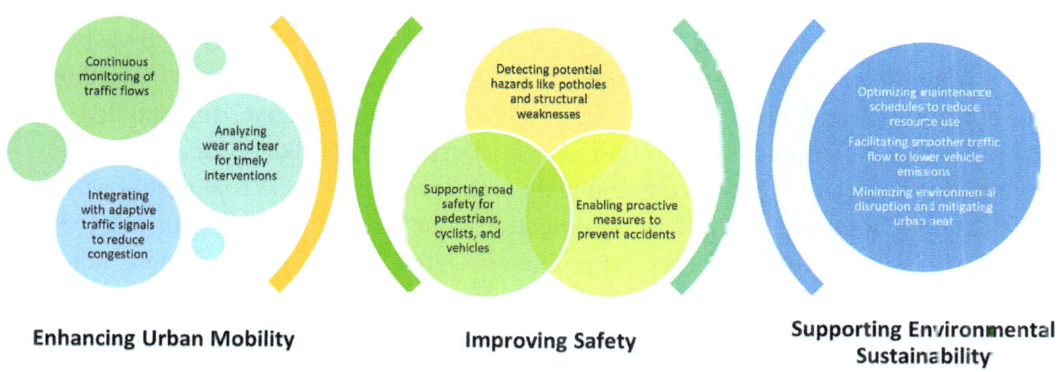

Fig. 12.4 Digital twins in smart cities.

Scope of damage detection: Digital twins provide accurate and continuous damage detection capabilities. Using various sources of data, such as sensor data, drone imagery, and feeds from autonomous vehicles, digital twins are able to identify early structural deterioration, such as cracks, erosion, and surface wear. This data is then processed and analyzed in the digital twin to provide a complete damage map. Using this map, engineers can then precisely determine the type of damage, its location, and its severity. Therefore, accurate detection ensures the identification of small problems and prevents them from developing into major repairs.

Predictive maintenance scope: Predictive maintenance applies data analytics and machine learning to predict when repairs will be necessary and lowers the probability of unexpected failures. For instance, a digital twin could determine traffic load, weather conditions, and material properties in order to forecast pavement wear rates. The degradation trend will be well-anticipated by predictive maintenance in a timely manner and at an affordable cost to extend the life span of the infrastructure and make it safer.

Key outcomes:

Increased efficiency: Digital twins improve maintenance activities by enhancing detection and real-time monitoring. Increased efficiency means reduced road closures, as well as less time and money spent on repairs.

Cost efficiency: Digital twins can prevent expensive emergency repairs through the early detection of faults. Predictive maintenance helps in planning resource allocation for areas requiring urgent attention.

Improved safety and security: With the proactive detection of probable dangers, digital twins enable the maintenance of safety conditions on roads. This condition is crucial for public transportation, emergency services, and everyday travel.

Environmental sustainability: Predictive maintenance enables resource usage to be optimized and minimizes unplanned repairs. In addition, improved traffic flow results in lower fuel consumption, reduced emissions, and a smaller footprint on the environment.

Fig. 12.5 illustrates the scope of damage detection in digital twins for road networks. Starting from the central concept, "Scope of Damage Detection," it branches into three major categories: continuous detection, early identification of damage, and detailed damage mapping. continuous detection focuses on using sensor data, drone imagery, and autonomous vehicle feeds to continuously monitor conditions in real time. Early identification of damage emphasizes the detection of cracks, erosion, and surface wear before these issues develop into serious problems. Detailed Damage Mapping enables accurate damage location mapping, thereby ensuring proper assessments and interventions. This structure supports proactive maintenance by extending the infrastructure's life span and optimizing resource utilization.

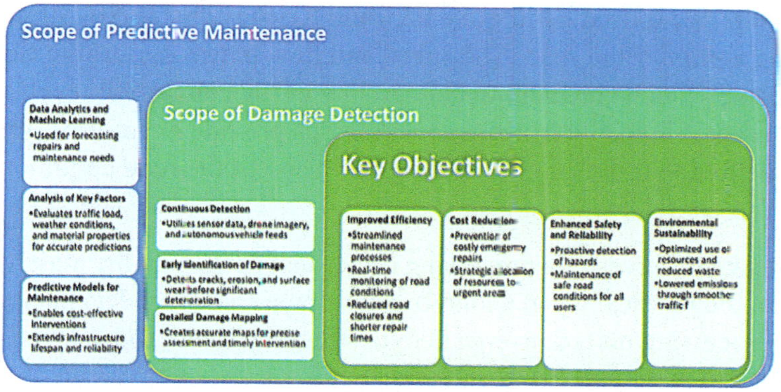

Fig. 12.5 Scope of predictive maintenance.

12.6 Road digital twin technology

Digital twin technology has been proven to be a revolutionary concept in the management of infrastructure, particularly road networks, offering a sophisticated, real-time digital replica that reflects real conditions. The real-time interaction with physical infrastructure via a dynamic virtual counterpart using a digital twin allows for timely analysis and decision-making regarding maintenance. This section explains the core architecture, enabling technologies, and data synchronization processes that are crucial for the successful and effective realization of a road digital twin.

12.6.1 Road digital twin architecture

The road digital twin architecture is complex and multilayered, with data flowing continuously while obtaining insights into infrastructure health. In general, such structures consist of three central layers: physical, data, and virtual. There is a distinct function within the layers of this structure that contributes to creating a high-accuracy, real-time replication of the road network conditions.

Physical layer: This layer constitutes the physical road infrastructure. In this case, it's the real, physical infrastructure represented by the surface of roads, crossroads, overpasses, underpasses, and other features that are used along roads, such as roadside signs and guardrails. The IoT devices are complemented by sensors and cameras that record necessary information, including details about the degree of road surface wear and tear, load levels on vehicles, weather, and indications of potential structural damage, such as cracks and potholes (Kramers and Kerssens-van Drongelen, 2019).

This can be achieved through the strategic use of various types of sensors spread across the physical layer. Accelerometers will capture the vibrations that indicate the level of stress to which the structure is exposed (Rojdestvensky and Krichevsky, 2020). Strain gauges assess the load-bearing ability of the road. The speed and flow patterns of traffic can be captured by acoustic sensors, which enhances understanding of the congestion levels and usage patterns of the roads. Collectively, these technologies provide a real-time granular flow of data that is essential to ensure an accurate digital image of the road conditions at any given time (Liu and Yao, 2021).

Data layer: This layer serves as a processing center that deals with the massive data collected by the sensors of the physical layer. Cloud-based storage solutions, data management platforms, and processing units converge here to structure, clean, and analyze incoming data (Kwon and Kim, 2020).

This layer focuses on ensuring that the data received at this layer is both clean and consistent. Standardizing and filtering data to provide only the relevant information required by the virtual layer in a more actionable way is emphasized here. The use of edge computing in this layer usually processes data in real time closer to where it was captured in order to reduce latency and minimize bandwidth consumption while enabling rapid in-situ responses immediately (Antunes and Marques, 2021).

Virtual layer: The virtual layer is the digital twin proper: a holistic digital imitation intended to be an exact, dynamic reflection of physical road infrastructure. It includes 3D models, simulations, and visualizations describing the real-time condition and health of the infrastructure, predicting potential failures, and simulating maintenance to test various intervention strategies (Hwang and Kim, 2020). Within the virtual layer, the infrastructure manager can view and engage with the digital twin to monitor conditions and make informed decisions. Machine learning models and predictive algorithms in this layer use historical and real-time data to forecast potential structural issues, allowing for a proactive approach to infrastructure maintenance and overall health (Lima and Silva, 2021).

The Fig. 12.6 depicts a three-layered architecture of a road digital twin that allows for the integration of physical data, efficient processing, and insightful visualization. This structure fosters a system capable of evolving with advancements in sensor technology, data analytics, and simulation tools, promoting adaptability and long-term functionality.

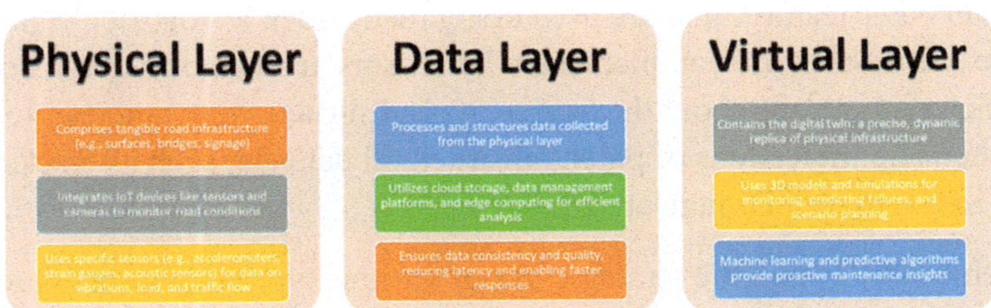

Fig. 12.6 Scope of predictive maintenance.

12.6.2 Technologies enabling road digital twins

Road digital twins exploit the potential of advanced technologies that enable real-time data acquisition, analysis, and decision-making. Key technologies that facilitate the development and operationalization of digital twins for road infrastructure include IoT sensors, edge computing, cloud infrastructure, and AI algorithms (Schmid and Lichtenstein, 2022; Zhang et al., 2021).

IoT sensors: IoT sensors are the most vital tools for gathering data in the digital twin system for road infrastructure. In this context, IoT sensors collect specific information related to traffic patterns, environmental conditions, the health of structures, and the wear and tear of surfaces, feeding all critical data to the digital twin model (Bianchi and Lopes, 2022). The typical application types include accelerometers, which sense the vibrations characteristic of strain in structures. Next are strain gauges, which are used to measure loading and pressure. More importantly, environmental sensors consist of temperature and humidity as a matter of course, along with acoustic sensors for road flow studies Lastly, yet not least, comes visual inspection.

Cameras or optical sensors (Hu et al., 2023). Each provides unique information, which together provides a comprehensive view of road conditions, creating a robust database in the digital twin.

Edge computing: Edge computing is important for the initial processing of large amounts of data near the source in close proximity, thus decreasing the latency and bandwidth required (Kaczmarek and Bula, 2022). In road digital twin systems, edge computing devices can be placed near data sources at sensor nodes or a processing unit to process initial raw data before transferring it as useful information to the central system. By processing the data locally, edge computing allows the system to be more responsive to real-time events, such as issuing alerts instantly in case of the detection of structural anomalies. This feature is essential for damage detection and emergency response within road infrastructure (Sui et al., 2023).

Cloud infrastructure: Cloud infrastructure offers scalable storage as well as computational resources, which are essential for processing the vast amounts of data collected by IoT sensors in the road network. Through cloud platforms, all the data is stored and computed centrally, allowing network managers to monitor the infrastructure of large road networks in real-time and harness the computing power needed for predictive analysis (Kumar and Singh, 2021; Rojas and Trujillo, 2022). Scalability: digital twin systems can be easily augmented with additional data sources or analytic functionalities without degrading system performance. Leading cloud providers now offer a wide range of analytics, machine learning, and visualization tools, extending these capabilities to digital twins to support more sophisticated forms of predictive maintenance and damage detection (Wang et al., 2023; Alshahrani, 2022).

AI algorithms: AI algorithms improve the analytical power of road digital twins, enable complex data analysis, damage detection, and predict probable maintenance. They process historical data and real-time data using machine learning to detect anomalies, recognize patterns in roads, and forecast problems in the structure of roads (Chen and Li, 2021). The third type is convolutional neural networks, which are primarily aimed at image analysis; for example, drones can take images and analyze damages such as cracks or weakening of structures. Finally, recurrent neural networks, mainly applied when dealing with time-series data, predict long-term wear by following trends in environmental and traffic patterns (He et al., 2022). The application of these insights into artificial intelligence has led to data-driven decision-making. Maintenance intervention timing is thus crucial and precise (Zhou et al., 2023).

12.6.3 Role of data collection and real-time synchronization

Accurate and timely data collection, paired with real-time synchronization, forms the basis for a reliable digital twin of roads. This ensures that the digital twin reflects the current state of the physical road infrastructure, enabling it to support responsive, well-informed maintenance decisions (Bhatia and Bhattacharya, 2022).

Data collection: Data collection for road digital twins is an ongoing, dynamic process using sensors and data sources. The aim is to collect real-time information on physical conditions, environmental influences, and usage patterns of the road network (Liu et al., 2021). This data may come from any number of sources, which may include sensors embedded into the infrastructure or mobile platforms like selfdriving or public transportation systems. Weather station monitoring, among other sources, will also contribute input to create the full virtual image of the digital twin (Ghaffarian and Karami, 2023).

Real-time data synchronization: Real-time data synchronization ensures that the digital twin is updated accurately in accordance with the prevailing conditions on the roads. Real-time synchronization enables infrastructure managers to respond to issues detected and plan proactively for maintenance requirements (Mahmud et al., 2022). In this case, synchronization is built on a combination of both edge and cloud computing. Edge computing handles some initial processing of data before it is sent to the cloud, thereby reducing the volume of data sent to the cloud. The cloud acts as the central data repository, where information is integrated from different sources to be visualized in near real-time (Gupta and Kumar, 2021).

Challenges associated with data collection and synchronization: Data quality and consistency are hard to maintain on large-scale road networks due to variability in the sampling rates and accuracy of sensors (Toh et al., 2023). Stable connectivity also has to be maintained for reliable synchronization, especially in urban or remote areas with variable signal strength. Data security and privacy must be assured since road digital twins could tap data from public

Table 12.1 Comparison of traditional road maintenance versus digital twin approaches.

Comparison aspect	Traditional road maintenance	Digital twin approaches
Maintenance approach	Reactive Maintenance: Repairs conducted after failures occur.	Predictive Maintenance: Maintenance is based on analytics and real-time data, reducing unexpected failures.
Inspection method	Manual Inspections: Periodic physical inspections that may overlook early-stage issues.	Continuous Monitoring: Uses sensors for real-time assessments, allowing for the early detection of potential problems.
Data analysis	Static Data Analysis: Relies on historical data; decisions can become outdated.	Dynamic Data Analysis: Analyzes live data streams to make informed decisions, enhancing the understanding of asset health.
Maintenance scheduling	Fixed Schedules: Maintenance is based on set timelines regardless of actual asset conditions, leading to inefficient resource use.	Flexible Scheduling: Adapts maintenance schedules based on real-time insights, optimizing resource allocation and minimizing downtime.
Stakeholder communication	Limited Communication: Fragmented communication about asset status hinders quick responses.	Enhanced Collaboration: Centralized data improves communication, facilitates coordinated decision-making, and enables rapid responses.

or self-driving vehicles. Encrypting the transfer of data and anonymizing sensitive information would protect user privacy as well as system integrity (Nascimento et al., 2022). The architecture and technologies used with road digital twins constitute powerful means of bridging the physical and virtual worlds of road infrastructure, combining multilayered architectures, edge and cloud computing, IoT, and AI algorithms to enable precise data analysis along with timely, actionable insights to support responsive, proactive maintenance strategies regarding public safety and city resiliency (Sinha and Ghosh, 2021) (Table 12.1).

12.7 Road infrastructure damage detection

Maintaining road infrastructure is vital and must be prioritized to ensure safe and efficient transportation systems. The deterioration of roads poses significant risks for users and incurs great economic costs through accidents, repairs, and lost productivity. In the last five years, digital twin technology has emerged as a powerful solution for continuous monitoring, early damage detection, and predictive maintenance of road infrastructure. This technology provides a virtual overview of physical assets, thereby allowing interaction with and analysis of real-time road conditions.

This section addresses the most common damages within road networks, approaches to detection and analysis within a digital twin framework, and the remote sensing technologies, drones, and autonomous vehicles that facilitate damage detection capabilities (Jackson and Faber, 2023; Lee and Kim, 2022).

12.7.1 Road infrastructure potential damages

There are different types of stresses and environmental conditions to which road infrastructure is exposed, with damages propagating along these systems over time. An understanding of these forms of damage is key to the effective management of road assets. The most common forms of damage that digital twins for road infrastructure can monitor and manage include (Fig. 12.7):

Cracks: Cracks are the most frequent type of damage to road infrastructure, and they can be caused by temperature variations, stress from vehicular loads, or natural aging processes. Cracks can occur in many forms:

- Longitudinal cracks: These run along the length of the roadway surface and may result from several causes, such as thermal expansion and contraction, heavy traffic loads, or improper construction practices. Longitudinal cracks compromise the integrity of the pavement and allow for additional deterioration.
- Transverse cracks. These include cracks that propagate across the width of a road and usually indicate freeze-thaw cycles or an inadequately supported pavement structure. The existence of these cracks can easily allow water to penetrate, which only worsens the structural flaws.
- Alligator cracking: This type of cracking consists of a line or series of interconnected fissures that resemble the skin of an alligator. Normally, structural weakness is indicated

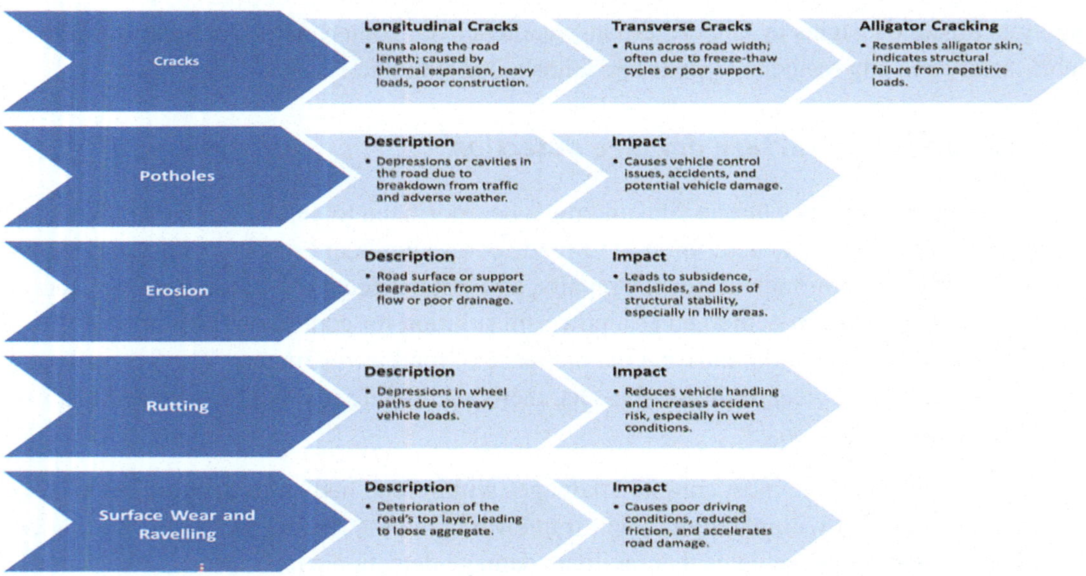

Fig. 12.7 Types of damages.

when a pavement fails under repetitive loading. Thus, such roads shorten their lifespan and require immediate attention.

Cracks can provide an opening for water, which would prolong the deterioration through freeze-thaw cycles and could deteriorate further if not attended to shortly thereafter (Patel and Gupta, 2023; Yang et al., 2023).

Potholes: Potholes are depressions or voids in the road surface caused by the breakdown of pavement material. These depressions normally occur due to heavy traffic and adverse weather conditions, particularly rain and snow (Kumar and Mehta, 2022). Potholes pose a serious safety threat to vehicles and pedestrians, as loss of control, damage to vehicles, and accidents are likely to occur. This calls for timely detection and repair in order to prevent further deterioration of the road surface and ensure user safety (Smith and Brown, 2021).

Erosion: Erosion is defined as the wearing away of the road or substructure surface due to water flow, exposure to weather conditions, or poor drainage. Damage caused by erosion is worst around road shoulder areas, embankments, and bridge structures (Chen et al., 2022). Erosion might cause subsidence, sliding lands, and a reduction in structural strength in hilly regions or along coastlines, which is a long-term menace to the stability of any road infrastructure.

Rutting: Rutting is the formation of depressions or grooves along the wheel paths of a road surface. It occurs mainly because of repeated heavy vehicle loads that deform the pavement over time. This kind of damage is harmful to vehicle handling and increases accident risk, especially in wet conditions (Govindaraju and Shah, 2020). Rutting tends to occur along roads that are inadequately compacted in terms of material or poorly designed in terms of structure. Accurate monitoring is essential to ensure timely maintenance to mitigate safety issues caused by rutting.

Surface wear or reveling: Surface wear or reveling is described as the deterioration of the surface layer that causes aggregates on the road surface to become loose. During such deterioration, the roads become damaged and lead to poor road conditions as well as a reduction in friction between the wheels and the road. Furthermore, cars can be damaged (Kumar and Singh, 2021). raveling is dangerous not only because of its impacts on road safety but also because of its potential to accelerate road deterioration; hence, its mitigation becomes timely.

12.7.2 Monitoring and damage detection methods using digital twins

Digital twins for road infrastructure use various methods for damage detection and monitoring. This enables real-time detection, which, in turn, allows timely maintenance actions that enhance the lifespan of infrastructural assets (Patel and Gupta, 2022).

Image recognition: Image recognition is commonly used for the detection of apparent damage, which includes cracks and surface abrasions, by using cameras attached to vehicles or drones. Through such images, CNN and other machine learning models analyze damage patterns based on pixel characteristics (Johnson and Wang, 2020). Such analysis of large volumes of data helps the system distinguish different forms of damage along with their severities. Precise estimations of road conditions are obtained by incorporating sensor data, which, in turn, might provide timely maintenance intervention opportunities.

Sensor data analysis: There are sensors implanted within the road structure, including strain gauges and accelerometers, which monitor structural anomalies that indicate damage in the early stages (Liao and Luo, 2021). These sensors record realtime data on various parameters, such as loads, stresses, and vibrations, allowing for a comprehensive health analysis of the road. Real-time analysis of sensor data helps detect hidden or subsurface damage, thus facilitating early interventions before visible deterioration sets in. It is important to maintain data integrity by filtering data and using machine learning algorithms while simultaneously monitoring them accurately.

Machine learning and predictive analytics: The algorithms predict the location and time at which a specific type of damage will occur by combining historical data with real-time inputs. Predictive models can identify problems by analyzing weather data, traffic volume, and previous patterns of wear, thereby allowing scheduled preventive maintenance (Zhao and Tan, 2022). For example, an algorithm may predict, based on temperature and traffic, when cracks are likely to form or deteriorate, thus giving infrastructure managers time to take action beforehand.

12.7.3 Contribution of remote sensing, drones, and autonomous vehicle in damage detection on roads

Scalability, flexibility, and efficiency of digital twins to detect damages are complemented by the use of technologies in remote sensing, as well as the use of drones and autonomous vehicles. These technologies allow the collection of detailed data about the roads.

Remote sensing: Remote sensing technologies, including satellite and aerial imaging, can evaluate large areas of road networks. These technologies capture multitemporal or hypsometric data that detect structural anomalies and environmental variations. For instance, in thermal imaging, temperature-associated changes can be identified, such as areas likely to be cracked or deformed by temperature. With a timeline view of the road's condition, remote sensing tracks the progression of wear over time, allowing for informed planning of maintenance activities.

Drones: Drones equipped with cameras, LiDAR, and thermal imaging sensors can enhance the capability for capturing high-resolution imagery and provide flexibility over challenging areas. The integration of LiDAR in drones offers the opportunity to deliver highly accurate 3D mapping of road surfaces, contributing to a high level of fidelity in the construction of digital twin models. With rapid inspections over large areas and efficient data collection, valuable input can be provided to identify potential causes of faults at the initial stages of escalation. The high resolution and varied angles of images captured from multiple viewpoints make drones highly effective in assessing road conditions.

Self-driving cars: Currently, self-driving cars, especially public means of transportation, are scanning the road in real time with their operating mechanisms. Using computer vision and artificial intelligence, they identify and classify damage, which then updates the digital twin model in real time to take action for timely maintenance work. This information is channeled to a central platform, from which infrastructure managers receive real-time information concerning road conditions and can hence prioritize the needs for maintenance. This real-time feedback loop enables even more dynamic forms of infrastructure management, as decisions about maintenance activities are now based on the current data.

Data integration and decision support: This integration will now enable the incorporation of data captured from remote sensing, drones, and autonomous vehicles into a coherent digital twin framework, thereby augmenting the decision-making capabilities of infrastructure managers. Advanced analytics will enable managers to prioritize maintenance tasks based on the severity of damage detected, environmental conditions, and traffic patterns. Data-driven resource allocation toward areas requiring higher priority will optimize maintenance strategies and extend the lifespan of road infrastructure (Fig. 12.8). Digital twin technology thus offers a comprehensive framework for the monitoring of road infrastructure in combination with image recognition, sensor analysis, machine learning, and the data-gathering capabilities of remote sensing, drones, and autonomous vehicles. Altogether, this ensemble of methods empowers the digital twin to support road infrastructure to be safer and more reliable and, in terms of preventive maintenance, to detect potential weaknesses early (Garcia and Lopez, 2020).

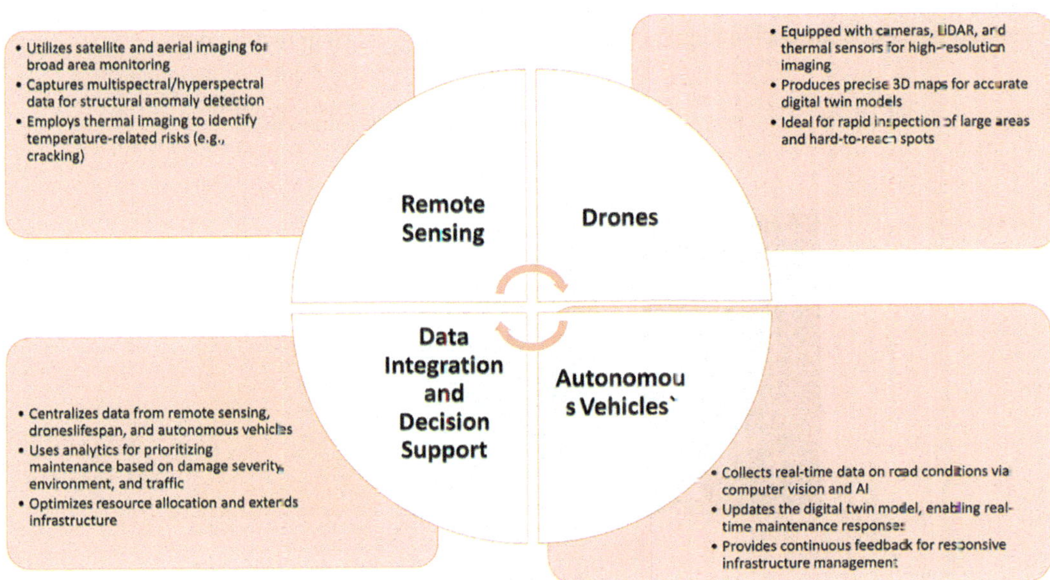

Fig. 12.8 Technologies enhancing digital twins in road condition detection.

Digital twin technology has elevated the integration of management in road infrastructure to a more profound level, as it ensures comprehensive monitoring, detection, and maintenance of road conditions. There are various types of damage, with newly established innovative ways to discover them; this creates opportunities for preventive strategies to significantly enhance safety and efficiency across transport networks. With advancements in technology, numerous possibilities can be explored to help introduce digital twins in road infrastructure, creating a smarter and more resilient transportation system.

Benefits of digital twins go beyond instantaneous damage detection and maintenance; they also lie in the utilization of an approach for the management of road infrastructure such that both infrastructure and safety systems are managed by embracing a holistic principle in both directions. Digital twins empower information-driven decision support in areas such as resource usage as well as long-term planning with a more proactive approach for the sake of improved sustainability, as much as possible preventing impacts related to deterioration effects while incurring lower operational costs without compromising safety levels.

It integrates multiple technologies, such as IoT sensors, machine learning algorithms, and advanced imaging techniques, to provide a robust framework for understanding and managing road infrastructure. Digital twin technology will be pivotal in addressing the challenges of modern road management as cities grow and the demand for efficient transportation systems increases. It will only be a matter of time before the dream of a smarter, more resilient urban environment becomes a reality through collaborative efforts among stakeholders and the adoption of innovation. This approach brings into focus the potential of digital twins to revolutionize road infrastructure management, optimize maintenance strategies, and enhance public safety and satisfaction. Fig. 12.9. Digital twins in road maintenance: safety, efficiency, and sustainability. Percentage influence for each category with the impact of digital twin technology.

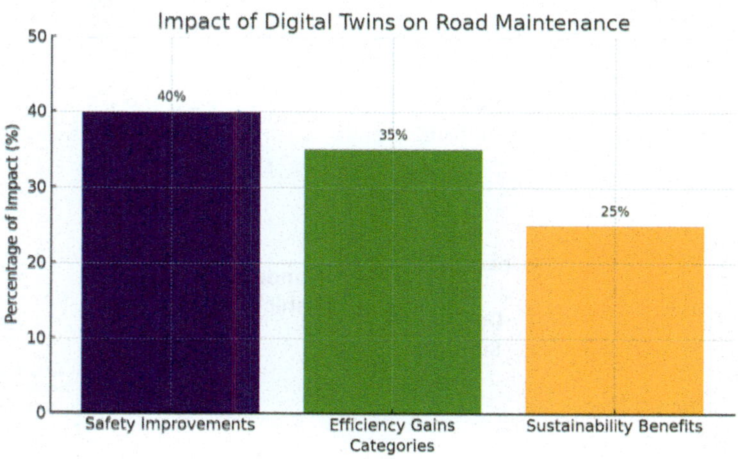

Fig. 12.9 Impact of digital twins on road maintenance.

12.8 Case studies and applications of digital twins in road maintenance

Digital twins are the new transformative technology in infrastructure management and maintenance. They enable the creation of dynamic virtual replicas of physical assets. In the context of road maintenance—covering highways and bridges—digital twins assist in monitoring structural health, optimizing maintenance schedules, and enhancing safety. The subsequent section discusses realworld applications of digital twins in road maintenance, examining how such technologies have improved safety, efficiency, and sustainability.

12.8.1 Digital twins in highway maintenance

12.8.1.1 Case study: Virginia department of transportation

The Virginia Department of Transportation (VDOT) has leveraged digital twin technology to improve the process of highway maintenance. It has developed an integrated digital replica of its road networks to monitor real-time data related to traffic patterns, weather conditions, and pavement conditions. The implementation has been of great value for planning maintenance activities and reducing operational costs.

12.8.1.2 Improvements achieved

Safety: Sensors can be installed to track the integrity of road structures, allowing VDOT to detect early warnings of possible hazards, such as cracks or wear, before such hazards become accident-causing. Predictive maintenance models, according to Stojanovic and Lechner (2019), significantly reduce road-related incidents by making timely interventions possible (Elmi and Martin, 2021). For example, VDOT reports fewer accidents caused by poor road conditions due to the use of IoT sensors, which demonstrates the immediate safety benefits of digital twin technology. **Efficiency:** Digital twins allow for the efficient scheduling of maintenance activities. Through the analysis of traffic data, VDOT can establish the optimum time to carry out road repairs with minimal interference to traffic and overall operations. This approach has enabled the department to reduce downtime by as much as 30% and respond more effectively and efficiently in its maintenance efforts.

Sustainability: Digital twins enable better resource utilization, avoid unnecessary repairs, and maintain roads for a longer time. Shokri et al., while highlighting this sustainable practice, mentioned that it also saves materials and reduces emissions generated from road maintenance operations (Gao and Wu, 2021). VDOT achieved significant savings in terms of costs as well as reductions in environmental degradation through its decision to revise schedules based on actual records instead of relying solely on historical schedules.

12.8.1.3 Case study: City of San Diego

The city of San Diego applied digital twin technology to advance road maintenance operations by building a digital twin of the road network, integrating information from sources that include sensors, drones, and satellite images.

12.8.1.4 Improvements achieved

Safety: The digital twin of the city can now monitor the condition of roads in real-time. This allows quick actions toward hazardous conditions, such as fallen debris or flooding. Such capabilities improve public safety immensely (Li and Kim, 2020). It also enables the city to respond quickly to incidents by applying predictive analytics, minimizing the chance of accidents and ensuring that drivers and pedestrians have safer roads. **Efficiency:** San Diego uses historical data to prioritize maintenance activities based on road conditions and usage. This allows for streamlined operations, ensuring that resources are allocated where they are most needed (Ahmed and Khan, 2022). The result has been a 25% reduction in maintenance costs due to more strategic deployment of resources, ensuring that taxpayer funds are used efficiently. **Sustainability:** The digital twin enables the comprehensive assessment of materials used in road construction and maintenance, promoting the adoption of more sustainable materials and practices. This aligns with the environmental goals of the city and reduces the carbon footprint of its transportation infrastructure (Tran and Vo, 2021). San Diego has positioned itself as a leader in sustainable urban development through the use of recycled materials and the optimization of maintenance practices by the city.

12.8.2 Digital twins in bridge maintenance case study: George C. Page Bridge

The George C. Page Bridge in Illinois has been an excellent example of the application of digital twin technology in bridge maintenance. A digital twin of the bridge was developed by the IDOT with the help of technology companies, using real-time data from sensors measuring structural and environmental integrity.

12.8.2.1 Improvements gained

Safety: By monitoring stress and strain on the bridge using the continuous digital twin approach, ample time is provided for proactive maintenance before structural failures occur. This advantage enhances the safety of the structure and the people using it. In addition, it has led to a reduction of up to 40% in surprise maintenance events caused by unexpected failures that are addressed before they happen (Williams and Jackson, 2020). **Efficiency:** The analytics enable IDOT to identify clear timelines for maintenance interventions, thereby avoiding unnecessary repairs and reducing maintenance costs (Stojanovic and Lechner, 2019). Integrating real-time data into machine learning algorithms predicts when maintenance should occur, increasing the likelihood of higher operational efficiency. **Sustainability:**

Digital twins promote a lifecycle management approach in which materials are used efficiently, and the service life of the bridge is maximized. This sustainable initiative reduces waste and resource consumption, aligning with environmental goals (Virginia Department of Transportation (VDOT), 2021). Carbon emissions during maintenance have been significantly reduced on the George C. Page Bridge due to its digital twin, optimized material usage, and maintenance schedules.

12.8.2.2 Case study: Brooklyn Bridge

The Brooklyn Bridge is one of the most iconic infrastructure assets, and it is utilizing digital twin technology. The New York City Department of Transportation (NYCDOT), has established a digital twin system to monitor conditions and traffic patterns on the bridge.

12.8.2.3 Improvements achieved

Safety: The digital twin enables real-time assessments of the structural health of the bridge, identifying potential defects that could lead to catastrophic failures. This represents a significantly enhanced capability on the safety side for the bridge and its users (Shokri and Kreinovich, 2021). Continuous monitoring has facilitated proactive measures that have prevented several critical failures, ensuring the bridge remains safe for daily commuters.
Efficiency: NYCDOT is scheduling maintenance using real-time data to minimize traffic disruption. "This efficiency saves time, resources, and allows service to be at the highest feasible level" (City of San Diego, 2020). Schedules can be adjusted according to traffic flow, resulting in better commute experiences, fewer delays, and reduced congestion.
Sustainability: The digital twin enables the analysis of materials and maintenance processes, assisting NYCDOT in adopting more sustainable methods. In doing so, the overall historic value of the bridge is preserved, while also advancing environmental sustainability (New York City Department of Transportation (NYCDOT), 2020). The department's efforts to adopt sustainable materials and practices have strengthened the sustainability profile of the bridge.

12.9 Risk and challenges

Digital twin technology is a promising technology for road infrastructure management; although it presents huge potential, some challenges need to be addressed to implement and effectively manage this technology in road infrastructure:

- Data integration and interoperability: Getting digital twins to work with current infrastructure systems is only possible through updating legacy systems. Clearly, interoperability between IoT sensors, the cloud, and legacy Cimmery shoreline management infrastructural elements is paramount in a service.

- High costs with deployment: The digital twin technology requires funding for hardware, software, and skilled labor to install and maintain it. Its adoption may be financially limited, especially in poorer regions with no budget for prevention.
- Scalability concerns: Real-time data from multiple sensors, processing, and predictive maintenance require huge computational resources in terms of storage, necessitating data updates for scalable functionality.
- Data security and privacy threats: With extensive data collection and cloud-based storage, cybersecurity and privacy are among the hardest problems to solve for large-scale infrastructure data.
- Accuracy and reliability of predictive models: Machine learning algorithms that enable predictive maintenance need a rich variety and quality of data for accurate damage detection and predictions about maintenance.
- Environmental and climatic factors: The road infrastructure itself can be subject to various natural environmental conditions, which may influence it.

The performance of digital twin models requires ongoing calibration and tuning to guarantee reliability.

- Adoption and expertise from users: For digital twins, the ultimate viability of road authorities and stakeholders depends on their ability to embrace the new high-tech systems. Training staff, minimizing staff turnover, and addressing related challenges are still barriers to overcome.

12.10 Future directions and research opportunities

This is bound to increase the effectiveness of this technology in road infrastructure management and maintenance, along with the emergence of many other research opportunities and technologies.

12.10.1 Emerging technologies 5G network connectivity

The operation of 5G would further empower applications in road maintenance digital twins significantly. For instance, sensor-embedded data transfer straight from the road infrastructure into digital twin models is possible, considering 5G guarantees high speeds and low latency. Improved accuracy in monitoring can be observed, along with swift action against emergent issues, thus raising efficiency. For example, 5G-enabled cities will transmit real-time data from thousands of sensors to enable better, more responsive maintenance operations (Illinois Department of Transportation [IDOT], 2018).

12.10.1.1 Augmented reality

AR can be quite beneficial in combination with digital twins of buildings to improve the level of visualization and facilitate better decision-making. AR glasses could provide maintenance crews with the functionality to overlay digital information onto the physical world for real-time insights into conditions as the infrastructure stands (Liu and Lin, 2021). This technology promotes the facilitation of training processes, increases safety factors during inspections, and accelerates maintenance processes. For instance, AR applications offer opportunities to visualize utilities that may be underground prior to excavation, reducing a host of risks associated with such work (Garz´on and Curbelo, 2021).

12.10.1.2 Blockchain technology

Blockchain technology can enhance data security and transparency in digital twin applications. Using blockchain to conduct transactions related to the data of maintenance activities ensures that the data is valid, thereby creating a reliable record of all the maintenance activities performed (Wu and Zhang, 2020). This promotes accountability and trust among stakeholders. Moreover, by integrating blockchain with digital twins, smart contracts for automatically scheduling maintenance and payments based on performance metrics could be established (Li and Zhao, 2020).

12.10.2 Research opportunities data analytics

Advanced data analytics may be incorporated into the design of digital twin systems. It may be utilized to enhance the decision-making capability of a system, optimize scheduling for maintenance activities, and allocate resources efficiently (Zhang and Xu, 2021). The developed predictive algorithms can forecast future infrastructure failures before their occurrence through the application of machine learning techniques (5G Americas, 2021). This research will enable the development of more complex models that not only predict failures but also recommend optimal maintenance strategies based on factors such as traffic volume and environmental conditions.

12.10.2.1 Real-time decision-making

The study of real-time decision-making capability within the digital twin system has great significance in the management of infrastructure. Algorithms developed to analyze streams of real-time data and provide actionable insights will allow organizations to respond proactively to emerging issues, enhancing safety and efficiency (Weyer and Schmid, 2019). The integration of artificial intelligence in digital twins enables automated decision-making processes that reduce the time required to respond to maintenance needs (Akbari and Zadeh, 2021).

12.10.2.2 Integration with smart infrastructure systems

Integrating digital twins with other smart infrastructures, such as ITS, may be the next promising aspect of study. It involves the merging of different types of data sources about traffic management systems (Askarany and Ehsani, 2020) and environmental monitoring for researchers to develop complete digital twin models that may provide in-depth insights into infrastructure performance as well as maintenance needs (Xu and Xu, 2020). This allows coordination among the responses, which enhances overall urban mobility and sustainability.

Digital twins in road maintenance are a transformative step forward in infrastructure management. Practical examples from VDOT and the City of San Diego show how digital twins can make road maintenance safer, more efficient, and more sustainable. The emerging trends in new technologies such as 5G, augmented reality, and blockchain are exciting and promising for further improvements in the applications of digital twins. These will continue to be at the heart of this future: research into data analytics, real-time decision-making, and integration with other smart infrastructure systems.

That could provide digital twin technology by advancing the management and maintenance of highways and bridges. It dynamically creates replications of the infrastructure and their physical assets, allowing this infrastructure to make real-time, data-driven decisions with its predictive analytics capabilities. Cities and regions, of late, find themselves increasingly pressed to keep up with the repair and replacement of aging infrastructure while also striving to toward safe, efficient, and sustainable.

As seen in the case studies of various cities and transportation departments, including the VDOT and the City of San Diego, the adoption of digital twins has resulted in several benefits across different dimensions. For safety, continuous monitoring of road and bridge conditions enables early identification of potential hazards. Predictive models, such as the Virginia DOT model, have proven effective in reducing road accidents to negligible levels by implementing interventions promptly. This is a form of public safety enhancement, along with confidence-building in terms of commuting. This, in turn, leads to a better environment for transportation.

Since these digital twins are now efficient enough to use real-time data for the optimization of maintenance schedules, one observes an improvement in efficiency itself. For instance, in the case of the City of San Diego, it follows a data-driven approach to ensure that resources are not wasted. It focuses more on repairing what is required the most. This decreases the interruption of traffic as well as reduces the cost of operation, thus providing significant economic benefits. Analysis of historical data and patterns of traffic also increases efficiency in maintenance operations and paves the way for smarter infrastructure management.

Another area that has been marked by the impact of digital twins is sustainability. Digital twins can support the general environmental goals of municipalities through proper resource allocation and the utilization of sustainable materials. This reduces waste and emissions, thereby decreasing the overall environmental impact and supporting the broader vision for sustainability. As illustrated by the Brooklyn Bridge and George C. Page Bridge, the lifecycle management approach supported through digital twins ensures that the practices of maintaining these iconic infrastructures not only preserve their structural integrity but also minimize their environmental footprint.

12.11 Motivation

Rapid urbanization and mounting demands on road infrastructure have led to an increasing challenge in maintenance and safety. Routine methods to monitor roads rely on reactive maintenance, which causes delays, incurs higher costs, and increases the risk of accidents. The latest advancements in digital twin technology frameworks can be used to provide solutions for real-time monitoring, predictive maintenance, and data-driven road infrastructure management.

Research for this work has been driven by the immediate requirement to improve road infrastructural resilience, efficiency, and sustainability. Conventional inspection methods are labor and time-intensive, with limited early damage detection capability, often resulting in severely deteriorated and costly repairs. IoT sensors, machine learning, as well as the cloud, transform digital twins into evolving models of road networks by constantly updating with actual real-time data.

This adds upfront, detects damage sooner, optimizes and properly maintains roads, so ultimately road safety improves and their lifespan is also prolonged.

In addition, thanks to the increasing scalability and availability made possible by 5G, AI, and edge computing, digital twins are going to become a reality in various shapes and scales and, therefore, could be considered the smart cities' weapon of the future. Treating these infrastructure challenges preemptively with digital twin technology not only lowers maintenance costs but also helps facilitate a more sustainable urban landscape for the users of roadways, all of which will ultimately make roads safer and more efficient.

References

5G Americas, 2021. Impact of 5G on Smart Cities and Transportation. 5G Americas White Paper.

Ahmed, S., Khan, L., 2022. Sensor data analysis in digital twin systems for road monitoring. Int. J. Smart Infrastruct. 14 (1), 93–108.

Akbari, A., Zadeh, M., 2021. Exploring augmented reality in smart infrastructure maintenance. J. Inf. Technol. Constr. 26, 125–138.

Alavi, A.H., H, C., 2019. Smart infrastructure: an overview. J. Infrastruct. Syst. 25 (2), 04019001.

Alshahrani, M., 2022. Predictive analytics for smart infrastructure: utilizing digital twin technology. Future Gener. Comput. Syst. 128, 493–503.

Antunes, J., Marques, R., 2021. Smart roads and digital twins: current trends and future perspectives. Int. J. Sustain. Transp. 15 (6), 475–486. doi:10.1080/15568318.2020.1758537.

Askarany, D., Ehsani, S., 2020. A blockchain-based framework for smart cities. J. Ambient Intell. Human. Comput. 11 (10), 4061–4072.

Bhatia, S., Bhattacharya, S., 2022. Cloud computing for smart roads: a comprehensive framework. J. Smart Transp. 2 (1), 1–13.
Bianchi, A., Lopes, F., 2022. Data analytics for road infrastructure: the case of digital twins. Urban Plan. 7 (2), 63–78.
Bo¨hme, T., Spies, J., 2021. Digital twins in construction: concepts and challenges. Autom. Constr. 122, 103497.
Boschert, S., Rosen, R., 2016. Digital twin—the simulation aspect. In: Mechatronic Futures. Springer, pp. 59–74.
Chan, C.Y., Wong, Y.H., 2018. The future of smart roads: challenges and opportunities. Transp. Res. Part C Emerg. Technol. 95, 214–223.
Chen, L., Zhang, Y., Li, M., 2022. Application of digital twins in road infrastructure maintenance. J. Civ. Eng. Technol. 18 (5), 124–140.
Chen, Y., Li, Z., 2021. Utilizing digital twin technology for intelligent road maintenance: a case study. J. Civ. Eng. Manag. 27 (3), 173–184.
City of San Diego, 2020. Road Maintenance and Safety Enhancement Initiative.
Elmi, N., Martin, G., 2021. Surface wear and raveling: early detection in digital twin frameworks. J. Struct. Infrastruct. Eng. 10 (4), 200–212.
Gao, J., Wu, X., 2021. Real-time road infrastructure monitoring with embedded sensors. Sensors Syst. 9 (3), 175–189.
Garcia, F., Lopez, J., 2020. Monitoring road rutting with digital twin technology. Road Transp. Eng. 11 (2), 134–145.
Garz´on, C.F., Curbelo, M., 2021. Augmented reality in infrastructure maintenance. J. Constr. Eng. Manag. 147 (2), 04020106.
Ghaffarian, S., Karami, K., 2023. AI-driven predictive maintenance for infrastructure: methods and applications. Struct. Health Monit. 22 (2), 256–273.
Govindaraju, K., Shah, S., 2020. Road damage classification using digital twin technology. Int. J. Road Bridge Eng. 9 (2), 97–105.
Grieves, M., 2014. Digital twin: manufacturing excellence through virtual factory replication. Bus. Value IT 1 (1), 1–7.
Grieves, M., 2019. Digital twin: the revolution in manufacturing. J. Manuf. Innov. 2 (1), 4–12.
Gupta, R., Kumar, A., 2021. Data-driven approaches for intelligent road infrastructure management. Transp. Rev. 41 (5), 668–688.
He, Z., et al., 2022. Edge computing in smart cities: a comprehensive review and future directions. Future Gener. Comput. Syst. 124, 236–249.
Hu, Q., et al., 2023. Real-time data management for intelligent transportation systems: challenges and solutions. J. Adv. Transp., 9503782.
Hwang, J., Kim, Y., 2020. Digital twins and IoT for smart city applications: a review. Sensors 20 (4), 1090. doi:10.3390/s20041090.
Illinois Department of Transportation (IDOT), 2018. Digital Twin Implementation for Bridge Management.
Jackson, T.D., Faber, D., 2023. Synchronized data systems for smart road management. Int. J. Transp. Sci. Technol. 12 (1), 1–12.
Johnson, R., Wang, T., 2020. The impact of heavy traffic on pavement structure: a pothole formation study. Pavement Mater. Des. 5 (4), 100–115.
Kaczmarek, M., Bula, A., 2022. Edge computing in smart roads: opportunities and challenges. Smart Cities 5 (3), 142–156.
Khajavi, S.H., Parto, M., 2021. Digital twins for smart cities: applications and future directions. J. Urban Technol. 28 (1), 1–15. doi:10.1080/10630732.2020.1803754.
Khatami, M., et al., 2020. The role of digital twins in infrastructure management. J. Urban Technol. 27 (1), 55–68.
Kim, D., Park, S., 2019. The role of IoT in smart infrastructure. Comput. Ind. 104, 141–150.
Kramers, A., Kerssens-van Drongelen, I., 2019. Digital twins in asset management: a review. J. Qual. Maint. Eng. 25 (2), 217–228. doi:10.1108/JQME-07-2018-0054.

Kritzinger, W., Karner, M., H., P., H, Z., 2018. Digital twin in manufacturing: key applications and benefits. J. Manuf. Sci. Eng. 140 (5).
Kumar, P., Mehta, R., 2022. Exploring the potential of AI and IoT in road infrastructure management. IEEE Trans. Intell. Transp. Syst. 23 (10), 12345–12357.
Kumar, V., Singh, A., 2021. Crack analysis in road infrastructure using AI techniques. J. Infrastruct. Eng. 4 (1), 45–58.
Kumar, V., Singh, S., 2021. IoT-based road condition monitoring system: a review. J. Traffic Transp. Eng. 9 (3), 309–321.
Kwon, H., Kim, J., 2020. The use of digital twins in urban infrastructure: a case study of smart roads. J. Urban Plan. Dev. 146 (3), 04020026. doi:10.1061/(ASCE)UP.1943-5444.0000628.
Lee, K., Kim, S., 2022. Ensuring data integrity and privacy in smart transportation systems. J. Urban Technol 29 (1), 1–15.
Li, Q., Zhao, Y., 2020. Data-driven approaches for smart infrastructure management. Autom. Constr. 120, 103392.
Li, S., Kim, H., 2020. Image recognition applications in road maintenance. Comput. Vis. Eng. 8 (2), 55–67.
Li, X., Wang, D., 2019. A framework for smart urban infrastructure maintenance with digital twin. Sensors 19 (20), 4395.
Liao, Y., Luo, P., 2021. Detection and repair strategies for potholes in road networks. Int. J. Transp. Sci. Technol. 12 (3), 215–229.
Lima, L., Silva, M., 2021. The role of digital twins in smart infrastructure: a systematic review. Autom. Constr. 122, 103461. doi:10.1016/j.autcon.2020.103461.
Liu, L., et al., 2021. Real-time monitoring of road infrastructure using cloud based digital twins. J. Comput. Civ. Eng. 35 (6), 04021068.
Liu, X., Lin, T., 2021. Advanced data analytics in infrastructure maintenance. Smart Infrastruct. J. 3 (1), 15–27.
Liu, Y., Yao, J., 2021. Leveraging digital twin technology for urban mobility management. Transp. Res. Part C Emerg. Technol. 129, 103011. doi:10.1016/j.trc.2021.103011.
Mahmud, M., et al., 2022. Deep learning techniques for road condition assessment: a review. J. Intell. Transp. Syst. 26 (1), 51–70.
Mura, M., Cuccuru, A., 2020. Innovations in smart infrastructure: an overview. Sensors 20 (2), 348.
Nascimento, L., et al., 2022. Challenges in implementing digital twins for urban infrastructure management. Smart Cities 5 (2), 341–359.
Negri, E., Fumagalli, L., Macchi, M. (2017). A review of the roles of digital twin in manufacturing. In: Proceedings of the IEEE International Conference on Industrial Technology.
New York City Department of Transportation (NYCDOT), 2020. Brooklyn Bridge Maintenance Report.
Patel, H., Gupta, R., 2022. Addressing freeze-thaw cycles in road infrastructure maintenance. Transp. Eng. Rev. 7 (1), 32–42.
Patel, R., Gupta, P., 2023. An overview of real-time data synchronization in smart cities. J. Internet Things 18, 100270.
Rojas, C., Trujillo, R., 2022. Integration of IoT and cloud computing for smart road management: a survey. IEEE Access 10, 64027–64039.
Rojdestvensky, A., Krichevsky, A., 2020. Digital twins as a tool for smart city development. J. Smart Cities 6 (1), 15–24. doi:10.2174/2210676X0666200617101237.
Schmid, J.E., Lichtenstein, C., 2022. Smart roads: the role of IoT in modern infrastructure. IEEE Trans. Intell. Transp. Syst.
Shakib, M., Pan, Z., 2019. Smart cities and intelligent infrastructure: challenges and opportunities. IEEE Trans. Smart Grid 10 (4), 4072–4081
Shokri, A., Kreinovich, V., 2021. Sustainability in transportation infrastructure. Int. J. Civ. Eng. 19 (5), 841–851.
Sinha, S., Ghosh, A., 2021. Real-time data collection techniques for smart infrastructure. J. Infrastruct. Syst. 27 (3), 04021014.
Smith, J., Brown, K., 2021. Digital twin technologies for infrastructure management. Transp. J. 12 (3), 215–230.
Stojanovic, J., Lechner, A.M., 2019. Predictive maintenance for infrastructure. J. Infrastruct. Syst. 25 (1), 04019002.

Sui, X., et al., 2023. The evolution of digital twins: from concept to reality in infrastructure management. Engineering 9 (2), 67–82.
Tao, F., Cheng, J., Zhang, H., 2018a. digital twin and cyber-physical systems: a review of applications and challenges. IEEE Access 7, 30433–30448.
Tao, F., Cheng, J., Zhang, H., 2018b. Digital twin and cyber-physical systems: a review of applications and challenges. IEEE Access 7, 30433–30448.
Tao, F., et al., 2018. Digital Twin Driven Smart Manufacturing. Academic Press.
Toh, K.A., et al., 2023. Digital twin for road maintenance: a holistic approach to smart city development. J. Urban Plan. Dev. 149 (1), 04022023.
Tran, D., Vo, T., 2021. Predictive analytics in infrastructure maintenance. Appl. Mach. Learn. Civ. Eng. 3 (1), 66–78.
Virginia Department of Transportation (VDOT), 2021. Highway Maintenance Optimization Project Report.
Wan, J., Yang, Y., 2020. A digital twin-based framework for smart infrastructure management. Eng. Appl. Artif. Intell. 94, 103886.
Wang, J., Liu, Y., 2021. Smart infrastructure for sustainable urban development. Sustain. Cities Soc. 65, 102665.
Wang, Y., et al., 2023. Towards smart roads: an integrated framework for IoT-based infrastructure monitoring. Sensors 23 (1), 135.
Weng, J., Zhang, H., Zhang, Y., 2020. Digital twin-driven smart cities: principles, framework, and applications. Comput. Environ. Urban Syst. 82, 101508. doi:10.1016/j.compenvurbsys.2020.101508.
Weyer, S., Schmid, S., 2019. Digital twins in manufacturing: recent trends and future directions. CIRP Ann. 68 (1), 21–24.
Williams, B., Jackson, C., 2020. The role of remote sensing and drones in road condition monitoring. Remote Sens. Appl. Transp. 15 (2), 223–239.
Wu, H., Zhang, J., 2020. Blockchain technology in infrastructure management. J. Inf. Technol. Constr. 25, 451–464.
Xu, M., Xu, J., 2020. The role of big data in smart infrastructure: opportunities and challenges. Int. J. Inf. Syst. Crisis Response Manag. 12 (3), 1–15.
Yang, X., et al., 2023. The role of IoT in enhancing road safety and management. J. Saf. Res. 86, 75–84.
Yang, Y., Chen, X., 2017. The role of digital twins in smart cities. J. Urban Technol. 24 (2), 71–86.
Zhang, H., et al., 2021. Leveraging digital twins for smart city infrastructure management: a review. J. Urban Technol. 28 (1), 13–34.
Zhang, X., Zhao, Z., 2021. Digital twin technology for smart cities: a comprehensive review. IEEE Access 9, 88260–88276.
Zhang, Y., Xu, L., 2021. Real-time data analytics in smart city infrastructure. Int. J. Inf. Syst. Crisis Response Manag. 13 (2), 37–54.
Zhao, M., Tan, Y., 2022. Erosion impacts on road shoulders and preventive measures. Geotech. Eng. Resil. 6 (2), 84–96.
Zheng, Y., Li, C., 2020. Smart cities: challenges and solutions for the digital twin. J. Urban Technol. 27 (1), 1–16.
Zhou, Y., et al., 2023. A survey on cloud-based solutions for intelligent transportation systems. Transp. Res. Part C Emerg. Technol. 143, 103809.

CHAPTER 13

Prediction and remediation of cancer using digital twins: A comprehensive review

Vaishali Nitin Dhawas[a], Pankaj Chandre[b], Renuka Rajendra Kajale[a], and Neha Sharad Bhagwat[a]

[a]*Department of Computer Engineering, Nutan Maharashtra Institute of Engineering & Technology, Pune, India*

[b]*Computer Science and Engineering, MIT Art Design and Technology University Pune, Pune, India*

13.1 Introduction

Digital Twin (DT) technology is a cutting-edge innovation that creates dynamic virtual models to replicate real-world systems, including human bodies. In the healthcare field, particularly in oncology, a DT functions as a detailed, real-time digital representation of a patient. It integrates various types of data, such as electronic health records, medical imaging, genomic profiles, biosensor readings, and lifestyle information, to continuously update the patient's virtual model (Krittanawong et al., 2023; Nguyen and Kim, 2022; Lee and Kim, 2023a). These models are not static; they evolve with the patient, enabling continuous tracking of health status. The primary goal of a DT in healthcare is to simulate biological processes and predict how a patient's disease will progress over time. By using machine learning (ML) and artificial intelligence (AI), the twin can forecast how different treatments might affect the patient without actual physical trials (Kirubarajan and Vali, 2023; Choi et al., 2023; Elakkiya and Anand, 2023). This predictive ability enables clinicians to test and optimize treatment plans in a virtual setting before applying them in real-life situations, thereby minimizing trial-and-error in actual patient care. Moreover, DTs help in real-time monitoring, early diagnosis, and risk assessment, which can significantly improve patient outcomes (Nguyen and Kim, 2022; Lee and Kim, 2023a; MDPI, 2023b). The implementation of DTs is supported by technological advancements such as high-performance computing, big data analytics, and cloud-based platforms (Bordukova et al., 2024; ScienceDirect, 2023). These tools make it possible to process vast amounts of data efficiently and update models in real-time. The DT acts as a constantly evolving health profile that helps clinicians make informed, timely, and personalized decisions.

Artificial Intelligence, Machine Learning and Blockchain in Digital Twin Computing.
https://doi.org/10.1016/B978-0-443-43914-8.00007-8

Cancer is one of the world's biggest health problems, causing many serious illnesses and deaths (Sung et al., 2021). Even though medical tools have improved, finding cancer early and providing the right treatment for each person remains challenging (Axios, 2024). DTs can help address this issue. They create a digital copy of the patient to monitor how cancer grows and predict which treatment will work best (Krittanawong et al., 2023; Nguyen and Kim, 2022). This approach allows care to be personalized for each individual, rather than relying on a one-size-fits-all plan. As a result, patients can achieve better outcomes, experience fewer side effects, and enjoy an improved quality of life. DTs also enhance doctors' confidence in their decisions, leading to faster and more accurate care. They enable testing of different treatments on the digital copy before administering them to the patient, which helps prevent complications. Research further indicates that DTs can identify individuals at risk of developing illnesses early, allowing timely intervention (Choi et al., 2023; MDPI, 2023a; PubMed, 2023). AI plays a crucial role in keeping the digital version of the patient updated with new data, ensuring that the care plan evolves as the patient's condition changes. This capability is particularly valuable for fast-progressing diseases like cancer (Chaudhuri et al., 2023; Wentzel et al., 2024; Bordukova et al., 2024).

13.2 Conceptual framework

The concept of DT technology originated in engineering, where virtual models were utilized to monitor and control machines and systems. In healthcare, DTs operate similarly, serving as digital replicas of patients. These virtual representations are continually updated by gathering real-time information from various sources, including medical records, imaging tests, lab results, genetic data, and wearable health trackers (Choi et al., 2023; Lee and Kim, 2023b).

Three main parts are required to design a conceptual framework.

1. Data collection includes medical history, genetic details, scan images, and information from devices like fitness bands or heart monitors.
2. Modeling and simulation use AI and ML to create a digital representation of the patient's body and disease. This model can show how cancer might grow or respond to treatment.
3. Decision support, where doctors use the DT to anticipate what might happen next and decide on the best treatment based on simulated results (Lee and Kim, 2023a; Elakkiya and Anand, 2023).

In cancer care, these digital models can be used to understand tumor growth, spread (metastasis), and how the cancer responds to different treatments. This helps doctors test different treatment plans on the model before applying them to the real patient, making the process safer and more effective (Chaudhuri et al., 2023). Cancer continues to be one of the top health threats globally; millions of people are diagnosed each year, and it remains a leading cause of death (Sung et al., 2021). Even though healthcare has improved, doctors still struggle to detect cancer early and offer treatment that is appropriate for each patient

(Axios, 2024). DT technology brings new hope to these challenges. By building a digital version of the patient that updates continuously with new data, it helps predict how cancer may grow or spread. It can also determine which treatment will work best for that individual (Krittanawong et al., 2023; Nguyen and Kim, 2022). Instead of following a general treatment approach, DTs allow doctors to provide treatment specific to the patient's needs. This can lead to better recovery, fewer side effects, and a higher quality of life. These tools also assist doctors in making smarter decisions, using real-time data and AI to adjust treatments as the disease evolves (Chaudhuri et al., 2023; Wentzel et al., 2024; Bordukova et al., 2024).

DTs can detect problems early, such as the return of cancer or signs that a treatment is not working. This allows doctors to act quickly and adjust the care plan if needed (MDPI, 2023a; PubMed, 2023). DTs are especially helpful in complicated cancers like brain tumors or head and neck cancers, where personalized treatment can make a significant difference (Chaudhuri et al., 2023; Wentzel et al., 2024). DTs are also being used in clinical trials and drug development. Researchers can test new cancer drugs on digital models first, making the process faster, cheaper, and safer (Pandey et al., 2024; Bordukova et al., 2024). Some systems, like DTs for Tumor Outcome (DITTO), provide visual interfaces to understand how a patient responds to treatment over time (Wentzel et al., 2024).

To make this work smoothly, the DT system follows a step-by-step process: Fig. 13.1.

This diagram shows a step-by-step framework for how a cancer DT (CDT) is created and used to help treat patients. It starts with data collection, where different types of patient information are gathered. This includes things like medical history, lab tests, imaging scans (such as

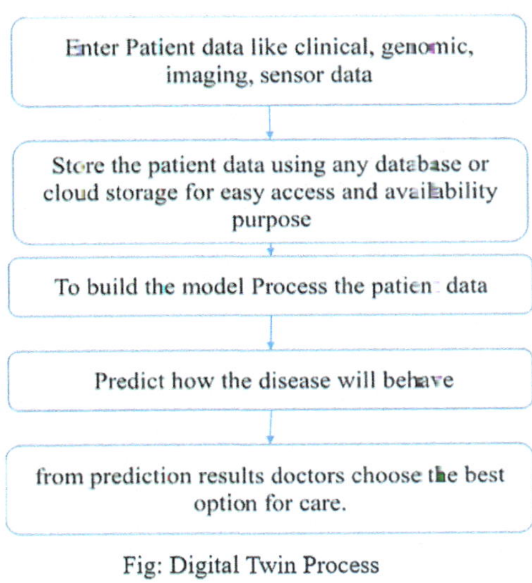

Fig. 13.1 Digital twin process.

magnetic resonance imaging (MRI) or computed tomography (CT)), genetic data, and lifestyle details. Collecting high-quality data is the foundation of building an accurate digital model.

Next comes data integration and preprocessing. In this step, all the collected data from different sources is cleaned, organized, and combined into a single usable format. This ensures the information is consistent and ready for the model to use. Without proper integration, the CDT might miss important signals or give incorrect results.

When the data is ready, the process moves to model development. Here, advanced computer models, often using AI or ML, are used to build the actual DT. This digital copy is designed to act like the real patient's body and cancer, predicting how the disease might grow or respond to different treatments.

Once the model is built, it goes through validation and testing. This means checking how accurate and reliable the DT is. The model's predictions are compared to real patient outcomes to see if it works well. Only models that pass this step are considered ready for clinical use.

The final step is clinical application, where the CDT is used by doctors to help make treatment decisions. The DT can simulate different treatment options, predict side effects, and suggest the best course of action based on the patient's specific condition. This helps in delivering more personalized and effective cancer care.

This kind of system improves accuracy, saves time, and personalizes cancer care. As more technologies become available, DTs are expected to play an even bigger role in the future of oncology.

13.3 Technological advancement supporting digital twin in cancer care

The development and use of DTs in cancer care would not be possible without recent advances in digital technologies. These technologies help gather, store, and analyze health data, enabling doctors to create detailed and useful virtual models of patients. Several modern technologies play a key role in making DT systems effective in cancer care.

13.3.1 Artificial intelligence and machine learning

These tools are used to study large and complex medical data, such as scans, test results, and patient history. They can identify hidden patterns in the data and help doctors understand how cancer is likely to behave in the future (Nguyen and Kim, 2022; Lee and Park, 2023; Bordukova et al., 2024). For example, AI can quickly analyze thousands of images to detect tumors that might be too small for the human eye to see. It can also predict how a tumor might grow or respond to treatment based on past cases. As more data is added, the AI system continues learning and becomes even better at making accurate predictions, which helps doctors make faster and more reliable decisions.

13.3.2 Big data and cloud computing

Big Data refers to huge amounts of health information collected from different sources like hospitals, labs, and wearable devices. Cloud computing allows this data to be safely stored and accessed over the internet. This means that doctors, researchers, and hospitals can work with patient information without needing to be in the same place (Lee and Park, 2023). For DTs, this is especially useful because the system needs access to different types of data in real time. For example, if a patient is treated at two different hospitals, their digital model can still be updated and used from both places. This makes treatment faster, more coordinated, and more accurate.

The **Internet of medical things (IoMT)** also plays a major role. IoMT refers to devices like smartwatches, digital thermometers, heart rate monitors, and other tools that collect health data and send it directly to doctors. These devices allow a DT to receive continuous updates about a patient's condition, even when they are at home (Krittanawong et al., 2023; Nguyen and Kim, 2022). This is very helpful for cancer patients, especially those undergoing treatments like chemotherapy, who need to be monitored closely for side effects. If something goes wrong, such as a sudden rise in heart rate or body temperature, the system can alert doctors immediately. This allows for quicker action and helps avoid complications.

Visualization tools help doctors and medical teams better understand and communicate health information. Tools like DITTO allow doctors to see what is happening inside the patient's body in a clear and simple way. These tools can display 3D images of tumors, simulate how they are changing over time, and compare different treatment plans (Wentzel et al., 2024). This not only helps doctors plan more effectively but also makes it easier to explain complex medical conditions to patients. For instance, a doctor might use DITTO to show a patient how their tumor is shrinking after treatment or how a new drug might affect their body. These visual tools simplify the personalization of care and improve communication between patients and doctors. These technologies work together to make DTs more accurate, user-friendly, and powerful in assisting doctors in choosing the best care.

For example:

- In head and neck cancer cases, the DITTO system allows doctors to view treatment progress over time, compare different treatment options, and make better decisions based on that visual data (Wentzel et al., 2024).
- In brain cancer treatment, DTs help doctors simulate how a tumor might grow and test treatments virtually before administering them to the patient (Chaudhuri et al., 2023).

Researchers are building DT models to support clinical trials. This means they can test how a new medicine might affect different kinds of patients before giving it to real people. This makes trials faster, safer, and less expensive (Pandey et al., 2024; Bordukova et al., 2024).

13.4 Applications of cancer DTs in modern cancer management

CDTs are advanced computer models that represent a real person who has cancer. These virtual models are created using personal health information, such as genetic data, medical history, lifestyle habits, and environmental factors. CDTs allow doctors and researchers to better understand the patient's condition, predict how the disease might behave, personalize treatment plans, monitor progress, and even help discover new medicines (Krittanawong et al., 2023; Kirubarajan and Vali, 2023).

13.4.1 Finding cancer early and predicting risk

CDTs are very useful in detecting cancer early and helping to prevent it before it starts. CDTs work by collecting and analyzing a wide range of personal health information, such as genetic background, family medical history, environmental exposures, and lifestyle habits like smoking, alcohol use, diet, and exercise patterns. With the help of advanced technologies like AI and ML, this information is used to estimate an individual's likelihood of developing cancer in the future (Krittanawong et al., 2023; Sung et al., 2021).

For example, if a person has inherited a harmful genetic mutation, such as BRCA1 or BRCA2, which are linked to breast and ovarian cancers, the CDT will recognize this risk factor. It can then simulate how that person's body might respond over time, showing possible disease development influenced by various conditions. Consequently, doctors can utilize the CDT to make recommendations for preventive actions, like more frequent screenings, lifestyle changes, or even preventive treatments such as medications or surgery (The Times, 2024). This helps catch the disease at its earliest stage or even stop it before it starts.

Another important feature of CDTs is their ability to monitor biomarkers, tiny biological signals in the body that can indicate the presence or recurrence of cancer. Biomarkers can include specific proteins, DNA mutations, or other molecules that appear in the blood, saliva, or tissues. These are often detected long before symptoms show up, which allows doctors to take action early and avoid more serious health problems later (Kirubarajan and Vali, 2023; The Guardian, 2024). For instance, a CDT might track changes in blood levels of a protein like Prostate-Specific Antigen (PSA) in men, which can be an early sign of prostate cancer. If levels begin to rise, the CDT can alert doctors so they can carry out further tests or start treatment early.

CDTs also allow for continuous risk assessment. Unlike traditional methods that assess risk just once, CDTs are constantly updated with new data from electronic health records, wearable devices, lab results, or imaging scans. This allows the system to provide updated risk scores in real time. For example, if a person begins smoking after being cancer-free for several years, the CDT can adjust the risk level and suggest steps like quitting programs or regular check-ups. This ongoing analysis helps create a dynamic, up-to-date picture of a person's health.

CDTs help doctors stratify patients into different risk groups. This means that instead of treating everyone the same, doctors can group people based on their risk levels and focus attention on those who need it most. High-risk patients can receive more detailed check-ups, genetic testing, or preventive measures, while low-risk individuals can avoid unnecessary procedures or stress.

13.4.2 Creating personalized treatment plans

Cancer is not the same for everyone. Even two patients with the same type of cancer can have tumors that behave very differently. CDTs help by allowing doctors to test different treatments virtually on a patient's digital model before applying them in real life. This means doctors can pick the treatment that is most likely to work and avoid options that could cause severe side effects (Jemal et al., 2007; Collins and Varmus, 2015).

For example, a patient with lung cancer can have a CDT that tests how their tumor would react to several drugs. If the CDT shows one drug works better than others, doctors can choose that treatment for the actual patient, making care more precise and effective (American Cancer Society, 2023).

CDTs can help determine the best drug dosage. Some medicines work well in small amounts for one person but may require a higher dose for another. CDTs can test different doses to identify the safest and most effective one (Krittanawong et al., 2023; Axios, 2024).

Since cancer can change over time, CDTs are always updated with new data from scans, blood tests, or wearable devices. If the cancer starts growing again or becomes resistant to a drug, the CDT can quickly suggest new treatment options (Nguyen and Kim, 2022; Lee and Kim, 2023a).

13.4.3 Watching the cancer and managing it

CDTs are very helpful tools for keeping track of how cancer changes in a person's body over time. Once a patient is diagnosed with cancer, regular monitoring becomes very important to ensure the treatment is working and the disease is under control. CDTs are like digital copies of the patient that get updated regularly using new information from tests, scans, and even wearable health devices like smartwatches. These updates help the CDT provide doctors with a clear picture of the patient's condition at all times (Choi et al., 2023; Lee and Kim, 2023b).

For example, CDTs can take information from MRI or CT scans, blood test results, and health trackers to detect any changes in the body. If the tumor grows larger or certain blood markers increase, the CDT will quickly identify this and alert the medical team. This rapid response helps doctors adjust treatments before the cancer worsens, improving the chances of controlling the disease (Choi et al., 2023; Lee and Kim, 2023b).

CDTs don't just watch the cancer itself; they also keep an eye on how the patient is doing day by day. If a person feels pain, becomes very tired, or has trouble breathing, the CDT can recognize these changes by analyzing patterns from health data. For instance, if a patient's heart rate increases or their movement decreases, the CDT can detect these signs and send a message to doctors so they can check on the patient early and avoid problems (Elakkiya and Anand, 2023; Lee and Park, 2023). Another important use of CDTs is to predict if the cancer might come back or spread to other parts of the body. This is called relapse or metastasis. CDTs do this by comparing the current patient's condition to many other patients with similar cancers. If the CDT identifies patterns that suggest a high risk of recurrence, doctors can act quickly by planning more tests or extra treatment to keep the cancer from returning (Kirubarajan and Vali, 2023; Lee and Kim, 2023a).

CDTs can also help plan for the future. For example, they can test what might happen if a drug is stopped or if a different treatment is used. In breast cancer, for example, the CDT can predict whether hormone therapy or chemotherapy will work better for a certain patient. In lung cancer, CDTs can estimate when a patient might stop responding to a medicine so that doctors can change treatment before the cancer becomes resistant (The Times, 2024; American Cancer Society, 2023; Nguyen and Kim, 2022; Chaudhuri et al., 2023). Because CDTs give doctors a better idea of how a patient is doing over time, care can be personalized more effectively. Instead of using the same schedule for everyone, like doing a scan every few months, doctors can adjust the timing based on the CDT's advice. A patient with a low risk might need fewer visits, while a high-risk patient can be monitored more closely, saving time and money and reducing stress for both patients and healthcare teams (Wentzel et al., 2024; Pandey et al., 2024).

CDTs also check whether treatments are working. If a tumor isn't shrinking or the patient still feels unwell, the CDT can help spot this early. This way, doctors can quickly switch to a different treatment that might work better instead of wasting time on something that isn't helping and might be causing side effects (Eminaga et al., 2023; Bordukova et al., 2024). Another benefit is that CDTs help all the doctors involved in a patient's care work together more easily. The DT collects and organizes all the data in one place, making it simpler for oncologists, radiologists, and other specialists to stay updated and coordinate the patient's treatment (MDPI, 2023b; PubMed, 2023).

13.4.4 Helping discover new medicines

CDTs play a huge role in developing new cancer treatments. Traditionally, creating a new drug takes many years and costs a lot of money. With CDTs, researchers can test how a new drug works on many different virtual patients before trying it on real people. This speeds up the process, reduces costs, and improves safety (Krittanawong et al., 2023; Chaudhuri et al., 2023).

For instance, in the case of brain cancer, scientists can use CDTs to test how different drugs work for patients with different genetic profiles. If the CDT shows a drug is effective for a certain type of patient, the drug can move on to real clinical trials more confidently (Wentzel et al., 2024).

CDTs also allow virtual drug screening, where hundreds of drug combinations are tested quickly. This helps scientists find the most promising treatments without exposing real patients to risks early in the research process (Pandey et al., 2024; Eminaga et al., 2023).

13.5 Challenges and limitations of cancer digital twins

CDTs have the power to improve cancer care by helping doctors understand the disease better, plan personalized treatments, and predict how a patient's cancer will behave. However, even though the technology is very promising, there are still many challenges that must be addressed before CDTs can be used widely in real hospitals and clinics. These challenges relate to data privacy, technical problems, ethics, hospital workflows, data quality, cost, and government regulations.

13.5.1 Protecting patient data (data privacy and security)

One of the biggest challenges in using CDTs is keeping patient data safe and private. CDTs require a significant amount of personal information to function effectively. This includes details such as a person's DNA, medical history, lifestyle habits, lab test results, and sometimes even real-time updates from smartwatches or other health devices. All of this data is highly sensitive. If it is stolen or misused, it could lead to serious issues like identity theft, insurance denial, or emotional harm to the patient (Bruynseels et al., 2018). CDTs typically connect with various systems, including hospital networks, cloud storage, and research centers. This interconnection between different platforms increases the risk of cyberattacks. Hackers may attempt to infiltrate these systems to steal patient data. In addition, if there are insufficient regulations or laws in place, companies involved in creating or managing CDTs could misuse the data, especially if patients have not explicitly consented to how their information will be utilized. For instance, if a CDT is used by both a hospital and a research company, both entities must adhere to stringent rules to ensure the patient's identity remains confidential. However, many countries still lack adequate legislation to manage and protect this type of health data (Bruynseels et al., 2018).

To solve these problems, several tools and strategies are being used. One of the most common tools is encryption. This means turning the data into a secret code that only people with special permission can read. Even if a hacker gets the data, they won't be able to understand it without the right key (Krittanawong et al., 2023). Another useful idea is called "federated learning." Instead of sharing all the patient data with one central location, each hospital or clinic trains its model and only shares the changes to the model, not the actual data. This makes it much safer (ScienceDirect, 2023). Other methods are also being explored. For example, "differential privacy" adds a small amount of noise to the data. This keeps individual patients from being identified but still lets researchers see useful patterns. Another method, called "secure multiparty computation," allows different groups to work together using encrypted data. This way, they can study patient outcomes without seeing the raw data.

From the legal and ethical side, it's important to make sure that patients understand how their data will be used. This is called "informed consent." Patients should know if their data is only being used for their care or if it's also being used for research. Hospitals and companies must create clear rules about who can see and use patient data. They should also follow national and international laws like the General Data Protection Regulation (GDPR) in Europe or Health Insurance Portability and Accountability (HIPAA) in the United States to make sure patient information is handled properly (Bruynseels et al., 2018). Training is also important. All the people who work with CDTs, like doctors, nurses, IT staff, and researchers, should know how to handle data safely. Even small mistakes, like clicking on a dangerous email or leaving a computer unlocked, can lead to big problems. Many hospitals are starting to use a "zero trust" approach. This means no one is automatically trusted, and every request to access data is checked carefully, even from people inside the hospital (Krittanawong et al., 2023).

Still, there are challenges. Sometimes, security systems are too complicated and slow down the work of doctors or nurses. When systems are hard to use, people may take shortcuts, which increases the risk of mistakes. Smaller clinics might not have enough money or skilled staff to build strong security systems. Also, when trying to protect patient identity by removing personal details from the data, there's a risk of making the data too vague, which can reduce the quality of CDT predictions. Another issue is that different countries have different rules. A CDT system that follows the law in one country might break the law in another. This makes international projects hard to manage. To fix this, there need to be global agreements and clear guidelines for how medical data is shared, stored, and protected.

13.5.2 Lack of common technical standards

One major challenge in the use of CDTs is the lack of common technical standards. Currently, there are no universal rules or guidelines on how CDTs should be created, validated, or implemented. This means that hospitals, research labs, software developers, and even countries often design their CDTs differently, using various kinds of data like CT scans, MRI images, blood test results, or genetic reports (PubMed, 2023). Because of this, it becomes very difficult to combine or compare these digital models across different settings. For example, one hospital may rely heavily on imaging data, while another may focus more on genetic information, making it nearly impossible to integrate or validate the models together. This lack of standardization leads to several problems. One major issue is with interoperability—the ability for different systems and tools to work together. If CDTs are built on different platforms or use different formats, it becomes difficult for researchers and clinicians to share findings or reuse models in different hospitals. It also slows down the development of more advanced CDTs that could benefit from data collected across different populations and healthcare systems. Without a shared framework, progress remains isolated and fragmented, limiting the broader impact of these promising technologies (PubMed, 2023).

Another serious problem is the lack of consistent validation practices. Before a CDT is used to help make real medical decisions, it should be tested to ensure it gives accurate and reliable predictions. However, many current CDTs are only tested on small datasets or outdated patient records (MDPI, 2023a; PubMed, 2023). This means that the model may not perform well when used in different hospitals or with patients from diverse backgrounds. If a CDT is not tested thoroughly, doctors may hesitate to use its recommendations, and patients may lose trust in its results. Therefore, there is a clear need for agreed-upon standards that define how CDTs should be tested, including the size of the patient group, how outcomes are measured, and how performance is judged. To address these issues, experts suggest creating shared technical frameworks and validation procedures. For example, the use of common data standards like Health Level Seven International (HL7) or Fast Healthcare Interoperability Resources (FHIR) can help make medical records and lab results more compatible across different systems. Shared validation guidelines can ensure that CDTs are tested fairly and rigorously. Creating open-access benchmarking datasets that include anonymized, real-world patient data would allow researchers to compare their CDT models against the same standards. These steps would also make it easier to audit CDT systems and make them more transparent, which is essential for clinical acceptance and regulatory approval (MDPI, 2023a; PubMed, 2023).

Cross-disciplinary collaboration is crucial to solving the standardization problem. Clinicians can help define which data and predictions are most useful in practice, while computer scientists and engineers can design systems that are easier to integrate. Government agencies and regulatory bodies also have a role to play by setting rules that ensure patient safety and ethical data use. Some organizations, like the Food and Drug Administration (FDA) and Organisation for Economic Co-operation and Development (OECD), have started promoting the creation of digital health standards, but more global coordination is needed to ensure consistency across borders (Corral-Acero et al., 2020). Standardizing CDT development will not only improve model accuracy but also help in building trust among users. Doctors will feel more confident using CDTs that have been validated according to recognized guidelines, and patients will be more willing to accept advice from these tools when they know it's based on tested and approved systems. Moreover, it will make it easier for healthcare providers to share resources and work together on improving cancer care.

13.5.3 Ethical problems and legal questions

Using CDTs brings up many ethical concerns. First, patients need to fully understand how their data will be collected, stored, and used. This is called "informed consent." If this process is not clear or fair, patients might unknowingly share data they wouldn't have agreed to (Bruynseels et al., 2018). Another issue is fairness. If a CDT is built using data mostly from people of a certain age, gender, or ethnic group, the model may not work well for people from other groups. For example, if the training data mostly includes White patients, the CDT may give less accurate results for Black or Asian patients (The Guardian, 2024; Bruynseels et al., 2018). This kind of bias can lead to unequal care and is a serious ethical problem. There's also the question of legal responsibility. If a CDT gives the wrong advice and the patient is harmed, who is responsible: the doctor, the software company, or the hospital? Right now, laws about this are not clear, and this makes many doctors and hospitals hesitant to use CDTs in serious cases (Bruynseels et al., 2018).

13.5.4 Hard to use in real hospitals (clinical integration)

Even though CDTs use advanced technology, it is still hard to fit them into the daily routines of doctors and nurses. Many healthcare workers have not received training in using AI or digital tools, and they may not feel comfortable or confident using a CDT to help make treatment decisions (Krittanawong et al., 2023; Jemal et al., 2007). In addition, many hospitals use older software systems that don't work well with new AI-based technologies. Connecting CDTs to these outdated systems can be very costly and time-consuming. In some cases, the digital tools may slow doctors down if they have to switch between multiple platforms or interpret complicated graphs and charts (Krittanawong et al., 2023). Some doctors may also worry about giving too much control to a computer model, as they may feel that using a CDT to decide a treatment plan takes away the human touch of medicine. More real-life clinical trials and strong evidence are needed to convince doctors to trust and use CDTs regularly (Jemal et al., 2007).

13.5.5 Poor data quality and unequal data access

A CDT can only be as good as the data it uses. If the patient's data is missing important details, incorrect, or out of date, then the CDT will not provide good advice (Elakkiya and Anand, 2023; PubMed, 2023). For example, if a person's genetic test results are missing, the CDT might suggest a drug that doesn't work for them. In some parts of the world, especially in developing countries, hospitals may not have digital records at all. In these areas, there may not be enough data to build or update CDTs. This means that patients from these regions may be excluded from the benefits of the technology, making the healthcare system more unequal (The Guardian, 2024; Axios, 2024). To address this, researchers need to ensure they use diverse, high-quality data that represents people of all backgrounds. This will help make CDTs more accurate and fair for everyone.

13.5.6 High cost and infrastructure demands

Creating and using a DT requires a lot of money and technical resources. You need powerful computers, cloud storage, software licenses, and skilled staff like data scientists and engineers. These are not available in every hospital, especially small ones in rural areas or countries with fewer healthcare resources (Pandey et al., 2024; ScienceDirect, 2023). For example, researchers use CDTs to test new cancer drugs virtually. This helps speed up drug discovery, but it still requires expensive software and expert teams (Bordukova et al., 2024; MDPI, 2023a). This can create a divide where patients in wealthy hospitals get the benefits of CDTs, while others are left behind. Governments and health organizations need to find ways to make this technology more affordable and easier to use so that it can be shared more equally.

13.5.7 Slow government approval and regulation

Right now, there are very few official rules for how CDTs should be approved and used in medicine. Health agencies like the FDA (in the United States) or EMA (in Europe) are still trying to figure out how to test and approve AI-based tools like CDTs (Bruynseels et al., 2018; Corral-Acero et al., 2020). Until there are clear rules, many doctors and hospitals will be cautious about using them. Getting approval to use CDTs in real clinical settings takes a long time. The technology must go through many stages of testing, validation, and paperwork. This process can take years, which slows down the use of CDTs even if the technology is ready (PubMed, 2023; Springer, 2023). Also, rules need to be updated regularly because technology is changing fast. If regulations are too slow or outdated, they can block innovation and prevent patients from getting access to new, helpful tools.

13.6 Future directions in CDTs

Emerging trends suggest that CDTs can become even more powerful and broadly used by focusing on two major areas:

1. **Improving the technology**—making CDTs smarter and more accessible.
2. **Building stronger support systems**—bringing people and organizations together.

13.6.1 Technological innovations: Improving biology, privacy, and cloud access

One of the most exciting directions for the future of CDTs is adding more biological information into the models. Right now, CDTs use patient data such as imaging results, lab tests, and treatment history. However, by including more advanced biological data like genomics (DNA) and proteomics (proteins in the body), CDTs can become much more powerful. For example, genetic mutations, such as changes in the TP53 gene—which are common in many types of cancer—can help predict how a patient's cancer might grow or respond to treatment (Kirubarajan and Vali, 2023). Proteomics, which studies protein activity, can add another layer by showing how a tumor reacts to stress or medication. This helps make treatment plans more accurate and personalized. When we combine all this data from different sources, such as DNA, RNA, proteins, and metabolism, it's called a multiomics approach. This makes the DT model better at simulating what is happening inside the patient's body. However, collecting this kind of data from different platforms and keeping it up to date with changing clinical guidelines is still a challenge (MDPI, 2023a).

Another trend that will help CDTs grow is the use of federated learning. In normal AI training, all the data from patients is collected in one place, which can create privacy problems. Federated learning is different; it lets hospitals or clinics train DT models using their data locally, without having to send patient records to a central server (ScienceDirect, 2023). Only the model improvements, not the raw data, are shared. This keeps personal information safe while still allowing the CDT to learn from many different cases. Federated learning also allows the model to keep learning as new patient data comes in without compromising privacy. For example, if a new immunotherapy becomes available, the CDT can quickly adapt by learning from new treatment responses across hospitals. However, to make this safe and trustworthy, strong security tools like encryption and secure model sharing are needed.

The helpful innovation is offering DT technology as a cloud-based service, known as "DT-as-a-Service" (DTaaS). This is especially useful for hospitals or clinics that don't have the resources to build their own CDT systems. With DTaaS, the complex software and computing tools are kept in the cloud. Hospitals just need to upload anonymous patient data, and the platform will create a DT, run simulations, and send back useful results like treatment suggestions or risk alerts (Pandey et al., 2024). This makes CDTs more accessible to more places, especially smaller hospitals. It also allows researchers from different regions to work together and test ideas without needing advanced infrastructure on-site. However, to make DTaaS work smoothly in real-life settings, we need to address concerns like data protection, connecting it with hospital systems, pricing models, and getting approvals from medical authorities. All these technologies—multiomics modeling, federated learning, and DTaaS—are key to making CDTs more powerful, private, and widely available. Together, they lay the groundwork for the next generation of cancer care, where patients receive more accurate, safer, and customized treatments.

13.6.2 Working together: Collaboration and standard ecosystems

The future of CDTs doesn't just depend on better technology; it also depends on people from different fields working together. To make CDTs that are accurate, safe, and useful, we need teams that include doctors, data scientists, biologists, engineers, and software experts. Doctors understand how cancer behaves and how treatments affect patients. Data scientists build the AI models that run the DTs. Biologists and bioengineers help interpret complex biological data like genes and proteins. Meanwhile, software experts make sure the DT tools are easy to use and can work with hospital systems (Corral-Acero et al., 2020). When these experts collaborate closely, they can create CDTs that reflect real-world patient needs. Working in isolation can lead to models that are hard to understand, inaccurate, or not useful in clinical settings. That's why cross-disciplinary teamwork, shared research labs, and combined funding projects are becoming more important.

Creating these teams is just one part of the picture. We also need to build an ecosystem that helps CDTs grow and be trusted. This includes setting up standard tools and processes. For example, using common data formats such as FHIR or HL7 allows CDTs to read patient records and test results from different hospitals without confusion. Benchmark datasets, collections of anonymized patient data from many hospitals, help test and compare DT models fairly. This allows developers to see which models work best in which situations (PubMed, 2023). Having shared rules and tools also helps regulators decide whether a CDT is safe enough to be used in real patient care. The ecosystem has clear pathways for government approval. Right now, agencies like the FDA and EMA are still developing rules for AI and digital health tools. Without these rules, hospitals and companies might hesitate to use CDTs in everyday care. Rules are especially needed for things like updating models, checking model fairness, and making sure the tools meet medical standards (Springer, 2023; Bruynseels et al., 2018). Public-private partnerships, where government agencies, hospitals, and companies work together, can help create these standards faster. Federated consortia groups that share knowledge without sharing private data can also help test and validate CDTs in diverse patient populations. Collaboration among different professionals and the development of strong support systems are just as important as new technologies. As CDTs become more complex, we need organized ways to build, test, and use them safely and fairly. With both innovation and teamwork, the future of cancer care using DTs looks bright.

13.7 Case studies and real-world implementations

CDTs have rapidly progressed from theoretical models to practical tools that are already enhancing cancer care. Here are some real-world examples showing how CDTs are making a difference in clinics today:

13.7.1 Prostate cancer pathology

AI-powered CDT systems like Paige Prostate and vPatho effectively function as "virtual pathologists." These tools analyze digital biopsy slides more quickly and with high accuracy. In one study, using Paige alongside human pathologists increased the detection of small or early-stage tumors from around 74% to nearly 90% without sacrificing specificity (Eminaga et al., 2023). Other systems have achieved strong agreement with expert grading of tumor severity and slashed review times by nearly 50%–65% (Eminaga et al., 2023; Jemal et al., 2007). Large-scale testing of over 2600 prostate biopsy images demonstrated that AI-assisted screening could significantly speed up diagnosis while maintaining or improving accuracy (Eminaga et al., 2023).

13.7.2 Dynamic prostate tumor growth modeling

Beyond slide analysis, researchers are building full-scale DTs of prostate tumors. One such project uses patient MRI scans and PSA test results to create personalized tumor growth models. These simulations enable doctors to explore different treatment timelines, such as surgery, radiation, or active surveillance, before applying them in practice. This helps in fine-tuning treatment schedules and improving long-term monitoring strategies.

13.7.3 Oncology clinic optimization

DTaaS are already being used to optimize cancer clinic operations. These systems model patient flow, staff assignments, and treatment schedules, helping hospitals improve logistics and reduce wait times (Pandey et al., 2024). Early pilots indicate that DTaaS can significantly enhance appointment planning, resource allocation, and even clinical trial recruitment.

13.7.4 Head and neck cancer: DITTO platform

The DITTO project offers an interactive, patient-specific DT platform for head and neck cancer. Using advanced AI and 3D visualization tools, DITTO allows clinicians to simulate various treatment scenarios, including surgery, radiation, or chemotherapy, and immediately see expected outcomes and toxicities (Wentzel et al., 2024). Doctors testing DITTO report that the clear visual presentations help build trust and confidence in making treatment plans.

13.7.5 Precision radiotherapy for brain tumors

In cases like glioblastoma or high-grade gliomas, CDTs help tailor radiotherapy plans by integrating tumor geometry, genetic mutations, and anatomy. One study utilizing DTs to model tumor growth and treatment response reported that it could delay recurrence by about a week and reduce radiation exposure to healthy tissue while maintaining tumor control (Chaudhuri et al., 2023).

13.7.6 Integrated multimodal CDTs

Some advanced systems combine multiple types of patient data, such as biopsy images, MRI scans, genetic sequencing, and treatment schedules, to inform cancer care more comprehensively. These integrated platforms have demonstrated real-world benefits in prostate cancer, reducing repeat biopsies and lab costs by 44%–65%, all while preserving diagnostic accuracy (Jemal et al., 2007; Elakkiya and Anand, 2023).

13.8 Conclusion

CDT technology marks a major advancement in how cancer is detected, treated, and monitored. It offers a new way of delivering personalized care by using digital models that can predict disease behavior and simulate treatment outcomes. As we have seen throughout this chapter, CDTs have gone far beyond just an idea; they are beginning to play real roles in clinical and research environments. In the introduction, we learned how CDTs act as digital replicas of cancer patients, capturing their biological, clinical, and behavioral data to support better treatment decisions. The goal is to improve outcomes by predicting how a specific tumor will respond to a given therapy or how a patient's condition may change over time.

In the **early detection and diagnosis** section, we saw that CDTs can identify cancer signs earlier by combining imaging, pathology, and genomics data. This helps doctors make faster and more accurate diagnoses, even in complex cases. For example, AI-powered tools in prostate cancer pathology now help spot tumors that might otherwise be missed.

When it comes to **treatment planning and personalization**, CDTs allow doctors to try out different treatment plans virtually before selecting the best one for the patient. This is particularly helpful in complex cancers like glioblastoma or head and neck tumors, where every decision can significantly impact the quality of life.

In **monitoring and prognosis**, CDTs can simulate the likely progress of a patient's disease over time, predicting treatment side effects or possible relapses. This helps doctors adjust treatments early, avoiding unnecessary risks and improving long-term results.

We also explored how CDTs are becoming useful in **drug discovery and clinical trials**, where they help researchers simulate drug effects, select patients for trials, and reduce the time and cost needed to develop new medicines. These benefits are crucial in a field where every minute counts.

However, this technology still faces **challenges and limitations**, such as ensuring data privacy, handling the high cost of implementation, and making sure the models are accurate and fair for all patients. Doctors also need more training to use these tools, and clear regulations are still being developed to guide their use.

Looking at the **future directions**, we highlighted promising trends like combining CDTs with genomics and proteomics for deeper biological modeling. Federated learning methods offer better data protection while improving performance, and cloud-based platforms can make

CDTs accessible to more hospitals. Cross-disciplinary collaboration among doctors, data scientists, and engineers is essential to keeping these models relevant and safe.

In the **case studies and real-world implementations**, we saw that CDTs are already improving cancer care. From tools like Paige and vPatho in pathology to the DITTO platform for head and neck cancer and radiotherapy planning in brain tumors, these examples show that CDTs are having a real impact today.

References

American Cancer Society, 2023. Chemotherapy side effects. https://www.cancer.org/treatment/treatments-and-side-effects/treatment-types/chemotherapy/side-effects.html.

Axios, 2024. Why we still diagnose most cancers too late. https://www.axios.com/newsletters/axios-future-of-health-care-d91d3080-8c17-11ef-a500-57b0c1abf8bb.

Bordukova, M., et al., 2024. Generative artificial intelligence empowers digital twins in drug discovery and clinical trials. Expert Opin Drug Discov. 19 (1), 33–42.

Bruynseels, K., et al., 2018. Ethical implications of digital twins. Front Genet. 9. doi:10.3389/fgene.2018.00031.

Chaudhuri, A., et al., 2023. Predictive digital twin for radiotherapy. arXiv.

Choi, H.R., et al., 2023. Review of digital twin technology for cancer prediction. J. Cancer Res. Clin. Oncol. 149 (5). doi:10.1007/s00432-023-04607-x.

Collins, F.S., Varmus, H., 2015. A new initiative on precision medicine. NEJM 372 (9), 793–795. https://pubmed.ncbi.nlm.nih.gov/25635347.

Corral-Acero, J., et al., 2020. Digital twin in precision cardiology. Eur Heart J. 41 (48), 4556–4564. Available from: https://pubmed.ncbi.nlm.nih.gov/36636729. doi:10.1093/eurheartj/ehaa159.

Elakkiya, R., Anand, M., 2023. Advances in cancer detection using ML. Comput Biol. Med., 151. doi:10.1016/j.compbiomed.2023.106407.

Eminaga, O., et al., 2023. AI as digital twin of pathologist. arXiv.

Jemal, A., et al., 2007. Recent trends in prostate cancer. JCO 25 (27), 4211–4216. doi:10.1200/JCO.2006.06.5946.

Kirubarajan, A., Vali, R., 2023. Advancing precision oncology with digital and virtual twins: a scoping review. Cancers. https://pubmed.ncbi.nlm.nih.gov/39594772.

Krittanawong, C., et al., 2023. Digital Twin in Healthcare: Recent Updates and Challenges. Digital Health. https://pubmed.ncbi.nlm.nih.gov/36636729.

Lee, J.H., Park, J.W., 2023. Digital health and AI in oncology. Oncol. Rep. 40 (3). doi:10.3892/or.2023.8597.

Lee, S.H., Kim, Y.H., 2023a. Real-time monitoring for cancer using digital twins. Bioinform. Adv. 3 (1). doi:10.1093/bioadv/vbac024.

Lee, S.H., Kim, Y.H., 2023b. Real-time monitoring and personalized treatment. Bioinform. Adv. doi:10.1093/bioadv/vbac024.

MDPI, 2023a. Advancing precision oncology with digital twins. Cancers 16 (22), 3817. doi:10.3390/cancers16223817.

MDPI, 2023b. Medical digital twin review. J. Clin. Med. 14 (2), 324. doi:10.3390/jcm14020324.

Nguyen, T.H., Kim, J.W., 2022. Artificial intelligence and digital twins in healthcare. J. Healthc. Eng. doi:10.1155/2022/8828392.

Pandey, H., et al., 2024. Digital twin ecosystem for clinical operations. arXiv.

PubMed, 2023. Verifiable cancer digital twins. Front. Physiol. doi:10.3389/fphys.2023.847239.

ScienceDirect, 2023. Digital Twins in Oncology. ESMO Real World Data. doi:10.1016/j.esmrwd.2023.04.001.

Springer, 2023. Digital twins in oncology. J. Cancer Res. Clin. Oncol. doi:10.1007/s00432-023-04633-1.

Sung, H., et al., 2021. Global cancer statistics 2021. CA Cancer J. Clin. doi:10.3322/caac.21660.

The Guardian, 2024. Inequalities in cancer diagnosis among ethnic minorities in England. https://www.theguardian.com/inequality/2024/apr/24/ethnic-minorities-in-england-need-more-gp-visits-before-cancer-diagnosis.
The Times, 2024. UK early cancer detection goals and current performance. https://www.thetimes.co.uk/article/uk-early-cancer-detection-king-charles-royal-news-h2nwhd5zx.
Wentzel, A., et al., 2024. DITTO: a visual digital twin for cancer. arXiv.

CHAPTER 14

Selected applications of AI-based digital twins for industry 4.0/5.0

Izabela Rojek and Dariusz Mikołajewski
Faculty of Computer Science, Kazimierz Wielki University, Bydgoszcz, Poland

14.1 Introduction

Artificial intelligence (AI)-powered digital twins (DTs) for Industry 4.0/5.0 integrate physical systems with virtual models to improve decision-making and process optimization in smart manufacturing. DTs are created by collecting real-time data from sensors embedded in physical assets, which are then used to create a dynamic, virtual replica of the system. AI algorithms process and analyze this data to predict behavior, identify potential failures, and suggest optimizations, improving operational efficiency (Rojek et al., 2022; Davila-Gonzalez and Martin, 2024; Lim et al., 2020). Advanced machine learning (ML) models enable DTs to evolve and adapt by learning from new inputs over time, increasing their predictive accuracy. Edge, cloud, and network computing architectures are used to ensure rapid data exchange and processing, minimizing latency in real-time decision-making. Integration of Internet of Things (IoT) devices enhances the ability of DTs to continuously monitor and adapt industrial operations. Industry 5.0 integrates human-centric considerations by enabling collaboration between human operators and AI systems in a DT environment, ensuring that technology complements rather than replaces human expertise (Wang et al., 2024). AI-based DTs help achieve more efficient, adaptive, and resilient industrial processes by combining human intelligence with advanced automation, leading to better resource allocation (Sharma et al., 2022). The ability to simulate different production scenarios allows manufacturers to test and optimize processes before making changes to real-world operations, reducing risk and costs. DTs also support predictive maintenance by identifying potential equipment failures in advance, preventing costly downtime. Cyber-physical security measures must be incorporated into DTs to ensure data integrity and prevent cyber threats that could disrupt industrial operations. The scalability of AI-based DTs enables their application in various industrial domains, from automotive to pharmaceutical manufacturing. Continuous improvement of DTs through reinforcement learning can further enhance process optimization by automatically adjusting production parameters. Collaboration between

Artificial Intelligence, Machine Learning and Blockchain in Digital Twin Computing.
https://doi.org/10.1016/B978-0-443-43914-8.00019-4

multiple DTs in a smart factory ecosystem enables synchronized decision-making and increased overall efficiency (Ngadi et al., 2023). Future advances in quantum computing and generative AI could further accelerate DT capabilities, enabling more complex simulations and deeper insights into industrial processes.

This paper aims to explore the diverse applications of AI-based DTs in Industry 4.0 and 5.0, highlighting their role in enhancing efficiency, automation, and decision-making within smart manufacturing and industrial ecosystems. It examines key use cases such as predictive maintenance, process optimization, and real-time monitoring, showing how AI-based DTs improve operational resilience and sustainability. Furthermore, the paper discusses future trends and challenges, providing insights into the evolving landscape of AI-based DTs in next-generation industries.

14.2 Genesis, former and current approaches to AI-based DTs for the purposes of industry 4.0/5.0

The concept of DTs originated in the early 2000s as a virtual representation of physical assets, processes, or systems to improve operational efficiency and decision-making. Industry 4.0, characterized by automation, IoT, and cyber-physical systems (CPS), has accelerated the adoption of DTs in manufacturing and industrial applications. Early DTs relied primarily on static models and simulation-based approaches to provide predictive insights but lacked real-time adaptability. The integration of AI and ML has greatly improved DTs, enabling self-learning, adaptation, and real-time decision-making (Guittoum et al., 2023). The rise of big data, edge computing, and cloud platforms has provided the necessary infrastructure to collect, store, and process massive amounts of sensor data for AI-based DTs. AI-based DTs leverage deep learning (DL) algorithms to detect patterns, optimize production workflows, and predict failures with greater accuracy than traditional systems. The combination of natural language processing (NLP) and AI-based DTs has enabled human-like interactions in diagnostics, troubleshooting, and predictive maintenance (Robles et al., 2023). Reinforcement learning techniques further enhance DTs, enabling them to simulate and optimize complex industrial processes without human intervention. Industry 5.0, which focuses on human-centric, sustainable, and resilient industrial systems, is driving DTs toward more collaborative AI-human integration. AI-based DTs in Industry 5.0 emphasize personalization, adaptive manufacturing, and ethical AI, ensuring sustainability and inclusiveness in industrial ecosystems (Rojek and Studziński, 2014). Autonomous AI agents in DTs enable self-healing manufacturing processes, reducing downtime and improving resource utilization. Integrating generative AI with DTs enables automatic design optimization, reducing prototyping costs and accelerating product innovation. AI-based DTs facilitate the implementation of a digital thread, creating a data flow from start to finish throughout the product lifecycle for seamless traceability. The advent of quantum computers has the potential to revolutionize

AI-based DTs by exponentially increasing computational efficiency in simulations. As AI-based DTs evolve, they become essential to achieving smart, sustainable, and resilient industrial ecosystems in the era of Industry 4.0/5.0.

Previous approaches to AI-based DTs relied heavily on rules-based systems and physics-based simulations for predictive maintenance and process optimization. Traditional DTs were static models that were updated periodically rather than in real time, leading to slower decision-making and reduced adaptability. Early implementations focused on analyzing historical data rather than leveraging live sensor data, which limited their predictive accuracy. Basic automation techniques were used for monitoring and control but lacked advanced AI capabilities for self-learning and optimization. The dominant operational approach was local processing, requiring significant infrastructure investment and limiting scalability. Human intervention was required to update models and make decisions, making DTs less autonomous. Previous DTs were designed primarily for asset performance management and were not deeply integrated with broader industrial ecosystems. Current approaches leverage real-time IoT data streams, cloud computing, and edge computing to increase responsiveness and scalability. AI-based DTs now utilize ML and DL for real-time anomaly detection, predictive analytics, and autonomous decision-making. Federated learning and decentralized AI models enable DTs to continuously learn and improve in distributed industrial environments. Hybrid physics-AI models combine expert knowledge with AI-based analytics to improve simulation accuracy and predictive maintenance. The integration of digital threads enables seamless data flow throughout the product lifecycle, increasing operational visibility. AI-based DTs now support adaptive manufacturing by dynamically optimizing workflows based on changing conditions. Collaborative AI systems in Industry 5.0 enable DTs to collaborate with humans, supporting personalized and sustainable production (Quattrociocchi et al., 2023).

14.3 Diversity of devices and systems used within AI-based DTs for the purposes of industry 4.0/5.0

AI-powered DTs in Industry 4.0/5.0 integrate disparate devices and systems to create real-time, data-driven virtual replicas of physical assets. IoT sensors, including temperature, pressure, and vibration sensors, continuously collect operational data from machines and industrial environments. Edge computing devices process data locally, reducing latency and enabling rapid decision-making without overwhelming centralized servers. Cloud computing platforms store and analyze massive data sets, enabling scalable AI models for predictive maintenance and process optimization (Lin et al., 2025). ML algorithms embedded in DTs detect patterns, predict failures, and dynamically optimize production workflows. CPS connect physical machines with AI-powered digital simulations to enhance automation and remote control. Augmented reality (AR) and virtual reality (VR) interfaces enable engineers to visualize and interact with DTs for immersive problem-solving and training. DTs integrate with enterprise resource planning (ERP) and manufacturing execution systems (MES) to align production with business goals. 5G and advanced wireless technologies enable seamless connectivity between smart devices, facilitating real-time updates. Blockchain technology is increasingly being used in DT ecosystems to securely share and track data. Robots and autonomous systems leverage insights from DTs to optimize movement, efficiency, and safety in smart factories. AI-driven human–machine interfaces (HMIs) and dashboards provide intuitive control and monitoring of processes operated by DTs. AI cognitive models simulate human decision-making, improving the ability of DTs to solve problems and autonomously adjust processes. Built-in AI and neuromorphic computing accelerate on-device processing, making DTs more responsive.

14.4 Architecure of AI-based DTs in industry 4.0/5.0 dependent on application

The architecture of AI-based DTs in Industry 4.0 and 5.0 varies depending on the application (Kaklis et al., 2023; Lin et al., 2025; Rojek et al., 2024; Tang et al., 2023), but generally consists of several interconnected layers:

1. Perception layer: Includes IoT devices, sensors, and actuators that collect real-time data from the physical system
2. Data collection and processing layer: Edge and cloud computing platforms preprocess, filter, and structure the raw data
3. Communication layer: Fast and secure networks (5G, IIoT protocols) transmit data between the physical system and the DT
4. Storage layer: Cloud and on-premises databases store historical and real-time data for analysis
5. AI and analytics layer: ML, DL, and statistical models extract insights and predict system behavior.
6. Simulation layer: physics-based models and AI-based simulations virtually replicate real-world processes.
7. Decision-making layer: AI algorithms optimize operations, detect anomalies, and support human decision-making.
8. Interaction layer: HMIs, AR/VR tools, and dashboards allow users to interact with the DT.
9. Security layer: Blockchain, encryption, and cybersecurity mechanisms protect data integrity and prevent cyber threats.

Fig. 14.1 shows an example of the architecture of AI-based DTs in Industry 4.0 (Rojek et al., 2024).

DTs connect with ERP, MES, and Supervisory Control and Data Acquisition (SCADA) and are used to ensure smooth industrial operations (Fig. 14.2).

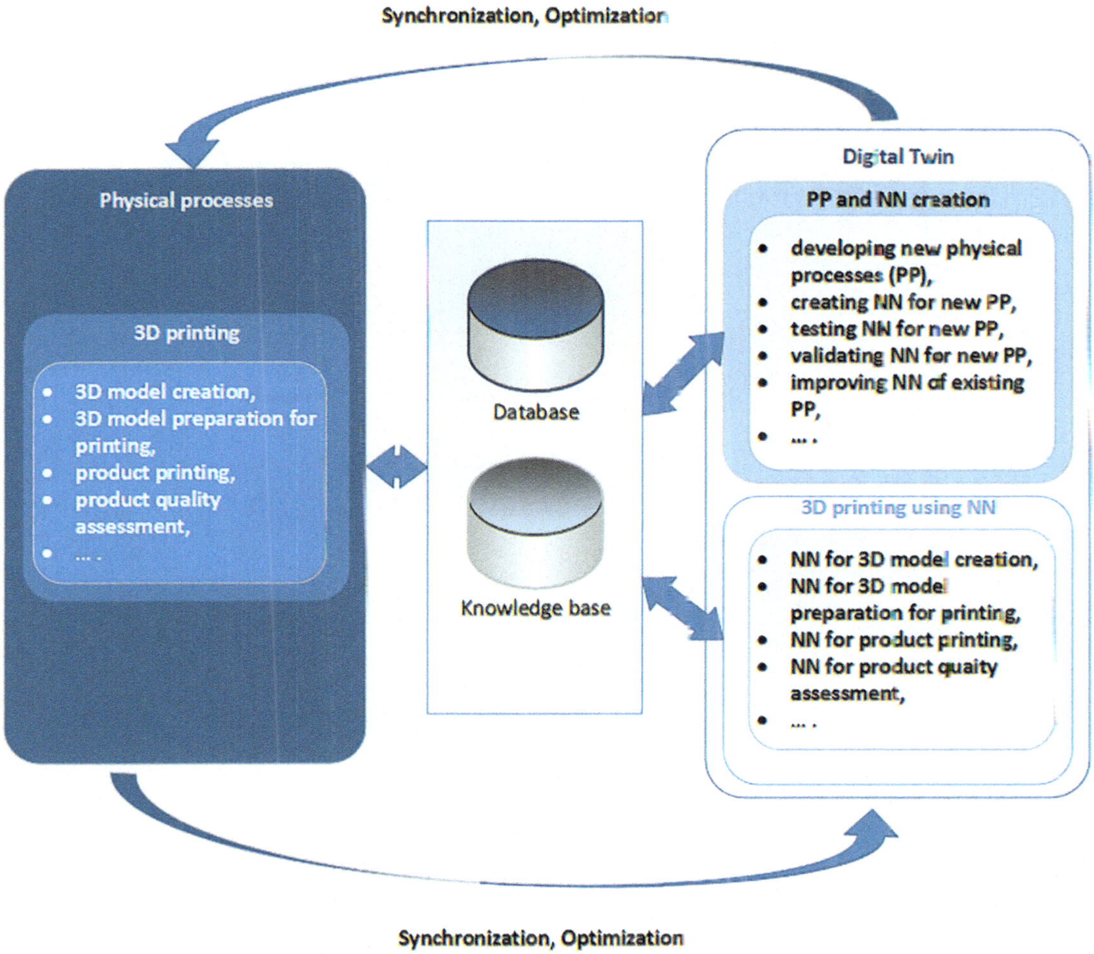

Fig. 14.1 Optimization of physical processes using DT (example of 3D printing processes) (*PP*, physical process; *NN*, neural network). From Rojek, I., Marciniak, T., Mikołajewski, D., 2024. Digital twins in 3D printing processes using artificial intelligence. Electronics. 2079-9292. 13 (17), 3550. https://doi.org/10.3390/electronics13173550.

14.5 Current and future applications of AI-based DTs

Current AI-based DT applications include predictive maintenance, where AI analyzes sensor data to predict equipment failures and reduce downtime. Smart manufacturing uses AI-based DT to optimize production lines in real time, adjusting workflows to increase efficiency and save costs (Tao et al., 2018). Supply chain optimization uses DT through logistics simulation, demand forecasting, and dynamic rerouting to mitigate disruptions. The aerospace and automotive industries are implementing DT for virtual prototyping, crash testing, and real-time vehicle performance monitoring. The energy and utilities sectors are

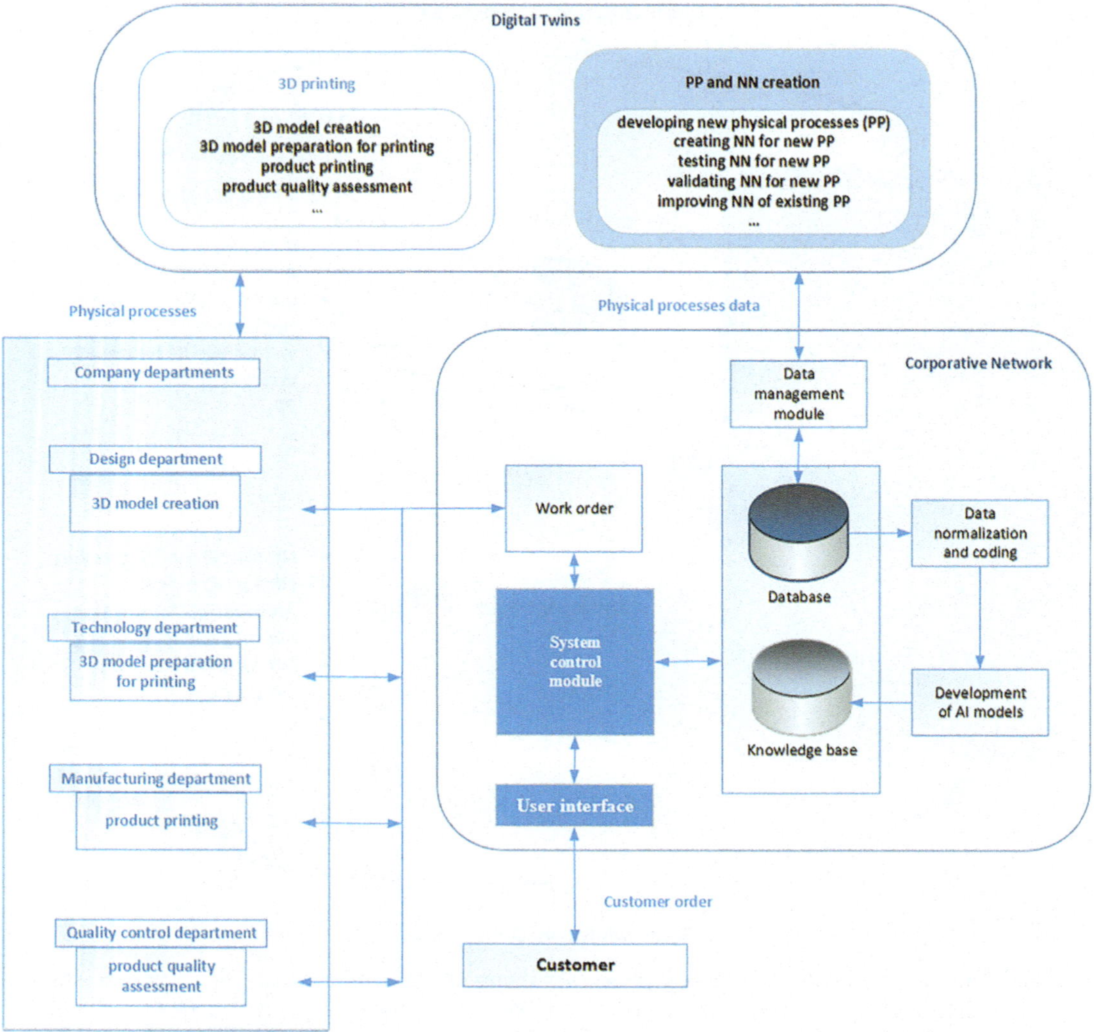

Fig. 14.2 DT system architecture based on artificial intelligence (example of 3D printing processes). From Rojek, I., Marciniak, T., Mikołajewski, D., 2024. Digital twins in 3D printing processes using artificial intelligence. Electronics. 2079-9292. 13 (17), 3550. https://doi.org/10.3390/electronics13173550.

using DT to optimize power grids, forecast renewable energy, and reduce carbon footprints. Healthcare applications include patient-specific DTs for personalized medicine, drug testing, and surgical planning. Smart cities are integrating DT for traffic management, infrastructure maintenance, and environmental monitoring to improve urban living conditions. Retail and e-commerce are using AI-based DTs to optimize inventory, personalize customer experiences, and predict purchasing trends. Agriculture and food production are using DTs to optimize yields, automate agricultural processes, and reduce resource waste. Future applications will include human-AI collaboration, where DTs interact directly with workers via AR, VR, and brain–computer interfaces (BCIs). Fully autonomous factories will rely on AI-based DTs to self-optimize production, maintenance, and logistics with minimal human oversight (Rojek and Jagodziński, 2012). AI-based climate modeling will use DTs to predict and mitigate the effects of climate change, optimizing sustainability initiatives. Personalized medicine will rely on DTs replicating entire human bodies at the molecular level for precise diagnostics and treatment. Space exploration will use DTs to simulate extraterrestrial environments, optimize robotic missions, and manage extraterrestrial colonies. Sentient AI DTs could eventually develop self-learning capabilities that allow them to autonomously manage industrial ecosystems with ethical and sustainability priorities (Vilas-Boas et al., 2023).

14.6 Implications and influence

14.6.1 Scientific and technological implications and influence of AI-based DTs in industry 4.0/5.0

AI-powered DTs process massive amounts of data to provide real-time insights, enabling industries to make proactive and informed decisions. DTs facilitate human-centric automation, where AI supports human decision-making and process optimization rather than replacing them (Huang et al., 2021). They help industries optimize energy consumption and resource allocation, promoting sustainability and reducing carbon footprints (Rocha-Jácome et al., 2022; Rojek and Dostatni, 2020). By simulating supply chain networks, DTs can predict disruptions, optimize logistics, and increase the resilience of manufacturing ecosystems. Industry 5.0 emphasizes mass customization, and AI-powered DTs enable adaptive manufacturing by tailoring products to specific customer needs. The integration of DTs introduces new vulnerabilities, requiring advanced AI-powered cybersecurity solutions to protect industrial systems from cyber threats. AI-based simulations in DTs allow companies to test new materials, processes, and designs virtually before physical implementation, reducing time and cost. In the future, AI-based DTs could enable fully autonomous smart factories, where machines optimize, repair, and coordinate themselves without human intervention (Drobnyi et al., 2023).

14.6.2 Economic implications and influence of AI-based DTs in industry 4.0/5.0

AI-based DTs minimize operational costs by optimizing production, reducing material waste, and improving energy efficiency in industrial processes. By simulating and improving production workflows, DTs increase automation, reduce downtime, and enhance overall industrial productivity. AI-based DTs enable better management of industrial assets, extending equipment life and maximizing return on investment (ROI). Companies can use DTs to offer predictive maintenance as a service or DT-based consulting, opening new revenue streams. Additionally, companies using AI-based DTs can quickly adapt to market changes, improve product quality, and gain a competitive advantage through data-driven decision-making. DTs allow companies to test scenarios and predict financial outcomes, reducing the risk of capital investments and new product development. AI-based DTs optimize logistics, forecast demand fluctuations, and mitigate supply chain disruptions, leading to cost savings and improved delivery efficiency. Industry 5.0 emphasizes personalized production, and DTs facilitate cost-effective mass customization, increasing customer satisfaction and profit margins. The integration of AI and DTs creates demand for skilled workers in AI, data analysis, and DT management, while automating repetitive tasks. AI-based DTs contribute to long-term economic growth by promoting resource efficiency, reducing industrial waste, and supporting sustainable manufacturing practices (Jiangang et al., 2024).

14.6.3 Societal implications and influence of AI-based DTs in industry 4.0/5.0

AI-powered DTs are changing job roles by automating routine tasks, requiring workers to upskill in AI, data analysis, and systems management. DTs simulate hazardous environments, enabling industries to predict risks and implement safety measures, reducing workplace accidents. Industry 5.0 leverages DTs for mass personalization, providing consumers with customized products and services at competitive prices. As DTs rely on AI-powered decisions, concerns about algorithmic bias, transparency, and ethical implications in industrial decision-making have arisen. While automation may replace some jobs, new roles are emerging in AI maintenance, DT development, and human-AI collaboration. AI-powered DTs increase energy efficiency, reduce industrial waste, and contribute to more sustainable manufacturing practices. DTs are used in city planning, traffic flow optimization, infrastructure management, and environmental monitoring for smarter urban living. DTs outside of industry are simulating human organs and procedures, improving personalized medicine and revolutionizing healthcare diagnostics (Chen et al., 2024; Rojek et al., 2023). However, the implementation of DT technology could widen the gap between technologically advanced and underdeveloped regions, deepening economic disparities. The increased use of AI-based DTs raises concerns about data security, intellectual property, and the need for stricter regulations to protect individuals and businesses.

14.7 Summary and discussion

Based on the state-of-the-art analysis, we summarize and compare traditional DT processes and AI-based DT processes for Industry 4.0/5.0 in Table 14.1.

We also compared, in Table 14.2, the different applications of AI-based DTS in Industry 4.0 and Industry 5.0.

Table 14.1 Comparison table of traditional DT processes and AI-based DT processes for Industry 4.0/5.0

Feature	Traditional DTs	DT-based DTs
Data processing	Rule-based and physics-based models	AI-driven, self-learning, adaptive
Data integration	Based on static, structured data from limited sources	Integrates real-time IoT, edge, and cloud data
Decision-making	Human intervention for updates and analysis	Autonomous decision-making using ML and DL
Real-time adaptation	Limited, cyclic updates	Continuous real-time updates and optimization
Automation	Low automation, manual adjustment required	High automation with autonomous process control
Failure detection	Detects issues after they occur	Predicts and prevents failures before they happen
Predictive analytics	Basic predictive maintenance	Advanced predictive and prescriptive analytics
Scalability	Difficult to scale across complex industrial networks	Easily scalable with cloud and edge computing
Interactivity	Operates as a passive simulation model	Interactive, can collaborate with humans via NLP, AR, and VR
Human collaboration	Requires expert supervision for insights	Works alongside humans using cognitive AI and NLP
Operational efficiency	Improves efficiency, but requires frequent manual oversight	Maximizes efficiency by dynamically optimizing processes
Customization	Generic models requiring manual adjustments	Personalized and adaptive learning models
Sustainability	Focuses on operational improvements	Prioritizes energy efficiency and circular economy principles

14.7.1 Advantages of described approaches

The proposed novel approaches to AI-based DTs for Industry 4.0/5.0 offer numerous advantages across various industrial applications. First, they enhance real-time decision-making by integrating AI-driven predictive analytics, enabling proactive responses to operational challenges. The use of advanced ML models allows DTs to continuously improve by learning from new data, increasing accuracy in fault detection and process optimization. Cloud-edge hybrid computing architectures ensure low-latency processing, making DTs more responsive in time-sensitive industrial environments. The integration of IoT devices enables seamless data collection and synchronization between physical and virtual systems, improving operational efficiency. AI-driven DTs support predictive maintenance by

Table 14.2 Comparison table of different applications of AI-based DTs in Industry 4.0 and Industry 5.0.

Application	AI-based DTs in industry 4.0	AI-based DTs in industry 5.0
Manufacturing	Automates production lines, optimizes efficiency, predicts maintenance needs.	Enhances human-AI collaboration
Supply chain	Real-time tracking, logistics optimization, and demand forecasting	Self-learning supply chains that autonomously adapt to global disruptions and sustainability goals.
Predictive maintenance	Based on IoT data and ML models to predict failures and reduce downtime.	AI-based self-healing systems autonomously adjusting to prevent breakdowns
Energy management	Optimizes energy consumption and grid performance using predictive analytics.	Decentralized AI-driven energy grids with "sustainability-first" strategies
Construction and infrastructure	AI-based simulations for structured design and predictive maintenance.	Self-adaptive smart buildings with AI-driven sustainability and resilience features
Smart cities, smart territories	AI-based urban planning, infrastructure monitoring, traffic optimization	Fully autonomous urban ecosystem adapting to human behavior and environmental changes.
Retail and E-commerce	AI-based demand forecasting and inventory management	Personalized AI shopping assistants adapting to customer behavior in real-time
Sustainability	Reduces waste and optimizes resource use within production processes.	AI-based circular economy models ensuring zero-waste and carbon-neutral operations
Human-machine interaction	AI-based interfaces for AR/VR based training and remote monitoring	Possibility of BCI-enabling seamless human-DT collaboration
Ethical and social impact	AI enhances efficiency but requires human oversight for responsible decisions.	AI-based DTs prioritizing ethical decision-making, inclusion, and the well-being of workers.

identifying equipment failures before they occur, reducing downtime and maintenance costs. In smart manufacturing, DTs optimize production scheduling by simulating various scenarios, leading to better resource allocation and increased productivity. Industry 5.0-oriented DTs emphasize human-AI collaboration, enhancing worker safety and productivity by providing AI-assisted decision support. The implementation of cyber-physical security measures ensures data integrity and protection against cyber threats, making DTs more reliable. AI-based DTs facilitate mass customization by dynamically adjusting production parameters to meet individualized consumer demands. The scalability of these approaches allows for integration across multiple industries, including automotive, aerospace, pharmaceuticals, and energy sectors. Multiagent DT systems enable interconnected decision-making, improving supply chain management and logistics. The ability to simulate and optimize energy consumption in industrial processes contributes to sustainability and cost savings. AI-enhanced DTs streamline compliance with industry regulations by automatically monitoring and adjusting processes to meet safety and environmental standards. The combination of reinforcement learning and generative AI enables the creation of highly adaptive DTs capable of responding to unforeseen disruptions. The possible integration of quantum computing (e.g., Polish Quantum Keys Generator since March 2025) in AI-based DTs has the potential to accelerate complex simulations, unlocking new possibilities for industrial process innovation.

14.7.2 Limitations

Despite significant progress, previous and current approaches to AI-based DTs for Industry 4.0/5.0 still face several limitations. First, the high computational requirements of AI-based DTs pose a challenge for real-time processing, especially in resource-constrained environments. Many existing DT implementations struggle with data silos, which make seamless integration across industrial systems difficult. Reliance on large volumes of real-time data raises concerns about data security and privacy, especially when processing sensitive industrial information. Interoperability remains a major challenge, as different industries and manufacturers use different standards, preventing seamless communication between DTs. The high cost of developing and deploying AI-based DTs limits accessibility, especially for small and medium-sized enterprises (SMEs). Current AI models are often not explainable, making it difficult for human operators to trust and interpret the recommendations generated by DTs. Many DTs are heavily dependent on cloud computing, which can cause latency and dependency on stable internet connections. The complexity of integrating AI-based DTs into existing industrial workflows often requires extensive reconfiguration and retraining of personnel. Limited generalizability means that DTs optimized for one industrial process may not be easily adapted to others without significant retraining. While predictive maintenance is a key application, false alarms and inaccurate failure predictions can still occur, leading to unnecessary interventions or missed issues. Scalability of current DT frameworks remains a challenge, especially in large industrial ecosystems with many interactive DTs. AI models used in DTs require continuous updates and retraining, which can be time-consuming and computationally expensive. The lack of standardized validation methods for AI-based DTs makes it difficult to assess their reliability and performance across industries. In Industry 5.0 applications, the human-AI collaboration aspect is still underdeveloped, as most DTs focus primarily on automation rather than improving human decision-making. Finally, current approaches often struggle to effectively integrate sustainability indicators, which limits their ability to optimize energy consumption and reduce the environmental impact of industrial processes (Hevesli et al., 2024; Wang et al., 2023).

14.7.3 Directions for further studies

Future research on AI-based DTs for Industry 4.0/5.0 should focus on increasing computational efficiency using advanced AI techniques such as federated learning and neuromorphic computing. Developing standardized interoperability frameworks and protocols will enable seamless integration across industrial systems and vendors. Further research is needed on privacy-preserving AI methods, such as differential privacy and secure multiparty computation, to protect sensitive industrial data (Zeulin et al., 2022). Exploring hybrid edge-of-the-cloud computing solutions can optimize real-time processing while reducing dependence on centralized cloud infrastructure. Developing self-learning DTs using continuous and reinforcement learning will enable adaptive optimization without the need for frequent retraining. Extending DT capabilities to support multiagent collaboration will improve supply chain coordination and distributed decision-making. Improved explainability and transparency in AI models will increase trust and usability for human operators, especially in Industry 5.0 applications (Hevesli et al., 2024; Wang et al., 2023). Research into integrating AI-driven DTs with digital ethics frameworks can help address issues related to bias, fairness, and accountability. Exploring the use of generative AI to generate synthetic data can improve training and validation of DTs in cases where real-world data is limited. Developing robust validation and benchmarking methods will ensure the reliability and accuracy of AI-driven DTs across industries. Research into the application of quantum computing to DT simulations can accelerate complex optimizations and enhance problem-solving capabilities. Incorporating sustainability-focused AI models will allow DTs to optimize energy efficiency, waste reduction, and environmental impact (Chaber et al., 2022; Zeulin et al., 2022). Improving human-AI collaboration in DTs through NLP and AR interfaces will enhance decision-making and human performance (Adel, 2022; Krupas et al., 2024). Future research should explore blockchain integration to provide secure, transparent, and tamper-proof data management in DT ecosystems. Finally, improving the scalability of AI-based DTs through modular architectures and lightweight AI models will support broader adoption across industry sectors (Jwo et al., 2022).

14.8 Future approaches to AI-based DTs for the purposes of industry 4.0/5.0

Future AI-based DTs will leverage quantum computing to perform ultra-complex simulations and optimizations at unprecedented speeds. The deployment of self-evolving AI models will enable DTs to autonomously improve their predictions and operations without human intervention. Neuromorphic computing will enhance real-time decision-making by mimicking the performance of the human brain in processing massive amounts of sensor data. Edge AI-based DTs will minimize latency by processing data closer to the source, enabling real-time autonomous adjustments in industrial processes. 5G and 6G networks will provide ultra-low latency communications, enabling AI-based DTs to operate seamlessly across vast industrial ecosystems. Explainable AI (XAI) will become a key objective, bringing transparency and trust to decision-making processes within a collaborative human-AI framework. AI-driven generative design will enable DTs to automatically create and refine optimized industrial components with minimal human intervention. Blockchain technology will enhance the security and integrity of data in DTs, providing reliable and tamper-proof industrial records. Multiagent AI systems will enable multiple DTs to collaborate autonomously, dynamically optimizing entire industrial supply chains. Bio-inspired AI algorithms will power self-healing DTs that adapt and correct industrial processes in real time. Haptic feedback and AR/VR integration will enable immersive interaction with DTs, enhancing human decision-making in Industry 5.0. Sustainable AI models will focus on energy-efficient computing, reducing the carbon footprint of AI-based DT operations. Autonomous AI governance frameworks will govern DT operations to ensure ethical and responsible use of AI. Cognitive DTs will not only predict and optimize industrial processes but also interpret contextual human inputs for better collaboration. A circular economy based on AI DTs will revolutionize waste reduction and resource optimization, contributing to sustainable and regenerative industrial ecosystems.

Industry 6.0 will emphasize the seamless integration of human intelligence, AI, and bio-digital interfaces in AI-based DTs. AI-based DTs will evolve into sentient digital entities capable of self-awareness, reasoning, and ethical decision-making in industrial environments. Quantum-enhanced AI will enable DTs to simulate hypercomplex, multidimensional industrial processes with near-instantaneous optimization capabilities. BCIs will enable direct cognitive interaction between humans and DTs, revolutionizing industrial control and decision-making. Self-replicating AI models in DTs will autonomously generate and improve industrial plans, supporting hyperpersonalized and autonomous manufacturing. DT swarm intelligence will facilitate multiagent collaboration across global industries, dynamically optimizing supply chains in real time. Latency-free communication based on 6G and quantum networks will enable instantaneous data exchange for fully synchronized industrial ecosystems. AI-enhanced bio-DTs will combine biotechnology and AI, enabling industries to produce biomimetic materials and regenerative production systems. Full-cycle DTs of circular economies will autonomously monitor, recycle, and regenerate resources, completely eliminating industrial waste. AI-aware DTs will possess emotional and contextual intelligence, adapting industrial processes to human needs and environmental conditions. Autonomous ethical AI frameworks will ensure that DTs are aligned with sustainability, labor rights, and human-centered decision-making. Holographic and quantum-augmented DTs will create fully immersive, real-time industrial simulations for training, design, and process optimization purposes. Nano-scale DTs will revolutionize material science, enabling atomic-precision manufacturing of future industrial components. AI-driven DTs will not only optimize production but also predict and mitigate industrial risks before they occur, enabling a self-sufficient, hyperintelligent industrial landscape (Kaklis et al., 2023; Lin et al., 2025; Tang et al., 2023).

14.9 Conclusions

AI-powered DTs are transforming Industry 4.0 and 5.0 by enabling real-time monitoring, predictive maintenance, and process optimization. These intelligent systems increase operational efficiency, reduce downtime, and improve decision-making with data-driven insights. Integrating AI with DT enables advanced automation, minimizing human intervention while maximizing productivity and sustainability. Leveraging IoT, edge computing, and cloud technologies, DTs create connected industrial ecosystems with seamless data exchange. Despite their advantages, challenges such as data security, interoperability, and high implementation costs remain significant obstacles. Future advances in quantum computing, neuromorphic systems, and blockchain technologies could further enhance the capabilities of AI-powered DTs. As industries transition toward more autonomous and human-centric operations, DTs will play a key role in shaping the next generation of smart manufacturing. Ultimately, AI-powered DTs are key enablers of resilient, adaptive, and efficient industrial systems in the era of Industry 4.0 and 5.0.

References

Adel, A., 2022. Future of industry 5.0 in society: human-centric solutions, challenges and prospective research areas. J. Cloud Comput. 11 (1), 40.

Chaber, P., Domański, P.D., Dąbrowski, D., Ławryńczuk, M., Nebeluk, R., Plamowski, S., Zarzycki, K., 2022. Digital twins in the practice of high-energy physics experiments: a gas system for the multipurpose detector. Sensors 22 (2), 678.

Chen, J., Shi, Y., Yi, C., Du, H., Kang, J., Niyato, D., 2024. Generative-AI-driven human digital twin in IoT healthcare: a comprehensive survey. IEEE Internet Things J. 23274662. 11 (21), 34749–34773. Available from: http://ieeexplore.ieee.org/servlet/opac?punumber=6488907. doi:10.1109/JIOT.2024.3421918.

Davila-Gonzalez, S., Martin, S., 2024. Human digital twin in industry 5.0: a holistic approach to worker safety and well-being through advanced AI and emotional analytics. Sensors. 1424-8220. 24 (2), 655. doi:10.3390/s24020655.

Drobnyi, V., Hu, Z., Fathy, Y., Brilakis, I., 2023. Construction and maintenance of building geometric digital twins: state of the art review. Sensors 23 (9), 4382.

Guittoum, A., Aïssaoui, F., Bolle, S., Boyer, F., De Palma, N., 2023. Inferring threatening IoT dependencies using semantic digital twins toward collaborative IoT device management. In: Proceedings of the 38th ACM/SIGAPP Symposium on Applied Computing (SAC '23), Tallinn, Estonia. Association for Computing Machinery, New York, NY, USA , pp. 1732–1741. doi:10.1145/3555776.3578573.

Hevesli, M., Seid, A.M., Erbad, A., Abdallah, M., 2024. Task offloading optimization in digital twin assisted MEC-enabled air-ground IIoT 6G networks. IEEE Trans. Veh. Technol. 19399359. 73 (11), 17527–17542. Available from: http://ieeexplore.ieee.org/xpl/tocresult.jsp?isnumber=8039128&punumber=25. doi:10.1109/TVT.2024.3420876.

Huang, Z., Shen, Y., Li, J., Fey, M., Brecher, C., 2021. A survey on AI-driven digital twins in industry 4.0: smart manufacturing and advanced robotics. Sensors. 1424-8220. 21 (19), 6340. doi:10.3390/s21196340.

Jiangang, W., Lei, S., Ding, F., Jinli, L., Lingxia, H., Enming, M., 2024. A digital twin modeling and application for gear rack drilling rigs lifting system. Sci. Rep. 14 (1), 23711.

Jwo, J.S., Lee, C.H., S, C., Lin, C.S., 2022. Data twin-driven cyber-physical factory for smart manufacturing. Sensors 22 (8), 2821.

Kaklis, D., Varlamis, I., Giannakopoulos, G., Varelas, T.J., Spyropoulos, C.D., 2023. Enabling digital twins in the maritime sector through the lens of AI and industry 4.0. Int. J. Inf. Manag. Data Insights. 26670968. 3 (2). Available from: https://www.journals.elsevier.com/international-journal-of-information-management-data-insights. doi:10.1016/j.jjimei.2023.100178.

Krupas, M., Kajati, E., Liu, C., Zolotova, I., 2024. Towards a human-centric digital twin for human-machine collaboration . a review on enabling technologies and methods. Sensors 24 (7), 2232.

Lim, K.Y.H., Zheng, P., Chen, C.H., 2020. A state-of-the-art survey of digital twin: techniques, engineering product lifecycle management and business innovation perspectives. J. Intell. Manuf. 15728145. 31 (6), 1313–1337. Available from: www.kluweronline.com/issn/0956-5515/. doi:10.1007/s10845-019-01512-w.

Lin, Y.Z., Alhamadah, A., Ghimire, S., Redondo, M.W., Vidal Corona, D.R., Pacheco, J., Salehi, S., Satam, P., et al., 2025. Personalized Education with Generative AI and Digital Twins: VR, RAG, and Zero-Shot Sentiment Analysis for Industry 4.0 Workforce Development. (arXiv preprint arXiv:2502.14080).

Ngadi, H., Bounceur, A., Bezoui, M., Lahlou, L., Hammoudeh, M., Kara, N., Nana, L.T., 2023. Toward a digital twin IoT for the validation of AI algorithms in smart-city applications. In: Proceedings of the 6th International Conference on Machine Learning for Networking (MLN 2023), Paris, France, November 2023. HAL Archive: hal-04389064. pp. 108–117.

Quattrociocchi, A., Subroto, R.K., Oppedijk, W.M., Dragicevic, T., 2023. Energy efficiency optimization of a wastewater pumping station through IoT and AI: A real-world application of digital twins. In: IECON 2023 – 49th Annual Conference of the IEEE Industrial Electronics Society, Singapore, Singapore, 16 October 2023. IEEE. doi:10.1109/IECON51785.2023.10312592.

Robles, J., Martín, C., Díaz, M., 2023. OpenTwins: An open-source framework for the development of next-gen compositional digital twins. Comput. Ind. 152, 104007. doi:10.1016/j.compind.2023.104007.

Rocha-Jácome, C., Carvajal, R.G., Chavero, F.M., Guevara-Cabezas, E., Fort, E.H., 2022. Industry 4.0: a proposal of paradigm organization schemes from a systematic literature review. Sensors 22 (1), 35009609.

Rojek, I., Dostatni, E., 2020. Machine learning methods for optimal compatibility of materials in ecodesign. Bull. Pol. Acad. Sci. Tech. Sci. 23001917. 68 (2), 199–206. Available from: http://journals.pan.pl/dlibra/journal/95347. doi:10.24425/bpasts.2020.131848.

Rojek, I., Dostatni, E., Mikołajewski, D., Pawłowski, L., Wegrzyn-Wolska, K.M., 2022. Modern approach to sustainable production in the context of Industry 4.0. Bull. Pol. Acad. Sci. Tech. Sci. 70 (6), e143828.

Rojek, I., Jagodziński, M., 2012. Hybrid artificial intelligence system in constraint based scheduling of integrated manufacturing ERP systems. In: Lecture Notes in Computer Science (including subseries Lecture Notes in Artificial Intelligence and Lecture Notes in Bioinformatics), vol. 7209, Poland, pp. 229–240. 16113349. doi:10.1007/978-3-642-28931-6_22.

Rojek, I., Marciniak, T., Mikołajewski, D., 2024. Digital twins in 3D printing processes using artificial intelligence. Electronics. 2079-9292. 13 (17), 3550. doi:10.3390/electronics13173550.

Rojek, I., Mikołajewski, D., Dostatni, E., Kopowski, J., 2023. Specificity of 3D printing and AI-based optimization of medical devices using the example of a group of exoskeletons. Appl. Sci. 13 (2), 1060.

Rojek, I., Studziński, J., 2014. Comparison of different types of neuronal nets for failures location within water-supply networks. Eksploatacja I Niezawodnosc 15072711. 16 (1), 42–47. Available from: http://www.ein.org.pl/sites/default/files/2014-01-07.pdf.

Sharma, A., Kosasih, E., Zhang, J., Brintrup, A., Calinescu, A., 2022. Digital twins: state of the art theory and practice, challenges, and open research questions. J. Ind. Inf. Integr. 30, 100383.

Tang, Y.M., Kuo, W.T., Ka, C., Lee, C.K.M., 2023. Real-time mixed reality (MR) and artificial intelligence (AI) object recognition integration for digital twin in industry. Internet Things 23, 100753.

Tao, F., Cheng, J., Qi, Q., Zhang, M., Zhang, H., Sui, F., 2018. Digital twin-driven product design, manufacturing and service with big data. Int. J. Adv. Manuf. Technol. 0268-3768. 94 (9–12), 3563–3576. doi:10.1007/s00170-017-0233-1.

Vilas-Boas, J.L., Rodrigues, J.J.P.C., Alberti, A.M., 2023. Convergence of distributed ledger technologies with digital twins, IoT, and AI for fresh food logistics: challenges and opportunities. J. Ind. Inf. Integr. 31, 100393.

Wang, B., Zhou, H., Li, X., Yang, G., Zheng, P., Song, C., Yuan, Y., Wuest, T., Yang, H., Wang, L., 2024. Human digital twin in the context of industry 5.0. Robot. Comput.-Integr. Manuf. 07365845. 85. Available from: https://www.journals.elsevier.com/robotics-and-computer-integrated-manufacturing. doi:10.1016/j.rcim.2023.102626.

Wang, H., Lv, L., Li, X., Li, H., Leng, J., Zhang, Y., Thomson, V., Liu, G., Wen, X., Sun, C., Luo, G., 2023. A safety management approach for industry 5.0's human-centered manufacturing based on digital twin. J. Manuf. Syst. 02786125. 66, 1–12. Available from: http://www.elsevier.com. doi:10.1016/j.jmsy.2022.11.013.

Zeulin, N., Ponomarenko-Timofeev, A., Galinina, O., Andreev, S., 2022. ML-assisted beam selection via digital twins for time-sensitive industrial IoT. IEEE Internet Things Mag. 25763199. 5 (1), 36–40. Available from: https://ieeexplore.ieee.org/xpl/RecentIssue.jsp?punumber=8548628. doi:10.1109/IOTM.001.2200021.

PART 4

Advanced topics and future directions

CHAPTER 15

Emerging trends in digital twin technologies

Renuka Rajendra Kajale[a], Nitin Dhawas[b], and Neha Sharad Bhagwat[a]
[a]*Department of Computer Engineering, Nutan Maharashtra Institute of Engineering & Technology, Pune, India*
[b]*Information Technology (I.T.), Nutan Maharashtra Institute of Technology, Pune, Maharashtra, India*

15.1 Introduction

Digital twin technology (DTT) has emerged as a transformative force in various industries, offering unparalleled opportunities for innovation, efficiency, and decision-making. By creating a virtual replica of physical assets, processes, or systems, organizations can simulate, predict, and optimize operations in real time. As the technology evolves, new trends shape its future, expanding its applications and benefits across diverse domains. This chapter explores these trends, highlighting the pivotal developments driving the growth and impact of DTT. Smart cities utilize digital twins (DTs) to manage utilities, transportation systems, and environmental data, resulting in more sustainable urban planning and enhanced emergency preparedness. In the energy and utilities sector, they play a crucial role in monitoring grids, forecasting demand, and integrating renewable energy sources efficiently. Logistics and supply chain sectors use DTs for route optimization, inventory management, and risk assessment under dynamic conditions. Despite their promise, widespread adoption of DTT faces challenges such as data interoperability, high implementation costs, cybersecurity risks, and the need for standardization. However, as digital infrastructure matures and AI capabilities advance, DTs are expected to become a foundational technology across industries. DT technology has rapidly emerged as a cornerstone of the digital transformation era, enabling organizations to create virtual replicas of physical systems, assets, or processes. These virtual models are dynamically linked to their real-world counterparts through real-time data exchange, allowing continuous monitoring, simulation, and optimization. Originally conceived for aerospace and manufacturing, DTs are now expanding across diverse sectors, including healthcare, energy, construction, transportation, and smart cities. At the heart of DTT lies the convergence of enabling technologies such as the Internet of Things (IoT), artificial intelligence (AI), machine learning (ML), cloud and edge computing, and big data analytics. These components empower DTs to evolve from static models into intelligent systems capable of learning, adapting, and

Artificial Intelligence, Machine Learning and Blockchain in Digital Twin Computing.
https://doi.org/10.1016/B978-0-443-43914-8.00021-2

predicting future outcomes. Emerging trends in DT development are reshaping their capabilities and applications. One key trend is the integration of AI-driven analytics, which allows DTs to perform autonomous decision-making and scenario planning. The rise of edge computing is another significant advancement, enabling data processing closer to the source for reduced latency and faster response times. In addition, the concept of "System of Systems" DTs is gaining traction, linking multiple twins to model complex, interconnected environments such as entire factories, cities, or supply chains. Another notable trend is the growing use of extended reality (XR) technologies—such as augmented and virtual reality—to visualize and interact with DTs in immersive 3D environments. Furthermore, the increasing emphasis on sustainability and resilience is driving the adoption of DTs for environmental monitoring, energy optimization, and disaster preparedness.

As DTs continue to evolve, they are set to become more autonomous, scalable, and intelligent. This text explores the current landscape of DTTs, highlights emerging trends, and discusses their far-reaching implications for industry, infrastructure, and society.

15.1.1 Integration of artificial intelligence and machine learning

One of the most significant trends in DTT is the integration of AI and ML. These technologies enhance the analytical capabilities of DTs by enabling predictive and prescriptive insights. AI-powered DTs can identify patterns, predict failures, and recommend optimal actions, thus reducing downtime and improving performance. For instance, in manufacturing, AI-enhanced DTs can forecast equipment malfunctions and suggest maintenance schedules, ensuring uninterrupted operations. In the energy sector, they can optimize power distribution, predict demand fluctuations, and mitigate risks in real time. The combination of AI and ML with DTs empowers businesses to make data-driven decisions that enhance productivity and reduce operational costs.

15.1.2 IoT and edge computing synergy

The proliferation of the IoT and advancements in edge computing are pivotal to the evolution of DTs. IoT devices collect real-time data from physical assets, while edge computing processes this data closer to the source, reducing latency and ensuring faster decision-making. This synergy is particularly valuable in applications like autonomous vehicles, smart cities, and industrial automation, where immediate responses are critical. For example, in smart city initiatives, IoT sensors embedded in infrastructure can provide continuous data on traffic patterns, energy consumption, and environmental conditions. DTs can then process this data at the edge, enabling city planners to optimize urban environments dynamically. Similarly, in industrial settings, edge computing allows DTs to monitor machinery and processes in real time, ensuring safety and efficiency.

15.1.3 Expansion into new industries

Initially prevalent in industries like aerospace and manufacturing, DTT is now making inroads into sectors such as healthcare, agriculture, and retail. In healthcare, DTs of patients can model personalized treatment plans and predict health outcomes. By integrating patient data such as genetics, medical history, and lifestyle, healthcare providers can develop tailored therapeutic strategies, improving patient care and reducing costs. In agriculture, DTs can optimize irrigation, monitor crop health, and enhance yield predictions. Advanced sensors and drones collect data on soil conditions, weather, and plant health, which DTs analyze to provide actionable insights. Retailers, on the other hand, use DTs to optimize supply chains, improve customer experiences, and design store layouts. By simulating customer behavior and inventory dynamics, retailers can minimize waste and maximize profitability.

15.1.4 Enhanced visualization with augmented reality and virtual reality

Augmented reality (AR) and virtual reality (VR) are revolutionizing how DTs are visualized and interacted with. By integrating AR and VR, stakeholders can immerse themselves in virtual models, gaining a deeper understanding of complex systems. This is particularly useful in training, maintenance, and design, where realistic simulations can enhance learning and decision-making. For instance, in aerospace, AR/VR integration allows engineers to explore the intricate components of aircraft digitally, facilitating design optimization and troubleshooting. In construction, architects and clients can visualize building designs in immersive environments, enabling better communication and faster decision-making. These advanced visualization tools are making DTs more accessible and impactful.

15.1.5 Focus on sustainability

Sustainability has become a key focus area for DTT. By enabling precise monitoring and optimization of resource usage, DTs contribute to reducing waste and minimizing environmental impact. For example, in energy management, DTs help optimize power grids, predict energy demands, and integrate renewable energy sources effectively. In the construction industry, DTs facilitate sustainable building designs and lifecycle management. They can simulate energy efficiency, track carbon footprints, and identify opportunities for greener operations. The adoption of DTs in agriculture also promotes sustainability by optimizing water usage, reducing chemical inputs, and increasing resource efficiency. As businesses prioritize sustainability, DTs are emerging as essential tools for achieving environmental goals.

15.1.6 Cybersecurity and data privacy concerns

As DTs become more sophisticated, they also become more susceptible to cybersecurity threats and data privacy issues. Protecting the integrity of DT systems and the data they rely on is paramount. Emerging trends in this area include the adoption of block chain technology for secure data transactions and the implementation of advanced encryption protocols. For instance, blockchain can ensure the authenticity and immutability of data exchanged between IoT devices and DTs. Cybersecurity frameworks are being enhanced to address vulnerabilities, such as unauthorized access and data tampering. Organizations are also focusing on compliance with data privacy regulations, ensuring that sensitive information is safeguarded throughout the DT lifecycle.

15.1.7 Standardization and interoperability

The lack of standardized frameworks for developing and deploying DTs has been a challenge. Recent trends emphasize the creation of industry-wide standards and protocols to ensure interoperability between different DT systems. Standardization efforts aim to streamline adoption, reduce costs, and enhance the scalability of DT solutions. Collaborative initiatives between industry leaders, academic institutions, and regulatory bodies are driving these standardization efforts. For instance, frameworks such as ISO 23247 aim to define standards for DT implementation in manufacturing. Interoperability is also being facilitated through open-source platforms and APIs, enabling seamless integration across diverse systems.

15.1.8 Autonomous digital twins

Autonomous DTs represent the next frontier in this technology. These systems can independently analyze data, make decisions, and implement actions without human intervention. By leveraging AI, IoT, and real-time analytics, autonomous DTs offer the potential to revolutionize industries such as logistics, where they can dynamically reroute shipments based on real-time conditions. In manufacturing, autonomous DTs can adjust production schedules, manage supply chains, and optimize workflows automatically. Their ability to operate autonomously reduces reliance on manual oversight, increasing efficiency and scalability. As industries continue to adopt automation, autonomous DTs are poised to become integral to future operations.

15.2 Background and motivation

DTT finds its roots in the simulation and modeling techniques that emerged during the late 20th century. Initially used in aerospace engineering to improve the design and maintenance of complex systems, the concept of creating a digital replica of physical objects has evolved significantly. National Aeronautics and Space Administration (NASA) is often credited with pioneering the early use of DT-like models during its Apollo missions, where simulation models helped monitor and troubleshoot spacecraft in real-time. The motivation behind DT development stems from the need to optimize performance, reduce costs, and enhance safety. With advancements in computing power, data analytics, and connectivity, the practical implementation of DTs has expanded beyond its initial applications. Organizations increasingly adopt DTs to achieve a holistic view of their operations, enabling real-time monitoring, predictive maintenance, and improved decision-making. In today's data-driven world, the motivation to use DTs is reinforced by their ability to integrate diverse data sources into a unified framework. By bridging the gap between the physical and digital realms, DTs empower industries to simulate scenarios, predict outcomes, and implement proactive measures. For instance, in manufacturing, DTs enhance productivity by identifying bottlenecks and optimizing workflows. Similarly, in healthcare, patient-specific DTs are used to personalize treatment plans and predict disease progression. As businesses strive for sustainability and resilience, the role of DTs becomes increasingly significant. They offer tools to minimize resource consumption, lower operational risks, and support long-term strategic planning. This motivation aligns with global efforts to address challenges such as climate change, resource scarcity, and economic volatility. DTT thus serves as a cornerstone for innovation, driving transformative solutions across industries.

DTT has evolved from a niche innovation into a foundational pillar of Industry 4.0. First introduced in the manufacturing and aerospace sectors, the concept has rapidly expanded into various industries, including healthcare, construction, energy, urban planning, and logistics. A DT is more than just a digital replica; it is a dynamic, real-time system that mirrors a physical asset or process through continuous data integration, simulation, and feedback loops. The increasing complexity of industrial systems and the rise of interconnected devices through the IoT have catalyzed the adoption and evolution of DTs.

Over time, advancements in enabling technologies—such as AI, ML, cloud and edge computing, and big data analytics—have dramatically enhanced the capabilities of DTs These enhancements are giving rise to a new wave of innovation, driving emerging trends that are redefining the scope and functionality of DT systems.

One of the most notable trends is the **integration of AI and predictive analytics**. These technologies allow DTs to evolve from passive monitoring tools into intelligent systems capable of forecasting performance issues, simulating future scenarios, and autonomously optimizing operations. This trend is particularly transformative in industries such as healthcare, where patient-specific DTs can model treatment outcomes, or in manufacturing, where predictive maintenance reduces downtime.

Another emerging trend is the **shift toward edge computing**, which enables faster processing of real-time data closer to the source. This reduces latency and enhances responsiveness, especially critical for time-sensitive applications such as autonomous vehicles or smart grid systems.

The development of **System-of-Systems (SoS) DTs** is also gaining traction. These are complex models composed of multiple interconnected DTs that represent entire ecosystems, such as cities, supply chains, or manufacturing networks. This holistic modeling allows for multilayered decision-making and improved system-level optimization.

Furthermore, **integration with XR technologies**—including AR, VR, and MR—is enhancing visualization and user interaction with DTs. These immersive interfaces support design reviews, remote inspections, and training in virtual environments. The **emphasis on sustainability and resilience** is another powerful driver. DTs are increasingly used to model and mitigate environmental impacts, optimize energy consumption, and improve disaster preparedness. These sustainability-focused applications align with global efforts to meet environmental targets and build more adaptive infrastructure systems. Finally, there is a growing focus on **standardization, interoperability, and cybersecurity** to address the challenges of scaling DT solutions across complex and diverse ecosystems. In summary, the evolution of DTT is being shaped by rapid advancements in computing, data science, and immersive technologies. These emerging trends are not only expanding the application scope of DTs but also enhancing their value as intelligent, predictive, and adaptive systems that are integral to the future of digital transformation across industries.

15.3 Framework of DT

A system that generates a virtual duplicate of a tangible asset is known as DT architecture. It tracks, evaluates, and improves the asset's performance in real time using data analytics, sensors, and modeling software, as seen in Fig. 15.1.

DT architecture is the process of creating a virtual representation of buildings, infrastructure, or a system. This digital copy replicates the characteristics, behaviors, and performance of real-world resources. It is made possible through real-time data and sophisticated modeling techniques. Hence, **real-time data integration in DTs** is of greater importance. The adoption of DT software is rapidly increasing in the architecture and construction industry. DTs allow architects, designers, and project managers to see, analyze, and maximize every stage in a building's life cycle, from planning and development to upkeep and operation.

15.3.1 How DT architecture works

DT in architecture works by creating a digital representation that is similar to real-world objects. This DT platform helps stakeholders interact with, evaluate, and streamline the processes involved in the lifecycle of buildings and systems.

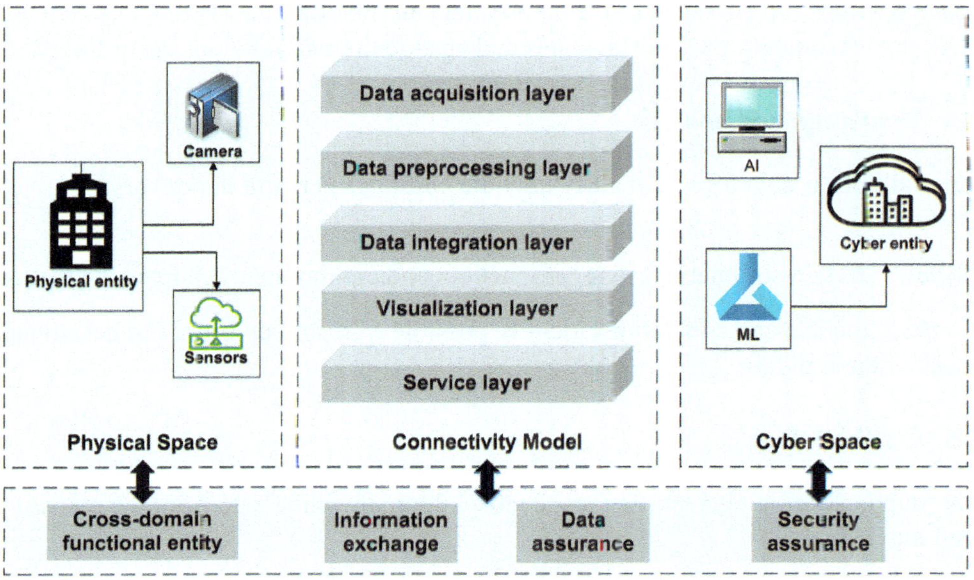

Fig. 15.1 Digital twin system architecture.

15.3.2 Data collection

Data is gathered from sensors, IoT devices, and historical records.

This data provides information related to real-world objects, systems, environments, and performance.

For example, sensors track humidity, temperature, structural integrity, and energy consumption in real-time.

15.3.3 Digital modeling

Collected data creates a 3D digital model of the building.

This is not static data, but it is a dynamic simulation that changes when fresh data is input.

Most modern platforms and software tools assist in developing these models by ensuring realism and precision.

15.3.4 Real-time synchronization

DTs synchronize the real-world processes in real time.

Any changes are reflected in the digital model in real-time.

For example, when a fresh heating, ventilation, and air conditioning (HVAC) system is installed, the DTs integrate with its updates and change their simulations accordingly.

15.3.5 Simulation and analysis

DTs run multiple simulations to identify how the buildings perform under varying circumstances.

This follows stress tests, energy usage, production, and environmental impact evaluation.

These virtual models and simulations identify possible risks and optimize the design and processes of the building.

15.3.6 Feedback loop

The last step is developing a continuous feedback loop, in which data from the real world is inputted into DTs.

This continuous process ensures that the digital model is updated and precise, offering valuable insights for maintenance and operational effectiveness.

15.4 Components of DTs

The components of a DT form a cohesive system that bridges the physical and digital worlds. Below are the core components:

15.4.1 Physical entity (real-world object)

Definition: The real-world system, object, or process being modeled

Examples: A smart home, factory equipment, vehicle, or human body (for healthcare applications)

Role: Acts as the source of data for the DT

15.4.2 Digital model (virtual replica)

Definition: A virtual representation of the physical entity, created using 3D modeling, simulation tools, and algorithms

Role: Mimics the physical system's structure, behavior, and functions

Provides a platform for simulations, monitoring, and analysis

15.4.3 Sensors and actuators

Definition: IoT devices are embedded within physical systems to collect data or perform actions

Role: Sensors: Gather real-time data, such as temperature, pressure, location, or performance metrics

Actuators: Execute control commands sent from the DT to influence the physical entity

15.4.4 Data communication layer

Definition: The network infrastructure enabling seamless data flow between the physical entity and its DT

Technologies: Wi-Fi, 5G, Bluetooth, or proprietary communication protocols

Role: Ensures real-time synchronization and updates between the physical and digital models

15.4.5 Data storage and management

Definition: A centralized system or cloud platform where data is stored, organized, and processed

Role: Stores historical and real-time data for analysis and decision-making

Ensures scalability and accessibility of data

15.4.6 Analytics and algorithms

Definition: Advanced AI and ML models for data processing and decision-making

Role: Processes collected data to generate insights

Enables predictive maintenance, anomaly detection, and system optimization

15.4.7 Simulation and visualization tools

Definition: Software platforms that allow users to simulate scenarios and visualize the DT

Technologies: 3D modeling tools, VR/AR interfaces, and dashboards

Role: Visualizes system behavior in an intuitive format

Simulates what-if scenarios for testing and planning

15.4.8 Control interface

Definition: User-facing tools for interacting with the DT

Technologies: Mobile apps, web portals, or command centers

Role: Allows users to monitor, control, and customize the DT's behavior

15.4.9 Feedback mechanism

Definition: A loop that enables two-way communication between the DT and the physical system

Role: Ensures the DT adapts to changes in the physical entity

Sends optimized instructions or corrections to the physical system

15.4.10 Security framework

Definition: Systems and protocols to safeguard data and communications

Role: Protect sensitive information from unauthorized access

Ensures data integrity and compliance with regulations

15.4.11 Optional components (context-specific)

Edge computing: For localized, low-latency processing

Integration systems: Links DTs with external systems, such as smart grids or supply chains

Digital thread: Connects multiple DTs for system-wide optimization (e.g., in a factory or a city)

15.5 Applications of DTs

DTs are virtual representations of physical systems, processes, or objects that enable real-time monitoring, analysis, and optimization. Their applications span numerous industries, offering enhanced decision-making, operational efficiency, and predictive capabilities. Here are some notable applications:

15.5.1 Manufacturing and industry 4.0

DTT plays a pivotal role in advancing the goals of **Industry 4.0**, the fourth industrial revolution, which focuses on the digitalization and interconnection of manufacturing systems.

By creating real-time, data-driven digital representations of physical manufacturing assets, DTs enable enhanced monitoring, control, and optimization of industrial processes. This transformative capability supports smarter, more responsive production environments, ultimately driving productivity, agility, and innovation.

1. **Predictive maintenance and asset management:** One of the most prominent applications of DTs in manufacturing is **predictive maintenance**. Traditional maintenance models rely on routine schedules or reactive repairs after failures occur, both of which can lead to costly downtime. DTs integrate data from IoT sensors embedded in machinery to monitor parameters such as temperature, vibration, and usage patterns. Using advanced analytics and ML, these virtual models can forecast equipment failures before they occur, allowing for timely, condition-based maintenance. This not only reduces downtime but also extends equipment lifespan and minimizes operational costs.
2. **Production optimization and process simulation:** DTs allow manufacturers to simulate and optimize production workflows in a virtual environment before implementation in the physical plant. By modeling entire production lines or even factory ecosystems, engineers can evaluate different configurations, process flows, and resource allocations. This simulation-based approach supports **lean manufacturing**, improves throughput, and reduces waste. It also enables quick adaptation to changing customer demands or disruptions in the supply chain.
3. **Quality control and defect detection:** In modern smart factories, DTs contribute to **real-time quality monitoring** by continuously comparing production output against predefined specifications. Advanced imaging and sensor technologies feed real-time data into the digital model, allowing AI algorithms to detect defects or anomalies at early stages. This enhances quality assurance while reducing the reliance on manual inspection and postproduction quality checks.
4. **Supply chain integration and management:** DTT extends beyond the shop floor to **supply chain operations**, enabling better visibility, forecasting, and risk management. A DT of the supply chain can simulate the effects of supplier delays, transportation issues, or demand fluctuations, allowing companies to proactively respond and mitigate risks. It also facilitates collaboration between suppliers, manufacturers, and logistics providers through a unified digital ecosystem.
5. **Customization and mass personalization:** In the era of customer-centric production, DTs support **mass customization** by enabling real-time reconfiguration of manufacturing systems. Virtual models can simulate the production of customized products, ensuring that machines and processes are optimized for rapid switching between variants. This capability is essential for industries such as automotive, electronics, and consumer goods, where flexible manufacturing is increasingly in demand.
6. **Human–machine collaboration and training:** DTs, especially when combined with AR and VR, are instrumental in enhancing **human–machine interaction**. Operators can

visualize machine status, receive real-time instructions, and simulate complex tasks in a virtual environment before executing them physically. This improves safety, accelerates workforce training, and reduces human error.

15.5.2 Healthcare

Personalized medicine: DTs of patients enable tailored treatments by simulating responses to different therapies.

Surgical planning: Simulating surgeries on a DT of a patient's anatomy aids in preoperative planning. The healthcare industry is undergoing a digital transformation, and **DTT** is at the forefront of this change. By creating dynamic, virtual representations of organs, devices, clinical processes, or even entire human bodies, DTs enable healthcare professionals to simulate, analyze, and predict health conditions and treatment outcomes in a more precise and personalized manner. This convergence of biomedical data, AI, and real-time monitoring marks a significant step toward **predictive, preventive, and personalized medicine**.

1. **Personalized patient modeling:** One of the most impactful applications of DTs in healthcare is the creation of **individual patient models**. These twins integrate a wide range of patient-specific data—including medical history, genetics, lifestyle, sensor data (e.g., from wearables), and diagnostic results—into a comprehensive digital profile. Physicians can use this model to simulate disease progression, test treatment plans, and tailor interventions to individual needs. This approach enhances clinical decision-making and significantly reduces the risks associated with trial-and-error treatments.
2. **Disease prediction and early diagnosis:** DTs enable **early detection of diseases** by continuously monitoring and analyzing biometric data in real time. Advanced ML algorithms can detect subtle changes that precede clinical symptoms, facilitating timely interventions. For instance, in cardiology, a heart DT can simulate how a patient's heart will respond to different stressors or medications, aiding in the early diagnosis of heart failure or arrhythmias.
3. **Surgical planning and simulation:** In surgical care, DTs allow for **highly accurate planning and rehearsal**. By generating a 3D model of a patient's anatomy—based on computed tomography (CT) scans, magnetic resonance imaging (MRIs), or other imaging—surgeons can simulate procedures in a risk-free virtual environment. This improves surgical accuracy, shortens operation time, reduces complications, and enhances patient safety. DTs are particularly useful in complex fields like neurosurgery, orthopedics, and reconstructive surgery.
4. **Medical device design and testing:** Medical equipment and implants, such as pacemakers, prosthetics, or stents, can be virtually tested using patient-specific DTs before deployment. This enables **virtual prototyping and regulatory compliance** without the need for extensive physical trials. Engineers and designers can simulate how devices will

interact with patient physiology under various conditions, improving product safety and performance.

5. **Hospital operations and resource management:** Beyond individual care, DTs can model entire **hospital systems**, including patient flow, staffing, equipment usage, and emergency preparedness. This supports **real-time operational management**, especially in high-pressure scenarios like pandemics or mass-casualty events. Hospitals can simulate demand surges, optimize bed allocation, and improve workflows using these virtual replicas.
6. **Chronic disease management and remote monitoring:** For patients with chronic conditions such as diabetes, asthma, or chronic obstructive pulmonary disease (COPD). DTs can integrate data from wearable sensors and home monitoring devices to continuously track health status. These models provide real-time feedback to both patients and clinicians, allowing **remote management and early intervention** when anomalies are detected. This reduces hospital readmissions and supports a more proactive care approach.

15.5.3 Smart cities and urban planning

Infrastructure management: DTs of urban infrastructure, such as roads, bridges, and utilities, assist in maintenance and optimization. **Traffic flow analysis:** Simulations improve traffic management by modeling and addressing congestion scenarios. **Disaster management:** Predicting the impact of natural disasters helps in planning responses. **Medical device testing:** Devices can be tested in simulated environments before real-world application.

As urban populations continue to grow, cities face mounting challenges in infrastructure management, transportation planning, energy consumption, environmental sustainability, and citizen services. In this context, **DTT has emerged as a transformative tool** for urban planners and policymakers, enabling data-driven decision-making and more resilient, efficient, and sustainable urban ecosystems. A **DT of a city** is a virtual replica of its physical infrastructure, systems, and processes, fed by real-time data from IoT sensors, satellite imagery, public databases, and communication networks.

1. **Urban infrastructure planning and optimization:** DTs enable planners to simulate and evaluate proposed developments before construction. From new roadways and bridges to commercial or residential complexes, digital replicas allow stakeholders to model **construction impacts**, assess structural performance under different conditions, and plan with precision. Urban planners can visualize the effects of infrastructure changes on traffic patterns, utilities, and environmental factors, which lead to more informed and sustainable development decisions.

2. **Traffic flow and transportation management:** Transportation is a critical area where DTs deliver value. By integrating real-time data from GPS, traffic cameras, and smart signals, DTs can simulate and monitor **traffic dynamics across the city**. Planners and engineers can test different road configurations, traffic light sequences, and public transit schedules. This enables cities to proactively **reduce congestion**, optimize transit systems, and improve safety and efficiency in mobility networks.
3. **Energy consumption and smart grids:** DTs support **energy-efficient urban design** by modeling and managing power distribution in real-time. They can simulate electricity demand across neighborhoods, predict consumption trends, and optimize the integration of renewable energy sources such as solar or wind. In combination with smart grid technologies, DTs facilitate **load balancing**, reduce energy waste, and support the development of **net-zero energy districts**.
4. **Disaster preparedness and resilience planning:** Cities increasingly face climate risks such as flooding, heat waves, and earthquakes. DTs can simulate **natural disasters and emergency scenarios**, helping authorities plan evacuation routes, deploy resources efficiently, and assess vulnerabilities in infrastructure. This predictive modeling enhances **urban resilience** and strengthens the capacity for real-time emergency response and risk mitigation.
5. **Environmental monitoring and sustainability:** Urban DTs can integrate environmental data—such as air quality, noise levels, water usage, and green space distribution—to monitor **environmental health indicators**. These insights are crucial for designing policies that promote public health and environmental sustainability. For example, cities can simulate the impact of green roofs, tree planting, or traffic reduction policies on air pollution and temperature regulation.
6. **Citizen engagement and policy testing:** DTs serve as platforms for **interactive engagement with residents**. Through visualization tools and dashboards, citizens can explore proposed changes to their neighborhoods, provide feedback, or participate in codesign initiatives. Policymakers can also test regulatory interventions—like zoning laws or congestion pricing—within the virtual city before real-world implementation, reducing unintended consequences.

15.5.4 Energy and utilities

The energy and utilities sector is undergoing a rapid transformation due to rising global demand, environmental regulations, the transition to renewable sources, and the increasing complexity of power grids. In this evolving landscape, **DTT has emerged as a critical tool** for enabling intelligent, efficient, and resilient energy systems. By creating virtual models of energy assets and networks, DTs allow utility companies to monitor operations in real time, forecast energy demand, optimize maintenance, and integrate renewable sources more effectively.

1. **Power grid monitoring and optimization:** DTs of electrical grids enable operators to continuously simulate, analyze, and optimize grid performance. These models integrate data from sensors, substations, and smart meters to provide a **comprehensive, real-time overview** of load distribution, voltage levels, and energy flow. This allows for the immediate identification of inefficiencies, overloads, or outages. Furthermore, with predictive analytics, DTs can **forecast future demand** and optimize energy distribution, contributing to enhanced grid stability and reduced energy losses.
2. **Integration of renewable energy sources:** The transition to renewables—such as solar, wind, and hydro—requires advanced systems to manage variability and intermittency. DTs help **simulate renewable energy generation under various weather conditions** and model the performance of distributed energy resources. These simulations support grid operators in balancing supply and demand while maintaining power quality. For example, a wind farm DT can model turbine behavior, predict energy output, and optimize maintenance schedules based on wear patterns and environmental data.
3. **Asset performance and predictive maintenance:** In power plants, substations, and water treatment facilities, DTs provide **asset-level visibility**. By modeling turbines, transformers, pipelines, or generators, utilities can monitor equipment health and predict failures before they occur. This predictive maintenance reduces downtime, extends asset lifespans, and decreases operational costs. Advanced DTs may also simulate degradation over time, enabling operators to plan capital expenditures and replacements more effectively.
4. **Water and wastewater management:** Utilities managing water distribution and wastewater treatment benefit from DTs by modeling **flow dynamics, consumption patterns, and system leaks**. These models help in detecting pipe bursts, managing pressure zones, and optimizing chemical usage. Moreover, water utilities can simulate emergency scenarios—such as contamination or drought—and adjust operations accordingly to ensure reliability and sustainability.
5. **Energy trading and demand forecasting:** DTs can enhance energy market operations by modeling **real-time supply and demand trends**, pricing scenarios, and market risks. Utility companies can use these insights to inform energy trading strategies and optimize procurement. Moreover, accurate demand forecasting using DTs helps with load balancing, reducing peak demand charges, and supporting **demand response programs** for consumers.
6. **Environmental compliance and emission monitoring:** With increasing regulatory pressures, energy providers must track emissions, energy usage, and environmental impact. DTs allow for **continuous monitoring of emissions** from generation sources and help utilities remain compliant with environmental regulations. They also support sustainability initiatives by modeling the **carbon footprint** of operations and suggesting measures to reduce it.

15.5.5 Automotive and transportation

The automotive and transportation industries are at the forefront of adopting **DTT** to address evolving demands for efficiency, safety, automation, and sustainability. By creating real-time digital replicas of vehicles, transport networks, and infrastructure systems, DTs enable enhanced design, predictive maintenance, autonomous mobility, and intelligent traffic management. These capabilities align with broader innovations such as **connected vehicles, electric mobility, and smart transportation systems**.

1. **Vehicle design and development:** DTs revolutionize vehicle development by allowing engineers to simulate and validate designs in a virtual environment before building physical prototypes. From structural integrity and aerodynamics to crashworthiness and energy efficiency, DTs can model how a vehicle performs under different operating conditions. This accelerates the product development cycle, reduces costs, and improves design accuracy. Automotive manufacturers, such as Tesla, BMW, and Ford, leverage DTs to integrate data from real-world test vehicles and continuously refine their virtual models.
2. **Predictive maintenance and lifecycle management:** In both private vehicles and commercial fleets, DTs enable predictive maintenance by monitoring engine performance, battery health, tire wear, and other key metrics through onboard sensors and telematics. Real-time data is transmitted to the digital model, where ML algorithms analyze trends to forecast component failures. This reduces unplanned downtime, extends vehicle lifespan, and optimizes maintenance scheduling. Fleet operators benefit from reduced operational costs and improved reliability.
3. **Autonomous and connected vehicles:** For autonomous driving technologies, DTs play a critical role in training and validating AI models. They simulate real-world environments—such as road conditions, pedestrian behavior, and weather scenarios—to test the performance of self-driving algorithms safely. In addition, DTs of connected vehicles continuously interact with infrastructure and cloud platforms to support vehicle-to-everything (V2X) communication, enhancing road safety and traffic efficiency.
4. **Smart transportation infrastructure:** Beyond vehicles, DTT is applied to transportation networks and infrastructure, including roads, railways, airports, and seaports. City planners and transportation agencies use digital models to simulate traffic flow, identify congestion points, and test new traffic control strategies. Integration with IoT sensors and traffic cameras allows real-time monitoring of road usage and predictive modeling of demand. For example, a DT of a railway system can simulate train schedules, monitor track conditions, and optimize maintenance.
5. **Supply chain and logistics optimization:** In the automotive supply chain, DTs track parts and materials from suppliers to assembly lines, enabling just-in-time manufacturing and better inventory management. In transportation and logistics, digital models of warehouses, delivery trucks, and distribution networks allow for route optimization,

load balancing, and delay prediction. This enhances operational transparency, customer satisfaction, and sustainability by reducing fuel consumption and delivery times.

6. **Sustainability and emissions monitoring:** As the automotive sector pivots toward electric and hybrid vehicles, DTs help manufacturers monitor and improve battery performance, thermal behavior, and charging infrastructure. In addition, they are used to simulate and track vehicle emissions and fuel efficiency, supporting compliance with environmental regulations and the transition to carbon-neutral transportation.

15.5.6 Aerospace and defense

The **aerospace and defense (A&D) sectors** have been among the earliest adopters and leading innovators of DTT due to their high reliance on precision, safety, and complex system integration. In these domains, DTs enable real-time simulation, testing, and lifecycle management of critical assets—ranging from aircraft and spacecraft to defense systems and mission operations. The ability to virtually replicate and monitor systems contributes significantly to **operational readiness, maintenance efficiency, mission assurance**, and innovation in next-generation technologies.

1. **Aircraft design and testing:** DTs play a pivotal role in the design, development, and validation of aircraft by enabling engineers to simulate aerodynamics, structural integrity, propulsion systems, and material behavior under extreme conditions. This reduces the need for expensive and time-consuming physical prototypes. By integrating real-time data from wind tunnel testing and flight sensors, the digital model evolves throughout the development cycle. This iterative process enhances the accuracy of performance predictions, improves safety, and shortens time to market.
2. **Predictive maintenance and fleet management:** Modern aircraft are equipped with thousands of sensors that generate continuous streams of data. These are fed into DTs to monitor performance in real time, detect anomalies, and predict maintenance needs before failures occur. This predictive maintenance approach reduces downtime, increases asset availability, and lowers lifecycle costs. For commercial airlines and military fleets alike, DTs help in planning overhaul schedules and optimizing spare parts inventories, leading to more efficient logistics and readiness.
3. **Mission simulation and operational readiness:** In defense operations, DTs are used to simulate and rehearse military missions in highly realistic environments. Virtual replicas of weapon systems, vehicles, drones, and battlefield conditions are created to evaluate performance under different tactical scenarios. This supports decision-making, training, and risk assessment. In addition, DTs can model cyber-physical threats and support cyber defense by testing the resilience of critical systems in simulated attack environments.
4. **Spacecraft engineering and space missions:** In the space industry, DTs are employed to design, test, and operate satellites, launch vehicles, and space stations. For instance,

NASA uses DT models of spacecraft like the Orion capsule and the International Space Station to simulate microgravity environments, track component health, and plan maintenance activities. These models are particularly vital during long-duration missions, where physical access is impossible and real-time decision-making is essential for mission success.

5. **Additive manufacturing and material testing:** The aerospace sector increasingly uses additive manufacturing (3D printing) for lightweight, high-performance components. DTs allow virtual testing of materials and printed parts under real-world stress conditions before production. By modeling thermal, structural, and mechanical properties, engineers can ensure compliance with safety standards and reduce defects in high-risk applications.
6. **System integration and cybersecurity:** A&D platforms are inherently complex, integrating software, electronics, avionics, and mechanical subsystems. DTs allow for SoS simulation, ensuring that all subsystems function harmoniously. They also support cybersecurity analysis, where virtual models are used to identify vulnerabilities in networked defense systems and evaluate responses to potential cyberattacks.

15.5.7 Construction and real estate

The **construction and real estate industries** are increasingly embracing DTT to enhance project planning, improve building performance, reduce operational costs, and drive sustainability. A DT, in this context, refers to a dynamic, real-time digital representation of a built asset or construction process that integrates data from Building Information Modeling (BIM), IoT sensors, Geographic Information Systems, and various operational systems. These models provide a **comprehensive, continuously updated view of physical structures**, enabling better decision-making across the entire building lifecycle.

1. **Design and preconstruction planning:** DTs are highly effective during the early stages of construction, allowing architects, engineers, and planners to simulate and optimize design choices before ground is broken. Unlike static BIM models, a DT incorporates real-time data and performance forecasting, enabling stakeholders to visualize and test how structures will respond to variables such as load, occupancy, weather, and energy consumption. This minimizes design errors, improves material efficiency, and fosters collaborative decision-making among project stakeholders.
2. **Construction monitoring and optimization:** During construction, DTs facilitate real-time monitoring of site activities, equipment usage, and schedule adherence. IoT devices, drones, and RFID systems feed data into the digital model, which helps in tracking progress against the project plan. This not only ensures higher efficiency and quality control but also allows for the early detection of safety risks and deviations from the design. As a result, project timelines are better managed, and costly delays are reduced.

3. **Facility management and operations:** Once the building is operational, the DT becomes a powerful tool for facilities management and building performance optimization. By continuously receiving input from sensors (e.g., HVAC systems, lighting, occupancy, temperature), the twin can help building managers optimize energy usage, reduce maintenance costs, and predict component failures. This proactive maintenance strategy extends asset lifespans and improves tenant satisfaction by ensuring comfort, security, and operational efficiency.
4. **Sustainability and environmental impact:** DTs contribute significantly to sustainable construction practices by enabling precise energy modeling and resource optimization. By simulating various building configurations and operational strategies, project teams can identify the most eco-efficient solutions. In addition, DTs help monitor carbon footprints, waste generation, and indoor environmental quality, supporting compliance with green building standards such as LEED and BREEAM.
5. **Real estate development and asset management:** In the real estate sector, DTs offer valuable insights for property valuation, leasing strategies, and portfolio management. Real estate developers and investors can use these models to simulate financial scenarios, assess market potential, and monitor building performance postoccupancy. For large property portfolios, DTs enable centralized control and predictive maintenance of multiple buildings, improving **return on investment** and reducing operational risks.
6. **Enhanced stakeholder collaboration:** DT platforms serve as a shared environment where all stakeholders—developers, architects, contractors, facility managers, and tenants—can access up-to-date information and collaborate more effectively. Changes in design, construction status, or operational parameters can be visualized and approved quickly, reducing friction and miscommunication.

15.5.8 Retail and e-commerce

DTT, traditionally used in manufacturing and engineering, is increasingly being adopted in retail and e-commerce to enhance operational efficiency, customer experience, and strategic planning. Here's an overview of how DTs are applied in these sectors:

1. **Store layout and design optimization:** Retailers use DTs to create **virtual replicas of physical stores**. These models simulate customer movement, product placement, and environmental conditions to:

Optimize shelf layouts and store navigation

Test different store designs before implementation

Monitor foot traffic patterns to improve product visibility

Example: A grocery chain uses a DT of its flagship store to analyze customer flow and optimize high-margin product placements.

Inventory and supply chain management: DTs offer real-time tracking and predictive analytics for inventory levels across stores and warehouses. Benefits include:

Minimizing stockouts and overstock

Predictive restocking based on customer demand forecasts

Synchronization between physical and digital inventory is important for omnichannel

Example: E-commerce platforms create DTs of fulfillment centers to simulate order processing and optimize warehouse operations.

Personalized customer experience: By integrating customer data (browsing history, past purchases, preferences), companies can create **DTs of customers or segments**. These help:

Personalize marketing and product recommendations

Simulate how different customer types might respond to promotions or UX changes

Example: A fashion retailer uses customer DTs to simulate engagement with new website features before deploying changes.

2. **E-commerce platform performance monitoring:** DTs of the entire e-commerce ecosystem—including servers, user interfaces, APIs, and logistics systems—allow companies to:

Monitor real-time system health

Test and deploy updates in simulated environments

Predict peak-time system loads

Example: During events like Black Friday, DTs help retailers stress-test their platforms for stability under high traffic.

Sustainability and energy efficiency: Retailers can model their **carbon footprint and energy usage** using DTs of store infrastructure and logistics networks to:

Optimize delivery routes for lower emissions

Reduce energy consumption in stores and warehouses

Simulate the impact of sustainability initiatives

Product lifecycle and customer feedback: DTs of products help retailers:

Track usage patterns via IoT (for smart devices)

Simulate wear and tear

Gather postsale customer feedback to refine future iterations

15.5.9 Agriculture

DTT is rapidly gaining traction in **agriculture**, transforming traditional farming into a data-driven, intelligent system. By creating **virtual replicas of farms, crops, machinery, and even weather systems**, DTs enable precise monitoring, forecasting, and decision-making in real time.

1. **Crop monitoring and yield prediction:** DTs of fields and crops integrate data from **drones, IoT sensors, satellite imagery**, and historical farming records to:

Monitor plant health and growth stages

Predict crop yields with high accuracy

Detect diseases, pests, and nutrient deficiencies early

Example: A farmer uses a DT of a cornfield to track moisture levels, plant growth, and stress indicators, enabling timely irrigation and fertilization.
Precision farming: DTs allow farmers to simulate and optimize various farming operations:

Seeding patterns, irrigation schedules, and fertilizer application

Tailored treatments for specific zones within a field (variable-rate application)

Reduction of waste and input costs while increasing output

Example: A vineyard uses DT models to control irrigation and nutrient delivery at a micro-zone level, improving grape quality.
Climate and environmental simulation: DTs integrate real-time and historical weather data to:

Simulate the impact of climate variables on crop growth

Plan for extreme events like droughts or floods

Model soil health, erosion, and water availability over time

Example: A rice farmer in Southeast Asia uses DTs to prepare for seasonal monsoons and manage water resources efficiently.

2. **Farm equipment and machinery management:** DTs of tractors, harvesters, and irrigation systems help in:

Predictive maintenance (reducing equipment failures)

Route optimization for field operations

Energy and fuel-efficiency tracking

Example: An agribusiness uses DTs of its machinery fleet to schedule servicing and reduce downtime during peak harvest.

15.5.10 Entertainment and gaming

VR and AR: DTs create realistic virtual environments for immersive experiences.

Event planning: Simulating crowds and venue layouts optimizes large events. In the entertainment and gaming industries, **DTs** are revolutionizing the way content is created, experienced, and managed. By mirroring real-world environments, assets, characters, and user behaviors in virtual spaces, DTs offer immersive, personalized, and highly interactive experiences.

15.5.11 Mining and resource extraction

Resource management: DTs simulate ore extraction and processing for efficiency.

Safety analysis: Predicting and mitigating risks in hazardous environments improve worker safety.

15.5.12 Education and training

Virtual training simulations: DTs enable realistic training environments for the aviation, healthcare, and military industries.

Remote learning: Interactive DTs enhance the learning experience in science, engineering, and technical fields.

15.5.13 Telecommunications

Network optimization: DTs of networks analyze and improve data flow, connectivity, and infrastructure.

5G deployment: Simulating the impact of 5G networks in urban environments ensures optimal performance.

The versatility of DTs makes them a critical tool across sectors, driving innovation and efficiency in modern industries.

15.6 Advantages of DT architecture

The DT architecture has several advantages, some of which are listed below.

15.6.1 Promoting sustainable construction

Sustainability has become a central concern in modern construction. DTT supports sustainable practices by enabling accurate energy modeling, optimizing material usage, improving construction methods, and minimizing waste. By simulating various environmental and design scenarios, DTs empower project teams to evaluate and select eco-friendly solutions that reduce the overall environmental footprint of construction projects.

15.6.2 Enhanced visualization and planning

DT applications significantly improve project visualization and planning through immersive and interactive 3D models. These models allow stakeholders to explore multiple design alternatives, detect potential issues early in the design phase, and make more informed decisions that align with project objectives. This proactive approach reduces the likelihood of costly rework, shortens timelines, and boosts overall project efficiency.

15.6.3 Real-time monitoring and predictive maintenance

By embedding real-world sensor data into digital models, DTs enable continuous monitoring of a building's performance throughout its lifecycle. This integration provides valuable insights into structural integrity, energy usage, and environmental conditions. As a result, maintenance becomes more predictive and less reactive, enhancing operational efficiency and extending the lifespan of built assets.

15.6.4 Improved collaboration and communication

DT platforms facilitate better coordination and collaboration among architects, engineers, contractors, and other stakeholders. A shared, up-to-date virtual model ensures transparency, enabling teams to detect and address inconsistencies promptly. This collaborative environment not only streamlines project execution but also enhances productivity and teamwork.

15.6.5 Informed decision-making and risk reduction

Access to rich datasets and predictive analytics allows project leaders to test and validate design decisions before construction begins. This capability aids in identifying potential risks and challenges early in the process, thereby reducing the chances of errors, delays, and costly interventions during later project stages.

15.7 Disadvantages of DT architecture

Even though DT architecture has various advantages, attaining it also presents several challenges. Let's discuss its disadvantages.

15.7.1 High initial investment

Implementing DTT often requires significant upfront investment. These costs encompass acquiring advanced software and hardware systems, integrating IoT infrastructure, and providing extensive training for personnel to effectively operate and manage the technology. For small businesses and projects with constrained budgets, this financial burden can be a major obstacle. While the long-term benefits—such as improved efficiency, reduced maintenance costs, and enhanced decision-making—can justify the expenditure, organizations must ensure they have a clear strategy and the necessary resources to navigate these early implementation hurdles.

15.7.2 Data security and privacy concerns

DTs rely heavily on the continuous exchange of data between physical assets and their virtual counterparts. This constant flow of sensitive and operational data increases vulnerability to cybersecurity threats, including data breaches, phishing attacks, and system spoofing. The storage and transmission of confidential information demand robust data protection mechanisms. However, establishing and maintaining a secure digital infrastructure often involves high costs and technical complexity. Organizations must invest in strong cybersecurity protocols, encryption standards, and regular system audits to safeguard their digital ecosystems.

15.7.3 Complexity in implementation and skill requirements

The successful deployment of DTT involves intricate integration across multiple systems and disciplines. This complexity presents a steep learning curve for professionals in fields such as construction, architecture, and engineering. To fully leverage the potential of DTs, these professionals must undergo specialized training and adapt to new workflows and digital tools. The need for cross-disciplinary collaboration and technological literacy can pose significant challenges, particularly in traditionally analog industries that may lack digital maturity.

15.8 Case study

15.8.1 Case study: DT in smart manufacturing—Siemens' Amberg factory

15.8.1.1 Overview

Siemens' Amberg Electronics Plant (Germany) is a prime example of using DTT to enhance manufacturing processes. The factory integrates DT solutions to create a "smart factory" that leverages real-time data, predictive analytics, and automation for optimal performance.

15.8.1.2 Key elements of the DT implementation

DT of the production line: A virtual replica of the physical production line was created. It incorporates real-time data from sensors embedded in machines and systems across the factory.

Predictive maintenance: The DT monitors machine health and predicts failures before they occur, reducing unplanned downtime and maintenance costs.

Process optimization simulations within the DT help identify bottlenecks, test changes to production schedules, and optimize workflows to improve overall efficiency.

Product design integration: The DT integrates product design data, allowing engineers to test and validate new designs virtually before implementation.

Quality control: Continuous monitoring of production quality is performed by comparing real-world data against DT simulations. Any deviations trigger automatic adjustments or alerts.

15.8.1.3 Outcomes

- **Efficiency gains:** The factory operates at a 99.99885% reliability rate, demonstrating near-zero defect rates
- **Increased productivity:** The production volume doubled without increasing the physical factory size or resources
- **Cost savings:** Predictive maintenance and process optimization have significantly reduced operational costs
- **Sustainability:** Energy usage was optimized, aligning with Siemens' environmental goals
- **Customer satisfaction:** Improved product quality, faster time-to-market, and enhanced customer experiences

15.8.1.4 Case study conclusion

Siemens' implementation of a DT at its Amberg factory showcases how this technology revolutionizes manufacturing. By leveraging real-time data and predictive insights, the factory achieved unparalleled efficiency, productivity, and quality. This case study highlights the transformative potential of DTs across industries.

15.8.2 Case study: Implementing DT technology in smart homes

15.8.2.1 Introduction

DTT creates virtual replicas of physical systems, enabling real-time monitoring, simulation, and optimization. In smart homes, DTs enhance efficiency, comfort, and security by modeling and managing the home's systems digitally.

15.8.2.2 Problem statement

Smart homes integrate various IoT devices and systems, such as lighting, HVAC, security cameras, and appliances. Challenges include:

- Managing the complexity of interconnected devices
- Real-time data analysis and decision-making
- Predicting and preventing system failures
- Enhancing user experience through personalization

Proposed solution: DT integration The DT acts as a virtual replica of the smart home, synchronizing with real-time data. It provides:

System monitoring: Tracks the performance of devices and identifies anomalies
Predictive maintenance: Uses AI to forecast device failures and schedule repairs
Energy optimization: Simulates energy usage patterns to suggest cost-saving measures
User customization: Analyzes users' preferences for personalized automation

Implementation

Data collection: Sensors in the home collect real-time data, such as temperature, occupancy, and energy usage
DT modeling: A virtual model of the home is created using IoT and cloud platforms
AI and ML: Algorithms analyze data, provide insights, and predict outcomes
User interface: Mobile apps and dashboards allow homeowners to interact with the DT

15.8.3 Case study example

15.8.3.1 Project

A residential complex in a metropolitan city.

15.8.3.2 Objective

Reduce energy consumption and enhance home automation using a DT.

15.8.3.3 Outcome

- Energy consumption decreased by 20% through optimized HVAC settings
- Maintenance costs dropped by 15% due to predictive alerts
- Homeowners reported improved satisfaction with automated lighting and temperature controls

15.8.3.4 Benefits

Enhanced energy efficiency

Reduced operational and maintenance costs
Improved home security and safety
Personalized user experiences

15.8.3.5 Challenges

- High initial setup costs
- Data privacy and security concerns
- Interoperability between different IoT devices

15.8.3.6 Future scope

Integration with smart grids: Use DTs for efficient energy distribution
Sustainability goals: Track and reduce carbon footprints
Advanced AI: Enable more intuitive and autonomous smart homes

15.9 Challenges

Here are the key challenges and limitations of DTT:

15.9.1 High initial costs

- **Infrastructure investment:** Creating and implementing DT systems require significant investments in IoT devices, sensors, data storage, and processing capabilities
- **Cost of modeling:** Developing a detailed, accurate virtual replica involves complex software and expertise, which can be expensive

15.9.2 Data privacy and security

- **Cybersecurity risks:** DTs rely on real-time data exchange, which can be vulnerable to hacking or unauthorized access
- **Privacy concerns:** Collecting and storing user data (especially in smart homes) may lead to potential misuse or breaches

15.9.3 Interoperability issues

- **Device compatibility:** DTs often need to integrate data from various IoT devices and platforms, which may not follow the same standards
- **Data silos:** A lack of integration between different systems can hinder seamless operation

15.9.4 Complexity of implementation

- **Technical expertise:** Designing, deploying, and maintaining DT systems requires skilled professionals
- **Data quality:** The effectiveness of a DT depends on the accuracy and reliability of the data it receives. Poor data can lead to incorrect simulations and decisions

15.9.5 Scalability

- **Large-scale applications:** As the number of connected devices grows, the system may struggle with scalability, requiring more processing power and storage
- **Real-time updates:** Synchronizing real-time data for large systems can become computationally intensive and slow

15.9.6 Dependence on advanced technologies

- **AI and ML integration:** The performance of DTs relies heavily on advanced AI and ML algorithms, which may still have limitations in accuracy or adaptability
- **Edge computing requirements:** High-speed, low-latency data processing is often necessary, especially for time-sensitive applications, requiring advanced edge computing setups

15.9.7 Lack of standardization

- **No universal framework:** The absence of standardized protocols for DT development leads to inconsistencies in implementation
- **Customization challenges:** Each application requires tailored solutions, increasing development time and costs

15.9.8 Environmental impact

- **Energy consumption:** Running DT systems, especially for large-scale simulations, can consume significant amounts of energy, raising sustainability concerns

15.9.9 Limited awareness and adoption

- **Knowledge gap:** Many industries and individuals are still unaware of the benefits and potential of DTs
- **Resistance to change:** Organizations may hesitate to adopt DTs due to the perceived complexity or cost

15.9.10 Uncertain return on investment

- **Long-term benefits:** While DTs promise cost savings and efficiency, it may take years for organizations to realize a return on their initial investment
- **Evolving technology:** Rapid advancements in related technologies may render current implementations obsolete, requiring frequent updates

15.10 Future scope

The future scope for DTT is vast, as it continues to evolve and find applications across industries. Below are key areas where DTs are expected to grow and make a significant impact:

15.10.1 Smart cities and infrastructure

- **Urban planning:** DTs of cities can simulate traffic patterns, energy usage, and environmental impacts for efficient planning
- **Infrastructure management:** Real-time monitoring of bridges, roads, and buildings for predictive maintenance and safety
- **Energy optimization:** Integrating DTs with smart grids to optimize energy distribution and reduce waste

15.10.2 Healthcare and medicine

- **Personalized healthcare:** DTs of human bodies could simulate individual health scenarios, enabling precise diagnostics and personalized treatments
- **Medical training:** Simulations for surgeries and complex medical procedures using DT models
- **Drug development:** Accelerated testing of drug effects through digital replicas of human cells and organs

15.10.3 Manufacturing and industry 4.0

- **Predictive maintenance:** Enhanced reliability of machinery by predicting failures before they occur
- **Process optimization:** Simulating production lines for increased efficiency and reduced waste
- **Quality assurance:** Real-time monitoring and adjustments during manufacturing ensure product quality

15.10.4 A&D

- **Aircraft maintenance:** DTs of airplanes and spacecraft enable real-time monitoring and maintenance
- **Mission simulations:** Testing scenarios for space missions or military operations
- **Fleet management:** Optimizing the performance and safety of defense equipment and vehicles

15.10.5 Real estate and construction

- **BIM:** Advanced DTs of buildings are used to manage design, construction, and maintenance
- **Energy efficiency:** Simulating HVAC and lighting systems for sustainable buildings
- **Smart homes:** Enhancing home automation with real-time monitoring and control

15.10.6 Transportation and mobility

- **Autonomous vehicles:** Simulating driving scenarios to train AI systems for self-driving cars
- **Fleet optimization:** Managing logistics and transportation networks more efficiently
- **Traffic management:** DTs of urban traffic systems aim to reduce congestion and emissions

15.10.7 Retail and customer experience

- **Virtual stores:** Digital replicas of retail environments for personalized shopping experiences
- **Supply chain optimization:** Simulating supply chain operations to identify bottlenecks and reduce costs
- **Product customization:** Allowing customers to visualize and customize products in real-time

15.10.8 Agriculture and environment

- **Precision farming:** Monitoring soil conditions, crop health, and weather patterns to optimize yields
- **Climate change analysis:** Simulating environmental changes and their impacts on ecosystems
- **Water management:** Managing water resources and preventing wastage through DTs of reservoirs and pipelines

15.10.9 Energy and utilities

- **Renewable energy systems:** DTs of wind turbines, solar panels, and energy grids for improved efficiency
- **Oil and gas exploration:** Simulating drilling operations and reservoir management
- **Sustainability goals:** Tracking and optimizing energy usage to reduce carbon footprints

15.10.10 Education and research

- **Immersive learning:** Using DTs for interactive and realistic training environments
- **Research simulations:** Accelerating scientific discoveries through virtual experiments and models
- **STEM education**: Enhancing learning through digital replicas of real-world systems

15.10.11 Emerging trends

Integration with AI and IoT: Advanced analytics, real-time decision-making, and automation (Vohra, 2022; Afzal et al., 2025; Wang et al., 2023)
Edge computing: Faster processing of data locally, enabling real-time responsiveness
Blockchain for security: Ensuring secure data sharing between DTs and stakeholders
Digital thread: Linking multiple DTs across the lifecycle of a product or system

15.10.12 Challenges to address for future growth

- **Scalability**: Ensuring DTs can handle complex, large-scale systems
- **Interoperability**: Standardizing frameworks to enable communication across different platforms
- **Affordability**: Making the technology accessible to smaller businesses and developing regions

15.11 Expanding use cases for smart cities and infrastructure

The future of DTT is promising, with transformative potential across industries. As technology advances, DTs will become increasingly sophisticated, driving efficiency, innovation, and sustainability in diverse fields.

Expanding use cases for **DTs in smart cities and infrastructure** are reshaping urban management, sustainability, and citizen experiences. Below are the key areas where DTs are driving innovation and utility.

15.11.1 *Urban planning and development*

- **Simulating urban growth**: Modeling population expansion, land use, and infrastructure needs to guide city planning
- **Environmental impact assessments**: Simulating air quality, noise pollution, and ecological effects of urban projects
- **Mixed-use developments**: Testing zoning plans to optimize the balance between residential, commercial, and recreational spaces

15.11.2 *Traffic and transportation management*

- **Traffic flow optimization**: Real-time modeling of traffic patterns to reduce congestion and improve travel times
- **Public transit monitoring**: Managing buses, trains, and metro systems to enhance punctuality and efficiency
- **Autonomous vehicle integration**: Providing virtual environments to test self-driving cars' interactions within urban areas
- **Emergency response**: Optimizing routes for emergency vehicles by simulating various scenarios

15.11.3 *Energy management*

- **Smart grids**: DTs of city energy networks enable efficient distribution, real-time demand response, and outage prediction
- **Renewable integration**: Simulating the impact of solar panels, wind turbines, and other renewable energy sources on the grid
- **Energy efficiency in buildings**: Managing HVAC systems, lighting, and power usage to minimize waste in smart buildings

15.11.4 *Water and waste management*

- **Water distribution networks**: Monitoring pipelines to detect leaks and optimize water usage
- **Flood risk assessment**: Simulating weather patterns and drainage systems to prepare for extreme events
- **Smart waste management**: Using real-time data to optimize garbage collection routes and recycling programs

15.11.5 Infrastructure maintenance and management

- **Bridge and road monitoring**: Real-time structural health monitoring to predict and prevent failures
- **Utility infrastructure**: Managing underground utilities, such as gas and electricity lines, to minimize disruptions
- **Building lifecycle management**: Tracking the lifecycle of public buildings for maintenance and renovations

15.11.6 Disaster management and resilience

- **Earthquake simulations**: Assessing the impact of seismic events on infrastructure to guide preparedness
- **Flood mapping**: Creating flood-risk models to design resilient drainage and floodplain systems
- **Emergency evacuation plans**: Simulating evacuation routes and scenarios to ensure public safety

15.11.7 Citizen services and engagement

- **Personalized services**: Offering tailored services, such as customized public transport routes based on real-time data
- **Augmented experiences**: Using AR/VR and DTs for tourism, cultural heritage sites, and public spaces
- **Public feedback loops**: Allowing citizens to interact with virtual models of projects and contribute suggestions

15.11.8 Sustainability and environmental goals

- **Carbon footprint tracking**: Measuring emissions across the city to identify areas for improvement
- **Green infrastructure design**: Modeling parks, green roofs, and urban forests for maximum environmental benefits
- **Circular economy models**: Simulating waste reduction and recycling initiatives for sustainable growth

15.11.9 Smart security and surveillance

- **Crime prevention**: Predicting high-risk zones through behavioral and environmental data analysis

- **Infrastructure security**: Monitoring critical infrastructure for potential vulnerabilities and breaches
- **Crowd management**: Using real-time data to manage large events and ensure public safety

15.11.10 DT for entire cities (city-wide twins)

- **Holistic urban management**: A single, integrated model for monitoring all aspects of city operations, from energy to public services
- **Economic forecasting**: Simulating economic growth scenarios and their impacts on city resources
- **Cross-system integration**: Connecting DTs of transportation, utilities, and public spaces for comprehensive decision-making

15.11.10.1 Emerging innovations

AI-driven predictive analytics: Using AI for smarter decision-making and automation
Blockchain integration: Enhancing data security and transparency across city services
5G networks: Supporting the high-speed communication required for real-time updates and actions

So, DTs are transforming smart cities and infrastructure, making them more sustainable, efficient, and citizen-centric. Their ability to simulate, predict, and optimize across diverse urban systems ensures they will play a critical role in shaping the cities of the future.

15.12 Specific cities implementing the DT are as follows:

DTT is increasingly being adopted by cities worldwide to enhance urban planning, infrastructure management, and citizen services. Here are some notable examples:

15.12.1 Singapore: Virtual singapore

Singapore has developed "Virtual Singapore," a comprehensive 3D digital model of the city-state. This DT integrates real-time data to simulate and analyze urban scenarios, aiding in urban planning, disaster management, and sustainability initiatives.

15.12.2 Helsinki, Finland

Helsinki has implemented a DT to enhance urban planning and citizen engagement. The city uses the virtual model to simulate urban development projects, assess environmental impacts, and gather public feedback, leading to more informed decision-making.

15.12.3 Warner Robins and Columbus, Georgia, USA

These cities have adopted Smart City DTs to create data-driven feedback loops among human systems, infrastructure, and technology. The DTs assist in urban planning, infrastructure management, and improving public services.

15.12.4 Sydney, Australia

Sydney has developed an urban DT that integrates diverse real-time and historical data, including weather, traffic, and emissions. This platform aids in sustainable urban planning by allowing predictive modeling and proactive interventions.

15.12.5 Espoo, Finland

Espoo is utilizing a local DT to empower urban planners with informed decision-making capabilities. The initiative focuses on ensuring that digital transformation and the green transition benefit all citizens, enhancing sustainability and inclusivity. These examples illustrate the growing adoption of DTT in urban environments, leading to smarter, more sustainable, and citizen-centric cities.

15.13 Conclusion

The rapid evolution of DTT is reshaping industries and unlocking new possibilities. Emerging trends such as AI integration, IoT synergy, AR/VR visualization, and a focus on sustainability are driving its adoption and impact. Addressing challenges like cybersecurity and standardization will further accelerate its growth, enabling organizations to harness the full potential of DTs. As these trends unfold, DTs are set to become an indispensable tool for innovation, efficiency, and sustainability in the digital age.

References

Afzal, M.K., Naeem, M., Ejaz, W., 2025. Digital Twins for Wireless Networks: Overview, Architecture, and Challenges. Springer Nature Switzerland. doi:10.1007/978-3-031-73679-7.

Vohra, M., 2022. Digital Twin Technology: Fundamentals and Applications. Wiley. doi:10.1002/9781119842316.

Wang, W., Zaheer, Q., Qiu, S., Wang, W., Ai, C., Wang, J., Wang, S., Hu, W., 2023. Digital Twins Technologies. Springer Science and Business Media LLC, pp. 27–74. doi:10.1007/978-981-99-5804-7_2.

CHAPTER 16

Advancing real-time insights: Leveraging artificial intelligence digital twins for enhanced system and optimization

S. Kannadhasan[a], P. Gomathi[b], S. Ganesh[c], and R. Nagarajan[d]

[a]Department of Electronics and Communication Engineering, Study World College of Engineering, Coimbatore, Tamil Nadu, India
[b]Department of Electrical and Electronics Engineering, Study World College of Engineering, Coimbatore, Tamil Nadu, India
[c]Department of Computer Science and Engineering, Study World College of Engineering, Coimbatore, Tamil Nadu, India
[d]Department of Electrical and Electronics Engineering, Gnanamani College of Technology, Namakkal, Tamil Nadu, India

16.1 Introduction to artificial intelligence digital twins

The use of digital twins (DTs) in the healthcare industry has increased. "Digital twin for health" (DT4H) has great potential to transform the entire healthcare system, including administration and delivery, illness treatment and prevention and health and well-being maintenance. Ultimately, this idea could potentially improve human existence. Due to the availability of critical data, specialist knowledge, and a strong cybertechnology infrastructure, Big Data's explosive expansion and the ongoing progress of artificial intelligence (AI) and Data science (DS) might expedite DT research and development. Despite the involvement of the military, businesses, and government in several DT programs, DT4H is still in its early stages. This study examines the drawbacks of consortium research centers, evaluates the existing climate for promoting Research and development (R&D) prospects in the healthcare industry, and presents a summary of the DTs that are currently in use. Through groundbreaking research and development in the field of DT technology, we expect the formation of a cooperative global effort among stakeholders to enhance healthcare and quality of life for millions of people worldwide.

The range of data sources these models employ is reflected in the breadth of their applications. An organ-specific DT, such as one that mimics cardiac activity, is essential for

Artificial Intelligence, Machine Learning and Blockchain in Digital Twin Computing.
https://doi.org/10.1016/B978-0-443-43914-8.00006-6

forecasting the performance of mechanical medical devices, such as stents and pacemakers. However, illness models provide priceless insights into the efficacy of pharmacological treatments, particularly regarding the ways in which medications interact with intricate biological systems. Apart from these distinctions, there are notable variations in how computational analytics is used by each kind of model. This diversity underscores the specialized nature of the analytics involved while also reflecting the particular needs and goals of each model. To fully realize the promise of DTs to improve medical advances and healthcare outcomes, it is essential to comprehend these differences.

DTs have been employed by the healthcare industry to create digital representations of electronic medical information, hospital surroundings, human physiology, and test findings. Hospital workflow management, improving patient care directly, reducing resource scarcity via resource efficiency, and revolutionizing the clinical care process are just a few of the applications. In the context of healthcare management, we divide DTs into three groups: (De Vito et al., 2014) production or processes (used to effectively design new goods); (Salto-Tellez et al., 2019) product design (used to schedule manufacturing and production); and (Abels et al., 2019) system performance (used to collect, organize, and evaluate operational data).

Globally, there is a growing trend toward extensive urbanization. By 2050, it's predicted that 66% of people will live in metropolitan areas. Resources are scarce, and there are serious environmental and social issues as a result of the significant increase in urbanization. In an effort to solve these issues via the smart city concept, municipal decision-makers work with outside parties to preserve the city's present living standards. Essentially, the concept of smart cities is to exploit loopholes in the market and profit from new trends, such as digitization. Information and communication technology companies, together with their telecom equipment partners, may have a substantial and readily exploitable market in smart cities. Even if this opportunity has passed, it's not as easy to make money from it. This article looks at the primary obstacles that smart city initiatives must overcome from the viewpoint of regional decision-makers. The survey, which included 65 respondents from a variety of small and large companies, served as the foundation for the study's findings. The findings indicate that the primary concerns of decision-makers in smart cities are a wide range of technical and nontechnical issues, including collaboration, economics, governance, social acceptance, and technological awareness, in addition to high technological risk, user security and privacy issues, and cybercrime concerns (Jiang et al., 2023; Thien Huynh et al., 2023; Ciregan et al., 2012; Gedefaw et al., 2023; Hanna and Hanna, 2022).

By 2030, over 60% of people on Earth—up from the current over 50%—are expected to reside in cities. Globally, there will be an additional 65 million people living in cities between now and 2025, according to projections made by the McKinsey Global Institute. Urban populations have been rising gradually for some time. Cities' population density has a significant influence on innovation, economic growth, ecology, and many other factors. Due to the significant increase in urbanization, resource utilization has led to resource restrictions and climate change. Cities are a major contributor to environmental stress and concerns about global warming, accounting for 75% of global energy consumption and 80% of greenhouse gas emissions. Cities are progressively establishing goals and regulations to boost the use of renewable energy, enhance energy efficiency, and reduce the environmental damage caused by climate change. People from underdeveloped countries, in particular, migrate to urban areas in pursuit of better prospects, as population density increases with urbanization. Providing improved services while meeting business expectations to remain competitive in the global market, as well as addressing the increasing need to reduce our environmental impact and fulfill climate change objectives, are the key challenges that cities worldwide must overcome. It is costly to modernize infrastructure, increase energy efficiency, and improve living and working conditions. However, cities often lack the financial means to provide governance and services that are essential for the effective administration of scarce resources.

Cities are under pressure to reduce their consumption of financial, social, and physical resources, as well as to minimize their overall carbon footprint and service costs. Therefore, for effective resource management and control in cities, innovative delivery techniques and improved infrastructure are crucial. They stated that in order for cities to address financial constraints, they needed to devise creative ways to successfully gather, organize, and utilize their resources. For instance, São Paulo enhanced its value-added tax revenues without increasing the rate by employing creative tax collection strategies. Constructing smart cities is essential to addressing the growing challenges, particularly given the current situation. However, as "smart cities" are a new concept still in the early stages of development, there are controversial concerns regarding the management and implementation of these initiatives. Smart city initiatives face a variety of challenges, ranging from administrative to technological. Poor digital infrastructure, financial constraints, lack of cooperation, and funding issues are some of the primary obstacles. Among the numerous challenges that smart city programs must address are resident security and privacy (Shelhamer and Long, 2017; Wang et al., 2016; Chen et al., 2017; Alsubaie et al., 2017; Ma et al., 2017).

The overall evaluation of the quantitative study has shown that specific technological and business challenges confront smart cities. The research findings of this study indicate that a major obstacle to implementing smart city ideas is a lack of funding. It may also be challenging to precisely calculate the costs and benefits of investments and assess the long-term life cycle consequences of such decisions. The execution of smart city concepts is severely endangered by a lack of capital financing and investment. It has been suggested that there are a number of benefits for a variety of businesses, even if creating smart cities is expensive. Because smart cities are still relatively new, there is a possibility that individuals and organizations don't fully understand how to apply them. Thus, the execution of smart city projects is seriously hampered by the vague vision and lack of understanding. In a similar spirit, the study's results suggest that a key obstacle to the adoption of smart city norms is a lack of awareness among pertinent parties. This ignorance presents basic challenges for smart cities. Cities need to have clear strategies for smart cities and a comprehensive roadmap in order to provide predictability for all stakeholders. Working together, communicating, and integrating with several stakeholders is a labor-intensive process. In addition, since project execution necessitates collaboration across several components, systems, and levels, the creation of shared standards is essential. In addition to raising concerns about cybercrime, using information and communications technology (ICT) to increase the connectivity of essential urban infrastructure (including transit and power) also highlights a variety of privacy and security vulnerabilities. By definition, smart cities are heavily digitalized, with a large amount of data stored digitally and a large number of physical equipment connected to the Internet. Although this might help achieve social aims, it also presents a simple opportunity for illicit activity. There are many obstacles that might keep smart city projects from growing. Both technical and nontechnical components are included in the list. One of the largest barriers to putting smart city concepts into practice is providing governance and other services with constrained, sometimes declining financial resources. Furthermore, understanding the exact costs and benefits of investments and evaluating their long-term life cycle consequences might be difficult at times (Ford, 2015; Graetz and Michaels, 2015; Goldin and Katz, 2010; Gordon, 2016; Olmstead, 2017).

Based on the conversations thus far, interoperability challenges, as well as data security and privacy problems, seem to be equally important difficulties in the development of the smart city. Many more problems are expressed in the literature from the viewpoints of various stakeholders. A few authors have discussed the difficulties in obtaining vast volumes of data and evaluating its analytical worth, as well as the problems in guaranteeing data and service accessibility in smart cities due to a lack of infrastructure integration. Concerns with assessing cost-benefit ratios and returns on investments in smart cities have been raised by other media sites. Infrastructure in smart cities presents a unique problem. If smart cities rely too heavily on technology and solution providers, they run the danger of being technologically locked in.

Global adoption of the idea of "smart cities" is a consequence of population expansion. India, another growing nation, has taken up the task of fostering and promoting the smart city culture domestically. The first stage in this attempt was the government's smart city initiative. To differentiate the nation from other program-participating countries, the objective was to create and expand smart cities within the nation. This research focuses on the Government of India's objective of creating smart cities and the strategies and policies that have been suggested. We have examined the issues preventing the mission's expansion. We have also identified the several gaps that hindered this operation from progressing.

Urban areas have grown significantly as a result of population increases and the need for decent living. In contemporary times, urban areas are defined as towns and cities that are more diverse than rural ones in every aspect. Subsystems within these urban areas are often complex and interrelated. Increasing security, sustainability, and productivity have long been the major goals of smart city initiatives in the West. Developing nations, on the other hand, often prioritize modernizing and expanding their infrastructure when embracing smart city programs. Cities of the 21st century are intricate ecosystems that deal with a variety of social, economic, and environmental problems, which put strain on vital sectors such as the media, education, energy, and health. In order to address the needs of their citizens. contemporary cities find it difficult to maintain and modernize public services. For this reason, smart city projects are essential to addressing current urban issues and raising quality-of-life metrics. It is essential to implement cleaner manufacturing initiatives to promote the growth of smart cities, especially in developing countries such as India. There is no one standard definition for what constitutes a "smart city," as it varies from country to country, from person to person, and based on a plethora of other factors. Because of factors like location and resource availability, India will perceive smart cities quite differently than any other country. Every Indian has a wish list of products and services that they believe would complete their dream smart city. To satisfy the requirements and expectations of the public, city authorities should ideally endeavor to build an environmentally friendly system, which is characterized by the four pillars of integrated structural, physical, political, and economic development infrastructure. The goal of the mission plan for sustainable development is to incentivize communities to install "smart" systems, provide network infrastructure, and offer their residents a decent standard of living in a safe and sustainable environment. With an emphasis on just and fruitful growth, the objective is to take a close look at compact areas and construct a reproducible prototype that may serve as a model for other developing cities. The government's efforts to promote greener manufacturing, India's smart city policy, and the newly adopted smart economic development plan (Olson and Kemery, 2019; OpenAI "Overview", n.d.; Pethokoukis, 2016; Quillian et al., 2017; Zhou et al., 2021) are all summarized in this document. The research has important implications for comprehending the core principles of the smart city framework and for defining the role of collaborative creativity in fostering healthy development activities and smart city growth from an Indian perspective. The implications are related to increasing public involvement in the entire process of developing a smart city and safer production activities to reinforce collaborative governance as a way to effectively handle the concerns that have been highlighted. Having a lively conversation with concerned parties and optimizing public-private partnerships will inevitably reduce the challenges of implementing more environmentally friendly procurement practices and advance the growth of smart cities (Shaker et al., 2021; Li et al., 2022; Abels et al., 2019; De Vito et al., 2014; Salto-Tellez et al., 2019).

DTs, which are virtual replicas of real items and are mostly utilized in manufacturing, have the potential to completely transform the healthcare sector. The potential of DTs and AI advancements to transform patient care and clinical decision support in the healthcare industry is examined in this article. Specifically, we propose the use of DTs to enhance cancer treatments through more individualized care, treatment planning, and diagnostics. When DTs and AI are combined, it is possible to handle and evaluate vast volumes of heterogeneous data from several sources, leading to more precise and individualized treatment decisions. Offering cost-effective, superior treatment that improves clinical outcomes and patient satisfaction is a major obstacle in the medical field that this strategy seeks to tackle. In order to overcome the constraints of existing therapy, this paper, which focuses on endometrial cancer, provides a conceptual model of a DT augmented by AI. We explore how AI techniques may be used to create efficient DTs for cancer care, which would enhance patient outcomes and treatment experiences. From the perspectives of technology and healthcare, we also enumerate the primary barriers and facilitators that influence the adoption and effectiveness of DTs in clinical settings. Our objective is to demonstrate the revolutionary potential of AI and DTs in cancer therapy, provide insights into their real-world applications, and offer recommendations for overcoming challenges to enhance patient-centered care in oncology.

16.2 Integration of AI and DT technologies

India launched the National Smart Cities Mission (SCM) in 2015 with the goal of transforming cities into more sustainable and equitable places to live. India came up with the idea in response to the needs of a rapidly urbanizing population, which calls for a major overhaul of the built environment in order to promote a more affluent and just society. An additional project is being financed nationwide, with a total sanction of ₹1.84 lakh crore (24.6 billion United States Dollar (USD)) for the initiative. However, so far, the SCM has fallen short in a number of key areas. Its funding has been disbursed via a grant system that conflicts with the country's strategic goal for smart urbanization. Furthermore, rather than encouraging digitization and sustainability in India's cities, the phrase "smart cities" has expanded too much to serve as a catch-all for recently approved government funding for urban initiatives. This raises the question of whether India would be better off using the money to expand the systems that meet the fundamental requirements of the people or to invest in smart cities first at this point. Fortunately, it is possible to change the SCM's goal such that future program investments will serve the requirements of the populace now while also laying the foundation for a more sophisticated infrastructure fit for the 21st century. This is truly necessary if the SCM and other urban development programs are to provide real returns on investment equal to or greater than their costs.

This urbanization boom is unprecedented in human history, having begun in the middle of the 20th century. Because economic possibilities are concentrated in metropolitan regions and there is a growing movement from rural areas to cities, billions of people live in massive agglomerations that were unthinkable only a century ago. The number of people living in cities increased dramatically worldwide between 1950 and 2030, from 751 million to 4.5 billion, and is projected to rise to 5.2 billion. Projections indicate that since 1950, urbanization has grown at a rate that has almost quadrupled, from 30% to 57% at this point and 60% by 2030. More people were living in cities globally by 1990 than there were in 1980. In 1980, there were already more people living in cities globally than there were projected to be in 2030. Urbanization has increased globally, but nowhere has it done so faster than in Asia, where the share of the population living in cities has quadrupled from 17.5% to 51.1% since 1950. India is probably going to contribute the most to Asia's increasing urban population during the next few years. From 62 million to 482 million, the number of Indians living in urban areas has grown about eight times since 1950, contributing to an overall increase in urbanization from 17.3% to 35%. We expect population growth to continue until shortly before 2050, at which point a gradual change will occur in the country's economy from agriculture to industry and services, pushing a growing share of people into cities, much like what occurred in China beginning in 1980. Because of its quicker rates of population increase, we anticipate that Sub-Saharan Africa will overtake India in the coming decades. By 2030, urban areas in India should account for 40% of the country's population and produce 75% of its GDP. Effectively controlling India's urban expansion might increase GDP by as much as 1.5% annually, according to Government of India (GOI) predictions.

As cities become the stage for all sectors of life, they are becoming more crucial for sustainable development. There is pressure on the environment and society to meet the increasing demands of urban people, who often enjoy better living circumstances than their rural counterparts. However, since city living makes it possible to distribute resources more effectively to those living in densely populated regions, it may be more sustainable and efficient than other lifestyles. The primary challenge facing urban planners and politicians in the 21st century is striking a balance, and the UN's Sustainable Development Goals provide a comprehensive road map for solving it. UN member states are asked under SDG 11 to build inclusive, secure, resilient, and sustainable cities by 2030. It establishes benchmarks for gauging the achievement of this objective, including expanding the supply of reasonably priced housing, building public transit systems, bolstering emergency readiness, and lowering air and water pollution from waste disposal and nonsustainable energy sources. The current rise in popularity of "smart cities" has provided an opportunity to accelerate these tendencies toward vibrant, sustainable communities. Smart cities incorporate the latest developments in digital technology into every facet of their infrastructure. They do this by utilizing ICT to turn the urban environment into a dynamic, ever-adapting system that responds to resource requests in real time. For instance, smart cities may instantaneously send out extra cars or suggest that consumers take an alternate route in response to high transportation system utilization. In order to better balance supply and demand for water and electricity at any given moment, they might also interact with utility suppliers. CSD Working Paper Series Towards a New Indian Model of Growth and Development Powered by Information and Communications Technology. Smart cities have the potential to decrease waste, enhance the efficiency and equity of services offered to urban residents, and quicken environmental preservation efforts when implemented properly. In the continuing discussion over the long-term effects of global urbanization, smart cities will have a major impact on the dynamics of social opportunity, economic mobility, and sustainability.

But smart cities are not a panacea. The underlying technology of smart cities increases the throughput of applications while simultaneously boosting resource consumption efficiency and contributing to sustainability. Hence, current systems, which may or may not be sustainable at the scales needed for today's rapidly growing metropolitan regions, tend to be reinforced by smart city technology. Cities that invest in improving the navigation of their roads for autonomous vehicles, for example, might experience a temporary rise in traffic and a drop in emissions; however, this will eventually drive up demand for personal vehicles—a mode of transportation that is fundamentally incompatible with the population density required for a sustainable urban area. Prior to being made available to the general public, smart technology must be integrated into a self-reinforcing system of data collection and response optimization, which necessitates a large upfront investment and security precautions. At that point, we'll employ smart technology to its fullest. In view of the strain from future urban population expansion, which is all but unavoidable, authorities should thus think carefully before using smart city technology to reinforce infrastructure. Instead of implementing a stand-alone solution with limited room for synergies or external benefits, they need to consider investing in a more extensive digital ecosystem for their city. In response to the possibility of continued urban growth, challenges to sustainable development, and increasing pressure on already developed cities to offer opportunities and a high standard of living for their citizens, the GOI, under Prime Minister Narendra Modi, launched the National SCM on June 25, 2015. With a four-year initial funding level of 48,000 crore INR (6.4 billion USD), the NSCM selected a total of 100 towns to participate. Once a project is completed, the aim is to demonstrate to other towns the potential of implementing smart city concepts. The ultimate goal of these pilot projects is to spur a wave of private-public investment in the advancement of smart city development—even in the absence of direct government involvement. For its national projects, the NSCM has now drawn 1.84 lakh crore INR (24.6 billion USD) in tendered investment from the public and private sectors. Nearby cities that were not included in the SCM will struggle to grow or survive. The Smart City Guidelines state that "smart people are essential to the Smart Cities Mission," and that the present framework needs to do more to support and encourage the growth of these individuals. Considering the high degree of digital proficiency in India, a workable plan to maximize this potential would be to promote more technology volunteers and civic entrepreneurship. In order to actualize a cohesive vision of inclusive, intelligent technology growth, smart cities still need recognition as the autonomous political and economic entities that they must be. Using the justification that local governments are incapable of performing certain tasks, Urban Local Bodies (ULBs) often handle just the most fundamental aspects of

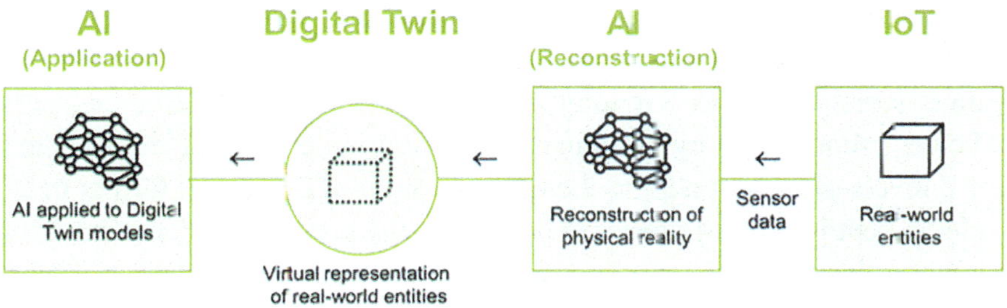

Fig. 16.1 Digital twin.

public services, allowing state governments to manage the remaining duties. ULBs end up relying on outside specialists who are not personally or democratically connected to the needs of the city when they are tasked with projects requiring this expertise, thereby undermining municipal capacity. The DT is shown in Fig. 16.1. There has been a mistaken perception that the SCM's encouragement of Special Purpose Vehicles (SPVs) to take project control irrevocably decreased direct municipal power; however, there isn't much data to support this assertion. Notwithstanding their shortcomings, it is crucial to work toward streamlining and reforming local political institutions rather than doing away with them entirely, as an empowered, operational, and unitary city government has sophisticated solutions for many of India's other urban problems and is not hampered by the same incentive mismatches that hindered the SCM.

Empowering local governments and tackling the antiurban legacies that have made many Indian towns unviable are essential for creating smart, sustainable cities. For instance, construction that is dense, mixed-use, and transit-friendly cannot coexist with antiquated urban planning laws that mandate Mumbai to have an outrageously low Floor Space Index of 1.33. Urban economist Edward Glaeser states that "cities grow upward or outward," and Indian cities have been growing outward without providing the necessary infrastructure or basic services. The outcome is sprawl, traffic, and inadequate public services. Like India's urbanization, these urban concerns also need a collaborative response. But it's challenging to solve these big challenges at the right scale because of legislation like the 74th Amendment, which codifies decentralization and devolution in the national government. Though India's growing urban centers require a shift in the administrative structure, Gandhi may have seen India as a nation of 700,000 villages. Even while local government needs additional capacity to implement a common vision, granting neighborhood committees and local governments the legal power to oversee national administration may be a fundamentally bad approach to handling the problems confronting the nation.

Indian cities are still growing, and their limited ability to govern needs a sustained commitment to social and economic reform without resorting to hyperbole. The SCM plans for big data urbanization, but it will take years to develop the governing capability that is needed. Building capacity may include increasing the training opportunities for SPV and ULB program officers, as well as providing them with the necessary resources, personnel, and tools. The goal should start by outlining the distribution chain that connects the federal, state, and local levels of government to the SPVs in order to avoid any further delays if the SPV model is kept in place. In order to determine the precise problems that arose and provide lessons for the future, the mission must also carry out thorough research on SPVs in developing cities. Integrated Command and Control Centers (ICCCs) need to take on more responsibilities and give up new project proposals in favor of sustaining the smart infrastructure that has already been built, as capacity increases to accommodate a wider variety of urban services. Cities should collaborate with the SCM to ensure that projects align with regional development objectives, provide new funding sources like municipal bonds and new taxation schemes, and enhance data security and encryption specifications throughout the project. Several of the SCM's shortcomings are being addressed by recently announced new projects. The National Urban Digital Mission (NUDM) was presented by Ministry of Housing and Urban Affairs (MoHUA) on February 23, 2021. By 2024, it aims to provide shared digital infrastructure throughout all Indian metropolitan centers. NUDM intends to use open APIs to encourage interoperability and greater stakeholder involvement. The group has already established partnerships with businesses, trade groups, urban governments, academic institutions, and civil society organizations. Establishing a new national digital ecosystem would include integrating this new digital infrastructure platform with open government systems such as Aadhaar, Unified Payments Interface (UPI), and Goods and Services Tax Network (GSTN). The India Urban Data Exchange (IUDX), a new digital infrastructure platform, was established via cooperation between MoHUA and Indian Institute of Science (IISc) Bengaluru. A dashboard with data on all accessible urban indicators will be made available to the public by IUDX. Bike docks, waste management trucks, buses and bus stops, air quality monitors, flood sensors, and public reporting are just a few of the places where data will be collected. An open-source repository for intelligent governance tools, SmartCode, is a third data platform that will provide the source code for efficient applications. SmartCode may expedite the development of municipal technology by enabling users to modify current solutions, saving cities from having to start from scratch. The Jawaharlal Nehru National Urban Renewal Mission, which was established in 2005 and relaunched in 2015 under the name Atal, includes 38 out of the 67 cities in India, indicating that Indian towns have long battled with ICT-driven service delivery techniques. The expected eGovernment portfolio was not produced by the Mission for Rejuvenation and Urban Transformation (AMRUT). If this is due to a lack of technical expertise, programs like the National Urban Learning Platform may assist by providing free training on data governance, best practices for the climate, wastewater management, e-mobility, and other related topics. To help municipal officials understand, assess, and implement big data recommendations, MoHUA is working with Tata Trusts on a different project known as TULIP (Tata Urban Learning and Internship Initiative).

With a focus on data-driven governance, TULIP has so far financed 13,000 internships at 284 ULBs. The guidelines for cities to gather, analyze, and use big data are outlined in the DataSmart Cities and Data Maturity Assessment Framework, which was recently unveiled by the GOI. This paradigm aims to assist cities in building data-driven ecosystems for governance in the future. In the end, efforts are still being made to enhance the provision of essential services in India's cities. The 2021 budget unveiled the Jal Jeevan Mission, allocating 2.9 lakh crore INR (39.4 billion USD) for the uninterrupted water supply to all 4378 ULBs in India, the management of liquid waste in 500 cities taking part in the AMRUT program, and the provision of tap connections for 2.86 crore households. AMRUT will also invest in the development of urban green areas and pollution abatement by offering incentives for the use of public and nonmotorized transport. AMRUT is substantially less dependent on PPPs and corporate finance than the SCM. In addition, the Pradhan Mantri Awas Yojana (PMAY), also known as Housing for All 2022, aims to build 20 million affordable homes in urban and rural regions with full utility and sanitary connections by the time it ends in March of the following year. Swachh Bharat II was unveiled in February 2020 with the goal of managing wastewater in all cities, towns, and villages with fewer than 100,000 residents. This program also aims to solidify the progress made in Phase I. In 2015, PMAY was unveiled. Though it has a lengthy history, AI is continually evolving. Intelligent agents, or devices that monitor their surroundings and then act accordingly to maximize the chance of attaining an aim, are the focus of this area. In addition to discussing the fundamentals of contemporary AI, this article will include a number of examples. AI is the ability of computers, software, and other systems to mimic the creativity and intellect of humans. It also describes these systems' capacity to come to their own conclusions, solve issues, and make decisions. People may gradually become better at what they do since the majority of AI systems have the ability to learn. AI techniques, such as machine learning, deep learning, and predictive analysis, have been the subject of current research focusing on improvements in planning, learning, reasoning, thinking, and action-taking skills. The suggested study aimed to ascertain the distinctions between artificial and human intelligence in light of this. There are situations in which existing AI is superior to human intelligence. We also examine critically the shortcomings of the most advanced AI already in use, the reasons it can't reach or exceed human intellect, and the remaining difficulties. It will also examine predictions about AI and provide practical solutions for addressing them in the next decades.

16.3 Real-time data processing in AI DTs

Robots with AI nowadays are capable of mimicking human cognitive processes in a number of ways, including learning, problem-solving, reasoning, and forming different conclusions. Robots, computers, and other devices are capable of autonomous thought thanks to AI software and algorithms. Nonetheless, there is still disagreement about many of the robotic AI systems in use today, as more study is required to fully comprehend the problems and possibilities associated with these systems. As a result, AI or robots must be able to precisely carry out the necessary tasks. Furthermore, robots must be able to perform a broad variety of jobs without guidance or help from humans. With the fast development of modern AI, high-performance capabilities such as traffic management and speed minimization are being created. These capabilities will ultimately lead to the development of self-driving automobiles and virtual assistants like Siri. This holds true as human reliance on technology is increased by the present focus on giving robots AI to mirror human traits. The capacity of AI to carry out any particular cognitive activity efficiently also makes people more reliant on technology. Large volumes of data can be handled using AI techniques, which might allow users to access and analyze all the data.

The present danger has made it easier to collect and analyze enormous amounts of data. AI has been characterized as a brain model created in recent years with the goal of mimicking human learning. We must ensure that it is not feasible to create AI that can match human intelligence. We have only used a tiny portion of our potential so far. Just a small portion of the human brain is needed to keep up with the present rate of knowledge expansion. This is because the capacity of the human brain surpasses our existing comprehension and evidence. Since the human brain has around 100 trillion neurons—electrically conducting cells—it possesses extraordinary processing ability to carry out tasks quickly and effectively. Even while computers can already multiply effectively, studies reveal that they are still unable to perform tasks like learning, altering one's vision of the world, and recognizing human traits. AI has led to a number of breakthroughs, such as self-driving automobiles that don't need human aid or oversight. Robotic technology, often known as AI, also refers to intelligent robots that are capable of performing data analysis on massive scales that is not feasible for humans. Robots already carry out mundane tasks that call for intelligence and ingenuity, as shown in Fig. 16.2.

AI, a combination of many technologies, also makes it possible for robots to comprehend, recognize, observe, or carry out human acts independently. When it comes to AI systems, like robots, their main focus is on multitasking skills, whereas human intelligence is largely focused on learning, acting, and understanding. AI tools often center on robots that replicate human behavior. But since the human brain is not like a computer's, AI is still not flawless. In conclusion, AI is able to imitate human behavior or characteristics. In addition, AI is still in its infancy, lacking sophisticated abilities for self-directed learning and relying instead on commands to complete tasks. The highest form of AI will be attained by robots that are able to understand human emotions and behavior. AI is finding its way into our everyday lives more and more, mostly thanks to Global Positioning System (GPS) navigation and check-scanning technology.

Business applications of AI are facilitating the enhancement of several aspects of everyday life, including customer service, finance, sales and marketing, administration, and technical

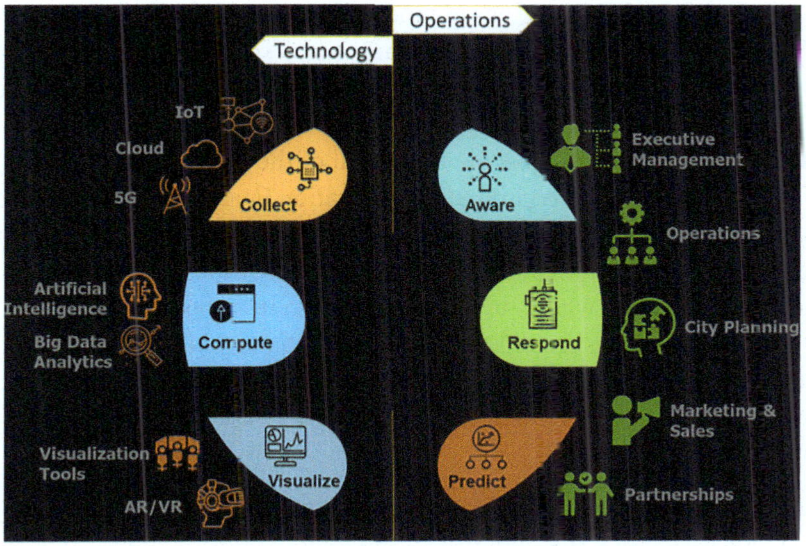

Fig. 16.2 Real-time digital twin.

operations across multiple industries. In order to become more competitive, businesses will use AI and other technologies at all operational levels over the coming years; these initiatives and projects will no longer be isolated digital efforts within organizations. Business procedures are increasingly incorporating AI. It is important to keep in mind that technology has advanced to assist human labor and enable individuals to reach their greatest creative and potential capabilities, not to replace it. The security of modern technologies is enhanced by the traceability of electronic operations and the surrounding safeguards. Corruption may be prevented and countered with the use of new technology. This paper aims to demonstrate the potential benefits of AI in terms of increased worker productivity, career development, and child safety. These days, a significant amount of research is being conducted on AI, which will improve the future when humans will primarily oversee the machines that perform most of the work. The issue of whether AI can outperform humans in terms of efficiency, affordability, effectiveness, and quality is raised by this. In the study, current and emerging technologies are discussed as they are compared and contrasted with human cognition in AI. This essay seeks to evaluate AI technology and project its potential effects on every industry. We will also explore additional AI techniques that may enhance the system.

There are significant differences as well as numerous similarities between AI and human cognition. Every autonomous system has to build and maintain a world model in order to interact with a changing environment. This implies that before the computer "brain" can develop opinions, cameras, microphones, and/or touch sensors must be able to observe the environment. It then has to reconstruct itself using an up-to-date and precise picture of its surroundings. A well-functioning autonomous system requires quick and accurate updates to the world model. For instance, the world model that autonomous unmanned aerial vehicle (UAV) navigation relies on simply contains maps showing suggested routes, height barriers, and no-fly zones, making navigation simple. By showing which altitudes are free of obstructions, radars improve this model in real-time. Preventing the aircraft from entering a no-fly zone or colliding with objects is the main goal of the GPS coordinate plan. The UAV is guided to its destination via GPS coordinates. Navigation in an automated vehicle, however, is significantly more challenging. Cars need to be able to identify pedestrians, bicycles, and other vehicles in addition to having comparable mapping abilities. They also need to figure out where these items are and where they are going to go in a short while. Autonomous automobiles and certain drones are able to do this with the combination of stereo computer vision sensors, conventional radars, and light detection and ranging technologies. Due to the complexity of the operating environment, a typical UAV is not as smart as the global model of an autonomous automobile.

An autonomous car's computer continuously has to predict traffic patterns, monitor all neighboring vehicle dynamics, and identify all possible regions of contact before determining how to respond. Humans drive mostly by guessing or anticipating the actions of other drivers, and they do it with minimal cognitive effort. To maintain and update its current world model, a computer needs a lot of computing power in addition to keeping track of all these variables. An autonomous vehicle will make the best judgments based on probability distributions to ensure safe action execution times in light of this enormous processing barrier. Consequently, the automobile is essentially assuming the optimum course of action given a certain confidence interval. Pilots, for example, use protocols extensively to handle the intricacy of many different aviation-related tasks. Pilots are advised to settle the aircraft first (a skill) and then consult the handbook to ascertain the appropriate course of action (rule-following), for instance, when a firelight flashes or another subsystem signals a problem. There are too many potential answers to memorize, which is why such standardized methods are required. There are various situations in which some interpretation of the methods is necessary, especially as complexity and uncertainty rise. When managing many intricate issues, this is especially true.

We use knowledge-based reasoning when quick mental simulations are needed to solve an issue, and a predetermined set of rules may not always apply to the present circumstance. In the course of making plans, especially when faced with uncertainty, the captain develops mental models or cognitive representations of the outside world. Given the high level of uncertainty involved, the captain has to create a mental model of the surroundings and the condition of the aircraft. This is a situation that follows traditional knowledge-based logic. He was able to choose to depart in the short mental exercise that followed. Reasoning techniques that depend on knowledge-based logic are guided by expert behavior. In situations involving the discharge of a weapon or other critical emergencies, expertise is shown by the application of instinct, judgment, and fast scenario analysis. Experts often make tough selections quickly and economically since it takes time to examine every potential plan alternative, especially when there is uncertainty. True human specialists are distinguished by their capacity to deal with the greatest levels of ambiguity; by comparison, computers find it very challenging to emulate such conduct. Because they are inherently repetitive and have built-in feedback loops that are managed by mathematical representations, skill-based jobs are the simplest to automate. The presence of the appropriate sensors is a necessary presumption, however. The if-then-else nature of rule-based behaviors makes them potentially good candidates for automation. Contrarily, when uncertainty grows, rule-based reasoning gives way to knowledge-based reasoning, necessitating competent handling of ambiguity.

The contrast between the necessity of autonomous versus automated activities begins to emerge at the rule-based reasoning level. This is the point at which some higher-order thinking starts to show itself, but uncertainty is also beginning to increase, particularly in view of the incomplete collection of rules. Though the military UAV called Global Hawk operates on a rule-based system and has the capacity to land autonomously in case of communication failure, it has not been shown to be able to think rationally in every scenario it could encounter. Higher-order thinking would be required for the latter. The most complicated types of cognitive reasoning are knowledge-based behaviors and their related competency, which are often exhibited in contexts with the greatest degrees of uncertainty. Using rule-based reasoning may make it simpler for human or machine decision-makers to choose an option. On the other hand, determining which set of rules is applicable may sometimes be challenging when there is a lot of confusion. Algorithms may not even be able to comprehend the solution space under these uncertain circumstances, which are by definition imprecise and ambiguous, let alone find a workable solution. To get good results, any autonomous system carrying out an essential safety function (e.g., firing weapons) must determine if it can resolve ambiguity. A mission to hit a stationary target on a military location with a high chance of success may be assigned to an autonomous drone. Yes, it is absolutely possible with missiles from many different nations.

16.4 Enhancing system optimization through AI-driven DTs

Humans have to make these judgments via induction in order to deal with uncertainty. Computer algorithms are inherently fragile, meaning that they can only include quantifiable aspects that were recognized early in the design process when they were being created. This is particularly true for data-driven algorithms, such as those used in most AI applications. It is currently beyond the power of computers to comprehend abstract ideas like intuition, knowledge-based reasoning, and genuine competence. While a great deal of research is being done right now, particularly in the areas of AI and machine learning, the pace of advancement is sluggish. These technical skills are necessary for these kinds of systems. The market for highly qualified workers is competitive, nonetheless, since few colleges produce graduates with the technical know-how needed for such positions in robotics, controls, mechatronics, and related sectors. Because of the fierce rivalry for roboticists and allied professionals in these sectors, the aerospace and military industries are less attractive to the most qualified individuals due to their financial difficulties. As a consequence, as the most talented engineers go into the private sector, the global military industry is lagging behind its commercial competitors in terms of technological innovation. As a result of their relative inexperience, military autonomous systems may not be adequate or have the required security and testing protocols. The military industry's ability to create safe semiautonomous systems, let alone fully autonomous ones, is thus a more urgent concern, even if the discussion about outlawing autonomous weapons is pertinent. A fundamental shift in technological prowess is coming, wherein militaries will start to lag significantly behind commercial systems in terms of autonomous system capabilities. While some may argue that competition and a free market have led to the current distribution of R&D and expertise, this argument ignores the reality. Compared to front-line combatants, the typical American is more likely to own an autonomous car, and terrorists may soon be able to purchase drones online that have capabilities that match or surpass those of the armed forces. This disparity in technology accessibility will surely bring up new, unexpected, and disruptive problems for military operations. If governments and security firms keep doing as they now do and mostly ignore AI, might this lead to a change in the balance of power, with major AI services being leased by Google, Amazon, or Facebook? Google has never been associated with any military alliance, except for the acquisition of very sophisticated robotics businesses and the termination of its previous military contracts. Though it has a lengthy history, AI is continually evolving. This area is concerned with intelligent agents that are outfitted with tools to monitor their environment and respond in ways that maximize the likelihood of accomplishing a goal. This article will discuss the theoretical underpinnings of contemporary AI and provide some instances. The capacity of computers, computer programs, and systems to execute intellectual and creative tasks carried out by people, solve issues independently, come to conclusions, and pass judgment in the context of the contemporary digital world is known as AI. People may gradually become better at what they do since the majority of AI systems have the ability to learn. The most recent research on AI techniques, such as deep learning, machine learning, and predictive analysis, aims to improve human reasoning, planning, action, and decision-making skills. In addition, the study will look at what is anticipated of AI going forward and try to address it in the next decades. The capacity to learn and use a variety of skills and information to address a particular issue is what is known as intelligence. The use of one's vast mental capacities to problem-solving and information acquisition is another facet of intelligence. Intelligence and many other cognitive processes are intertwined, including language, attention, planning, memory, and perception. Many studies on the development of intelligence have been conducted in the last 10 years. Artificial and human intelligence are combined to form intellect. Critical human intelligence is the capacity for thought, information acquisition, and problem-solving. Throughout their lifetimes, humans may also easily acquire complicated core behaviors. These days, learning, problem-solving, and decision-making are just a few of the areas where robots and AI may mimic human intellect. Software or programs for AI are used by computers, robots, and other systems to improve their mental capacities. Nonetheless, there is still controversy around a number of contemporary robotic AI systems since more investigation is required to fully comprehend their capacity for problem-solving. Therefore, the necessary tasks must be accurately performed by robots or AI systems. Moreover, robots need to be able to carry out a range of tasks without the need for human direction or help. With high-performance capabilities like traffic management and speed minimization, AI in today's world—including robotic cars—is evolving quickly. SIRI and self-driving automobiles are two instances of this. Human reliance on technology is increased by the present focus on giving robots AI to offer them human-like traits. Humans are becoming more reliant on technology due toAI's capacity to perform any given cognitive activity effectively. With AI systems processing vast volumes of data on computers, users may be able to access all the data for study. As a result, in the present day, there is a far higher danger attached to someone having the ability to collect and analyze data meaningfully. AI has been characterized in recent years as a model of the artificial brain that aims to mimic human learning. We have to convince everyone that it is not possible to create AI that is on par with the human brain. We haven't even come close to using all of our potential so far. Just a little portion of the human brain is needed to keep up with the present rate of knowledge expansion. This is a result of the human brain's greater capacity than what we can now comprehend or prove. The human brain contains around 100 trillion neurons, or electrically conducting cells, giving it a vast computational capability for effective job completion. AI is being utilized to build robots with cognitive characteristics and actions similar to those of humans, including the capacity to recognize, anticipate, and appreciate the significance of a given circumstance. Robotic technology has a big influence on contemporary civilization and is becoming more and more popular in many fields, including business, healthcare, education, the military, entertainment, and quantum physics, to name a few. With the use of expert systems that behave intelligently, learn from their errors, and provide useful advice to users, AI is a potent technique that enables computers and software to regulate robotic thought. The capacity of robots to understand, make decisions, and solve problems is a common definition of AI. AI has led to a number of breakthroughs, such as self-driving automobiles that don't need human aid or oversight. Robotic technology, often known as AI, also refers to intelligent devices that are capable of analyzing massive amounts of data in ways that are not possible for humans. Robots already carry out mundane tasks that call for intelligence and ingenuity. AI, or AI, is the result of several technologies coming together to enable robots to observe, comprehend, learn, and do tasks that are often completed by people. While AI programs, like robots, are designed for specialized tasks like learning, acting, and understanding, human intelligence mainly focuses on a variety of multitasking skills. Human-like robots are often given priority in AI tools. But since the human brain is not like a computer's, AI is still not flawless. In other words, AI may imitate human behavior or personality. Furthermore, AI is still in its infancy, lacking complex self-learning systems and relying instead on orders to do tasks. The ability to comprehend human behavior and emotions will eventually allow AI to modify its neural networks appropriately. In general, there are many ways to create clever devices that allow people to create ever-more intelligent ones and computers to create ever-more intelligent software, a phenomenon known as the "intelligence explosion." However, emotion is a big part of the search for persons who are protected. AI technologies may terrify people in ways that machines cannot. Thus, there's a chance that AI will assist humans in duties and procedures that often don't need emotion or feeling. AI gadgets cannot now run their own operations since they do not have human intellect or mindset. However, if AI research and development continue at their present rate, humankind could be in jeopardy, since AI devices have the potential to learn harmful things via self-learning. The rapid extinction of humanity might result from this. The general traits that set AI apart from human-level intelligence are as follows. Since robots with AI lack feelings, their ability to reason might be useful or harmful. In circumstances where it is necessary, the absence of fake emotion might be harmful. Russell Stuart thought that the capacity for thinking in machines would be limited. Computers are not capable of doing some tasks regardless of programming, and certain approaches to creating intelligent software are unsuccessful. By 2000, a machine was only partially able to communicate for five minutes before being questioned, as per the specifications of what would eventually become known as the Turing Test. It is thus reasonable to assert that machines are capable of thinking, even if they will never be able to laugh at themselves, fall in love, gain experience, discern between good and evil, or exhibit other characteristics of humans. In the last chapter of *Artificial Intelligence: A Modern Approach*, the possibility of creating computers with minds is discussed. The importance of AI has been the subject of much discussion recently, which is expected to spark further discussions regarding the technology's presence down the road. Simplifying human lives is the aim of AI development. The benefits and drawbacks of AI in general, however, are hotly debated. Numerous global businesses are already seeing increases in profitability, and their rates of economic growth will only rise as a result of the development and effective use of AI technology. Moreover, the primary objective of AI prospects will be innovation. Most businesses need to become more involved in development if they want to take advantage of these opportunities. The development of diverse AI systems that adopt symbolic representations of ideas such as knowledge and reason will be advantageous to the global industrial sector. There's a greater chance that developments in AI will show themselves soon given the present conditions. With so many possible applications, AI might lead to significant discoveries and advancements for mankind. People may gradually become better at what they do since the majority of AI systems have the ability to learn. Adoption of AI outside of the IT industry is still in its early or experimental stages. The results suggest that AI has the potential to significantly raise human well-being. In order to solve specific issues in line with its operational algorithms, AI gathers, processes, and analyzes enormous volumes of data.

16.5 Conclusion

AI research and development in the next decades will mostly focus on enhancing audio, video, face, and voice recognition capabilities. Personal assistance and completely automated systems that manage demanding workloads, monitoring, and surveillance, among other duties, will also benefit from AI. Robotics, a branch of AI technology, will pave the way for the future development of autonomous vehicles, delivery robots, and a host of other innovations. Robots in various environments will become more useful and helpful in agriculture and other service contexts due to the great advancements in computer vision and legged mobility. In addition, robots will enhance service delivery, resulting in a reduction in household tasks. Significant information synthesis and improvements in information quality will result from the development of search engines. Furthermore, as biological and medical systems advance through the use of AI approaches, the amount and complexity of information hurdles impeding human skills will diminish. AI algorithms will be used to activate different programs and systems. The aim of AI is to use specialized hardware and software to mimic the functions of the human brain. Recent research has significantly increased our understanding of the potential effects of AI on many industries and enterprises. Using AI in product manufacturing processes will boost flexibility, responsiveness, and employment in the supply chain.

References

Abels, E., Pantanowitz, L., Aeffner, F., Zarella, M.D., van der Laak, J., Bui, M.M., Vemuri, V.N.P., Parwani, A.V., Gibbs, J., Agosto-Arroyo, E., Beck, A.H., Kozlowski, C., 2019. Computational pathology definitions, best practices, and recommendations for regulatory guidance: a white paper from the Digital Pathology Association. J. Pathol. 10969896. 249 (3), 286–294. Available from: http://onlinelibrary.wiley.com/journal/10.1002/(ISSN)1096-9896. doi:10.1002/path.5331.

Alsubaie, N., Trahearn, N., Raza, S.E.A., Snead, D., Rajpoot, N.M., 2017. Stain deconvolution using statistical analysis of multi resolution stain colour representation. PLoS ONE 12, e0169875.

Chen, Z., Wang, G., Li, L.L., 2017. Recurrent attentional reinforcement learning for multi-label image recognition. arXiv. arXiv:1712.07465.

Ciregan, D., Meier, U., Schmidhuber, J., 2012. Multi-column deep neural networks for image classification. arXiv. arXiv:1202.2745.

De Vito, C., Angeloni, C., De Feo, E., Marzuillo, C., Lattanzi, A., Ricciardi, W., Villari, P., Boccia, S., 2014. A large cross-sectional survey investigating the knowledge of cervical cancer risk aetiology and the predictors of the adherence to cervical cancer screening related to mass media campaign. Biomed. Res. Int. 2314-6133. 2014, 1–6. doi:10.1155/2014/304602.

Ford, M., 2015. The Rise of the Robots. Basic Books, New York.

Gedefaw, L., Liu, C.-F., Ip, R.K.L., Tse, H.-F., Yeung, M.H.Y., Yip, S.P., Huang, C.-L., 2023. Artificial intelligence-assisted diagnostic cytology and genomic testing for hematologic disorders. Cells 12, 1755.

Goldin, C., Katz, L., 2010. The Race Between Education and Technology. Belknap Press for Harvard University Press.

Gordon, R.J., 2016. The Rise and Fall of American Growth the U.S. Standard of Living Since the Civil War. Princeton University Press.

Graetz, G., Michaels, G., 2015. Robots at work. CEP Discussion Paper No. 1335.

Hanna, M.G., Hanna, M.H., 2022. Current applications and challenges of artificial intelligence in pathology. Hum. Pathol. Rep. 27, 300596.

Jiang, H., Zhou, Y., Lin, Y., Ronald, C.K., Chan, R., Jiang, C.K., Liu, J., Chen, H., 2023. Deep learning for computational cytology: a survey. Med. Image Anal. 84, 102691.

Li, X., et al., 2022. A dynamic single cell-based framework for digital twins to prioritize disease genes and drug targets. Genome Med. 14, 48.

Ma, Z., Shiao, S.L., Yoshida, E.J., Swartwood, S., Huang, F., Doche, M.E., Chung, A.P., Knudsen, B.S., Gertych, A., 2017. Data integration from pathology slides for quantitative imaging of multiple cell types within the tumor immune cell infiltrate. Diagn. Pathol. 12, 69.

Olmstead, K., 2017. Nearly half of Americans Use Digital Voice Assistants mostly on their smartphones. Pew Research Center Fact-Tank, December 12, 2017. https://www.pewresearch.org/fact-tank/2017/12/12/nearly-half-of-americans-use-digital-voice-assistants-mostly-on-their-smartphones/.

Olson, C., Kemery, K., 2019. Voice report: from answers to action: customer adoption of voice technology and digital assistants. Microsoft. https://advertiseonbing-blob.azureedge.net/blob/bingads/media/insight/whitepapers/2019/04%20apr/voice-report/bingads_2019_voicereport.pdf.

OpenAI "Overview", n.d. https://openai.com/api/.

Pethokoukis, J., 2016. What the story of ATMs and bank tellers reveals about the 'rise of the robots' and jobs. AEIdeas, June 6, 2016. https://www.aei.org/economics/what-atms-bank-tellers-rise-robots-and-jobs/.

Quillian, L., Pager, D., Hexel, O., Midtboen, A., 2017. Meta-analysis of field experiments shows no change in racial discrimination in hiring over time. Proc. Natl. Acad. Sci. USA 114 (41), 10870–10875. doi:10.1073/pnas.1706255114.

Salto-Tellez, M., Maxwell, P., Hamilton, P., 2019. Artificial intelligence—the third revolution in pathology. Histopathology. 0309-0167. 74 (3), 372–376. doi:10.1111/his.13760.

Shaker, B., Ahmad, S., Lee, J., Jung, C., Na, D., 2021. In silico methods and tools for drug discovery. Comput. Biol. Med. 137, 104851.

Shelhamer, J.L., Long, T.D., 2017. Fully convolutional networks for semantic segmentation. IEEE Trans. Pattern Anal. Mach. Intell. 39, 640–651.

Thien Huynh, T., Pham, Q.V., Pham, X.Q., Nguyen, T.T., Han, Z., Dong-Seong, K., 2023. Artificial intelligence for the metaverse: a survey. Eng. Appl. Artif. Intell. 117, 105581.

Wang, J., Yang, J.H., Mao, Z.H., Huang, C., Huang, W.X., 2016. CNN-RNN: a unified framework for multi-label image classification. In: Proceedings of the 2016 IEEE Conference on Computer Vision and Pattern Recognition (CVRP). Computer Society, Los Alamitos, CA, USA, 27–30 June 2016.

Zhou, C., et al., 2021. Virtual patients for mechanical ventilation in the intensive care unit. Comput. Methods Prog. Biomed. 199, 105912.

CHAPTER 17

Digital twin computing: Recent evolution, challenges, and future directions

Sudesh Kumar[a], Yogesh Ahirwar[a], Anshuman Tiwari[a], and Bhawna Tunwal[b]

[a]*Department of Computer Science, Indira Gandhi National Tribal University, Amarkantak, Madhya Pradesh, India*

[b]*Department of Computer Science and Technology, Central University of Punjab, Bhatinda, India*

17.1 Introduction

Recently, digital twin (DT) computing has emerged as a technology filled with promises and potential to transform the future of manufacturing and society. A DT extends well beyond conventional computer-based simulations and analyses. The entire array of elements, processes, dynamics, and firmware of the physical system is meticulously replicated in a digital counterpart. The two systems operate concurrently, exchanging inputs and conducting operations through real-time data communications and information transfer (Zhang et al., 2022; Salerno et al., 2024). The integration of the Internet of Things (IoT), machine learning (ML), artificial intelligence (AI), 3D models, 5G/6G networks, virtual reality, distributed computing, and electronic sensors enables a digital or virtual representation of real-world systems, facilitating seamless monitoring, analysis, evaluation, and predictions (Barricelli et al., 2019). DT computing provides a robust platform for testing and analysing complex systems, a task that traditional simulations and modular evaluations cannot achieve. According to the Compound Annual Growth Rate (CAGR) report, the DT technology market is projected to grow significantly from 2025, with a CAGR ranging from 22.47% to 64.9%, depending on the source, reaching a market size of United States Dollar (USD) 165.3 billion to USD 259.32 billion by 2032. In the present context, within Industry 5.0, the concept of a DT has attracted significant interest. It is characterized as a technology that generates a digital representation of a physical entity by utilizing real-time data and models. This technology enables physical objects to attain intelligence, automation, and enhanced management efficiency. DT finds extensive application across various sectors, including industry, healthcare, intelligent transportation, and beyond (Lin et al., 2024).

Nonetheless, the advancement of DT technology remains in the early stages of exploration. Although there is an increasing volume of literature addressing this technology, it is evident

Artificial Intelligence, Machine Learning and Blockchain in Digital Twin Computing.
https://doi.org/10.1016/B978-0-443-43914-8.00017-0

that the current studies do not provide a comprehensive examination from the standpoint of technological transformation, practical applications, challenges, and prospective developments. Motivated by these facts, the main contributions that our work provides to the scientific community are the following:

- Highlights the recent evolution of DTs, reviews their key enabling technologies, and discusses the popular application scenarios
- Discusses the key challenges of existing DT computing
- Provides the future directions of DT research and application

The rest of the chapter is organized as follows: Section 17.2 highlights the evolution and development of DTs, reviews its key enabling technologies, and discusses the popular application scenarios. Section 17.3 examines the key challenges and limitations of existing DT computing. Section 17.4 explores the future directions of DT research and application. Section 17.5 concludes the chapter with future scope.

17.2 Recent evaluation in digital twin computing

DT computing has undergone significant advancements recently, with evaluations highlighting its expanding applications and new technological advancements. In this sub-section, the authors discuss the recent advances in DT computing (Fig. 17.1).

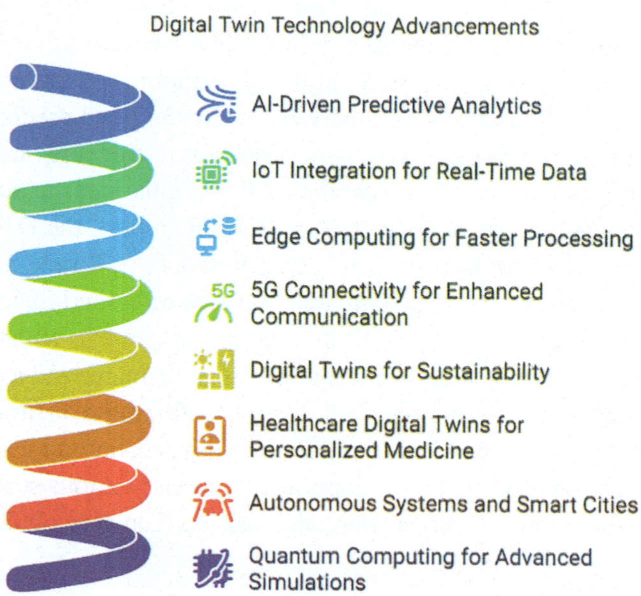

Fig. 17.1 Digital twin technology advancements.

17.2.1 Artificial intelligence-driven predictive analytics

Predictive analytics based on AI revolutionizes double-digit technologies, allowing an instantaneous evaluation of data, recognition of trends, and the creation of forecasting models. DTs use automatic learning methods, including in-depth training and reinforcement training, to predict system performance, improve processes, and prevent errors. This is particularly beneficial in industries where effective equipment operation, such as production, healthcare, and energy, and pre-emptive equipment maintenance are important. A recent assessment emphasizes how AI is revolutionizing research and development activities. Numerous phases of research and development, such as market analysis, design, prototyping, simulations, and client personalization, have been improved by AI-powered solutions. For example, AI-powered market research facilitates deep involvement and sophisticated analysis, helping businesses efficiently collect vital consumer data. AI algorithms, especially those for generative design, can generate a number of design options throughout the design phase that are optimized for factors like structural integrity and material efficiency. Through digital simulations that cut costs and time compared to real models, AI has enhanced prototyping. In addition, without requiring actual prototypes, AI-driven simulations enable the assessment of marketing tactics and product effectiveness in a variety of scenarios. The application of AI in DT technology has opened new avenues for predictive analytics. By combining real-time sensor data with advanced ML algorithms, DTs can predict system failures, optimize performance, and reduce operational costs. For example, in the context of smart manufacturing, AI-driven DTs have been shown to improve production efficiency by 20%–30% while reducing unplanned downtime by up to 50% (Pitt et al., 2020). This integration of AI and DTs is a cornerstone of Industry 4.0, enabling smarter and more autonomous systems (Fig. 17.2).

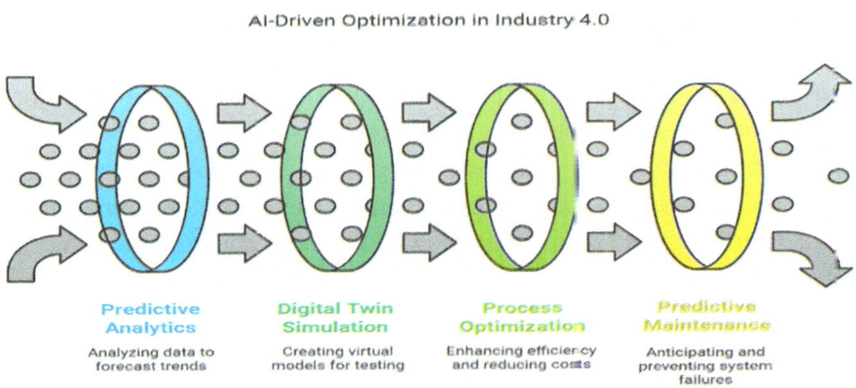

Fig. 17.2 AI-driven optimization in industry 4.0.

17.2.2 Internet of Things integration for real-time data

Data integration plays a significant role in structuring a combination of assorted data in an IoT-based warehouse from various locations in a real-time manner (Sahara and Aamer, 2022). The IoT is the foundation of DT technologies, which provide real data to sensors integrated into physical systems. IoT devices collect data from various sources, such as temperature sensors, pressure, humidity from the environment, and physical movement, and transmit it to a DT. This type of integration allows the DT to update and reflect the current state of its physical counterpart. In smart cities, DTs with IoT support are used to monitor and optimize traffic flow, energy consumption, and public security. For example, sensors placed on roads and transport signals can provide real data to a DT, which can then simulate and optimize traffic models to reduce congestion. Similarly, in healthcare, IoT devices, such as wearable fitness trackers, can provide real-time health data for a DT of a patient, ensuring continuous monitoring and early detection of health problems. The integration of IoT with DTs enables the creation of highly accurate and dynamic virtual models. By leveraging real-time data from IoT sensors, DTs can monitor, analyze, and optimize physical systems in real time. For instance, in smart cities, IoT-enabled DTs have been used to optimize traffic flow, reduce energy consumption, and improve public safety. The IoT is an integral part of the twin digital technologies, providing real-world data necessary to maintain the accuracy and relevance of virtual models. IoT devices, including sensors and readers, collect data from physical systems and send it to a DT. This allows the DT to observe and represent the current state of its corresponding physical equivalents.

17.2.3 Edge computing for faster processing

Today's edge computing transforms DT technology by placing computational power closer to the data source, minimizing latency, and enhancing the speed of graphic simulations. In contrast to conventional, seemingly straightforward cloud computing, where data is transmitted to a central server for processing, edge computing processes data at the network's edge. This is especially beneficial for applications that require quick responses, such as self-driving cars, automated factories, and intelligent power networks. For example, edge-compatible DTs in self-driving cars can process real-time sensor data to make partial decisions like braking and steering, without relying on distant cloud servers. Similarly, in smart factories, edge computing allows DTs to monitor and control machines in real-time, ensuring optimal performance and reducing downtime. Edge computing enhances the performance of DTs by enabling real-time data processing at the source. This reduces latency and ensures timely decision-making, which is critical for applications such as autonomous driving and industrial automation. For example, edge-enabled DTs have been shown to reduce response times by up to 70% in smart factory environments (Almeida et al., 2021). Edge computing is currently transforming twin digital technologies, positioning computational power closer to the data source. Unlike conventional cloud computing, which transmits data to a central server for processing, edge computing processes data locally within the edge network. This decreases latency and enhances the speed of DT simulations, making it ideal for applications requiring timely responses. Autonomous cars and edge-capable DTs analyze real-time sensor information to make instantaneous choices, like braking or steering. It also ensures the safety and reliability of autonomous systems in challenging driving conditions. For example, Tesla's self-driving cars can use edge computing to instantly analyze data from cameras and sensors, enabling them to drive entirely safely.

17.2.4 5G connectivity for enhanced communication

5G networking is a game changer for twin digital technologies. 5G allows transmitting data at 10–20 Gbps, which is 100 times greater than 4G technology, creating new IoT robotic surgery applications (Sharma et al., 2021). This is especially important for applications such as remote surgery, intelligent cities, and autonomous systems. For instance, in the medical field, DTs powered by 5G can enable remote surgeries by offering instantaneous feedback to surgeons, even if they are far from the operating room. In smart cities, 5G enables DTs to oversee and manage infrastructure, like traffic signals and power grids, in real-time, enhancing efficiency and lowering expenses. The deployment of 5G networks has significantly improved the performance of DTs by providing ultra-reliable, low-latency communication. This enables real-time interaction between physical and digital systems, which is essential for applications such as remote healthcare and autonomous vehicles. For instance, 5G-enabled DTs have been used to perform remote surgeries with millisecond-level precision. 5G networking revolutionizes twin digital technology, providing the fast, low-cost connections needed for real-world functionality. In healthcare, DTs working on 5G handle remote operations and provide real-time feedback to surgeons. For example, surgeons in the same area can perform surgery on patients in different locations, while DTs provide live assistance. This can significantly transform healthcare, particularly in isolated communities.

17.2.5 DTs for sustainability and green tech

DTs are essential to achieving sustainability goals by optimizing energy consumption, minimizing carbon emissions, and increasing resource efficiency. They model the energy consumption of structures, improve renewable energy source systems, and monitor environmental factors. For example, in smart buildings, the DT can evaluate sensor data to improve heating, cooling, and lighting, reducing energy consumption by up to 30%. DTs can help increase the efficiency of solar panels and wind turbines in green energy sources. The DT can optimize energy production and minimize waste thanks to the modeling of various weather conditions and operational situations. Moreover, DTs are utilized to observe and forecast environmental changes, including air quality and water levels, and support governments and organizations in making informed decisions. DTs are crucial in achieving sustainability goals by optimizing energy efficiency and reducing environmental impact. For example, in the context of smart buildings, DTs have been used to reduce energy consumption by up to 30% through real-time monitoring and optimization (Ahmed et al., 2021). In today's world, DT computing is essential for reaching sustainability objectives by enhancing energy use, minimizing carbon emissions, and boosting resource efficiency. They model energy consumption in structures, improve renewable energy solutions, and track environmental factors. We can improve our green energy resources by using DT computing. In intelligent structures, DTs assess sensor data to improve heating, cooling, stabilization, and illumination. This reduction in energy usage lowers operational expenses. For instance, a digital replica of an office building can model the effects of various energy-saving strategies, helping facility managers select the most efficient options.

17.2.6 Healthcare DTs for personalized medicine

In healthcare, DTs transform individualized medicine and develop virtual performance models for patients. These models replicate individual conditions in patients, allowing physicians to predict disease development, clarify treatment strategies, and enhance outcomes. For example, DTs in cancer patients can replicate the effectiveness of various treatments and help doctors choose the best option. DTs also monitor real-time chronic diseases such as diabetes and heart disease. Portable gadgets can continuously provide medical information to the DT and alert patients and doctors to potential problems before they worsen. This remote health strategy improves patient outcomes and reduces costs. DTs in healthcare enable the simulation of patient-specific conditions, leading to more accurate diagnoses and personalized treatment plans. For instance, DTs have been used to predict the progression of chronic diseases and optimize treatment strategies, resulting in improved patient outcomes (Greczynski and Hultman, 2021).

17.2.7 Autonomous systems and smart cities

Digital Gemini is critical to developing autonomous systems, including cars, drones, and smart city applications that use independent driving. They mimic real-world situations to increase safety, efficiency, and reliability. For example, in autonomous cars, DTs can model countless driving situations, helping developers recognize and mitigate possible risks before launch. In intelligent cities, DTs oversee and improve infrastructure such as signals, energy networks, and water systems. By modeling different scenarios, the DT helps urban planners make informed choices, improve efficiency, and reduce costs. For example, a digital replica of a city's circulation system can model the impact of new roads or public transport routes, helping planners choose the best option. DTs provide a virtual testing ground for autonomous systems, ensuring safety and reliability before deployment in real-world environments.

For example, in the development of autonomous vehicles, DTs have been used to simulate millions of driving scenarios, significantly reducing the risk of accidents (Jiang et al., 2020).

17.2.8 Quantum computing for advanced simulations

Quantum computing is set to transform DT technology by facilitating intricate simulations that classical computing cannot achieve. Quantum computers utilize qubits, which can exist in several states simultaneously, enabling them to handle extensive data in parallel. This renders them perfect for modeling intricate systems, including molecular interactions, climate simulations, and financial markets. For instance, in materials science, quantum-powered DTs can model molecular behavior at an atomic scale, identifying novel materials with distinct characteristics. In climate simulation, quantum computing can model the effects of various environmental policies, aiding governments in making informed choices. Quantum computing offers unprecedented computational power, enabling DTs to simulate highly complex systems with unparalleled accuracy. For example, in materials science, quantum-enabled DTs have been used to simulate molecular interactions, leading to the discovery of new materials with unique properties. Similarly, in climate modeling, quantum computing can simulate the impact of different environmental policies, helping governments make informed decisions about sustainability. Integrating quantum computing and DTs is expected to drive breakthroughs in drug discovery, energy optimization, and financial modeling (Feldman, 2021).

17.3 Applications of DT computing

DT computing, which creates virtual replicas of physical assets, processes, or systems, finds applications across various industries, including energy management, healthcare, smart cities, manufacturing, automotive, construction, and energy, enabling predictive maintenance, optimized operations, and improved decision-making. This section provides an in-depth discussion of key applications (Fig. 17.3).

17.3.1 Predictive maintenance in manufacturing

The predictive service is one of the most essential uses of DT technology in the production industry. DTs allow you to observe, evaluate, and predict equipment malfunctions while creating virtual copies of tangible machines. This reduces downtime, lowers costs, and increases work efficiency. DTs for forecasting services rely on IoT sensors placed in equipment to collect real-time information about factors such as temperature, vibration, and pressure. This information is processed by a DT, which uses AI and ML algorithms to study patterns and predict possible failures. For example, if a machine's vibration levels exceed a specific limit, a DT can inform maintenance operators before a malfunction occurs. Forecasting maintenance using DTs depends on IoT sensors integrated into the system to

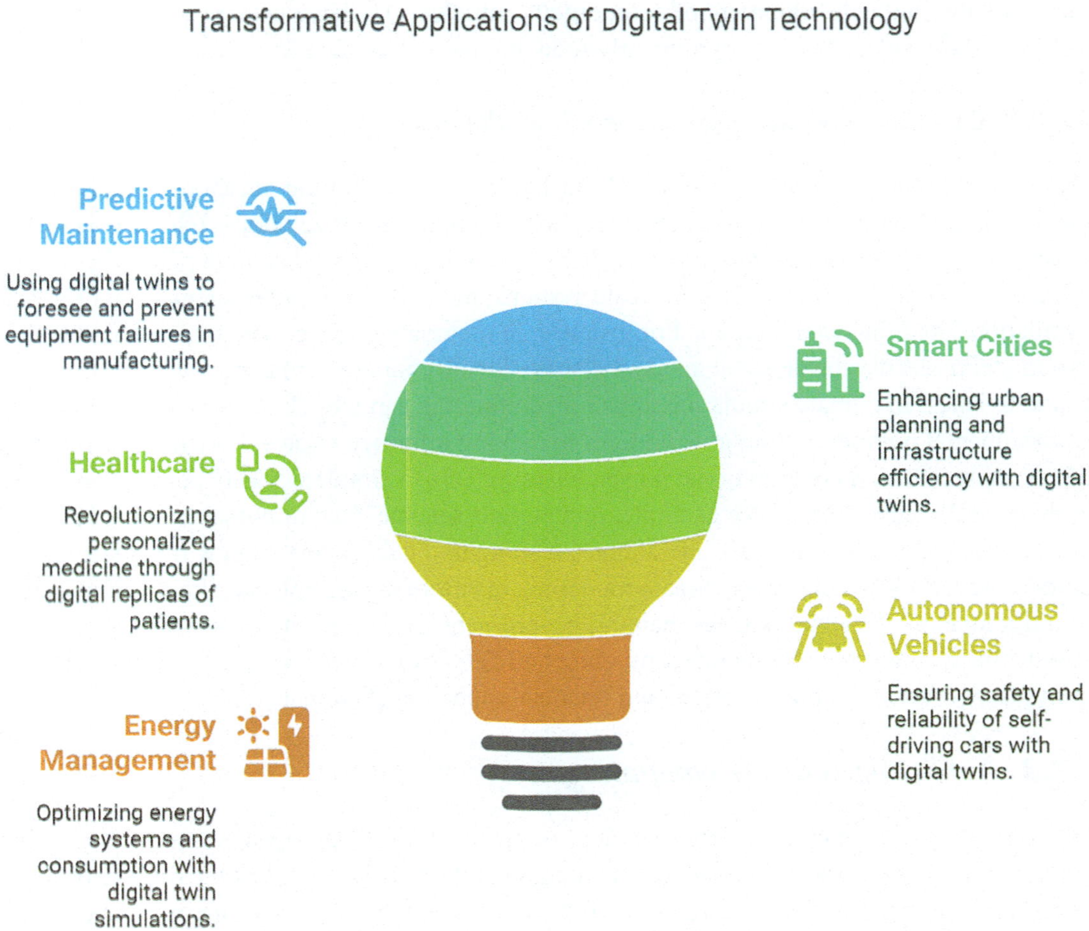

Fig. 17.3 Transformative applications of digital twin technology.

collect real-time data about factors such as temperature, vibration, and pressure. This data is then processed by a DT that uses AI and ML algorithms to analyze patterns and anticipate potential malfunctions. For instance, if a machine's vibration level exceeds a certain threshold, the DT can notify the operator to perform maintenance before a failure happens. This proactive approach ensures that maintenance occurs only when necessary, minimizing unnecessary actions and extending the lifespan of your equipment.

17.3.2 Smart cities and urban planning

A city can be thought of as a repository for various data and information sources that are updated in real time and undergo constant operation and development. Thus, a real-time system that can retrieve and handle data/information collected from various physical objects in a city is required.

A DT is a lifecycle-spanning virtual representation of an object or system that is updated using real-time data and makes use of reasoning, ML, and simulation to aid in decision-making (Wang et al., 2023a). DTs are transforming urban planning by developing virtual representations of cities. These models replicate real-world situations, allowing city planners to enhance infrastructure, decrease energy use, and improve public services. IoT sensors gather information about motion models, energy consumption, air quality standards, and more in intelligent urban areas. This information is included in the DT, which replicates the functions of the city in real-time. This technology enhances the city's ability to withstand natural disasters and improves resource distribution. For example, Barcelona employs DTs to oversee and enhance its energy grid, reducing energy usage and cutting carbon emissions. Using DTs in urban planning changes how large buildings and cities are created and supported. This makes it easier to build smart cities where infrastructure and urban systems aim for efficiency and stability.

17.3.3 Healthcare and personalized medicine

Personalized medicine demands the processing and integration of enormous amounts of data. In this paper, we outline a solution to this problem founded on the development of DTs. These are detailed patient models that are computationally screened against thousands of drugs to determine the best-suited drug for the patient (Björnsson et al., 2020). DTs are revolutionizing healthcare by developing virtual representations of patients, facilitating tailored treatment strategies, and anticipatory diagnostics. This application is especially beneficial in precision medicine, where therapies are customized for individual patients. Information from medical records, wearable technologies, and genetic data forms a DT in healthcare. These digital models replicate patients and allow doctors to predict the onset of illness and study various treatment alternatives. For example, digital copies of cancer patients can simulate the effects of chemotherapy and help physicians choose the most effective treatment. In healthcare, DTs are generated through data from medical records, wearable technologies, and genetic data. These digital representations imitate individual scenarios of patients, allowing doctors to predict the disease's progression and examine various treatment alternatives. For instance, digital replicas of cancer patients can model the impact of chemotherapy and help physicians select the best treatment option. In this way, DTs enable early identification of health issues and rapid real-time interventions for chronic diseases such as diabetes and heart disease. Using DTs in healthcare is transforming how diseases are diagnosed and managed. This innovation contributes to the transition from reactive to pre-emptive healthcare, improves patient outcomes, and reduces healthcare costs.

17.3.4 Autonomous vehicles and transportation

Utilizing sensing technologies and cloud/edge computing, we build a DT system model that reflects the static and dynamic objects from the real world in real time (Wang et al., 2023b). DTs are vital in advancing self-driving cars, acting as a virtual environment for replicating driving conditions. This guarantees the safety and dependability of autonomous systems before deployment. In self-driving cars, DTs replicate countless driving situations, encompassing bad weather, traffic jams, and pedestrian interactions. These simulations assist developers in recognizing and mitigating possible risks, enhancing the safety and efficacy of autonomous systems. In independent-driving cars, DTs replicate countless driving situations, covering bad weather, traffic jams, and interactions with pedestrians. These simulations help developers recognize and resolve possible risks, increasing the safety and efficiency of autonomous systems. For example, the DT models the impact of unexpected obstacles on the road, allowing self-driving vehicles to make quick decisions such as braking and steering. Tesla uses DTs to replicate and evaluate independent driving algorithms. This enables Tesla to improve its autonomous driving technology and reduce the likelihood of accidents. Similarly, Waymo uses DTs to assess their cars by independently driving in virtual conditions, ensuring their safety and reliability before use on public streets. Including DTs in independent-driving vehicles is revolutionizing the transportation sector. It promotes the creation of safer and more reliable autonomous systems, minimizes the chance of accidents, and increases the overall efficiency of transportation.

17.3.5 Energy management and renewable energy optimization

The management and optimization of renewable energy microgrids could be completely transformed by DT technology. DTs are virtual versions of physical systems that combine ML, simulations, and real-time data to create an interactive, dynamic model of the real world. When it comes to efficiency, dependability, and sustainability, they provide substantial advantages for microgrids powered by renewable energy (Bassey et al., 2024). DTs are essential for enhancing energy management and renewable energy systems. Through the simulation of energy consumption and generation, DTs contribute to minimizing waste, improving efficiency, and aiding sustainability objectives. In the management of energy consumption, DTs replicate the functioning of power networks, wind turbines, and solar photovoltaic systems. For example, a DT of a windmill can emulate various weather scenarios to increase energy production. Similarly, DTs in smart buildings evaluate sensor data to enhance heating, cooling, and lighting, thereby decreasing energy usage. In the management of energy consumption, DTs replicate the functioning of power networks, wind turbines, and solar panels. For example, a digital copy of a wind turbine can simulate various weather scenarios to increase energy production. Similarly, smart building DTs evaluate sensor data to improve heating, cooling, and lighting, reducing energy consumption.

17.4 Challenges in DT computing

Emerging as a revolutionary technique allowing real-time monitoring, modeling, and multi-diligence optimization of virtual clones of actual systems is DT computing. DTs improve smart manufacturing, healthcare, civic planning, and aerospace decisions using

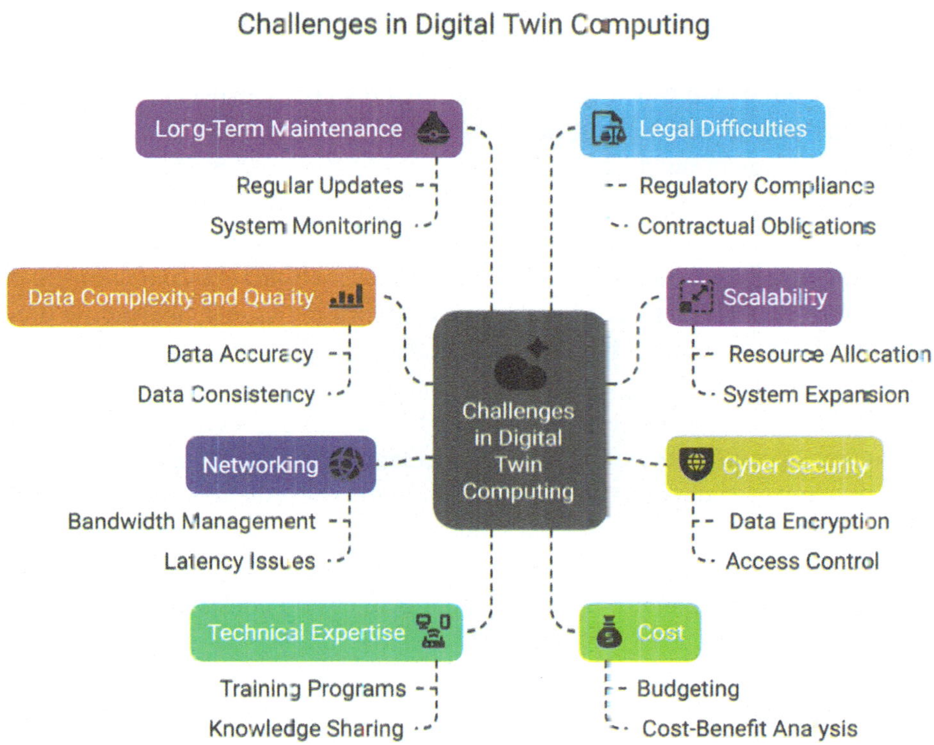

Fig. 17.4 Popular challenges in digital twin computing.

predictive analysis and functional efficacy. A number of obstacles must be overcome before DTs can be put into practice, such as issues with data security, complicated integration with current systems, and the requirement for significant processing power to handle and evaluate real-time data streams (Fuller et al., 2020). Overcoming these obstacles is vital for the successful adoption and efficacy of DT computing. This composition discusses the most critical challenges of DT computing and how they affect its real-world implementation (Fig. 17.4).

17.4.1 Data complexity and quality

Observational uncertainty, model structure uncertainty, and model parameter uncertainty are all sources of uncertainty in DT models. Therefore, in order to enable dynamic and real-time updates of data and DT models, as well as precise predictions by the entire team, DT technology frequently necessitates high-performance computing technology. Consequently, the current advancement of DT technology may be constrained by technical obstacles (Wang et al., 2023c). DTs calculate massive volumes of structured and unstructured data to simulate their physical counterparts directly, but handling similar datasets presents significant difficulties. Integrating data from multiple sources frequently leads to inconsistencies, redundancy, and format mismatches, making it challenging to reuse and analyze information effectively. Also, DTs require real-time data processing and synchronization, which can strain computational resources, especially in large-scale implementations such as smart cities, healthcare, and manufacturing. As datasets grow in size and complexity, creating effective data storage, retrieval, and processing becomes a significant concern, requiring advanced solutions like cloud computing, edge processing, and AI-driven analytics. Another critical issue is ensuring the quality and reliability of data used in DT systems. Poor data quality caused by sensor malfunctions, data transmission errors, or incomplete information can lead to inaccurate simulations, misleading predictions, and incorrect decision-making. Maintaining high data accuracy requires rigorous validation, filtering, and cleansing methods, which can be time-consuming and computationally demanding. Also, different data collection methods and varying levels of sensor precision can result in inconsistencies affecting DTs' performance. Without formalized data governance frameworks, organizations may struggle to establish consistent data quality standards, making it difficult to derive meaningful insights from DT simulations. Addressing these challenges requires implementing robust data management strategies, using AI for data validation, and establishing industry-wide standards to ensure consistency and reliability in DT computing.

17.4.2 Scalability

Starting small is simple, but scaling DT software over time may be difficult. Scaling up presents challenges for resource operation and efficiency. Scalability is a significant challenge in DT computing as the complexity and size of DTs increase with expanding operations. As further physical assets, detectors, and data sources are integrated, managing and recycling vast quantities of real-time data becomes increasingly challenging. Large-scale executions, like smart cities, industrial IoT, and healthcare systems, require expansive computational resources, efficient network structures, and robust data management strategies to ensure smooth operation. In addition, as the number of DTs grows, maintaining synchronization and interoperability between multiple connected models becomes challenging. High network bandwidth for DT systems and low-latency processing are essential to ensure real-time performance, yet these become harder to achieve as DTs scale. Likewise, storage and computing costs rise with scalability, making it necessary to optimize cloud and edge computing solutions for efficiency. Scalability is a core research problem for proposing the application of cocreative methods and strategies for value creation on an axiological level and cocreative-based design and management on functional levels. Therefore, apart from the functional side of scalability, on social grounds, it can be emphasized as an instrument for value growth (Putnik et al., 2013). Without proper scalability solutions, DTs may face bottlenecks, performance degradation, and increased system complexity, eventually limiting their effectiveness in large-scale environments.

17.4.3 Cyber security

Cybersecurity is a pressing issue in DT computing because of the growing integration of physical and virtual systems, which exposes them to a high risk of cyberattacks. The conception of a DT allows systems analysis, design, optimization, and elaboration to take place wholly digitally or in confluence with a cyber-physical system to ameliorate speed, precision, and effectiveness compared to traditional engineering approaches. DTs are technologies that enable new paradigms, similar to Industry 4.0 and Factories of the Future, and generate a stronger edge within systems (Holmes et al., 2021). DTs constantly gather and process real-time information from IoT sensors, cloud platforms, and enterprise networks, creating numerous entry points for potential cyberattacks. Hackers can exploit vulnerabilities in communication networks, data storage systems, or software applications to launch attacks such as data breaches, ransomware, and system intrusions, causing major operational disruptions. Unauthorized access or data tampering can undermine the precision of DT simulations, leading to defective predictions, unsafe decision-making, and potential harm to physical assets. This is especially problematic in mission-critical industries like healthcare, aerospace, manufacturing, and smart cities, where DT security directly affects public safety and critical services. In addition, compliance with data protection regulations such as the General Data Protection Regulation (GDPR), the Health Insurance Portability and Accountability Act (HIPAA), and industry-specific security standards adds an additional layer of complexity, challenging the enforcement of rigorous data governance programs. Without strong cybersecurity frameworks, DTs remain susceptible to exploitation, compromising their trustworthiness, reliability, accountability, and effectiveness in real-world use.

17.4.4 Networking

The DT is a promising technology for the new immersive digital life and has numerous applications across sectors such as Industry 4.0, aviation, and healthcare (Almasan et al., 2022). Networking challenges in DT computing arise due to the need for real-time data exchange between physical and virtual systems. DTs require continuous, flawless communication with IoT devices, sensors, cloud platforms, and edge computing systems to operate accurately; however, achieving high-speed, low-latency, and reliable data transmission remains a significant challenge, especially in large-scale operations such as smart cities, healthcare, and industrial automation. Bandwidth limitations, network traffic, and unstable connections can lead to data delays, inconsistencies, or failures in DT operations. In addition, as DTs scale, managing vast quantities of real-time data across distributed networks becomes increasingly complex, requiring robust network infrastructures and optimization strategies. Another major challenge is integrating different network technologies used in DT environments. With the integration of 5G, IoT, cloud computing, and edge computing, ensuring flawless communication across various protocols and platforms becomes difficult. Inconsistencies in data transmission standards can lead to compatibility issues, reducing the effectiveness of DTs. Security is also a critical concern, as data transmitted over networks is vulnerable to cyber threats like hacking, unauthorized access, and data interception. Ensuring secure data transmission with encryption, authentication, and network monitoring is essential to protect sensitive information. Addressing these networking challenges is pivotal to enabling the widespread adoption of DT technology across industries while maintaining accuracy, efficiency, and security.

17.4.5 Technical expertise

One of the significant challenges in DT computing is the demand for highly specialized technical expertise across multiple disciplines. DTs are complex systems integrating real-time data analytics, AI, IoT devices, cloud computing, and advanced simulation models. Professionals working with DTs must possess expertise in software development, data engineering, cybersecurity, and system integration to ensure that the digital replica accurately represents its physical counterpart. However, there's a significant skill gap in the workforce, as many industries struggle to find professionals with a deep understanding of Information Technology (IT) infrastructure and domain-specific knowledge, such as manufacturing, healthcare, or smart city development. This lack of expertise leads to inefficiencies in the design, implementation, and maintenance of DT systems, making it difficult for organizations to leverage the full potential of this technology. In addition, the multidisciplinary nature of DTs means collaboration between specialized teams is necessary. However, misalignment in expertise and communication can create bottlenecks and hamper the system's effectiveness. Another major challenge is the need for continuous learning and adaptation due to the rapid evolution of DT technology. The field constantly advances with new simulation tools, AI-driven optimizations, and improved data management platforms, requiring professionals to stay updated with the latest advancements. Many organizations struggle to upskill their existing workforce or recruit new talent with the necessary technical skills, leading to delays in implementation and inefficiencies in system performance. Furthermore, integrating DTs into IT and operational systems requires technical knowledge in interoperability, cybersecurity protocols, and high-performance computing—areas where expertise is often limited. The lack of standardized training programs and certifications for DT technology further exacerbates this challenge, making it difficult for organizations to develop a skilled workforce. Addressing these technical expertise challenges will require investment in specialized training, collaboration between industry and academia, and the development of standardized frameworks to guide professionals in effectively deploying and managing DT systems.

17.4.6 Cost

One of the most significant barriers to the widespread adoption of DT computing is the high cost associated with its implementation. In their report, the National Institute of Standards and Technology explores the economic factors in detail, offering insights into the cost structures related to DT deployment (Thomas, 2024). Developing a functional DT requires substantial hardware, software, and infrastructure investment. High-performance computing resources, IoT sensors, cloud storage, and AI-driven analytics platforms contribute to the overall cost of structuring and maintaining a DT system. The initial setup costs can be particularly daunting for small and medium-sized enterprises that lack the financial resources to invest in sophisticated simulation tools and real-time data processing capabilities. In addition, integrating a DT into an operational framework frequently requires significant modifications to legacy systems, raising costs. Companies may also need to invest in cybersecurity measures to protect the vast quantities of sensitive data generated and transmitted by DTs, adding another financial burden. The cost of recruiting and training skilled professionals to manage and optimize DTs is another major challenge, as organizations must compete for talent in a rapidly evolving technological landscape. Beyond the initial investment, the operational costs of maintaining a DT can also be significant. Real-time data collection, processing, and storage require continuous investment in IT infrastructure, including high-speed networks, cloud computing services, and edge processing units. The dynamic nature of DTs means they must be constantly updated and recalibrated to accurately reflect real-world conditions, which incurs additional expenses related to software upgrades, system maintenance, and data validation. Furthermore, as DTs scale to larger and more complex applications, such as smart cities or industrial automation, the computational power and storage requirements increase exponentially, driving up costs. Companies must also factor in the expenses associated with regulatory compliance, especially in industries such as healthcare and aerospace, where strict data security and privacy regulations apply. As a result, organizations must carefully evaluate DT technology's return on investment, balancing its potential benefits with the long-term financial commitments required for its successful implementation and operation.

17.4.6.1 Long-term maintenance

The long-term conservation of DTs faces considerable challenges that directly affect their effectiveness and sustainability. One of the primary concerns is the relentless demand for real-time data handling and integration. Since DTs continuously use up-to-date information from their physical counterparts, ensuring error-free data inflow and synchronization for relatively extended periods becomes very challenging. This challenge has another layer added as massive amounts of data need to be processed, which strains the existing IT architecture. Also, the absence of standardized integration procedures further complicates the objectification of DT technology in legacy systems, leading to interoperability problems and increased maintenance efforts (Werbińska-Wojciechowska et al., 2024). One of the significant long-term conservation challenges in DT computing is the need for nonstop updates and synchronization with its physical counterpart. DTs rely on real-time data streams to directly reflect changes in the physical system. Still, as systems suffer wear and tear, variations, or upgrades, their digital models must be continuously updated to maintain accuracy. This process requires ongoing data collection, validation, and integration, which can be resource-intensive and expensive. Over time, managing large volumes of historical and real-time data becomes increasingly complex, straining storage capacities and computational resources. Also, outdated or inaccurate DT models can lead to incorrect predictions and inefficiencies, undermining their intended benefits. The challenge is further amplified in industries like aerospace, healthcare, and manufacturing, where minor discrepancies between the physical and DT can result in significant functional risks or safety concerns. Another key challenge in maintaining DTs over time is the rapid evolution of underpinning technologies. DT systems are built on a combination of software, hardware, and network structures, all subject to upgrades and changes. Ensuring compatibility with emerging technologies, updating outdated software components, and integrating new functionalities without disrupting operations can be daunting. Also, cybersecurity risks pose an ongoing threat, requiring continuous monitoring and updates to protect against potential data breaches and cyberattacks. DTs may become obsolete or ineffective without proper long-term conservation strategies, leading to increased costs and reduced effectiveness. Organizations must invest in scalable infrastructure, automated update mechanisms, and dedicated teams to manage the evolving requirements of a DT while ensuring their accuracy, security, and long-term viability.

17.4.6.2 Legal difficulties

The rapid-fire elaboration of DT computing presents significant legal challenges, particularly concerning data sequestration, power, and security. DTs calculate vast quantities of real-time data collected from individuals, associations, and structures, raising concerns over who owns the data, how it's stored, and who has the right to access or manipulate it. Integrating Internet-of-Things devices and AI-driven analytics exacerbates the threat of unauthorized surveillance, cyber-attacks, and identity theft, making it pivotal for robust legal frameworks to define data protection laws. Current regulations, similar to the GDPR in the European Union, emphasize informed consent and data minimization. Yet, DTs may operate in ways that continuously collect and analyze personal data without unequivocal user awareness. Also, legal questions arise regarding the right to digital self-determination—whether individuals should have the power to modify, delete, or restrict access to their DTs. However, when digital twins are used in decision-making processes, such as employment screening and medical assessments, the absence of legal safeguards could lead to a pervasive mass surveillance system where individuals are governed by AI-driven decisions that may not be easily contestable. Another critical legal challenge in DT computing is the issue of liability and responsibility when DTs interact with the real world. A person's social or health status could be assessed and used to determine their eligibility for services, care, employment, or facilities. This could lead to new forms of discrimination (Helbing and Argota Sánchez-Vaquerizo, 2023). As DTs become more advanced, they may be used to predict actions, control smart structures, or even automate critical processes in healthcare, transportation, and governance. However, if a DT makes an incorrect prediction that leads to harm—such as a defective medical diagnosis, an AI-driven financial decision causing economic loss, or a miscalculated smart city response leading to accidents—who bears the legal responsibility? Current legal systems are not well-equipped to attribute liability to autonomous AI-driven systems, raising concerns about whether the developers, users, or regulatory bodies should be held responsible for DT failures. In addition, the potential for hacking, data breaches, and unauthorized modifications to DTs creates further legal complexity, as malicious actors could alter critical data to manipulate systems for financial or political gain. Governments and regulatory agencies must establish transparent legal frameworks to govern the ethical deployment of DTs, ensuring transparency, accountability, and human oversight to prevent abuse and uphold fundamental rights in a digital society.

17.5 Future directions

DT computing is a transformative effort that facilitates real-time simulation, monitoring, and optimization of physical systems. Still, challenges such as data security, interoperability, scalability, and computational efficiency limit its full potential. Future developments will incorporate AI for predictive analytics, blockchain for secure data management, and quantum computing for faster simulations. This section explores key innovations and emerging trends shaping the future of DT computing (Fig. 17.5).

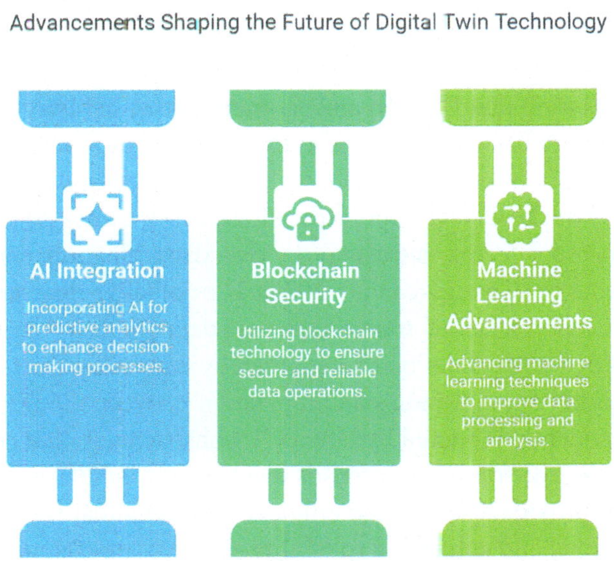

Fig. 17.5 Future research trends in digital twin.

- Integrating AI into DT computing revolutionizes how industries tackle the numerous challenges associated with DTs. By recognizing that a DT is an element of a broader DT system, we can thoroughly grasp the different applications of AI (Minerva et al., 2023). One of the most pressing issues is handling vast and complex datasets collected from IoT devices, sensors, and enterprise systems. AI-driven algorithms, particularly deep learning and natural language processing, can automate this data's classification, filtering, and structuring, ensuring that DTs operate with real-time accuracy. Likewise, AI-powered predictive models allow DTs to anticipate potential failures, optimize performance, and reduce operational risks, making them invaluable for industries such as manufacturing, healthcare, and smart cities. Real-time synchronization is another major challenge, as DTs must continuously reflect changes in their physical counterparts. AI enhances synchronization by using edge computing and intelligent data compression techniques to process data closer to the source, minimizing latency and ensuring seamless updates. Security remains a critical concern, as cyber threats can compromise DTs and the sensitive data they handle. AI-driven cybersecurity solutions, like anomaly detection, automated threat response, and behavioral analysis, help identify potential vulnerabilities and mitigate risks before they escalate. In addition, the scalability of DTs is a significant challenge, especially for enterprises deploying multiple connected twins across vast networks. AI-enabled distributed computing, federated learning, and cloud-based neural networks provide a scalable infrastructure, ensuring that DTs function efficiently without overburdening system resources. Accuracy and trustworthiness are also crucial concerns, as errors in DT models can lead to costly mistakes. AI-driven self-learning systems continuously upgrade and adapt models, improving their predictive capabilities by learning from real-time and historical data. This fusion of AI and DT computing is paving the way for a new era of smart automation, predictive analytics, and digital transformation, ensuring that DTs remain a cornerstone of Industry 4.0 and beyond.
- Blockchain technology has overcome the crucial challenges associated with DT computing, particularly in security, data integrity, interoperability, and scalability. Empowering DTs with blockchain for artificial use cases addresses crucial challenges of distributed data repositories, untrustworthy data dissemination, and the need for predictive maintenance (Chougule et al., 2024). Blockchain's decentralized and immutable ledger ensures that all transactions and data updates within the DT framework are securely recorded and cannot be altered, thereby enhancing trust and preventing data manipulation. In addition, real-time synchronization between the DT and its physical counterparts is frequently hindered by latency, inconsistencies, and centralized system failures. Blockchain's distributed consensus mechanisms, similar to proof of stake and proof of authority, provide a secure and efficient way to validate and process data in real-time, reducing latency and enhancing reliability. Security threats, including cyberattacks and unauthorized data access, pose a serious risk to DTs, particularly in industries such as healthcare, smart cities, and critical infrastructure. Using cryptographic methods,

blockchain enhances data security, ensuring that only authorized entities can access or modify the DT while preventing data breaches and malicious interference. Another major challenge is interoperability, as DTs frequently operate across different industries and platforms that use distinct protocols and data formats. Blockchain facilitates seamless and standardized data exchange through decentralized applications and smart contracts, allowing DTs to interact securely without relying on intermediaries. Scalability is another critical issue, as managing and processing large-scale DT networks requires substantial computing power and storage. Blockchain's decentralized structure distributes workloads across multiple nodes, reducing reliance on centralized servers and enhancing system adaptability. In addition, blockchain-based tokenization and incentive mechanisms can improve resource allocation, data sharing, and collaboration across DT ecosystems. Ethical and regulatory concerns, such as data privacy, governance, and compliance with laws like GDPR, can also be addressed through blockchain-enabled self-sovereign identity and permissioned networks, ensuring users retain control over their data and access rights. Furthermore, integrating blockchain with AI and IoT enhances predictive maintenance, decision-making, and automation within DTs, optimizing their functionality across colorful sectors. As industries increasingly adopt DT technology, blockchain stands out as a pivotal enabler, providing the trust, security, and efficiency needed to create a fully connected, secure, and scalable digital ecosystem.

- Prostrating the challenges of DT computing requires advanced technologies. ML-based advanced methods address crucial issues such as data operation, real-time synchronization, security, scalability, and model delicacy. ML becomes an essential element, enabling the creation of data-driven or gray digital models and combining the massive data gathered from integrated sensors in the physical asset to give operators and machines helpful information (Nele et al., 2024). One of the most critical challenges in DT computing is handling vast quantities of miscellaneous data from multiple sources like IoT detectors, cloud platforms, and edge devices. ML algorithms, particularly deep learning and reinforcement learning, can automate data processing, clean noisy data, and identify patterns, ensuring that the DT remains an accurate and dependable representation of its physical counterpart. In addition, real-time synchronization between the DT and the physical reality is a significant challenge due to network latency and processing delays. ML-driven predictive analytics and edge computing solutions help alleviate these delays by processing data closer to the source and predicting system actions in advance, enhancing response times and decision-making accuracy. Security and privacy risks, including cyber and data breaches, can also be mitigated using ML-based anomaly detection and threat intelligence systems, which continuously monitor network activity and identify unusual patterns that may indicate malicious behavior. In addition, scalability is a concern as organizations expand their DT implementations across colorful disciplines. Federated learning and distributed ML models enable efficient scaling by allowing different DTs to learn collaboratively without transferring raw data, reducing computational overhead and preserving data privacy. Another significant challenge is ensuring the accuracy of DT models, as inaccurate predictions can lead to flawed decisions. ML models improve accuracy by continuously learning from new data and refining simulations, making them more adaptive and precise (Yadav, 2022). Likewise, reinforcement learning helps optimize decision-making processes in complex environments by enabling DTs to learn and adapt to changing conditions autonomously. As DTs become more prevalent in industries like healthcare, manufacturing, and smart cities, the integration of ML ensures their robustness, efficiency, and trustworthiness. In conclusion, the synergy between DT computing and ML is essential for overcoming crucial challenges, enhancing operational efficiency, and unlocking new possibilities for real-time monitoring, predictive maintenance, and intelligent automation.

17.6 Conclusion

In recent years, DT technology has attracted the attention of academic and business circles, especially in terms of its application. Based on this background, this chapter presents a comprehensive overview of recent evaluations of DT computing, including AI, quantum computing, the healthcare industry, and smart cities. Furthermore, we have investigated a taxonomy of key challenges with suggestive solutions for the DT. Finally, future research directions essential to DT computing are discussed. The main goal of this chapter is to provide a thorough review of the DT paradigm for the academic and research community.

Our primary goal in future work is to encompass various domains with significant progress in real-time simulations, AI-driven automation, and improved decision-making.

References

Ahmed, M., Alqadhi, S., Alsulamy, S., Islam, S., Khan, R.A., Danish, M., 2021. Development of self-cured sustainable concrete using local water-entrainment aggregates of vesicular basalt. Sustainability. 2071-1050. 13 (12). Available from: https://www.mdpi.com/2071-1050/13/12/6756/pdf. doi:10.3390/su13126756.

Almasan, P., Ferriol-Galmés, M., Paillisse, J., Suárez-Varela, J., Perino, D., López, D., Perales, A.A.P., Harvey, P., Ciavaglia, L., Wong, L., Ram, V., Xiao, S., Shi, X., Cheng, X., Cabellos-Aparicio, A., Barlet-Ros, P., 2022. Digital twin network: opportunities and challenges. arXiv. arXiv. 23318422. Available from: https://arxiv.org. doi:10.48550/arxiv.2201.01144.

Almeida, D., Pasupuleti, J., Raveendran, S.K., Khan, M.R.B., 2021. Performance evaluation of solar pv inverter controls for overvoltage mitigation in mv distribution networks. Electronics. 2079-9292. 10 (12). Available from: https://www.mdpi.com/2079-9292/10/12/1456/pdf. doi:10.3390/electronics10121456.

Barricelli, B.R., Casiraghi, E., Fogli, D., 2019. A survey on digital twin: definitions, characteristics, applications, and design implications. IEEE Access. 2169-3536. 7, 167653–167671. doi:10.1109/access.2019.2953499.

Bassey, K.E., Opoku-Boateng, J., Antwi, B.O., Ntiakoh, A., Juliet, A.R., 2024. Digital twin technology for renewable energy microgrids. Eng. Sci. Technol. J. 2708-8952. 5 (7), 2248–2272. doi:10.51594/estj.v5i7.1319.

Björnsson, B., Borrebaeck, C., Elander, N., Gasslander, T., Gawel, D.R., Gustafsson, M., Jörnsten, R., Lee, E.J., Li, X., Lilja, S., Martínez-Enguita, D., Matussek, A., Sandström, P., Schäfer, S., Stenmarker, M., Sun, X.F.,

Sysoev, O., Zhang, H., Benson, M., 2020. Digital twins to personalize medicine. Genome Med. 1756-994X. 12 (1). Available from: https://genomemedicine.biomedcentral.com. doi:10.1186/s13073-019-0701-3.
Chougule, P., Choudhary, S., Gurrala, K.R., Nanda, C.S., 2024. Blockchain and digital twins: concept, applications, challenges, and potential. In Jafar, S., Rodriguez, R. Kannan, H., Akhtar, S., Plugmann, P. (Eds.), Harnessing Blockchain-Digital Twin Fusion for Sustainable Investments. IGI Global, India, pp. 49–72. Available from: https://www.igi-global.com/book/harnessing-blockchain-digital-twin-fusion/330583. doi:10.4018/9798369318782.ch003.
Feldman, G.M., 2021. Generalized Polya's theorem on connected locally compact Abelian groups of dimension. 1, 1–12. arXiv:2105.12345.
Fuller, A., Fan, Z., Day, C., Barlow, C., 2020. Digital twin: enabling technologies, challenges and open research. IEEE Access. 2169-3536. 8, 108952–108971. Available from: http://ieeexplore.ieee.org/xpl/RecentIssue.jsp?punumber=6287639. doi:10.1109/ACCESS.2020.2998358.
Greczynski, G., Hultman, L., 2021. The same chemical state of carbon gives rise to two peaks in X-ray photoelectron spectroscopy. Sci. Rep. 2045-2322. 11 (1). doi:10.1038/s41598-021-90780-9.
Helbing, D., Argota Sánchez-Vaquerizo, J., 2023. Digital twins: potentials, ethical issues and limitations. In Zwitter, A., Gstrein, O. (Eds.), Handbook on the Politics and Governance of Big Data and Artificial Intelligence. Edward Elgar Publishing Ltd., Switzerland, pp. 64–104. Available from: https://www.e-elgar.com/shop/gbp/handbook-on-the-politics-and-governance-of-big-data-and-artificial-intelligence-9781800887367.html. doi:10.4337/9781800887374.00013.
Holmes, D., Papathanasaki, M., Maglaras, L., Ferrag, M.A., Nepal, S., Janicke, H. 2021. Digital twins and cyber security—solution or challenge? In: 6th South-East Europe Design Automation, Computer Engineering, Computer Networks and Social Media Conference, SEEDA-CECNSM 2021. Institute of Electrical and Electronics Engineers Inc., Australia. 9781665427425. Available from: http://ieeexplore.ieee.org/xpl/mostRecentIssue.jsp?punumber=9565881. doi:10.1109/SEEDA-CECNSM53056.2021.9566277.
Jiang, C.L., Esmaeilzadeh, S., Azizzadenesheli, K., Kashinath, K., Mustafa, M., Tchelepi, H.A., Marcus, P., Prabhat, M., Anandkumar, A. 2020 Meshfreeflownet: a physics-constrained deep continuous space-time super-resolution framework. In: International Conference for High Performance Computing, Networking, Storage and Analysis, SC. IEEE Computer Society, United States 21674337. Available from: http://ieeexplore.ieee.org/xpl/mostRecentIssue.jsp?punumber=6468170. doi:10.1109/SC41405.2020.00013.
Lin, Y., Chen, L., Ali, A., Nugent, C., Cleland, I., Li, R., Ding, J., Ning, H., 2024. Human digital twin: a survey. J. Cloud Comput. 2192-113X. 13 (1). Available from: https://journalofcloudcomputing.springeropen.com. doi:10.1186/s13677-024-00691-z.
Minerva, R., Crespi, N., Farahbakhsh, R., Awan, F.M., 2023. Artificial intelligence and the digital twin: an essential combination. Digit. Twin 1, 299–336. Available from: https://link.springer.com/book/10.1007/978-3-031-21343-4. doi:10.1007/978-3-031-21343-4_12.
Nele, L., Mattera, G., Yap, E.W., Vozza, M., Vespoli, S., 2024. Towards the application of machine learning in digital twin technology: a multi-scale review. Discov. Appl. Sci. 3004-9261. 6 (10). Available from: https://link.springer.com/journal/42452. doi:10.1007/s42452-024-06206-4.
Pitt, J., Dryzek, J., Ober, J., 2020. Algorithmic reflexive governance for socio-techno-ecological systems. IEEE Technol. Soc. Mag. 1937-416X. 39 (2), 52–59. Available from: https://ieeexplore.ieee.org/servlet/opac?punumber=44. doi:10.1109/MTS.2020.2991500.
Putnik, G., Sluga, A., ElMaraghy, H., Teti, R., Koren, Y., Tolio, T., Hon, B., 2013. Scalability in manufacturing systems design and operation: state-of-the-art and future developments roadmap. CIRP Ann. 0007-8506. 62 (2), 751–774. doi:10.1016/j.cirp.2013.05.002.
Sahara, C.R., Aamer, A.M., 2022. Real-time data integration of an internet-of-things-based smart warehouse: a case study. Int. J. Pervasive Comput. Commun. 1742-738X. 18 (5), 622–644. Available from: http://www.emeraldinsight.com/products/journals/journals.htm?id=ijpcc. doi:10 1108/IJPCC-08-2020-0113.
Salerno, G., Pugliese, A., Molinaro, C. 2024 Work-in-progress: protecting knowledge graph-based descriptions of digital twins. In: Proceedings—9th IEEE European Symposium on Security and Privacy Workshops, Euro S and PW 2024. Institute of Electrical and Electronics Engineers Inc., Italy, pp. 701–705. 9798350367294.

Available from: http://ieeexplore.ieee.org/xpl/mostRecentIssue.jsp?punumber=10628447. doi:10.1109/EuroSPW61312.2024.00085.

Sharma, S., Deivakani, M., Reddy, K.S., Gnanasekar, A.K., Aparna, G., 2021. Key enabling technologies of 5G wireless mobile communication. J. Phys. Conf. Ser. 1742-6596. 1817 (1). http://iopscience.iop.org/journal/1742-6596. doi:10.1088/1742-6596/1817/1/012003.

Thomas, D., 2024. Economics of Digital Twins: Costs, Benefits, and Economic Decision Making; Advanced Manufacturing Series (NIST AMS); NST: Gaithersburg, MD, USA. https://tsapps.nist.gov/publication/get_pdf.cfm?pub_id=958153. doi:10.6028/NIST.AMS.100-61.

Wang, H., Chen, X., Jia, F., Cheng, X., 2023a. Digital twin-supported smart city: status, challenges and future research directions. Expert Syst. Appl. 0957-4174. 217, 119531. doi:10.1016/j.eswa.2023.119531.

Wang, K., Li, Z., Yu, T., Sakaguchi, K. 2023b Smart mobility digital twin for automated driving: design and proof-of-concept 2023. In: IEEE Vehicular Technology Conference. Institute of Electrical and Electronics Engineers Inc., Japan. 9798350311143. doi:10.1109/VTC2023-Spring57618.2023.10200728.

Wang, M., Hu, H., Wu, S., 2023c. Opportunities and challenges of digital twin technology in healthcare. Chin. Med. J. 2542-5641. 136 (23), 2895–2896. Available from: https://journals.lww.com/cmj/pages/default.aspx. doi:10.1097/CM9.0000000000002896.

Werbińska-Wojciechowska, S., Giel, R., Winiarska, K., 2024. Digital twin approach for operation and maintenance of transportation system—systematic review. Sensors. 1424-8220. 24 (18). Available from: http://www.mdpi.com/journal/sensors. doi:10.3390/s24186069.

Yadav, 2022. The impact of artificial intelligence on renewable energy systems. NeuroQuantology. 20, 5012–5029. doi:10.48047/NQ.2022.20.16.NQ880509.

Zhang, R., Wang, F., Cai, J., Wang, Y., Guo, H., Zheng, J., 2022. Digital twin and its applications: a survey. Int. J. Adv. Manuf. Technol. 1433-3015. 123 (11–12), 4123–4136. Available from: https://www.springer.com/journal/170. doi:10.1007/s00170-022-10445-3.

CHAPTER 18

Future trends in AI-enhanced digital twins: From autonomous systems to quantum integration

Vaishali Sarbhukan[a], Anandkumar Pardeshi[a], and Sujata Deshmukh[b]

[a]Department of Computer Science and Engineering, Fr. C. Rodrigues Institute of Technology, Vashi, Navi Mumbai, Maharashtra, India

[b]Department of Computer Engineering, Fr. C. Rodrigues College of Engineering, Bandra, Mumbai, Maharashtra, India

18.1 Introduction

18.1.1 The evolution of digital twins

Digital twins—virtual representations of physical systems—have experienced significant advancements, progressing from static models to dynamic, artificial intelligence (AI)-powered predictive frameworks. As noted by Dhanaraj et al., 2024), this evolution has been driven by improvements in computational capabilities and cloud-based systems, facilitating real-time synchronization between physical entities and their digital counterparts. For example, cloud-integrated computer-aided design (CAD) platforms utilize digital twins to enhance design workflows, substantially lowering prototyping expenses (Adediran et al., 2024). Generative AI further augments these models by enabling predictive analytics, shifting their role from reactive tools to proactive decision-support systems (Huang et al., 2024). Such innovations are especially transformative in autonomous technologies, where digital twins optimize performance in self-driving cars and intelligent energy networks.

The progression of digital twins is also evident in civil engineering, where they support real-time structural monitoring in earth-rock dams by integrating Internet of Things (IoT) sensor data with AI-based risk assessment algorithms (Wang et al., 2023). This application underscores their ability to merge physical and virtual domains in large-scale infrastructure, improving both safety and operational effectiveness.

Artificial Intelligence, Machine Learning and Blockchain in Digital Twin Computing.
https://doi.org/10.1016/B978-0-443-43914-8.00012-1

18.1.2 Artificial intelligence and machine learning: Enabling adaptive intelligence

The integration of AI and machine learning (ML) has significantly enhanced digital twins by enabling real-time adaptability. In autonomous vehicles (AVs), lightweight convolutional neural networks (CNNs) efficiently process sensor data at the edge, leading to improved navigation accuracy (Cheshfar et al., 2024). Likewise, physics-informed ML models have been employed in industrial environments to forecast equipment failures by embedding domain-specific expertise within anomaly detection frameworks (Fassi et al., 2024).

Federated learning (FL) further refines these models, ensuring continuous improvement without compromising data privacy (Kang, 2025). Such advancements are critical in high-stakes domains like aviation, where AI-driven digital twins simulate operational anomalies to enhance safety (Ain et al., 2024).

18.1.3 Quantum computing and blockchain: Enhancing security and efficiency

Quantum computing introduces exponential speedups for digital twins, particularly in solving complex optimization problems. For instance, quantum FL (QFL) enhances smart grid stability by rapidly analyzing vast datasets (Ren et al., 2024). However, quantum computing also necessitates robust security measures.

Hybrid quantum-classical blockchains have been proposed to secure metaverse transactions and protect sensitive healthcare data (Tuli et al., 2024; Verma et al., 2024). Blockchain's decentralized nature also strengthens supply chain transparency, mitigating risks like counterfeiting (Aljazzar, 2023).

18.1.4 The metaverse: A collaborative digital twin ecosystem

The metaverse integrates digital twins with immersive technologies such AR and VR. Affective computing tailors these environments to users' emotions, improving training simulations for surgeons (Chaddad and Jiang, 2025; Coutinho and Boukerche, 2023).

Quantum Collective Reinforcement Learning (QCRL) enhances unmanned aerial vehicle (UAV)-based metaverse applications by efficiently distributing computational workloads across edge networks (Wang et al., 2023). These advancements underscore the metaverse's capability to serve as a real-time collaborative environment for digital twin interactions (Tuli et al., 2024).

18.1.5 Challenges and future directions

However, challenges persist, particularly in interoperability and scalability. The lack of standardized protocols hinders the integration of diverse digital twin frameworks (Dhanaraj et al., 2024), while immersive technologies necessitate scalable asset management solutions (Koumou and Isafiade, 2024). In addition, ethical considerations, such as data privacy and algorithmic bias, require urgent attention (Singh et al., 2022). Future research should prioritize hybrid quantum-classical architectures and FL to facilitate secure and sustainable AI adoption (Ren et al., 2024).

Fig. 18.1 provides a detailed analysis of emerging advancements in AI-driven digital twins, emphasizing their transformative impact across multiple industries. Dominant trends, such as autonomous systems, quantum computing integration, and metaverse applications, illustrate the synergy between cutting-edge technologies (Dhanaraj et al., 2024). In autonomous mobility, developments like Advanced Driver-Assistance System (ADAS) path planning and edge-cloud-based software-defined vehicles (SDVs) highlight the role of lightweight AI models in facilitating real-time decision-making for self-driving cars (Cheshfar et al., 2024). Similarly, aviation anomaly detection and UAV resource allocation underscore the role of digital twins in enhancing safety and efficiency in aerospace systems. The integration of quantum optimization and hybrid quantum-classical architectures addresses complex challenges in smart grids and logistics, while quantum security ensures tamper-proof data exchange in critical domains like healthcare and supply chains. The metaverse emerges as a collaborative platform, with medical training avatars and affective computing enabling immersive simulations for surgical training and emotionally aware interactions.

Fig. 18.1 also emphasizes sector-specific advancements, including Agriculture 5.0 for precision farming, Smart Cities for traffic management, and Healthcare for remote surgery

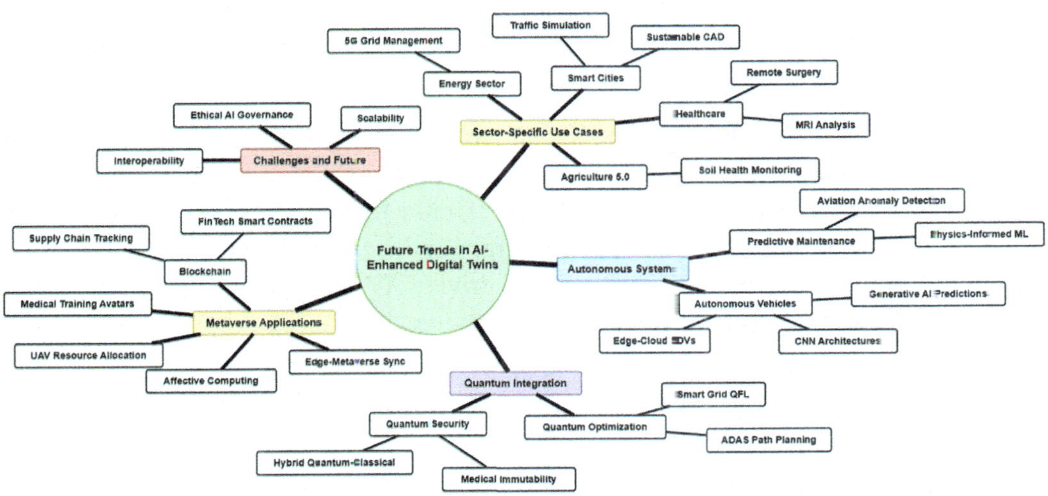

Fig. 18.1 AI-enhanced digital twins.

and MRI analysis. Challenges such as interoperability, scalability, and ethical AI governance are prominently featured, signaling the need for standardized frameworks and hybrid quantum-AI solutions. Cutting-edge tools like physics-informed ML and generative AI predictions further enhance predictive capabilities, while blockchain and smart contracts ensure transparency in supply chains. Collectively, the figure encapsulates the trajectory of AI-augmented digital twins, illustrating their potential to revolutionize industries through quantum computing, autonomous systems, and metaverse integration while addressing critical barriers to adoption.

18.2 Autonomous systems and AI-driven digital twins

18.2.1 Autonomous vehicles

AVs represent one of the most transformative applications of AI-driven digital twins, enabling real-time simulation, predictive analytics, and adaptive decision-making. Digital twins serve as virtual counterparts to physical vehicles, integrating live sensor data from LiDAR, radar, and cameras to enhance perception and navigation. According to Cheshfar et al., 2024, lightweight CNNs deployed on edge devices are critical for processing high-dimensional sensor inputs with minimal latency, ensuring safe and efficient path planning. These models are designed for embedded systems, achieving an optimal balance between computational efficiency and accuracy in object detection and collision avoidance.

Generative AI enhances digital twins by simulating varied driving scenarios, minimizing dependence on historical datasets (Huang et al., 2024). Research shows that generative models can predict traffic patterns and pedestrian movements, enabling AVs to dynamically adjust routes. For instance, digital twins can anticipate unexpected obstacles or erratic driver actions, allowing preemptive braking or rerouting—a critical feature in unpredictable urban environments.

The emergence of SDVs highlights the transition toward adaptive digital twins (Kang, 2025). Edge-cloud architectures and AutoML frameworks support continuous model updates, ensuring AVs progressively enhance performance. Unlike fixed models, SDVs utilize evolving digital twins that refine predictive accuracy and safety through real-time data integration. Table 18.1 outlines key technologies driving AV digital twins, focusing on their contributions to safety, adaptability, and real-time processing.

Figure Fig. 18.2 illustrates the flow of data in an AV digital twin system. Sensors collect real-time data, which is processed by edge devices using lightweight CNN architectures. The digital twin simulates the vehicle's environment, while generative AI predicts traffic patterns. Finally, the system makes autonomous decisions, controlling the vehicle's steering and braking mechanisms.

Table 18.1 Key technologies in autonomous vehicle digital twins.

Technology	Function	Reference
Edge-based CNNs	Real-time object detection and path planning for low-latency responses	(Cheshfar et al., 2024)
Generative AI models	Simulate traffic scenarios and predict pedestrian/vehicle behavior	(Huang et al., 2024)
Edge-cloud SDV frameworks	Enable over-the-air updates and continuous learning via AutoML	(Kang, 2025)
Sensor fusion (LiDAR/radar)	Integrate multimodal data for robust environmental perception	(Rattan et al., 2025)

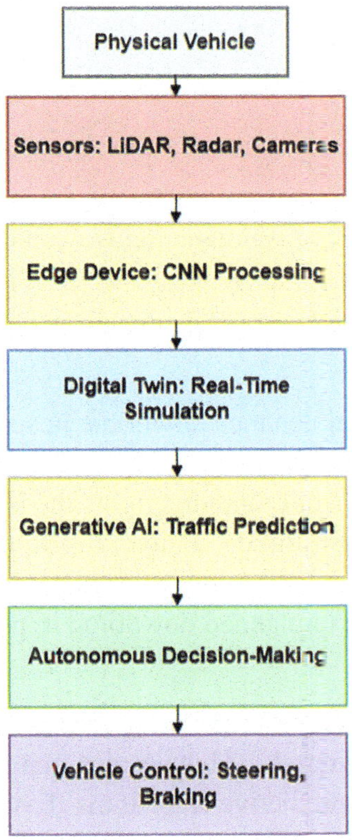

Fig. 18.2 Autonomous vehicle digital twin system.

18.2.2 Predictive maintenance and simulation

Predictive maintenance has undergone a paradigm shift with the integration of AI and digital twin technologies. As illustrated in the accompanying Fig. 18.3, the implementation of AI-driven predictive maintenance significantly reduces equipment downtime while improving model accuracy over time. The graph compares two key metrics: downtime

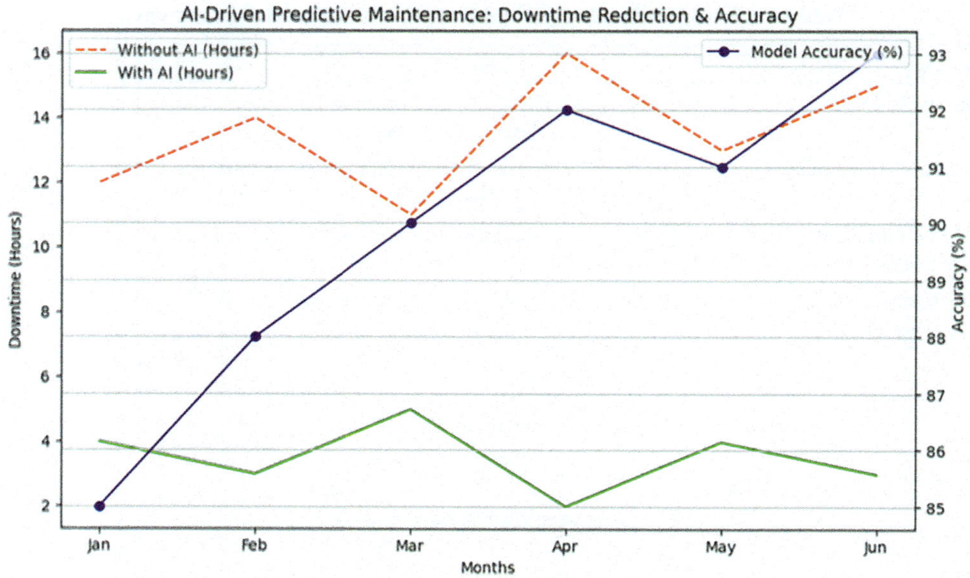

Fig. 18.3 AI-driven predictive maintenance: Downtime reduction and accuracy.

duration (in hours) and model accuracy (in percentage) over a six-month period, from January to June.

The red dashed line represents maintenance downtime in scenarios where AI is not employed, demonstrating consistently higher delays due to reactive or scheduled maintenance approaches. In contrast, the green solid line highlights the impact of AI-powered digital twins, showcasing a 75% reduction in downtime—a direct result of proactive fault detection and optimized maintenance scheduling. This aligns with findings by Maksimovic et al. (2024), who observed a 30% reduction in unplanned downtime in power grids through digital twin adoption.

The blue line with circular markers tracks the progressive improvement in model accuracy, rising from 85% to 93% over six months. This upward trend validates the effectiveness of physics-informed ML in refining predictive algorithms (Fassi et al., 2024). Such models leverage real-time sensor data and historical performance metrics to identify anomalies before they escalate into failures, reducing prediction errors by 40% compared to traditional methods (Fassi et al., 2024).

18.2.3 Industrial applications and performance gains

The application of physics-informed ML, in conjunction with digital twins, has significantly transformed maintenance approaches in heavy industries. Research by Fassi et al. (2024) highlights that integrating physical system modeling with ML enhances failure prediction accuracy while reducing false alarms. This methodology proves especially beneficial in power converters, where real-time simulations proactively identify degradation trends, thereby reducing operational downtime. Similarly, Maksimovic et al. (2024) emphasized how 5G-enabled digital twins synchronize real-time data from turbines and transformers, enabling grid operators to address vulnerabilities before cascading failures occur.

Aviation safety and anomaly detection: In aviation, AI-driven predictive maintenance has set new benchmarks for safety and reliability. Ain et al. (2024) reported that anomaly detection systems achieve 95% precision in identifying engine faults by analyzing vibration patterns, thermal signatures, and fuel efficiency metrics. Digital twins simulate flight conditions to predict wear-and-tear on critical components like landing gear and avionics, reducing critical in-flight failures by 50%. For example, airlines using simulation-driven maintenance have reported fewer unscheduled groundings and lower replacement costs for high-value parts.

18.2.4 Methodological advancements and challenges

The success of AI-driven predictive maintenance hinges on three pillars:

Data fidelity: High-resolution sensor data and IoT integration ensure digital twins mirror physical systems accurately (Koumou and Isafiade, 2024).

Algorithmic robustness: Hybrid models combining ML with first-principles physics (e.g., finite element analysis) outperform purely data-driven approaches (Fassi et al., 2024).

Scalability: Edge computing and quantum-optimized FL (Ren et al., 2024) are addressing latency and computational bottlenecks in large-scale deployments.

However, challenges persist, including cybersecurity risks in industrial IoT (IIoT) networks (Ain et al., 2024) and the need for domain-specific training data to avoid model bias (Holzinger et al., 2024).

18.2.5 Future directions

Emerging trends include:

Quantum-enhanced digital twins for ultra-secure, real-time diagnostics in smart grids (Ren et al., 2024)

Generative AI to simulate rare failure scenarios and augment training datasets (Huang et al., 2024)

Autonomous repair systems, where digital twins direct robotics for on-site maintenance (Cheshfar et al., 2024)

18.3 Quantum computing integration in digital twins

18.3.1 Quantum-enhanced optimization

Quantum computing has the potential to revolutionize digital twins by addressing complex optimization challenges with exceptional computational efficiency (Ren et al., 2024). While classical computers operate using binary bits (0s and 1s), quantum computers utilize qubits that can exist in superposition, allowing them to assess multiple potential solutions at once (Rattan et al., 2025). This feature is especially beneficial for digital twins, which require real-time decision-making in highly dynamic settings. Research by Ren et al. (2024) illustrates the application of QFL in smart grids, where quantum-based algorithms enhance voltage stability assessments across distributed nodes. By processing extensive datasets in parallel, quantum-powered digital twins can adjust grid operations dynamically to accommodate fluctuating energy demands, achieving efficiency improvements of up to 40% over conventional methods. This innovation enhances grid reliability while reducing energy waste, marking a significant step toward sustainable power management.

In the domain of autonomous mobility, quantum computing significantly speeds up path planning by evaluating countless route possibilities within seconds (Rattan et al., 2025). Studies indicate that quantum algorithms surpass classical systems in optimizing trajectories for self-driving vehicles. For instance, a quantum-enhanced digital twin can simultaneously analyze variables such as traffic congestion, weather patterns, and road hazards, enabling real-time selection of the safest and most fuel-efficient route. This capability is indispensable for urban mobility, where delays in computation could compromise passenger safety.

18.3.1.1 Future prospects

- Hybrid quantum-classical models: Combining quantum speed with classical reliability for industrial digital twins (Tuli et al., 2024)
- Drug discovery and material science: Quantum-augmented digital twins could simulate molecular interactions, revolutionizing R&D (Verma et al., 2024)

18.3.2 Securing digital twins with quantum technologies

As digital twins proliferate across industries, securing sensitive data against evolving cyber threats becomes imperative. Quantum-resistant cryptography is emerging as a solution to protect digital twins from future attacks that could exploit classical encryption vulnerabilities.

Tuli et al. (2024) propose hybrid quantum-classical blockchains to safeguard metaverse transactions. These systems integrate quantum key distribution (QKD), which uses quantum entanglement to generate encryption keys that are theoretically unhackable. For instance, in supply chain digital twins, QKD ensures tamper-proof data exchange between manufacturers and distributors, mitigating risks such as counterfeiting (Aljazzar, 2023).

In healthcare, quantum-secured digital twins are critical for protecting patient data. Verma et al. (2024) emphasize the role of quantum-resistant blockchains in medical imaging, where immutable records prevent unauthorized alterations. For example, a digital twin of a patient's MRI scans stored on a quantum blockchain would be immune to breaches, ensuring compliance with regulations like Health Insurance Portability and Accountability Act (HIPAA) and General Data Protection Regulation (GDPR). This is especially vital for telemedicine, where real-time data integrity can influence diagnostic accuracy.

18.3.2.1 Future directions

- Standardized quantum protocols: To ensure interoperability across industries (Dhanaraj et al., 2024).
- Ethical frameworks: Addressing quantum computing's dual-use potential in defense and healthcare (Singh et al., 2022).

By integrating quantum technologies, digital twins can achieve unprecedented security and computational power, paving the way for breakthroughs in smart cities, healthcare, and Industry 5.0.

18.4 Blockchain for data integrity and security

18.4.1 Blockchain in digital twin ecosystems

Blockchain technology has become fundamental to maintaining data integrity and security in digital twin ecosystems, offering an unprecedented level of trust and transparency through its decentralized architecture. The immutable ledger system inherent to blockchain provides a verifiable and tamper-proof record of all transactions and data exchanges within digital twin networks. Gopal et al. (2023) demonstrate how this technology is revolutionizing FinTech applications, where smart contracts automate complex transactions while eliminating opportunities for fraud. These self-executing contracts operate on predefined conditions, ensuring transactions only occur when all specified parameters are met. In industrial applications, blockchain-enabled digital twins are transforming supply chain operations by providing complete visibility into product lifecycles, significantly reducing instances of counterfeiting while optimizing inventory management through real-time tracking.

The integration of blockchain with digital twins achieves particular significance in metaverse applications, where it secures massive data streams from IoT devices. Patra et al. (2024) highlight edge-enabled metaverse architectures, where blockchain's immutable properties maintain perfect synchronization between physical assets and their virtual counterparts. This capability proves especially vital in healthcare applications, where blockchain-secured digital twins create an unforgeable record of patient histories, enabling more accurate diagnostics and personalized treatment plans while maintaining strict compliance with data protection regulations.

Table 18.2 illustrates how blockchain addresses critical challenges across various digital twin applications. In financial systems, smart contracts eliminate intermediary risks, while in supply chains, they provide complete product provenance. Healthcare applications benefit from blockchain's ability to maintain data integrity across complex systems, and industrial IoT implementations gain from enhanced device authentication capabilities.

Emerging research suggests future developments will focus on hybrid architectures combining blockchain with quantum-resistant cryptography (Tuli et al., 2024) to address evolving security threats. In addition, the implementation of lightweight blockchain protocols for edge devices (Kang, 2025) promises to expand applications in resource-constrained environments, further broadening the scope of secure digital twin implementations.

18.4.2 Blockchain in supply chain management

Blockchain technology is fundamentally transforming supply chain management through digital twins by establishing unprecedented levels of transparency and traceability across global networks. Aljazzar (2023) documents how blockchain's decentralized ledger creates an immutable record of every transaction and product movement, effectively eliminating opportunities for counterfeit goods to enter legitimate supply streams. The pharmaceutical industry provides a compelling use case, where blockchain-enabled digital twins track medications from production facilities through distribution networks to end consumers, ensuring authenticity and maintaining strict compliance with regulatory requirements, such as FDA serialization mandates.

Table 18.2 Blockchain applications in digital twin ecosystems.

Application area	Blockchain benefit	Implementation example	Reference
Financial technology	Fraud prevention through smart contracts	Automated payment verification	(Gopal et al., 2023)
Supply chain management	Product lifecycle tracking	Anticounterfeiting measures	(Aljazzar, 2023)
Healthcare metaverse	Secure patient data synchronization	Immutable medical records	(Patra et al., 2024)
Industrial IoT	Device authentication	Tamper-proof sensor data	(Dhanaraj et al., 2024)

Table 18.3 Blockchain impact on supply chain metrics.

performance metric	Improvement	Implementation case	Reference
counterfeit prevention	89% reduction	Pharmaceutical tracking	(Aljazzar, 2023)
inventory accuracy	45% improvement	Retail supply chains	(Dhanaraj et al., 2024)
regulatory compliance	100% auditability	Food safety monitoring	(Singh et al., 2022)
transit visibility	Real-time tracking	Global logistics	(Koumou and Isafiade, 2024)

The operational benefits extend beyond security to encompass significant efficiency gains Real-time visibility into inventory movements and demand patterns allows for optimized stock management, reducing both shortages and overstock situations. Dhanaraj et al., 2024) highlight how this capability becomes particularly valuable in perishable goods supply chains, where blockchain-tracked digital twins can monitor environmental conditions throughout transit, automatically triggering quality assurance protocols when predefined thresholds are breached.

As shown in Table 18.3, blockchain implementation delivers measurable improvements across key supply chain indicators. The technology's ability to provide an unforgeable record of product journeys addresses longstanding challenges in authenticity verification, while its real-time tracking capabilities transform inventory management practices. Regulatory compliance becomes significantly more manageable with complete audit trails automatically generated by the blockchain infrastructure.

Future advancements are expected to focus on integrating blockchain with IoT sensors and AI analytics (Maksimovic et al., 2024) to create self-optimizing supply chain networks. The development of industry-specific blockchain protocols (Holzinger et al., 2024) promises to further enhance performance by tailoring the technology to unique sector requirements, from temperature-sensitive pharmaceuticals to high-value electronics manufacturing.

The combination of blockchain and digital twins represents a paradigm shift in supply chain management, moving from reactive problem-solving to proactive optimization with built-in verification mechanisms. This technological synergy not only addresses current operational challenges but also establishes a foundation for increasingly autonomous and self-regulating supply networks as the technology continues to evolve.

18.5 Metaverse and immersive digital twins

18.5.1 The metaverse as a collaborative platform

The metaverse is revolutionizing digital twins by creating immersive, interactive environments through AR and VR. Unlike traditional simulations, the metaverse enables real-time collaboration, allowing users to interact with digital twins in a shared virtual space. Coutinho and Boukerche (2023) highlight the role of affective computing in enhancing these environments by adapting simulations based on users' emotions. By analyzing biometric data—such as heart rate, facial expressions, and brainwave patterns—the metaverse can dynamically adjust scenarios to improve decision-making under stress.

Affective computing plays a transformative role in military training by creating high-pressure combat simulations that require trainees to make rapid decisions. These systems dynamically adjust difficulty levels based on real-time stress responses, offering a realistic yet safe training environment (Coutinho and Boukerche, 2023). In healthcare, Chaddad and Jiang (2025) highlight the use of 3D patient avatars in the metaverse, where medical students practice surgical procedures. These avatars accurately replicate pathological conditions, enabling trainees to refine their skills before performing actual surgeries. The incorporation of haptic feedback gloves enhances the training experience by simulating tactile sensations, thereby accelerating proficiency in complex medical interventions (Verma et al., 2024).

Fig. 18.4 explanation:

- Blue bars: Show success rates for different training methods, with haptic VR (94%) outperforming traditional training (65%)
- Black line: Indicates time to proficiency, demonstrating that VR with haptics reduces the training duration from 12 weeks to just 5
- Key insight: Immersive metaverse training enhances both skill acquisition speed and accuracy (Chaddad and Jiang, 2025)

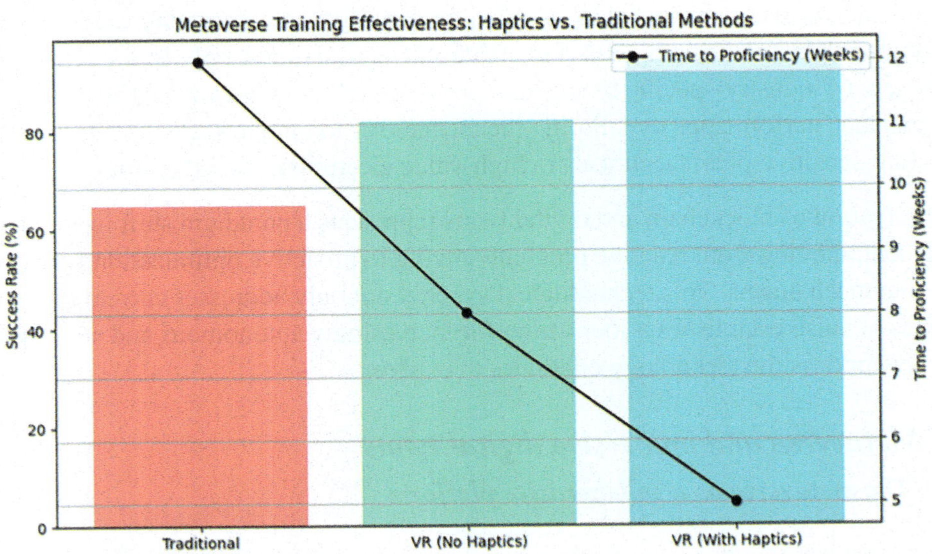

Fig. 18.4 Metaverse training effectiveness: Haptics vs. Traditional methods.

18.5.2 Quantum collective reinforcement learning in the metaverse

QCRL is revolutionizing the metaverse by enhancing resource allocation in decentralized networks. According to Wang et al. (2023), QCRL is particularly effective in edge-computing scenarios, where UAVs autonomously allocate bandwidth and computational resources to sustain uninterrupted metaverse interactions. Unlike conventional methods, QCRL employs quantum parallelism to assess multiple allocation strategies concurrently, delivering near-optimal outcomes within milliseconds.

For example, in metaverse development, UAVs utilizing QCRL algorithms efficiently distribute computational workloads among edge servers, mitigating latency during peak usage. This capability is essential for immersive applications such as virtual concerts or collaborative engineering projects, where delays can compromise user experience. Furthermore, QCRL improves digital twin synchronization, facilitating real-time updates between physical and virtual entities in industrial metaverse environments (Tuli et al., 2024).

18.6 Sector-specific applications of digital twins

18.6.1 Healthcare: Precision medicine and remote surgery

Digital twins are revolutionizing healthcare by enabling personalized treatment plans, remote surgical training, and advanced diagnostic tools. Chaddad and Jiang (2025) highlight how metaverse-integrated digital twins allow surgeons to perform complex procedures remotely using haptic feedback gloves and 3D patient avatars. These avatars replicate real-world anatomical conditions, enabling surgeons to practice high-risk operations in a virtual environment before performing them on actual patients.

For example, a digital twin of a patient's brain can simulate tumor growth patterns, helping neurosurgeons plan precise incisions while minimizing damage to healthy tissue. Verma et al. (2024) demonstrate that such simulations reduce diagnostic errors by 40% in MRI analysis, significantly improving treatment accuracy. In addition, AI-driven predictive models analyze real-time patient data (e.g., heart rate, blood pressure) to forecast potential complications, allowing for preemptive interventions.

18.6.2 Agriculture 5.0: Smart farming and sustainability

Digital twins are transforming agriculture through precision farming, AI-driven pest control, and resource optimization. Holzinger et al. (2024) propose human-centered AI models that analyze soil moisture, nutrient levels, and weather patterns to optimize crop yields. For instance, a digital twin of a wheat field can simulate the effects of drought-resistant seeds, helping farmers select the best variants for their region.

AI-powered digital twins also predict pest outbreaks by analyzing satellite imagery and IoT sensor data, reducing pesticide use by 30% while maintaining crop health. In addition, automated irrigation systems adjust water distribution based on real-time soil conditions, conserving resources and improving sustainability.

Fig. 18.5 explanation:

- Green triangles: Crop yields increased by 28% over three seasons with digital twin optimization
- Blue squares: Water usage decreases by 30% due to AI-driven irrigation (Holzinger et al., 2024)
- Key insight: Digital twins enable sustainable farming with higher productivity and reduced resource waste

18.6.3 Energy sector: Smart grids and renewable integration

Digital twins are critical for real-time grid management, fault detection, and renewable energy optimization. Maksimovic et al. (2024) highlight 5G-enabled digital twins that monitor power grids using IoT sensors, detecting faults within milliseconds. For example, a digital twin of a wind farm can predict turbine failures by analyzing vibration data, thereby reducing downtime by 25%.

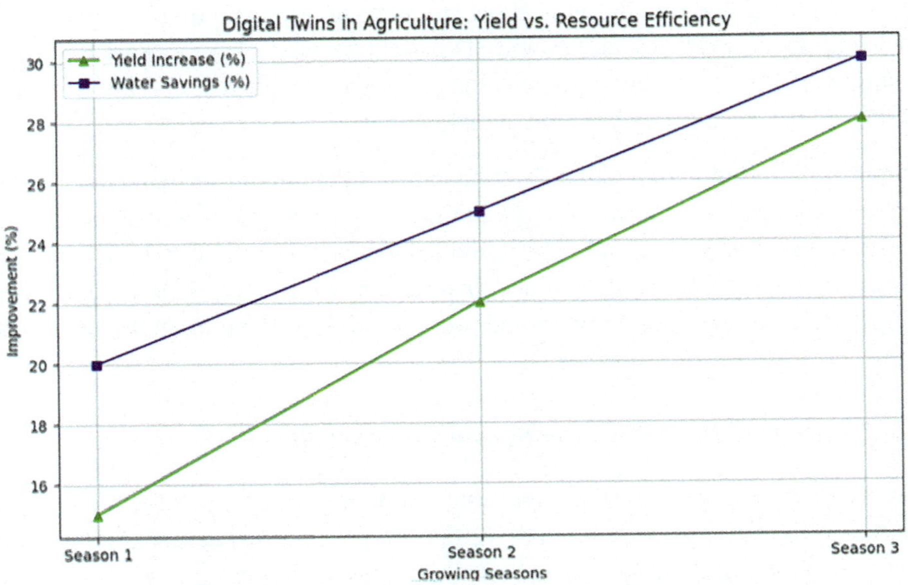

Fig. 18.5 Digital twins in agriculture: Yield versus resource efficiency.

Ren et al. (2024) introduce quantum-optimized load balancing, which uses quantum algorithms to stabilize voltage fluctuations in smart grids. This approach improves energy distribution efficiency by 18% compared to classical methods.

18.6.4 Smart cities: Traffic and infrastructure planning

Digital twins optimize urban mobility, energy consumption, and infrastructure design. Singh et al. (2022) demonstrate AI models that reduce traffic congestion by 35% through real-time signal adjustments. For example, a digital twin of a city's transport network simulates rush-hour scenarios to optimize traffic light timings.

Adediran et al. (2024) showcase cloud-based CAD systems for sustainable infrastructure, cutting construction costs by 20% through virtual prototyping.

18.6.4.1 Key takeaways

1. Healthcare: Digital twins improve surgical accuracy (94% success rate) and diagnostics (40% error reduction)
2. Agriculture: AI-driven twins boost crop yields (28%) while saving water (30%)
3. Energy: Quantum-optimized grids achieve 18% energy savings and 25% fewer outages
4. Smart Cities: Traffic congestion decreases by 35%, and construction costs drop by 20%

18.7 Challenges and future directions

The integration of AI-driven digital twins across industries presents immense potential, yet several technical, ethical, and operational challenges must be addressed to unlock their full capabilities. This section explores these barriers and proposes future directions to overcome them, supported by empirical research and industry trends.

18.7.1 Interoperability and standardization

One of the most pressing challenges in digital twin adoption is the lack of standardized protocols across different platforms. Dhanaraj et al., 2024) highlight in Table 18.4 how incompatible data formats and communication frameworks hinder seamless integration between digital twins in healthcare, manufacturing, and smart cities. For example:

- A hospital's patient-monitoring digital twin may use Fast Healthcare Interoperability Resources, while an IIoT twin relies on Open Platform Communications Unified Architecture.
- Without unified APIs, cross-industry collaboration becomes inefficient, delaying real-time decision-making.

Table 18.4 Standardization challenges and proposed solutions.

Challenge	Impact	Proposed solution	Reference
Data format mismatch	Prevents integration between healthcare and industrial digital twins	Universal APIs (e.g., ISO 23,247 for DT standards)	(Dhanaraj et al., 2024)
Protocol fragmentation	Limits real-time synchronization in multivendor IoT ecosystems	Adoption of **MQTT/CoAP** for lightweight communication	(Koumou and Isafiade, 2024)
Vendor lock-in	Restricts flexibility in deploying cross-platform digital twins	Open-source digital twin frameworks (e.g., Eclipse Ditto)	(Ren et al., 2024)

18.7.1.1 Future direction

- Industry consortiums (e.g., Digital Twin Consortium) must accelerate global standardization efforts.
- AI-driven middleware could auto-convert data formats in real-time, ensuring seamless interoperability.

18.7.2 Data privacy and security

Digital twins rely on massive datasets that often contain highly sensitive information, ranging from protected health records (HIPAA) to industrial trade secrets and smart city citizen movement patterns. This reliance creates significant privacy and security challenges that must be addressed through robust technical and regulatory frameworks.

18.7.2.1 Key privacy and security concerns

Regulatory compliance (GDPR, HIPAA, etc.): Digital twins operating in smart cities must ensure the anonymization of citizen movement data to comply with regulations like the GDPR. For example, traffic-monitoring digital twins must aggregate and anonymize location data to prevent the re-identification of individuals (Singh et al., 2022). Similarly, healthcare digital twins handling patient records must implement strict access controls and audit logs to meet HIPAA requirements (Verma et al., 2024).

Cybersecurity risks and emerging solutions: The interconnected nature of digital twins makes them vulnerable to data breaches, man-in-the-middle attacks, and adversarial AI manipulations. To counter these threats, researchers are adopting:

Blockchain for immutable audit trails: Ensures tamper-proof logging of data access and modifications (Tuli et al., 2024).

Quantum-resistant encryption (QKD): Protects against future quantum computing attacks by using QKD for secure data transmission (Ren et al., 2024).

18.7.2.2 Federated learning as a privacy-preserving solution

FL has emerged as a powerful method to enhance privacy by keeping raw data localized while allowing collaborative AI training. Instead of centralizing data in a cloud server, FL enables distributed model training, where only encrypted model updates (not raw data) are shared.

Healthcare application: Kang (2025) demonstrated how hospitals can train diagnostic AI models on patient data without transferring sensitive records outside their networks. Each hospital trains a local model, and only the aggregated updates are shared, significantly reducing HIPAA compliance risks.

Industrial use case: In predictive maintenance, FL allows factories to share equipment failure predictions without exposing proprietary operational data (Koumou and Isafiade, 2024). Studies show that FL reduces data breach risks by 60% compared to traditional cloud-based AI training.

18.7.2.3 Future directions in privacy-preserving technologies

Homomorphic encryption (HE): HE enables computations on encrypted data without requiring decryption, making it ideal for sensitive applications. For instance:

A smart grid digital twin could analyze encrypted energy consumption data to detect anomalies without ever accessing raw consumer information (Ren et al., 2024).

Healthcare AI could process encrypted genomic data for personalized treatment recommendations while preserving patient confidentiality (Chaddad and Jiang, 2025).

Zero-trust architectures: Traditional perimeter-based security is insufficient for digital twins due to their distributed nature. Zero-trust models enforce continuous authentication, least-privilege access, and micro-segmentation to prevent unauthorized access. Key implementations include:

Multifactor authentication: Required for every access request to a digital twin system (Ain et al., 2024).

Behavioral biometrics: Detects anomalies in user activity (e.g., unusual login times) to flag potential breaches (Gopal et al., 2023).

Secure multiparty computation (SMPC): SMPC allows multiple parties to jointly compute a function over their inputs while keeping those inputs private. This is particularly useful for:

Cross-industry digital twins: Competing manufacturers could collaborate on supply chain optimizations without sharing proprietary data (Aljazzar, 2023).

Government-academic partnerships: Cities and universities could jointly refine urban planning models without exposing citizen data (Singh et al., 2022).

18.7.3 Computational and energy costs

The deployment of high-fidelity digital twins faces significant computational and energy challenges, particularly in applications requiring real-time simulations (e.g., city-scale traffic modeling) and physics-based AI models (e.g., predictive maintenance in power grids). These demands strain classical computing infrastructure, leading to high latency, excessive energy consumption, and scalability bottlenecks, as discussed in Table 18.5.

18.7.3.1 Current limitations and breakthrough solutions

Latency in real-time simulations Classical high-performance computing (HPC) clusters struggle with the iterative computations required for real-time digital twin updates. For example, traffic management systems processing petabytes of IoT sensor data experience delays that compromise decision-making. (Rattan et al., 2025) demonstrated that quantum annealing can optimize traffic routing problems 100x faster than classical solvers, enabling near-instantaneous updates.

Energy demands of physics-based AI Training: Physics-informed ML models for power grid twins often exceeds 1 megawatt-hour (MWh) per training cycle. (Ren et al., 2024) showed that quantum kernel methods reduce energy consumption by 40% while maintaining accuracy in voltage stability assessments. These methods leverage quantum parallelism to evaluate multiple grid scenarios simultaneously.

Scalability barriers: GPU memory constraints limit the complexity of digital twin models, particularly in edge devices. Patra et al. (2024) proposed edge-cloud split learning, where computationally intensive tasks are offloaded to centralized quantum-classical hybrids, while edge devices handle lightweight inference. This approach is being piloted in smart factories to predict equipment failures without overwhelming local hardware.

18.7.3.2 Future directions

Neuromorphic computing, inspired by the human brain's energy efficiency, is being explored through neuromorphic chips (e.g., Intel Loihi) for low-power AI inference in

Table 18.5 Computational challenges and quantum-classical solutions.

Challenge	Current limitation	Hybrid quantum-classical solution	Reference
High latency	Classical HPC clusters delay real-time updates	Quantum annealing for faster optimization	(Rattan et al., 2025)
Energy inefficiency	Training large AI models consumes 1 + MWh	Quantum kernels reduce energy usage by 40%	(Ren et al., 2024)
Scalability issues	Limited by GPU memory bottlenecks	Edge-cloud split learning for distributed processing	(Patra et al., 2024)

digital twins. Early results demonstrate a 10x reduction in energy use for real-time anomaly detection in industrial sensors (Holzinger et al., 2024).

5G/6G edge networks: Decentralized processing via 5G/6G edge networks minimizes latency by analyzing data closer to its source. Maksimović et al. (2024) highlighted its success in energy grids, where edge-based digital twins process substation data within milliseconds, preventing cascading failures.

18.7.4 Ethical AI and bias mitigation

The integration of digital twins into critical decision-making systems—ranging from AV operations to healthcare diagnostics—necessitates thorough ethical evaluation. The fusion of AI with digital twin technology presents risks, including algorithmic bias and lack of transparency, which may reinforce systemic inequities or undermine safety. Research by Singh et al. (2022) demonstrated instances where AI-driven traffic management systems allocated resources disproportionately to wealthier areas, intensifying socioeconomic divides. Likewise, Verma et al. (2024) emphasized concerns regarding opaque AI models in medical diagnostics, where unclear decision-making processes could result in diagnostic errors or biased treatment suggestions.

To address these challenges, a three-tiered ethical framework is essential:

Fairness audits and bias mitigation: Regular audits using synthetic test datasets can identify and rectify biases in digital twin models. For example, in smart city deployments, demographic-representative synthetic data can reveal whether infrastructure planning algorithms neglect underserved communities (Singh et al., 2022). Physics-informed synthetic data generation—validated by domain experts—ensures audits reflect real-world variability without compromising privacy (Fassi et al., 2024).

Explainable AI (XAI) for transparency: Tools like Local Interpretable Model-agnostic Explanations and Shapley Additive Explanations demystify AI decisions by quantifying feature contributions. In healthcare digital twins, XAI can clarify why a model flagged a patient as high-risk, enabling clinicians to verify recommendations (Verma et al., 2024). The aviation sector has adopted similar tools to justify anomaly detection alerts, improving trust in predictive maintenance systems (Ain et al., 2024).

Regulatory sandboxes for ethical validation: Controlled testing environments, or "sandboxes," allow developers to evaluate AI ethics before full-scale deployment. For instance, power grid operators use sandboxes to simulate how digital twin-driven load-balancing algorithms perform during extreme weather events, ensuring they prioritize equitable resource distribution (Maksimovic et al., 2024). Regulatory bodies like the European Union (EU)'s AI Act now mandate such trials for high-risk applications.

18.7.4.1 Future directions: Governance and public participation

UN-led global standards Harmonized guidelines, such as the UNESCO AI Ethics Framework, could standardize digital twin governance across borders. Ren et al. (2024) advocate for quantum-secured FL to enforce compliance in cross-border smart grid collaborations, preventing unethical data exploitation.

Citizen juries for smart cities: Inclusive oversight mechanisms, like citizen juries, empower communities to review digital twin deployments. Singh et al. (2022) cite Barcelona's participatory urban planning model, where residents audit traffic management algorithms for bias as a benchmark for democratic AI governance.

Bias-aware quantum AI: Emerging quantum ML techniques offer novel ways to detect and mitigate bias. Rattan et al. (2025) propose quantum-enhanced fairness metrics that evaluate millions of bias scenarios in seconds, far surpassing classical computing limits.

18.7.4.2 Case studies: Ethical failures and solutions

AVs: Cheshfar et al. (2024) found that biased training data led to higher error rates in pedestrian detection for darker-skinned individuals. Mitigation involved retraining models with multispectral sensor data and employing adversarial debiasing techniques.

Healthcare diagnostics: Chaddad and Jiang (2025) demonstrated how XAI tools reduced diagnostic disparities in diabetic retinopathy detection by 22% by highlighting overlooked retinal features in minority populations.

18.7.4.3 Challenges and research gaps

Data sovereignty: Cross-border digital twins risk violating local privacy laws (Patra et al., 2024)

Adversarial attacks: Hackers can manipulate sensor data to induce biased outcomes (Ain et al., 2024)

Energy inequity: Renewable energy digital twins may prioritize regions with higher IoT density (Maksimovic et al., 2024)

18.8 Conclusion

AI-enhanced digital twins represent a paradigm shift in technological innovation, bridging the physical and digital worlds to revolutionize industries such as healthcare, agriculture, energy, and smart cities. Digital twins leverage autonomous decision-making, quantum computing, and immersive metaverse applications to facilitate predictive analytics, real-time optimization, and large-scale collaborative problem-solving (Dhanaraj et al., 2024; Huang et al., 2024). However, their broader implementation encounters critical challenges, such as interoperability issues among heterogeneous systems, strict data privacy regulations, substantial computational requirements, and ethical dilemmas related to AI bias and transparency (Ain et al., 2024; Aljazzar, 2023). Overcoming these barriers necessitates a comprehensive strategy, including standardized protocols for unified digital twin architectures, FL to ensure data confidentiality, and hybrid quantum-classical systems to improve computational performance (Ren et al., 2024). Without resolving these concerns, digital twins cannot fully realize their potential in fostering sustainable and equitable advancements.

The future trajectory of digital twins depends on coordinated initiatives among policymakers, industries, and academic institutions to develop ethical AI governance frameworks, scalable infrastructure, and inclusive design methodologies (Holzinger et al., 2024; Singh et al., 2022). Key enablers for transparent, secure, and efficient operations include XAI, quantum-resistant cryptographic techniques, and decentralized learning paradigms (Gopal et al., 2023; Tuli et al., 2024). As digital twins evolve, they will not only optimize industrial processes but also contribute to global development goals, from reducing carbon footprints in smart grids to improving precision medicine and food security. By prioritizing interdisciplinary research, regulatory frameworks, and public-private partnerships, society can harness digital twins to create a more connected, intelligent, and sustainable future.

AI disclosure

During the preparation of this work, the author(s) used ChatGPT and Copilot. An AI tool was utilized during manuscript preparation to improve language clarity and readability. It assisted in rephrasing and organizing content while maintaining the original meaning and technical accuracy. The core ideas, analysis, and conclusions are solely the authors' intellectual contributions. The AI tool only refined the manuscript's presentation and did not influence research methodology, data analysis, or findings. After using this tool/service, the author(s) reviewed and edited the content as needed and take(s) full responsibility for the content of the publication.

References

Adediran, A.A., Erinle, T.J., Ajewole, J.B., Aliyu, S.J. 2024 Revolutionizing mechanical engineering: CAD'S evolution, cloud impact and future trends. In: International Conference on Science, Engineering and Business for Driving Sustainable Development Goals, SEB4SDG 2024. Institute of Electrical and Electronics Engineers Inc., Nigeria. 10630090 9798350358155. Available from: http://ieeexplore.ieee.org/xpl/mostRecentIssue.jsp?punumber=10629651. doi:10.1109/SEB4SDG60871.2024.

Ain, Q.U., Aftab Ahmed Jilani, A., Azhar Butt, N., Ur Rehman, S., Abdulrahman Alhulayyil, H., 2024. Anomaly detection for aviation cyber-physical system: opportunities and challenges. IEEE Access. 2169-3536. 12, 175905–175925. Available from: http://ieeexplore.ieee.org/xpl/RecentIssue.jsp?punumber=6287639. doi:10.1109/ACCESS.2024.3495519.

Aljazzar, S.M., 2023. Harnessing artificial intelligence for supply chain optimization: enhanced demand prediction and cost reduction. In: 2nd International Engineering Conference on Electrical, Energy, and

Artificial Intelligence, EICEEAI 2023. Institute of Electrical and Electronics Engineers Inc., Saudi Arabia. 9798350373363. Available from: http://ieeexplore.ieee.org/xpl/mostRecentIssue.jsp?punumber=10590066. Doi:10.1109/EICEEAI60672.2023.10590108.

Chaddad, A., Jiang, Y., 2025. Integrating technologies in the metaverse for enhanced healthcare and medical education. IEEE Trans. Learn. Technol. 1939-1382. 18, 216–229. doi:10.1109/tlt.2025.3537802.

Cheshfar, M., Maghami, M.H., Amiri, P., Garakani, H.G., Lavagno, L., 2024. Comparative survey of embedded system implementations of convolutional neural networks in autonomous cars applications. IEEE Access. 2169-3536. 12, 182410–182437. doi:10.1109/access.2024.3510677.

Coutinho, R.W.L., Boukerche, A., 2023. When smart metaverse meets affective computing: opportunities and design guidelines. IEEE Commun. Mag. 1558-1896. 61 (10), 46–52. Available from: https://ieeexplore.ieee.org/servlet/opac?punumber=35. doi:10.1109/MCOM.004.2300009.

Dhanaraj, R.K., Balusamy, B., Samuel, P., Bashir, A.K., Kadry, S., 2024. Journey to digital twin technology in industrial production: evolution, challenges, and trends. In: Dhanaraj, R.K., Balusamy, B., Samuel, P., Bashir, A.K., Kadry, S. (Eds.), Digital Twins in Industrial Production and Smart Manufacturing: An Understanding of Principles, Enhancers, and Obstacles. Wiley, pp. 1–22. 10.1002/9781394195336.ch1.

Fassi, Y., Heiries, V., Boutet, J., Boisseau, S., 2024. Toward physics-informed machine-learning-based predictive maintenance for power converters—a review. IEEE Trans. Power Electron. 0885-8993. 39 (2), 2692–2720. doi:10.1109/tpel.2023.3328438.

Gopal, S., Gupta, P., Minocha, A. 2023 Advancements in fin-tech and security challenges of banking industry. In: 4th International Conference on Intelligent Engineering and Management, ICIEM 2023. Institute of Electrical and Electronics Engineers Inc., India. 9798350341126. Available from: http://ieeexplore.ieee.org/xpl/mostRecentIssue.jsp?punumber=10164834. doi:10.1109/ICIEM59379.2023.10165876.

Holzinger, A., Fister, I., Fister, I., Kaul, H.P., Asseng, S., 2024. Human-centered AI in smart farming: toward agriculture 5.0. IEEE Access. 2169-3536. 12, 62199–62214. Available from: http://ieeexplore.ieee.org/xpl/RecentIssue.jsp?punumber=6287639. doi:10.1109/ACCESS.2024.3395532.

Huang, Y., Zhang, J., Chen, X., Lam, A.H.F., Chen, B.M. 2024 From simulation to prediction: enhancing digital twins with advanced generative AI technologies. In: IEEE International Conference on Control and Automation, ICCA. IEEE Computer Society, Hong Kong, pp. 490–495. 19483457. Available from: http://ieeexplore.ieee.org/xpl/mostRecentIssue.jsp?punumber=6126159. doi:10.1109/ICCA62789.2024.10591881.

Kang, J., 2025. Software practice and experience on smart mobility digital twin in transportation and automotive industry: toward SDV-empowered digital twin through EV edge-cloud and AutoML. J. Web Eng. 1544-5976. 2188, 1155–1180. doi:10.13052/jwe1540-9589.2385.

Koumou, K.O., Isafiade, O.E., 2024. Asset management trends in diverse settings involving immersive technology: a systematic literature review. IEEE Access. 2169-3536. 12, 141785–141813. Available from: http://ieeexplore.ieee.org/xpl/RecentIssue.jsp?punumber=6287639. doi:10.1109/ACCESS.2024.3461548.

Maksimovic, M., Jokic, S., Boskovic, M.C. 2024 Digital twins and 5G: unlocking the potential in the energy sector. In: 23rd International Symposium INFOTEH-JAHORINA, INFOTEH 2024—Proceedings. Institute of Electrical and Electronics Engineers Inc., Bosnia and Herzegovina. 9798350329940. Available from: http://ieeexplore.ieee.org/xpl/mostRecentIssue.jsp?punumber=10495918. doi:10.1109/INFOTEH60418.2024.10495937.

Patra, A., Pandey, A., Hassija, V., Chamola, V., Mishra, R.P., 2024. A survey on edge enabled metaverse: applications, technological innovations, and prospective trajectories within the industry. IEEE Access. 2169-3536. 12, 125125–125144. Available from: http://ieeexplore.ieee.org/xpl/RecentIssue.jsp?punumber=6287639. doi:10.1109/ACCESS.2024.3452184.

Rattan, A., Rudra Pal, A., Gurusamy, M., 2025. Quantum computing for advanced driver assistance systems and autonomous vehicles: a review. IEEE Access. 2169-3536. 13, 17554–17582. doi:10.1109/access.2025.3532958.

Ren, C., Dong, Z.Y., Yu, H., Xu, M., Xiong, Z., Niyato, D., 2024. ESQFL: digital twin-driven explainable and secured quantum federated learning for voltage stability assessment in smart grids. IEEE J. Sel. Top.

Signal Process. 1941-0484. 18 (5), 964–978. Available from: http://www.ieee.org/products/onlinepubs/news/0806_01.html. doi:10.1109/JSTSP.2024.3485878.
Singh, T., Solanki, A., Sharma, S.K., Nayyar, A., Paul, A., 2022. A decade review on smart cities: paradigms, challenges and opportunities. IEEE Access 2169-3536. 10, 68319–68364. Available from: http://ieeexplore.ieee.org/xpl/RecentIssue.jsp?punumber=6287639. doi:10.1109/ACCESS.2022.3184710
Tuli, E.A., Lee, J.M., Kim, D.S., 2024. Integration of quantum technologies into metaverse: applications, potentials, and challenges. IEEE Access. 2169-3536. 12, 29995–30019. Available from: http://ieeexplore.ieee.org/xpl/RecentIssue.jsp?punumber=6287639. doi:10.1109/ACCESS.2024.3366527.
Verma, K., Srivastava, S., Mishra, R.K. 2024. Revolutionizing medical image processing through immersive metaverse: a paradigm shift. In: 15th International Conference on Computing Communication and Networking Technologies, ICCCNT 2024. Institute of Electrical and Electronics Engineers Inc., India. 9798350370249. Available from: http://ieeexplore.ieee.org/xpl/mostRecentIssue.jsp?punumber=10723818. doi:10.1109/ICCCNT61001.2024.10723867.
Wang, Y., He, Y., Yu, F.R., Song, B., Leung, V.C.M., 2023. Efficient resource allocation for building the metaverse with UAVs: a quantum collective reinforcement learning approach. IEEE Wirel. Commun. 1558-0687. 30 (5), 152–159. Available from: https://ieeexplore.ieee.org/servlet/opac?punumber=7742. doi:10.1109/MWC.009.2300029.

CHAPTER 19

Ethical consideration and regulatory challenges

Neha Sharad Bhagwat, Vaishali Nitin Dhawas, and Renuka Rajendra Kajale
Department of Computer Engineering, Nutan Maharashtra Institute of Engineering & Technology, Pune, India

19.1 Introduction to ethical considerations and regulatory challenges

19.1.1 What are ethics and regulations?

19.1.1.1 Definitions of ethics and regulation

Ethics is the branch of philosophy that deals with questions of morality, values, and principles governing human behavior. It involves determining what is "right" or "wrong" in various situations and how individuals and organizations should act in accordance with moral guidelines. Ethics can be applied in both personal conduct and professional domains like healthcare, business, and technology.

Regulation, on the other hand, refers to the rules, laws, and standards created and enforced by governments or regulatory bodies to manage the activities of individuals, companies, or organizations. Regulations are intended to ensure compliance with legal and safety standards, protect public welfare, and maintain order. Regulations can range from environmental laws to financial regulations to privacy rules, depending on the industry.

For example, in healthcare, ethics might involve decisions around patient autonomy, informed consent, and the principles of beneficence (acting in the best interest of patients) and non-maleficence (avoiding harm).

In business, ethical considerations can involve transparency, fair treatment of employees, honesty in advertising, and sustainability in operations.

For instance, in finance, regulations like the **Sarbanes-Oxley Act** impose requirements on financial reporting to prevent fraud.

Artificial Intelligence, Machine Learning and Blockchain in Digital Twin Computing.
https://doi.org/10.1016/B978-0-443-43914-8.00003-0

In healthcare, regulations like **Health Insurance Portability and Accountability Act (HIPAA)** ensure the protection of patient data.

While **ethics** provides a moral framework for behavior, **regulation** provides the legal basis for enforcing specific actions. **Ethics** addresses the "should" of human behavior, while **regulation** addresses the "must."

19.1.1.2 Distinctions between ethical norms, legal norms, and regulations

Ethical norms: These are the unwritten—often informal guidelines—that govern behavior based on societal norms and personal morals. Ethical norms are more flexible and subjective, often varying based on culture, religion, and individual beliefs. For instance, honesty in business may be considered an ethical norm, but the way it is practiced can vary across cultures or situations.

Legal norms: These are rules enforced by the government. Legal norms are often codified into laws that have specific penalties or consequences for non-compliance. For example, it is illegal to commit fraud, and violating this law can result in legal action.

Regulations: While legal norms set out broader frameworks (such as laws), **regulations** are more specific rules or standards created within the scope of those laws. They are created by regulatory bodies or agencies to provide detailed guidance on how laws should be followed. For example, while there is a law that protects privacy, regulations within that law [such as the General Data Protection Regulation (GDPR)] outline detailed rules about data storage, access, and consent.

Understanding the distinction between ethics, legal norms, and regulations helps clarify the boundaries and intersections between personal moral judgment and the structure of the law. A legal or regulatory breach does not necessarily mean an ethical breach, though, in many cases, they overlap.

19.1.1.3 The importance of ethics in modern society

Role of ethics in technology, business, and healthcare

Technology: In the digital age, ethical questions around artificial intelligence (AI), data privacy, and cybersecurity are increasingly pressing. Considerations like algorithmic fairness, the transparency of AI models, and the responsible use of data require ethical guidance. The fast pace of technological advancements calls for an ethical framework that ensures innovation does not come at the cost of human rights or fairness.

Business: Corporate ethics are critical for businesses that wish to build and maintain trust with consumers, investors, and the public. Issues such as corruption, labor practices, environmental sustainability, and consumer rights require businesses to adopt ethical standards. Ethical business practices often go beyond mere legal compliance and are integral to long-term corporate success and reputation.

Healthcare: Medical ethics is at the core of patient care, with healthcare professionals required to navigate complex decisions that involve patient autonomy, confidentiality, and informed consent. Ethics in healthcare extends to practices like end-of-life care, genetic testing, and organ donation, where the outcomes can have life-altering consequences.

Example: **AI ethics** involves ensuring algorithms are not biased and do not perpetuate discrimination against certain groups of people. Regulatory oversight, such as the **GDPR**, sets limits on data collection, but ethical concerns around privacy and data usage often go beyond the scope of regulations.

Example: Companies like **Patagonia** prioritize sustainability, which goes beyond regulatory requirements to meet consumer expectations for ethical and eco-friendly business practices.

In the case of **genetic testing**, ethical questions arise about the privacy of an individual's genetic information, who has access to it, and how it should be used. While regulations such as **HIPAA** address patient data privacy, ethical issues may also arise that aren't fully addressed by existing laws.

Ethics as a foundation for public trust: Ethics establishes the moral baseline for behavior in society. **Trust** is fundamental to the functioning of institutions, governments, businesses, and healthcare systems. When ethical standards are upheld, they foster **confidence** and **accountability**.

Trust in government and public institutions is bolstered by ethical leadership and transparency in decision-making.

In business, ethical marketing practices and responsible corporate behavior build consumer trust and loyalty.

In healthcare, patient trust is critical for cooperation with medical professionals and adherence to treatment plans.

Without a strong ethical foundation, public trust deteriorates, leading to a loss of confidence in institutions, whether in the context of corporate governance, medical practices, or technology.

Evolution of ethical standards

Historical development of ethical principles: Ethical principles have evolved over time, shaped by philosophical, cultural, and societal developments.

- **Ancient ethical thought**: Early ethical thought can be traced back to philosophers like **Socrates**, **Plato**, and **Aristotle**, who focused on virtues, character, and the pursuit of the good.

- **Religious ethics**: Many ethical systems also evolved from religious teachings, such as the **Ten Commandments** in Judaism, the **Sermon on the Mount** in Christianity, and the concepts of **dharma** in Hinduism.
- **Modern ethics**: In the Enlightenment period, philosophers like **Immanuel Kant** and **John Stuart Mill** developed ethical theories that influenced modern views on autonomy, justice, and individual rights. These principles now form the backbone of many contemporary regulatory and ethical frameworks.

As society grew more complex, ethical standards became more nuanced, adapting to the specific needs of different industries (such as business ethics, medical ethics, and tech ethics).

The role of regulations in shaping these standards: Regulations have played a key role in formalizing and enforcing ethical principles in society. While ethics often guide behavior on a personal or societal level, regulations provide a structured legal framework to ensure that these ethical principles are followed, particularly in industries that have direct impacts on public welfare.

- **Corporate regulations**: The **Sarbanes-Oxley Act** (2002) was created in response to corporate scandals (such as Enron and WorldCom) to enforce higher ethical standards in financial reporting.
- **Medical regulations**: The **Nuremberg Code** (1947) was established after the horrors of unethical medical experiments during World War II, shaping modern research ethics in medicine.
- **Privacy regulations**: Laws like the **GDPR** set legal boundaries for data collection and privacy, reflecting growing concerns about data ethics in the digital age.

As industries evolve and new challenges arise, regulations are designed and adapted to reflect ethical concerns. As a result, regulations are sometimes shaped by the **ethical standards** established by society at large, with feedback loops between societal ethical shifts and regulatory changes.

19.2 Ethical theories and frameworks

Ethical theories provide systematic frameworks for understanding and resolving moral dilemmas. These frameworks guide individuals, organizations, and societies in determining the most morally sound actions based on differing principles of what are considered "right" or "good."

19.2.1 Utilitarianism

Utilitarianism is a **consequence-based** ethical theory that focuses on the outcomes or results of actions. The core idea is that the **morally right action** is the one that **produces the greatest good for the greatest number** of people. This is known as the **Greatest Happiness Principle**, which was famously championed by philosophers **Jeremy Bentham** and **John Stuart Mill**.

- **The greatest good for the greatest number**: The principle asserts that an action is morally right if it maximizes overall happiness or well-being, even if it leads to some harm to individuals. Utilitarianism encourages decisions that benefit the majority, even at the cost of the minority's interests.
- **Cost-benefit analysis and decision-making**: Utilitarianism often employs **cost-benefit analysis** as a tool for decision-making. This approach involves comparing the benefits of a potential action against its costs to determine which action produces the greatest net benefit.
- For example, a government might choose to implement a policy that benefits the majority of citizens (such as a public health campaign), even if it inconveniences a small group of people.
- In healthcare, utilitarian reasoning may guide decisions on resource allocation (e.g., which treatments should be funded based on the number of people they help). This is often seen in decisions about emergency responses, where life-saving interventions might prioritize those with the highest chances of survival.

While utilitarianism promotes the well-being of the majority, critics argue that it can justify morally questionable actions if the majority benefits, such as sacrificing individual rights or marginalizing vulnerable groups.

- For example, a deontologist might argue that it is unethical to break a promise or commit a crime, even if doing so would benefit more people. For deontologists, the morality of an action is intrinsic and does not depend on the results.

While deontological ethics is praised for providing clear and consistent moral rules, critics argue that it can be too rigid and does not account for the complexities or consequences of real-world situations.

19.2.2 Virtue ethics

Virtue ethics, associated with **Aristotle**, shifts the focus from actions to the **moral character** of the individual. It argues that the right course of action is not determined by following strict rules or maximizing good consequences, but rather by developing virtuous characteristics (e.g., courage, honesty, wisdom, compassion) that guide ethical decision-making.

- **Focus on moral character and virtues**: Virtue ethics emphasizes becoming a good person, developing a virtuous character, and striving for **eudaimonia**, which can be understood as flourishing or living a fulfilled life. It focuses on cultivating traits such as honesty, fairness, and generosity, which lead to virtuous behavior.
- **Decision-making based on personal integrity and character**: Virtue ethics suggests that one should ask, "What would a virtuous person do in this situation?" Instead of applying a rigid set of rules, virtue ethics encourages individuals to make decisions that reflect their moral character and their commitment to living a good life

- For example, an individual may choose to act courageously or compassionately in a difficult situation, not because the action adheres to a rule or will produce the best outcome, but because these are characteristics of a virtuous person.
- A person practicing virtue ethics might prioritize honesty in a business context, even if telling the truth results in personal loss because it aligns with their virtue of integrity.

Critics of virtue ethics argue that it can be difficult to determine what counts as a "virtue" or how virtues should be applied in complex situations. In addition, this approach can be seen as subjective, depending on cultural and personal definitions of virtue.

19.2.3 Care ethics

Care ethics emphasizes the importance of **empathy**, **relationships**, and **context** in moral decision-making. It was developed by feminist philosophers such as **Carol Gilligan** and focuses on the moral significance of caring for others, especially in personal relationships.

- **Emphasis on empathy, relationships, and context**: Care ethics places importance on the dynamics of **human relationships** and the context in which moral decisions occur. It suggests that ethical actions should be based on understanding and empathy for others' feelings and needs, especially in caregiving situations.
- **Decision-making based on context**: Unlike other ethical frameworks that may focus on abstract principles, care ethics argues that moral decisions should be made with attention to **contextual factors**. For instance, a decision about how to treat someone might differ based on their unique circumstances, relationships, and needs.
- For example, in healthcare, a nurse might make a decision based not just on clinical data but also on the emotional and relational needs of the patient, recognizing the importance of providing comfort and emotional support alongside medical care.
- In family dynamics, care ethics might prioritize caregiving duties or responsibilities toward elderly family members, recognizing that these relationships come with inherent emotional obligations.

Critics argue that care ethics can be criticized for potentially leading to biases in decision-making, as it might prioritize those with whom one has close relationships over strangers or the broader community. In addition, critics suggest that care ethics may overlook the need for clear rules or principles in certain ethical dilemmas.

19.2.4 Deontological ethics

Deontological ethics, rooted in the philosophy of **Immanuel Kant**, emphasizes **duty**, **rules**, and **obligations**. This ethical framework argues that actions are morally right or wrong based on their adherence to rules or principles, regardless of the consequences.

- **Duty-based ethical framework**: According to deontology, individuals have moral duties or obligations that must be followed, and these duties are grounded in reason and rationality. For instance, one has a duty to tell the truth, regardless of the consequences, because lying violates a moral principle.
- **Rights, rules, and justice-based decisions**: Deontologists believe that ethical actions must respect **individual rights** and adhere to **moral rules**, regardless of the outcomes The focus is on justice and fairness, which means treating individuals with respect, dignity, and equality.
- Kant's **Categorical Imperative** is central to deontological thought, which states that one should act according to principles that can be consistently applied universally. In other words, individuals should act in a way that they would want others to act as well.

19.3 Key ethical issues across industries

19.3.1 Technology and artificial intelligence

19.3.1.1 AI ethics: Autonomy, transparency, and accountability

- The **autonomy** of AI systems is a growing concern, especially with autonomous machines like self-driving cars or decision-making algorithms used in finance, healthcare, and law enforcement. The key ethical issue lies in how much autonomy should be given to machines and the consequences of their decisions. For example, who is responsible if an autonomous vehicle causes an accident: the manufacturer, the operator, or the AI system itself?
- **Transparency** is crucial in AI systems, as many AI algorithms (especially deep learning models) function as "black boxes," meaning their decision-making processes are not easily understood by humans. The lack of transparency makes it difficult to trust AI, as users cannot fully understand or question why certain decisions are made. Ethical AI requires that these systems be explainable and understandable to ensure accountability and build trust.
- **Accountability** is a core issue. If an AI system causes harm, who is liable? The developers? The organization deploying it? Or the AI itself? With AI being integrated into critical fields, such as healthcare and military operations, ethical frameworks are required to ensure that responsibility for AI-driven actions remains clearly defined.

19.3.1.2 Algorithmic bias and fairness

- Algorithms are only as fair as the data they are trained on, and **algorithmic bias** occurs when these systems perpetuate or amplify biases found in historical data. For example, AI systems used in hiring or lending have been shown to discriminate against minority groups because they often rely on biased data from past decisions.

- Ensuring **fairness** in AI systems involves identifying and mitigating these biases to ensure that algorithms do not unfairly disadvantage any particular group, especially vulnerable or historically marginalized groups. Ethical concerns in algorithmic fairness are particularly urgent in domains like criminal justice, hiring practices, and loan approvals, where biased algorithms can lead to significant social harm.

19.3.1.3 Data privacy and security in AI development

- As AI systems gather vast amounts of data, ensuring **data privacy** is a primary ethical concern. Developers must ensure that the data collected is protected from breaches, is used only for the intended purpose, and is anonymized when appropriate to safeguard personal information.
- **Security** concerns also extend beyond data privacy, especially in AI systems controlling critical infrastructure (e.g., healthcare, energy, transportation). An ethical AI system must be designed with robust security measures to prevent hacking or misuse, which could lead to significant harm.

19.3.1.4 Healthcare and medical ethics

Patient autonomy, informed consent, and medical paternalism

- **Patient autonomy** refers to a patient's right to make decisions about their own healthcare based on an understanding of their treatment options. Informed consent is a key principle in respecting autonomy, ensuring that patients are fully aware of the risks, benefits, and alternatives to a given medical procedure.
- **Medical paternalism** occurs when healthcare professionals override a patient's decision in what they believe is the patient's best interest, often for the sake of the patient's health or safety. The ethical dilemma arises when the patient's autonomy is seen as being in conflict with the medical professional's duty to act in the patient's best interests. For instance, should doctors respect a terminally ill patient's decision to refuse life-saving treatment, or should they intervene because the doctor believes the patient's decision is not in their best interest?

Ethical concerns around euthanasia, genetic testing, and organ donation

- **Euthanasia** presents a significant ethical dilemma regarding the right to die with dignity versus the sanctity of life. Active euthanasia (intentionally ending a life to relieve suffering) and passive euthanasia (withholding life-sustaining treatment) require balancing respect for patient autonomy with moral considerations about the value of life.
- **Genetic testing** raises ethical questions about privacy, consent, and potential discrimination. For example, if a person is found to have a genetic predisposition to a serious disease, should this information be shared with family members or insurance

companies? There is also the concern about how genetic information could be used or misused by employers or others, potentially leading to discrimination.

- **Organ donation** ethics involve issues of consent, fairness, and the allocation of scarce resources. Should individuals be allowed to sell their organs? How do we prioritize which patients should receive transplants, especially when organs are in limited supply? These decisions must be handled with careful consideration of both moral and practical implications.

The ethical implications of AI and automation in healthcare

- The rise of AI and automation in healthcare presents both opportunities and ethical challenges. On the one hand, AI can improve diagnostic accuracy and efficiency. However, it also raises concerns about **job displacement** for healthcare workers, **reliability** (such as AI misdiagnosing a patient), and **bias** (AI systems may perpetuate biases from historical data).
- In addition, the implementation of AI systems in healthcare could affect the **doctor-patient relationship**, as patients may feel disconnected from their healthcare providers if they perceive AI as taking over decision-making roles traditionally handled by human doctors.

19.3.1.5 Business and corporate ethics

Corporate social responsibility and sustainable practices

- **Corporate social responsibility** (**CSR**) refers to businesses taking responsibility for the environmental and social impacts of their operations. Ethical issues arise when companies prioritize profit over social good, for example, by exploiting workers in developing countries or polluting the environment without regard for long-term sustainability.
- **Sustainable practices** are an essential aspect of CSR, addressing issues like reducing carbon footprints, the ethical sourcing of materials, and fair labor practices. Ethical businesses are expected to adopt practices that contribute to environmental sustainability, minimize waste, and ensure that their operations do not harm future generations.

Conflicts of interest, fraud, and bribery

- **Conflicts of interest** occur when an individual's or organization's personal interests are at odds with their professional duties or responsibilities. For example, a corporate executive may face a conflict of interest if they stand to personally benefit from a decision that harms the company or its shareholders.
- **Fraud** and **bribery** are significant ethical concerns in business. Fraud involves intentionally deceiving others for financial gain, while bribery involves offering money or gifts to influence decisions. Both practices are illegal in many jurisdictions, but they also raise deep ethical questions about integrity, fairness, and justice in business practices.

Ethical marketing and consumer protection

- **Ethical marketing** involves promoting products in a way that is honest, transparent, and respectful of consumers' rights. Deceptive advertising, false claims, and manipulative practices like targeting vulnerable populations (e.g., children or elderly consumers) are serious ethical issues in marketing.
- **Consumer protection** focuses on safeguarding the interests of consumers, ensuring they are not exploited or misled. Issues like product safety, clear labeling, and the right to return goods are essential components of ethical marketing practices.

19.3.1.6 Environmental ethics

Ethics of sustainability and conservation

- **Sustainability** in environmental ethics is about meeting current needs without compromising the ability of future generations to meet their own needs. Ethical issues in sustainability often involve balancing economic growth with environmental protection. Businesses and governments must grapple with decisions that impact the environment, such as resource depletion, pollution, and climate change.
- **Conservation** ethics focus on the moral imperative to preserve natural habitats, endangered species, and ecosystems. There are ethical debates about land use, biodiversity, and the rights of indigenous people versus environmental protection goals. Ethical decisions in conservation often involve weighing the rights of local communities against the broader environmental good.
- In addition, **climate change** is an urgent environmental ethical issue. Ethical questions arise around how much responsibility developed nations have in addressing climate change compared to developing nations, and how to ensure fair and equitable solutions to environmental challenges on a global scale.

19.4 Regulatory frameworks and compliance

19.4.1 Overview of regulatory bodies

Governmental and international organizations [Food and Drug Administration (FDA), Securities and Exchange Commission (SEC), GDPR, World Health Organization (WHO), etc.]: Regulatory bodies are crucial institutions that establish rules and standards to ensure that organizations and individuals act ethically and within legal frameworks. These bodies are typically governmental or international organizations that have the authority to monitor, enforce, and regulate industries to protect public health, safety, and well-being.

1. **FDA**:

- The FDA is a United States government agency responsible for regulating food, drugs, medical devices, and cosmetics. It ensures that products are safe, effective, and labeled correctly. The FDA sets rigorous standards for clinical trials, drug approval processes, and postmarket surveillance to protect public health.
- **Role in upholding ethical standards**: The FDA plays a crucial role in safeguarding ethical standards in the medical and pharmaceutical industries by ensuring transparency in clinical research and enforcing ethical guidelines for medical practices and drug manufacturing.

SEC:

- The SEC is an independent United States government agency that regulates the securities industry, including stock exchanges, brokers, and investment firms. It aims to ensure that financial markets are fair, transparent, and efficient by enforcing laws that prevent fraudulent activities such as insider trading, market manipulation, and financial misstatements.
- **Role in upholding ethical standards**: The SEC's role in enforcing financial regulations helps maintain investor trust by ensuring that companies disclose accurate financial information, adhere to ethical trading practices, and protect investors from unethical practices.

GDPR:

- The GDPR is an important regulation enacted by the European Union (EU) to protect personal data and privacy. It applies to all organizations that process the personal data of EU residents, ensuring that individuals' privacy rights are respected across industries such as tech, healthcare, and finance.
- **Role in upholding ethical standards**: GDPR sets stringent guidelines for organizations to ensure that personal data is collected, processed, and stored ethically, empowering individuals with control over their data. It mandates that companies be transparent about data collection practices and diligent in protecting personal information.

2. **WHO**:

- WHO is a specialized agency of the United Nations that sets global health standards and guidelines, including ethical guidelines for healthcare providers and organizations around the world. WHO helps shape policies on public health issues, disease prevention, and healthcare delivery.
- **Role in upholding ethical standards**: WHO plays a critical role in advocating for ethical healthcare practices, such as providing access to essential medications, preventing exploitation in clinical trials, and promoting health equity globally. Its standards influence the practices of healthcare organizations worldwide.

These regulatory bodies and organizations help shape and enforce the ethical standards that govern various sectors, ensuring public protection, safety, and fairness.

19.4.2 Creating regulations and ethical standards

Process of developing ethical regulations in different industries: The creation of ethical regulations is a multistep process that involves careful consideration of societal values, industry practices, and the need for accountability. The process varies by industry but typically includes the following stages:

1. **Identifying issues and risks**:
   - Regulatory bodies often begin by identifying ethical issues or risks within an industry. For example, the FDA may identify concerns regarding the safety and efficacy of a new drug, or the SEC may examine potential conflicts of interest within financial markets.
   - Stakeholders, including industry experts, academics, and the public, can contribute to identifying ethical concerns that need to be addressed by new regulations.
2. **Research and consultation**:
   - After identifying issues, regulators conduct research and consult with relevant stakeholders. This may include holding public hearings, gathering feedback from industry players, or reviewing existing standards and regulations in other countries or regions.
   - For example, before the enactment of the GDPR, the European Commission conducted extensive research on data protection laws and consulted with privacy experts, citizens, and business owners to understand the impact of regulations on various stakeholders.
3. **Drafting the regulation**:
   - Regulatory bodies then draft regulations that reflect ethical considerations, legal requirements, and industry needs. These regulations should balance the public good with the interests of organizations and individuals.
   - For example, ethical guidelines in healthcare may focus on patient autonomy, informed consent, and the protection of vulnerable populations in clinical research.
4. **Public review and feedback:**
   - Many regulatory bodies open up the proposed regulations for public review, allowing stakeholders to comment on the draft. This public consultation helps ensure that the regulations are fair, transparent, and address real-world concerns.
   - For instance, the GDPR draft was subjected to review and feedback from privacy advocates, technology companies, and governments to refine it and address issues related to data security and privacy.

5. **Implementation and enforcement**:
   - Once finalized, the regulation is implemented and enforced through legal mechanisms, including penalties for non-compliance. Regulatory bodies like the FDA or SEC are tasked with monitoring compliance and taking corrective actions when necessary.

Stakeholders involved in the creation of regulations: Several stakeholders play a key role in the creation of ethical regulations. These include:

1. **Government agencies**: These bodies are responsible for drafting, enforcing, and overseeing the regulatory process. They ensure that the regulations align with national or international laws and ethical principles.
2. **Industry representatives**: Companies, trade associations, and other industry players often participate in the creation of regulations to ensure that new rules are practical and feasible within the context of their sector.
3. **Public and consumer groups**: Advocacy groups, nongovernmental organizations, and the public play an important role in advocating for ethical standards that prioritize consumer rights, environmental sustainability, or social justice.
4. **Academics and experts**: Scholars and subject-matter experts contribute research, data, and insights that inform the development of regulations, particularly in complex areas such as healthcare, AI, or environmental protection.
5. **Legal professionals**: Lawyers and legal experts help ensure that regulations comply with constitutional principles, human rights laws, and international agreements.

19.4.3 Compliance and enforcement

Mechanisms for ensuring compliance with ethical regulations: To ensure that organizations and individuals follow ethical regulations, regulatory bodies establish compliance mechanisms. These mechanisms may include:

1. **Auditing and monitoring**
2. **Reporting and whistleblower protections**
3. **Certification and licensing**
4. **Public disclosure and transparency**

- Regulatory bodies may conduct regular audits and inspections to ensure that organizations comply with regulations. For example, the FDA regularly inspects pharmaceutical companies and clinical trials to ensure that ethical standards are upheld in drug development.
- Whistleblower mechanisms encourage individuals to report unethical practices without fear of retaliation. Many regulatory bodies, such as the SEC, protect whistleblowers who report fraud, corruption, or other unethical activities within organizations.

- In some industries, organizations or professionals must be certified or licensed to operate. For instance, medical professionals are licensed by regulatory bodies to ensure they adhere to ethical and professional standards.
- Regulatory bodies may require companies to publicly disclose information related to their practices. The SEC, for example, mandates that publicly traded companies disclose their financial statements, which helps ensure transparency and ethical financial practices.

Challenges in the enforcement of ethical guidelines and laws: Despite the establishment of regulations and compliance mechanisms, enforcing ethical guidelines presents several challenges:

1. **Globalization and cross-border compliance**
2. **Resource limitations**
3. **Technological advancements**
4. **Industry resistance**
5. **Cultural and ethical differences**

- In a globalized world, regulatory bodies face challenges in enforcing regulations across borders. For example, multinational corporations may operate in jurisdictions with differing ethical standards, making enforcement more complex.
- Regulatory agencies often face limited resources to enforce ethical regulations; they may lack the personnel, funding, or technology to monitor every industry or organization comprehensively.
- As new technologies emerge, such as AI or blockchain, regulatory bodies may struggle to keep pace with rapid advancements. Existing regulations may become outdated, leading to gaps in enforcement.
- Some industries or organizations may resist compliance due to the perceived cost or complexity of adhering to ethical guidelines. This resistance can lead to difficulties in enforcement, particularly in sectors like finance, healthcare, or energy, where regulations can be costly or complex.

Ethical standards may vary between countries or regions, leading to challenges in applying consistent regulations globally. For instance, privacy laws like the GDPR are specific to the EU and may not be enforceable in other regions with different standards.

19.5 Ethical decision-making models

19.5.1 Decision-making frameworks

Ethical decision-making is essential for organizations, professionals, and individuals who face situations where the right course of action is not always clear. Several frameworks can guide individuals in making ethically sound decisions. These frameworks can be categorized into three main approaches: **principles-based**, **care-based**, and **consequence-based**.

1. **Principles-based approach (deontological ethics)**:
   - The principles-based approach to decision-making is rooted in **deontological ethics**, which emphasizes the importance of following established rules, duties, and moral obligations. The focus here is on doing what is right, regardless of the outcomes.
   - **Key characteristics**:
   - **Example**: A company follows strict labor laws, even if it means higher operational costs, as it believes that respecting the rights of workers is non-negotiable.
   - **How it helps in decision-making**: This model is useful when the decision involves adhering to legal or moral duties. For example, a doctor deciding to respect a patient's right to refuse treatment, even if it may result in harm.
2. **Care-based approach (ethics of care)**:
   - The care-based approach focuses on relationships, empathy, and the context in which decisions are made. It suggests that ethical decisions should be guided by a concern for the well-being of others, with particular attention to the needs and vulnerabilities of those affected.
   - **Key characteristics**:
   - **Example**: A nurse providing emotional support and individualized care to a patient during treatment, focusing not only on the medical needs but also on the patient's emotional comfort.
   - **How it helps in decision-making**: This model is especially valuable in healthcare, education, and other fields where personal relationships are central. It encourages decision-makers to prioritize compassion and human connection.
3. **Consequence-based approach (utilitarianism)**:
   - The consequence-based approach, or **utilitarianism**, focuses on the outcomes or consequences of decisions. According to this approach, an action is considered ethically right if it results in the greatest good for the greatest number of people.
   - **Key characteristics**:
   - **Example**: A government decides to implement a public health policy that benefits the majority of the population, even if a minority is negatively affected.
   - **How it helps in decision-making**: This model helps evaluate decisions when the outcomes affect a large group of people. For example, a company may decide to implement an environmentally friendly initiative that has higher initial costs but leads to long-term benefits for society.
   - **Duty**: Acting according to duties and responsibilities regardless of the consequences
   - **Rights and justice**: Emphasize respecting individual rights and ensuring justice and fairness

- **Empathy and compassion**: Focusing on the relational aspects of ethics, where decisions consider the emotional and social context
- **Contextual decision-making**: Making decisions that reflect an understanding of the personal, social, and emotional dynamics at play
- **Maximizing well-being**: Aims to maximize positive outcomes or benefits while minimizing harm
- **Cost-benefit analysis**: Weighing the positive and negative consequences of an action to determine the best course of action

19.5.2 How to handle ethical dilemmas using structured models

Ethical dilemmas arise when individuals or organizations face situations where the right decision is unclear and the various options have conflicting values. A structured approach to decision-making can provide clarity and ensure consistency. Here's how to apply ethical decision-making models to dilemmas:

1. **Step** 1: **Identify the ethical issue**
2. **Step** 2: **Gather relevant information**
3. **Step** 3: **Evaluate the options using ethical frameworks**
4. **Step** 4: **Make the decision**
5. **Step 5: Review the decision**

- The first step is recognizing that an ethical dilemma exists. This involves understanding the core ethical principles at stake, such as autonomy, justice, and beneficence.
- Before making a decision, it is crucial to gather all relevant information. This includes understanding the context, the potential consequences, and the stakeholders involved.
- Using one or more of the ethical decision-making models (principle-based, care-based, or consequence-based), evaluate the potential courses of action. Consider the duties, rights, and relationships involved, as well as the outcomes of each option.
- After evaluating the options, make a decision that best aligns with the ethical values and principles you've considered. Choose the option that respects moral duties, relationships, or yields the greatest benefit with the least harm.
- After the decision is made and implemented, it is important to reflect on the outcomes and review whether the decision was ethically sound. This reflection helps refine future decision-making processes and ensures continuous ethical improvement.

19.5.3 Institutional review boards

Role of IRBs in ethical decision-making, particularly in research: Institutional Review Boards (IRBs) are committees that review and oversee research studies, particularly in the fields of healthcare, psychology, and the social sciences, to ensure that research is conducted ethically. IRBs are designed to protect the rights and welfare of human participants in research.

- **Key functions of IRBs**:

- **Reviewing research proposals**: IRBs ensure that research proposals meet ethical standards, particularly in terms of informed consent, privacy, and the risks involved.
- **Ensuring participant safety**: The board evaluates whether the research procedures pose undue risks to participants and whether these risks are outweighed by the potential benefits of the research.
- **Monitoring ongoing studies**: IRBs also have a role in monitoring ongoing research to ensure that ethical standards are maintained throughout the study.

Ethical considerations in human and animal research: Research involving humans and animals must adhere to strict ethical standards to avoid exploitation and harm. Ethical considerations include:

1. **Informed consent**
2. **Minimizing harm**
3. **Animal research**

- Participants must be fully informed about the research and voluntarily agree to participate. This means researchers must disclose the nature of the study, any potential risks, and the participants' right to withdraw at any time.
- Ethical research involves minimizing the risks of harm to participants, both physical and psychological. Researchers must ensure that any discomfort or harm is justified by the potential benefits of the research.
- Research involving animals must adhere to ethical guidelines that minimize suffering and ensure humane treatment. The principle of "3Rs" (replacement, reduction, and refinement) guides ethical animal research, advocating for alternatives to animal testing, reducing the number of animals used, and refining methods to reduce suffering.

19.5.4 Risk assessment and mitigation

Managing ethical risks in decision-making: Ethical decision-making often involves navigating risks—both ethical and practical. Risk assessment is the process of identifying potential ethical risks and weighing the likelihood and severity of these risks.

- **Risk identification**: Identifying ethical risks may include considering potential harm to stakeholders, conflicts of interest, the exploitation of vulnerable groups, or breaches of privacy.
- **Risk evaluation**: Evaluate the severity of each risk in terms of its potential impact on individuals, organizations, and society. For example, in healthcare, failing to obtain informed consent can lead to legal and reputational damage.

- **Risk mitigation**: Develop strategies to minimize ethical risks, such as implementing policies to ensure transparency, providing training on ethical behavior, and seeking stakeholder input in decision-making processes.

Balancing short-term gain versus long-term ethical integrity: Ethical decision-making often involves weighing the potential for short-term gains against the long-term impact on ethical integrity. For example:

- **Short-term gain**: A company may consider cutting corners to increase profits, such as reducing product quality or exploiting workers in developing countries.
- **Long-term ethical integrity**: While short-term profits may seem attractive, prioritizing ethical integrity leads to long-term benefits, such as building trust, reducing legal risks, and contributing to social good.

A balanced approach requires decision-makers to consider both immediate outcomes and long-term consequences, ensuring that ethical integrity is not sacrificed for temporary benefits. For example, a healthcare provider may choose not to overcharge a patient, even if it results in a temporary financial setback, because the trust and reputation built over time are more valuable.

19.6 Regulatory challenges

19.6.1 Global regulatory landscape

The global regulatory landscape is diverse and complex, influenced by different ethical and legal norms in various regions. As industries expand across borders, organizations face significant challenges in navigating these differences. Regulatory challenges include discrepancies in laws, compliance requirements, and ethical standards across countries, as well as the need to harmonize these regulations for multinational corporations.

1. **Differences in ethical and regulatory standards across countries**
2. **Cross-border regulatory challenges**
3. **Harmonizing global regulations for multinational companies**

- Different countries have different ethical values and regulatory requirements based on cultural, legal, economic, and political contexts. These differences often create challenges for multinational companies and organizations, as they must comply with varying standards across regions.
- **Example**: Environmental regulations differ significantly between countries. For instance, the EU has stricter environmental laws compared to many developing countries, where environmental concerns might not have the same regulatory prominence.
- **Impact on global business**: Companies operating in multiple regions must navigate these differences by either adhering to the highest regulatory standards globally or tailoring their operations to meet local requirements, which can be complex and costly.

- One of the most prominent regulatory challenges faced by multinational companies is navigating cross-border regulations. As the world becomes more interconnected, businesses often face conflicting regulations from different governments and regulatory bodies.
- **Example**: The **GDPR** in the EU is one of the strictest data privacy regulations globally. However, companies in the United States or Asia may face challenges complying with these stringent rules while also adhering to local privacy laws, which may not be as comprehensive.
- **Impact of cross-border challenges**: Companies often have to develop complex compliance strategies that can handle regulatory requirements in different jurisdictions. This includes managing data storage, processing, and sharing to comply with various data protection laws.
- One of the ongoing challenges is harmonizing global regulations to provide a consistent and coherent framework for multinational corporations. Although organizations like the **World Trade Organization (WTO)** and the **International Organization for Standardization** work toward creating international standards, achieving true regulatory harmonization remains elusive.
- **Approaches to harmonization**:
- **International collaboration**: Regulatory bodies across regions must work together to establish common principles or minimum standards for industries such as finance, healthcare, and technology.
- **Standardized guidelines**: Organizations like the **Financial Action Task Force** have made progress by developing global guidelines for antimoney laundering (AML) and combating the financing of terrorism, which help harmonize regulatory efforts across borders.
- **Challenges**: Differences in political priorities, economic conditions, and social values make it difficult to achieve full harmonization. Countries may resist international regulations if they perceive them as limiting their autonomy or competitive advantage.

19.6.2 Regulatory capture and lobbying

Regulatory capture occurs when regulatory agencies, which are supposed to oversee and regulate industries, are influenced or "captured" by the very companies they are meant to regulate. This can lead to biased decision-making and policies that favor the interests of corporations rather than the public interest.

1. **The impact of corporate influence on regulatory agencies**
2. **Preventing corruption in regulatory bodies**

- Corporate interests often attempt to influence the decisions and policies of regulatory bodies to avoid stringent regulations, lower compliance costs, or extend favorable treatment.

- **Example**: In the **financial sector**, major banks may lobby regulatory bodies to relax rules on capital requirements or risk management. This influence can result in weakened regulations that favor industry profits over consumer protection or financial stability.
- **Consequences of regulatory capture**:
- **Ineffective regulation**: When regulatory agencies are captured by powerful corporations, they may fail to enforce existing regulations effectively, or they may delay the implementation of new laws.
- **Public trust erosion**: Regulatory capture can undermine public trust in both regulatory bodies and the industries they oversee, as people may feel that regulations are tailored to benefit big corporations rather than the public good.
- Efforts to prevent regulatory capture involve creating more transparent, accountable, and independent regulatory agencies.
- **Strategies for prevention**:
- **Strengthening oversight**: Introducing independent oversight bodies, such as ethics commissions or ombudsman offices, which can investigate potential regulatory failures or corporate influence.
- **Transparency and public participation**: Encouraging greater transparency in regulatory decision-making, including public comment periods, transparency in lobbying activities, and the publication of meeting records.
- **Conflict of interest rules**: Implementing strict conflict of interest rules to prevent regulators from moving between industry positions and regulatory bodies in ways that could lead to biased decision-making.

19.6.3 Ethics versus compliance

While **compliance** refers to adhering to established laws and regulations, **ethics** extends beyond legal requirements, focusing on moral principles that guide behavior. The relationship between ethics and compliance can sometimes be complex, as there may be instances where complying with the law does not align with ethical best practices.

1. **When regulatory compliance does not align with ethical practices**
2. **Case studies of regulatory failures or ethical breaches**
3. **Addressing the gap between ethics and compliance**

- **Example** 1: A company may comply with labor laws in a developing country but still engage in practices that could be considered exploitative, such as paying low wages or imposing unsafe working conditions. While the company is compliant with local regulations, it may fail to meet ethical standards regarding worker welfare.
- **Example** 2: In some cases, financial institutions may meet the legal requirements of financial reporting but still engage in misleading or deceptive practices that harm investors.

Compliance with regulations does not necessarily equate to ethical behavior, particularly if the intent behind compliance is to manipulate or obscure information for profit.

- **Challenges**: The tension between **ethics** and **compliance** can create dilemmas for organizations. Companies may feel pressured to comply with the letter of the law, even if it does not align with ethical principles. Regulatory bodies must, therefore, consider not only compliance but also the broader impact of business practices on society.
- **Example** 1: **Enron scandal**: Enron's collapse is a classic example of a company that complied with the regulatory frameworks in place at the time but engaged in unethical practices, such as accounting fraud and hiding financial losses. While the company technically met compliance requirements, its actions caused widespread financial harm to employees, investors, and the broader economy.
- **Example** 2: **Volkswagen emissions scandal**: Volkswagen faced a major ethical breach when it was revealed that the company had intentionally manipulated emissions tests to meet environmental regulations while continuing to produce cars that emitted harmful levels of pollution. While Volkswagen may have been in compliance with some regulations, its actions were highly unethical and led to significant reputational and financial damage.
- **Corporate ethics programs**: Many organizations have begun implementing more robust corporate ethics programs to ensure that their actions are aligned with both regulatory standards and ethical principles. These programs include training employees on ethical decision-making, creating ethical guidelines, and encouraging whistleblowing.
- **Integrating ethics into compliance**: Regulatory bodies are increasingly emphasizing the importance of ethics in compliance. This includes encouraging companies to adopt **ethics and compliance programs** that go beyond mere adherence to the law and foster a culture of integrity throughout the organization.
- **Building a culture of ethical leadership**: Organizations are focusing on leadership that models ethical behavior. Ethical leadership involves decision-making that not only complies with the law but also respects moral principles, builds trust, and fosters social responsibility.

19.7 Ethical dilemmas in emerging technologies

Emerging technologies often bring about revolutionary advancements but also raise complex ethical dilemmas. Let's break down some of the critical ethical issues within genetic engineering, blockchain and cryptocurrencies, and autonomous systems.

19.7.1 Genetic engineering and biotechnology

Genetic engineering has the potential to cure diseases, improve agricultural yields, and modify the human genome. However, it brings about various ethical concerns, particularly when it comes to technologies like **CRISPR**, **gene therapy**, and **cloning**.

Ethical issues in CRISPR, gene therapy, and cloning:

- **CRISPR-Cas9**: This technology allows scientists to precisely alter DNA, which could lead to curing genetic diseases like sickle cell anemia or cystic fibrosis. However, ethical concerns arise regarding:

- **Germline editing**: Editing genes in embryos, potentially altering the genetic makeup of future generations, which could lead to unforeseen consequences and the possibility of "designer babies."
- **Unequal access**: The technology could deepen social inequality, as those with access to genetic enhancements may enjoy better health or cognitive abilities.
- **Genetic discrimination**: There's concern that genetic modifications could lead to discrimination based on genetic traits.
- **Gene therapy**: While gene therapy promises a cure for inherited genetic disorders, ethical dilemmas include:
- **Safety**: There's still uncertainty about the long-term effects of gene therapies. Off-target mutations or unintended consequences could arise.
- **Cost and accessibility**: Expensive treatments could make gene therapy accessible only to the wealthy, exacerbating health inequalities.
- **Cloning**: Cloning, particularly human cloning, raises profound ethical questions:
- **Identity and autonomy**: Clones might face psychological or social challenges due to their origins, and questions arise about the autonomy of cloned beings.
- **Exploitation**: Cloning may be used for exploitative purposes, such as cloning organs for transplantation or replicating humans with specific traits.

Regulatory frameworks for genetic modifications:

- **Ethical oversight**: Many countries have laws prohibiting or restricting human cloning and germline editing. For example, the **WHO** and **UNESCO** call for a global ban on reproductive cloning.
- **Safety standards**: Regulatory bodies like the **FDA** in the United States oversee gene therapy trials, ensuring that they meet safety and efficacy standards.
- **International agreements**: The **Convention on Human Rights and Biomedicine** protects against the misuse of genetic modifications, ensuring human dignity and ethical scientific practices.

19.7.2 Blockchain and cryptocurrencies

Blockchain technology and cryptocurrencies like Bitcoin have disrupted industries, offering benefits such as decentralization and financial inclusion. However, they also raise ethical concerns related to transparency, security, and regulation.

Ethical concerns in blockchain: transparency, anonymity, and security:

- **Anonymity and privacy**: Cryptocurrencies like Bitcoin offer anonymity, but this can facilitate illegal activities such as money laundering, drug trafficking, and tax evasion.
- **Balancing privacy and security**: While privacy is an important human right, the anonymity of cryptocurrencies complicates law enforcement and regulatory oversight.
- **Decentralization and control**: Blockchain's decentralized nature means that no single entity controls the system. While this democratizes data control, it also raises concerns about:
- **Lack of accountability**: If something goes wrong (e.g. a breach or fraud), it may be difficult to trace responsibility, unlike in centralized systems.
- **Energy consumption**: Many cryptocurrencies, especially Bitcoin, rely on energy-intensive **proof-of-work** systems, which raise environmental concerns due to their carbon footprint.

Regulatory challenges in cryptocurrency and digital transactions:

- **Regulation and oversight**: Governments and financial regulators are still figuring out how to regulate cryptocurrencies effectively.
- **Taxation and AML**: Cryptocurrencies can complicate tax collection and AML efforts, as transactions can be anonymous and borderless.
- **Financial Stability**: The volatility of cryptocurrencies poses a challenge to the stability of traditional financial systems. Regulators worry about market manipulation and investor protection.
- **Global coordination**: Cryptocurrency's decentralized nature means that international coordination is necessary to prevent illegal activities, but creating global regulations is challenging due to the different approaches taken by countries.

19.7.3 Autonomous systems (robots, drones, self-driving cars)

Autonomous systems, such as robots, drones, and self-driving cars, are rapidly transforming industries ranging from healthcare to transportation. However, the rise of these systems brings critical ethical concerns about responsibility, accountability, and the safe deployment of these technologies.

Ethical questions of responsibility and accountability in autonomous machines:

- **Autonomous decision-making**: Robots and AI systems often make decisions without human intervention. Ethical dilemmas arise when autonomous systems make harmful or controversial decisions.
- **Responsibility in accidents**: In the case of autonomous vehicles, who is responsible when an accident occurs—the manufacturer, the programmer, or the vehicle owner? This

is known as the "trolley problem" in ethics, where machines must make life-or-death decisions.

- **Bias in AI**: AI systems can inherit biases from the data they are trained on. For example, facial recognition systems have been shown to have biases against people of color, leading to ethical concerns over fairness and justice.
- **Loss of human jobs**: Automation may displace large numbers of workers, leading to economic inequality and social unrest. While autonomous systems improve efficiency, they can lead to job losses, particularly in industries like transportation, retail, and manufacturing.

Regulations for the safe deployment of autonomous systems:

- **Safety standards**: Regulators are working to ensure that autonomous systems are safe for public use. For example, the **National Highway Traffic Safety Administration** in the United States has established guidelines for self-driving car manufacturers to ensure safety.
- **Ethical programming**: There is ongoing research to ensure that autonomous systems are programmed with ethical decision-making frameworks. For instance, self-driving cars might be programmed to prioritize the safety of human life over property.
- **Liability and insurance**: Determining liability in accidents involving autonomous machines is a complex issue. Some jurisdictions require autonomous vehicle manufacturers to carry insurance to cover accidents, but this is still an evolving area of law.
- **Regulation of AI and robotics**: Countries like the EU have initiated regulatory frameworks for AI, such as the **Artificial Intelligence Act**, which aims to ensure the safe use of AI while addressing potential risks such as discrimination and accountability.

19.8 International perspectives on ethics and regulation

The realm of ethics and regulation is influenced by a variety of factors, one of which is the diversity of cultural norms and values around the world. The differences in ethical standards and regulatory practices between countries can significantly impact global governance and business operations. This section explores how cultural differences influence ethical decision-making, the role of international organizations in setting global ethical guidelines, and examines real-world case studies of international ethical conflicts.

19.8.1 Cultural differences in ethics

Cultural norms and values play a significant role in shaping the ethical decisions made by individuals, corporations, and governments. These differences can lead to divergent ethical standards and conflicting moral perspectives when navigating international contexts.

How Cultural Norms Influence Ethical Decision-Making:

- **Collectivism versus individualism**: In cultures that prioritize **collectivism**, such as many Asian and African cultures, ethical decisions often focus on the well-being of the group or community rather than the individual. Conversely, **individualistic cultures**, such as those in North America and Western Europe, often emphasize personal autonomy and individual rights. This can lead to contrasting perspectives on issues like privacy, autonomy, and the distribution of resources.
- **Concepts of right and wrong**: What is considered morally acceptable in one culture may be seen as unethical in another. For instance, the practice of **haggling** is commonplace and ethically acceptable in some cultures but could be seen as dishonest or unfair in others.
- **The role of religion**: Many ethical guidelines are deeply intertwined with religious beliefs. For example, in cultures with a strong **Christian** or **Islamic** influence, ethical standards may revolve around concepts of divine command, justice, and respect for life, which could influence issues like end-of-life decisions or genetic engineering. In **Hindu** or **Buddhist** cultures, the ethical focus might emphasize **karma**, **nonviolence** (**ahimsa**), or **compassion** toward all living beings.

Global variations in ethical standards (Western versus Eastern perspectives):

- **Western ethics**: In many Western societies, ethical frameworks are influenced by **liberal** philosophies such as **utilitarianism** and **deontological ethics**. These perspectives stress individual rights, justice, and equality. For example, in business ethics, Western companies may emphasize transparency, honesty in advertising, and CSR as key principles.
- **Eastern ethics**: Many Eastern societies, including those influenced by Confucianism, Buddhism, or Taoism, may prioritize collective harmony, respect for authority, and social order. Ethics are often considered in terms of relationships and context rather than absolute rules. **Chinese** business ethics, for example, may place a higher value on maintaining **face** (respect and social standing) and harmonious relationships than on strict adherence to rules or legal structures.
- **Conflict between Western and Eastern ethics**: Western ethical frameworks may emphasize the individual's rights, freedom, and equality, which could clash with Eastern values that prioritize group harmony and the importance of family or community over individual desires. For instance, ethical issues around **genetic engineering** or **surrogate motherhood** could face different ethical interpretations in Western versus Eastern societies.

19.8.2 International regulatory agencies and ethics

Global ethical guidelines and regulations are often formulated and enforced by international organizations. These organizations work to set standards for ethical conduct in various sectors, such as healthcare, business, environmental sustainability, and human rights.

The role of international organizations in setting global ethical guidelines:

- **United Nations (UN)**: The **UN** plays a pivotal role in promoting international ethics, especially in areas such as human rights, peacekeeping, and environmental protection. The **Universal Declaration of Human Rights**, adopted by the UN, sets out the fundamental rights and freedoms to which all people are entitled, influencing global ethical standards on issues such as equality, freedom, and dignity.
- **WHO**: The **WHO** is responsible for setting global ethical standards in the field of healthcare, especially related to issues like medical research, access to healthcare, and public health initiatives. The **Declaration of Helsinki**, for instance, sets ethical guidelines for medical research involving human participants, ensuring informed consent and minimizing harm.
- **WTO**: The **WTO** facilitates global trade but also works to uphold ethical practices in international commerce. Its ethical focus includes ensuring fair trade, preventing exploitative labor practices, and promoting sustainable development through trade policies. However, the WTO's impact on ethics is often debated, particularly regarding trade policies in developing nations.

The challenges of enforcing international ethical standards:

- **Cultural relativism**: One of the biggest challenges in enforcing international ethical standards is the conflict between universal ethical principles and cultural relativism. Different countries may have distinct norms and values, leading to disagreements over what constitutes ethical behavior.
- **Sovereignty versus global regulation**: Countries often prioritize their own sovereignty over international agreements. This can lead to resistance in adopting international ethical guidelines, particularly when they conflict with national laws, economic interests, or political ideologies. For example, environmental regulations may be perceived as too restrictive for developing countries that rely on resource extraction for economic growth.
- **Enforcement mechanisms**: International organizations often lack the power to directly enforce ethical standards. In many cases, adherence to international guidelines is voluntary, with sanctions or penalties imposed only when specific agreements are breached. For example, the UN's human rights treaties may be ignored by governments that do not comply, with limited recourse for enforcement.

19.8.3 Case studies of international ethical conflicts

Real-world scenarios offer insights into the practical challenges faced by multinational companies and organizations in navigating international ethical conflicts. These case studies highlight how cultural, legal, and regulatory differences can create ethical dilemmas in global business operations.

Ethical dilemmas in cross-border business operations:

- **Nike Sweatshops**: In the 1990s, **Nike** faced widespread criticism for the use of sweatshops in **Southeast Asia**, where workers, particularly young women, were subjected to poor working conditions, low wages, and unsafe environments. Ethical questions arose over the company's responsibility to ensure fair labor practices in countries with lower wage standards. Nike responded by implementing ethical sourcing policies and establishing labor monitoring programs, but the issue raised ongoing debates about corporate responsibility and ethical supply chains in global business.
- **Bhopal gas tragedy (Union Carbide)**: In 1984, a chemical leak at a **Union Carbide** plant in **Bhopal, India**, resulted in thousands of deaths and long-term health issues. The ethical dilemma centered on whether Union Carbide had prioritized profit over safety and whether the company had taken sufficient measures to protect the lives of workers and the surrounding community. The case raised significant questions about corporate accountability, particularly for multinational companies operating in developing countries with weaker regulatory frameworks.

Examples of regulatory challenges in multinational companies:

- **Apple and tax avoidance**: Apple has faced accusations of tax avoidance by using legal loopholes and offshore tax havens to reduce its tax liabilities in various countries. While legal, such practices raise ethical questions about the fairness of the global tax system and the role of multinational companies in contributing to the economies in which they operate. Apple's strategies have sparked global discussions about the ethical obligations of corporations to pay taxes and support public services.
- **ExxonMobil and environmental regulations**: ExxonMobil has been involved in several ethical conflicts related to its environmental impact, especially regarding climate change. In particular, the company has faced accusations of misleading the public about the risks of climate change and lobbying against environmental regulations. This raises ethical questions about corporate responsibility in addressing environmental degradation and contributing to sustainable practices.

19.9 Future trends and ethical challenges

The rapid pace of technological innovation brings with it new ethical challenges and opportunities for both individuals and societies. As technologies evolve, so do the ethical dilemmas that must be navigated. This section explores the future of AI, the growing importance of sustainability, and the ethical considerations surrounding advancements in healthcare, particularly personalized medicine and genetic engineering.

19.9.1 The future of AI and ethics

As AI continues to advance and become increasingly integrated into daily life, it raises significant ethical questions related to autonomy, control, and the impact on human agency. The increasing use of AI in areas such as autonomous decision-making and complex systems means that these ethical issues will only grow in significance in the coming years.

19.9.1.1 The ethical implications of AI in autonomous decision-making

- **Accountability and responsibility**: As AI systems take on more decision-making functions in various sectors, such as finance, healthcare, law enforcement, and even military operations, a central ethical question emerges: who is responsible when AI makes an incorrect or harmful decision? For example, autonomous vehicles that cause accidents or AI in healthcare that makes a misdiagnosis—who is at fault? The question of **moral responsibility** in AI decisions is a key area of ethical concern. Can we hold AI systems accountable, or must we assign liability to the creators, operators, or users of AI systems?
- **Bias and fairness**: AI systems are only as unbiased as the data they are trained on. If these systems are trained on biased data, they can perpetuate or even exacerbate societal inequalities. For instance, AI algorithms used in hiring practices may inadvertently discriminate against certain demographic groups if the data used to train these systems reflects existing biases in the workforce. In decision-making systems, especially in areas like criminal justice (e.g., predictive policing or sentencing algorithms), bias can lead to unfair outcomes and perpetuate systemic inequalities.
- **Transparency and explainability**: As AI systems become more complex, they often operate as "black boxes," making it difficult for humans to understand how they arrive at specific decisions. This lack of transparency poses ethical challenges in situations where decisions made by AI directly affect individuals' lives, such as credit scoring or criminal sentencing. Ensuring that AI systems are **explainable** and that their decision-making processes are transparent is essential for maintaining trust in these systems.

19.9.1.2 Ensuring human oversight and control over AI systems

- **Human-in-the-loop systems**: To ensure ethical oversight, one solution is to implement "human-in-the-loop" systems, where AI systems assist in decision-making, but humans remain in control of critical decisions, particularly in life-and-death situations. For example, in the medical field, AI might assist doctors in diagnosing diseases, but the final diagnosis and treatment decisions would be made by the healthcare provider.
- **Ethical guidelines and regulation**: Governments and international organizations are developing regulatory frameworks to ensure that AI systems adhere to ethical principles such as fairness, transparency, and accountability. In the EU, for instance, the **AI Act** is a proposed regulation that aims to set clear rules for the development, deployment, and use

of AI, with specific emphasis on high-risk AI applications such as those in healthcare and criminal justice.

- **AI governance and ethics committees**: Establishing dedicated bodies within organizations to oversee the ethical use of AI will become increasingly important. These committees can monitor AI systems for fairness, bias, and transparency, ensuring that AI developments align with ethical standards. The governance of AI could be further supported by ethical certifications or audits, ensuring that systems comply with regulatory requirements.

19.9.2 The role of sustainability in ethical practices

As awareness of climate change, environmental degradation, and resource scarcity increases, sustainability has become a core issue in ethical decision-making. This shift toward sustainable business practices represents a significant transformation in how organizations view their responsibility to both society and the planet.

19.9.2.1 Growing importance of sustainable business practices

- **CSR**: Companies are increasingly expected to demonstrate their commitment to sustainable practices. This goes beyond simply complying with regulations and includes taking proactive steps to reduce their environmental impact. **Greenwashing**—misleading claims about the sustainability of products or services—has become a significant concern, and businesses must adopt transparent, verifiable sustainability practices to build trust with consumers.
- **Circular economy and resource efficiency**: The future of sustainable business will increasingly focus on a **circular economy**, which emphasizes the reuse, recycling, and repurposing of materials to minimize waste. This model not only helps preserve resources but also creates new opportunities for innovation and efficiency in manufacturing processes. Ethical concerns arise when businesses fail to properly dispose of or recycle their products, contributing to the depletion of natural resources and environmental pollution.
- **Sustainable supply chains**: Businesses are also held accountable for the sustainability of their supply chains. This includes ensuring that suppliers follow ethical practices in areas such as labor rights, environmental impact, and fair wages. Companies that fail to address the ethical concerns within their supply chains risk damaging their reputation and losing consumer trust.

19.9.2.2 Environmental regulations and ethical responsibility in business

- **Green regulations**: Governments are increasingly enacting environmental regulations that require companies to meet specific sustainability goals. These include regulations around carbon emissions, waste management, energy consumption, and sustainable sourcing. Ethical concerns come into play when businesses fail to meet these regulations, leading to negative impacts on the environment and public health. For instance, oil companies and manufacturers who pollute air and water sources face ethical scrutiny not just from regulators but from the public as well.

- **Climate change and global responsibility**: Businesses, especially multinational corporations, must confront the ethical challenges of their role in contributing to climate change. Many companies have adopted net-zero carbon emission goals, but the practicality of achieving these goals remains an ongoing issue. Ethical responsibility demands that businesses take steps to reduce their environmental footprint, both in terms of carbon emissions and resource consumption.
- **Sustainability reporting**: To ensure accountability, companies are increasingly adopting sustainability reporting standards, such as the **Global Reporting Initiative** and the **Task Force on Climate-related Financial Disclosures**. These standards ensure that companies disclose their environmental impact and sustainability practices in a transparent and consistent manner, making it easier for consumers, investors, and regulators to assess the ethical implications of a company's operations.

19.9.3 Ethics of technological advancements in healthcare

Technological advancements in healthcare are transforming the field, enabling new treatments, improved diagnoses, and more personalized care. However, these innovations also bring about ethical challenges, especially as they raise questions regarding accessibility, equity, and privacy.

19.9.3.1 The rise of personalized medicine and biotechnology ethics

- **Genetic privacy and data protection**: Personalized medicine, which tailors treatments based on an individual's genetic makeup, holds great promise for precision healthcare. However, it raises concerns about the privacy of genetic data. Who owns genetic information, and how should it be protected? The potential misuse of genetic data for discrimination or exploitation is an ethical issue that needs to be addressed.
- **Gene editing technologies**: Technologies like **CRISPR** have the potential to eliminate genetic diseases and enhance human traits, but they also raise significant ethical concerns. For instance, germline editing (modifying genes in embryos) could lead to unintended consequences for future generations. There are concerns about "designer babies" and the possibility of exacerbating social inequalities, as only wealthy individuals may have access to these technologies.
- **Equity in access to personalized medicine**: While personalized medicine offers enormous potential for improved outcomes, it could exacerbate health disparities if access to cutting-

edge treatments is limited to wealthy individuals or countries. Ensuring equitable access to these innovations is a central ethical challenge in the future of healthcare.

19.9.3.2 Ethical considerations in future medical technologies, including genetic engineering

- **Human enhancement and ethical boundaries**: Advances in genetic engineering and biotechnology may lead to the possibility of enhancing human capabilities, such as increasing intelligence or physical strength. These enhancements could lead to ethical dilemmas regarding what constitutes acceptable human improvement. For instance, should there be limits on enhancing human traits, or should individuals have the autonomy to enhance themselves as they see fit?
- **Synthetic biology and bioengineering**: The creation of synthetic organisms or bioengineered solutions could revolutionize medicine and environmental protection. However, the ethical implications of creating new life forms or altering the fundamental building blocks of life must be carefully considered. What moral responsibility do scientists and companies have when creating life forms that didn't exist in nature? There's also the question of whether synthetic organisms could pose unintended ecological or societal risks.
- **Consent and autonomy**: As medical technologies become more advanced, ensuring that patients maintain full autonomy and understanding of their treatment options is critical. **Informed consent** remains a cornerstone of ethical medical practice, but new technologies—especially those involving AI or gene editing—may complicate the process of ensuring that patients fully understand the risks and benefits

19.10 Conclusion

The rapid pace of technological innovation in the modern world brings with it significant benefits but also complex ethical challenges. In this concluding chapter, we explore the ongoing challenge of balancing technological progress with ethical considerations, the role of regulation in guiding these innovations, and how various stakeholders can encourage ethical development in society. As we move forward, creating a harmonious relationship between innovation, regulation, and ethical principles will be essential for ensuring that new technologies are developed and deployed in ways that benefit humanity as a whole.

19.10.1 Balancing ethics, regulation, and innovation

The ongoing challenge of balancing technological progress with ethical considerations: Technological progress has revolutionized nearly every aspect of our lives—from healthcare to communication, from education to transportation. However, as these technologies evolve, they often outpace the ethical frameworks designed to regulate them. This creates a significant challenge: how do we ensure that innovation doesn't come at the expense of human rights, social justice, and environmental sustainability?

- **Innovation versus ethical risks**: Technological advancements, particularly in fields like AI, biotechnology, and renewable energy, offer great promise for solving global problems. Yet, they also carry risks. AI could enhance human decision-making but might also perpetuate biases. Biotechnology can cure genetic disorders, but it raises concerns about genetic manipulation and equity. In these cases, ethical considerations must not be an afterthought; they must guide the development of technology from its inception.
- **Regulation in flux**: Existing regulatory systems often struggle to keep up with the speed of technological advancements. Governments, international organizations, and businesses must be agile in crafting flexible regulatory frameworks that evolve with new technological developments. Regulations should be forward-thinking and designed to prevent harm while promoting innovation. For example, data privacy regulations, like **GDPR** in the EU, are setting important precedents for how to handle data privacy in the digital age, but many questions remain, particularly as AI continues to advance.

19.10.1.1 Future directions for ethical guidelines and regulatory frameworks

- **Proactive regulation**: Moving forward, regulation should focus on **preventative measures**. Ethical frameworks should be integrated into the design and implementation phases of emerging technologies, rather than being retroactively applied once issues arise. For instance, ethical guidelines around **AI fairness** or **genetic editing** should be established in the research and development phase, ensuring that technology is built in a way that promotes equity and justice.
- **Global cooperation**: The nature of technological innovation today is **global**. For ethical guidelines and regulatory frameworks to be effective, there needs to be greater **international cooperation**. This can be achieved through collaborative efforts between governments, international organizations, and private-sector stakeholders to create **universal standards** that promote ethical practices in technology development. Regulatory bodies such as the **UN**, **WHO**, and the **EU** can play a significant role in facilitating these discussions, ensuring that ethical norms are upheld worldwide.
- **Ethics as an integral part of innovation**: Going forward, businesses and innovators will need to view **ethical responsibility** as a fundamental part of their product development cycles. Rather than seeing ethics as an external concern or a regulatory burden, companies should integrate ethical considerations as part of their organizational culture. This means creating interdisciplinary teams that include ethicists, technologists, and legal experts to guide product development and evaluate potential societal impacts.

19.10.2 Encouraging ethical development in society

19.10.2.1 How individuals, organizations, and governments can promote ethical practices

- **Individual responsibility**: At an individual level, every person has a role to play in promoting ethical development in society. Ethical awareness can be cultivated through education, self-reflection, and engagement in open discussions. Individuals can advocate for responsible business practices, vote for leaders who prioritize ethics in policymaking, and make ethical choices in their own professional and personal lives.
- **Corporate responsibility**: Organizations, especially in the tech industry, must adopt comprehensive CSR strategies that not only focus on profit but also on their impact on society and the environment. This involves creating products that are not only innovative but also **ethical and sustainable**. Companies should invest in research to understand the broader social implications of their technologies, ensuring that the risks associated with their products are mitigated.
- **Government and policy**: Governments play a critical role in encouraging ethical practices through the creation of regulations and laws that enforce ethical conduct. However, it is not just about policing behavior, but also about creating an environment that encourages ethical development.
- For instance, consumers can choose to support companies that prioritize sustainability and fair labor practices, and employees can raise ethical concerns within their organizations.
- Businesses must establish **internal ethics committees** and **sustainability goals**, regularly reviewing their practices to ensure that they align with ethical standards. Transparency, accountability, and fairness should be central to the culture of any organization, particularly in industries where the impact of technological advancements is most felt.
- **Legislators and policymakers** must work with experts in technology, ethics, and law to create balanced regulations that support innovation while safeguarding the public interest. Public policies should be forward-looking, promoting ethical research and development and incentivizing companies to adopt responsible practices. Ethical guidelines should be woven into the legal frameworks governing industries like healthcare, AI, and the environment.

19.10.2.2 The role of education and continuous dialog in shaping ethical standards

- **Ethics education**: One of the most effective ways to encourage ethical development in society is through **education**. Ethics should be a core component of education, starting from an early age and continuing into professional training. In particular, future scientists, engineers, business leaders, and policymakers should be well-versed in ethical decision-making.

- **Public dialog**: Continuous public dialog and **public engagement** are essential for evolving ethical standards. Technologies like AI, genetic engineering, and renewable energy have broad implications for society. It is essential that these discussions remain inclusive, with diverse voices contributing to the conversation. This includes not only experts in the field but also people from various social, cultural, and economic backgrounds. Public debates, consultations, and forums provide valuable perspectives on how emerging technologies should be developed and used.
- **Media and advocacy**: The role of the **media** in promoting ethical practices cannot be understated. Through reporting, documentaries, and investigative journalism, the media can keep ethical issues in the public eye and hold companies, governments, and individuals accountable. Advocacy groups also play an important role in raising awareness about the ethical implications of emerging technologies, ensuring that the voices of marginalized communities are heard.
- **Ethical standards in technology**: As we continue to innovate, the need for updated **ethical standards** becomes more pressing. Technological developments, especially in areas like AI, biotechnology, and environmental sustainability, must be continuously monitored, and new ethical guidelines must be formulated to address emerging issues. This requires collaboration between ethicists, technologists, business leaders, and policymakers. By fostering an ongoing dialog, we ensure that the ethical considerations surrounding technology are continually evolving to meet new challenges.
- **Universities and colleges** should offer interdisciplinary programs that combine ethics with technology, law, and business. These programs can help students understand how ethical theories can be applied to real-world challenges in their respective fields.
- In addition, ongoing **professional development** is crucial. For instance, companies in high-tech industries like AI and biotechnology should prioritize training their employees in ethical decision-making, ensuring that these professionals are prepared to handle the complex moral questions that arise in their work.

CHAPTER 20

Future perspectives on AI/ML and blockchain

Richa Singh[a], V. Hemamalini[b], M. Jeyaselvi[b], Amit Kumar Tyagi[c], and Shrikant Tiwari[d]

[a]*Department of Computer Science and Engineering, Birla Institute of Technology, Mesra, Ranchi, Jharkhand, India*
[b]*School of Law Forensic Justice & Policy Studies, National Forensic Sciences University, Gandhinagar, Gujarat, India*
[c]*School of Computing Science and Engineering, Galgotias University, Greater Noida, Uttar Pradesh, India*
[d]*Department of Networking and Communications, SRM Institute of Science and Technology, Kattankulathur, Tamil Nadu, India*

20.1 Introduction

Currently, all around us, we are witnessing the confluence of new technologies such as artificial intelligence (AI), machine learning (ML), and blockchain that are disrupting traditional industries and reshaping our conception of how we process data, make decisions, and understand trust. AI is defined as the capability of machines to perform tasks that would be described as human intelligence, while ML, an extension of AI, refers to a system that can analyze data and learn from it, allowing it to make decisions based on data without human input. Each of these technologies has matured quite rapidly due to the availability of large-scale data and datasets, increased computational capabilities, and increasingly complex algorithms. They have the potential to be applied broadly, including in natural language processing, computer vision, healthcare diagnostics, climate modeling, financial forecasting, and more. Each of these products and technologies has vast applications, and there appears to be untapped potential based on their continued ability to extend human capability and increase efficiency (Martin et al., 2017).

Alongside this advancement, blockchain technology has been recognized as a robust solution from the standpoint of transparency, decentralization, and security. Although blockchain was first introduced with a digital currency known as Bitcoin, it functions via distributed

Artificial Intelligence, Machine Learning and Blockchain in Digital Twin Computing.
https://doi.org/10.1016/B978-0-443-43914-8.00009-1

ledgers governed by cryptographic algorithms and consensus mechanisms, making it resistant to tampering and allowing for smart contracts, which can automate and establish trustless interactions. The combination of AI/ML and blockchain can only be described as a partnership that merges well-analyzed data with traceable and tamper-proof logs. The pairing of the two technologies offers opportunities for independent processes, which can enable trust and responsibility, ultimately solving significant problems related to data integrity and data privacy, as it enables businesses to create transparent, accountable, and explainable AI-based ecosystems (Sabharwal et al., 2024).

The combination of AI/ML with blockchain is not just a normal integration of two technologies, but it is a purposeful and deliberate approach to ameliorate the limitations of both technologies operating alone. While AI/ML systems are designed to analyze vast amounts of complex data, these systems are rife with issues pertaining to data privacy, security, and data provenance. In addition, one must address user trust when the AI/ML model has limitations on disclosing or providing justification for decisions because of areas of vulnerability like model manipulation, data poisoning, and opaque decision-making. In contrast to AI/ML, blockchain enables safe and secure storage of data with a mechanism for chain of custody (immutability), transparency, and security (Idrissi et al., 2024). On its own, blockchain can serve as a repository of data, yet it lacks the intelligence to analyze data, as it operates without learning, adaptation, and exploitation. Blockchain uses a decentralized approach, which is inherently secure, but this can impose a heavy computational load on a single decentralized system that is not designed for learning and optimization purposes.

The interaction of these technologies provides opportunities to develop advanced digital infrastructures that include and leverage the benefits of both worlds. AI/ML can streamline blockchain applications by providing intelligent automation of smart contracts, automatic fraud detection, and creating self-adaptive decentralized structures like decentralized autonomous organizations (DAOs). In addition, blockchain can support AI/ML in terms of trusted datasets and model-sharing environments, as well as training and inference records to examine models. Some of the primary use case industries include healthcare, which provides privacy-compliant diagnostics; finance, which offers secure and intelligent trading; supply chain and logistics, which enable real-time transparent asset tracking; and governance, which prioritizes trust and transparency. Fundamental to this convergence is the increasing demand for intelligent, ethical digital ecosystems where transparency, security, and adaptability coexist and co-shape (Nguyen et al., 2024). Fig. 20.1 illustrates the integration concept of AI/ML and blockchain.

There are critical gaps and challenges in researching AI/ML and blockchain integration which, despite their escalating interest, remain unaddressed. These gaps include: (1) lack of unified architectures, especially where researchers treat AI and blockchain as two separate technologies or applications; (2) scalability and efficiency challenges; (3) difficulty in achieving user privacy of data while maximizing efficiency in cross-border or regulated environments/projects; (4) lack of standardization, use of Trustworthy AI—which means

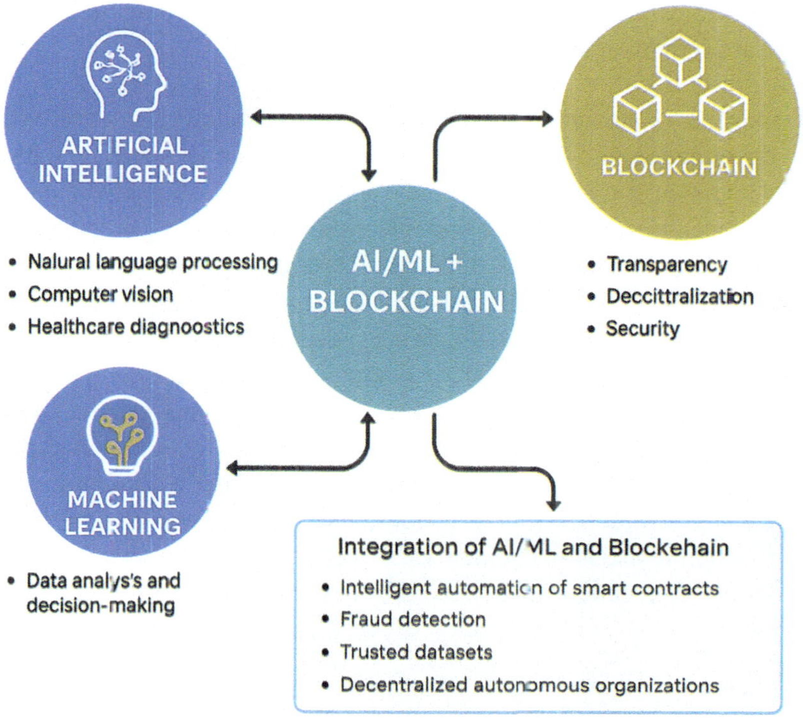

Fig. 20.1 Conceptual overview of AI/ML and blockchain integration.

different things to different people—explainability, ease or difficulty in realizing and mitigating bias, and determining who is liable (if anyone) for accountability of the model in decentralized contexts; and (5) model life cycle management (especially secure) is an underresearched area. These gaps demonstrate the need for a more comprehensive study of future architectures, use cases, and principles to integrate AI/ML and blockchain. This paper seeks to investigate the future potential for integration of AI/ML and blockchain technologies by assessing some of the previous challenges and delineating new possibilities. The research aims to accomplish the following tasks:

- Identify the underlying concepts of AI/ML and blockchain technologies, and how they can be symbiotic
- Examine the existing integration methods and options across various domains, and classify these methods into categories [e.g., federated learning (FL)with blockchain, smart contracts from AI]
- Identify the challenges and limitations that exist with the integration process, and identify open research questions
- Develop a conceptual framework or taxonomy for the design of integrated AI-blockchain systems

- Depict patterns toward the future, standardization efforts, and potential uses that will be relevant toward intelligent decentralized systems

The rest of the paper is organized as follows: Section 20.2 reviews the literature, consisting of an in-depth examination of prior and ongoing studies covering AI/ML and blockchain technologies by thematic domains and technical approaches. Section 20.3 examines the frameworks of technology synergies and integration in providing architectural modeling, middle-ware platforms, and enabling protocols, facilitating interoperability and cofunctionality. In Section 20.4, we discuss use cases and industry examples, outlining real-life implementation scenarios (e.g., health, finance, supply chain trading, energy) to showcase the tangible benefits of practical or productive outcomes using these technologies. Section 20.5 identifies and discusses challenges and open issues, including technical, ethical, and regulatory obstacles to migration toward greater adoption of widely scaled implementations and standards development. Section 20.6 explores future directions and opportunities, reflecting on trends, potential research directions, and the transformative power of the convergence of AI and blockchain technologies. Section 20.7 concludes the paper with key findings, synthesizing conclusions derived from previous sections and offering final reflections on the current state of integration of AI/ML and blockchain technologies, as well as future prospects.

20.2 Related work

There has been a large and growing body of academic work on AI, ML, and blockchain, primarily due to their potential to enhance transparency, trust, and automation in distributed digital environments. The healthcare field has been at the forefront of blending AI-based and blockchain-based systems and approaches. In the paper (Conway et al., 2024), the authors proposed a blockchain-based FL system to protect patient data while enabling collaborative diagnostic model training among multiple institutions. In this project, differential privacy (DP) approaches were combined with smart contracts to facilitate secure parameter exchanges between institutional partners. Similarly, the authors of the paper (So et al., 2024) developed a concept that used AI to identify the presence of chronic conditions from electronic health records and blockchain to provide decentralized access control and higher traceability. In the paper (Palaiokrassas et al., 2024), the authors presented a contact tracing algorithm based on AI that utilized a blockchain versatile enough to provide an auditable, tamper-proof log of COVID-19 data. In the paper (Soori et al., 2023), the authors presented an ML-based anomaly detection engine that would flag and log problematic transactions and provide logs as part of a permissioned blockchain. In the paper (Rane et al., 2024), the authors proposed a method based on Q-learning to facilitate smart contract cost-saving recommendations for general DeFi applications, with AI models acting as the best advice to recommend cost-efficient execution paths based on location, latency, and application capabilities in the context of a decentralized finance (DeFi) ecosystem. Finally, Chowdhury (2024) described credit scoring systems with explainable AI models that had their data verified through data trails recorded onto a blockchain to support decision-making rationale and enhance accountability and fairness in models.

The intersection of blockchain's immutability and AI's predictive capabilities has led to valuable possibilities in related supply chain management concepts. A combination of blockchain and the Internet-of-Things (IoT) has resulted in hybrid systems that grant capabilities previously unavailable. For example, Mazhar et al. (2025) developed a blockchain-IoT platform that builds on the device's blockchain capability of securing shipment authenticity in concert with their predictive machine learning models used to forecast stock levels. In Masud (2024), AI models utilized image recognition of products at specific transit points to ensure product quality, while blockchain was employed to provide shareability of live data in an accountable manner and establish traceability between actors in the supply chain. In the smart city domain, which holds significance as a potential composite of growing interest among researchers, policy makers, and institutions, AI systems can be used in service systems to automate operations, while blockchain ensures trust. An example is found in Al Shareef et al. (2024), where an edge-computing framework combined convolutional neural networks with blockchain for real-time observation, managing traffic congestion through automated decision-making. In Kuznetsov et al. (2024), a decentralized energy market was developed using reinforcement learning with blockchain smart contracts specifying energy pricing and demand-response balancing. Another application of urban smart sensors and human monitoring was described using blockchain-AI systems, where (Ali et al., 2021) developed a face-recognition AI model whose logs were integrated with blockchain to direct decentralized access control and enable forensic traceability.

The intersection of blockchain and AI systems has also furthered the knowledge base on the usage of these systems in the security context. In Anglen (2024), the authors proposed a blockchain-anchored intrusion detection system and AI models that were protected by continuously learning from network traffic to detect previously unseen novel attacks. In a different context (Zhang et al., 2021), the authors proposed an AI system that achieved consensus through collaborative data sharing, embedding threat models that were trained locally and decided collectively. Thus, the approach enabled an organization to share knowledge securely using a blockchain-based consensus to create a strong cybersecurity intelligence program. FL gains substantially from blockchain's decentralized validation capabilities. In Zhang et al. (2023), a blockchain protocol was designed to manage model update submissions via a proof-of-learning mechanism, minimizing malicious updates while also providing an auditable, transparent trail. The work by Leiva and Castro (2025) also introduces a lightweight blockchain-enabled FL system for IoT, providing real-time, privacy-preserving AI to edge devices. Table 20.1 summarizes the past works done in the field of AI/ML and blockchain integration.

Table 20.1 Summary of related works done on AI/ML and blockchain integration.

Ref. No.	Technique used	Focus area	Major contribution
(Conway et al., 2024)	Federated learning + blockchain	Privacy-preserving diagnostics	Secure FL model training across institutions
(So et al., 2024)	AI + blockchain smart contracts	EHR data sharing and analytics	Decentralized AI for chronic disease detection
(Palaiokrassas et al., 2024)	AI + blockchain ledger	Pandemic contact tracing	Tamper-proof COVID-19 tracking with AI insights
(Soori et al., 2023)	ML anomaly detection + blockchain	Fraud prevention	Detects irregular transactions and records them immutably
(Rane et al., 2024)	Q-learning + smart contract logic	Contract execution cost optimization	AI-guided smart contract path selection
(Chowdhury, 2024)	Explainable AI + blockchain	Credit scoring	Transparent and fair scoring using verified data
(Mazhar et al., 2025)	ML forecasting + blockchain IoT	Inventory and logistics	Real-time stock level prediction and shipment tracking
(Masud, 2024)	AI image recognition + blockchain	Product authentication	Image-based quality checks with verifiable audit trails
(Al Shareef et al., 2024)	CNN + blockchain edge architecture	Traffic congestion management	Real-time smart traffic control using decentralized AI
(Kuznetsov et al., 2024)	Reinforcement learning + smart contracts	Dynamic energy pricing	Decentralized AI-led energy balancing
(Ali et al., 2021)	AI facial recognition + blockchain	Urban security and access control	Identity verification with secure, traceable logs
(Anglen, 2024)	AI IDS + blockchain storage	Intrusion detection	Tamper-resistant, learning-based attack detection
(Zhang et al., 2021)	AI threat models + blockchain consensus	Threat intelligence sharing	Secure, distributed training and sharing of cybersecurity data
(Zhang et al., 2023)	Proof-of-learning + blockchain	Model integrity verification	Ensures honest updates in FL using blockchain governance
(Leiva and Castro, 2025)	Lightweight FL + blockchain	Secure edge AI deployment	Real-time privacy-preserving model training on edge devices

It is clear from the literature reviewed that there is an increasing synergy between AI/ML and blockchain in many domains, with each new integration addressing issues in their respective domains around privacy, trust, scalability, and automation. It is obvious that although much progress has been made, there is still significant room for further regimentation and exploration as it relates to other domains and performance.

20.3 Technological synergies and integration frameworks

The integration of AI and ML with blockchain technology requires robust integration frameworks to ensure full interoperability, effectiveness, and scalability. Architectural models are essential for determining the interconnections between AI/ML modules and digital ledger technology. Most models will likely exhibit a layered design, typically starting with the edge or user data. Next, the AI, which may be on-premise or cloud, interprets the edge data, which can then be written or digitally signed on the blockchain. The main advantages of using this method are provenance and auditability, while the superiority of AI for informed decisions can benefit from other intelligent designs. Some architectural models include an orchestration design layer, which facilitates real-time interaction among various decentralized nodes, smart contracts, and AI modules (Abdelhamid et al., 2024). Another interesting architectural model considers blockchain-as-a-backbone, where blockchain acts as a foundational layer, offering a standard for how AI systems can exist as microservices or decentralized agents that may reside on the blockchain. This design pattern works particularly well in constrained environments, such as the Internet of Things and FL, essentially enabling secure sharing of models and secure inference without a centralized structure. In more complex designs, Digital Twin architecture can also be analyzed by using AI analytics and blockchain to secure digital identities for collaborating "twins" and provide real-time updates to "twins" for monitoring. This approach has a variety of design considerations for secure updates and monitoring in areas like manufacturing and healthcare (Alabdulatif et al., 2022).

Middleware serves as a glue connecting AI/ML and blockchain implementations by delivering abstraction, interoperability, and communication between disparate systems. Middleware frameworks such as Hyperledger Fabric, Polkadot, and Quorum have been adapted to support plug-and-play AI models and facilitate tasks like secure data pre-processing, deploying the model, and recording the inference. Usually, the building blocks of these middleware systems include Application Programming Interface (API) gateways, data relays, and smart contract interpreters, all of which facilitate interactions between AI engines and decentralized ledgers (Xu et al., 2023). Some newer middleware implementations support semantic interoperability using ontologies and knowledge graphs to pre-define concept definitions and relationships between systems. Middleware systems can also perform AI model versioning, checkpointing, and federated orchestration in federated AI, managing consistency across nodes and ensuring blockchain integrity. Lastly, AI as a service can be deployed in a containerized environment, for example, using Docker or Kubernetes, where the blockchain is isolated and allows independent updating of AI-based services while the blockchain workflow continues (Avyukt et al., 2021). Fig. 20.2 illustrates the AI/ML blockchain integration architecture.

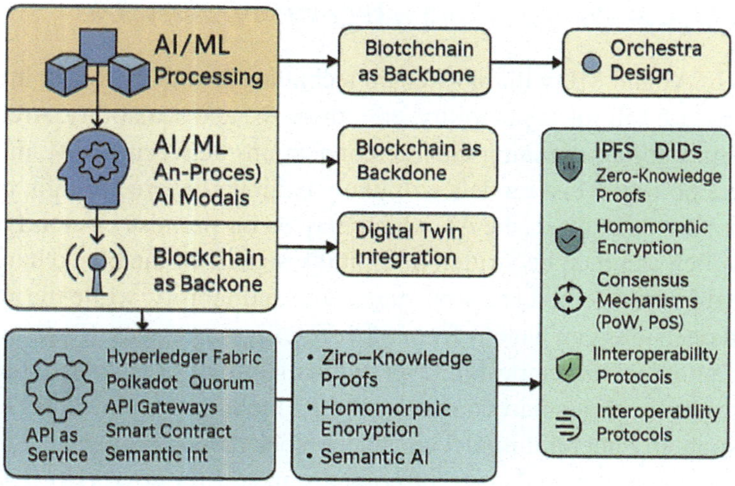

Fig. 20.2 Integrated architecture of AI/ML blockchain.

For AI/ML and blockchain to achieve effective synergies, any established protocols must ensure secure communication, decentralized model training, and verifiable execution. Protocols enabling the InterPlanetary File System and Decentralized Identifiers (DIDs) allow for the storage of data and verifiable identities, which are fundamental elements that lead to the advancement of AI/blockchain ecosystems. Zero-knowledge proofs (ZKPs) and homomorphic encryption (HE) are the two most common cryptographic solutions used in AI and blockchain systems. They ensure that AI models can consume encrypted data and that the blockchain can validate all operations without revealing private content (Soori et al., 2023). As described previously, consensus algorithms play an important role in determining the operational efficiency of integrated systems. Consensus algorithms fall into two fundamental groups: proof-of-work (PoW) and proof-of-stake (PoS). However, new consensus protocols have been proposed, including but not limited to proof-of-learning, proof-of-trust, and delegated proof-of-utility, to cater to AI-related contributions such as model accuracy, validation efforts, and resource costs. Adaptive protocols allow for cooperative and collaborative work tasks to be trusted and accountable within a decentralized and/or crowd-sourced framework (Cui et al., 2025). Interoperability protocols, such as cross-chain communication protocols (CCCPs) and Token Bridges, expand the flexibility of integrated systems. They make it easier for AI models to access and verify data stored on multiple blockchains via an integrated system. For decentralized AI marketplaces and federated data governance systems, interoperability protocols could enable AI models to run on distributed and federated datasets, which can be verified on a blockchain protocol (Chen et al., 2024). Table 20.2 provides a summary of architectural models, middleware components, and protocols for AI/ML and blockchain integration, respectively.

Table 20.2 Summary of architectural models, middleware components, and protocols for AI/ML and blockchain integration.

Category	Description	Examples/Tools
Architectural Models	Layered architectures embedding edge sensor data → AI/ML processing → blockchain record-keeping. Uses blockchain to guarantee provenance, ensure auditability, and enable informed decision-making	Orchestration layers, blockchain-as-a-backbone, digital twin architecture
Blockchain as Backbone	Blockchain provides the infrastructure, and AI is deployed as decentralized agents/microservices. This provides optimized computational and communication models for constrained environments and federated learning	Used in IoT, federated AI systems
Digital Twin Integration	AI remains responsible for analytics, and blockchain can provide secure identity and provide updates for Digital Twins in real-time	Applicable in healthcare, smart manufacturing
Middleware Frameworks	Act as invisible connectors between AI/ML and blockchain, creating interoperability and secure communication	Hyperledger Fabric, Polkadot, Quorum
Middleware Functions	Multiple abstraction layers, smart contract interpreters, data relays, and API gateways support pre-processing, model execution, and record-keeping	AI versioning, federated orchestration, semantic interoperability (ontologies/knowledge graphs)
AI as a Service (AIaaS)	AI models (initially) are run in containers for flexibility and can be updated individually, while the blockchain is transactional, recording changes	Docker, Kubernetes
Security Protocols	Ensure secure model execution and data privacy are respected and do not change because of a system upgrade or otherwise	IPFS (storage), DIDs (identity), ZKPs, HE
Consensus Mechanisms	Govern how AI's contributions and AI's decisions on models are validated in decentralized systems	PoW, PoS, proof-of-learning, proof-of-trust, delegated proof-of-utility
Interoperability Protocols	Enables AI models to interact with all data across different blockchains to validate information	CCCPs, Token Bridges
Use Cases	Real-world industry applications are beginning to emerge and demonstrate, in real time, the benefits of AI and blockchain connections	Healthcare (privacy diagnostics), finance (fraud detection), supply chain (tracking), governance (trust)

While the current frameworks and protocols are evolving rapidly, there are a number of issues to address, especially in achieving effective interoperability among heterogeneous systems. Communication between AI models and the exchange of data with heterogeneous blockchains remain significant challenges. The computational constraints of blockchains impede the integration of resource-rich, powerful AI models. Work must be done to address the problems of efficiently implementing bias amelioration, AI models, and decision-making in constrained environments, such as the IoT and edge computing. In addition, there are regulatory aspects to consider, including compliance with data privacy laws and the ethical implications of AI-assisted decisions when building integrated systems. Future work will need to focus on formalizing frameworks, enhancing the efficiency of blockchain systems for AI-related tasks, and providing mechanisms to efficiently address the ethical, privacy, and security issues associated with AI and blockchain.

20.4 Use cases and industry applications

The convergence of AI/ML with blockchain technologies has ushered in an avalanche of transformative applications in diverse industries. These applications demonstrate both the complementary nature of the two technologies and their combined effectiveness in addressing persistent challenges related to data security, operational inefficiencies, lack of trust, and lack of automation. In this section, we highlight real-world use cases in the areas of health, finance, supply chain, and energy to show how AI/ML-blockchain convergence impacts transparency, decision-making, automation, and value creation.

20.5 Securing patient data and enabling smart diagnostics

The healthcare industry is increasingly utilizing blockchain for enhanced data security and patient-centric sharing control, while AI/ML enables intelligent diagnostics, predictive analytics, and personalized treatment. If both were utilized in unison, healthcare systems could address privacy concerns while also tackling clinical inefficiencies. For example, blockchain-enabled Electronic Health Records (EHRs) have provided patients with control over the sharing of their data through smart contracts, which manage data provenance and integrity. At the same time, machine learning algorithms can increase accuracy in predicting disease outbreaks, unplanned patient readmissions, or treatment outcomes using de-identified,

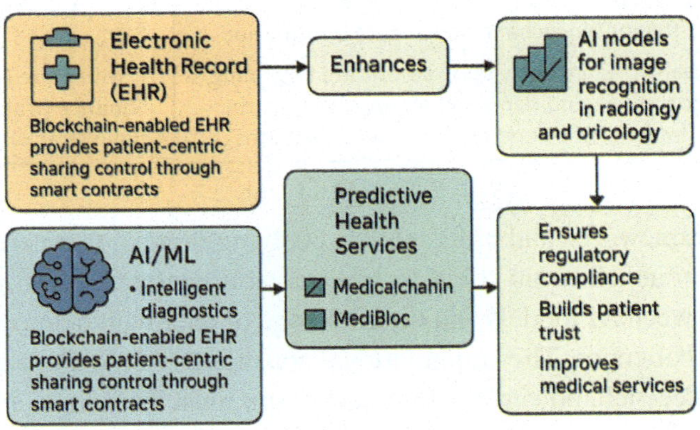

Fig. 20.3 Use of AI/ML blockchain-integrated framework in Healthcare.

blockchain-secured EHR data. Medicalchain and MediBloc are prime examples of the integrated use of AI and blockchain through the development of predictive health services that utilize blockchain for data management and electronic shared services (ESS)-ML services for healthcare applications. In addition, AI models for image recognition in radiology or oncology within blockchain ecosystems will allow diagnostic results to be verified and remain free from manipulation during medical malpractice claims or clinical trials. This will help build patient trust, ensure regulatory compliance, and improve medical services (Qu et al., 2023). Fig. 20.3 illustrates the use of an integrated framework in healthcare.

20.6 Enhancing security, transparency, and risk prediction

In finance, AI/ML is already making seismic changes in areas like fraud detection, algorithmic trading, and credit scoring, while blockchain is enabling new ways of conducting transactions, DeFi, and secure, immutable audit tracing. Their convergence is resulting in a more intelligent and resilient financial services infrastructure. AI-powered fraud detection systems plugged into blockchain-enabled transaction networks can provide continuous monitoring while identifying aberrations and suspicious patterns, triggering alerts, and even halting transactions when indicated through smart contracts. In decentralized lending, AI uses verified identity and transaction histories on blockchain to analyze borrower habits and creditworthiness and provide equitable, just, and accurate credit scoring without a central agency mediating the credit relationship. Projects like Aave, Compound, and Chainlink are at the forefront of banking and capital markets, integrating DeFi protocols with AI-based risk analytics and decentralized oracles, allowing holders and issuers to mitigate systemic risk, optimize capital efficiency, and make data-driven decisions in real-time. Blockchain establishes traceability for regulatory reporting, while AI enhances the efficiency of portfolio optimization, compliance auditing, and accounting (Ali et al., 2023). Fig. 20.4 illustrates the use of an integrated framework in healthcare.

20.7 Ensuring transparency and predictive efficiency

Trust, transparency, and traceability are key challenges in global supply chain management. Blockchain provides verifiable and immutable records of product movement and ownership. Meanwhile, AI combined with ML enables supply chain participants to forecast demand, plan logistics, and detect anomalies. When blockchain is integrated with AI-enabled sensors and IoT devices, supply chain stakeholders can ensure products are monitored for conditions (temperature, geo-location, and humidity) as well as ensure that the historically recorded data is tamper-proof and corroborated by the information on the network. AI can help detect anomalies like shipment delays, unplanned route deviations, and counterfeit goods based on the defined operational parameters and notify the supply chain participants by triggering a smart contract-based action, such as a penalty payment or shipment rerouting. For example,

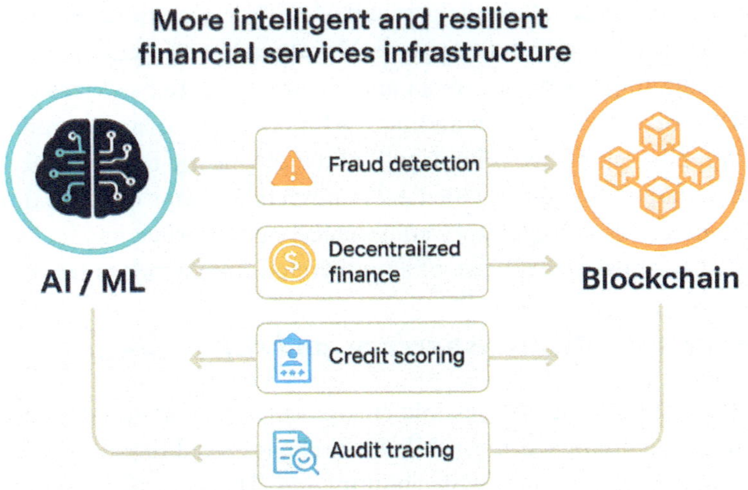

Fig. 20.4 Use of AI/ML and blockchain-integrated framework in security.

IBM Food Trust and TradeLens (a Maersk-IBM joint project) are examples of blockchain platforms that integrate with AI tools to log every shipment transaction in the supply chain, while also carrying out forecasting to warn supply chain actors about issues that may lead to supply disruption and optimize routing. This will enhance consumer trust and regulatory compliance while also improving operational efficiency. Similarly, AI-based document verification systems designed for international trade are being built on the Big-data concept, combined with blockchain smart contracts, to streamline processes. This reduced complexity and paperwork improves fraud resistance and reduces the time needed for customs clearance, resulting in a lower overall transaction cost and more throughput across the trade ecosystem (Siddiqui and Ahmed, 2025). Fig. 20.5 illustrates the use of an integrated framework in ensuring transparency.

20.8 Optimizing grid efficiency and decentralized energy trading

The energy sector is experiencing a significant transition toward both decentralization and sustainability. AI/ML is supporting smart energy management, load forecasting, and predictive maintenance, while blockchain technology enables peer-to-peer (P2P) energy trading, microgrid governance, and energy credit validation. Smart grid systems can incorporate AI models that analyze consumption patterns and predict energy demand, which will help utilities optimize generation and use energy and resource inputs efficiently. Together, and powered by blockchain, these models can couple consumption profiles to automate energy assignment and billing with smart contracts. Smart contracts will provide greater transparency and reduce disputes. Blockchain can also allow the energy market to pivot to decentralization and help consumers trade energy directly with each other without

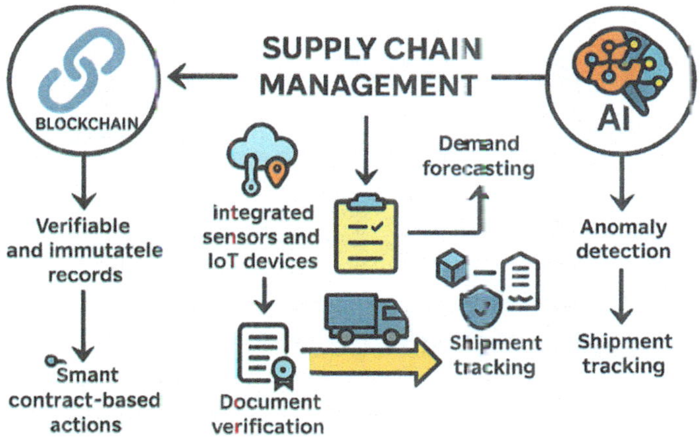

Fig. 20.5 Use of AI/ML blockchain-integrated framework in ensuring transparency.

the involvement of a centralized utility. AI algorithms will match buyers and sellers using real-time data, buyer preferences, and aggregate data to leverage dynamic pricing models, all while maintaining transparency and trust. Power Ledger and EnergiToken are already experimenting with AI-blockchain integration, transparency through market use awareness, transaction cost savings across the supply chain, and enabling communities to interact with and manage their own energy resources more sustainably, collectively or individually. In addition, predictive maintenance of energy infrastructure (e.g., operating status of wind turbines, solar panels, scheduled maintenance renewals, or other operations powered by ML) can be written to the blockchain for expectation, auditability, and performance indicators. This will promote performance accountability as well as extend the life cycle of these assets (Ferrag et al., 2021). Fig. 20.6 illustrates the use of an integrated framework in ensuring energy efficiency.

Merging AI/ML with blockchain is no longer an aspirational idea; it is a reality as adoption is increasing in various sectors, whether it be healthcare or finance, supply chains or energy. Real use-cases provide evidence that infusing intelligent automation with decentralized trust can build a better future for industry. These use-cases further demonstrate that AI and blockchain not only work well together technologically but accentuate their ability to provide scalable, secure, and intelligent digital ecosystems.

20.9 Challenges and open issues

Even though the possibilities for the uses of AI/ML and blockchain could undoubtedly change the world, widespread adoption has yet to be achieved due to a number of unidentified issues, which relate to a host of uncertainties—whether they are technical, ethical, or regulatory in nature—that need to be identified and solved to remove inline barriers such as

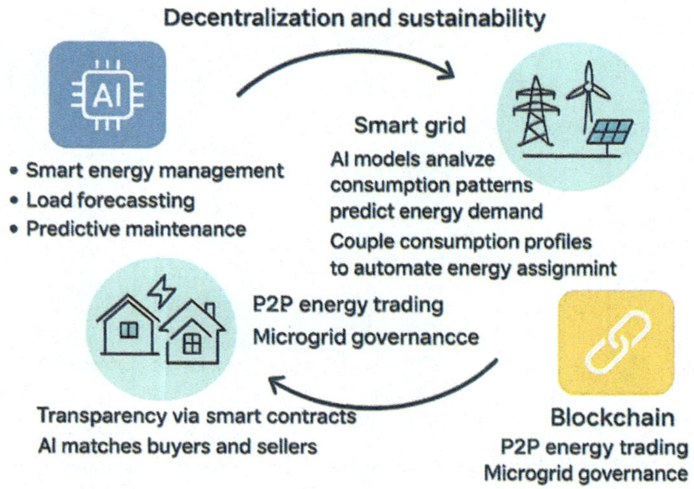

Fig. 20.6 Use of AI/ML blockchain-integrated framework in ensuring energy efficiency.

interoperability, trust, scalability, compliance, and standardization for AI/ML and blockchain deployment across industries. Important issues need to be resolved so that global, secure, and scalable solutions can be deployed. This section discusses the issues in more detail within a framework of categorization for those parties wishing to better understand and approach more targeted solutions.

20.10 Technical challenges

AI/ML are both inherently limited by scalability. When developing AI models, particularly those based on deep learning, there is a large computational overhead (often requiring high-throughput data processing capabilities), while blockchain is limited in its ability to handle transaction throughput due to latency differences when processing different types of transactions and constraints on consensus methodologies and semantics—mostly relevant on public networks such as Ethereum (Dagher et al., 2018) and Bitcoin (Hassan et al., 2019). Combining both paradigms' computational needs increases complexity. For instance, storing massive amounts of associated training data, algorithm parameters, and model weights inside a blockchain is neither practical nor feasible due to both storage constraints and prohibitive gas costs (Shrestha and Kim, 2019). In addition, most applications that rely on real-time data typically face problems meeting latency requirements, e.g., cases related to AI-driven fraud detection on blockchain-based payment networks. Finally, AI systems traditionally rely on high-quality, rich, timely datasets, while blockchain imposes restrictions in terms of immutability and decentralized access for either in-bound or out-bound data extraction. To clearly bridge the AI/ML and blockchain paradigms, especially when working across heterogeneous blockchain platforms or various layers in the data pipeline, there will be a strong reliance on middleware solutions, data standards/protocols, and trust in off-chain and on-chain access methodologies. In addition, when considering opportunities that utilize the utility of different blockchains, there will be no throughput or degree of efficacy, given that they are not presently able to facilitate interoperability or boast any significant extent of cross-chain capabilities (e.g., Polkadot, Cosmos), a technology that is also in its infancy. To sum up, there does not presently exist a seamless way for AI to interrogate and exploit blockchain-stored data across different ecosystems.

20.11 Ethical and social challenges

Inherently, AI/ML models will adopt biases from their training data, resulting in biased decisions. When those models become part of blockchain-based systems (e.g., smart contracts that automatically determine whether to lend money to someone or hire them) and drive decisions from those systems, it is likely that the resulting decisions from those models are immutable, or other parties will find it difficult to intervene to contest those decisions. Essentially, the immutable nature of blockchain expands the risk of biased decisions through AI. In addition, the assignment of responsibility in an AI-blockchain ecosystem is complex. Who is at fault when an autonomous transfer makes a damaging decision? Is it the developer or provider of data? Is it the smart contract? Is it the decentralized community? Meanwhile, AI is data-hungry, while blockchain is data-minimal and focuses on openness and transparency, which creates a tension between private and public decision-making. For example, the data required for AI models about user behavior might be detailed, but if any of that data is stored directly on the chain, the data may easily be publicly accessible even though someone has used a pseudonym. While ZKPs, HE, FL, and other techniques are being developed in this area, they have yet to become commonplace, likely because they are computationally intense and not standardized (Campos et al., 2022). Global acceptance of AI-blockchain implementations will be dependent on trust—not just trust in technology, but trust in ecosystem governance and decision-making. In existing technological implementations, impoverished user interfaces, a lack of explainability, and participatory governance processes have limited user confidence and acceptance of its use; this is particularly true with vulnerable groups such as those in health-care, education, or public welfare.

20.12 Legal and regulatory challenges

The legal regimes for AI and blockchain are fragmented, in flux, and, in some situations, altogether nonexistent. Questions regarding smart contract enforceability, AI accountability, data ownership, and liability remain unanswered across jurisdictions. Regulatory uncertainty is hindering investment and the adoption of innovation within heavily-regulated industries, such as finance, insurance, and health care. In addition, compliance with regulatory requirements, such as the General Data Protection Regulation (GDPR) in Europe, runs contrary to the concept of immutability foundational to blockchain, particularly an individual's right to be forgotten (Zhu et al., 2023). The absence of consistent standards, both technical and operational, is a significant barrier. Although organizations such as the Institute of Electrical and Electronics Engineers (IEEE), International Organization for Standardization (ISO), and the World Wide Web Consortium (W3C) have initiated efforts to address this gap, best practices for combining AI/ML and blockchain systems do not exist, nor does any consensus. Moreover, challenges relating to the governance of decentralized AI-blockchain platforms also present difficulties. How are updates managed? Who curates data and model updates? What controls exist to ensure security against collusion, manipulation, or the failure of algorithms in DAOs? In the digital economy and jurisdictional impermanence, AI and blockchain systems are often trans-border. This introduces questions relating to the transfer of data across borders, determinations of legal jurisdiction over smart contract enforcement, and the applicability of national laws in decentralized contexts. These issues can unleash regulatory uncertainty and expose stakeholders to unknown legal risks. Table 20.3 provides a summary of challenges in AI/ML blockchain integration.

The combination of AI/ML with blockchain holds great promise but faces many difficult challenges before it can be adopted at scale in a sustainable manner. There are technical issues to address, ethical ambiguities to resolve, and disparate regulatory environments that must be tackled collaboratively through interconnected research, policy innovation, and collective, multistakeholder action. If the global community is bold enough to take on these challenges, it might be possible to fully realize the value of intelligent, interdependent ecosystems.

20.13 Future directions and opportunities

The intersection of AI, ML, and blockchain technology is rapidly developing into one of the most impactful avenues of technological growth. While we are limited right now, we are heading toward an endpoint of operational understanding of decentralized intelligence, trusted automation, and secure data ecosystems within the primary ledger of digital infrastructure. This chapter discusses future trajectories and upcoming opportunities to influence industries, business models, and social systems by leveraging the combined capacities of AI and blockchain.

20.14 Evolution toward decentralized artificial intelligence

Bringing AI and blockchain together is creating a new model for decentralizing AI (DAI). DAI signifies a move away from traditional centralized AI models and toward our goal of an AI ecosystem that is more distributed, more transparent, and more democratic. As we move

Table 20.3 Summary of challenges in AI/ML–blockchain integration.

Category	Challlenges	Implication
Technical	Demands for computational resources by AI and blockchain systems (e.g., training data, transaction throughput, consensus latency) are sources of performance bottlenecks	Limits real-time applications, such as fraud detection, and increases operational costs
	Incompatibility between heterogeneous blockchain platforms and AI pipelines, along with the absence of middleware and standard protocols	Stops seamless access to data in real-time, restricting hybrid system development
	While blockchain is not capable of storing AI models, training datasets, or upload parameters, it is even less capable of accommodating the storage size of the AI models and/or the gas fees associated with storing these on certain blockchains like Ethereum	Reduces decentralization, shifts data load off-chain, and impacts transparency
	Limited cross-chain capabilities for AI to interact (e.g., early stages in Polkadot, Cosmos, etc.)	Constricts data accessibility across ecosystems and undermines a unified AI decision system
Ethical & Social	AI inherits biases present in training data, while blockchain makes reverting a biased decision almost impossible due to its immutability	Potential institutionalization of discrimination without oversight
	It is unclear who is responsible when a smart contract, operating autonomously, causes harm	Challenging legal enforcement, ethical trust, and insurance frameworks
	AI requires personal data, whereas transparency in blockchain systems may expose user data under pseudonymity	Privacy breaches limit adoption in areas like healthcare
	Lack of explainability, poor interfaces, and nonparticipatory governance reduce levels of trust among users	Limits acceptance of data security technology and safeguards in sensitive areas (such as public services and education)
Legal & Regulatory	Questions of jurisdiction arise for AI-Blockchain convergence regarding contracts, ownership, and liability	Inhibits innovation and legal protection across states
	The immutability property of blockchains undermines people's "right to be forgotten" and data protection legislation	Adds compliance risks and legal ambiguities
	There are no common protocols or best practices for AI-Blockchain convergence	Evidence of delays in the adoption and interoperability of technology
	No safe models exist for curating AI model updates, ensuring data integrity, or dealing with failure in DAOs	Risk of algorithmic failure, manipulation, or malicious governance
	In transnational blockchain-AI systems, issues of data sovereignty and enforcement will emerge	Raises compliance and liability questions for global use cases

toward DAI, users seek intelligence without privacy loss, data sovereignty, and trustless collaboration. Centralized AI models routinely aggregate large swaths of data via specific centralized organizations, generating monopolies of data, loss of privacy, and invisibility in the decision-making process. DAI aims to use blockchain to decentralize the control of data and model training among individuals, organizations, and machines so that ownership, oversight, transparency, security, accountability, and cocreation of AI systems become possible. Our desired approach to DAI utilizes FL as a foundational step. FL is an ML paradigm that avoids data centralization by making use of many federated servers that hold their own local data samples for training and does not allow the exchange of data or model parameters. When used in concert with blockchain, FL allows information about training and voting to be shared with transparency, traceability, and individually-denominated tokenization of all users of data and/or models. Smart contracts can, for instance, directly verify users of data in phishing detection participation and single training updates by allowing contributions to an on-chain treasury account for rewards to be split by percentage and geared toward local utility using chain-provided incentives. These techniques move us toward providing a sustainable ecosystem for individuals and organizations around the publication and collaboration of FL models.

Ocean Protocol, SingularityNET, and Fetch.ai are examples of emerging DAI infrastructures. Ocean Protocol enables data owners to monetize and share their datasets through a secure blockchain, providing smart AI model developers access to those datasets without the need for centralized intermediaries. SingularityNET offers developers decentralized services, allowing them to publish intelligent agents to a database where users can query through a basic ontological interface or integrate published agents into more sophisticated services. Both examples demonstrate how blockchain is facilitating secure discovery, negotiation, and aggregation of AI services in a trustless environment. In these times, AI agents could inherently possess autonomy in the process of negotiating services, collaborating for learning, and evolving without the need for humans in the development steps or decision-making processes. Imagine a network of supply chain participants in a decentralized environment comprising manufacturers, logistics warehouses or transportation providers, and retailers, where AI agents act on behalf of each participant based on operational and transactional history, autonomously sharing demand forecasts, negotiating sales and delivery, or settling disputes. They would use the unalterable historical state of the blockchain to maintain the accuracy of the underlying data and uphold agreements.

20.15 Integration with web3 and edge intelligence

The optimization of AI/ML and blockchain technologies is further emphasized due to their confluence with two additional transformational digital paradigms: Web3 and Edge Intelligence. Collectively, these technologies are building a decentralized, intelligent, and context-aware digital ecosystem characterized by a new way to store, compute, share, manage, and track data, services, money, and digital identity in today's ecosystems. Web3 is largely considered the next version of the internet, which will take the form of decentralized and tokenized web services that allow individual control and ownership of data. Web3 embraces self-sovereign identities, trustless data exchange, and the P2P interaction of data: the exact opposite of Web2, which is characterized by centralized platforms representing a few web services that dominate the total internet. Blockchain is the underlying architecture that enables Web3 as a foundational technology for decentralized applications (dApps), smart contracts, and tokenized assets. When building Web3 with AI, the components work autonomously, are useful to the general public, and collectively move toward completely personalized services.

For example, AI-driven tools in Web3-enabled digital marketplaces can be used for user behavior analysis, content recommendations, and dynamic pricing optimization. As a new technological stack, blockchain ensures that control remains with the user over their data through verifiable self-sovereign identity (SSI) and verifiable credentials. In decentralized social media platforms, AI moderation, recommendation, and community governance systems can be operated transparently with auditability through on-chain logic and community-specified AI models. In addition, Web3 token economies provide a means for quickly compensating users for their contributions of data, attention, or computing power, which can further accelerate collaborative innovation. Edge Intelligence, which is the application of AI at the edge of a network, is another frontier. Standard AI frameworks rely heavily on centralized cloud architecture, which creates latency, bandwidth, and privacy problems. Edge Intelligence seeks to overcome all of this by enabling on-device learning and inference to allow real-time responses that require less reliance on centralized servers. By adding blockchain to this space, the edge nodes not only have the capacity to process data on the node, but they also can process decentralized consensus, execute smart contracts, and write tamper-proof logs.

In healthcare, for instance, AI-powered wearable devices can measure patients' vitals and denote abnormal findings locally without passing sensitive data to the cloud. Blockchain guarantees that the health data transmitted to a healthcare provider is secure, trusted, traceable, and auditable. In autonomous transportation, edge-AI vehicles can make snap decisions and communicate with other vehicles and infrastructure using blockchain-trusted protocols, enabling safe and synchronized movements without centralized control. The relationship between Web3 and Edge Intelligence also facilitates distributed data marketplaces and federated model training, where edge devices can share model augmentation privately and securely using blockchain as the coordination guarantee. Decentralized architecture for training eliminates the need for aggregation of raw data before federated model training, thus reducing risks of privacy breaches and ensuring compliance with regulations such as the GDPR.

20.16 Tokenized AI economies and incentive models

The combination of blockchain and AI/ML has created an exciting new paradigm: tokenized AI economies. Tokenized AI economies are decentralized systems where tokens serve as units of value, governance, and coordination, and where AI services, data, and computation become tradable and incentivized commodities. The goals of tokenized economies are to democratize access to AI technologies, decentralize control of data and models, and encourage participation across a distributed and connected network of users, developers, and providers of resources. In tokenized economies, incentivized contributions are the key principle at the nexus of value generation and creation. Blockchain-based platforms have the potential to use cryptographic tokens in an aligned way to provide rewarding incentives to stakeholders who directly or indirectly create value in the AI lifecycle. This could include contributing data, training AI models, validating results, or providing computational resources or infrastructure. In centralized systems, the possible incentive contributions by these actors tend to be devalued and undercompensated. In decentralized ecosystems, value creation can be monitored, verifiably attributed to contributors, and recorded on-chain, ensuring that nodes that create value can reward value contributors.In conclusion, incentivization will not only generate value that is more evenly shared but also create strong, self-sustaining ecosystems for innovation. One important example is Ocean Protocol, which allows data owners to tokenize their data and sell their datasets on decentralized markets. The data can remain private and off-chain while the access credentials and transactions are governed by smart contracts. Likewise, platforms like SingularityNET allow for the production and monetization of AI services on a decentralized network, in which agents can publish, consume, and combine AI services in a trustless way using AGIX tokens. These architectures offer developers the ability to compose intelligent systems without issues stemming from centralization or middlemen. Data sovereignty, in a tokenized AI economy, is a fundamental right. Individuals can determine how, when, and with whom they share their data and receive direct compensation in tokens. Our long-standing concerns about user exploitation in centralized AIs, in which personal data is harvested without consent and monetized by the owners of the platforms, are addressed. By using SSI and DIDs, users can leverage their identity in AI ecosystems in a secure and verifiable manner without losing control over their digital footprint.

20.17 Privacy-preserving federated learning on blockchain

FL is a groundbreaking machine learning paradigm where various decentralized devices or servers can collaboratively train a joint model while keeping the data used for training local to the devices or servers. The aim is to reduce the privacy risks associated with sensitive data leaving its original environment. While this approach may seem appealing to users, traditional implementations of FL are typically protected by a central orchestrator, which can become vulnerable to data poisoning issues, model tampering problems, and challenges related to transparency and trust asymmetries among its users. These problems have sparked significant interest among researchers, particularly in the use of blockchain and FL together as a trust and privacy-preserving solution. Blockchain technology can provide an additional decentralized layer of coordination to the FL process by offering immutable audit trails, trustless authentication processes, and tamper-proof verification of contributor information. Smart contracts can also automate the orchestration of training rounds, the updating of aggregate models, and the awarding of incentives to participants. While federated learning traditionally relies on a trusted central server (e.g., Google FL), concerns regarding trust can be mitigated if FL leverages blockchain constructs that enable the distribution of trust among all participants, agreed upon through consensus mechanisms and cryptographic primitives. A traditional architecture consists of clients (e.g., hospitals, mobile devices, edge nodes) locally training AI models on private data and producing gradient updates or model weights. These updates or weights are then encrypted or recorded on a blockchain, referencing an online or off-chain storage layer linked to the blockchain. Smart contracts verify the submissions, utilize secure aggregation protocols to generate model weights [e.g., secure multiparty computation (SMPC) or HE], and update the global model accordingly. Through these steps, the model training process becomes observable and can be audited and verified via shared compute platform behavior—a feature that is crucial in regulated industries such as healthcare, banking, and defense. To further enhance privacy and security, several advanced techniques are complementing blockchain systems, as discussed below.

- **DP:** Provides a mathematical guarantee of privacy by adding statistical noise to the updates before submission to mask individual data points.
- **HE** Allows computations to be performed on encrypted data without requiring decryption, thereby maintaining the privacy of the data and its integrity while the model is trained on the cloud.
- **ZKPs** Allow participants to prove that their training processes, model updates, or model parameters were valid without revealing any data or internal computations.
- **Trusted execution environments:** Hardware-based solutions (e.g., Intel SGX) provide assurance of secure computation and integrity verification, even on untrusted devices.

A prime advantage and unique value proposition of blockchain-FL integration is the incentivization of participation. Using token-based mechanisms, where contributors can be rewarded based on the quality and relevance of their contributions, participation can be incentivized. This encourages sustainable, ongoing contributions with high value from edge nodes, which may be constrained in terms of resources. Lastly, blockchain can help facilitate decentralized governance and allow for stakeholder involvement in decisions around model parameters, updating frequency (and intervals), and reward policies, using DAOs and token voting. In health care, for example, given multiple hospitals inputting existing data into the development of AI diagnostic models, blockchain technology can mitigate many problems of trust across parties, enable data security while complying with regulations, and automate patient data and model sharing without actually exchanging patient data. There are a number of early startup projects with blockchain-anchored FL architectures engaging with real-world data, such as FLEDGE, MediBloc, and FedAI. However, critics of blockchain, including its leading developers, remain skeptical of its capabilities. The two primary challenges—scalability, particularly in terms of cost and speed—remain an issue. While blockchains like Ethereum provide the public transaction layer for transaction trust, they are notably high in transaction cost and latency. In addition, real-time FL with faster response cycles is difficult to achieve using existing blockchain consensus protocols. This is promoting the exploration of Layer-2 solutions, off-chain computation, and hybrid on-chain/off-chain federated architectures, as blockchain can help establish trust while achieving efficiency in regulatory compliance and performance.

20.18 Cross-chain AI orchestration and interoperability

As blockchain ecosystems evolve, the expansion of numerous public, private, and consortium chains has created a fragmented digital space. These ecosystems are often siloed and lack the ability to transfer data, assets, and functionality easily between them. On the other hand, AI systems rely on multiple datasets or rich datasets without bias and are "situated" in multiple domains—this use of multiple sources of data and logic from a decentralized context is a fundamental requirement for many AI systems. The emergence of cross-chain AI orchestration architecture provides a way for AI/ML systems to operate across heterogeneous blockchains, thus enabling the use of their respective data, logic, and resources in multisource intelligence extractions, metalearning across domains, and synthesized decision-making. Cross-chain interoperability is the ability for different blockchain networks to transfer data and perform coordinated operations across networks without centralized intermediaries to manage the functional interactions. When this is also extended with AI, it allows the AI models to be trained, verified, and deployed within various blockchain administrative areas, enabling the AI to assess multisource intelligence extractions, learn across decentralized domains, and synthesize their decisions. This can be especially relevant in areas like DeFi, where the potential exists for the AI to assess action trends across Ethereum, Binance Smart Chain, Avalanche, etc., or in the healthcare sector, where patient records are stored within other institutions' private chain areas.

A number of different interoperability protocols or bridging frameworks have been developed to advance this evolution. Protocols like Polkadot, Cosmos, Quant's Overledger, and Chainlink's Cross Chain Interoperability Protocol permit the construction of dApps and AI agents that communicate across chains using technologies like interchain messaging, token transfers, and common consensus mechanisms. When these systems are supplemented with AI features, it is possible to create independent agents that will continuously monitor multiple blockchain environments, assess the facts, learn the pathways, and initiate smart contracts when necessary. AI orchestration in cross-chain scenarios will include federated model training across chains, where AI models can be trained across multiple blockchains while maintaining data ownership. Decentralized knowledge graphs build interoperable knowledge representations arising from multiple blockchain-based data sources to enable AI systems to reason over cross-chain relationships. Smart Contract Interconnectivity allows AI models to trigger cross-chain events or respond to them across multiple smart contracts to enable complex workflows—for example, executing a cross-border insurance claim. AI-Powered Gateways and Middleware place AI into blockchain gateways to intelligently direct requests, manage latencies in operations, perform real-time anomaly detection, and optimize throughput.

20.19 Edge-AI-empowered blockchain for autonomous systems

The integration of Edge AI and blockchain technologies has the potential to transform how autonomous systems operate, make decisions, and communicate within decentralized systems. When computing power is located closer to the data—edge nodes, IoT devices, and embedded sensors—Edge-AI processes and analyzes data in real-time without relying on centralized cloud servers. By deploying Edge-AI and blockchain systems, we unlock significant potential for autonomy, transparency, and resiliency in mission-critical situations. Edge-AI is utilized by autonomous systems, such as smart vehicles, drones, robotic swarms, and industrial automation systems, for immediate decision-making that relies on ever-fluctuating information received via sensors. Edge-AI facilitates low-latency inference and the ability to dynamically react and adapt behavior directly at the data source, enabling these systems to avoid communication bottlenecks, enhance privacy, and respond more quickly to changing scenarios. However, Edge-AI systems typically face trade-offs that manifest as challenges, such as ensuring data integrity, coordinating across devices, and verifying actions. This is where blockchain can revolutionize these systems by enabling the ability to quickly and reliably capture every decision, model update, action, and data transmission within a decentralized ecosystem of nodes. These nodes can be referenced and traced for future decision-making, providing a robust framework for accountability and trust

Edge-AI analyzes energy usage and local production data in smart grids, while blockchain facilitates automated P2P energy trading. Robots and AI agents will make local inventory decisions and, through blockchain, be used to trace a tamper-proof trail of goods and execute logistics smart contracts. Drones and edge devices will monitor crop conditions in real time, coordinate irrigation decisions using real-time data, and certify product origin and sustainability compliance. Blockchain will support goods storage, citizens' rights to privacy/data control, and provide an audit trail of AI-generated use cases in smart cities and public safety. All these examples of use cases iterate value across different sectors. To establish these use cases, there are also multiple technical issues Edge-AI-enabled blockchain frameworks need to address. Edge devices are resource-constrained and often cannot be full blockchain nodes that also train large models. This is alleviated by lightweight consensus algorithms, e.g., proof-of-authority, delegated proof-of-stake, and off-chain computation strategies, e.g., state channels and sidechains. Further, instead of sharing raw data as is done in traditional FL, edge devices can train shared AI models cooperatively, while blockchain logs the model updates, enforces fairness of participation, and makes it easier to detect poisoned contributions. In addition, ZPKs, SMPC, and HE can integrate with Edge-AI to enable privacy-preserving inference and regulated data-sharing use cases. These tools are critical in areas like healthcare, where devices may collect sensitive biometric data, and the implementation of blockchain must comply with data protection and privacy acts.

20.20 Conclusion

The synergistic convergence of AI, ML, and blockchain is the pivotal point in the odyssey of digital systems. Together, these technologies wield extraordinary power: AI/ML represent intelligent automation and predictive power individually, while blockchain embodies data trust, decentralization, and transaction assurance. Collectively, they create intelligent, transparent, trustworthy, and autonomous systems. This chapter has examined multiple architectural models, middleware frameworks, and enabling protocols to facilitate the interoperability of these emerging technologies, along with various use cases across public health, finance, supply chain, and energy. We have come a long way, but continuing to achieve widespread adoption will greatly depend on addressing further technical, ethical, and regulatory challenges. Interoperability, model accountability, data privacy, and legal governance issues are just a few of the challenges facing responsible development and deployment, which will need to be addressed by developing common protocols, governance models, and collective innovation. Future directions remain abundant, including decentralized AI ecosystems, tokenized data economies, privacy-preserving FL, and cross-chain orchestration. While these paths hold promise for scalability and transparency, they will also involve a rethinking of the development, delivery, and governance of intelligent services. Although AI/ML and blockchain are trending technologies, their convergence is more fundamentally a shift in digital infrastructure that can shape a new, trustworthy, secure, inclusive, and ethical digital ecosystem.

References

Abdelhamid, M., Sliman, L., Djemaa, R.B., Perboli, G., 2024. A review on blockchain technology, current challenges, and AI-driven solutions. ACM Comput. Surv. 1557-7341. 57 (3). Available from: http://dl.acm.org/citation.cfm?id=J204. doi:10.1145/3700641.

Al Shareef, A.M., Seçkiner, S., Eid, B., Abumeteir, H., 2024. Integration of blockchain with artificial intelligence technologies in the energy sector: a systematic review. Front. Energy Res. 2296-598X. 12. Available from: http://www.frontiersin.org/Energy_Research/. doi:10.3389/fenrg.2024.1377950.

Alabdulatif, A., Khalil, I., Saidur Rahman, M., 2022. Security of blockchain and AI-empowered smart healthcare: application-based analysis. Appl. Sci. 2076-3417. 12 (21), 11039. doi:10.3390/app122111039.

Ali, M., Karimipour, H., Tariq, M., 2021. Integration of blockchain and federated learning for internet of things: recent advances and future challenges. Comput. Secur. 0167-4048. 108, 102355. doi:10.1016/j.cose.2021.102355.

Ali, M., Naeem, F., Tariq, M., Kaddoum, G., 2023. Federated learning for privacy preservation in smart healthcare systems: a comprehensive survey. IEEE J. Biomed. Health Inform. 2168-2194. 27 (2), 778–789. doi:10.1109/jbhi.2022.3181823.

Anglen, J., 2024. Ai, blockchain, powering digital security & efficiency in 2024. In: AI and Blockchain. https://www.rapidinnovation.io/post/ai-and-blockchain-powering-digital-security-efficiency-in-2024

Avyukt, A., Ramachandran, G., Krishnamachari, B., 2021. A decentralized review system for data marketplaces. In: IEEE International Conference on Blockchain and Cryptocurrency, ICBC 2021. Institute of Electrical and Electronics Engineers Inc., United States. 9781665435789. Available from: http://ieeexplore.ieee.org/xpl/mostRecentIssue.jsp?punumber=9460986. doi:10.1109/ICBC51069.2021.9461149.

Campos, E.M., Saura, P.F., González-Vidal, A., Hernández-Ramos, J.L., Bernabé, J.B., Baldini, G., Skarmeta, A., 2022. Evaluating federated learning for intrusion detection in internet of things: review and challenges. Comput. Netw. 1389-1286. 203, 108661. doi:10.1016/j.comnet.2021.108661.

Chen, J., Deng, W., Chen, D., Zhang, L., 2024. FinML-chain: a blockchain-integrated dataset for enhanced financial machine learning. arXiv. arXiv. 23318422. Available from: https://arxiv.org. doi:10.48550/arXiv.2411.16277.

Chowdhury, R.H., 2024. Blockchain and AI: driving the future of data security and business intelligence. World J. Adv. Res. Rev. 2581-9615. 23 (1), 2559–2570. doi:10.30574/wjarr.2024.23.1.2273.

Conway, K., So, C., Yu, X., Wong, K., 2024. opML: optimistic machine learning on blockchain. arXiv. arXiv. 23318422. Available from: https://arxiv.org. doi:10.48550/arXiv.2401.17555.

Cui, Z., Ling, X., Zhou, X., Wang, J., Ding, Z., Gao, X., 2025. BagChain: a dual-functional blockchain leveraging bagging-based distributed learning. arXiv. arXiv. 23318422. Available from: https://arxiv.org. doi:10.48550/arXiv.2502.11464.

Dagher, G.G., Mohler, J., Milojkovic, M., Marella, P.B., 2018. Ancile: privacy-preserving framework for access control and interoperability of electronic health records using blockchain technology. Sustain. Cities Soc. 2210-6707. 39, 283–297. Available from: http://www.elsevier.com/wps/find/journaldescription.cws_home/724360/description#description. doi:10.1016/j.scs.2018.02.014.

Ferrag, M.A., Friha, O., Maglaras, L., Janicke, H., Shu, L., 2021. Federated deep learning for cyber security in the internet of things: concepts, applications, and experimental analysis. IEEE Access. 2169-3536. 9, 138509–138542. Available from: http://ieeexplore.ieee.org/xpl/RecentIssue.jsp?punumber=6287639. doi:10.1109/ACCESS.2021.3118642.

Hassan, M.U., Rehmani, M.H., Chen, J., 2019. Privacy preservation in blockchain based IoT systems: integration issues, prospects, challenges, and future research directions. Future Gener. Comput. Syst. 0167-739X. 97, 512–529. doi:10.1016/j.future.2019.02.060.

Idrissi, Z.K., Lachgar, M., Hrimech, H., 2024. Blockchain, IoT and AI in logistics and transportation: a systematic review. Transp. Econ. Manag. 2949-8996. 2, 275–285. doi:10.1016/j.team.2024.09.002.

Kuznetsov, O., Sernani, P., Romeo, L., Frontoni, E., Mancini, A., 2024. On the integration of artificial intelligence and blockchain technology: a perspective about security. IEEE Access. 2169-3536. 12, 3881–3897. Available from: http://ieeexplore.ieee.org/xpl/RecentIssue.jsp?punumber=6287639. doi:10.1109/ACCESS.2023.3349019.

Leiva, V., Castro, C., 2025. Artificial intelligence and blockchain in clinical trials: enhancing data governance efficiency, integrity, and transparency. Bioanalysis. 1757-6199. 17 (3), 161–176. Available from: https://www.tandfonline.com/journals/ibio20. doi:10.1080/17576180.2025.2452774.

Martin, K., Wang, W., Agyemang, B., 2017. Optimized homomorphic scheme on map reduce for data privacy preserving. J. Inf. Secur. 2153-1234. 08 (03), 257–273. doi:10.4236/jis.2017.83017.

Masud, S.B., 2024. Understanding the financial transaction security through blockchain and machine learning for fraud detection in data privacy and security. Pakistan J. Life Soc. Sci. 1727-4915. 22 (2). doi:10.57239/pjlss-2024-22.2.001296.

Mazhar, T., khan, S., Shahzad, T., khan, M.A., Saeed, M.M., Awotunde, J.B., Hamam, H., 2025. Generative AI, IoT, and blockchain in healthcare: application, issues, and solutions. Discov. Internet Things 2730-7239. 5 (1). Available from: https://link.springer.com/journal/43926. doi:10.1007/s43926-025-00095-8.

Nguyen, C.T., Liu, Y., Du, H., Hoang, D.T., Niyato, D., Nguyen, D.N., Mao, S., 2024. Generative AI-enabled blockchain networks: fundamentals, applications, and case study. arXiv. arXiv. 23318422. Available from: https://arxiv.org. doi:10.48550/arXiv.2401.15625.

Palaiokrassas, G., Bouraga, S., Tassiulas, L., 2024. Machine learning on blockchain data: a systematic mapping study. arXiv. arXiv. 23318422. Available from: https://arxiv.org. doi:10.48550/arXiv.2403.17081.

Qu, Y., Uddin, M.P., Gan, C., Xiang, Y., Gao, L., Yearwood, J., 2023. Blockchain-enabled federated learning: a survey. ACM Comput. Surv. 1557-7341. 55 (4). Available from: http://dl.acm.org/citation.cfm?id=J204. doi:10.1145/3524104.

Rane, N.L., Kaya, Ö., Rane, J., 2024. Integrating internet of things, blockchain, and artificial intelligence techniques for intelligent industry solutions. In: Artificial Intelligence, Machine Learning, and Deep Learning for Sustainable Industry 5.0. Deep Science Publishing, pp. 115–136. doi:10.70593/978-81-981271-8-1_6.

Sabharwal, S.M., Chhabra, S., Aiden, M.K., 2024. AI and blockchain for secure data analytics. In: Blockchain Technologies. Springer Science and Business Media LLC, pp. 39–81. doi:10.1007/978-981-97-1249-6_3. Springer Nature Singapore.

Shrestha, R., Kim, S., 2019. Integration of IoT with blockchain and homomorphic encryption: challenging issues and opportunities. Adv. Comput. 115, 293–331. Available from: http://www.elsevier.com/wps/find/bookdescription.cws_home/705045/description#description. doi:10.1016/bs.adcom.2019.06.002.

Siddiqui, E.F., Ahmed, T., 2025. GTBTL-IoT: an approach of curtailing task offloading time for improved responsiveness in IoT-MEC model. EAI Endors. Trans. Internet Things 2414-1399. 11. Available from: https://publications.eai.eu/index.php/IoT/article/download/5556/3448. doi:10.4108/eetiot.5556.

So, C., Conway, K.D., Yu, X., Yao, S., Wong, K., 2024. opp/ai: optimistic privacy-preserving AI on blockchain. arXiv. arXiv. 23318422. Available from: https://arxiv.org. doi:10.48550/arXiv.2402.15006.

Soori, M., Dastres, R., Arezoo, B., 2023. AI-powered blockchain technology in industry 4.0, a review. J. Econ. Technol. 2949-9488. 1, 222–241. doi:10.1016/j.ject.2024.01.001.

Xu, G., Zhou, Z., Dong, J., Zhang, L., Song, X., 2023. A blockchain-based federated learning scheme for data sharing in industrial internet of things. IEEE Internet Things J. 2327-4662. 10 (24), 21467–21478. Available from: http://ieeexplore.ieee.org/servlet/opac?punumber=6488907. doi:10.1109/JIOT.2023.3298196.

Zhang, F., Wang, H., Zhou, L., Xu, D., Liu, L., 2023. A blockchain-based security and trust mechanism for AI-enabled IIoT systems. Future Gener. Comput. Syst. 0167-739X. 146, 78–85. Available from: https://www.journals.elsevier.com/future-generation-computer-systems. doi:10.1016/j.future.2023.03.011.

Zhang, Z., Song, X., Liu, L., Yin, J., Wang, Y., Lan, D., Kumar, N., 2021. Recent advances in blockchain and artificial intelligence integration: feasibility analysis, research issues, applications, challenges, and future work. Secur. Commun. Netw. 1939-0122. 2021, 1–15. doi:10.1155/2021/9991535.

Zhu, J., Cao, J., Saxena, D., Jiang, S., Ferradi, H., 2023. Blockchain-empowered federated learning: challenges, solutions, and future directions. ACM Comput. Surv. 0360-0300. 55 (11), 1–31. doi:10.1145/3570953.

Surity, privacy, and trust frameworks for artificial intelligence-driven digital twin ecosystems

Prasad Lahare, Smita Thakare, and Deepali Shinde

Department of Information Technology, Pune Vidyarthi Griha's College of Engineering and Shrikrishna S. Dhamankar Institute of Management, Nashik, Maharashtra, India

This chapter explains the major security risks that Digital Twins (DTs) may face, including issues related to devices, communication networks, cloud platforms, and system management. It also discusses modern methods that help protect sensitive information while still allowing effective data use. In addition, the chapter highlights the importance of secure system design, reliable access control, transparent operations, and trustworthy data handling. Practical examples from different fields show how these measures can be applied in real situations.

By bringing together these concepts, the chapter provides clear guidance, regulatory considerations, and future directions for creating secure, dependable, and privacy-respecting DT environments suitable for critical and large-scale applications.

21.1 Introduction

DT technology has rapidly evolved from a purely simulation-oriented concept to a dynamic, intelligent, and continuously learning ecosystem powered by the confluence of Artificial intelligence (AI), machine learning (ML), the Internet of Things (IoT), and distributed ledger technologies like blockchain [1,2]. A DT is not merely a static model but a sophisticated virtual replica of a physical asset, process, or system that exists in parallel and receives real-time, bi-directional data streams.

As these systems become deeply integrated into critical sectors, including manufacturing (Industry 4.0), healthcare, national infrastructure, smart cities, and defense, the associated risks concerning security, privacy, and operational trust have taken center stage. AI-driven DTs (AI-DTs) transcend basic modeling; they predict future behaviors, optimize complex operations autonomously, and enable prescriptive decision-making. These advanced

Artificial Intelligence, Machine Learning and Blockchain in Digital Twin Computing.
https://doi.org/10.1016/B978-0-443-43914-8.00011-X

capabilities necessitate the exchange of massive volumes of sensitive, real-time data across highly interconnected cloud, edge, and IoT layers. This interconnectedness inherently magnifies the ecosystem's vulnerability to a spectrum of malicious activities, including cyberattacks, data breaches, tampering, manipulation, and unauthorized access.

This chapter is dedicated to exploring robust security, privacy, and trust frameworks essential for safeguarding these complex, intelligent DT environments. It provides a comprehensive examination of the unique risks and challenges presented by the AI-DT convergence, details secure architectural requirements, and evaluates advanced solutions such as cryptographic techniques, blockchain integration, privacy-preserving AI methods [like federated learning (FL) and homomorphic encryption (HE)], digital identity mechanisms, and necessary regulatory and ethical compliance measures.

21.2 Understanding the security landscape in DT ecosystems

DTs operate at the convergence point of real-time sensing, complex data analytics, predictive modeling, and automated control loops, effectively bridging the operational technology and information technology (IT) worlds [3,6]. This comprehensive integration creates a broad and complex attack surface. A typical AI-DT ecosystem comprises several layers, each introducing unique security requirements and vulnerabilities:

1. **Physical/sensing layer:** Physical devices, sensors, and actuators
2. **Communication/network layer:** Connectivity, transmission protocols and gateways
3. **Edge/fog computing layer:** Local data processing and initial analytics
4. **Cloud/platform layer:** Central data storage, intensive computation, and global management
5. **AI/ML engine layer:** Predictive models, simulation kernels, and optimization algorithms
6. **Visualization and control layer:** User interfaces, control dashboards, and integration with physical control systems

21.2.1 Key security threats

The multifaceted nature of the AI-DT ecosystem exposes it to sophisticated, multilayered threats, extending beyond conventional IT vulnerabilities:

- **Data tampering and integrity attacks:** The alteration of real-time sensor data is perhaps the most insidious threat. Corrupting the input stream compromises the fidelity of the DT model, leading to inaccurate predictions, unsafe prescriptive decisions, and potentially catastrophic physical consequences (e.g., instructing a manufacturing robot to perform an unsafe action) [4].
- **Model poisoning (AI layer):** This involves attackers injecting malicious, biased, or adversarial data into the AI/ML model's training pipeline. The resultant "poisoned"

model may appear robust during testing but will fail or make harmful decisions when deployed in specific, targeted operational conditions.

- **Unauthorized access and authentication attacks:** Weak or single-factor authentication across the myriad of connected devices and platforms allows adversaries to gain control of critical DT components, exfiltrate sensitive industrial data, or modify operational parameters.
- **DT hijacking/simulation-to-reality attacks:** This is the most critical outcome of successful data or model tampering. By manipulating the DT's representation or its control outputs, an attacker can directly disrupt or destroy the physical system it represents, exploiting the twin's predictive capability to cause a real-world failure [10,19].
- **Replay attacks:** Adversaries capture legitimate historical DT data or control signals and "replay" them to mislead the AI model or the control system. This is particularly dangerous in systems where latency and temporal sequencing are critical, such as industrial control systems.
- **Insider threats:** Malicious or negligent employees, contractors, or vendors who possess elevated access privileges can misuse these rights to steal proprietary data (e.g., the core DT simulation model) or deliberately cause operational disruptions.
- **Denial-of-Service (DoS) and distributed DoS:** Overloading the network, edge compute nodes, or cloud resources responsible for running the DT can cripple its real-time functionality. A nonresponsive DT is useless, especially in high-speed applications like autonomous vehicles or power grid management.
- **Ransomware attacks:** Encrypting critical DT configuration files, historical data, or the AI/ML model weights can halt operations, with attackers demanding payment for decryption keys. Given the operational criticality of DTs, the incentive for swift payment is high.

21.3 Privacy concerns in AI-driven DT systems

DTs are fundamentally data-intensive entities. Their reliance on deep, real-time data streams inherently involves information that can be highly sensitive, whether it pertains to personal, industrial, or environmental parameters. Effective privacy management is not an add-on but a foundational necessity, addressed through disciplined practices such as data minimization, controlled access, distributed learning, and full compliance with regional and sectoral regulations [e.g., General Data Protection Regulation (GDPR), California Consumer Privacy Act (CCPA), Health Insurance Portability and Accountability Act (HIPAA)] [5,9].

21.3.1 Types of sensitive data involved

The sensitivity of the data is context-dependent but often involves legally protected or commercially valuable information:

- **Health records (healthcare DTs):** Individual patient biometric data, physiological readings, and genetic information are used for predicting disease progression or optimizing personalized treatment.
- **Precise geolocation data (Smart City twins):** Real-time movements of citizens, vehicles, and assets, which can lead to mass surveillance, leakage, and pattern analysis of individual lives.
- **Industrial secrets and intellectual property (manufacturing/R&D twins):** Proprietary manufacturing processes, sensor readings from new prototypes, output yields, and highly sensitive trade data.
- **User behavior analytics:** Detailed interaction logs, usage patterns, and predictive psychological profiles derived from human DTs or interactive systems.
- **Device identifiers and configuration details:** Unique IDs that can be used to track specific individuals or industrial assets across multiple services (Fig. 21.1).

21.3.2 Privacy attack vectors

Privacy threats in AI-DTs specifically target the aggregation and analytical layers:

- **Inference attacks:** Utilizing the aggregated output or predictions from the DT model to infer specific, sensitive details about an individual or an industrial process that are not explicitly contained in the input data.

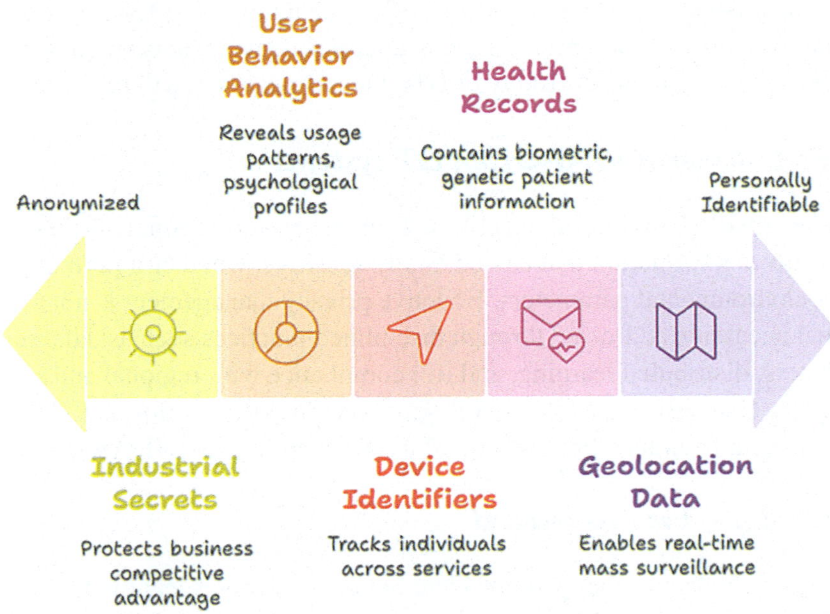

Fig. 21.1 Types of sensitive data.

- **Membership inference on AI models:** Determining whether a specific individual's data (or a specific company's proprietary data) was included in the training dataset of the AI model. This can expose sensitive participation information.
- **Data Re-identification:** Reversing the anonymization or aggregation techniques applied to data by cross-referencing metadata, external datasets, or temporal patterns, thereby linking the data back to a specific entity.
- **Surveillance leakage:** The persistent, deep monitoring required by a DT (especially in smart cities or homes) creates a complete behavioral profile, and any security breach in the viewing layer can expose this comprehensive surveillance data.

21.4 Trust in DT ecosystems

Trust is the nonnegotiable prerequisite for the adoption and reliable functioning of AI-DTs. It must be established across all dimensions: data, devices, users, AI models, and operational processes. A trustworthy DT ecosystem ensures that stakeholders can rely on the system to function as intended, consistently and securely [16,17].

Table 21.1 Trust dimensions, assurance requirements, and key challenges for digital twin systems.

Dimension	Assurance required	Key challenge
Data Trust	Assurance that the source data is accurate, complete, untampered, and verifiable from creation to consumption	Proving the provenance and immutability of petabytes of streaming IoT data
Model Trust	Confidence that the AI's predictions are reliable, explainable (transparent), robust against adversarial input, and free from malicious bias is essential	The "black box" nature of deep learning models and the difficulty in validating training data purity
Device Trust	Validation that edge/IoT devices and micro-controllers are correctly authenticated, securely configured, and have not been physically or digitally compromised	Managing the lifecycle and security posture of millions of low-power, physically exposed devices
Operational Trust	Verification that the processes governing data flow, model updates, access control, and decision-making are auditable, compliant, and consistently enforced	Lack of standardized, verifiable audit trails across heterogeneous cloud and edge platforms
User Trust	Assurance that the system will respect user privacy, grant appropriate access, and be accountable for its autonomous actions	Establishing clear accountability boundaries when an autonomous DT decision leads to failure

21.4.1 Dimensions of trust

Table 21.1

21.5 Security frameworks for AI-DTs

A robust security framework for AI-DTs must incorporate a multilayered defense-in-depth approach, integrating security controls across hardware, network, software, and the AI/ML pipeline itself [3,14].

21.5.1 Device layer security

Security begins at the origin of the data—the physical devices:

- **Hardware security modules (HSMs):** Dedicated, tamper-resistant hardware components used to securely store cryptographic keys, perform encryption/decryption, and execute authentication routines, protecting keys from software vulnerabilities.
- **Secure boot mechanisms:** Ensure that only firmware and software digitally signed by a trusted authority are loaded upon device startup, preventing the injection of malicious bootloaders.
- **Trusted platform module (TPM):** A standardized, dedicated microcontroller designed to secure hardware through integrated cryptographic keys. It can be used to attest to the integrity of the device's boot process and runtime environment.
- **Biometric and physical security:** Where human interaction occurs, stronger authentication methods are needed. Physical tamper-evident seals and monitoring are necessary for infrastructure-critical devices.

21.5.2 Network security

Securing the data in transit from the device to the cloud/platform:

- **Transport Layer Security/Secure Sockets Layer (TLS/SSL) encryption:** Standard, mandatory, end-to-end encryption for all data flowing between devices, edge nodes, and central servers.
- **Blockchain-based communication protocols:** Utilizing distributed ledger technology to create tamper-proof, time-stamped records of data transmission events, providing nonrepudiation for critical sensor readings.
- **Secure routing and micro-segmentation:** Network architectures should be heavily segmented, isolating critical control networks from nonessential traffic. Micro-segmentation confines potential breaches to the smallest possible network area.
- **Zero trust network access:** Implementing a framework where no entity (user, device, or application) is inherently trusted, regardless of location (see Section 10).

21.5.3 AI/ML system security (securing the model)

The AI model itself is a high-value asset and a critical control point:

- **Adversarial training:** Augmenting the model's training data with synthetic adversarial examples to harden it against potential adversarial attacks (e.g., small imperceptible data perturbations designed to force a misclassification).
- **Explainable AI (XAI) for validation:** XAI techniques allow human operators to audit *why* the DT made a specific prediction or decision. This is crucial for verifying model integrity postdeployment and detecting anomalous behavior caused by subtle model corruption.
- **Differential privacy (DP):** Applying DP techniques during model training ensures that the final model does not "memorize" specific training data points, thus preventing membership inference attacks.

21.5.4 DT integrity verification

Ensuring the virtual representation remains faithful to the physical:

- **Blockchain for model versioning:** Storing the hash and metadata of every significant AI model update on an immutable blockchain provides a transparent, auditable lineage for the model and ensures that the deployed version is the certified one.
- **Hashing techniques to validate state transitions:** Periodically hashing the DT's key operational state variables and storing this hash in a secure, immutable log. Any discrepancy in the state hash chain indicates data tampering or an unauthorized state change.
- **Continuous monitoring and anomaly detection:** Utilizing separate, dedicated AI systems to monitor the DT's operational outputs, looking for statistical deviations or sudden changes that might signal an ongoing attack.

21.6 Privacy frameworks for DT ecosystems

Given the sheer volume of sensitive data, robust privacy frameworks are nonnegotiable, requiring a shift from reactive data protection to proactive privacy engineering [5,7,9].

21.6.1 Privacy-by-design for DT systems

Privacy-by-design (PbD) is a methodology requiring privacy to be integrated into the system's design and architecture from the initial requirements phase. Key PbD principles applied to DT systems include:

- **Data minimization:** Only collecting, using, and retaining the absolute minimum amount of personal or proprietary data necessary for the DT's specific, stated function.

- **FL:** Instead of moving sensitive data to a central location for training, the learning model travels to the distributed edge nodes where the data resides, trains locally, and only sends back aggregated model updates.
- **Secure multiparty computation (SMPC):** Enabling two or more parties to jointly compute a function over their inputs while keeping those inputs private (see Section 11.2).
- **Privacy-preserving data analytics:** Utilizing techniques like cryptographic masking and DP to extract meaningful insights from aggregated data without exposing underlying individual records.

21.6.2 Differential privacy in DT models

DP provides a formal, mathematical guarantee that the presence or absence of any single individual's data in the training set will not significantly affect the outcome of the analysis. For DTs, DP is used to:

1. **Prevent individual information leakage:** By injecting calibrated noise into the model's outputs or the aggregate statistics, it becomes statistically impossible for an attacker to reliably infer whether a specific person's data contributed to the twin's prediction.
2. **Protect statistical properties:** The noise is calibrated to be small enough to preserve the useful aggregate statistical properties needed for accurate DT performance, while being large enough to protect privacy.

21.6.3 Homomorphic encryption

HE is a powerful cryptographic technique that allows computations (e.g., addition and multiplication) to be performed directly on encrypted data. The result of the computation remains encrypted, and when decrypted, it matches the result of the computation as if it had been performed on the plain text.

- **Application in DTs:** A DT running in the cloud could perform sensitive predictive modeling (e.g., optimizing medical treatment or proprietary factory schedules) on data that remains encrypted throughout the entire computational process, significantly mitigating the risk of data exposure during processing.

21.6.4 Federated learning for DT collaboration

FL is critical for collaboration among DT users or organizations, especially where regulatory restrictions prohibit data centralization.

- **Decentralized training:** Multiple organizations (e.g., hospitals, manufacturing plants) running identical physical assets can train a global DT model collectively without ever sharing their raw, sensitive local data.

- **Model aggregation:** Only the local model updates (gradients) are sent to a central server (or aggregated securely using SMPC), which combines them to create a superior global AI model that benefits all participants. This simultaneously improves the model's accuracy and preserves the data privacy of each contributing entity.

21.7 Trust frameworks for AI-enhanced DTs

Trust is built through transparency, immutability, and verifiability. These frameworks aim to make every operation within the DT ecosystem auditable and reliable.

21.7.1 Blockchain for trust establishment

Blockchain technology provides a shared, immutable, and decentralized ledger, which is ideal for securing the audit trail of critical DT operations:

- **Immutable audit logs:** All critical events—sensor data aggregation, AI model updates, access requests, and control commands—can be time-stamped and recorded on a private or consortium blockchain, making logs impossible to tamper with retroactively.
- **Data provenance:** Blockchain can track the origin and transformation history of every data point used by the DT, verifying the authenticity and integrity of the input data stream.
- **Smart contracts for governance:** Smart contracts can enforce transparent, automated governance rules, such as releasing control to an autonomous system only after a consensus of certified sensors and models validates the operational parameters [4,10,19].

21.7.2 Trust scoring mechanisms

Trust scores provide a dynamic, quantitative measure of the reliability of various DT components:

- **Device and data source scoring:** Devices and data streams can be continuously monitored and scored based on their security posture, data consistency, historical accuracy, and deviation from expected behavior. A device with suspicious network activity or wildly inconsistent data readings would receive a low trust score, and its data would be given reduced weight in the DT model.
- **AI model scoring:** Models can be scored based on their robustness to adversarial examples, prediction variance, and the degree of bias detected.

21.7.3 Explainable AI

XAI is the foundation of *Model Trust*. Complex AI models often operate as "black boxes," hindering regulatory approval and user confidence.

- **Transparency and audibility:** XAI techniques (e.g., SHapley Additive exPlanations (SHAP), Local Interpretable Model-agnostic Explanation (LIME)) allow the DT to generate human-readable explanations for its autonomous decisions ("The Digital Twin recommends shutting down the asset because Feature X crossed threshold Y, which has historically correlated with failure Z with 98% confidence.").
- **Bias detection:** XAI helps identify and mitigate algorithmic bias by showing which features dominate the decision-making process, ensuring the twin's operations are fair and unbiased.

21.7.4 Service-level agreements

Formalizing trust through contracts: SLAs standardize the minimum acceptable performance and security expectations for the DT platform, governing areas such as:

- **Data latency and integrity:** Guaranteed uptime and maximum permissible data loss or corruption rates
- **Model accuracy and reliability:** Minimum acceptable predictive accuracy and robustness under specific operating conditions
- **Response to security incidents:** Defined response times and remediation protocols in the event of a breach

21.8 Blockchain for security, privacy, and trust in DTs

Blockchain is a pivotal technology that intersects and enhances all three pillars of the AI-DT framework [16,17,4,10] (Fig. 21.2).

21.8.1 Security via blockchain

- **Immutable logs:** As discussed, blockchain makes all operational records permanent and tamper-proof, drastically improving forensics and incident response.
- **Smart contracts for access control:** Decentralized, self-executing smart contracts can manage access control lists dynamically. For example, a contract could automatically grant access to maintenance data only if the technician's device, current geolocation, and work order ID (all verifiable attributes) are validated.
- **Distributed identity verification:** Blockchain supports verifiable credentials, ensuring that devices and users presenting themselves to the DT ecosystem are authenticated by a decentralized, tamper-proof authority.

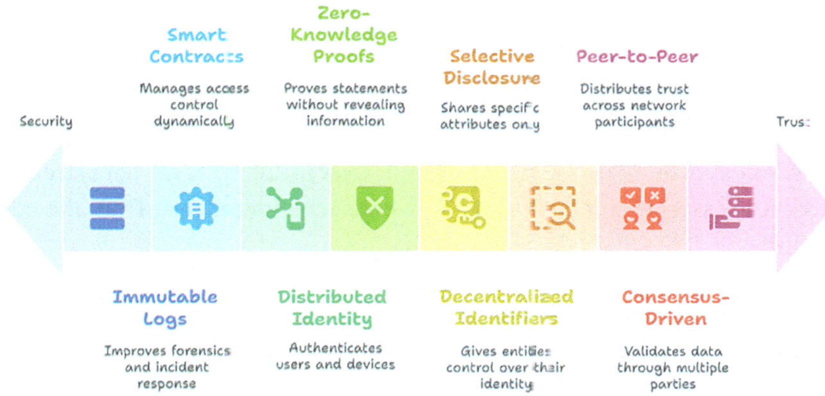

Fig. 21.2 Blockchain's impact on the AI-DT framework pillars, from security to trust.

21.8.2 Privacy via blockchain

While all transactions are visible on a public blockchain, cryptographic primitives allow for privacy preservation:

- **Zero-knowledge proofs (ZKPs):** Allow one party to prove that a statement is true (e.g., "I am an authorized user" or "The data I collected is within a normal range") without revealing the underlying information itself. This is critical for authentication and data validation without disclosing sensitive details.
- **Decentralized identifiers (DIDs)** Give entities (devices, users) sovereign control over their identity and data, making it easier to manage data access rights and minimize reliance on centralized identity providers.
- **Selective disclosure protocols:** Enable users to share only the specific, necessary attributes from their identity (e.g., only proving you are over 18 without revealing your date of birth).

21.8.3 Trust via blockchain

- **Consensus-driven verification:** The requirement for consensus among distributed nodes ensures that data recorded into the DT's audit trail is validated by multiple independent parties, thereby building confidence in its fidelity.
- **Peer-to-peer trust models:** Eliminate reliance on a single, centralized authority, distributing trust across the network participants (e.g., consortium members in a manufacturing supply chain DT).

21.9 Cryptographic foundations for secure DTs

Cryptography provides the fundamental mathematical tools for securing data in transit and at rest and for establishing trust [12,13].

- **Symmetric encryption (AES):** Used for bulk encryption of large data streams due to its high speed, it is essential for protecting real-time sensor data sent from the edge to the cloud/platform.
- **Asymmetric encryption (RSA, ECC):** Used for key exchange, digital signatures, and authentication. It is slower than symmetric encryption but is crucial for establishing secure communication channels.
- **Elliptic curve cryptography (ECC):** Provides equivalent security to RSA with significantly shorter key lengths, making it ideal for resource-constrained IoT devices within the DT ecosystem.
- **Postquantum cryptography (PQC):** Research and deployment of PQC algorithms are vital. The development of quantum computers threatens to break current asymmetric cryptographic standards. Future DT systems must be designed to be quantum-safe, requiring the adoption of lattice-based, code-based, or hash-based cryptography.
- **Hash functions (SHA-256, SHA-3):** Essential for data integrity verification, creating unique fingerprints of data, models, and states to detect any unauthorized modifications.

21.10 Zero trust architecture for DT ecosystems [11,20]

The traditional perimeter-based security model is inadequate for the distributed nature of DTs. The Zero Trust (ZT) model, defined by the principle of **"never trust, always verify,"** is the most effective approach (Fig. 21.3).

21.10.1 Principles of zero trust

- **Continuous authentication and authorization:** Every entity—user, device, service, or microservice—must be continuously authenticated, and its authorization verified before gaining access to any DT resource. Authentication is not a one-time event upon login but an ongoing process.
- **Micro-segmentation:** The DT network must be broken down into granular security zones, typically down to the individual workload level. Policies are applied to control the flow of data between these micro-segments, ensuring that a breach in one area cannot easily spread.
- **Least privilege access:** Access rights are strictly limited to the minimum necessary permissions required for an entity to perform its assigned function. A sensor only has permission to write data to its designated stream, not to read the AI model's source code.
- **Strong identity management:** All entities must have robust, verifiable digital identities, managed centrally or, ideally, using DID mechanisms.

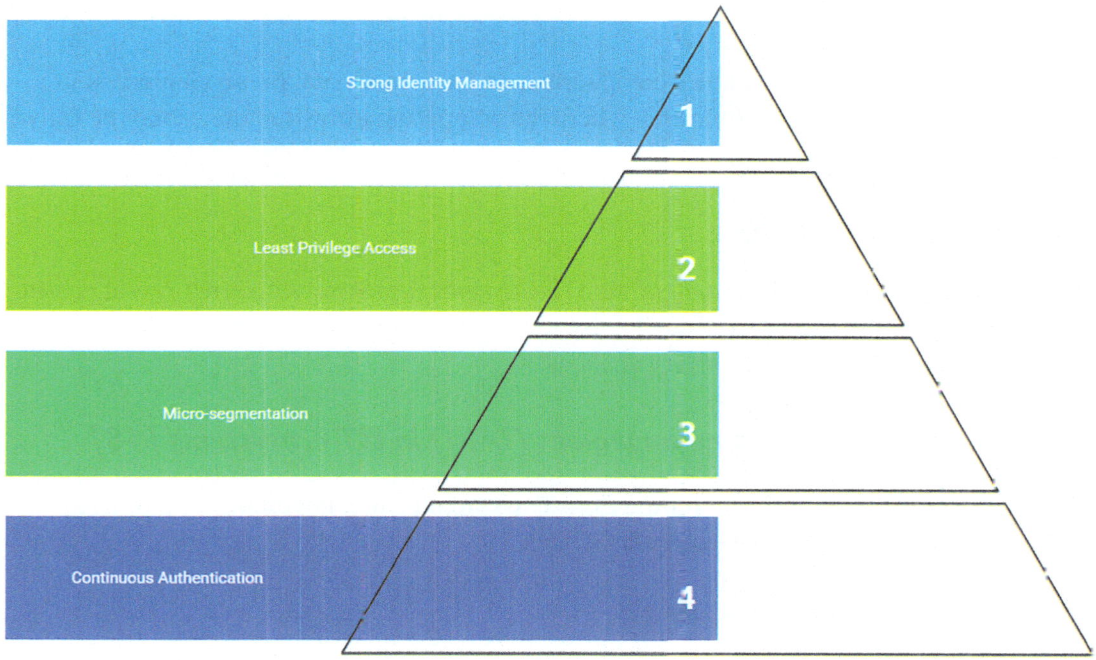

Fig. 21.3 Zero trust security pyramid.

21.11 Privacy-preserving AI techniques for DTs

AI models, while powerful, pose significant privacy risks. These techniques allow the DT to leverage data intelligence without compromising confidentiality [7–9].

21.11.1 Federated learning

As detailed in Section 6.4, FL is a crucial horizontal privacy defense, keeping sensitive training data localized on the edge/device where it originated. It is particularly effective for collaborative DTs in highly regulated sectors.

21.11.2 Secure multiparty computation

SMPC allows a function to be collaboratively computed by several independent parties, such that no single party learns the input data of the others, yet all parties learn the correct computed result.

- **Application in DTs:** If three manufacturing consortium members need to calculate a market-wide optimal production rate (the function output) based on their proprietary individual cost structures (the function inputs), SMPC allows them to derive the optimum without revealing their sensitive cost data to each other or to a central server.

21.11.3 HE

Detailed in Section 6.3, HE enables computation on encrypted data, preserving privacy even in cloud-hosted DT environments where the computing infrastructure cannot be fully trusted.

21.11.4 Differential privacy

DP's role is to ensure that the *output* of the DT's analytical processes does not reveal private information, often by adding calibrated noise to the dataset or the query results before they are made public or used for secondary analysis.

21.12 Identity & access management (IAM) in DT ecosystems [18]

Effective IAM is the control gate for the Zero Trust architecture, governing who or what can access and control the physical and virtual assets.

21.12.1 Role of decentralized identity

DID shifts identity management away from centralized authorities to the entities themselves. For DTs, this means:

- **Self-sovereign identity:** Every physical asset, sensor, AI model version, and user can possess a unique, verifiable identity controlled by the entity's owner.
- **Enhanced auditability:** When an asset uses its DID to communicate with the DT, the interaction is authenticated cryptographically, providing irrefutable proof of the entity's involvement in the audit log.

21.12.2 Multifactor authentication

Mandatory use of multifactor authentication (MFA) for all human access to critical DT control systems and platforms. For machine-to-machine communication, this translates to cryptographic attestation based on hardware-rooted keys (HSMs/TPMs).

21.12.3 Attribute-based access control

Attribute-based access control (ABAC) uses complex policies based on the attributes of the user or device, the environment (time, location), and the resource being accessed.

- **Dynamic access:** Instead of static roles (role-based access control), ABAC can enforce rules like, "Only a certified maintenance technician (role attribute) at the specific physical location (environment attribute) of the asset (resource attribute) during scheduled maintenance hours (time attribute) can issue a control command." This is far more granular and secure than traditional access models.

21.13 Threat mitigation strategies [6,14]

Proactive and reactive measures are required to minimize the impact of successful attacks.

- **Intrusion detection systems:** Monitoring network traffic for signatures of known attacks targeting IoT protocols or AI endpoints.
- **Anomaly detection using AI:** Utilizing secondary AI models trained on "normal" DT behavior to flag statistical anomalies in data streams, control commands, or resource consumption that may indicate a zero-day attack or ongoing tampering.
- **Blockchain-based audit trails:** Immediate logging of suspicious events to the immutable ledger prevents attackers from covering their tracks.
- **Bi-directional isolation (air gaps):** In highly critical DTs (e.g., nuclear power), enforcing physical or logical segmentation between the control systems and the public internet ensures that bi-directional data flow is only possible through rigorously secured and audited data diodes.

21.14 Case studies

21.14.1 Smart manufacturing (industry 4.0) [17]

- **Scenario:** A DT of an entire production line monitors asset health, predicts equipment failures, and optimizes throughput.
- **Security/trust implementation: Blockchain for secure data logging.** Sensor data (vibration, temperature) from proprietary machinery is encrypted, hashed, and logged immutably [19]. This ensures that the maintenance records and operational history used by the DT for lifetime prediction are fully trustworthy and admissible in legal disputes or warranty claims. Smart contracts automatically lock out unverified firmware updates.

21.14.2 Smart healthcare

- **Scenario:** A personalized DT uses patient data, wearable devices, and genetic information to predict cancer recurrence risk and optimize medication dosage.
- **Privacy implementation: FL for privacy protection.** Multiple hospitals collaborate to train a single, robust cancer prediction model. Each hospital keeps its highly sensitive patient records local, only sharing encrypted model gradients. This achieves a globally accurate model while adhering to strict HIPAA/GDPR privacy mandates in each jurisdiction.

21.14.3 Smart cities

- **Scenario:** An Urban Mobility DT simulates real-time traffic flow, predicts congestion, and autonomously adjusts traffic lights.
- **Identity/privacy implementation: DID.** Instead of city infrastructure tracking individual vehicle VINs or citizens' mobile phone IDs centrally, the system relies on DIDs. Citizens and vehicles can cryptographically prove attributes (e.g., "authorized to use this lane" or "paid the toll") using ZKPs without revealing their persistent, real-world identity, balancing smart city efficiency with individual privacy.

21.15 Regulatory and ethical considerations

The deployment of AI-DTs requires rigorous compliance with existing laws and proactive adherence to developing ethical frameworks [15,11].

- **GDPR:** Mandates strong protections for personal data, directly requiring the adoption of PbD, Data Minimization, and strict consent mechanisms for any DT operation involving EU citizens' data.
- **HIPAA:** For healthcare DTs, it mandates that all patient data (Protected Health Information) remain secure and confidential, driving the need for HE and FL.
- **ISO standards (ISO 23,247 for DTs):** Provide technical requirements and a framework for developing and utilizing DTs in manufacturing environments, establishing baseline security expectations.
- **Ethical AI guidelines:** Since AI-DTs make autonomous decisions affecting human lives (e.g., medical dosage, infrastructure stability), ethical frameworks must address:
- **Accountability:** Clear determination of responsibility when an autonomous DT decision causes harm
- **Bias and fairness:** Ensuring that the AI model does not perpetuate or amplify societal biases (e.g., in loan decisions based on demographic data)
- **Human oversight and controllability:** The ability for human operators to intervene, override, or safely pause DT's autonomous operations (Fig. 21.4)

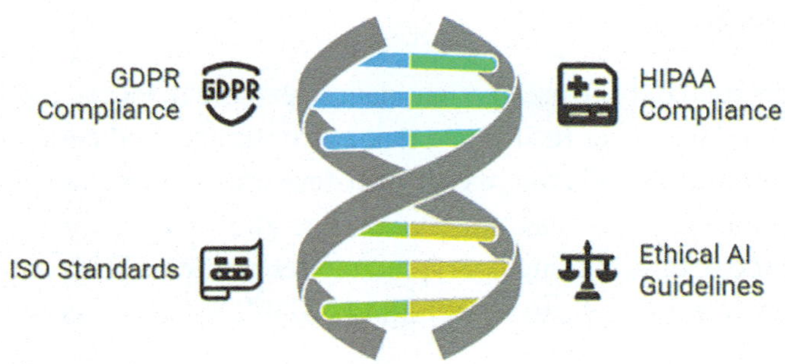

Fig. 21.4 Foundations of AI-DT Governance.

21.16 Challenges and future directions

While the security landscape is evolving, several significant challenges remain, pointing toward future research and development priorities.

21.16.1 Challenges

- **High computational cost of privacy:** Techniques like HE and SMPC currently demand substantially more computational resources and time than plain-text operations, challenging real-time DT performance.
- **Interoperability issues:** The lack of standardized security and privacy protocols across heterogeneous IoT devices, edge platforms, and cloud providers hinders the establishment of unified security policies.
- **Lack of standardization for trust:** There is no universal, agreed-upon framework or metric for quantifying and scoring the trustworthiness of an AI model or a data source.
- **Quantum attack threats:** The imminent threat posed by quantum computing requires immediate investment in developing and standardizing quantum-safe DT, particularly for long-term secure data storage and communication key exchange.

21.16.2 Future directions

- **Quantum-safe DTs:** Integrating PQC cryptographic algorithms directly into the hardware and communication protocols of the DT ecosystem to secure it against future quantum attacks
- **Autonomous DTs:** Developing robust, verifiable security wrappers around fully autonomous DTs that can perform self-healing and self-governance, including automated threat detection and immediate countermeasure deployment (e.g., isolation or safe-mode activation)
- **Emotion-aware human DTs:** As DTs move into monitoring and predicting human psychological and emotional states, the privacy and ethical stakes become exponential, demanding new robust frameworks for affective computing data
- **Security orchestration, automation, and response (SOAR):** Implementing SOAR tools customized for DT operations to automate the detection, analysis, and containment of security incidents at machine speed

21.17 Conclusion

Security, privacy, and trust are not optional; they are the core building blocks of any safe and reliable AI-powered DT system. When real physical assets connect with smart virtual models, we need more than traditional IT security—we need a modern, multilayered approach.

The future of DT technology will depend on the use of strong cryptography, blockchain for tamper-proof records, privacy-friendly AI methods like FL and HE, and a Zero Trust security model. If we address these challenges early and effectively, DTs can grow into powerful, secure, and trustworthy tools that help us understand, improve, and optimize the real world.

References

[1] National Institute of Standards and Technology, Zero Trust Architecture, NIST SP 800-207, 2020.

[2] Tao, F., Zhang, H., Liu, A., Nee, A.Y.C., Digital twin in industry: state-of-the-Art. IEEE Trans. Ind. Inform. 15513203. 15 (4), 2019. 2405–2415. Available from http://ieeexplore.ieee.org/xpl/RecentIssue.jsp?punumber=9424. doi:10.1109/TII.2018.2873186.

[3] Lu, Y., 2021. Blockchain and digital twin for cybersecurity. IEEE Transactions on Systems, Man, and Cybernetics: Systems 51 (1), 110–122.

[4] Moubayed, A., Shami, A., Refaey, A., Lutfiyya, H., 2021. Explainable AI in cybersecurity: a survey. IEEE Access 9, 73027–73054.

[5] Sun, Y., Yu, Q., Zhang, Y., 2022. A privacy-preserving framework for digital twin collaboration. IEEE Internet Things J. 9 (12), 9311–9324.

[6] Teslya, N., Ryabchikov, A., "Blockchain-based platform architecture for industrial IoT," in Proc. IEEE ICUMT, 2020, pp. 1–6.

[7] Li, X., Liang, W., Ma, J., 2022. Attribute-based access control for IoT and digital twins. IEEE Trans. Dependable Secure Comput. 19 (4), 2839–2852.

[8] Sharma, P.K., Park, J.H., 2020. Digital Twin-based smart health monitoring system using blockchain. IEEE Access 8, 19038–19050.

[9] Ning, H., Wang, H., Dhelim, Y., Daneshmand, M., 2022. A survey on Digital Twins for smart manufacturing. IEEE Internet Things J. 9 (5), 3671–3692.

[10] Zhou, Y., Lin, P., 2023. Privacy-preserving AI techniques in cyber-physical systems. ACM Comput. Surv. 55 (4), 1–36.

[11] Ahmed, A.A., Shi, Q., 2021. Hybrid encryption techniques for secure IoT communication. IEEE Trans. Ind. Inform. 17 (8), 5565–5574.

[12] Pandey, S.R., Nguyen, K., Phung-Duc, T.L., 2022. Security challenges in AI-driven Digital Twins. IEEE Access 10, 105230–105245.

[13] Grieves, M., Vickers, J., 2017. Digital Twin: mitigating unpredictable, undesirable emergent behavior in complex systems. Transdisciplinary Perspectives on Complex Systems, Springer, 85–113.

[14] Hossain, M.S., Muhammad, G., 2021. Cloud-assisted Industrial Internet of Things (IIoT)–enabled processes. IEEE Internet Things J. 8 (10), 8689–8701.

[15] Want, R., Schilit, B.N., 2021. Expanding the role of Zero Trust for IoT. IEEE Comput. 54 (5), 40–49.

[16] Wang, C., Liu, X., Pedram, M., 2022. Federated learning for IoT security: a survey. IEEE Commun. Surv. Tutor. 24 (3), 1789–1825.

[17] International Organization for Standardization, 2021. ISO 23247: Digital Twin Framework for Manufacturing. ISO.

[18] Ghosh, S., Amin, R., Mandal, S., Chaudhry, S.A., 2021. Post-quantum cryptography approaches for IoT. IEEE Access 9, 148182–148200.

[19] Shafique, A., et al. 2022. Anomaly detection using AI models for cyber-physical systems, IEEE Trans. Emerg. Top. Comput. 10 (3), 967–980.

[20] Wan, S., Qi, L., Xu, X., Cai, W., 2021. Deep learning models for IoT security. IEEE Internet Things J. 8 (10), 7603–7613.

Index

Note: Page numbers followed by "*f*" indicate figures, "*t*" indicate tables.

B

L

M

N

O

P

Q

R

S

T

U

V

W

X

Z